TRAUMATIC ABUSE
AND NEGLECT OF CHILDREN AT HOME

TRAUMATIC ABUSE AND NEGLECT OF CHILDREN AT HOME

edited by Gertrude J. Williams and John Money

The Johns Hopkins University Press
Baltimore and London

Manufactured in the United States of America

The Johns Hopkins University Press, Baltimore Maryland 21218
The Johns Hopkins Press Ltd., London

Library of Congress Catalog Card Number 79-3684
ISBN 0-8018-2231-9

Library of Congress Cataloging in Publication data will be found on the last printed page of this book.

To our parents

Belle Thorner Rubin, Barnet Rubin,
Frank Money, and Ruth Mary Read Money
and to all parents in our extended families
who do not abuse or neglect their children.

CONTENTS

PREFACE

Parental abuse and neglect of children have a long past, but efforts to curb and prevent these practices have a comparatively short history. In early times, children were battered, neglected, and abandoned by their parents. The existence of these practices was not only recognized but accepted, shrugged off, or even socially sanctioned.

The modern response—or rather, nonresponse—to child abuse and neglect has been denial, the primitive defense against awareness of realities too overwhelming to assimilate. Paradoxically, the evolvement of humanitarian ideals probably contributed to the denial of the existence of parental abuse and neglect of children and, hence, indirectly to their perpetuation. It was a humane ethos that spawned ideals that gradually became transformed into myths of the happy childhood, the maternal instinct, and home as always a haven for children. To become aware of the reality of child abuse and neglect at home—that childhood may be agonizing, that parents may torture their children, that home may be a chamber of horrors—threatens too profoundly those protective fictions that give consistency to and a basis for trust in the ideal of family life.

Like the Nazi holocaust and Hiroshima, parental cruelty to children stirs marginal awareness of the extremes of human suffering and helplessness, and one is impelled to flee from such an unbearably anguishing realization. Abuse and neglect by one's own parents is so macabre that until recently these practices had been relegated to the realm of folk tales, under the guise of wicked witches, cruel stepparents, and terrified children. Now, at last, the sciences, social work, and the law are beginning to catch up with folk wisdom; and public and professional consciousness has been awakened to the reality and frequency of traumatic abuse and neglect of children at home.

The academic forebear of this book, a special issue of the *Journal of Pediatric Psychology,* was guest-edited by Gertrude J. Williams under the title *Abused and Neglected Children.* This special issue, which dealt with the maltreatment of children by parents and society, contained a review article coauthored by John Money on abuse dwarfism, a newly recognized syndrome of child abuse in which the pituitary gland fails to secrete its daily quota of growth hormone (somatotropin) until the child is moved to another domicile.

After inspecting *Abused and Neglected Children,* the Director of The Johns Hopkins University Press became interested in publishing as a book an even more comprehensive anthology on the subject. Having agreed to this undertaking, the editors decided, in the interest of compactness and depth, to address themselves specifically to the traumatic abuse and neglect of children at home.

In addition to an extensive literature search, the editors solicited papers in various professional publications in order to obtain manuscripts from little known sources and unpublished manuscripts covering the most recent investigations. The chapters selected as meriting inclusion in this book are the result of screening nearly two-hundred published and unpublished articles. The editors wrote original chapters on important topics not covered in these articles.

The book does not cover abuse and neglect of children in courts, reformatories, child-care institutions, or other social structures outside the home. The role of government, industry, and the socioeconomic community in the mistreatment of children deserves a volume of its own. The term, traumatic, refers to the seriousness and chronicity of the child abuse and neglect dealt with in this book.

This anthology brings together from widely scattered sources a collection of papers dealing with major dimensions of child abuse and neglect at home. Papers were selected not only to present the subject matter from a variety of perspectives but also to illuminate the complexities and issues in this inchoate area. Chapter 1 describes some of the difficulties related to such basic problems as defining child abuse and neglect and determining their incidence. From Chapter 2 on, the book is organized into six major sections that form a logical framework within which to conceptualize this fragmented subject. The editors have made a special effort to give coherence to the volume by writing introductions to each major theme.

The papers in Part I illustrate the overt and covert social sanctions for violence against children that contribute to parental child abuse and neglect. In contrast, the papers in Part II provide a historical perspective on compassion and protectiveness, the bright side of attitudes toward children. Part III describes the characteristics of abusive parents, the earliest and largest focus of psychosocial investigations on child abuse. Part IV deals with a recently developing area that has profound implications for theory and practice related to the perinatal period: the characteristics of the victims that put them at risk for abuse or neglect. Parts V, VI, and VII deal with responses of the victim to abuse and neglect. Part V presents papers that give diverse perspectives on manifold psychobiological, developmental effects on children of abuse and neglect by their parents. The special feature of Part VI is the syndrome of abuse dwarfism, a newly discovered syndrome in which the effect of abuse and neglect is the arrest of statural growth and also of intellectual growth during the course of abuse and neglect. Both deficits are reversible once the child no longer encounters an abusive, neglectful environment. The special feature of Part VII is abuse and neglect with respect to the sexual organs and their use. Sexual abuse at home refers to incest. Child molestation and assault by strangers are not included. Part VIII presents a selection of papers on management, treatment and prevention. Some of them deal with approaches that emphasize rehabilitation of abusive parents. Other chapters deal with much less frequently applied interventions that focus on the child and on the provision of a new nonabusive, nonneglectful, nonparental environment.

ACKNOWLEDGMENTS

We appreciate the kindness and assistance of Barbara R. Abel, Los Angeles Children's Protective Services, and Shirley Goldberg, reference librarian, University City Library, St. Louis. In Baltimore, June Werlwas, Master of Mental Health, contributed many hours as a reader and a referee of articles for inclusion in this book. Sue M. Blair held the position of managing editor of the manuscripts from the beginning until they were ready for copy-editing and production. Nancy Middleton Gallienne was the copy editor. These three people dedicated themselves to the book with outstanding competence and devotion; as did Helen Cutler with the proofreading.

TRAUMATIC ABUSE
AND NEGLECT OF CHILDREN AT HOME

CHAPTER 1

Child Abuse and Neglect: Problems of Definition and Incidence

Gertrude J. Williams

Abuse and neglect consist of a multitude of varied physical and psychological traumas to children. Acts of abuse include such bodily violence as beating, squeezing, lacerating, binding, burning, suffocating, poisoning, or exposure to excess heat and cold. Abuse also includes such psychological traumas as sensory overload with light, sound, pain, itching, stench, aversive taste, or prevention of sleep and verbal overload with insults, accusations, or indoctrination.

Acts of neglect are also physically and psychologically damaging. Neglected children are deprived of such physiological necessities as nourishment, drink, clothing, shelter, and sanitation, and of such psychological needs for sensory stimulation as skin contact and motion, and for social communication by way of gestural and vocal language, training, and schooling.

Acts of abuse and neglect appear to be so distinct that defining these terms would seem to present no problems. Yet there is little uniformity in the definitions of child abuse and neglect or in the use of the terms to denote them. Sometimes different terms are actually synonymous; other times, identical terms refer to quite different acts. The variety of terms and definitions and the logical inconsistencies in their application reflect the manifold perspectives on these acts and the inchoate state of conceptualization. Medical, psychological, and sociological definitions abound, and legal definitions vary from state to state.

Some professionals, especially physicians, adhere to the fairly narrow definition of the "battered child syndrome" described in the classic publication of Kempe, Silverman, Steele, Droegemueller, and Silver (1962): ". . . the syndrome should be considered in any child exhibiting evidence of possible trauma or neglect (fracture of any bone, subdural hematoma, multiple soft tissue injuries, poor skin hygiene, or malnutrition) or where there is a marked discrepancy between the clinical findings and the historical data supplied by the parents" (p. 24).

Justice and Justice (1976) explain their preference for defining child abuse as physical maltreatment:

> . . . terms such as social, psychological, and emotional abuse or deprivation are so general that they mean different things to different people. We agree with Gelles' (1975) observation that "while broken bones can be identified by X-ray, how can we

identify a mental injury?"... We do not mean to minimize the problem of nonphysical abuse of children; we simply believe that physical child abuse, defined as nonaccidental injury is itself such a complicated problem that an understanding of the causes and what to do about them has only begun (p. 18).

The definition of emotional abuse and neglect is a thorny issue that is beginning to receive attention (Feshbach and Feshbach 1976) and that creates difficulties in conceptualization. For example, Whiting (1976) reports on a workshop designed to define emotional neglect. The tentative definition of the participants, professionals and paraprofessionals in child-related fields, was as follows: "emotional neglect of a child equals the parents' refusal to recognize and take action to ameliorate a child's identified emotional disturbance." Such a definition would meet with formidable problems if applied to some clinical situations.

For instance, some physically abusive parents cooperate with a family rehabilitation program involving counseling for themselves and medical treatment of the abused child's physical injuries. They no longer physically abuse the child, but they do interfere with professionally recommended psychotherapy for the child's emotional disturbance (Williams 1976). If the definition of child abuse excludes emotional neglect, the parents would be viewed as no longer abusing their child. If, however, the definition does include emotional neglect, then the parental abuse would be viewed as continuing, and the rehabilitation program would be viewed as helping the parents change to a less discernible form of child abuse. The law, too, is unclear in its references to emotional abuse or neglect. Although child abuse is a crime in all states, its definition varies. Some states define it narrowly as physical assault, whereas others include emotional abuse in their statutes, but do not define it.

Some investigators prefer to define child abuse as the gamut of abuses committed against children, including emotional abuse as well as the emotional effect of physical abuse and neglect. For example, Fontana (1971) uses the all inclusive term "maltreatment syndrome of children," because children "are often without obvious signs of being battered but (have) multiple minor physical evidences of emotional, and at times, nutritional neglect and abuse." He emphasizes that "only this awareness and recognition of the maltreated child can prevent the last phase of the battered child syndrome, many times avoiding permanent physical and emotional crippling as well as death" (Fontana 1966).

Helfer and Kempe (1976) prefer the more general term "child abuse and neglect" because "the problem is clearly not just one of *physical* battering.... The most devastating aspect... is the permanent adverse effects on the development process and the child's emotional well-being."

The definition cited in the Child Abuse Prevention and Treatment Act of 1974 is also all inclusive. It states: "... the term 'child abuse and neglect' means the physical or mental injury, sexual abuse, negligent treatment, or maltreatment of a child under the age of 18 by a person who is responsible for the child's welfare under circumstances which indicate that the child's health or welfare is harmed or threatened thereby" (see Chapter 10, this book).

Distinctions between physical abuse and neglect often present problems.

Although some children are both physically abused and neglected, others are subject to one form of maltreatment. For example, some abused children are not neglected and may, in fact, be well-nourished and well-clothed. On the other hand, some neglected children are not abused. Although HEW[1] (1976a) advises that "distinctions between abuse and neglect should have no place in decisions of whether to report a case of maltreatment," twelve states do not include child neglect in their reporting laws. Many investigators believe that reported cases of child neglect are grossly underestimated. The vagueness of the term and the fact that it is often subsumed under child abuse may contribute to this problem. Cheney (1966) contends that "neglect . . . is a concept which permits no degree of certainty, either in legal definitions or social applications."

Reference to the sexual abuse of children, a practice with no operational definition, also complicates the definitional problem. Sometimes the term refers to incest, other times to assault in connection with sexual overtures to a child. Still other times it is vaguely defined as molestation, exposure to sexual acts, or indecent liberties and may encompass actions toward children ranging from obscene language to rape (Jaffe, Dynneson, and TenBensel 1975). Kempe and Kempe (1978) refer to sexual abuse as a form of exploitation that includes pedophilia, rape, and all forms of incest, whether forceful or not. They state: "Sexual abuse is defined as the involvement of dependent, developmentally immature children and adolescents in sexual activities that they do not fully comprehend, to which they are unable to give informed consent, or that violate the social taboos of family roles" (p. 43).

Most states do not define sexual abuse, and others do not even subsume it under child abuse. Some investigators, such as Gil (1970), explicitly exclude sexual abuse from the definition of physical abuse of children.

Extending the definition of child abuse and neglect to include its social context produces formidable complexities. From a social perspective, responsibility for harm to the child is transferred from parents to society. Gil (1969, 1970) and Gelles (1973) are proponents of a view of child abuse and neglect as expressions of social pathology rather than psychopathology.

Alvy (1975) describes a comprehensive approach to the definition of child abuse and neglect that includes both family and social pathology. He defines "individual abuse" as "the physical and emotional abuse and neglect of children which results from acts of commission and omission on the part of parents and other individual caretakers."

Alvy (1975) extends the definition of child abuse and neglect to include "collective abuse," which refers to the gamut of destructive collective attitudes toward children, such as social class and race discrimination, and to "institutional abuse," which refers to socially sanctioned harmful practices against children, such as corporal punishment.

The comprehensive approach gives rise to a number of conceptual questions. For example, five million American children suffer from malnutrition that may

---

[1]Department of Health, Education, and Welfare.

affect their physical and psychological development more profoundly than nonaccidental injury or neglect. Should these children be defined as abused? If they should, who is the abuser in the many situations in which economic deprivation prevents parents from providing adequate nourishment and shelter for these children? If they should not, then child abuse and neglect are being defined in terms of the intention of the perpetrator without regard to the damaging impact on children. If the intention of the perpetrator is a criterion for defining child abuse, other conceptual difficulties arise. For example, if a parent blinds a child accidentally while physically punishing him or her and regrets the injury, then the child would be viewed as suffering from an accidental injury rather than child abuse.

In light of the problems related to the definition of child abuse and neglect and the inconsistencies in the use of terms to denote these acts, it is not surprising that estimates of incidence range from 60,000 to 4,000,000 cases annually. The variation and vagueness of definitions of child abuse and neglect are but one reason for the wide range of estimates.

The information on which estimates are based comes from many sources, including social agencies, hospitals, police reports, and national surveys, all of which are based on different kinds of samples and criteria of reporting. Moreover, many estimates are inferential or speculative. There is general agreement, however, that cases of child abuse and neglect are significantly under-reported.

A number of factors contribute to under-reporting. Many professionals still lack the skills to distinguish between accidents and abuse or neglect. Even if abuse or neglect is suspected, they may be reported as accidental or otherwise misdiagnosed. Despite mandatory reporting laws, physcans often fail to report child abuse or neglect for their middle and upper class patients. Some physicians may not even bring up the matter with the parents for fear of antagonizing them and jeopardizing their practice. Others refer the child to a hospital for treatment, in the hope or expectation that the hospital staff will report the abuse. HEW (1976*b*) indicated that 17 cases of child abuse and neglect were reported in Florida for a one-year period. After improvements in reporting were implemented during the following year, the figure rose to 19,000 reported cases.

Light (1973) describes distortions of the incidence of child abuse and neglect by under-reporting practices of private physicians. He states that, if every low-income family in which a child was abused or neglected were given $10,000 annually as a means of reducing child abuse, the incidence of abuse would appear to decrease as a function of improved economic resources. In reality, however, the apparent decrease would be an artifact, because "the child abuser will have purchased the private pediatrician's lower reporting rates."

The United States National Center on Child Abuse and Neglect estimates that there are approximately one million abused and neglected children in America, of which between 100,000–200,000 are physically abused, 60,000–100,000 are sexually abused, and the remainder are neglected (Besharov 1977).

According to the National Council of Organizations for Children and Youth (1976), which based estimates on 1970 census data, there are 580,000 cases of child abuse annually. Using other criteria and procedures, Newberger and Hyde (1975) estimated 200,000 cases a year, and Gil (1970) estimated a range of 2,500,000 to 4,000,000 annually. Levine (1974) estimated a range of 500,000 to 2,000,000 cases annually for child neglect alone.

Most investigators agree that child abuse and neglect are increasing. Helfer (1974) indicates that the rate of increase in the number of reports is 30 percent annually. Mitchell (1977) reports that "there is a rising incidence of child abuse in urban industrial communities which is only partially due to greater public sensitivity and more intensive ascertainment of cases." HEW (1976a) concludes that "reported cases [of child abuse and neglect] account for the visible tip [of the iceberg]. . . . Estimates suggest a problem of staggering proportions yet to be revealed."

REFERENCES

Alvy, K. T. "On child abuse: Values and analytic approaches." *Journal of Clinical Child Psychology* 4 (1975):36–37.

Besharov, D. J. "U.S. National Center on Child Abuse and Neglect: Three years of experience." *Child Abuse and Neglect: The International Journal* 1 (1977):173–77.

Cheney, K. B. "Safeguarding legal rights in providing protective services." *Children* 13 (1966):86–92.

Feshbach, N. D., and Feshbach, S. "Punishment: Parent rites versus children's rights." In G. P. Koocher (ed.), *Children's Rights and the Mental Health Professions*, pp. 149–70. New York: John Wiley & Sons, 1976.

Fontana, V. J. "An insidious and disturbing medical entity." *Public Welfare* 24 (1966): 235–39.

———. *The Maltreated Child: The Maltreatment Syndrome in Children.* Springfield, Ill.: Charles C Thomas, 1971.

Gelles, R. "The social construction of child abuse." *American Journal of Ortho-psychiatry* 45 (1975):365.

Gil, D. G. "Physical abuse of children: Findings and implications of a nationwide survey." *Pediatrics* 44 (1969), part 2:857–64.

———. *Violence against Children: Physical Child Abuse in the United States.* Cambridge, Mass.: Harvard University Press, 1970.

HEW. *Child Abuse and Neglect: An Overview of the Problem.* Vol. 1. Washington, D.C.: National Center on Child Abuse and Neglect, Publ. No. (OHD) 75–30073, 1976a.

HEW. *Child Abuse and Neglect: The Roles and Responsibilities of Professionals,* Vol. 2. Washington, D.C.: National Center on Child Abuse and Neglect, Publ. No. (OHD) 75–30074, 1976b.

Helfer, R. E. *A Self-Instructional Program on Child Abuse and Neglect.* Unit 4. Chicago: Committee on Infant and Preschool Child, American Academy of Pediatrics and Denver: National Center for Prevention of Child Abuse and Neglect, 1974.

Helfer, R. E., and Kempe, C. H. *Child Abuse and Neglect: The Family and the Community.* Cambridge, Mass.: Ballinger, 1976.

Jaffe, A. C., Dynneson, L., and TenBensel, R. "Sexual abuse of children: an epidemiologic study." *American Journal of Diseases of Children* 129 (1975): 689–92.

Justice, B., and Justice, R. *The Abusing Family*. New York: Human Sciences Press, 1976.

Kempe, C. H., Silverman, F. N., Steele, B. F., Droegemueller, W., and Silver, H. K. "The battered child syndrome." *Journal of the American Medical Association* 181 (1962):17–24.

Kempe, R. S., and Kempe, C. H. *Child Abuse*. Cambridge, Mass.: Harvard University Press, 1978.

Levine, A. "Child neglect: Reaching the parent." *Social Rehabilitation Record* 1 (1974):26–27.

Light, R. J. "Abused and neglected children in America: A study of alternative policies." *Harvard Educational Reveiw* 43 (1973):556–98.

Mitchell, R. G. *Child Health in the Community: A Handbook of Social and Community Paediatrics*. Edinburgh: Churchill Livingstone, 1977.

National Council of Organizations for Children and Youth. *America's Children*. Washington, D.C., 1976.

Newberger, E. H., and Hyde, J. N. "Child abuse: Principles and implications of current pediatric practice." *Pediatric Clinics of North America* 22(1975):695–715.

Whiting, L. "Defining emotional neglect." *Children Today* 5(1976):2–5.

Williams, G. J. "Editorial: Special issue on abused and neglected children." *Journal of Pediatric Psychology* 1(1976):3–5.

PART I

Social Sanctions for Child Abuse and Neglect

Although there was no doubt that . . . parents were also objects of punishment whether for religious or legal reasons, they at least had some leeway to avoid it. Children could not: they were always available to be punished. If they were not being whipped by slaves as in Roman times, they were being whipped by their parents who were "slaves" of other punishing systems of religion or law.

(Newman, 1978, p. 62)

Editor's Introduction

At first glance, child abuse and neglect appear to be repugnant, unnatural acts that are alien to everyday life. Yet when viewed from historical and social perspectives they lose their anomalous appearance, for child abuse and neglect have sturdy roots in the past and reflect current social sanctions favoring violence against children.

Since time immemorial, children have been treated with incredible cruelty and have had little recourse to the law, which regarded them as possessions of their parents or the state. Children have been tortured, burned, worked to death, terrorized, and flogged daily in order to "discipline" them, dipped in icewater and rolled in the snow in order to "harden" them, and buried alive with their dead parents. Their parents have exposed them to weather, starved or abandoned them, in order to avoid the burden of rearing them or dividing property into too small parts. DeMause (1974) contends that "there would be a point back in history where most children were what we would now consider abused."

In Roman law, the power of a father over his children was absolute: he could kill, sell, or offer them to sacrifice. The status of children as chattels of their fathers, a major foundation for social sanctions for child abuse, was affirmed even by Aristotle, preeminent proponent of democracy, who stated: "The justice of a master or a father is a different thing from that of citizen, for a son or slave is property, and there can be no injustice done to property."

Concern for the suffering of children abandoned by their parents did not enter into the considerations of Seneca, when he endorsed the mutilation of these children in order to exploit them for money:

> Look on the blind wandering about the streets leaning on their sticks, and those with crushed feet, and still again look on those with broken limbs. This one is without arms, that one has his shoulders pulled down out of shape in order that his grotesqueries may excite laughter. . . . Let us go to the origin of all those ills—a laboratory for the manufacture of human wrecks—a cavern filled with limbs torn from living children. . . . What wrong has been done to the Republic? On the contrary, have not these children been done a service inasmuch as their parents have cast them out? (DeMause 1974, p. 31)

Another major contributor to sanctions for child abuse is an interpretation of the Bible that views children as products of original sin, possessed of evil impulses that threaten to run wild. This viewpoint stresses that they also possess malleability that can enable them to be molded into virtuous adults through the rigorous, unremitting efforts of parents. "Withhold not correction from a child,"

Proverbs admonishes; "thou shalt beat him with a rod and deliver his soul from hell." Kings describes disobedient children being torn apart by bears, and Deuteronomy refers to unruly children being stoned to death. Beating a child, far from being viewed as an instance of child abuse, represented the discharge of the sacred duty of righteous parents to exorcize evil from children—literally, to beat the devil out of them—in order that good might triumph over evil (Sunley 1963).

The religious imperative to "break" children of their evil impulses was also expressed in the unquestioned right of parents to control them at any cost. Thus, in nineteenth century England, an opponent of a bill to protect the health of children working in factories stated that if a bill regulating child labor were passed, "parents would conceive it as a loss of the British birthright, that of control of a parent over his child" (Housden 1955). When a child challenged the authority of parents, the law intervened in behalf of the parents. For example, a law was passed in Illinois in 1819 that referred to crimes and punishments. Subsumed under this law is a section referring to the "disobedience of children and servants" that states: "... if any children or servants shall, contrary to the obedience due to their parents and masters, resist or refuse to obey their lawful commands, upon complaint thereof to any justice of the peace to send him or them so offending to the jail or house of correction, there to remain until they shall humble themselves to the said parents or masters' satisfaction" (Abbott 1938, p. 343).

The privacy of the home, expressed in the old Anglo-Saxon adage that "a man's home is his castle," has also contributed to social sanctions for child abuse. Regardless of what brutal practices took place there, the home has been off-limits to protective intervention. For example, in 1880 when Lord Shaftsbury's attention was called to parental child abuse, he replied: "The evils you state are enormous and indisputable, but they are of so private, internal and domestic a character as to be beyond the reach of legislation and the subject would not, I think, be entertained in either House of Parliament" (Allen and Morton 1961).

Social sanctions for child abuse cannot be dismissed as an archaic brutality that has vanished. The abuse of children continues to be sanctioned at home and at school under the guise of such euphemisms as corporal punishment or discipline. The Department of Health, Education and Welfare (HEW 1975) indicates that many abusive parents are characterized by a righteous belief in the value of harsh punishment as a means of preventing the child from being "spoiled." Helfer (1975) refers to "an intolerable situation which must be changed:" in some states, parents who base their abuse of their child on religious grounds are given more legal rights than those who do not.

A case pending in the Family Court of New York demonstrates that violence against children is still being socially sanctioned on Biblical grounds and highlights the equivalence of corporal punishment and child abuse (*Herald American/Post-Standard*, 1978). The minister of a fundamentalist church is appealing the court-ordered removal of his fourteen-year-old daughter after the county child protection agency charged him with child abuse. The child had run away from home after being beaten for "rebellious behavior" related to contact dancing, which her father believes leads to "a loss of purity." He denied having abused her and claimed that he "spanked her hard enough to break her will." He testified that "God provided a fleshy area of the body, the buttocks, to receive spankings." The abused child's mother, after thanking God "for the husband He's given me," testified, "I encouraged him to spank her because the Bible says, 'if thou beatest the child with a rod, he shall not die but shall be saved.'"

Research on the punishment practices of normative samples reveals the extent to which violence against children is still socially sanctioned. Gelles (1977) interviewed randomly selected American parents regarding violent practices toward their children. He found that during 1975, 1,000,000 children were kicked, bitten, or punched by their parents; 750,000 were beaten up by their parents; and 50,000 had a gun or knife "used" on them.

A ruling by the United States Supreme Court in the case of Ingraham vs. Wright (1977) illustrates that child abuse continues to be socially sanctioned. The plaintiff, Ingraham, a junior high school student, was in such pain from being "struck repeatedly with a wooden instrument" by Wright, the principal, that he was taken to a hospital for treatment. The Court record indicated that "plaintiff introduced evidence that he had suffered a painful bruise that required the prescription of cold compresses, a laxative, sleeping and pain-killing pills and ten days of rest at home and that prevented him from sitting comfortably for three weeks."

The Court ruled that "the administration of corporal punishment in public schools, whether or not excessively administered does not come within the scope of Eighth Amendment protection." That is, the Constitution's "cruel and unusual punishment" clause applies to the protection of incarcerated criminals, not children in public schools. Furthermore, the Court decreed that the constitutional right to "due process" guaranteed in the Fifth and Fourteenth Amendments does not apply to children. Unlike other citizens, a child is not assumed to be innocent until proven guilty. Thus, violence against children is legally sanctioned in the absence of prior notice or a hearing in connection with a school staff member's allegation against them.

A number of preposterous consequences emerge from this ruling. Children in American public schools currently receive less protection against violence and the violation of their constitutional rights than do criminals in prison. Furthermore, children placed in juvenile institutions under court order for the conviction of crimes receive more protection than do other children placed in the same institution for intellectual impairment and emotional problems. Finally, the highest court in the land now serves as a model of socially sanctioned violence against children.

Since ancient times, the use of violence has been sanctioned for selected groups of vulnerable persons, and its basis in morality has been dogmatically preached. Over the years, reason, justice, and mercy have triumphed over irrationality and tyranny. One hundred years ago the beating of wives and the flogging of sailors were banned. Employees are no longer whipped, and the beating of animals is illegal. Corporal punishment of criminals has been legally abolished. The use of violence has given way to nonviolent alternatives in all groups but one: children, the weakest members of the human species and the only group on whom the infliction of pain continues to be socially sanctioned.

Thus, child abuse and neglect are not inexplicable atrocities far removed from daily life. They become understandable as extreme points on a continuum of socially sanctioned cruelty to children that has deep historical moorings. Out of the mouths of babes comes wisdom, the old adage says, but the lips of children have, in reality, been sealed. Although history has chronicled the lives of adults, it has bypassed children who, over the centuries, were expected to be seen, not heard, and who were incapable of writing about their plight. A new field, the psychohistory of childhood, records the affairs of this heretofore historically neglected group. In Chapter 2, DeMause, founder of the psychohistory of childhood, discusses why "the history of childhood is a nightmare from which we have only recently begun to awaken." Cameronchild's paper (chapter 3) is a first-person account of her recent, nightmarish childhood of abuse and neglect by middle-class, professional parents. Ignored by a number of professionals and other community representatives, the maltreatment continued until the author's emotional problems led to her placement in a psychiatric hospital where the abuse and neglect continued under the guise of treatment. In Chapter 4, Hyman, director of the National Center for the Study of Corporal Punishment and Its Alternatives, examines the Supreme Court's legal sanction of corporal punishment at school and discusses the ramifications of this decision for the abuse of children at home.

G. J. W.

REFERENCES

Abbott, G. *The Child and the State*, Vol. II. Chicago: University of Chicago Press, 1938.
Allen, A., and Morton, A. *This Is Your Child*. London: Routledge-Kegan Paul, 1961.
DeMause, L. *The History of Childhood*. New York: Psychohistory Press, 1974.
Gelles, R. J. "Violence toward Children in the United States." Paper presented at the convention of the American Association for the Advancement of Science, Denver, Colorado, February 1977.
HEW. *Child Abuse and Neglect: An Overview of the Problem*. Vol. 1. Washington, D.C.: National Center on Child Abuse and Neglect. DHEW Publ. No. (OHD) 75-30073, 1975.
Helfer, R. E. *Child Abuse and Neglect: The Diagnostic Process and Treatment Programs*. Washington, D.C.: U.S. Dept. of Health, Education and Welfare, Publ. No. (OHD) 75-69, 1975.
Herald American/Post-Standard. "Discipline or Child Abuse?"; "Rally to Back Minister in Battle with State." Syracuse, N.Y., July 2 and 3, 1978.
Housden, L. G. *The Prevention of Cruelty to Children*. London: Jonathan Cape, 1955.

Ingraham vs. *Wright*, 498 F. 2d 248 (5th Cir. 1977).

Newman, G. *The Punishment Response*. Philadelphia: Lippincott Co., 1978.

Sunley, R. "Early Nineteenth-century American Literature on Child Rearing." In M. Mead and M. Wolfenstein, eds., *Childhood in Contemporary Cultures*. Chicago: University of Chicago Press, 1963.

CHAPTER 2

Our Forebears
Made Childhood a Nightmare

Lloyd DeMause

For most people in our society, infants and children are small people to whom we should try to offer aid and comfort whenever possible. This attitude is new. A search of historical sources shows that until the last century children were instead offered beatings and whippings, with instruments usually associated with torture chambers. In fact, the history of childhood is a nightmare from which we have only recently begun to awaken.

The newness of the ability to feel empathy toward children is clear from a five-year study that my colleagues and I have just completed. The further back in history we went, the lower the level of child care we found, and the more likely children were to have been killed, abandoned, whipped, sexually abused and terrorized by their caretakers.

A child's life prior to modern times was uniformly bleak. Virtually every childrearing tract from antiquity to the 18th century recommended the beating of children. We found no examples from this period in which a child wasn't beaten, and hundreds of instances of not only beating, but battering, beginning in infancy.

One 19th-century German schoolmaster who kept score reported administering 911,527 strokes with a stick, 124,000 lashes with a whip, 136,715 slaps with his hand and 1,115,800 boxes on the ear. The beatings described in most historical sources began at an early age, continued regularly throughout childhood, and were severe enough to cause bruising and bloodying. It took centuries of progress in parent-child relations before the West could begin to overcome its apparent need to abuse its children.

PERSONALITY, NOT TECHNOLOGY

I believe that the major dynamic in historical change is ultimately neither technology nor economics. More important are the changes in personality that grow from differences between generations in the quality of the relationship between parent and child. Good parenting is something that has been achieved only after centuries as generation after generation of parents tried to overcome the abuse of their own childhoods by reaching out to their children on more mature levels of relating.

Throughout history, an adult has had three major reactions to a child who needs its care. The projective reaction consists of using the child as a receptacle for the adult's unconscious feelings. The reversal reaction occurs when the adult uses the child as a substitute for an adult figure who was important in his own childhood. The empathic reaction, a late historical acquisition, occurs if the adult is able to empathize with and satisfy the child's needs.

The first two reactions occurred simultaneously in parents in the past, producing a strange double image of the child in which it was at once both bad (projective) and needed (reversal). The further back in history you look, the more evident are these reactions and the more bizarre the prevailing attitudes toward children.

Century after century of battered children grew up and battered their own children in turn. John Milton's wife complained that she hated to hear the cries of his nephews as he beat them. Beethoven whipped his piano pupils with a knitting needle. Even royalty was not exempt—little Louis XIII was whipped upon awakening for his previous day's misdemeanors.

Even infants were often beaten. John Wesley's wife Susannah said of her babies, "When turned a year old (and some before), they were taught to fear the rod, and to cry softly." Rousseau reported that young babies were often beaten to keep them quiet. An early American mother wrote of her battle with her four-month-old infant: "I whipped him 'till he was actually black and blue, and until I *could not* whip him any more, and he never gave up a single inch."

SALTED AND SWADDLED

If the newborn was allowed to live, parents would salt it and then bathe it in ice water to "harden" it. The baby was tied up tightly in swaddling bands for its first year, supposedly to prevent it from tearing off its ears, breaking its legs, touching its genitals or crawling around like an animal. Traditional swaddling, as one American doctor described it, "consists of entirely depriving the child of the use of its limbs by enveloping them in an endless bandage, so as to not unaptly resemble billets of wood, and by which the skin is sometimes excoriated, the flesh compressed, almost to gangrene . . . "

Swaddled infants were not only more convenient to care for, since they withdrew into themselves in sleep most of the day, but they were also more easily laid for hours behind hot ovens, hung on pegs on the wall, and, wrote one doctor, "left, like a parcel, in every convenient corner." In addition, they were often thrown around like a ball for amusement. In 16th-century France, a brother of Henri IV, while being tossed from one window to another, was dropped and killed. Doctors complained of parents who broke the bones of their children in the "customary" tossing of infants. Nurses often said that the stays that encased children beneath their swaddling bands were necessary because they could not "be tossed about without them."

Adults in the past, like contemporary child batterers, regularly succumbed to urges to mutilate, burn, freeze and drown infants. The Huns used to cut the cheeks of newborn males, Italian Renaissance parents would "burn in the neck with a hot iron, or else drop a burning wax candle" on newborn babies, and it was common to cut the string under the newborn's tongue, often with the midwife's fingernail. In every age, the deliberate mutilization of children's bones and faces prepared them for a lifetime of begging.

As late as the 19th century in Eastern Europe, baptism was not a matter of simple sprinkling, but an ice-water ordeal that often lasted for hours and sometimes caused the death of the infant. The regular practice of the plunge bath involved nearly drowning the infant over and over again in ice-cold water "with its mouth open and gasping for breath." The dipping of infants in cold rivers has been considered therapeutic since Roman times and, as late as the 19th century, children were often put to bed wrapped in cold wet towels to make them hardy. With such beginnings, it is not surprising that 18th century pediatrician William Buchan said "almost one half of the human species perish in infancy by improper management or neglect."

Although there were many exceptions to the general pattern, the average child of parents with some wealth spent his earliest years in the home of a wet nurse, returned home at age three or four to the care of other servants, and was sent out to service, apprenticeship, or school by age seven, so that the amount of time parents of means actually spent raising their children was minimal.

Since antiquity, wet nurses have been acknowledged to have been thoroughly unreliable—Jacques Guillimeau described how the child at nurse might be "stifled, overlaid, be let fall, and so come to an untimely death, or else be devoured, spoiled, or disfigured by some wild beast." A clergyman told one British doctor about his parish which was "filled with suckling infants from London, and yet, in the space of one year, he buried them all except two." Of 21,000 children born in Paris in 1780, 17,000 were sent into the country to be wet-nursed, 3,000 were placed in nursery homes, 700 were wet-nursed at home and only 700 were nursed by their own mothers. Even those mothers who kept their infants at home often did not breastfeed them, giving them pap (water and grain) instead. One 15th-century mother, who had moved from an area in which nursing infants was common, was called "swinish and filthy" by her Bavarian neighbors for nursing her child herself, and her husband threatened to stop eating if she did not give up this "disgusting habit."

TERRORS OF THE NIGHT

As the child grew out of swaddling clothes, parents found it terribly frightening to care for, having projected their own unconscious needs into the child. As a result, children were always felt to be on the verge of turning into actual demons, or at least to be easily susceptible to "the power of the Devil." To keep their small devils cowed, adults regularly terrorized them with a vast army of ghostlike figures, from the Lamia and Striga of the ancients, who ate children raw, to the witches of Medieval times, who would steal bad children away and suck their blood. One 19th-century tract described in simplified language the tortures God had in store for children in Hell: "The little child is in this red-hot oven. Hear how it screams to come out . . . It stamps its little feet on the floor." The need to personify punitive figures was so powerful that this terrorizing of children did not stop at imaginary figures. Dummies were actually made up to be used in frightening children. One English writer, in 1748, describes how:

"The nurse takes a fancy to quiet the peevish child, and with this intent, dressed up an uncouth figure, makes it come in, and roar and scream at the child in ugly disagreeable notes, which grate upon the tender organs of the ear, and at the same time, by its gesture and near approach, makes as if it would swallow the infant up."

Another method that parents used to terrorize their children employed corpses. A common moral lesson involved taking children to visit the gibbet, where they were forced to inspect rotting corpses hanging there as an example of what happens to bad children when they grow up. Whole classes were taken out of school to witness hangings, and parents would often whip their children afterwards to make them remember what they had seen.

SEXUAL ABUSE

The sexual abuse of children was also far more prevalent in the past than it is today. Growing up in Greece and Rome often included being used sexually by older men. Boy brothels flourished in every city in antiquity, and slave boys were commonly kept for homosexual use. Sexual abuse by pedagogues and teachers of small children was a common complaint, and even Aristotle thought that adult homosexuality must be a result of "those who were abused from childhood."

Erotic drawings often show nude children waiting on adults in sexual embrace, and Quintilian said that even noble children "hear us use such words, they see our mistresses and minions; every dinner party is loud with foul songs, and things are presented to their eyes of which we should blush to speak." Tiberius "taught children of the most tender years, whom he called his *little fishes*, to play between his legs while he was in his bath. Those which had not yet been weaned, but were strong and hearty, he set at fellatio." Castrated children were considered as especially arousing in antiquity, and infants were often castrated in the cradle for use in brothels.

The sexual use of children continued until early modern times. Servants were commonly known to be child molesters, and even parents would masturbate their children "to make their yards grow longer." Little Louis XIII was often hauled into bed by his parents and others and included in their sexual acts. By the

18th century, however, parents began instituting severe punishments for childhood sensuality, perhaps in an unconscious maneuver to control their own sexual desires. By the 19th century, parents and doctors began waging a frenzied campaign against childhood masturbation, threatening to cut off the child's genitals, performing circumcision and clitoridectomy without anesthesia as punishment, making children wear spiked cages and other restraints, and opening anti-masturbation sanatoria all over Europe.

GOOD NEWS

Despite the bleakness of this general historical picture of childhood, there is good evidence that childrearing modes have continuously evolved over the past two millennia in the West. An independent source of change lies within the parent-child relationship itself, as each generation of parents attempts anew to go beyond the abuses to which it has been subjected, producing a psychological advance in each period of history.

Consider, for instance, the long struggle against infanticide. In antiquity infanticide was so common that every river, dung-heap and cesspool used to be littered with dead infants. Polybius blamed the depopulation of Greece on the killing of legitimate children, even by wealthy parents. Ratios of boys to girls in census figures ran four to one, since it was rare for more than one girl in a family to be spared. Christians were considered odd for their opposition to infanticide, although even that opposition was mild, with few penalties. Large-scale infanticide of legitimate babies continued well into medieval times, with boy-girl ratios in rich as well as poor families often still running two to one. As late as 1527, one priest admitted that "the latrines resound with the cries of children who have been plunged into them." Yet infanticide was increasingly confined to the killing of illegitimate babies, and there is similar evidence of a continuous decrease in beating and other abusive practices through the centuries.

EVOLUTIONARY TRENDS

The following six evolutionary modes seem to describe the major trends of parent-child relations in the more advanced parts of the West:

Infanticidal mode (Antiquity). The image of Medea hovered over childhood in antiquity, not only because parents resolved their anxieties about taking care of children by infanticidal acts, but also because the lives of those children who were allowed to live were constantly threatened by severe abuse.

Abandonment mode (Medieval). The parents who accepted the right of the child to live but whose immaturity made them still unable to care for it, abandoned the child either to a wet nurse, foster family, monastery, nunnery, other home (as servants) or simply through severe emotional neglect by the parents themselves.

Ambivalent mode (Renaissance). A closer relationship with the child produced ambivalent parents, fearful that their child's insides were full of evil so that they had to be purged with continuous enemas, yet close enough to express both love and hate, often in bewildering juxtaposition.

Intrusive mode (18th century). A decrease of ambivalence now enabled the parent actually to make the intrusive control of the child's insides part of their own defense system. The child was no longer so full of dangerous projections, and was therefore not swaddled, nor sent out to wet-nurse, nor given enemas, but was instead toilet-trained, prayed with but not yet played with, and disciplined as much through guilt as by beating. As empathy grew, pediatrics could be invented, and the general improvement in child care reduced infant mortality greatly.

Socializing mode (19th century to now). Still the major mode of parents today, socializing involves thinking of the child as someone who needs continuous training and guidance in order to become civilized. Most discussions of child care still take place within the socializing mode, and it has been the source of all contemporary models of the psyche from Freud to Skinner. In practice, it involves giving up most of the severe beating and other overt forms of abuse while using covert methods of manipulation, guilt, and a general detached quality of parenting to sustain the long periods of contact with children whose increasing needs are simply too much for the parents.

Helping mode (just beginning). The helping mode starts with the proposition that the child knows better than the parent what it needs at each stage of its life, and involves both parents fully in the child's daily life as they help it with its expanding needs. The helping mode requires enormous time, energy and emotional maturity on the part of both parents, especially in the first six years of the child's life, as they play with it, tolerate its regressions, and discuss its needs and conflicts in an effort to keep pace with its emotional and intellectual growth.

Studies of contemporary American families show children being cared for by parents included in all six of these modes. In fact, when psychiatrists arrange family types on a scale of decreasing health, they are actually listing historical modes of childrearing, with the lower part of the scale describing parents who behave like evolutionary arrests, psychological fossils stuck in personality modes from a previous historical period when most parents used to batter children. The finding that most child abusers were themselves abused as children supports this picture.

Even though childhood for many is now more humane than at any other time in history, functional equivalents of earlier modes remain with us. Children are not sent out to wet nurses at birth, or to be servants at seven, but we do abandon them to hosts of nurseries, teachers, camps, and baby sitters for major portions of their young lives. Intrusive parents still find ways to restrict their baby's movements, such as swaddling and corsets did, and parents continue to emotionally abandon, betray, manipulate and hurt their children both overtly and covertly.

Because psychic structure is passed from generation to generation through the narrow gap of childhood, the childrearing practices of a society are more than just another item on a list of cultural traits. The history of childhood in fact determines which elements in all the rest of history will be transmitted and which will be changed. By studying the history of childhood we can gain an understanding of the personality traits on which our adult society rests, and perhaps even alter those historical group fantasies like war that threaten us most.

CHAPTER 3

An Autobiography of Violence

Jessica Cameronchild

Being a Battered Child Means . . .

Hoping that maybe your parents will be in a good mood, but knowing you couldn't trust them even if they were.

Hoping that you can just get through breakfast and off to school without any altercations.

Hoping no one will notice the stitches and black eye you have tried to hide behind your hair.

Wanting to be "as good of a bike rider as the rest of the kids," but still rehearsing the laugh you will present with the explanation that you hurt your arm by falling off your bike.

Hoping someone will care enough not to believe the incessant explanations you offer to account for your injuries.

Feeling that everything will be alright "if only *you* . . . "

Feeling guilty and confused when you make a mistake and other adults tell you: "It's alright." "They understand." "It's just a mistake."

Teachers like you because you're so well behaved.

The kids don't like you because all the teachers do and you don't know how to play anyway.

Never knowing the consequences of a gesture, facial expression, or request. Sometimes a gift of flowers is received affectionately and somtimes it's dashed down with a shove and a tirade of abuse. Sometimes a request for a piece of gum is a "good idea" and sometimes it's "proof of your horrid greediness and irresponsible lack of concern for the cost of dental care." Sometimes looking sad is met with friendly concern, and sometimes you're berated and punished for being ungrateful. But you just never know . . .

Worrying when you're away from home, about what might be happening to brothers and sisters at home.

These thoughts are dedicated to Eleanor Fairchild with sincere gratitude for her compassion, strength, and insight.
Reprinted with permission from *Child Abuse and Neglect: The International Journal* 2(1978):139–49. Copyright 1978.

Trying to find a safe explanation for why you never bring your friends home.

Trying to figure out what you did to "deserve" to be born into the family situation you were born into; trying desperately to be a "good" person who doesn't "deserve" the abuse you keep getting.

Being careful not to cry or laugh too loudly.

Feeling guilty that you're a burden to your parents, and sorry that you were ever born. "Knowing" they feel the same way about you.

Hoping maybe you were adopted and that you could find your "real" parents and convince them you'll be good if only they'll take you back. But worrying about who would take care of your "present" parents if you were rescued.

Lying awake at night, listening to a brother or sister crying and feeling sad. But wishing they would cry a little more softly so they won't "get it" again.

Somehow feeling your parents could love you if only you were sorry enough . . .

Living in constant fear that you or one of your brothers or sisters will be killed.

Hoping the doctor won't believe your parents' explanation for your injuries, but knowing she/he will.

Wishing the problem was alcoholism or a chemical imbalance so the problem could be cured.

Developing your sensitivity so as to intuit threatening mood changes, but more often feeling that heightened sensitivity is more painful than helpful.

Wishing they could just touch you, or hold you without hurting you, but sensing that they really need to be held, too.

At times hating them bitterly, but soon being reduced to tears because you know "they didn't mean to" or "they're just having a bad day" or "you shouldn't have been so loud" or . . .

Wishing that there was someone gentle and caring that you could talk to, but knowing that if the subject ever came up, you would defend them loyally. They're your parents and you love them, and you need to believe they love you.

A FRAGILE PEACE

*"How am I to face the odds of man's bedevilment and God's,
I, a stranger and afraid in a world I never made?"* [1]

Neither of my parents are "animals" or malicious people by nature. They are both very proud, rigid people with enormous needs for approval, nurturance and control. Though neither was abused as a child, their parents were extremely strict and totally conditional in their love. Both of my parents were raised in

[1]A. E. Housman, *Last Poems*, XII.

homes where children were seen as vehicles for meeting their parents' needs and were saddled with the burden of feeding their parents' enormous prides.

I have four brothers: one, a year my senior, a twin, another one year younger than I, and the youngest who is five years my junior. Both of my parents are college educated and hold advanced degrees. My mother taught learning-disabled children before she met my father; she had experience with small children, but was unequipped to deal with five children under six years of age without support. My father, the actively abusing parent and spouse, once confided to me that he had wanted "companions" and knew nothing about small children. His feeling was that we "just kept coming."

Several common characteristics in abusing parents evident in my personal experience are outlined below:

—The emotional deprivation and strong need for control and nurturance experienced by both my parents.
—The denial of responsibility on my father's part.
—The lack of a support system experienced by both parents.
—The fact that there were two people, one active and one passive, involved in our abuse.
—My parents' view of us as companions and primary sources of approval and affection, rather than as children with our own needs.

Therapists have suggested that abusers have a character dysfunction that allows aggressive impulses to be expressed without control. There also seems to be some evidence that abusive spouses and parents possess relatively little empathy and, therefore, may be unresponsive to the signs of pain in their victims. Drug use (alcohol included) was not a factor in the abuse that occurred in my home.

I distinguish between two kinds of abuse in my own experience. Oftentimes, there were calmly enforced, sadistic rituals, defined as "discipline," as well as totally unpredictable outbursts of violence. The former can be exemplified by my recollections of being forced to kneel upright, with piles of books in our outstretched arms for hours, of being made to "shove out" (to maintain a posture as if were were sitting on a chair, without a chair to support us) and to "eat a square meal" (to face straight ahead, without looking down at your plates) while eating. For years we were lined up and spanked with a stick before school in the morning and again when our father returned home in the evening. Sometimes we were put in a cold shower in the middle of the night if our parents went out for the evening. If one of us was told to sweep the driveway, we would be spanked with a stick for each leaf our father discovered when he inspected the job.

The second type of abuse that I distinguish was that of unpredictable outbursts of rage. I recall incidents such as the time our father dumped over a fully-set kitchen table because our mother had served two starches with dinner. There was also the time he nailed me to the wall by my braid for laughing too loudly. Allowing a door to slam, dropping a utensil at dinner, being too slow, using the "wrong" tone of voice, failing to maintain eye contact, not standing up straight enough, and laughing too loudly were all likely to incur severe beatings.

We were slapped and spanked with a stick daily and every few months received injuries that required medical attention.

Verbal abuse was incessant. We were constantly demeaned and insulted, told how stupid and unloveable we were and threatened with murder and torture. Sometimes our parents threatened to abandon us. Occasionally, our father threatened to commit suicide because we were such a burden. We just kept trying to be perfect and to minimize our demands so that they would love us.

As I alluded to earlier, our mother was also the victim of our father's impulsiveness and frustration. Every few months she received broken ribs, black eyes, and cut lips.

All of this illustrates the atmosphere that pervaded our house—that of unreliable, inconsistent messages and unpredictable outbursts of violence. There seemed to be unknown rules about everything. For example, I once was asked to change the roll of toilet paper in our parents' bathroom. I put the new roll on so that it led out from the bottom instead of over from the top. For this infraction I was thrown down two flights of stairs. Needless to say, this inconsistency and explosiveness instilled great fear and insecurity in all of us, but we had to be very careful not to communicate our timidity for fear of punishment. It was too easy to cause our father to feel inadequate and unloved.

We were made to witness the violence inflicted upon each other, either as a result of proximity or because our father felt it would deter us from like "transgressions." We couldn't help each other nor could we communicate our sympathy for fear of being the next target. This instilled a philosophy of "everyone for himself," and set up a detachment between the members of our family as a means of self-preservation.

For awhile I was able to switch back and forth between the obvious need for total control at home and a somewhat less guarded affect when there were no penalties for laughing or yelling with excitement. However, over time, I could not maintain the dual affect. Eventually, I became extremely passive and self-controlled at all times.

We felt betrayed by our mother's failure to intervene on our behalf, but we frequently witnessed our father's mistreatment of her and realized that she could not risk interfering. We also felt guilty at our inability to defend our own mother. Our mother's passive position served to reinforce our view of our father's omnipotence; even another "grown-up" could not protect us from him.

Another pervasive theme in our home was the message that "If you're careful enough, you can be perfect." There was no such thing as an accident or a mistake in our home. Once one of my brothers fell off a ten-story building and broke his ankle. When our father learned about it, he beat my brother with his crutch for getting hurt. Our father punished my brother for getting hurt in the fall, but also because he felt inadequate and helpless in the face of my brother's discomfort and pain. This is also a tragic example of the role-reversal which is so common in abusive families. The children are expected to take care of their parents.

We were all under constant pressure. Three of my brothers handled their frustration and anger by following our father's violent example. At home they would pick up the nearest object and beat on another sibling with it if they were crossed. This is understandable both in light of our father's ever-present example, and because we couldn't yell and argue like other siblings. That type of behavior would get my parents involved, and that meant trouble.

One of my brothers and I had learned to equate anger with violence. As we learned to abhor violence, we denied and suppressed our anger. We were passive and depressed.

My parents both felt very inadequate and frequently set up double binds to test our preference for one over the other. We usually chose to live with our mother's inflicted guilt rather than with our father's fist. However, our mother would inevitably induce our father to punish us for her hurt feelings.

There was real confusion in our feelings for our parents, especially toward our father. We were as much controlled by our sympathy for him as we were by our fear of his violent behavior. He was a terrifying abuser on the one hand and a frustrated, fragile repenter on the other. His ambivalence can be graphically illustrated by an incident in which he split my head open with a hammer because I wasn't smiling. He injured me because he felt frustrated and inadequate when he sensed I was unhappy.

Through all these years we were attending the same school, with many of the same teachers. We also visited the same pediatrician month after month. He was a friend of our father's and was usually given plausible explanations for our injuries. It is usually the "trouble-maker" who gets attention at school, but we were all straight "A" students and extremely well-behaved. No one seemed to recognize that there was something unhealthy about our model behavior. No one questioned how such capable children could hurt themselves so often, just as no one seemed to wonder how someone as capable as our mother could "walk into doors" as she so often explained to account for her bruises.

Finally, my younger brother began having trouble with school. He was extremely bright and bored with school. His teacher suggested he skip several grades, but our parents felt it would be unhealthy for him. He began misbehaving in class and getting sent home from school. His teachers suggested that he was in need of some counseling. After shaving his head, making him sleep outside, forbidding any of us to establish eye contact with him, spanking him 50–75–100 times with a stick, our father finally called our local mental health department. When our mother learned of the appointment, she canceled it, because she knew the head of the department. This blindness to alternatives led our parents to revert to their earlier position that there was nothing wrong with my brother "that a good thrashing couldn't take care of." He continued to be sent home from school. While I am not intending to level ultimate blame, it is clear that ignorance of our home situation led the school personnel to set my brother up for increased violence.

Finally, my brother was again sent home from school, and this time when he arrived home he shot his head off with a rifle. He was eleven years old. There was no question about his death being suicide; he left a note and the trigger was rigged. The coroner, our pediatrician, our police chief and a police officer all saw his body and yet chose to "leave the family alone." I found his body; it was a powerful sight. I emphasize this to point out the incredible level of denial that was used to ignore the desperation and futility inherent in my brother's act.

I think there were several influences operating to support such denial. We were an upper-class family and money buys privacy. We are all familiar, no doubt, with the term "suspect" categories. I believe that there are also unconscious "exempt" categories; I believe that the misconception that "things like that don't happen in 'nice' families" (both our abuse and my brother's suicide) worked against us.

Living in a small town, as we did, sets up an "isolation of familiarity" that is just as futile as the isolation found in big cities. There wasn't anyone our parents didn't know and that they felt they could afford to "lose face with."

My brother and I had talked about turning our father in for child abuse, but we thought that abused children were children whose parents didn't love them. If we were abused children, that meant our parents didn't love us, which meant that we were unlovable. We weren't ready to admit that. Also, who could we tell? The police chief, our pediatrician, and teachers were all friends or acquaintances of our parents. We were aware of their refusal to become involved. I have often heard people say that any child who doesn't get what he/she wants thinks he/she is an abused child. If we told someone, we were sure that they wouldn't believe us. We were convinced that we would be killed by our father if a single word was spoken. Our father's omnipotence (in our eyes) made it seem that nothing could change things, anyway.

Finally, we had denied our abuse to ourselves as well as to others. We always rationalized our situation by saying: "He's having a bad day," or "We were too loud anyway," etc. We never saw it as a life-long pattern, but treated each incident as an isolated one. We forever hoped that if we could just be careful enough, remember all of the old rules, and anticipate all of the new ones, that we could make the violence stop.

Most of us didn't have many friends; we were too well-behaved to be much fun to play with. It's hard to be close to people when you're hiding such a big part of your life. Also, as I mentioned earlier, we were our parents' chief sources of companionship and affection, so we spent very little time with other people.

No one ever told us to lie about our injuries, though there was some intimation about not "airing dirty laundry in public." Somehow, we always lied about our stitches and bruises. There was a sense of shame connected with admitting that we were being hurt at home, because it implied our own guilt and intimated that we were unlovable. There was also a sense of duty in protecting our father (again, the role-reversal in operation).

Following my brother's suicide our father took his pain and frustration out on our mother more than on us, but essentially nothing changed. In fact, the guilt and added pressure raised the tension at home. For me, the guilt stemmed from the detachment I needed to maintain in order to helplessly watch his daily abuse. I wasn't his friend or his ally—just another silent witness.

My brother's suicide reinforced my sense of isolation and insecurity. I had spent thirteen years preoccupied with our father's mood changes, to the exclusion of all else. When my brother killed himself, I felt that life was truly unmanageable and unpredictable. The many professionals involved failed to intervene or to recognize the tragic statement that my brother was trying to make. Their lack of involvement seemed to condone all that we had experienced, as well as to reinforce our sense of helplessness.

Two years later I told a high school teacher that I had tried to kill myself. At the time it was a purely impulsive action, but retrospectively I realize that I had to imply the possibility of an act equally as drastic as my brother's suicide to insure that some intervention was instituted. My teacher referred me to the school psychiatrist, who had me psychologically tested. The tests showed that I was very angry, unhappy, had minimal self-esteem, and was afraid of violence. These findings, combined with her assumption that a child my brother's age could not kill himself unless he was acting out the suicidal impulse of a parent, led her to contact our parents.

She told our parents that I would kill myself if I wasn't hospitalized, and that I would make fifty percent slower progress if they weren't in therapy, too. I became the pivotal contact with our family as the identified patient. Strategically this was an understandable move on the psychiatrist's part. Our parents were over a barrel, as they had refused therapy for my brother. Had they consented to therapy perhaps his suicide could have been averted. But I question whether it was really necessary to lock me up in an acute care child-adolescent psychiatric ward.

INSTITUTIONAL ABUSE

"Children's talent to endure stems
from their ignorance of alternatives." [2]

When I was admitted to the psychiatric unit with a diagnosis of "adjustment reaction to adolescence," the psychiatrist withdrew from the case explaining that her caseload was too full, and stating that she felt I would benefit more if I dealt with a male therapist. She saw each of my parents once a week for individual therapy and every other week for marital counseling. There was no mention of family therapy. No treatment was offered to my brothers, and there was no expressed concern for the effect my hospitalization or parents' therapy might have on my brothers at home.

After two months of hospitalization, I was following the ward routine and posing no problems for the staff. My therapist told me that I wasn't working on my problems of depression and low self-esteem. Having had no prior experience with therapy, I didn't know what "working on my problems" meant. Knowing that I would be going home when I was discharged did not encourage me to be

[2]M. Angelou, *I Know Why the Caged Bird Sings* (New York: Random House, 1970).

the spontaneous, assertive, outgoing person that they envisioned as the "new me." Even if I had grasped the principles of therapy, I knew what I was going home to.

So I was put on an "harassment" or so-called Rage Reduction Program, which was actually a Rage Induction Program. The rationale for the program was that depression is anger turned inward and that soon I would rebel against my harassment. Once angry, I would no longer be depressed and could be returned home with no threat of suicide. From 7:00 A.M. until 11:00 P.M. every day, I was on my hands and knees, scrubbing the outline of a linoleum square in a counterclockwise motion. I couldn't change hands or sit back on my calves unless I was willing to suffer the consequences, such as missing a meal, staying up an extra hour, sitting under a ledge which was 2½ feet off the ground, or scrubbing behind my head with a toothbrush. Another punishment used was called going into "sheets," which is a procedure in which male staff members wrap the patient from neck to ankles in layers of sheets and then tie the patient to his/her bed. The result is absolute restriction of movement. If I went into "sheets" on this program, the minimum stay was four hours. I went into "sheets" approximately sixty times. I ate alone, facing the wall, kneeling up at a tray that was on a chair. Frequently, my assigned staff would give me an impossible time limit, allowing me to eat only with my left hand or with both hands behind my back. If I refused to eat under these conditions, I was threatened with tube feeding while in "sheets."

I had a conference with my parents, assigned staff, and therapist once a week. I also had two half-hour individual sessions with my assigned staff each day, and three sessions with my therapist each week. However, I had to continue scrubbing the floor, remain in "sheets," or perform some other bizarre task during these interactions. I wasn't allowed to interact with anyone but these people, but was harassed by any staff member who felt so inclined.

That was my life for the first month of the program. As inconceivable as it seems to me now, after the first month I felt bored by the program, but didn't really mind what they did to me. It just served to reinforce established patterns from my home situation. Having experienced such ritualistic abuse since early childhood, I had long since buried any impulse to react against it.

My parents allied themselves with my therapist and the staff and harassed me during our conferences instead of concentrating on vital family counseling. Because I failed to respond to this milder form of harassment, the staff pushed me harder. I was assigned to two male staff members with this routine: I had fifteen minutes to get up, get dressed, put my bed and linen away, go to the bathroom, and be back at the wall. This all required that I literally not be out of arm's length of a staff member. Staff would frequently refuse to help me and if I was late I'd be put in "sheets" until I could explain why I was late. Often I was made to polish my assigned staff member's tennis shoes with a dry cloth.

At this point I was made to stand up and face a door that was in full view of all ward residents, staff, or visitors and scrub three raised wooden numbers, clockwise with a dry rag in one hand and counterclockwise with a toothbrush in the other hand, simultaneously. These numbers were about three inches higher than I could reach comfortably, but I went into "sheets" or was given some other task if I raised my heels off the ground. I had to convince my assigned staff that I was hungry, had to go to the bathroom, or wanted to go to bed or these "privileges" were uncomfortably extended. Convincing the staff usually meant yelling and swearing in a sufficiently outraged tone of voice, but the staff harassed me for disturbing the unit if I did. I had to face straight forward at all times, but the staff would often squirt me in the ear with a water gun, clap their hands, or pop paper bags next to my ears. If I turned my head, or was accused of doing so, I went into "sheets."

Someone suggested that I keep time for the unit, so while scrubbing the numbers I was made to say, "At the sound of the tone the time will be ten fifty-two and ten seconds . . . Beep," for sixteen hours a day. A staff member would call, "Time," and if I was more than a minute off, I went into "sheets." I dreamed and talked the time for three weeks. If I refused to do this or any other task, I was put in "sheets" for a four-hour time minimum, until I agreed to resume the task. This was because quitting a task was considered to be "symbolic suicide." While in "sheets" staff frequently ratted my hair, rubbed food in my face and hair, and tickled my restrained feet. I'd eventually get fed up with the cramped, hot sheets and the staffs' harassment of me and agree to resume the task. When I got out of "sheets," I had to make up another "sheet bed." My assigned staff member would tear it up and demand that I make up another one, which he would then tear up. This would go on for nearly an hour.

Once a staff member brought in a book about the life of Teddy Roosevelt. Each day I was given several facts to memorize, complete with punctuation. They were only stated once, but on command I was expected to recite all the facts I had memorized. If I made any errors or refused to cooperate, I was put in "sheets." This intense treatment resulted in acute tachycardia and high blood pressure. However, I remained on the program. At this time, my chief harasser confided that until I began manifesting these psychosomatic symptoms, he couldn't understand why I was in the hospital!

As incredible as it may seem, most of the staff members who worked with me liked me very much. I like many of them. They have since shared their guilt and self-recrimination with me and are retrospectively bewildered that they could have participated in such a program. They have further confided that they saw no justification for either my hospitalization or my treatment program and could not have recognized signs of "improvement" in me because they didn't really understand the purpose of the program. Yet, these people all participated fully in my degradation and harassment. To me, this illustrates the incredibly destructive things that compassionate people can be led to do when they feel relieved of responsibility for their actions (as was graphically illustrated by Stanford University's "Zimbardo" experiment and Princeton University's "Millgram" experiment).

The functioning of the unit was based on a rigid hierarchy, with a staff that neither approved of nor understood what their purpose in my treatment was.

They participated because the ultimate responsibility for my treatment plan lay with my private therapist.

My parents are both intellectual, educated people who demanded a well-rationalized, clearly visible treatment program. They didn't question this program as they feared that they might be looked down upon or considered ignorant by the professionals involved.

During the third month things really tightened up. I learned to cry, which the staff viewed as manipulative behavior, so they increased my tasks. I was trying to do what the staff wanted me to do. I didn't want to learn that yelling and swearing would be rewarded; such behavior would have gotten me expelled from school and beaten at home.

The two staff members then started to work together. One told me to scrub the numbers on the door, the other told me to scrub the linoleum square on my hands and knees. I switched back and forth between the two tasks until one staff member put me in "sheets" for not doing as he had requested. I stayed in "sheets" for four hours. The other staff member then put me back in "sheets" for being in "sheets" rather than doing what he had requested. This went on for several days. Finally, I refused to deal with either of them and was left in "sheets" while one staff member took two days off. When he came back, I was more than eager to comply with any request.

Somewhere along the line I developed insomnia and was given strong medication that drugged me until noon. I still had to perform my tasks and remember Teddy Roosevelt facts. When I tried to protest, I was threatened with a forced injection, as this refusal was viewed as self-destructive behavior.

During these previous two weeks my ward doctor and one of my assigned staff members left. This was a problem, as their replacements had viewed the tactics, but missed the alleged purpose of the program. My continued lack of responsiveness led the staff to more desperate measures. I was made to scrub the top right hinge of a door clockwise with a dry cloth and a corresponding spot on the left hand side of the door counterclockwise with a toothbrush simultaneously. Both were just out of my reach in height. After fifteen minutes of this, I was in real pain but couldn't seem to convince the staff of this. I stayed in this position for two days. If I quit, the two staff would physically force me to continue. I always associate this memory with a crucifixion.

I felt that the staff were trying to break me rather than following the original purpose of the program. I recognized that the staff were frustrated and that my apathy was going to get me hurt. My parents were harassing me about money; our insurance was running out; further hospitalization would cost them $150 a day. I asked what it was I had to do to get off the program. I was told that I had to convince my assigned staff and therapist that I resented the treatment that I had received. I also was to develop an alternate program for myself that would demonstrate my awareness of my problems.

I never really believed that I shouldn't have been treated that way. It was uncomfortable, at times painful, and boring, but my orientation toward authority figures, particularly males, along with my apathy and lack of self-esteem, supported the program. It was confusing to me. I believed that I was basically worthless. (My family and hospitalization further reinforced my opinion of myself.) But, if pretending that I was otherwise would get me off the program, I was willing to try.

I had to earn the time to work on my alternate program while on the Harassment Program. I had a lot of information with which to develop an alternate program. Staff members' indirect suggestions and an invaluable list of my strengths and weaknesses given to me the *fifth* day of my hospitalization gave me the guidelines. I developed a "Scheduled-Involvement" Program and began mentally rehearsing my speech of "rage." After two weeks I managed to convince my assigned staff members that I was "truly too worthwhile a person to be treated so inhumanly." It took an additional three weeks to convince my therapist. It I raised my voice or swore at him, he'd dismiss me, telling me that when I could be "appropriate," we'd discuss it again. Already the behavior that I had been rewarded for on the program was creating conflicts.

Finally, after four months, I switched to my "Scheduled-Involvement" Program and was allowed to go outside into a fenced play area for the first time in seven months. After ten days on my new program my insurance ran out and I was discharged and sent home with no transition period and a new diagnosis of "acute undifferentiated schizophrenia." I started my junior year in high school two days late, feeling totally alone, depressed, and somewhat in culture shock.

It is incomprehensible that the realities of my home situation were totally ignored in the affixing of my diagnoses, as well as in the formulation and implementation of my treatment program. My brothers recount that the pressures caused by my hospitalization and parents' therapy resulted in an intolerable increase in violence at home.

It seems pathetically ironic that I came from a highly abusive, confusing home situation and was placed on a program managed by highly abusive, confusing caretakers. This had a destructive effect on my future perceptions of authority figures, as well as my self-esteem. The psychiatrist and hospital staff were, in fact, setting up a very futile and destructive double bind by putting me on a program that required me to give up defenses that were vital to my survival at home. My perception of reality was further confused by the pressure put on me to establish warm and trusting relationships with my tormentors, and the labeling of my failure to do so as a "character deficiency." Again, my failure to be open and confrontive with my father was viewed to be symptomatic of my "adjustment reaction to adolescence."

As I acknowledged earlier, I was very controlled and apathetic; I *did* need therapy. But I grew out of those defenses when it was safe to do so. I can see the logic of the psychiatrist labeling me as the patient in order to force my parents into treatment. However, the course of my treatment exacerbated the violence for my brothers at home, condoned our parents' past mistreatment of us, reinforced their denial, and augmented my futile view of the world in general. My hospital caretakers are not malicious people, as my parents are not. While there were some sadists and self-serving opportunists on staff, most were reasonable, honorable people. No one was willing or able to analyze my behavior in relation to the oppressiveness of my family life. They were able to espouse the naive theories of depression used to justify my treatment only because they carefully avoided looking at what was really going on.

My parents remained in therapy for about a year. With the support my father got from his therapy, he was able to control almost all of his abusive impulses. As my mother is a very private person, she greatly resented therapy's requirement for self-disclosure. She kept her appointments, but was determined not to change. She viewed my father and me as the ones with problems. I finished my junior year in high school and then applied for early admission to college away from home. I am presently a 23-year-old doctoral candidate working in a city near my home; two of my brothers are in graduate school; the third is in college. My brothers are all gentle, compassionate men. Like myself, they have each had to find their own role models from which to learn about healthy male-female relationships. They all struggle with feelings of inadequacy and have some difficulty with intimacy. Like myself, they have had to learn healthy responses to aggression in themselves and others; we have all learned that it's okay to be happy.

Our parents are living alone now; I have never known them to get along so well together. My guess is that not having to compete with five children for each other's attention has made the difference. We deal more formally with our parents than most offspring, but despite the usual value clashes found in any family, we get along well. Our relationships with our parents are based on our independent, adult status. There is no evident shadow of our years of abuse as children. We've been through a lot, and they've been through a lot. We deal with each other as we are now, with unspoken respect for each other's private struggles.

That isn't to say that all is forgiven. I spoke with my older brother about this once, and he expressed his feelings, which reflect my own. He said, "I care for them very much, but even though it doesn't interfere with our day-to-day interactions, I know that deep down, I can never forgive them for what they did to us."

I am a very intense, intuitive woman. I am somewhat untrusting and my tolerance for intimacy is low. Through observation and experimentation I am learning that anger and aggression are not synonymous with violence, though I am still hypersensitive when witnessing anything more than mild discord. While to others I project an air of self-reliance, the truth is that I carry a very hurt child within me. It is too late for me to have the accepting, loving "parents" I privately searched for for years. At times, that same need is translated into an impulse to have a child of my own. I fantasize that a baby would give me the unconditional love that I never got. However, I recognize this as the same destructive expectation my parents held.

I have given therapy another try. It's hard to go through all of that old pain again, but I would like to have a child some day, and I see enough of my parents in me to believe in the multi-generational effects of child abuse. I am a surprisingly hopeful person and while at times I feel angry and futile in my struggles to repair the damage, I have strengths which grew from the broken places; I believe that in time I will learn how to love and to be loved.

CHAPTER 4

Corporal Punishment in the Schools: America's Officially Sanctioned Brand of Child Abuse

Irwin A. Hyman

On April 19, 1977, the United States Supreme Court in a 5 to 4 decision decided that school children are not protected under the Eighth Amendment to the Constitution, which forbids the use of cruel and unusual punishment (Ingraham v. Wright 1977). This case began when James Ingraham and Roosevelt Andrews, students in Charles R. Drew Junior High School, Dade County, Florida, filed a complaint in the United States Supreme Court for the Southern District of Florida. While Ingraham and Andrews filed for damages for personal injuries resulting from paddling incidents, they also filed a class suit to stop the use of corporal punishment in the Dade County School System.

The incident that resulted in this suit occurred on October 6, 1970. A number of students, including fourteen-year-old James Ingraham, were slow to leave the stage of the school auditorium at Drew. When asked to move faster by the teacher, they apparently did not move fast enough and they were taken to Mr. Wright, the principal of Drew. When confronted, Ingraham claimed that he had left the stage when requested and refused to allow Mr. Wright to paddle him. Wright refused to accept Ingraham's statements of innocence and requested the help of Lemmie Deliford, the assistant principal, and Solomon Barnes, his administrative assistant. Barnes held Ingraham's legs and Deliford held his arms while Wright spanked him on the buttocks with a two-foot long wooden paddle. Ingraham received twenty strokes of the paddle and then was told by Wright to wait outside the office or Wright would "bust him on the side of [his] head."

Despite Wright's order, Ingraham went directly home. After examining the black and purple buttocks, his mother took him to the local hospital, where the physician diagnosed the injury as a hematoma. The doctor prescribed pills to relieve the pain, a laxative, sleeping pills, and ice packs and advised him to stay home for at least a week. Ingraham, as a result, was out of school for eleven days

Edited version of a paper presented at the Second Annual National Conference on Child Abuse and Neglect, Houston, Texas, April 18, 1977. Parts of this paper were written under funding by the National Institute of Education Contract NIE-P-77-0079.

33

and he claimed that he could not sit comfortably for approximately three weeks. Many other cases of officially sanctioned child abuse had occurred in Drew High School during previous years; as a result the class action suit was filed. Obviously, what has occurred in schools under the rubric of the "proper maintenance of discipline" would be legally defined as child abuse if it had occurred in the home.

While the Supreme Court did not approve of the extent of force used on Ingraham, it is also evident that they felt that the Constitution does not protect children from this type of abuse. The majority expressed the opinion that, since schools are open institutions and teachers are bound by rules of reasonable conduct, parents could sue under criminal law for assault in the types of cases described. Clearly, the Supreme Court decision supports and in many ways encourages the daily practice by teachers and administrators of hitting, paddling, pinching, punching, strapping, shoving, throwing, kicking, and verbally abusing children in the schools throughout the "land of the free and the home of the brave." The documentation for this practice is maintained at the National Center for the Study of Corporal Punishment and Alternatives in the Schools at Temple University. At the Center, a press clipping service provides the material for constant updating of a case book that classifies the various types of excessive use of corporal punishment at school. Since information is received only on cases that either go to court or are reported in the press because of formal parent complaints, reported cases represent the tip of the iceberg.

By not allowing constitutional protection for school children against the use of corporal punishment, the Supreme Court has indirectly endorsed the legitimization of the use of physical force in the changing of behavior, thus further reinforcing a Judeo-Christian ethic of "spare the rod and spoil the child." The history of the use of force on children reveals a long tradition of excessive beatings of children in order to improve behavior and exorcise the evil in them. The majority of the Supreme Court was extremely short-sighted in terms of the long-term implications of their decision. Their sanction of the use of physical force in the schools can only reinforce the already existing acceptance of this practice, which, in many cases, leads to frequent child abuse, which is documented. Children can be raised without the use of physical force; research indicates that once a person accepts the use of positive and humane approaches, superior learning takes place (Hyman, McDowell and Raines 1978).

In Western culture, children have historically been granted few, if any, rights (Williams 1976). In societies where violence and lack of due process are common, the family mirrors the cultural milieu in relation to the use of force. A recent theoretical paper by Babcock (1977), a member of the staff of the Center, suggests that there is some basis for predicting family use of physical force for discipline as a function of various facets of the culture. Babcock, in reviewing cross-cultural studies, found a correlation of characteristics of culture where corporal punishment could easily exist and those where corporal punishment would be incongruent with other characteristics. The major potential predictors for family use of corporal punishment and consequent child abuse were (1) belief in aggressive gods, (2) the infliction of pain on infants by the primary caretaker, (3) the generation of high anxiety in socializing children, (4) low indulgence of children and (5) increasing complexity of cultural traits. It is not the purpose of this chapter to present a detailed analysis, but it is important to recognize that America is not the child-loving nation that it is claimed to be. It was not until 1900 that American law even recognized that anyone within the family other than the father and husband had any rights at all (Drinan 1973). American attitudes toward children are reflected in the fact that nine years *after* the founding of the Society For the Prevention of Cruelty to Animals, a group in New York organized the first Society for Prevention of Cruelty to Children. One is led to the almost indisputable conclusion that the majority of Americans really do not like children (Keniston 1975). This conclusion is not new, but it is almost always rejected when presented to the average citizen.

The evidence adds up to one of two conclusions; at the least, we are a society that does not understand the difference between what we believe we do for our children and what we actually do for them. At worst, we know that large numbers of children, some in the shadow of our nation's capital, are deprived of basic human rights; but we do not care as long as we can assure the health and safety of our own. This is not to condemn our society, for the dilemma is really a matter of cognitive dissonance that has never been resolved. After all, we are surely a nation of optimists who believe in our own good will. And, in truth, we periodically evidence that good will through generosity toward an unequaled system of private charities, international relief, and the acceptance of a continuing stream of immigrants and political refugees from the dictatorships and highly controlled countries that now make up much of the world. Despite the continued corruption of our politicians, the avarice of big business and the apparent never ending growth of bureaucracy, American democracy still muddles on and cleanses itself periodically.

There is a paradox, however, in our view of ourselves and in others' view of us. As a society, we are often criticized from within and without as being overly child oriented and permissive. Yet, in this same society, child abuse accounts for more childhood deaths than any disease (Hyman and Schreiber 1975), and we permit American educators to use often barbaric methods of discipline. Infant mortality is quite high when compared with other Western democracies, and when we consider infant mortality among minority groups alone, it is shockingly high (Coles 1975). Perhaps one of the best historical anecdotes illustrating our treatment as viewed by others was related in the *Wall Street Journal* (Chase 1975). It seems that a great Nez Perce Indian chief was on a peace mission to a white general. He rode through a white man's encampment when he happened to observe a soldier hitting a child. The chief reined in his horse and said to his companion: ''There is no point in talking peace with barbarians. What could you say to a man that would strike a child?'' The chief's diagnosis of our society in the 1800s, if only peripherally based on his observations of an accepted practice toward children, was unfortunately and amazingly accurate especially considering the eventual fate of his tribe and that of others. But then our twentieth-century society has a long series of "broken treaties" with its children.

It is surprising that the public school is the last remaining institution where a citizen may be assaulted by authorities. The police, the military, and prison officials are not allowed to use physical force as a method of punishment. The legal restraints on the use of physical force carry two messages. First, and most obvious, is that our society will no longer tolerate the use of barbaric methods by officials. These are considered unconstitutional because they rob the recipients of benefits proscribed by the Constitution. However, the second and more subtle message is that our civilization has rejected the use of these methods for changing the behavior of the recipients.

The Supreme Court, in refusing constitutional protection of school children from the use of physical force, reinforces a traditional concept that physical force is an acceptable way to change the behavior of children. Once this premise is accepted there is little doubt that the society therefore accepts that use by parents with their own children. The next and unfortunate logical step for the procorporal punishment parent is that, since society accepts the use of force for change in behavior, then there must be some gradient. The gradient is translated into the fact that many people believe that the more severe the punishment, the more effective it will be. Another translation is that the more extreme the misdemeanor by the child, the more extreme must be the penalty.

Finally, woven into the fabric of the thinking of the advocate of corporal punishment, reinforced by the Supreme Court's decision, is the fact that no one yet has ever been able to legislate tempers. As a result, acceptance of the use of physical force, which supposedly will be reasonable, is the first step in releasing the anger, frustration, and hostility of parents, so that when they do lose their temper, they have only gone "a little too far" in a behavior that is sanctioned by American society. Until Americans accept the premise that physical force is ineffective, barbaric, and counterproductive, we will continue to believe that only a few disturbed and sick individuals carry the use of corporal punishment to the extent where it becomes child abuse.

The relationship between corporal punishment and child abuse is illustrated by the press clippings of cases of corporal punishment in schools throughout the country. Very often when children are clearly abused by teachers or administrators and a legal suit ensues, the community is more supportive of the abuser than of the child or parent. In a Missouri case, administrators gave several boys a choice between eating cigarettes or being paddled. Two of the children ate the cigarettes and were hospitalized. After the parents sued the school board, members of the community harassed the parents. One school board member who delivered water in the community refused to deliver water to the parents. On a number of occasions community members buzzed by the home of the parents making a great deal of noise with motorcycles, trucks, etc. (Hyman, McDowell, and Raines 1977).

Incongruencies involved in attitudes and practices that have resulted in a codified pattern of institutional violence in our society are enmeshed in a confusion of causes. It is important, therefore, to approach the problem by separating the main etiological and conceptual frameworks within which the practice of corporal punishment is intertwined. The following discussion considers corporal punishment from the three approaches related to legal, moral, and scientific issues.

LEGAL ISSUES

The general definition of corporal punishment stems from a legal frame and indicates it to be the infliction of pain or loss or the confinement of the human body as a penalty for some offense (Barnhart 1963). *Black's Law Dictionary* (1968) defines corporal punishment as "physical punishment as distinguished from pecuniary punishment or a fine; any kind of punishment of or inflicted on the body, such as whipping or the pillory. The term may or may not include imprisonment according to the individual case." Educationally, corporal punishment has been generally defined as, "the infliction of pain by a teacher or other educational official upon the body of a student as a penalty for doing something which has been disapproved of by the punisher" (Wineman and James 1967).

Corporal punishment in the schools is not implied when (1) the teacher uses force to protect himself or herself, the pupil, or others from physical injury; (2) to obtain possession of a weapon or other dangerous object; or (3) to protect property from damage.

There are two main areas in which the constitutionality of corporal punishment is argued (Reitman, Follmann, and Ladd 1972). One focus, that corporal punishment is cruel and unusual, is based on the Eighth Amendment to the Constitution. This rests on a number of grounds, most importantly the concept that the application of physical punishment to children violates democratic freedom and the dignity of the individual. The other argument, based on the Fifth and Fourteenth Amendments to the Constitution, is that corporal punishment violates due process of law. This is divided between substantive due process and procedural due process. Under the substantive issue, it is argued that corporal punishment is often conducted in an arbitrary and capricious manner and does not bear a reasonable relationship to a societal purpose. Under the procedural issue, it is argued that before being punished, one is entitled to certain procedural safeguards, such as a notice of charge, right to a fair hearing, etc. (Friedman and Hyman 1977).

Currently, forty-six states allow or specifically endorse the use of corporal punishment through state legislation as a means of disciplining children in public schools (Friedman and Hyman 1977). Some states, such as Hawaii, currently are reviewing their statutes and have imposed temporary bans on the use of physical punishment. Maine has a new statute, but its meaning is unclear. In contrast with the United States, other countries have abolished corporal punishment in schools.

These include Luxembourg, Holland, Austria, France, Finland, Sweden, Denmark, Belgium, Cyprus, Japan, Ecuador, Iceland, Italy, Jordan, Qatar, Mauritius, Norway, Israel, The Philippines, Portugal, and all communist block countries (Reitman, Follmann, and Ladd 1972; Bacon and Hyman 1976).

MORAL ISSUES

Puritan and Calvinist traditions of American society and the early medical realities of infant and childhood mortality resulted in the attitudes that are abhorrent to modern thinking concerning children. Estimates of mortality suggest that occurrences of measles, typhoid, small pox, diphtheria, dysentery, and respiratory ailments resulted in one-third of all infants dying each year (Coles 1975). For most of those who did survive, childhood certainly had its pleasures, but pleasure was generally considered by religious society as evil. Even if one did not subscribe to the Calvinistic belief that "children were imps of darkness," the historical precedent for maltreatment of children goes back even to the schools of Sumer 5,000 years ago (Radbill 1974). The most severe practice of corporal punishment leads to murder, and the concept of state supported infanticide or murdering children is not new. As late as the sixteenth century, the belief in inherent evil in children was so strong that Martin Luther, assuming that they must be inhabited by the devil, indicated that retarded children should be drowned (Radbill 1974).

In America, the practice of corporal punishment has been overt and publicly sanctioned from colonial days. The "spare the rod and spoil the child" philosophy of that colonial era was reflected in the schooling of the times. Manning (1959) reports that a schoolhouse, constructed in 1793 in Sunderland, Massachusetts, had an ominous whipping post built into the floor. Erring young students were securely tied to the post and whipped by the schoolmaster in the presence of their classmates. Manning (1959) also reports, in a similar vein, on "paddling" devices being prominent implements of the classroom in the 1800s. Paddling rods, canes, and sticks were placed conspicuously in the classroom, easily accessible to the teacher.

The issue of moral lessons taught by paddling in schools is currently illustrated in the state of Maine. The Maine legislature enacted a law forbidding the use of corporal punishment in all schools. Shortly after passage, a number of groups of educators began lobbying for the return of corporal punishment. Especially vociferous have been teachers, parents, and students from Maine Christian Schools (Connally 1977). Ralph I. Yarnell, executive director of the Northeastern Regional American Association of Christian Schools, claimed that spankings, paddlings, and whippings teach students "obedience, thrift and other virtues." An elementary school principal from Bangor Christian School stated that paddling does "wonders for helping a student mature."

Bongiovanni (1977), a member of the staff at the National Center for the Study of Corporal Punishment and Alternatives in the Schools, completed an extensive and exhaustive review of the research on punishment during the last ten years. His findings were as follows:

> The use of corporal punishment by school personnel provides the child with a real-life model of aggressive behavior which has been demonstrated to be imitated by young children (Bandura 1962; Bandura, Ross, and Ross 1961; 1963). Not only do children imitate such aggressive behavior, but, they also tend to employ these aggressive behaviors when faced with frustration in their own lives. In a study in which children observed a model being punished, a learned fear reaction was demonstrated to have occurred, although they were not recipients of any punishment (Berger 1962). The implication for school personnel is that the use of corporal punishment may provide a living model of aggression which may be imitated by the classroom children. Such a model may provide a problem-solving method which can be utilized by the child in various settings. In addition, by visibly punishing a child in the presence of others, the other children may become fearful and anxious. Such conditions are not conducive to socialization or learning.
>
> The available research on punishment, when applied to schools, suggests that it is ineffective in producing durable behavior change, is potentially harmful to students and personnel, and, is highly impractical in the light of the controls necessary for maximal effectiveness. The maximal effectiveness of corporal punishment can only be achieved by close adherence to the basic principles and factors which have been shown to influence its ultimate effectiveness as a behavior-reducing method. In light of the role of school personnel in education, and the welfare for the student, corporal punishment appears to be impractical, time consuming, and contrary to the goals of education.
>
> The potential for social disruption constitutes the primary disadvantage of punishment. In light of these negative side effects, the possible reduction of undesirable behavior should clearly be secondary in importance. The need for discipline and adherence to rules is a necessary part of education. However, there are many alternatives to corporal punishment which may be utilized by school personnel.
>
> Those who defend the use of corporal punishment as a practical method, tend to view the practicality issue from the prospective of school personnel only. As a method, it can be applied to anyone, there is no need for any type of specialized training, it can be applied to all settings, and no special equipment except a paddle is necessary. The fact that most school personnel are physically stronger than the children makes corporal punishment especially attractive. In defense of corporal punishment, Killory (1973) cites four criteria of punishment to be considered: First, it should result in the greatest behavior change; second, it should demand the least effort on the part of the user; third, it should result in behavior that is relatively permanent; and fourth, it should produce minimal side effects. This writer contends that none of these criteria, by the research evidence available, supports the use of corporal punishment in the schools as a method for obtaining durable behavior change (p. 10).

Not only is punishment an ineffective and inefficient method of teaching, in more severe forms it decreases learning.

An extensive review of Rosenshine and Furst (1971) considered seventeen studies that were based on counts of teacher use of criticism. Criticism in all studies was generally defined as negative statements, demeaning students or their actions, and/or the use of threats. Almost all of the studies reviewed indicated a negative relationship between teacher criticism and student achievement. In ten of the seventeen studies, stronger rather than milder forms of criticism were clearly negatively correlated with achievement. Rosenshine and Furst (1971) conclude that "teachers who use extreme amounts and forms of criticism usually have classes that achieve less in most subject areas" (p. 51). Although all of the studies cited are correlational, there is certainly enough evidence against the use of severe criticism and threats.

Research indicates that the use of corporal punishment is much more extensive than many believe (Hyman, McDowell, and Raines 1977). During the 1971–72 school year, the Dallas Public Schools reported an average of 2,000 incidents of physical punishment per month (*Nation's Schools* 1972). In the Houston public schools, Dr. J. Boney, an administrator, reported that during a two-month period in 1972, 8,279 paddlings were administered (Elardo 1977). With a student population of about 200,000 children this averages about four incidents of teacher violence against children per child per year.

Finally, there is some evidence that increasing use of corporal punishment tends to increase the rate of school vandalism. Lee Hardy and Virginia Miller (Hyman et al. 1977) made a study of twelve schools on the outskirts of Portland, Oregon, and found that rates of the use of corporal punishment appeared to be correlated with increases in the cost per pupil of vandalism against school property. Although the study is limited, it certainly suggests a fruitful area for further investigation.

IS CORPORAL PUNISHMENT A FORM OF CHILD ABUSE?

This chapter summarizes some of the literature collected by the staff at the National Center for the Study of Corporal Punishment and Alternatives in the Schools, which suggests that the practice of corporal punishment is a particularly insidious form of child abuse that few take seriously. It is hoped, however, that child-abuse workers will realize the importance of this issue. It is difficult to measure to what extent family attitudes support or cause the use of corporal punishment in the schools and to what extent the official practice encourages the use of force in the home; the two practices are certainly closely woven into the fabric of our society.

There is some evidence that home-school practices of child rearing go hand in hand. An intercultural study of aggression by Bellack and Antell (1974) considered the playground behavior of children in Germany, Italy, and Denmark. Observers recorded aggressive behavior by adults and children. The results indicated a correlation between adult and child aggression that also reflected cultural beliefs about child rearing. The greater aggressiveness in German institutions and child rearing results in greater peer aggressiveness. The belief in force as a method of discipline in Germany was reflected in a poll that showed that 60 percent of parent respondents believed not only in spanking but in actually beating their children (Bellack and Antell 1974). Whereas Germans practice corporal punishment in the schools, the Danes and Italians do not. Their rate of interchild aggression on the playground was much less than that of Germans. While the study is limited, it reflects the belief by some scientists that part of man's inhumanity to man is his revenge for the indignities suffered in childhood and that children do model aggressive behavior as a manner in which to solve problems.

Several American studies indicate that a large percentage of parents and educators favor the use of corporal punishment in the schools either as a regular method of discipline or as a last resort (Hyman et al. 1977). In fact, everyone seems to strongly favor corporal punishment except those who receive it. And among those who receive it, perhaps the best explanation is given in another study by Elardo (1977), who interviewed elementary school children. Most said that some would prefer paddling to other forms of punishment in order to "get it over with." They also felt it did no good in changing behavior. One articulate child said: "Sometimes you get accused falsely of doing something. If you get paddled and later prove you did not do it, you can't get unpaddled. But if you lose an activity, maybe by the time the activity should occur you can prove your innocence and still get your activity" (Elardo 1977, p. 18).

It is clear that the legal use of corporal punishment in the schools has led to actual physical acts that are abusive to school children. How can we expect parents not to use violence against children when we officially sanction its use in education? Although we have not measured the extent to which school corporal punishment encourages its use at home, it is reasonably clear from the evidence presented that there is a relationship.

In summary, there is little doubt that corporal punishment is as American as apple pie, motherhood, and the flag. It is a cherished tradition, most often defended on the grounds of religious belief and the need to maintain order. It has only been eliminated when citizens, legislatures, and judges have examined the data. The majority of Americans still support the belief that corporal punishment is helpful when applied with "love and moderation." Child abuse in the home and its officially sanctioned counterpart in school have reached proportions that call for a public reexamination of our traditional beliefs about child rearing and education. However, as long as the public schools in this country, especially those in the south and southwest, staunchly defend the use of corporal punishment, there will be no change in the public attitude sufficient to turn the tide. The evidence suggests that degrees of "moderation" in the infliction of pain on school children vary according to the feelings of too many people. We cannot legislate subjectively determined moderation or permit the law to sanction a practice that depends so much on individual tempers. Inasmuch as the Supreme Court has closed a major route for the elimination of the public practice of hitting, other more creative approaches to the prevention of the use of physical force on children must be found. As long as the public endorses hitting children, it is unlikely that parents will give up this centuries old, destructive practice. Consequently, child abuse will continue in a society that officially recognizes the use of physical force to control the behavior of children.

REFERENCES

Babcock, A. "A Cross Cultural Examination of Corporal Punishment." Paper presented at the Conference on Child Abuse; Children's Hospital National Medical Center, Washington, D.C., February 19, 1977.

Bacon, G., and Hyman, I. Brief of the American Psychological Association Task Force on the Rights of Children and Youth as amicus curiae in support of petitioners, The Supreme Court of the United States, No. 75-6527, 1976.

Bandura, A. "Social Learning through Imitation." In M. R. Jones, ed., *Nebraska Symposium on Motivation*. Lincoln: University of Nebraska Press, 1962.

Bandura, A., Ross, D., and Ross, S. A. "Transmission of aggression through imitation of aggressive models." *Journal of Abnormal Social Psychology* 63(1961):575-82.

Bandura, A., Ross, D., and Ross, S. A. "Imitation of film-mediated aggressive models." *Journal of Abnormal Social Psychology,* 66(1963):3-11.

Barnhart, C. L. *American College Dictionary*. New York: Random House, 1963.

Bellak, L., and Antell, M. "An intercultural study of aggressive behavior on children's playgrounds." *American Journal of Orthopsychiatry* 44(1974):503-11.

Berger, S. M. "Conditioning through vicarious instigation." *Psychological Review* 69(1962):450-66.

Black, Henry C. *Black's Law Dictionary*. St. Paul, Minn.: West Publishing Co., 1968, 4th edition, p. 408.

Bongiovanni, A. "A Review of Research of the Effects of Punishment." Paper presented at Conference on Child Abuse, Children's Hospital National Medical Center, Washington, D.C., February 19, 1977.

Chase, N. F. "Corporal punishment in the schools." *Wall Street Journal,* November 11, 1975.

Coles, R. "Growing up in America—then and now." *Time,* December 29, 1975, pp. 27-29.

Connally, M. "Corporal punishment bill is heard." *Kenne Journal* (Augusta, Maine), March 16, 1977.

Drinan, R. F. "The Rights of Children in Modern American Family Law." In A. E. Wilkerson, ed., *The Rights of Children*. Philadelphia: Temple University Press, 1973.

Elardo, E. "Implementing Behavior Modification Procedures in an Elementary School: Problems and Issues." Paper presented at the annual meeting of the American Educational Research Association, New York City, April 1977.

Friedman, R., and Hyman, I. "An Analysis of State Legislation Regarding Corporal Punishment." Paper presented at the Conference on Child Abuse, Children's Hospital National Medical Center, Washington, D.C., February 20, 1977.

Hyman, I., McDowell, E., and Raines, B. "Corporal Punishment in the Schools: An Overview of Theoretical and Practical Issues." Paper presented at the Conference on Child Abuse, Children's Hospital National Medical Center, Washington, D.C., February 20, 1977 (partially supported by NIE Contract NIE-P-77-0079).

Hyman, I., and Schreiber, K. "Selected concepts and practices of child advocacy in school psychology." *Psychology in the Schools* 2(1975):50–58.

Ingraham v. Wright, 498 F. 2d 248 (5th Cir. 1977).

Keniston, K. "Do Americans really like children?" *Today's Education,* November–December 1975, pp. 16–21.

Killory, J. F. "In defense of corporal punishment." *Psychology Reports* 35(1974):575–81.

Manning, John. "Discipline in the good old days." *Phi Delta Kappan,* December 1959.

Nation's Schools. "It's time to hang up the hickory stick," 90 (November 1972).

Radbill, S. X. "A History of Child Abuse and Infanticide." In R. F. Helfer and C. II. Kempe, eds., *The Battered Child* (2nd edition). Chicago: University of Chicago Press, 1974.

Reitman, A., Follmann, J. and Ladd, E. T. "Corporal Punishment in the Public Schools: The Use of Force in Controlling Student Behavior. New York: American Civil Liberties Union, 1972.

Rosenshine, B., and Furst, N. "Research in Teacher Performance Criteria," In B. O. Smith, ed., *Research in Teacher Education.* Englewood Cliffs, N.J.: Prentice Hall, 1971.

Williams, G. J. "Origins of filicidal impulses in the American way of life." *Journal of Clinical Child Psychology* 3(1976):2–11.

Wineman, O., and James, A. Policy Statement—Metropolitan Detroit Branch of the ACLU of Michigan. "Corporal Punishment in the Public Schools," 1967.

PART II

Protection of Children against Abuse and Neglect: Historical Background

In stable, closely knit communities, informal supports and restraints contributing to the protection of children were exercised by public opinion and by concerned relatives, friends, and neighbors, who were aware of problems within the family group. The absence of these supports and restraints, related to the anonymity made possible in mobile, urban populations, has created a vacuum. The community can no longer rely completely upon public opinion, relatives, friends and neighbors to provide protection to the child whose health and life are in danger.

(Boardman, 1963, p. 8)

Editor's Introduction

The protection of children against abuse and neglect by their parents is usually viewed as a product of the last two decades because of extensive media coverage and legislation during that era. Yet as far back as 1735, Massachusetts had passed a statute for the city of Boston which provided that when parents: "were unable, or neglected to provide necessaries for the sustenance and support of their children... and where persons bring up their children in such gross ignorance that they do not know, or are not able to distinguish the alphabet, or twenty-four letters, at the age of six years, the overseers might bind out such children to good families for a decent and Christian education" (Folks 1902, p. 167).

Although English common law set forth the rights of parents and their duty to support and educate their children, "the status of the duties as 'imperfect' (or unenforceable) obligations under common law rendered them of limited utility to the child or to others who sought enforcement, in his or their own behalf" (Rosenheim 1977, p. 428).

It was not until the nineteenth century that intervention by authorities into the home to protect children against parental cruelty and neglect received stronger social sanction and improved legislation, making enforcement of the law possible. Three important factors contributed to improvements in child-protection legislation. One, of course, was humanitarianism. Altruistic concern for the suffering of children was especially prominent in the writings of poets and novelists. The following poem written in the early 1800s by Elizabeth Barrett Browning illustrates this concern:

> But the young, young children, O my brothers
> They are weeping bitterly!
> They are weeping in the playtime of others
> In the country of the free.

Another more complicated contributor to the enactment of stronger child-protection legislation was ideological: the vision of a classless, participatory democracy in the United States. This vision could only be implemented by prohibition of child labor and the establishment of a system of compulsory education, so that the literacy of America's future citizens would be insured. Attitudes toward child labor ranged from repudiation to social sanction. William Blake's poem, *The Chimney Sweep*, written in 1788, indicates the humanitarian attitude toward the practice:

When my mother died I was very young,
And my father sold me, while yet my tongue
Could scarcely cry weep, weep, weep.
So your chimneys I sweep and in soot I sleep.

Social sanctioning of child labor continued, however, even as late as the turn of the twentieth century. "In the silk mills children were generally taken about 7, but some as early as 6, principally, it was said, to oblige their parents. . . . 'If there was a restriction as to the work of children under 10 years of age,' said William Sedgwick, a cotton spinner, 'I think parents would be injured thereby because many children under 10 aid the sustaining of their family by their wages'" (Housden 1955, p. 81).

In addition to having to surmount social sanctions for child labor, nineteenth-century reformers faced formidable problems in budgeting and administering inspection of factories to implement laws protecting employed children. Consequently, they "sought to tie the child labor ban to compulsory education laws so that the two sets of law would be mutually reinforcing" (Rosenheim 1977, p. 433). Rosenheim states: ". . . it can be argued that the roots of the American child labor and compulsory education movements are found in American political ideology, rather than in humanitarian reaction to the evils themselves. The ideal of representative government elevates literacy to prominence; political participation presumes discourse and communication" (p. 433). Thus, the struggle to prohibit abuse of children in the workplace, coupled with the compulsory education movement, gave impetus to legislation to prohibit abuse of children in the home.

Finally, the wish to protect impressionable children against the immorality and other forms of deviance of their parents played a role in the development of child-protection legislation. Two English custody cases exemplify this motivation. In 1817 in *Shelley vs. Westbrook,* the court denied the poet, Shelley, custody of his children on the basis of his unconventional behavior and belief in atheism. In *Wellesley vs. The Duke of Beaufort* in 1827 and *Wellesley vs. Wellesley* in 1828, "the scandalous conduct of Wellesley, proved by financial irresponsibility, adultery, and coarse language vented in his children's presence, resulted in the victory of his deceased wife's relatives over the father's claim of custody" (Rosenheim 1977, p. 430).

The zeal for moral reform of individuals greatly influenced legislation and law enforcement on behalf of children in the United States during the latter half of the nineteenth century. Under the charismatic leadership of Henry Bergh, founder of the Society for the Prevention of Cruelty to Animals, the Society for the Prevention of Cruelty to Children was established and given legally sanctioned police powers. Some members, such as Bergh, acted from purely humanitarian motives. Platt (1969) views "the child savers" as motivated primarily by the desire to control deviancy among the children of the poor. Their purpose was to save the souls of indigent, urban children through placement in Christian homes and institutions where they could receive education, religious and moral training, and rescue from the temptations of city living. Thus, the first and major targets of the enforcement of legislation to protect children against parental abuse and neglect were poor families. In describing the origins of child-protection law Rosenheim (1977) states:

> It presupposes passivity of children as its ideal. It permits the possibility that the passive can become corrupted and misguided. Child protection thus encompasses the tasks of both salvation and reeducation. There are the underlying purposes of legislation for children. Together with the older law (English common law) of parent and child laid down over seven centuries, they form the modern legal framework for the definition and implementation of permissible standards of behavior by and toward children (p. 438).

Had urbanization not taken place in the United States, child-protective legislation and services might not have been necessary. With urbanization, however, came the loss of informal community regulation of family relationships. Child-protection agencies now substitute for this lost social network. As Henry (1965) stated:

> There is minimal social regulation of parent-child relations in our culture; this is, above all, what makes lethal child-care practices possible. In a primitive culture, where many relatives are around to take an active interest in one's baby, where life is open, or in large households, where many people can see what a mother is doing and where deviations from traditional practice quickly offend the eye and loosen critical, interested tongues, it is impossible for a parent to do as he or she pleases with his child. In a literal sense, a baby is often not even one's own in such societies, but belongs to a lineage, clan, or household—a community—having a real investment in the baby. It is not private enterprise (p. 332).

The chapters in this part give varied glimpses of the history of child protection. The first three papers, little known in the child abuse field, are uniquely relevant to the topic. The brief essay by James Kent, chief justice of the New York Supreme Court, is one of his many lectures that were published in four volumes from 1826 to 1830. It indicates that even Roman law, permissive in granting great power to the father over his children, nevertheless, required parents to support them, a requirement Kent characterizes as a precept of "universal law." Despite the emphasis on children's rights during the last two decades, the enlightened view that parental rights result from carrying out their duties to their children was assumed by jurists during the early 1800s.

The case of Kaspar Hauser, described by Simon in Chapter 6, has no parallel in the history of child abuse and neglect. He had lived in a dungeon under conditions of extreme cruelty and social isolation—the circumstances resulting in this confinement still remain a mystery—until he was found in Nuremberg, Germany, in 1828, when he was seventeen years old. In all likelihood, he suffered from psychosocial (abuse) dwarfism (discussed in Part VI by Money), for he grew more than two inches in height after a few weeks during his stay with his devoted teacher (von Feuerbach 1966, p. 329). Simon discusses the significance of Kaspar's acquisition of language after such prolonged, intense deprivation, a topic which is also discussed in the Editor's Introduction to Part VI and in Chapter 22. The special compassion and active interest in his development shown by many in Kaspar's short life—the reasons for his assassination at age twenty-one are unknown—are highlights in the history of child protection.

Kaspar Hauser's story would be incomplete without the inclusion of his poignant dialogue with von Feuerbach (1966), a distinguished jurist whose book on Kaspar published in 1832 was originally subtitled, *An Instance of a Crime against the Life of the Soul (the Development of All Its Intellectual, Moral and Immortal Parts) of Man*. Kaspar said:

> I was just thinking how many beautiful things there are in the world, and how hard it is for me to have lived so long and to have seen nothing of them; and how happy children are who have been able to see all these things from their earliest infancy, and can still look at them. I am already so old, and am obliged to learn what children knew long ago. I wish I had never come out of my cage; he who put me there should have left me there. Then I should never have known and felt the want of any thing; and I should not have experienced the misery of never having been a child, and of having come so late into the world (p. 355).

Von Feuerbach replied that

> . . . in respect to the beauties of nature, there was no great cause for regretting his fate in comparison with that of other children and men, who had been in the world since their childhood. Most men, having grown up amidst these glorious sights, and considering them as common things which they see every day, regard them with indifference; and retaining the same insensibility throughout their whole life, they feel no more at beholding them, than animals grazing in a meadow. For Kaspar who had entered upon life as a young man, they had been preserved in all their freshness and purity and hereby no small indemnification was given him for the loss of his earlier years; and he has thus gained a considerable advantage over them. Kaspar answered nothing and seemed, if not convinced, yet somewhat comforted. But it will never be possible, at any time, entirely to comfort him respecting his fate. He is a tender tree, from which the crown has been taken, and the heart of whose root is gnawed by a worm (p. 355).

Chapter 7 is a little known speech given by novelist Charles Dickens in behalf of the Hospital for Sick Children in London in 1858. In Chapter 34, Gardner describes the Dickensian terrors of child abuse, especially psychosocial dwarfism. Dickens, himself a product of parental abuse and neglect, transformed his early terrifying existence into artistic creations. His novels incited the humanitarian spirit and contributed greatly to social reform during the 1800s. There is an ironic sidelight related to this particular expression of child advocacy. It was at the Hospital for Sick Children, just a few years after Dickens gave his impassioned speech, that a physician (Johnson 1868) puzzled over the frequency of repeated fractures in children. Although he attributed them to rickets, Kempe and Kempe (1978) assert that, in all cases he described, the children had been abused.

In Chapter 8, Williams describes the one-hundred-year era from the founding of the Society for the Prevention of Cruelty to Children to the enactment of the Child Abuse Prevention and Treatment Act. History has indeed repeated itself, for over a century ago there was furor over parental maltreatment of children, sensational newspaper accounts, and strong child-protective legislation. These earlier social reforms were followed, however, by waning interest in the problem of cruelty to children. This state of affairs is also seen in the waxing and waning of public attention to other social problems. For example, the muckrakers in the early 1900s also incited public support for the passage of federal laws to protect the public against contaminated food, misbranding of drugs, and other threats to public health. Although significant reforms took place, the movement dissipated until it was revived many decades later by Ralph Nader and the consumer advocacy movement. It is to be hoped that the recent movement against child abuse and neglect will not meet a similar fate—to lie dormant once again for several decades after its novelty and sensationalism wear off.

The article presented in Chapter 9 on "the battered child syndrome" published in 1962 by Kempe and his associates represents a watershed in the history of child protection. Their findings belied the belief that the mistreatment of children by their parents was a practice of the past and that child-protection agencies were successfully treating the infrequent occurrences of child abuse and neglect at home. Their nationwide survey demonstrated that the syndrome was not rare and that it was a frequent cause of death or permanent brain injury in infants and young children. Their article accomplished a great deal more than indicating the continued existence and high incidence of the battered child syndrome. It emphasized the abuse and neglect of reality by physicians who denied its existence and by social workers who believed that casework was curbing and preventing it.

The publication of the article and subsequent work on the problem by Kempe (1971) and others (De Francis 1963; Young 1964; Paulsen 1966; Elmer 1967; Helfer and Kempe 1968; Steele and Pollack 1969; Gil 1970; Fontana 1971) gave impetus to the conducting of Senate hearings, in 1973, chaired by then Senator Walter F. Mondale, on a bill "intended to be a vehicle for a thorough study of the medical, legal and sociological aspects of child abuse" (p. 2). The outcome of the hearings was the passage of the Child Abuse Prevention and Treatment Act of 1974, presented in Chapter 10. This legislation is a milestone in the history of child protection because it was the first time parental abuse and neglect of children had been dealt with at a national level.

G. J. W.

REFERENCES

Boardman, H. E. "Who Insures the Child's Right to Health?" In *The Neglected and Battered Child Syndrome*. New York: Child Welfare League of America, 1963.

De Francis, V. *Child Abuse—Preview of a Nationwide Survey.* Denver: American Humane Association, 1963.

Elmer, E. *Children in Jeopardy: A Study of Abused Minors and Their Families.* Pittsburgh: University of Pittsburgh Press, 1967.

Folks, H. *The Care of Destitute, Neglected and Delinquent Children.* New York: Macmillan Company, 1902.

Fontana, V. J. *The Maltreated Child,* 2nd edition. Springfield, Ill.: Charles C Thomas, 1971.

Gil, D. G. *Violence against Children: Physical Child Abuse in the United States.* Cambridge, Mass.: Harvard University Press, 1970.

Helfer, R. E., and Kempe, C. H. (eds.). *The Battered Child.* Chicago: University of Chicago Press, 1968.

Henry, J. *Culture against Man.* New York: Vintage Books, 1965.

Housden, L. G. *The Prevention of Cruelty to Children.* London: Jonathan Cape, 1955.

Johnson, A. A. W. *Lectures on the Surgery of Childhood.* London, 1868.

Kempe, C. H. "Paediatric implications of the battered baby syndrome." *Archives of Diseases of Children* 46(1971):28–37.

Kempe, R. S., and Kempe, C. H. *Child Abuse.* Cambridge, Mass.: Harvard University Press, 1978.

Mondale, W. F. Hearings before the Subcommittee on Children and Youth, 93rd Congress, on the Child Abuse Prevention Act (S. 1191), 1973.

Paulsen, M. B. "Legal framework of child protection." *Columbia Law Review* 66(1966):679–717.

Platt, A. *The Child Savers.* Chicago: University of Chicago Press, 1969.

Rosenheim, M. K. "The Child and the Law." In E. H. Grotberg, ed. *200 Years of Children.* Washington, D.C.: Office of Child Development, 1977.

Shelley vs. Westbrook, 37 Eng. Rep. 850 (Ch. 1817).

Steele, B. F., and Pollack, C. B. "A Psychiatric Study of Parents Who Abuse Infants and Small Children." In R. E. Helfer and C. H. Kempe, eds., *The Battered Child.* Chicago: University of Chicago Press, 1968.

von Feuerbach, P. J. A. "Kaspar Hauser." In J. A. L. Singh and R. M. Zingg, eds., *Wolf-Children and Feral Man.* New York: Archon Books, 1966. Originally published in German as *Beispiel eines Verbrechens am Seelenleben des Menschen.* Ansbach: 1832.

Wellesley vs. the Duke of Beaufort, 38 Eng. Rep. 236 (Ch. 1827).

Wellesley vs. Wellesley, 4 Eng. Rep. 1078 (H. L. 1828).

Young, L. R. *Wednesday's Children.* New York: McGraw–Hill, 1964.

CHAPTER 5

Duties and Rights of Parents under American Common Law, 1826

James Kent

I. OF THE DUTIES OF PARENTS

The duties of parents to their children, as being their natural guardians, consist in maintaining and educating them during the season of infancy and youth, and in making reasonable provision for their future usefulness and happiness in life, by a situation suited to their habits, and a competent provision for the exigencies of that situation.

(1) Of Maintaining Children

The wants and weaknesses of children render it necessary that some person maintain them, and the voice of nature has pointed out the parent as the most fit and proper person. The laws and customs of all nations have enforced this plain precept of universal law. The Athenian and the Roman laws were so strict in enforcing the performance of this natural obligation of the parent, that they would not allow the father to disinherit the child from passion or prejudice, but only for substantial reasons, to be approved of in a court of justice.

The obligation on the part of the parent to maintain the child continues until the latter is in a condition to provide for its own maintenance, and it extends no further than to a necessary support. The obligation of parental duty is so well secured by the strength of natural affection, that it seldom requires to be enforced by human laws. According to the language of Lord Coke, it is "nature's profession to assist, maintain, and console the child." A father's house is always open to his children. The best feelings of our nature establish and consecrate this asylum . . . .

All the provision that the statute law of New York has made on this subject applies to the case of necessary maintenance; and as the provision was borrowed from the English statutes of 43 Eliz. and 5 Geo. I., and is dictated by feelings

Reprinted from *Commentaries on American Law*, Part IV, Lecture 29, "Of Parent and Child," by James Kent (New York, 1826–30).

inherent in the human breast, it has probably been followed, to the extent at least of the English statutes, throughout this country. The father and mother, being of sufficient ability, of any poor, blind, lame, old, or decrepit person whomsoever, not being able to maintain himself, and becoming chargeable to any city or town, are bound, at their own charge and expense, to relieve and maintain every such person, in such manner as the overseers of the poor of the town shall approve of, and the court of general sessions shall order and direct. If the father, or if the mother, being a widow, shall abscond and leave their children a public charge, their estate is liable to be sequestered, and the proceeds applied to the maintenance of the children. The statute imposes a similar obligation upon the children, under like circumstances. This feeble and scanty statute provision was intended for the indemnity of the public against the maintenance of paupers, and it is all the injunction that the statute law pronounces in support of the duty of parents to maintain their adult children. During the minority of the child, the case is different, and the parent is absolutely bound to provide reasonably for his maintenance and education; and he may be sued for necessaries furnished, and schooling given to a child, under just and reasonable circumstances. The father is bound to support his minor children, if he be of ability, even though they have property of their own; but this obligation in such a case does not extend to the mother, and the rule, as to the father, has become relaxed. The courts now look with great liberality to the circumstances of each particular case, and to the respective estates of the father and children; and in one case, where the father had a large income, he was allowed for the maintenance of his infant children, who had still a larger income. The legal obligation of the father to maintain his child ceases as soon as the child is of age, however wealthy the father may be, unless the child becomes chargeable to the public as a pauper. . . .

And in consequence of the obligation of the father to provide for the maintenance, and, in some qualified degree, for the education of his infant children, he is entitled to the custody of their persons, and to the value of their labor and services. There can be no doubt that this right in the father is perfect, while the child is under the age of fourteen years. But as the father's guardianship, by nature, continues until the child has arrived to full age, and as he is entitled by statute to constitute a testamentary guardian of the person and estate of his children until the age of twenty-one, the inference would seem to be, that he was, in contemplation of the law, entitled to the custody of the persons, and to the value of the services and labor of his children, during their minority. . . .

The father may obtain the custody of his children by the writ of *habeas corpus,* when they are improperly detained from him; but the courts, both of law and equity, will investigate circumstances, and act according to sound discretion, and will not always, and of course, interfere upon *habeas corpus,* and take a child, though under fourteen years of age, from the possession of a third person, and deliver it over to the father against the will of the child. They will consult the inclination of an infant, if it be of a sufficiently mature age to judge for itself, and even control the right of the father to the possession and education of his child when the nature of the case appears to warrant it. . . .

2. OF THE RIGHTS OF PARENTS

The rights of parents result from their duties. As they are bound to maintain and educate their children, the law has given them a right to such authority; and in the support of that authority, a right to the exercise of such discipline as may be requisite for the discharge of their sacred trust. This is the true foundation of parental power; and yet the ancients generally carried the power of the parent to a most atrocious extent over the person and liberty of the child. The Persians, Egyptians, Greeks, Gauls, and Romans tolerated infanticide, and allowed to fathers a very absolute dominion over their offspring; but the Romans, according to Justinian, exceeded all other people, and the liberty and lives of the children were placed within the power of the father. It was not, however, an absolute license of power among the Romans, to be executed in a wanton and arbitrary manner. It was a regular domestic jurisdiction, though in many instances this parental power was exercised without the forms of justice. The power of the father over the life of his child was weakened greatly in public opinion by the time of Augustus, under the silent operation of refined manners and cultivated morals. It was looked upon as obsolete when the Pandects were compiled. Bynkershoek was of opinion that the power ceased under the Emperor Hadrian, for he banished a father for killing his son. The Emperor Constantine made the crime capital as to adult children. In the age of Tacitus, the exposing of infants was unlawful, but merely holding it to be unlawful was not sufficient. When the crime of exposing and killing infants was made capital, under Valentinian and Valens, then the practice was finally exterminated and the paternal power reduced to the standard of reason and of our own municipal law, which admits only the *jus domesticae emendationis,* or right of inflicting moderate correction, under the exercise of a sound discretion. In everything that related to domestic connections, the English common law has an undoubted superiority over the Roman. Under the latter, the paternal power continued during the son's life and did not cease even on his arriving at the greatest honors. The son could not sue without his father's consent or marry without his consent; and whatever he acquired, he acquired for the father's advantage; and in respect to the father, the son was considered rather in the light of property than a rational being. Such a code of law was barbarous and unfit for a free and civilized people; and Justinian himself pronounced it unhuman and mitigated its rigor so far as to secure to the son the property he acquired by any other means than by his father; and yet even as to all acquisitions of the son, the father was still entitled to the use.

The father (and on his death, the mother) is generally entitled to the custody of the infant children, inasmuch as they are their natural protectors, for maintenance and education. But the courts of justice may, in their sound discretion, and when the morals, or safety, or interests of the children strongly require it, withdraw the infants from the custody of the father or mother, and place the care and custody of them elsewhere. . . .

CHAPTER 6

Kaspar Hauser

Nicole Simon

CASE HISTORY

Arrival in Nuremberg

Kaspar Hauser was nineteenth-century Europe's most famous child (Peitler and Ley 1927). He was first noticed at Nuremberg's Haller Gate during the Whitsun holidays on May 26, 1828. He gave the appearance of a drunken peasant who seemed neither to know where he was nor to understand anything said to him. When asked what he wanted, who he was, where he came from, he would only repeat the last few words of each request. Or he would break into tears, responding with moans and unintelligible sounds. Sometimes he answered by reciting over and over the phrases: "Ä Sechtene möcht ih wähn, wie mei Vottä wähn is" ("I want to be a soldier, like my father"), "Reutä wähn, wie mei Vottä wähn is" ("Want to be a rider, like my father"), or "woas nit" ("don't know"). He held in his hand a letter addressed to the captain of the Chevaux Legers. The author of this letter claimed to have cared for Kaspar since October 7, 1812, after finding the infant boy on his doorstep. Enclosed was another note, supposedly written by the infant's mother. It stated that his name was Kaspar, gave his birth date as April 30, 1812, and said that his dead father had been a member of the Chevaux Legers, and that he should be sent to Nuremberg at age seventeen.

The stranger was placed in custody of the police. According to von Feuerbach (1832–1833), "He appeared neither to know nor to suspect where he was. He betrayed neither fear, nor astonishment, nor confusion; he rather showed an almost animal-like dulness, which either leaves external objects entirely unnoticed, or stares at them without thought" (p. 7). When questioned by the police, he responded to everything, again, with one of his phrases, "Ä Reutä

The research for this article was begun during the author's tenure as a fellow of the Radcliffe Institute supported by NIMH postdoctoral fellowship number 1 F22 MH00691-01. The author is grateful to Eckehard Simon, professor of German, Harvard University, for helpful comments on the manuscript.

Reprinted with permission from *Journal of Autism and Childhood Schizophrenia* 8(1978):209–17. Copyright 1978, Plenum Press.

wähn...," etc., "woas nit," or "Hoam weissa" ("know home"). He was 4 feet 9 inches tall; the first signs of a beard were beginning to appear around his lips and chin, but his wisdom teeth had not yet erupted (they first appeared in 1831, three years later). There were inoculation scars on both arms, usually a sign of high birth. The soles of his feet were lacking calluses; they were as soft as the palms of the hand and covered with blood blisters (which remained visible for several months). One of the officers decided to test him with pen and paper. With a sudden expression of delight, the stranger took the pen and wrote, to everyone's surprise, legibly and in a firm hand, *Kaspar Hauser*. The police officials concluded that he had a defective or demented mind and could not be released. He was confined in the tower at the Vestner Gate, the usual place of detention for felons and vagabonds.

During his first days in prison, Kaspar frequently cried out, "Ross" (horse). One of the tower guards brought him a toy horse. With tears of joy, Kaspar sat down on the floor beside the horse, stroked it, patted it, and kept his eyes fixed on it. He was soon given more toy horses and trinkets to play with. When observed through a concealed opening in the door, he was always found sitting on the floor in the same position, legs outstretched in front of him, decorating his toy horses with ribbons, strings, coins, bells, and bits of paper, or dragging them back and forth at his side. According to the guards, he spent every hour of the day engaged in this activity, without paying the least attention to anyone or anything else around him.

Adjustment to Civilization

After 4 or 5 days, the superintendent of the prison, whose name was Hiltel, took Kaspar into his own quarters in the tower. Kaspar remained with the Hiltel family for about two months. During this time, eleven-year-old Julius Hiltel became especially attached to Kaspar, and it was he who, with great zeal, first taught Kaspar to speak and to attach concepts to his utterances. Within one month Kaspar had acquired enough rudiments of speech to express, to some degree, his thoughts and previous experiences. Von Feuerbach first visited Kaspar on July 11, 1828, and described his speech as telegraphic and deficient in syntax, especially conjunctions, participles, and adverbs. The pronoun *I* occurred very rarely; he usually referred to himself in the third person or as *Kaspar*. He also addressed others by name rather than by the second-person pronoun. In speaking to him, one could not use the pronoun *you (du)* but had to say *Kaspar* to be immediately understood. The words that he could say were clearly enunciated without hesitation or stammering, although formulation of coherent speech was still beyond his capabilities. Often he would repeat a phrase over and over in an effort to extract its meaning (Pies 1925).

On July 18, 1828, Kaspar was placed in the care of Professor Daumer, a young teacher in the Gymnasium (high school). Daumer dedicated himself to the education of Kaspar in much the same way that Itard had devoted himself to teaching Victor of Aveyron (Daumer 1873; Pies 1925). But, unlike Victor, Kaspar soon displayed an astonishing memory and an immense curiosity, and he applied himself to learning with an almost inflexible perseverance. Writing and drawing soon took the place of the toy horses with which he had occupied his days in prison.

In February of 1829, nine months after his arrival in Nuremberg, Kaspar began to write his own story. This brief autobiography is repeated in Pies (1925, vol. 2, pp. 187–212); the vocabulary and style are simple enough to be easily read by anyone just beginning to learn German. In it Kaspar described how, for as long as he could remember, he had always lived in a small, dark room. Coarse dark bread and water were his only nourishment. Sometimes after awakening he would find that he had a clean shirt on and his fingernails had been cut. He had two toy horses and had always whiled away his time by running them back and forth at his side. Shortly before Kaspar was taken to Nuremberg, his caretaker brought some paper and a pencil into his dungeon and guided his hand through the motions of forming letters and words. From then on, copying the figures on paper replaced Kaspar's interest in his toy horses. Most interesting is Kaspar's description of how he reacted when his caretaker spoke to him for the first time. His companion pointed to his horses and said, "Ross." The man repeated this several times and Kaspar listened intently. Suddenly it occurred to Kaspar to try to imitate this sound himself. It took seven or eight attempts before he could begin to say it clearly. The man later taught him to recite the phrases, "Ä sechtene möcht ih wähn . . . ," etc. The man spoke these phrases over and over to Kaspar on several visits. When he was alone, Kaspar would practice by talking to his toy horses. Then, one day his caretaker carried him out of his prison. They began the journey to Nuremberg. Kaspar spent most of the way learning to walk, which was very painful and tiring, and practicing his phrases. Shortly before his caretaker left him outside of Nuremberg, the man changed Kaspar's clothes. Then he placed the letter in Kaspar's hand and disappeared.

Newspaper reports that Kaspar was preparing these memoirs for publication led to the first attempt on his life in October 1829 in the cellar of Daumer's house (Pies 1925). After this attempted murder, Kaspar was transferred to the home of a city councilor and kept under police guard. Because of the progress he had made with Daumer, Kaspar was sent to the Gymnasium to continue his schooling. There he experienced great difficulty both with his studies, Latin in particular, and in his relationships with the other students. In 1830, Kaspar was transferred to the guardianship of Baron von Tucher, with whom he enjoyed an excellent relationship for over a year.

In December 1831, Kaspar was officially adopted by Lord Stanhope, a well-to-do Englishman, who had him transferred to the home of a schoolmaster named Meyer in Ansbach. Kaspar never established the kind of close relationship with Meyer that he had with his previous guardians, Daumer and von Tucher. Stanhope and Meyer are thought to have been possible co-conspirators in the cover-up of Kaspar's past (Evans 1892). Meyer's opinions can be read in Pies (1925, vol. 1, pp. 281–301; 1928, pp. 18–21, 99–112). In October 1832, Kaspar began religious instruction with a Lutheran pastor named Fuhrmann, whose home became more and more a refuge for him. Fuhrmann's account (reprinted in Pies 1925, vol. 2, pp. 105–52) contains interesting examples of Kaspar's struggles to understand such concepts as original sin and free will and how to abide by the Ten Commandments. Kaspar was confirmed in May 1833. A few days later von Feuerbach died unexpectedly while on an excursion with a party of friends during the Whitsun holidays. This happened to be the fifth anniversary of Kaspar Hauser's appearance in Nuremberg. Von Feuerbach's unexplained and sudden death led many people to suspect that he was poisoned; according to Evans (1892), he may have been close to the solution of the mystery surrounding Kaspar Hauser's early imprisonment.

On Saturday, December 14, 1833, Kaspar spent the afternoon with Pastor Fuhrmann's family making Christmas gifts. Fuhrmann (Pies 1925, vol. 2, pp. 137–44) described the events of this final day in great detail. After leaving the pastor's house, Kaspar went to the public park, apparently to meet a man who claimed to have a document explaining his past. The man handed him a small purse containing a piece of paper with a riddle scribbled on it; then he stabbed him in the chest and fled. Kaspar died seventy-eight hours later on December 17.

Postmortem Examination

The medical reports concerning Kaspar Hauser's death and autopsy can be found in two published sources, Heidenreich's (1834) article and Pies's (1928) collection of legal transcripts. Heidenreich's article is also reprinted in Pies (1925, vol. 2, pp. 153–84). The postmortem examination was undertaken on December 19, by an officially appointed commission, thirty-five hours after death. First a thorough investigation of the extent of the stab wound was made. Both the tip of the heart and the left lung had been penetrated. Examination of the abdominal cavity revealed an unusually enlarged liver, the substance of which was very soft. The wound had pierced the diaphragm and penetrated the liver at least 2 inches. The wound also grazed the stomach wall and a quantity of digested food had escaped into the abdominal cavity. This was noted as the cause of death. Examination of the cranial cavity revealed unusually thick skull bones. The brain was examined by taking away successive layers. The cortical substance as well as the white matter appeared normal. There was a barely perceptible increase in fluid in the lateral ventricles. The cerebellum, cut in two, appeared normal as did the cerebrum (Pies 1928).

Heidenreich's (1834) description of the brain is somewhat more detailed and suggestive of possible pathology. Heidenreich states:

> On the whole, the brain was small but there were no noticeable abnormalities. However, the *cerebellum* ["das kleine Hirn"] appeared, in comparison with the *cerebrum* ["das grosse Hirn"] rather large and well developed; the *occipital lobe* ["hinter{e}n Lappen"] of the cerebrum did not cover the cerebellum as is usually the case. The cerebrum appeared in this respect somewhat small. Nothing particularly

abnormal was seen on horizontal sections. The *corpus callossum* ["grosse Commissur"] was fully developed, as were the *thalami* ["Sehhügel"]. The plexus chorioidei were normal. The *corpora quadrigemini* ["Vierhügel"] were very small. Convolutions of the cerebellum were clear and numerous. Nothing unusual or deviant was noted about the base of the brain or the cranial nerves. The separation between the *cerebral hemispheres* ["mittlere Hirnlappen"] at the bony base of the skull was, however, striking. These lay as in a rounded, deepened nest, because of the especially high *petrosal bone* ["Felsenbein"] and the equally very high swordlike continuation of the *sphenoid bone* ["Keilbein"] above. These bony formations were not symmetric; the depressions and elevations were larger and more pronounced on the right than on the left side. The cortical gyri did not appear very numerous or distinct, but were on the contrary, more compact and coarse. Single masses such as the corpus callossum, thalami, etc. appeared large and well developed. On the whole, however, the brain appeared not to have an especially fine and intricate structure (pp. 110–11).[1]

One is impressed by how much was already known in the early nineteenth century about the structure of the brain, despite the crudeness of the methods available at the time.

DISCUSSION

One major theory (Evans 1892; Pies 1925; Singh and Zingg 1942–1966) is that Kaspar Hauser had been born heir to the Duchy of Baden on September 29, 1812. As part of a scheme devised by his grandfather's second wife, he was kidnapped a little more than two weeks after his birth to make way for the succession of her own sons. The abducted prince was kept alive rather than put to death so that he could be produced as an embarrassment to his uncle, who might later claim more direct lineage to the throne. If this was the case, then for only the first two weeks after birth was he cared for in his own family. If not downright hostile, his environment from earliest infancy would have lacked the security of a warm maternal protector. That this was the case has far more support (Evans 1892) than can be advanced for the theory that Victor of Aveyron had been abandoned before the *critical age* for language development (four to five years of age).

Kaspar Hauser's enlarged liver provides substantial evidence the he had indeed been subjected to malnutrition and to prolonged confinement. Dr. Albert, who was head of the autopsy commission, pointed out in his court testimony (Pies 1928) that Kaspar Hauser's enlarged liver was like those of geese kept in confinement to produce plump livers for good pâté. Although he was only 4 feet 9 inches tall when he first arrived in Nuremberg, the fact that he grew 2 inches taller after meat was added to his diet (von Feuerbach 1832–1833) is further evidence that his small stature was due more to malnutrition than to heredity. Although the neuroanatomical data are crude, the pathology of the brain is also consistent with a history of malnutrition during childhood. Aside from the cor-

---

[1]For the italicized Latin and English translations of the older German anatomical terms, I referred to Flechsig (1883), Pfeifer (1911), and Schüller (1905).

pora quadrigemini, other subcortical centers, such as the thalamus, were well developed. The cerebral cortex, on the other hand, had fewer than normal gyri, which appeared somewhat shrunken and coarse. This pattern of pathology is consistent with normal prenatal development (normal subcortical growth), but selective retardation of growth of cortex can follow severe malnutrition in infancy and early childhood (Winick, Rosso, and Waterlow 1970).

Kaspar's social development was discussed in graphic terms by von Feuerbach (1832–1833):

> If Kaspar, who may now be reckoned among civilized and well behaved men, were to enter a mixed company without being known, he would strike everyone as a strange phenomenon. . . . [I]ncapable of uttering a single pleasantry, or even of understanding a figurative expression, he possesses dry, but thoroughly sound common sense, . . . in respect to things which directly concern his person and which lie within the narrow sphere of his knowledge and experience, he shows an accuracy, and an acuteness of judgement, which might shame and confound many a learned pedant. . . . [H]e often utters things, which coming from any other person of the same age would be called stupid or silly; but which coming from him, always force upon us a sad compassionate smile. . . . Neither childish tricks and wanton pranks, nor instances of mischief and malice, can be laid to his charge . . . he possesses too much seriousness (pp. 154–59).

Kaspar Hauser was accused by a few of being a clever swindler; a discussion of these accusations can be found in Daumer (1873) and Evans (1892). The behavior described by von Feuerbach (1832–1833), Daumer (1873), and Fuhrmann (Pies 1925) might be hard to mimic unless the swindler had had some opportunity to analyze the intellectual and social deficiencies of children recovering from early language handicaps. The evidence supporting minimal brain pathology would also imply that Kaspar probably was not clever enough to perpetrate such a swindle. Kaspar certainly remained somewhat backward. Nevertheless, his development went far beyond that of Victor of Aveyron, despite the underdevelopment of the cerebral cortex, which was most likely due to malnutrition. His ability to learn language past the onset of adolescence does not lend support to the theory of a "critical period" beyond which language cannot develop.

Kaspar Hauser's case is unique, but if any of the studies of abandoned children in history has significance, the carefully compiled records that exist on Kaspar Hauser have special significance. His case cannot properly be ignored in any discussion of the effects of environmental deprivation on later development, especially those that cite the work of Itard with Victor of Aveyron. .

REFERENCES

Bettelheim, B. "Feral children and autistic children." *American Journal of Sociology* 64(1959):455–67.

Cohen, D. J. "Itard's pupil." *Science* 194(1976):311–12.

Daumer, G. F. *Kaspar Hauser. Sein Wesen, seine Unschuld, seine Erduldungen und sein Ursprung in neuer, gründlicher Erörterung und Nachweisung.* Regensburg: Verlag von Alfred Coppenrath, 1873.

Evans, E. E. G. *The Story of Kaspar Hauser, from Authentic Records.* London: Swan Sonnenschein, 1892.

Flechsig, P. *Plan des menschlichen Gehirns.* Leipzig: Verlag von Veit, 1883.

Heidenreich, F. W. "Kaspar Hausers Verwundung, Krankheit und Leichenöffnung." *Journal der Chirurgie und Augen-Heilkunde* 21(1834):91–123.

Peitler, H., and Ley, H. *Kaspar Hauser: Über tausend bibliographische Nachweise.* Ansbach: C. Brügel, 1927.

Pfeifer, R. A. *Das menschliche Gehirn: Nach seinem Aufbau und seinen wesentlichen Leistungen.* Leipzig: Verlag von Wilhelm Engelmann, 1911.

Pies, H. *Kaspar Hauser: Augenzeugenberichte und Selbstzeugnisse* (2 vols.). Stuttgart: Robert Lutz Verlag, 1925.

Pies, H. *Die amtlichen Aktenstücke über Kaspar Hausers Verwundung und Tod.* Bonn: Kulturhistorischer Verlag, 1928.

Schüller, A. *Archiv und Atlas der normalen und pathologischen Anatomie in typischen Röntgenbildern, Ergänzungsband 11: Die Schädelbasis im Röntgenbilde.* Hamburg: Lucas Gräfe & Sillem, 1905.

Singh, J. A. L., and Zingg, R. M. *Wolf-Children and Feral Man.* Denver: University of Denver, 1942. (Reprinted by Archon Books, 1966.)

von Feuerbach, A. [*Kaspar Hauser. An account of an individual kept in a dungeon, separated from all communication with the world, from early childhood to about the age of seventeen*] (H. G. Linberg, Trans.). Boston: Allen & Ticknor, 1833. (Originally published, 1832.)

Winick, M., Rosso, P., and Waterlow, J. "Cellular growth of cerebrum, cerebellum, and brainstem in normal and marasmic children." *Experimental Neurology* 23(1970):393–400.

CHAPTER 7

Speech on Behalf of the Hospital for Sick Children

Charles Dickens

At Freemasons' Hall, February 9th, 1858.

"Ladies and Gentlemen,

"It is one of my rules in life not to believe a man who may happen to tell me that he feels no interest in children. I hold myself bound to this principle by all kind consideration, because I know, as we all must, that any heart which could really toughen its affections and sympathies against those dear little people must be wanting in so many humanising experiences of innocence and tenderness, as to be quite an unsafe monstrosity among men; therefore I set the assertion down, whenever I happen to meet with it—which is sometimes, though not often—as an idle word, originating possibly in the genteel languor of the hour, and meaning about as much as that knowing social lassitude, which has used up the cardinal virtues and quite found out things in general, usually does mean. I suppose it may be taken for granted that we, who come together in the name of children, and for the sake of children, acknowledge that we have an interest in them; indeed, I have observed since I sat down here that we are quite in a childlike state altogether, representing an infant institution, and not even yet a grown up company. A few years are necessary to the increase of our strength, and the expansion of our figure; and then these tables, which now have a few tucks in them, will be let out, and then this hall, which now sits so easily upon us, will be too tight and small for us. (Cheers and laughter.) Nevertheless, it is likely that even we are not without our experience now and then of spoilt children. I do not mean of our own spoilt children, because nobody's own children ever were spoilt—(laughter)—but I mean the disagreeable children of our particular friends. (Laughter.) We know by experience what it is to have them down after dinner, and, across the rich perspective of a miscellaneous dessert, to see, as in a black dose darkly, the family doctor looming in the distance. (Much laughter.) We know—I have no doubt we all know—what it is to assist at those little maternal anecdotes and table entertainments, illustrated with imitations and descriptive dialogue, which might not be inaptly called, after the manner of my friend Mr. Albert Smith, the toilsome ascent of Miss Mary and the eruption (cutaneous) of Master Alexander.

(Laughter.) We know what it is when those children won't go to bed; we know how they prop their eyelids open with their forefingers when they will sit up; how, when they become fractious, they say aloud that they don't like us, and our nose is too long, and why don't we go? And we are perfectly acquainted with those kicking bundles which are carried off at last protesting. (Cheers and laughter.) An eminent eye-witness told me that he was one of a company of learned pundits who assembled at the house of a very distinguished philosopher of the last generation, to hear him expound his stringent views concerning infant education and early mental development, and he told me that, while the philosopher did this in very beautiful and lucid language, the philosopher's little boy, for his part, edified the assembled sages by dabbling up to the elbows in an apple pie which had been provided for their entertainment, having previously anointed his hair with the syrup, combed it with his fork, and brushed it with his spoon. (Renewed laughter.) It is probable that we also have our similar experiences, sometimes, of principles that are not quite practice, and that we know people, claiming to be very wise and profound about nations of men, who show themselves to be rather weak and shallow about units of babies.

"But, ladies and gentlemen, the spoilt children whom I have to present to you after this dinner of today are not of this class. I have glanced at these for the easier and lighter introduction of another, a very different, a far more numerous, and a far more serious class. The spoilt children whom I must show you are the spoilt children of the poor in this great city—the children who are, every year, forever and ever irrevocably spoilt out of this breathing life of ours by tens of thousands, but who may, in vast numbers, be preserved, if you, assisting and not contravening the ways of Providence, will help to save them. (Cheers.) The two grim nurses, Poverty and Sickness, who bring these children before you, preside over their births, rock their wretched cradles, nail down their little coffins, pile up the earth above their graves. Of the annual deaths in this great town, their unnatural deaths form more than one-third. I shall not ask you, according to the custom as to the other class—I shall not ask you, on behalf of these children, to observe how good they are, how pretty they are, how clever they are, how promising they are, whose beauty they most resemble—I shall only ask you to observe how weak they are, how like death they are! And I shall ask you, by the remembrance of everything that lies between your own infancy and that so mis-called second childhood, when the child's graces are gone, and nothing but its helplessness remains,—I shall ask you to turn your thoughts to *these* spoilt children, in the sacred names of Pity and Compassion.

'Some years ago, being in Scotland, I went with one of the most humane members of the humane medical profession, on a morning tour among some of the worst-lodged inhabitants of the old town of Edinburgh. In the closes and wynds of that picturesque place—I am sorry to remind you what fast friends picturesqueness and typhus often are—we saw more poverty and sickness in an hour than many people would believe in a life. Our way lay from one to another of the most wretched dwellings—reeking with horrible odours—shut out from the sky—shut out from the air—mere pits and dens. In a room of one of these foul places, where there was an empty porridge-pot on the cold hearth, with a ragged woman and some ragged children crouching on the bare ground near it—where, I remember as I speak, that the very light, reflected from a high damp-stained and time-stained house wall, came trembling in, as if the fever which had shaken everything else there had shaken even it—there lay, in an old egg-box, which the mother had begged from a shop, a little feeble, wasted, wan, sick child. With his little wasted face, and his little hot worn hands folded over his breast, and his little bright attentive eyes, I can see him now, as I have seen him for several years, looking steadily at us. There he lay in his little frail box, which was not at all a bad emblem of the little body from which he was slowly parting—there he lay quite quiet, quite patient, saying never a word. He seldom cried, the mother said; he seldom complained; 'he lay there seeming to woonder what it was a' aboot. God knows I thought, as I stood looking at him, he had his reasons for wondering—reasons for wondering how it could possibly come to be that he lay there, left alone, feeble and full of pain, when he ought to have been as bright and as brisk as the birds that never got near him—reasons, for wondering how he came to be left there, a little decrepid old man, pining to death, quite a thing of course, as if there were no crowds of healthy and happy children playing on the grass under the summer's sun within a stone's throw of him, as if there were no bright, moving sea on the other side of the great hill overhanging the city; as if there were no great clouds rushing over it; as if there were no life, and movement, and vigour anywhere in the world—nothing but stoppage and decay. There he lay looking at us, saying in his silence, more pathetically than I have ever heard anything said by any orator in my life, 'Will you please to tell me what this means, strange man? and if you can give me any good reason why I should be so soon so far advanced upon my way to Him who said that children were to come into His presence, and were not to be forbidden, but who scarcely meant, I think, that they should come by this hard road by which I am travelling—pray give that reason to me, for I seek it very earnestly, and wonder about it very much;' and to my mind he has been wondering about it ever since. Many a poor child, sick and neglected, I have seen since that time in this London; many a poor sick child I have seen most affectionately and kindly tended by poor people, in an unwholesome house and under untoward circumstances, wherein its recovery was quite impossible; but at all such times I have seen my poor little drooping friend in his egg-box, and he has always addressed his dumb speech to me, and I have always found him wondering what it meant, and why, in the name of a gracious God, such things should be!

"Now, ladies and gentlemen, such things need not be, and will not be, if this company, which is a drop of the life-blood of the great compassionate public heart, will only accept the means of rescue and prevention which it is mine to offer. Within a quarter of a mile of this place where I speak, stands a courtly old house, where once, no doubt, blooming children were born, and grew up to be men and women, and married, and brought their own blooming children back to patter up the old oak staircase which stood but the other day, and to wonder at the old oak carvings on the chimney-pieces. In the airy wards, into which the old state drawing-rooms and family bedchambers of that house are now converted, are such little patients that the attendant nurses look like reclaimed giantesses, and the kind medical practitioner like an amiable Christian ogre. Grouped about the little low tables in the centre of the rooms are such tiny convalescents that they seem to be playing at having been ill. On the dolls' beds are such diminutive creatures, that each poor sufferer is supplied with its tray of toys; and, looking around, you may see how the little tired, flushed cheek has toppled over half the brute creation on its way into the ark; or how one little dimpled arm has mowed down (as I saw myself) the whole tin soldiery of Europe. On the walls of these rooms are graceful, pleasant, bright childish pictures. At the beds' heads, are pictures of the figure which is the universal embodiment of all mercy and compassion,—the figure of Him who was once a child Himself, and a poor one. Besides these little creatures on the beds, you may learn in that place that the number of small out-patients brought to that house for relief, is no fewer than ten thousand in the compass of one single year. In the room in which these are received, you may see against the wall a box, in which it is written, that it has been calculated, that if every grateful mother who brings a child there will drop a penny into it, the Hospital funds may possibly be increased in a year by so large a sum as forty pounds. And you may read in the Hospital report, with a glow of pleasure, that these poor women are so respondent as to have made, even in a toiling year of difficulty and high prices, this estimated forty, fifty pounds. (Cheers.) In the printed papers of this same Hospital, you may read with what a generous earnestness the highest and wisest members of the medical profession testify to the great need of it; to the immense difficulty of treating children in the same hospitals with grown-up people, by reason of their different ailments and requirements; to the vast amount of pain that will be assuaged, and of life that will be saved through this Hospital—not only among the poor, observe, but among the prosperous too, by reason of the increased knowledge of children's illnesses, which cannot fail to arise from a more systematic mode of studying them. Lastly, gentlemen, and, I am sorry to say, worst of all—(for I must present no rose-colored picture of this place for you—I must not deceive you), lastly—the visitor to this Children's Hospital, reckoning up the number of its beds, will find himself perforce obliged to stop at very little over thirty;* and will learn, with sorrow and surprise, that even that small number, so forlornly, so miserably diminutive, compared with this vast London, cannot possibly be maintained, unless the Hospital be made better known; I limit myself to saying better known, because I will not believe that in a Christian community of fathers and mothers, and brothers and sisters, it can fail being better known, to be well and richly endowed. (Cheers.) Now, ladies and gentlemen, this, without a word of adornment—which I resolved when I got up not to allow myself—this is the simple case. This is the pathetic case, which I have to put to you; not only on

---

*The liberal response made to this appeal enabled the Committee to increase the number of beds for in-patients from 32 to 41. In the summer of 1865, additional wards were opened, and the number of in-patients increased to 75.

behalf of the thousands of children who annually die in this great city, but also on behalf of the thousands of children who live half-developed, racked with preventible pain, shorn of their natural capacity for health and enjoyment. If these innocent creatures cannot move you for themselves, how can I possibly hope to move you in their name?

The most delightful paper, the most charming essay, which the tender imagination of Charles Lamb conceived, represents him as sitting by his fireside on a winter night, telling stories to his own dear children, and delighting in their society, until he suddenly comes to his own solitary batchelor self, and finds that they were but dream-children, who might have been but never were. 'We are nothing,' they say to him; 'less than nothing and dreams. We are only what might have been, and we must wait upon the tedious shore of Lethe, millions of ages, before we have existence and a name.' 'And immediately awaking,' he says, 'I found myself in my arm-chair.' The dream-children whom I would now raise, if I could, before every one of you, according to your various circumstances, should be the dear child you love, the dearer child you have lost, the child you might have had, the child you certainly have been. Each of these dream-children should hold in its powerful hand one of the little children now lying in the Child's Hospital, or now shut out of it to perish. Each of these dream-children should say to you, 'O, help this little suppliant in my name; O, help it for my sake!' Well!—and immediately awaking, you should find yourselves in the Freemasons' Hall, happily arrived at the end of a rather long speech, drinking 'Prosperity to the Hospital for Sick Children,' and thoroughly resolved that it shall flourish.'' (Loud cheers.)

CHAPTER 8

Cruelty and Kindness to Children: Documentary of a Century, 1874–1974

Gertrude J. Williams

> The largest part of that history which we commonly call ancient is
> practically modern, as it describes society in a stage analogous to
> that in which it now is, while on the other hand most of what is
> called modern history is practically ancient, as it relates to a state
> of things that has passed away.
>
> *(Arnold, 1830, p. 636)*

According to popular belief, child abuse and neglect at home were discovered and vehemently opposed in the 1960s and 1970s. Yet more than a century ago, American society was indeed "in a stage analogous to that in which it now is" in regard to child abuse and neglect. The current clamor parallels the public outrage, extensive media coverage, legislation, and zealous protection of children that characterized an earlier era. The scenarios were similar too: a climate favorable for social reform, a devoted leader, and a responsive press.

SOCIOHISTORICAL BACKGROUND OF CHILD PROTECTION

The child protection movement—or child-rescuing, as it was called in the earlier era—began during the latter part of the nineteenth century, a period dubbed "the confident years" (Andrist, Russell, and Harwood 1969). The Industrial Revolution, spurred on by military production during the Civil War, promised hope and prosperity for all. Historian Charles Beard used to quote the remark of an old Indiana farmer to illustrate the exuberance of the times: "You can see it in people's faces, you can feel it in the air. Everybody and everything's going places" (Goldman 1952, p. 3).

Everybody, indeed, was going places—or was viewed as capable of doing so. Spurred on by tales of unlimited opportunity for all, immigrants poured into the new promised land. The immutable class and caste system of Europe, "the old country," contrasted dismally with the democratic ethos of the United States: faith in the possibility of achievement for anyone, regardless of origin. The American Experience, success through initiative and hard work, was embodied in the Horatio Alger stories—*Brave and Bold, Luck and Pluck*—depicting the rise of the hero of humble beginnings from rags to riches. Fiction imitated life.

Living in the White House was military hero and president, Ulysses S. Grant, earlier an insignificant clerk in the army, a failure with a drinking problem. Steel tycoon and millionaire Andrew Carnegie had once been an immigrant messenger boy. Famed writer, Mark Twain, had dropped out of school at twelve to become a printer's apprentice. "Yesterday I wasn't worth a cent," boasted an oil speculator just a few years after immigrating from Ireland, "and bejabbers, today I'm worth thousands upon thousands" (Operholtzer 1917, p. 258).

True, crushing poverty existed in the midst of opulence. Yet the vital belief that wrongs could and would be righted persisted. It was a time of sensitivity to injustice, a time of reform and social activism. The 13th Amendment had put an end to slavery. The right to "due process" had been assured to all citizens by the passage of the 14th Amendment. The Woman's Suffrage Movement, officially begun at the Seneca Fall Convention and interrupted by the Civil War, had been revitalized in 1869 by Susan B. Anthony, Elizabeth Cady Stanton, and Lucy Stone (Hole and Levine 1971). Labor unions were forming. Socialism and populism were on the rise. It was a time of change. It was a time of perpetual motion. Fittingly, the rocking chair became extremely popular in American homes, a symbol of a time when "you moved while sitting still" (Goldman 1952, p. 4).

FROM ANIMAL PROTECTION TO CHILD PROTECTION

Henry Bergh, whose leadership gave impetus to the child protection movement in the United States, was a preeminent representative of this peripatetic period. "Inspirer, advocate, diplomatist, lecturer, writer, administrator, fund raiser, and tireless propagandist for the protest against the abuse of animals" (Carson 1972, p. 97), Bergh had founded the Society for the Prevention of Cruelty to Animals (SPCA) in 1866 and was its first president. He became aware of the plight of animals when he served as secretary for the American legation in Russia, which had no laws protecting animals against cruelty. Dismissed by a supervisor who was envious of his popularity with the Russians, Bergh returned to America via England, where he visited the Royal Society for the Prevention of Cruelty to Animals, the world's first humane society, which had been responsible for the passage of the Cruelty to Animals Act of 1849 (Morse 1968, p. 190).

Although there were animal protection laws in New York and other states, the means for enforcing them were inadequate. Having found his calling—"At last I've found a way to utilize my gold lace" (Carson 1972, p. 98)—Bergh gathered together a number of leaders in law, politics, and finance in New York. Using the Royal Society and English anticruelty laws as models, the group was instrumental in getting legislation passed that protected animals from cruelty and in chartering a humane society that had police authority to implement the law, activities that laid down the pattern for later protection of children.

The cause of animal protection, known as "Bergh's war," was zealously promoted by Bergh and his fellow advocates known as "Bergh's agents." These militant advocates of animal protection stirred up arrests and lawsuits against individuals and companies connected with all manner of animal maltreatment, including the abuse of street car horses and dairy cows, cockfighting, the plucking of live chickens, and cruel methods of slaughtering food animals. As a result of the efforts of the SPCA, live birds were replaced with clay pigeons in trap shooting. Bergh continually pressured P. T. Barnum to improve the treatment of animals in his circus, including the live toads fed to the boa constrictor, which, at one point, had to be sent "to Hoboken in a suitcase to be fed beyond the reach of the Society" (Carson 1972, p. 102). The measure of Bergh's charisma is attested to by the fact that Barnum, who had eventually befriended Bergh, left a bequest in 1891 for the erection of a monument to him.

Bergh's magnetic personality, his opposition to cruel but popular practices, and his intense devotion to his cause resulted in a great deal of public attention and newspaper publicity. Ironically, the impetus for Bergh's efforts did not stem from a special liking for animals but from ethical principles. "This is a matter purely of conscience. It has no perplexing side issues," he asserted. "It is a moral question. . . . It is a solemn recognition of . . . mercy" (*New York Times* 1866). One journalist said of him: "He who doeth one thing is terrible!" (New York Public Library, no date).

It was from this formidable champion of the helpless that a charity worker sought help in the now legendary case of Mary Ellen Wilson, an eight-year-old girl who had been abused and neglected by step-parents. The time was ripe for social reform in behalf of children during the era just prior to the twentieth century, "the century of the child." Several states had established orphanages for children of military personnel killed in the Civil War. The Massachusetts Board of State Charities had subsidized foster homes for children. Public education was free in Michigan, and a national system of education had been proposed.

The progressive times, the ongoing groundwork in child advocacy, the participation of the influential Henry Bergh and a sensational case of brutality to an innocent child were powerful ingredients in mobilizing extensive press coverage, especially by the *New York Times,* whose reports of the case follow.

PRESS COVERAGE OF A CHILD ABUSE CASE, 1874

The first report published by the *New York Times* on April 19, 1874, depicts the "good press" of Bergh and the background of the case. Contrary to the views of some current writers, the case did not reach court because Mary Ellen was declared an animal and thus entitled to legal protection. Rather, it appears that the case was accepted by the court because the petition was brought by Bergh, "who recognized it as being clearly within the general laws of humanity." Furthermore, Henry Bergh acted as a "humane citizen" in this case, not as a representative of the Society for the Prevention of Cruelty to Animals, as some current writers allege, and as the following report indicates:

> *MR. BERGH ENLARGING HIS SPHERE OF USEFULNESS.* Inhuman Treatment of a Little Waif—Her Treatment—A Mystery to Be Cleared Up

It appears from proceedings had in Supreme Court . . . yesterday, in the case of a child named Mary Ellen, that Mr. Bergh does not confine the humane impulses of his heart to smoothing the pathway of the brute creation toward the grave or elsewhere, but that he embraces within the sphere of his kindly efforts the human species also. On his petition a special warrant was issued by Judge Lawrence, bringing before him yesterday the little girl in question, the object of Mr. Bergh being to have her taken from her present custodians and placed in charge of some person or persons by whom she shall be more kindly treated. In his petition Mr. Bergh states that about six years since Francis and Mary Connolly, residing at No. 315 West Forty-first street, obtained possession of the child from Mr. Kellock, Superintendent of the Department of Charities; that her parents are unknown; that her present custodians have been in the habit of beating her cruelly, the marks of which are now visible on her person; that her punishment was so cruel and frequent as to attract the attention of the residents in the vicinity of the Connolly's dwelling, through whom information of the fact was conveyed to Mr. Bergh; that her custodians had boasted that they had a good fortune for keeping her; that not only was she cruelly beaten, but rigidly confined, and that there was reason to believe that her keepers were about to remove her out of the jurisdiction of the court and beyond the limits of the State.

Upon this petition, Judge Lawrence issued, not an ordinary writ of habeas corpus, but a special warrant, provided for by section 65 of the Habeas Corpus act, whereby the child was at once taken possession of and brought within the control of the court. Under authority of the warrant thus granted, Officer McDougal took the child into custody, and produced her in court yesterday. She is a bright little girl, with features indicating unusual mental capacity, but with a care-worn, stunted, and prematurely old look. Her apparent condition of health, as well as her scanty ward-robe, indicated that no change of custody or condition could be much for the worse.

In his statement of the case to the court Mr. Elbridge T. Gerry, who appeared as counsel for Mr. Bergh, said the child's condition had been discovered by a lady who had been on an errand of mercy to a dying woman in the house adjoining, the latter asserting that she could not die happy until she had made the child's treatment known; that this statement had been corroborated by several of the neighbors; that the charitable lady who made the discovery of these facts had gone to several institutions in the vain hope of having them take the child under their care; that as a last resort she applied to Mr. Bergh, who, though the case was not within the scope of the special act to prevent cruelty to animals, recognized it as being clearly within the general laws of humanity, and promptly gave it his attention. It was urged by council that if the child was not committed to the custody of some proper person, she should be placed in some charitable institution: as, if she was to be returned to her present custodians, it would probably result in her being beaten to death.

The Connollys made no appearance in court, and on her examination the child made a statement as follows: My father and mother are both dead. I don't know how old I am. I have no recollection of a time when I did not live with the Connollys. I call Mrs. Connolly mamma. I have never had but one pair of shoes, but I cannot recollect when that was. I have had no shoes or stockings on this Winter. I have never been allowed to go out of the room where the Connollys were, except in the night time, and then only in the yard. I have never had a particle of flannel. My bed at night has been only a piece of carpet stretched on the floor underneath a window, and I sleep in my little under-garments, with a quilt over me. I am never allowed to play with any children, or to have any company whatever. Mamma (Mrs. Connolly) has been in the habit of whipping and beating me almost every day. She used to whip me with a twisted whip—a raw hide. The whip always left a black and blue mark on my body. I have now the black and blue marks on my head which were made by mamma, and also a cut on the left side of my forehead which was made by a pair of scissors. (Scissors produced in court.) She struck me with the scissors and cut me; I have no recollection of ever having been kissed by any one—have never been kissed by mamma. I have never been taken on my mamma's lap and caressed or petted. I never dared to speak to anybody, because if I did I would get whipped. I have never had, to my recollection, any more clothing than I have at present—a calico dress and skirt. I have seen stockings and other clothes in our room, but was not allowed to put them on. Whenever mamma went out I was locked up in the bedroom. I do not know for what I was whipped—mamma never said anything to me when she whipped me. I do not want to go back to live with mamma, because she beats me so. I have no recollection of ever being on the street in my life. . . . [Counsel stated further evidence would be produced] . . . as to the mysterious visits of parties to the house of the Connollys, which, taken together with the intelligent and rather refined appearance of the child, tends to the conclusion that she is a child of parents of some prominence in society, who, for some reason have abandoned her to her present undeserved fate . . . Counsel on behalf of Mr. Bergh, in his statement to the court, desired it to be clearly understood that the latter's action in the case has been prompted by his feelings and duty as a humane citizen; that in no sense has he acted in his official capacity as President of the Society for Prevention of Cruelty to Animals, but is none the less determined to avail himself of such means as the laws place within his power, to prevent the too frequent cruelties practiced on children.

The next two exerpts from the *Times* published April 11 and 14, 1874, demonstrate the extent to which children were pawns of uncaring citizens, professionals, and institutions. During her infancy, Mary Ellen was handed over to Mrs. Connolly, with no questions asked, by the superintendent of the institution where she was living and was perfunctorily uprooted, merely on the statement of a physician who served as a reference for the satisfactoriness of the subsequently abusive home.

(4/11/1874) THE MISSION OF HUMANITY. Continuation of the Proceedings Instituted by Mr. Bergh on Behalf of the Child, Mary Ellen Wilson

Quite a number of persons, including several ladies, were attracted to the court by the publicity which had been given to the proceedings had on the previous day, all of them evidently deeply sympathizing with the little neglected waif, whose cause had been espoused by Mr. Bergh. Ten o'clock in the morning, to which the hearing had been adjourned, found the little girl, Mr. Bergh and his counsel, Messrs. Elbridge T. Gerry and Ambrose Monell, and Mrs. Connolly, the former custodian of the girl, all present in court. The first witness put upon the stand was Mrs. Connolly, who testified as follows: I was formerly married to Thomas McCormack, and had three children by him, all of whom are dead. After Mr. McCormack's death I married Francis Connolly. Before my first husband died he told me he had three children by another woman, who was alive, but a good-for-nothing. I went with McCormack to Mr. Kellock, and got out the child, Mary Ellen, my husband signing the paper.

Here the paper referred to was produced, and which proved to be an "indenture" of the child, Mary Ellen Wilson, aged one year and six months, to Thomas

McCormack, butcher, and his wife, Mary, in February, 1866, and whereby they undertook to report once a year the condition of the child to the Commissioners of Charities and Correction. This indenture was indorsed by Commissioner Isaac Bell and Secretary Brown.

Witness continued as follows: I know this was one of my husband's illegitimate children. He selected this one. The mother's name, I suppose, is Wilson, because Mr. Kellock, the Superintendent, had the name down. Mr. Kellock asked no questions about my relation to the child. I told him I wanted this child. My husband never told me where the woman Wilson lived. We got the child out on the 2d of January, without any paper being served or any receipt for the child. This was the only paper we signed, and it was not signed until the 15th of February. Sometimes my husband told me the mother of the child lived down town. I learned from several people who knew my husband that the woman is still alive. I could not tell who they were. They were laborers who came from work with him and stopped there drinking. I have no way of knowing if the woman is still alive, or if she has any relatives. I never received a cent for supporting this child. At the time I took the child we were living at No. 866 Third avenue, and my husband said the mother left it there, and he would take it out until such time as she called for it. I have instructed the child according to the undertaking in the indenture—that there is a God, and what it is to lie. I have not instructed her in "the art and mystery of housekeeping," because she is too young. She had a flannel petticoat when she came to me, and I gave her no others.

At this point the witness grew somewhat excited at Mr. Gerry, the examining counsel, whom she assumed to be ignorant of the difficulties of bringing up and governing children, and concluded her testimony by an admission that on but two occasions had she complied with the conditions of the indenture requiring her to report once a year to the Commissioners of Charities and Correction the condition of the child.

(4/14/1874)

Mr. Geo. Kellock, Superintendent of Outdoor Poor, testified that a child named Mary Ellen Wilson was indentured from the Department of Charities in 1866, being then eighteen months old; that the records show the same to have been left there on the 21st of May, 1864, by a woman named Mary Score, giving her address as No. 235 Mulberry street, and who swore that until within three weeks of that time she had received $8 per month for the child's support; had no means of knowing who the child's parents were, and nothing was said by either Mr. McCormack or his wife, Mrs. Connolly, at the time, as to any relationship of either of them to the child; the $8 per month had been paid to Mary Score by the parties leaving the child with her, and it was when that payment stopped that she brought the child to his office. Reference was demanded from Mr. and Mrs. McCormack when they took the child, and they gave their family physician, Dr. Laughlin or McLaughlin, whose statement in reference to them was deemed satisfactory and an order for the delivery of the child was given accordingly.

The news report of April 22, 1874 described the stepmother's violent displacement of her frustration on to the child, a prominent characteristic of abusive parents. Legal issues specific to children apparently were not involved in the case, as some current writers claim. The abusive mother was tried for and found guilty of assault and battery.

MARY ELLEN WILSON. Mrs. Connolly, the Guardian, Found Guilty, and Sentenced One Year's Imprisonment at Hard Labor

Mary Connolly, the discovery of whose inhuman treatment of the little waif, Mary Ellen Wilson, caused such excitement and indignation in the community, was placed on trial before Recorder Hackett yesterday, in the Court of General Sessions. The prisoner, whose appearance is anything but prepossessing, sat immovable during the proceedings, never lifting her eyes from the ground, except when the child was first placed on the stand. Little Mary Ellen, an interesting-looking child, was neatly dressed in the new clothes provided for her by the humane ladies who have taken an interest in her, and has so much improved since her first appearance in the courts as to be scarcely recognized as the cowering, half-naked child rescued by Mr. Bergh's officers. The child was brought into court in charge of Mrs. Webb, the matron at Police Headquarters. Mr. Bergh occupied a seat beside District Attorney Rollins, and took an active part in the proceedings. There were two indictments against the prisoner, one for feloniously assaulting Mary Ellen Wilson with a pair of scissors on the 7th of April, and the other for a series of assaults committed during the years 1873 and 1874. The trial yesterday was on the indictment charging felonious assault.

The little child was put upon the stand, and having been instructed by Recorder Hackett in the nature and responsibility of an oath, was sworn. At first she answered the questions put to her readily, but soon became frightened and gave way to sobs and tears. She was soon reassured, however, by the kind words of the Recorder and District Attorney Rollins, and intelligently detailed the story of her ill-treatment. The scar on her forehead when taken from Mrs. Connolly's house, had been inflicted, she said by her "mamma" with a pair of scissors. Her "mamma" as she called Mrs. Connolly, had been ripping a quilt, which she held, and struck her with the scissors because she did not like how the quilt was held. The child stated that she had been repeatedly beaten with a long cane by her "mamma" without having done anything wrong. The general cruelty and neglect of Mrs. Connolly were also testified to by the child, as has already been published in the proceedings of the preliminary examinations. Mrs. Webb, Matron at Police Headquarters, Detective McDougall, Alonzo S. Evans, of Mr. Bergh's society, Mrs. Wheeler of St. Luke's Mission, Mrs. Bingham, from whom the prisoner rented apartments, Mrs. States, and Charles Smith, testified to the bruises and filth on the child's body when rescued from Mrs. Connolly's, and to the instances of ill-treatment which had come to their knowledge. After an able argument from District Attorney Rollins and a charge of characteristics clearness from the Recorder, the jury retired, and after twenty minutes deliberation, returned a verdict of guilty of assault and battery.

Recorder Hackett, addressing the prisoner, said that he had no doubt whatever of her guilt. She had been accorded every opportunity to prove her innocence, and the court was fully satisfied that she had been guilty of gross and wanton cruelty. He would have been satisfied if the jury had found her guilty of the higher offense charged. As a punishment to herself, but more as a warning to others, he would sentence her to the extreme penalty of the law—one year in the Penitentiary at hard labor. The prisoner heard her sentence without moving a muscle, and preserved the same hard, cruel expression of countenance displayed by her during the trial, while being conveyed to the Tombs.

A brother of Mrs. Connolly says that the child was legally adopted by the prisoner, who has the legal proofs in her possession, and will seek to gain the custody of the little one at the expiration of her term of punishment.

FOUNDING OF THE SOCIETY FOR THE PREVENTION OF CRUELTY TO CHILDREN

As exerpts from the *New York Times* on December 17 and 29, 1874 suggest, the Society for the Prevention of Cruelty to Children (SPCC) was founded for the same purpose as the parallel animal protection agency; namely, to meet the need for enforcement of existing laws. Henry Bergh continued to be a driving force in the society.

(12/17/1874)

The apprehension and subsequent conviction of the persecutors of little Mary Ellen, some time since, suggested to Mr. Elbridge T. Gerry, the counsel engaged in the prosecution of the case, the necessity for the existence of an organized society for the prevention of similar acts of atrocity. Upon expressing his views among his friends he found plenty of sympathizers with the movement, but no one sufficiently interested to attempt the formation of such a society. About this time he met Mr. John D. Wright, to whom he had stated his plan. The latter at once became warmly interested, and undertook the necessary steps toward effecting an organization. Invitations were extended to a large number of prominent citizens interested in the welfare of children to meet at Association Hall on Tuesday afternoon and many promptly responded. Mr. Gerry defined the object of the meeting which, he said, was to organize a society for the prevention of cruelty to children. There were in existence in this City and State, he said, many excellent institutions, some as charitable corps, and others as State reformatories and asylums, for receiving and caring for little children. Among these ought be cited the Children's Aid Society, Society for the Protection of Destitute Children, etc., and in addition each religious denomination had one or more hospitals and similar institutions devoted to the moral and physical culture of helpless children. These societies, however, only assured the care of their inmates after they had been legally placed in their custody. It was not in the province of these excellent institutions to seek out and rescue from the dens and slums of the City the little unfortunates whose lives were rendered miserable by the system of cruelty and abuse which was constantly practiced upon them by the human brutes who happened to possess the custody or control of them; and this was the defect which it was proposed to remedy by the formation of this society. There were plenty of laws existing on the statute books of the State, which provided for all such cases as had been cited but unfortunately no one had heretofore been held responsible for their enforcement. The Police and prosecuting officers were engaged in the prosecution and conviction of offenses of a graver legal character, and, although they were always ready to aid in enforcing the laws when duly called up to do so, they could not be expected to discover and prosecute those who claimed the right to ill-treat the children over whom they had an apparent legal control. This society proposed to enforce legally, but energetically, the existing laws and to secure the conviction and punishment of every violation of any of those laws. The society would not interfere with the numerous institutions already existing, but would aid them in their work. It did not propose to aid any religious denomination, and would be kept entirely free from any political influences. Its duty toward the children would be discharged when their future custody should be decided by the courts. The counsel for the society volunteers his gratuitous services in the prosecution of cases reported by its officers during the first year. The Secretary will be entitled to a moderate compensation, but no salary will be paid to the remaining officers. . . .

(12/29/1874)

The Society for the Prevention of Cruelty to Children met yesterday afternoon at No. 100 East Twenty-second street, Mr. John D. Wright presiding. There was a very large attendance, three-fourths of whom were ladies, and all evinced the deepest interest in the proceedings. The Chairman stated briefly the objects of the society, and said that they felt complimented at seeing so many ladies with them, which showed that they felt an interest in the objects of the society. He hoped that all of those present would, in common with the society, interest themselves in the matter, and become co-workers with them. The object was one which had long been overlooked in this City. Children have rights which parents and guardians should respect, and he was sure that the more the society became known the more interest would be felt in it.

Mr. Elbridge T. Gerry, counsel for the society, said that the press throughout the City, with one unimportant exception, had endeavored to do them justice. . . . The society claimed the sympathy of every woman in the community, the co-operation of every married man, and also the assistance of every young man. They had a case now pending where a woman was arrested for placing her own child on a red-hot stove, the result of which was that the child died. He hoped for the sake of humanity that the mother was insane. The law, said Mr. Gerry, does not authorize a brutal father to injure his child, and they would take such measures as would prevent it, if possible in the future. They proposed to receive complaints from any person, and such complaints will be promptly investigated. He alluded to the case of little Mary Ellen, who was beaten with a raw cow-hide for three months, and he was glad to say that the woman who inflicted the cruelty was sent to the Penitentiary for one year. What the society wanted was to find those persons who are ready to place the facts before them. He predicted that as soon as the habitual abusers of children learn that there is a law to reach them, there will be very few cases like that of Mary Ellen, or the red-hot stove case. He concluded by hoping that various institutions would give the society their aid and co-operation. . . .

Mr. Henry Bergh said he felt a great interest in the subject. There seemed to him "that there is a providence in the affairs of men, rough hew them as they may." The slaves were first freed from bondage; next came the emancipation of the brute creation, and next the emancipation of the little children was about to take place. He took exception to Mr. Gerry calling a father who ill treated his child a "brute." His (the speaker's) clients never got drunk and did not chastise in that way. While anxious to protect children from undue severity, he said he was in favor of good wholesome flogging, which he often found most efficacious. His connection with the society is only a slender one, the Chairman and Mr. Gerry being the active agents. There was, he said, a serious aspect to the question. These little waifs of society were destined at a future day to become the fathers and mothers of this Republic. If they were neglected the permanent interests of this Republic would be neglected. He drew attention to "baby farming," and said the question would receive the attention of the society. Policemen, too, who used their clubs would not be neglected, and one of these officers was now under arrest for injuring a child. He hoped every man and woman would aid this Christian and civilized work. . . .

Mr. Bergh said the society should be careful not to interfere in petty cases, as it would ruin their usefulness. It is only the atrociously bad cases that should engage their attention at first.

Media coverage of the plight of Mary Ellen culminated in the passage, in 1875, of "an Act of the incorporation of societies for the prevention of cruelty to children". The magnitude of the society's legal authority and community influence are clearly demonstrated in Sections 3 and 4:

> 3. Any society so incorporated may prefer a complaint before any court or magistrate having jurisdiction for the violation of any law relating to or affecting children, and may aid in bringing the facts before such court or magistrate in any proceeding taken.
>
> 4. All magistrates, constables, sheriffs and officers of police shall, as occasion may require, aid the society so incorporated, its officers, members and agents in the enforcement of all laws which now are or may hereafter be enacted, relating to or affecting children. (*Laws of New York,* 1881, p. 114.)

What happened to little Mary Ellen? The former darling of the press, having served her purpose, was "finally disposed of" by being reinstitutionalized, as this brief, but poignant report of December 27, 1874 indicates.

LITTLE MARY ELLEN FINALLY DISPOSED OF

In the matter of the child Mary Ellen Wilson, rescued from Mary Connolly, and whose grandparents were alleged to be residing in London, Judge Lawrence yesterday decided that the relatives not having been found, the child should be sent to "The Sheltering Arms." It was the case of little Mary Ellen which led to the formation of the Society for the Prevention of Cruelty to Children.

The secretary's report on the first year of the Society for the Prevention of Cruelty to Children (SPCC) attests to the militancy of these early child advocates:

We have agents about the city to look after poor children in the streets. In cases where we find children are hired to beg, we arrest the parties who hire them out. This is frequently done by Italian organ-grinders, of whom we arrested quite a number during the past month. The society in all its transactions in reference to children, brings them before the court having jurisdiction in the matter. If a complaint is made to us of any child being ill-used, we send an officer to investigate the case and see what can be done. If the child is very badly abused, we cause it to be taken away and put into an asylum or otherwise properly provided for. Children abandoned in the streets are likewise disposed of. We also give advice and information to all parties asking for it, relating to children, and a great many come to us for this purpose. When there is any offense committed against the child, like that of inducing a young girl to go into a house of ill-fame, we follow the case through to the end. (Letchworth 1876, p. 306).

In 1877, the American Humane Association was incorporated and established national headquarters in Denver, Colorado. By the turn of the century, its membership was comprised of 150 anti-cruelty or humane societies throughout the nation, most of which dealt with both child and animal protection (Bremner

1971, p. 201). The nature of the child maltreatment was indistinguishable from current cases. They differed, however, in the rapid disposition of cases and in the fact that some children, themselves, requested the Society's protection. The following is a sample of cases from the files of the Massachusetts Society for the Prevention of Cruelty to Children (1881):

> Man arrested for incestuous relations with his own daughter, 12 years of age. Sentenced to five years in State Prison. Girl adopted by good family.
>
> Girl, 9. Mother dead. Step-mother had severely whipped the girl. Had scars on head and face; had been placed on hot stove. Left naked in a cold room in winter. Difficult to obtain evidence. Child taught to conceal cruelty. To avoid publicity, father gave child to the Society.
>
> ... girl, 15, living with aunt who ... overworked and abused her by blows on the head, and by striking with hot poker. Girl sought our protection. We obtained guardianship and custody after a long contest.
>
> Six children, 4 months to 10 years. Father drunken and ugly, abused wife and children. Case investigated. Arrangements made to send wife and children to relatives in another State. Father repented, promised reform; mother accepted his promise. At last accounts doing well (pp. 31–33).

The right of the community to intrude in the home in order to protect children against cruel and abusive parents was asserted in 1882 by Elbridge Gerry, lawyer for Henry Bergh in the Mary Ellen Wilson case, legal advisor to the Society for the Prevention of Cruelty to Animals and president of the New York Society for the Prevention of Cruelty to Children from 1879–1901 (Bremner 1971, p. 190). After emphasizing the greater power of corporations, in this case the SPCC, over law enforcement agencies in protecting children, especially against wealthy or influential parents, he emphasized:

> [The Societies] interfere only when the law authorizes their interference for the benefit of the child; and they assert alike in their teaching and in their practice, the existence of the axiom that at the present day in this country, children have *some* rights, which even parents are bound to respect. ... No matter how exalted the offender, the Society has the right to confront him with its proofs; no matter how degraded the object of its mercy, the Society is bound by its corporate duty to stretch out its hand and rescue from starvation, misery, cruelty and perhaps death, the helpless little child who ought to have a protector, but for some reason, not its fault, has been deprived of advantage (pp. 129–30).

In a paper presented at the International Congress of Charities, Correction and Philanthropy in 1893, Fay described empathically the feelings of abusive parents whose children must be removed from them, an empathy that characterizes child abuse workers in current programs:

> It is a delicate duty to deprive parents of their children, and the work must be done with caution, and only in cases of necessity. The parents thus deprived are not destitute of affection; the liquids they imbibe do not quench parental love; and the tears they shed are as real as those flowing from the eyes of men and women who had had better opportunities in life, or who had better resisted temptation. But our duty demands that, while we appreciate the loss of the parents, we think of the gain to the child. We should strive

to be as kind in our action as a just enforcement of the law will permit, having a constant care, in cases of apparent neglect, to distinguish between the poor and destitute and the unworthy and dissolute. But we have a constant duty to remember that these neglected children have more years before them of happiness or misery than their parents, and have not lost their rights by their own bad conduct; so that, if there is to be suffering by the severing of the family tie, the parents should be the sufferers, and the child have the "right to life, liberty, and the pursuit of happiness."

FROM PRIVATE CHILD-RESCUING TO PUBLIC CHILD PROTECTION AGENCIES

The SPCC was the driving force behind significant reforms in behalf of children: The New York SPCC drafted an act to prevent baby farming, the practice of boarding infants in unlicensed private homes and institutions until their death or adoption. Another act prevented the *padrone* system, the business of purchasing children from their parents in Italy for the purpose of employing them in dangerous theatrical performances. The societies promoted the creation of temporary homes for children separated from their parents. They worked for the passage of child labor laws. And their efforts to prohibit the mingling of children detained by the court with adult criminals gave impetus to the establishment of juvenile courts (De Francis 1973; Lunderg 1947). Fundamental differences in viewpoint developed among the societies, however, which contributed to the demise of militant child protection. The New York SPCC implemented a philosophy of child-rescuing, whereas the Massachusetts SPCC and the majority of societies were concerned about the potential dangers of the police powers of the SPCC and wished to coordinate efforts with other agencies and to work toward treatment and prevention. Folks (1902) described the state of affairs:

> The influence of the "cruelty" societies as a whole has been in favor of the care of children in institutions, rather than by placing them in families. So far as known, none of the societies have undertaken the continued care of the children rescued by them, but all have turned them over to the care of institutions or societies incorporated for the care of children. By a vigorous enforcement of the laws authorizing the commitment of vagrant, begging, and various other classes of exposed children, they have very largely increased the numbers of children becoming wards of public or private charity. Usually they have not coöperated to any extent with placing-out societies, perhaps because of being continually engaged in breaking up families of bad character, but have rather become feeders of institutions, both reformatory and charitable. The New York society during 1900 placed six children in homes or situations; during the same period 2407 children were, upon its recommendation, committed to institutions. Constantly occupied with questions involving the custody of children, they have, not unnaturally, preferred to place the children rescued by them within the walls of institutions, where possession is at least nine points of the law, rather than to trust to a measure of uncertainty necessarily involved in the placing-out system. Without detracting from the great credit due to such societies for the rescue of children from cruel parents or immoral surroundings, it must be said that their influence in the upbuilding of very large institutions, and their very general

failure to urge the benefits of adoption for young children, have been unfortunate. Probably their greatest beneficence has been, not to the children who have come under their care, but to the vastly larger number whose parents have restrained angry tempers and vicious impulses through fear of "the Cruelty" (p. 174).

In addition to divergent philosophies within the anticruelty societies, social and governmental changes contributed to the shift from child-rescuing by private corporations to public child protection agencies. World War I had gradually deflected attention from the movement, and the Depression decreased the number of financial contributions to these private agencies. Furthermore, children did not always fare particularly well under the auspices of agencies devoted to the dual function of animal and child protection. For example, between 1920 and 1922, the society in Colorado handled 5,183 animal cases compared to only 1,118 cases of children (Shultz 1924, p. 223). Most important perhaps was the realization that the government, rather than the private sector, should be dealing with child protection. For example, the secretary of the Pennsylvania SPCC asserted: "This thing that we are doing is, after all, the job of the public authorities. The public ought to protect all citizens, including the children, from cruelty and improper care. As speedily as conditions admit, we should turn over to the public the things we are at present doing" (American Humane Association 1914, p. 25). Finally, public child welfare services became responsible for child protection because of the mandate in the Social Security Act of 1930, which required child welfare services for "neglected, dependent children, and children in danger of becoming delinquent" (De Francis 1973*a*, p. 303). The American Humane Association's Children's Division became the national association of child protective agencies, which includes in its membership state, local, public, and the few remaining private protection agencies, juvenile courts, and other child welfare services. It now provides consultation to public agencies, promotes public understanding of child protection, conducts research, and performs other services.

The backbone of child protective services became the field of social work, which, since the 1920s, had become increasingly professionalized. In accordance with this professionalism, and influenced by psychoanalysis, which emphasized a neutral stance with respect to the client, social work rejected the law-enforcement approach to child abuse and neglect and any judgment of wrong-doing on the part of the parents. In the words of De Francis (1973*b*), director of the Children's Division of the American Humane Association:

> In those early days, protective services for children was almost equated with law enforcement. The view was that if a parent was neglecting or abusing a child, this constituted violation of the law. Therefore, the approach was to rescue the child from the "bad" home and to prosecute the parents for violation of the law. This procedure was in practice for a substantial number of years. It was an era before the social sciences made themselves felt. It was before social work, as a profession, had come into being. . . . The advent of social services made an impact on these early child protection agencies. They began to question their approach in terms of asking, "Is it truly beneficial to the child to rescue the child from a bad home? Would it not make better sense if, instead, we rescued the home for the child? Would it not make better

sense if we provided services so that we made a 'good home' out of a bad home; so that we made responsible parents out of irresponsible people?'' (p. 323)

This shift in focus from the child to the family led to a view of the parent, rather than the child, as the primary client. As De Francis (1973*a*) has explained:

> Child Protective Services is a specialized area of Child Welfare. It is concerned with preventing neglect, abuse and exploitation of children by "reaching out" with social services to stabilize family life. It seeks to preserve the family unit by strengthening parental capacity for good child care. While it is child centered, the special focus is on the family where unresolved problems have produced visible signs of neglect or abuse and the home situation presents actual hazard or the potential for additional damage in the physical or emotional well-being of children (pp. 303–304).

This philosophical guideline, introduced by social workers in the 1920s, of keeping the family together while working with the parents continued, for good or ill, to dominate the treatment and prevention of child abuse and neglect.

Ironically, while for several decades social workers had been investigating and treating the maltreatment of children by their parents, medicine did not officially discover—or rather, rediscover—the problem until the 1950s. A little ground had been broken much earlier by physicians outside the United States. In 1868, Ambroise Tardieu, a professor of legal medicine in France, had described autopsy findings on several children who had been battered to death. That year physician Athol Johnson diagnosed rickets as the cause of repeated fractures in a group of children at the Hospital for Sick Children in London. "We now know that almost every case he described was, in fact, an abused child" (Kempe and Kempe 1978).

MEDICINE'S OFFICIAL DISCOVERY OF CHILD ABUSE AND NEGLECT BY PARENTS

There are a number of reasons for the delay by several decades in medicine's official acknowledgment of cases of child maltreatment seen in medical practice. In addition to psychological factors, to be discussed later, technological factors contributed to misdiagnoses. The diagnosis of "battered child syndrome," which eventually came to be associated with bone fractures in various stages of healing, could not readily be made until the relatively recent discipline of pediatric radiology had been established. According to Radbill (1968), infant x-rays had been studied in 1906, but it was not until 1926 that the first x-ray department in a children's hospital was established. It was not until 1935 that "the radiographic features of injuries to bones of infants and their repair were . . . described in any detail" (Silverman 1968, p. 59).

In 1946, John Caffey, a professor of pediatric radiology at Columbia University, described the occurrence in infants of unexplained fractures of the long bones accompanying subdural hematoma. He reported: "In each case unexplained fresh fractures appeared shortly after the patient had arrived home after discharge from the hospital. In one of these cases the infant was clearly unwanted by both parents and this raised the question of intentional ill-treatment of the infant; the evidence was inadequate to prove or disprove this point'' (p. 172). He concluded that ''the fractures appear to be of traumatic origin but the traumatic episodes and the causal mechanisms remain obscure'' (p. 173).

A paper by Silverman in 1953, which referred to Caffey's (1946) findings, raised the possibility of parent-caused injury of children: ''It is not often appreciated that many individuals responsible for the care of infants and children (who cannot give their own history) may permit trauma and be aware of it, may recognize trauma but forget or be reluctant to admit it, or may deliberately injure the child and deny it'' (p. 413).

Injuries of children by parents were viewed primarily as accidentally, not intentionally, inflicted, as the following indicates:

> How many times have we seen children lifted on or off street cars, vehicles, up and down steps by a well meaning but none the less potentially traumatic pull of an arm? How many children are swung by their arms or legs? How many children are saved from falls or other injuries which may have serious consequences by a quick grab by a custodian or parent? There is probably hardly a child who at some time during his infancy has not been exposed to trauma of this sort (p. 425).

In his summary, Silverman recommended that ''extreme care must be exercised not to overwhelm responsible custodians of the infants with feelings of guilt as the history is elicited'' (p. 426). In his discussion of Silverman's paper, Neuhauser (1953) flirted with the notion of child abuse in his description of injury to a child by an intoxicated parent of low intelligence. In referring to a ''type of trauma . . . incidental to ordinary family life,'' he stated: '' . . . the incidence of injury goes up in inverse proportion to the intelligence of the parents, and particularly to their addiction to inebriating liquors, because most of the ones we have seen have been where the father has come home intoxicated and wanted to play with the child and tossed it back and forth to a family friend'' (p. 427).

In 1955, Woolley and Evans described cases in which child abuse and neglect by parents were unequivocal. They concluded:

> The general environmental factors surrounding infants who suffer osseous discontinuity range from ''unavoidable'' episodes in stable households, through what we have termed an unprotective environment, to a surprisingly large segment characterized by the presence of aggressive, immature, or emotionally ill adults . . . they came invariably from unstable households with a high incidence of neurotic or frankly psychotic behavior on the part of at least one adult, and we have termed such situations injury-prone environments. When these infants were removed from such surroundings and treated as if their defects were due to adverse stresses, healing took place promptly and new lesions did not develop. . . . It is difficult to avoid the overall conclusion that skeletal lesions having the appearance of fractures . . . are due to undesirable vectors of force (pp. 542–43).

In a special invited lecture at the Annual Congress of the British Institute of Radiology, Caffey (1957) selected the topic of traumatic lesions in the bones of children. After reexamining his earlier (1946) data and those of other investigators, he concluded that intentional child abuse by parents was often the basis for the medical syndrome:

> The diagnosis of traumatic injury to infants and children is of more than academic interest, especially when the injuries are repeated and when the traumatic origin is denied by parents or other caretakers. The correct early diagnosis of injury may be the only means by which the abused youngsters can be removed from their traumatic environment and their wrongdoers punished. Correct early diagnosis of injury by the radiologist may be life-saving to some of these otherwise helpless youngsters, or it may prevent permanent crippling injuries to others. Early diagnosis may also prevent or stop unwarranted expensive medical investigations which ultimately prove embarrassing to the attending physician when the true story of simple trauma becomes known'' (p. 283).

By 1960, Elmer, a social worker at Children's Hospital in Pittsburgh, had published an article attributing the resistance of physicians to diagnosing child abuse to a repugnance for the problem felt by other professionals as well, and to the difficulty in assuming an objective attitude with abusive parents.

CHILD ABUSE AND NEGLECT REVISITED: THE SIXTIES AND SEVENTIES

Attention to the maltreatment of children by their parents was revitalized by the publication in 1962 of an article by Henry Kempe, chairman of the Department of Pediatrics at the University of Colorado School of Medicine, and by several medical colleagues. They coined the term "the battered child syndrome," a condition of high incidence, and emphasized the unwillingness of physicians to diagnose it. The article and subsequent workshops and conferences chaired by Kempe elicited extensive media coverage, public outrage, legislation, and the publication of hundreds of articles in professional and popular periodicals. But why the furor? Had not the maltreatment of children by their parents been discovered decades earlier? Had not protection of children against abuse been going on in America since the establishment of the anticruelty societies? What was the fuss about?

The hullabaloo was a response not only to the rediscovery of child abuse, but to other overwhelming discoveries. One was the harsh and embarrassing reality that personal factors were seriously interfering with the professional work of physicians regarding child abuse and neglect. Needless deaths and further injuries had been occurring because of failure to diagnose the battered child syndrome and take protective action by members of a profession dedicated to healing and saving lives. It is to the credit of the medical profession, however, that physicians, themselves, pointed out the failure. Helfer (1968), a pediatrician and collaborator of Kempe, asserted that physicians' unwillingness to diagnose the condition "cannot prevail much longer for the problem is too immense and the responsibilities too clear to be ignored" (p. 43). He then proceeded to spell out clearly some of the psychological bases for this unwillingness: "emotional ties to the family, lack of understanding of his legal (much less moral) obligations, denial of the facts, inability to obtain these facts, lack of experience, and 'busy attitude' '' (p. 44).

Another discovery was that parental abuse and neglect still continued with great frequency in the United States, despite the earlier enactment of laws and development of social work services in child protection. The movement in the sixties, according to Rosenheim (1977), reflected:

> . . . genuine alarm about the existence of a problem which, hitherto, had commonly been considered to be solved . . . statutory penalties against cruelty to children were among the first wave of modern child welfare enactments. Both the criminal laws prohibiting child cruelty and later statutes authorizing intervention by child-rescue societies in cases of suspected cruelty were nineteenth century events. It had been widely assumed that physical cruelty was a deplorable fact of the past—in the Western world, at least. It had been assumed, especially by those in child welfare disciplines (who presumably give most thought to these matters) that the modern challenge was preventing or curtailing the effects of *emotional* cruelty. Professional literature reflects the shift in emphasis from physical to emotional abuse between the 1870s and the 1950s (p. 453).

Just as physicians had denied the reality of child abuse, social workers were denying the reality that many abusive parents continued to abuse their children, despite case work provided by child protection agencies. In the words of Kempe (1968):

> It is regrettable that casework is often undertaken at the risk of further damage to a defenseless child in the mistaken belief that "there is no such thing as a person we cannot help." Indeed, there are clearly situations where a case worker has to face the fact that reliance principally on case work therapy alone will not prevent a repetitive injury to the child. Eisenberg has stated that social workers as a group tend to believe there is no such thing as "cancer of the soul" (p. 170).

Regarding the frequency of reabuse because of social workers' reluctance to remove abused children from the parental home while parents receive case work, Kempe (1968) stated:

> One of the serious problems protective services face in their management of child abuse relates to the disposition of those cases in which placement away from home is not accomplished and the decision to leave the child with the abusing parents has been made. . . . In the battered child syndrome under the situation prevailing and while the child remains an irritant and so liable to further injury, casework alone is apt to be a dangerous method of handling the problem, and protective services should be extremely cautious about assuming the responsibility for leaving the injured child in the home, especially if the child has been badly battered and is under three years of age (p. 170).

The realization that neither casework alone, nor medicine alone, could solve the intricate problem of parental child abuse and neglect led to the emphasis on the multidisciplinary approach to management, treatment, and prevention, an approach also pioneered in 1962 by Boardman, a social worker at Children's Hospital in Los Angeles.

It is not surprising that the discovery of the continuation of child abuse and its repression by professionals took place during the sixties. Like the earlier era when Henry Bergh held sway, the sixties was a time of keen sensitivity to injustice and radical social change, of serious questioning of once cherished ideologies and merciless probing of old truths. Child abuse and neglect were rediscovered in the midst of the rediscovery of the abuse and neglect of ethnic minorities, women, the old, the poor, and many others. Furthermore, defenses against the perception of violence were being inundated by manifold expressions of violence in American society: Vietnam, Watts, Selma, the assassinations of the Kennedys and Martin Luther King, and a host of other violences that stretched comprehension but could not be denied. In a decade distinguished by consciousness-raising, public consciousness was bound to be raised to violence in the home as well as in the streets, to repression by the professionals as well as by clients.

Like Henry Bergh many decades earlier, Henry Kempe was the driving force behind the child protection movement during a turbulent era. He described his role in publicizing the battered child syndrome:

> When I saw child abuse between 1956 and 1958 in Denver, our housestaff was unwilling to make this diagnosis. Initially I felt intellectual dismay at diagnoses such as "obscure bruising," "osteogenesis imperfecta tarda," "spontaneous subdural hematoma." When I served as a member of the program committee of the American Academy of Pediatrics in the late 1950s and became chairman of that committee in 1960, I discovered that one prerogative of this position was to plan one plenary session. The rest of the committee agreed to a multidisciplinary group presentation of child abuse, provided only that I came up with a title that would catch our membership's attention. That is how the emotive term, "the battered child syndrome" was born (1978, p. 256).

In July 1962, there appeared in the *Journal of the American Medical Association* an article entitled "The Battered-Child Syndrome," by Kempe, Silverman (the radiologist who in 1953 had suggested parent involvement in the development of children's fractures), Steele (a psychiatrist), Droegemueller (an obstetrician), and Silver (a radiologist). The authors presented findings on the incidence of child abuse based on a nationwide survey of hospitals, described the syndrome and characteristics of abusive parents, and discussed the reluctance of physicians to acknowledge the existence of parental child abuse. An editorial in that issue commented favorably on the article, referred to the probable high frequency of the syndrome, and exhorted physicians to be alert to the diagnosis and to take protective action when the syndrome was suspected:

> It is likely that (the battered-child syndrome) will be found to be a more frequent cause of death than such well recognized and thoroughly studied diseases as leukemia, cystic fibrosis, and muscular dystrophy, and it may well rank with automobile accidents and the toxic and infectious encephalitides as cause of acquired disturbances of the central nervous system. . . . The implication that parents were instrumental in causing injury to their child is often difficult for the physician to accept. . . . Despite the understandable hesitation of the physician in becoming involved in what may turn out to be a police action, the consequences of improper disposition

are often so tragic that the physician must, in good conscience, call on social agencies and legal authorities to make certain that proper protection is given the child (p. 42).

The speed of public and professional response, enhanced by media coverage, was incredible. The U.S. Children's Bureau invited Kempe to a conference that year to participate in drafting model legislation on child abuse. The following year the Children's Division of the American Humane Association drafted similar legislation, recommending that child abuse cases be referred to child protection agencies. In 1963 alone, eighteen bills to protect battered children were introduced in the U.S. Congress, and eleven of them passed the same year. The American Medical Association, the Council of State Governments, and the Committee on the Infant and Preschool Child of the American Academy of Pediatrics presented their recommendations from 1964 to 1966. By 1967, all states in the nation, as well as Washington, D.C. and the Virgin Islands, had passed child abuse reporting laws. "Few legislative proposals in the history of the United States," asserted Monrad Paulsen, Dean of the Law School of the University of Virginia, "have been so widely adopted in so little time" (1966, p. 47). The fact that professionals had to be legally mandated to report a child's injured condition attests to the intensity of resistance to the problem of child abuse, a situation that is unprecedented in the history of public health.

In March and April 1973, Senate hearings chaired by then Senator Walter Mondale took place on the Child Abuse Prevention Act, "to establish a National Center on Child Abuse and Neglect, to provide financial assistance for a demonstration program for the prevention, identification, and treatment of child abuse and neglect . . ." (p. 3). Part of the hearings were held in Denver because, according to Mondale, "it is well known that the team of witnesses about to testify before us, under the leadership of Dr. Kempe, consists of the finest effort being undertaken in the country today" (p. 164). Kempe and his associates presented the complicated issue of parental child abuse and neglect with clarity, wit and fervor. As Senator Jennings Randolph, a member of the Subcommittee on Children and Youth, said at the hearings, "Dr. Kempe, I wish you could be heard by millions of people. You are an ardent and very effective advocate" (p. 286).

And indeed, millions did hear about child abuse. Media coverage was as heart rending and as sensational as newspaper accounts in the Mary Ellen case decades earlier, as the following headlines indicate:

EXPERTS SAY MOST TEENAGE SLAYERS WERE ABUSED AS CHILDREN (*Washington Post*, 11/9/72) . . . RESCUING THE VICTIMS WHO CAN'T FIGHT BACK (*Washington Post*, 2/1/73) . . . THE CHILD-BEATERS: SICK BUT CURABLE; "MOTHERING," NOT PRISON, IS THE BEST HOPE FOR HELPING THESE PARENTS, EXPERTS SAY (*Denver Observer*, 3/24/73) . . . CHILD ABUSE—THE DARK SIDE OF FAMILY LIFE (*Sunday Star*, 3/25/73) . . . IMPASSIONED MONDALE WAGES WAR ON TRAGIC CHILD BEATINGS (*Christian Science Monitor*, 3/30/73). . . . (Senate Hearings, pp. 659–74)

The past scenario—a time of social change, a devoted leader, a responsive press—was being replayed. The Child Abuse Prevention and Treatment Act was signed into law in 1974, a century after the founding of the Society for the Prevention of Cruelty to Children.

REFERENCES

American Academy of Pediatrics, Committee on the Infant and Preschool Child. ''Maltreatment of children—The physically abused child.'' *Pediatrics* 37(1966):377–82.

American Humane Association. *38th Annual Report.* Denver, 1914.

American Humane Association. *Guidelines for Legislation to Protect the Battered Child.* Denver, 1963.

American Medical Association. Editorial. *Journal of the American Medical Association* 181(1962):42.

American Medical Association. ''Battered child legislation.'' *Journal of the American Medical Association* 188(1964):386.

Andrist, R. K., Russell, F., and Harwood, M. *History of the Confident Years.* New York: American Heritage, 1969.

Arnold, A. Appendix I. *Translation of Thucydides,* Vol. I. London: Oxford, 1830.

Boardman, H. ''A project to rescue children from inflicted injuries.'' *Social Work* 7(1962):43–51.

Bremner, R. H. *Children and Youth in America: A Documentary History,* Volume II. Cambridge, Mass.: Harvard University Press, 1971.

Caffey, J. ''Multiple fractures in the long bones of infants suffering from chronic subdural hematoma.'' *American Journal of Roentgenology,* 56(1946):163–73.

———. ''Some traumatic lesions in growing bones other than fractures and dislocations: Clinical and radiological features.'' The Mackenzie Davidson Memorial Lecture. *British Journal of Radiology* 30(1957):225–38.

Carson, G. *Men, Beasts, and Gods: A History of Cruelty and Kindness to Animals.* New York: Charles Scribner's Sons, 1972.

Children's Bureau. *The Abused Child: Principles and Suggested Language for Legislation on Reporting the Physically Abused Child.* Washington, D.C.: Government Printing Office, 1963.

Council on State Governments. *Physical Abuse of Children: Suggested State Legislation.* Washington, D.C., 1965.

De Francis, V. Testimony. Hearings before the Subcommittee on Children and Youth, 93rd Congress, on the Child Abuse Prevention Act (S. 1191), 1973*a*, pp. 301–14.

———. Protecting the abused child. Hearings before the Subcommittee on Children and Youth, 93rd Congress, on the Child Abuse Prevention Act (S. 1191), 1973*b*, pp. 323–31.

Elmer, E. ''Abused young children seen in hospitals.'' *Social Work* 5(1960):98–102.

Fay, F. B. Paper presented at the International Congress of Charities, Correction and Philanthropy. Chicago, 1893.

Folks, H. *The Care of Destitute, Neglected, and Delinquent Children.* New York: Macmillan, 1902.

Gerry, E. T. ''The relation of Societies for the Prevention of Cruelty to Children to child-saving work.'' *Proceedings of the National Conference of Charities and Correction* (1882): 129–30.

Goldman, E. *Rendezvous with Destiny: A History of Modern American Reform.* New York: Alfred A. Knopf, 1965.

Helfer, R. E. "The Responsibility and Role of the Physician." In R. E. Helfer and C. H. Kempe (eds.), *The Battered Child*. Chicago: University of Chicago Press, 1968.

Hole, J., and Levine, E. *Rebirth of Feminism*. New York: Quadrangle, 1971.

Johnson, A. A. W. *Lectures on the Surgery of Childhood*. London, 1868.

Kempe, C. H. "Some Problems Encountered by Welfare Departments in the Management of the Battered Child Syndrome." In R. E. Helfer and C. H. Kempe (eds.), *The Battered Child*. Chicago: University of Chicago Press, 1968.

————. "Child abuse—The pediatrician's role in child advocacy and preventive pediatrics." *American Journal of Diseases of Children* 132(1978):255-60.

Kempe, C. H., Silverman, F. N., Steele, B. F., Droegemueller, W., and Silver, H. K. "The battered child syndrome." *Journal of the American Medical Association* 181(1962):17-24.

Kempe, R. S., and Kempe, C. H. *Child Abuse*. Cambridge, Mass.: Harvard University Press, 1978.

Laws of New York. Albany, 1881.

Letchworth, W. P. *Extracts from the Ninth Annual Report of the State Board of Charities of the State of New York, Relating to Orphan Asylums and Other Institutions for the Care of Children*. Albany, 1876.

Lundberg, E. O. *Unto the Least of Them*. New York: Appleton–Century–Crofts, 1947.

Massachusetts Society for the Prevention of Cruelty to Children. *First Annual Report*, Boston, 1881.

Morse, M. *Ordeal of the Animals*. Englewood Cliffs, N.J.: Prentice-Hall, 1968.

New York Public Library. Miscellaneous papers, no date.

New York Times. Reportage, 1866, 1874.

Neuhauser, E. B. D. "Discussion of Dr. Silverman's paper." *American Journal of Roentgenology, Radium Therapy and Nuclear Medicine* 69(1953):426-27.

Oberholtzer, E. P. *History of the United States*. New York: Macmillan, 1917, Vol. I.

Paulsen, M. G. "Legal protection against child abuse." *Children* 13(1966):42-48.

Radbill, S. X. "A History of Child Abuse and Infanticide." In R. E. Helfer and C. H. Kempe (eds.), *The Battered Child*. Chicago: University of Chicago Press, 1968.

Rosenheim, M. K. "The Child and the Law." In E. H. Grotberg (ed.), *200 Years of Children*. Washington, D. C.: Office of Child Development, 1977.

Shultz, W. J. *The Humane Movement in the United States, 1910–1922*. New York: Columbia University Press, 1924.

Silverman, F. N. "The Roentgen manifestations of unrecognized skeletal trauma in infants." *American Journal of Roentgenology, Radium Therapy and Nuclear Medicine* 69(1953):413-42.

————. "Radiologic Aspects of the Battered Child Syndrome." In R. E. Helfer and C. H. Kempe (eds.), *The Battered Child*. Chicago: University of Chicago Press, 1968.

Subcommittee on Children and Youth. Hearings on the Child Abuse Prevention Act (S. 1191), 93rd Congress, 1973.

Tardieu, A. *Étude medico-legale sur l'infanticide*. Paris, 1868.

Woolley, P. V., and Evans, W. A. "Significance of skeletal lesions in infants resembling those of traumatic origin." *Journal of the American Medical Association* 158(1955):539-43.

CHAPTER 9

The Battered-Child Syndrome

C. Henry Kempe, Frederic N. Silverman, Brandt F. Steele, William Droegemueller, and Henry K. Silver

The battered-child syndrome, a clinical condition in young children who have received serious physical abuse, is a frequent cause of permanent injury or death. The syndrome should be considered in any child exhibiting evidence of fracture of any bone, subdural hematoma, failure to thrive, soft tissue swellings or skin bruising, in any child who dies suddenly, or where the degree and type of injury is at variance with the history given regarding the occurrence of the trauma. Psychiatric factors are probably of prime importance in the pathogenesis of the disorder, but knowledge of these factors is limited. Physicians have a duty and responsibility to the child to require a full evaluation of the problem and to guarantee that no expected repetition of trauma will be permitted to occur.

The battered-child syndrome is a term used by us to characterize a clinical condition in young children who have received serious physical abuse, generally from a parent or foster parent. The condition has also been described as "unrecognized trauma" by radiologists, orthopedists, pediatricians, and social service workers. It is a significant cause of childhood disability and death. Unfortunately, it is frequently not recognized or, if diagnosed, is inadequately handled by the physician because of hesitation to bring the case to the attention of the proper authorities.

INCIDENCE

In an attempt to collect data on the incidence of this problem, we undertook a nation-wide survey of hospitals which were asked to indicate the incidence of this syndrome in a one-year period. Among 71 hospitals replying, 302 such cases were reported to have occurred; 33 of the children died; and 85 suffered permanent brain injury. In one-third of the cases proper medical diagnosis was followed by some type of legal action. We also surveyed 77 District Attorneys who

Reprinted with permission from *JAMA* 181(1962):17–24. Copyright 1962, American Medical Association.

reported that they had knowledge of 447 cases in a similar one-year period. Of these, 45 died, and 29 suffered permanent brain damage; court action was initiated in 46% of this group. This condition has been a particularly common problem in our hospitals; on a single day, in November, 1961, the Pediatric Service of the Colorado General Hospital was caring for 4 infants suffering from the parent-inflicted battered-child syndrome. Two of the 4 died of their central nervous system trauma; 1 subsequently died suddenly in an unexplained manner 4 weeks after discharge from the hospital while under the care of its parents, while the fourth is still enjoying good health.

CLINICAL MANIFESTATIONS

The clinical manifestations of the battered-child syndrome vary widely from those cases in which the trauma is very mild and is often unsuspected and unrecognized, to those who exhibit the most florid evidence of injury to the soft tissues and skeleton. In the former group, the patients' signs and symptoms may be considered to have resulted from failure to thrive from some other cause or to have been produced by a metabolic disorder, an infectious process, or some other disturbance. In these patients specific findings of trauma such as bruises or characteristic roentgenographic changes as described below may be misinterpreted and their significance not recognized.

The battered-child syndrome may occur at any age, but, in general, the affected children are younger than three years. In some instances the clinical manifestations are limited to those resulting from a single episode of trauma, but more often the child's general health is below par, and he shows evidence of neglect, including poor skin hygiene, multiple soft tissue injuries, and malnutrition. One often obtains a history of previous episodes suggestive of parental neglect or trauma. A marked discrepancy between clinical findings and historical data as supplied by the parents is a major diagnostic feature of the battered-child syndrome. The fact that no new lesions, either of the soft tissue or of the bone, occur while the child is in the hospital or in a protected environment lends added weight to the diagnosis and tends to exclude many diseases of the skeletal or hemopoietic systems in which lesions may occur spontaneously or after minor trauma. Subdural hematoma, with or without fracture of the skull, is, in our experience, an extremely frequent finding even in the absence of fractures of the long bones. In an occasional case the parent or parent-substitute may also have assaulted the child by administering an overdose of a drug or by exposing the child to natural gas or other toxic substances. The characteristic distribution of these multiple fractures and the observation that the lesions are in different stages of healing are of additional value in making the diagnosis.

In most instances, the diagnostic bone lesions are observed incidental to examination for purposes other than evaluation for possible abuse. Occasionally, examination following known injury discloses signs of other, unsuspected, skeletal involvement. When parental assault is under consideration, radiologic examination of the entire skeleton may provide objective confirmation. Following diagnosis, radiologic examination can document the healing of lesions and reveal the appearance of new lesions if additional trauma has been inflicted.

The radiologic manifestations of trauma to growing skeletal structures are the same whether or not there is a history of injury. Yet there is reluctance on the part of many physicians to accept the radiological signs as indications of repetitive trauma and possible abuse. This reluctance stems from the emotional unwillingness of the physician to consider abuse as the cause of the child's difficulty and also because of unfamiliarity with certain aspects of fracture healing so that he is unsure of the significance of the lesions that are present. To the informed physician, the bones tell a story the child is too young or too frightened to tell.

PSYCHIATRIC ASPECTS

Psychiatric knowledge pertaining to the problem of the battered child is meager, and the literature on the subject is almost nonexistent. The type and degree of physical attack varies greatly. At one extreme, there is direct murder of children. This is usually done by a parent or other close relative, and, in these individuals, a frank psychosis is usually readily apparent. At the other extreme are those cases where no overt harm has occurred, and one parent, more often the mother, comes to the psychiatrist for help, filled with anxiety and guilt related to fantasies of hurting the child. Occasionally the disorder has gone beyond the point of fantasy and has resulted in severe slapping or spanking. In such cases the adult is usually responsive to treatment; it is not known whether or not the disturbance in these adults would progress to the point where they would inflict significant trauma on the child.

Between these two extremes are a large number of battered children with mild to severe injury which may clear completely or result in permanent damage or even death after repeated attack. Descriptions of such children have been published by numerous investigators including radiologists, orthopedists, and social workers. The latter have reported on their studies of investigations of families in which children have been beaten and of their work in effecting satisfactory placement for the protection of the child. In some of these published reports the parents, or at least the parent who inflicted the abuse, have been found to be of low intelligence. Often, they are described as psychopathic or sociopathic characters. Alcoholism, sexual promiscuity, unstable marriages, and minor criminal activities are reportedly common amongst them. They are immature, impulsive, self-centered, hypersensitive, and quick to react with poorly controlled aggression. Data in some cases indicate that such attacking parents had themselves been subject to some degree of attack from their parents in their own childhood.

Beating of children, however, is not confined to people with a psychopathic personality or of borderline socioeconomic status. It also occurs among people with good education and stable financial and social background. However, from the scant data that are available, it would appear that in these cases, too, there is a defect in character structure which allows aggressive impulses to be expressed too freely. There is also some suggestion that the attacking parent was subjected to similar abuse in childhood. It would appear that one of the most important factors to be found in families where parental assault occurs is "to do unto others as you have been done by." This is not surprising; it has long been recognized by psychologists and social anthropologists that patterns of child rearing, both good and bad, are passed from one generation to the next in relatively unchanged form. Psychologically, one could describe this phenomenon as an identification with the aggressive parent, this identification occurring despite strong wishes of the person to be different. Not infrequently the beaten infant is a product of an unwanted pregnancy, a pregnancy which began before marriage, too soon after marriage, or at some other time felt to be extremely inconvenient. Sometimes several children in one family have been beaten; at other times one child is singled out for attack while others are treated quite lovingly. We have also seen instances in which the sex of the child who is severely attacked is related to very specific factors in the context of the abusive parent's neurosis.

It is often difficult to obtain the information that a child has been attacked by its parent. To be sure, some of the extremely sociopathic characters will say, "Yeah, Johnny would not stop crying so I hit him. So what? He cried harder so I hit him harder." Sometimes one spouse will indicate that the other was the attacking person, but more often there is complete denial of any knowledge of injury to the child and the maintenance of an attitude of complete innocence on the part of both parents. Such attitudes are maintained despite the fact that evidence of physical attack is obvious and that the trauma could not have happened in any other way. Denial by the parents of any involvement in the abusive episode may, at times, be a conscious, protective device, but in other instances it may be a denial based upon psychological repression. Thus, one mother who seemed to have been the one who injured her baby had complete amnesia for the episodes in which her aggression burst forth so strikingly.

In addition to the reluctance of the parents to give information regarding the attacks on their children, there is another factor which is of great importance and extreme interest as it relates to the difficulty in delving into the problem of parental neglect and abuse. This is the fact that physicians have great difficulty both in believing that parents could have attacked their children and in undertaking the essential questioning of parents on this subject. Many physicians find it hard to believe that such an attack could have occurred and they attempt to obliterate such suspicions from their minds, even in the face of obvious circumstantial evidence. The reason for this is not clearly understood. One possibility is that the arousal of the physician's antipathy in response to such situations is so great that it is easier for the physician to deny the possibility of such attack than to have to deal with the excessive anger which surges up in him when he realizes the truth of the situation. Furthermore, the physician's training and personality usually makes it quite difficult for him to assume the role of policeman or district attorney and start questioning patients as if he were investigating a crime. The humanitarian-minded physician finds it most difficult to proceed when he is met with protestations of innocence from the aggressive parent, especially when the battered child was brought to him voluntarily.

Although the technique wherein the physician obtains the necessary information in cases of child beating is not adequately solved, certain routes of questioning have been particularly fruitful in some cases. One spouse may be asked about the other spouse in relation to unusual or curious behavior or for direct description of dealings with the baby. Clues to the parents' character and pattern of response may be obtained by asking questions about sources of worry and tension. Revealing answers may be brought out by questions concerning the baby such as, "Does he cry a lot? Is he stubborn? Does he obey well? Does he eat well? Do you have problems in controlling him?" A few general questions concerning the parents' own ideas of how they themselves were brought up may bring forth illuminating answers; interviews with grandparents or other relatives may elicit additional suggestive data. In some cases, psychological tests may disclose strong aggressive tendencies, impulsive behavior, and lack of adequate mechanisms of controlling impulsive behavior. In other cases only prolonged contact in a psychotherapeutic milieu will lead to a complete understanding of the background and circumstances surrounding the parental attack. Observation by nurses or other ancillary personnel of the behavior of the parents in relation to the hospitalized infant is often extremely valuable.

The following two condensed case histories depict some of the problems encountered in dealing with the battered-child syndrome.

REPORT OF CASES

CASE 1.—The patient was brought to the hospital at the age of 3 months because of enlargement of the head, convulsions, and spells of unconsciousness. Examination revealed bilateral subdural hematomas, which were later operated upon with great improvement in physical status. There had been a hospital admission at the age of one month because of a fracture of the right femur, sustained "when the baby turned over in the crib and caught its leg in the slats." There was no history of any head trauma except "when the baby was in the other hospital a child threw a little toy at her and hit her in the head." The father had never been alone with the baby, and the symptoms of difficulty appeared to have begun when the mother had been caring for the baby. Both parents showed concern and requested the best possible care for their infant. The father, a graduate engineer, related instances of impulsive behavior, but these did not appear to be particularly abnormal, and he showed appropriate emotional concern over the baby's appearance and impending operation. The mother, aged 21, a high school graduate, was very warm, friendly, and gave all the appearance of having endeavored to be a good mother. However, it was noted by both nurses and physicians that she did not react as appropriately or seem as upset about the baby's appearance as did her husband. From interviews with the father and later with the mother, it became apparent that she had occasionally shown very impulsive, angry behavior, sometimes acting rather strangely and doing bizarre things which she could not explain nor remember. This was their first child and had resulted from an unwanted pregnancy which had occurred almost immediately after marriage and before the parents were ready for it. Early in pregnancy the mother had made statements about giving the baby away, but by the time of delivery she was apparently delighted with the baby and seemed to be quite fond of it. After many interviews, it became apparent that the mother had identified herself with her own mother who had also been unhappy with her first pregnancy and had frequently beaten her children. Despite very strong conscious wishes to be a kind, good mother, the mother of our patient was evidently repeating the behavior of her own mother toward herself. Although an admission of guilt was not obtained, it seemed likely that the mother was the one responsible for attacking the child; only after several months of treatment did the amnesia for the aggressive outbursts begin to lift. She responded well to treatment, but for a prolonged period after the infant left the hospital the mother was not allowed alone with her.

CASE 2.—This patient was admitted to the hospital at the age of 13 months with signs of central nervous system damage and was found to have a fractured skull. The parents were questioned closely, but no history of trauma could be elicited. After one week in the hospital no further treatment was deemed necessary, so the infant was discharged home in the care of her mother, only to return a few hours later with hemiparesis, a defect in vision, and a new depressed skull fracture on the other side of the head. There was no satisfactory explanation for the new skull fracture, but the mother denied having been involved in causing the injury, even though the history revealed that the child had changed markedly during the hour when the mother had been alone with her. The parents of this child were a young, middle-class couple who, in less than two years of marriage, had been separated, divorced, and remarried. Both felt that the infant had been unwanted and had come too soon in the marriage. The mother gave a history of having had a "nervous breakdown" during her teens. She had received psychiatric assistance because she had been markedly upset early in the pregnancy. Following an uneventful delivery, she had been depressed and had received further psychiatric aid and four electroshock treatments. The mother tended to gloss over the unhappiness during the pregnancy and stated that she was quite delighted when the baby was born. It is interesting to note that the baby's first symptoms of difficulty began the first day after its first birthday, suggesting an "anniversary reaction." On psychological and neurological examination, this mother showed definite signs of organic brain damage probably of lifelong duration and possibly related to her own prematurity. Apparently her significant intellectual defects had been camouflaged by an attitude of coy, naïve, cooperative sweetness which distracted attention from her deficits. It was noteworthy that she had managed to complete a year of college work despite a borderline I.Q. It appeared that the impairment in mental functioning was probably the prime factor associated with poor control of aggressive impulses. It is known that some individuals may react with aggressive attack or psychosis when faced with demands beyond their intellectual capacity. This mother was not allowed to have unsupervised care of her child.

Up to the present time, therapeutic experience with the parents of battered children is minimal. Counseling carried on in social agencies has been far from successful or rewarding. We know of no reports of successful psychotherapy in such cases. In general, psychiatrists feel that treatment of the so-called psychopath or sociopath is rarely successful. Further psychological investigation of the character structure of attacking parents is sorely needed. Hopefully, better understanding of the mechanisms involved in the control and release of aggressive impulses will aid in the earlier diagnosis, prevention of attack, and treatment of parents, as well as give us better ability to predict the likelihood of further attack in the future. At present, there is no safe remedy in the situation except the separation of battered children from their insufficiently protective parents.

TECHNIQUES OF EVALUATION

A physician needs to have a high initial level of suspicion of the diagnosis of the battered-child syndrome in instances of subdural hematoma, multiple unexplained fractures at different stages of healing, failure to thrive, when soft tissue swellings or skin bruising are present, or in any other situation where the degree and type of injury is at variance with the history given regarding its occurrence or in any child who dies suddenly. Where the problem of parental abuse comes up for consideration, the physician should tell the parents that it is his opinion that the injury should not occur if the child were adequately protected, and he should indicate that he would welcome the parents giving him the full story so that he might be able to give greater assistance to them to prevent similar occurrences from taking place in the future. The idea that they can now help the child by giving a very complete history of circumstances surrounding the injury sometimes helps the parents feel that they are atoning for the wrong that they have done. But in many instances, regardless of the approach used in attempting to elicit a full story of the abusive incident(s), the parents will continue to deny that they were guilty of any wrongdoing. In talking with the parents, the physician may sometimes obtain added information by showing that he understands their problem and that he wishes to be of aid to them as well as to the child. He may help them reveal the circumstances of the injuries by pointing out reasons that they may use to explain their action. If it is suggested that "new parents sometimes lose their tempers and are a little too forceful in their actions," the parents may grasp such a statement as the excuse for their actions. Interrogation should not be angry or hostile but should be sympathetic and quiet with the physician indicating his assurance that the diagnosis is well established on the basis of objective findings and that all parties, including the parents, have an obligation to avoid a repetition of the circumstances leading to the trauma. The doctor should recognize that bringing the child for medical attention in itself does not necessarily indicate that the parents were innocent of wrongdoing and are showing proper concern; trauma may have been inflicted during times of uncontrollable temporary rage. Regardless of the physician's personal reluctance to become involved, complete investigation is necessary for the child's protection so that a decision can be made as to the necessity of placing the child away from the parents until matters are fully clarified.

Often, the guilty parent is the one who gives the impression of being the more normal. In two recent instances young physicians have assumed that the mother was at fault because she was unkempt and depressed while the father, in each case a military man with good grooming and polite manners, turned out to be the psychopathic member of the family. In these instances it became apparent that the mother had good reason to be depressed.

RADIOLOGIC FEATURES

Radiologic examination plays two main roles in the problem of child-abuse. Initially, it is a tool for case finding, and, subsequently, it is useful as a guide in management.

The diagnostic signs result from a combination of circumstances: age of the patient, nature of the injury, the time that has elapsed before the examination is carried out, and whether the traumatic episode was repeated or occurred only once.

Age.—As a general rule, the children are under 3 years of age; most, in fact are infants. In this age group the relative amount of radiolucent cartilage is great; therefore, anatomical disruptions of cartilage without gross deformity are radiologically invisible or difficult to demonstrate. Since the periosteum of infants is less securely attached to the underlying bone than in older children and adults, it is more easily and extensively stripped from the shaft by hemorrhage than in older patients. In infancy massive subperiosteal hematomas may follow injury and elevate the active periosteum so that new bone formation can take place around and remote from the parent shaft.

Nature of Injury.—The ease and frequency with which a child is seized by his arms or legs make injuries to the appendicular skeleton the most common in this syndrome. Even when bony injuries are present elsewhere, e.g., skull, spine, or ribs, signs of injuries to the extremities are usually present. The extremities are the "handles" for rough handling, whether the arm is pulled to bring a reluctant child to his feet or to speed his ascent upstairs or whether the legs are held while swinging the tiny body in a punitive way or in an attempt to enforce corrective measures. The forces applied by an adult hand in grasping and seizing usually involve traction and torsion; these are the forces most likely to produce epiphyseal separations and periosteal shearing. Shaft fractures result from direct blows or from bending and compression forces.

Time after Injury That the X-Ray Examination Is Made.—This is important in evaluating known or suspected cases of child-abuse. Unless gross fractures, dislocations, or epiphyseal separations were produced, no signs of bone injury are found during the first week after a specific injury. Reparative changes may first become manifest about twelve to fourteen days after the injury and can increase over the subsequent weeks depending on the extent of initial injury and the degree of repetition. Reparative changes are more active in the growing bones of children than in adults and are reflected radiologically in the excessive new bone reaction. Histologically, the reaction has been confused with neoplastic change by those unfamiliar with the vigorous reactions of young growing tissue.

Repetition of Injury.—This is probably the most important factor in producing diagnostic radiologic signs of the syndrome. The findings may depend on diminished immobilization of an injured bone leading to recurring macro- and microtrauma in the area of injury and healing, with accompanying excessive local reaction and hemorrhage, and ultimately, exaggerated repair. Secondly, repetitive injury may produce bone lesions in one area at one time, and in another area at another, producing lesions in several areas and in different stages of healing.

Thus, the classical radiologic features of the battered-child syndrome are usually found in the appendicular skeleton in very young children. There may be irregularities of mineralization in the metaphyses of some of the major tubular bones with slight malalignment of the adjacent epiphyseal ossification center. An overt fracture may be present in another bone. Elsewhere, there may be abundant and active but well-calcified subperiosteal reaction with widening from the shaft toward one end of the bone. One or more bones may demonstrate distinctly thickened cortices, residuals of previously healed periosteal reactions. In addition, the radiographic features of a subdural hematoma with or without obvious skull fracture may be present.

Differential Diagnosis.—The radiologic features are so distinct that other diseases generally are considered only because of the reluctance to accept the implications of the bony lesions. Unless certain aspects of bone healing are considered, the pertinent findings may be missed. In many cases roentgenographic examination is only undertaken soon after known injury; if a fracture is found, reexamination is done after reduction and immobilization; and, if satisfactory positioning has been obtained, the next examination is usually not carried out for a period of six weeks when the cast is removed. Any interval films that may have been taken prior to this time probably would have been unsatisfactory since the fine details of the bony lesions would have been obscured by the cast. If fragmentation and bone production are seen, they are considered to be evidence of repair rather than manifestations of multiple or repetitive trauma. If obvious fracture or the knowledge of injury is absent, the bony changes may be considered to be the result of scurvy, syphilis, infantile cortical hyperostoses, or other conditions. The distribution of lesions in the abused child is unrelated to rates of growth; moreover, an extensive lesion may be present at the slow-growing end of the bone which otherwise is normally mineralized and shows no evidence of metabolic disorder at its rapidly growing end.

Scurvy is commonly suggested as an alternative diagnosis, since it also produces large calcifying subperiosteal hemorrhages due to trauma and local exaggerations most marked in areas of rapid growth. However, scurvy is a systemic disease in which all of the bones show the generalized osteoporosis associated with the disease. The dietary histories of most children with recognized trauma have not been grossly abnormal, and whenever the vitamin C content of the blood has been determined, it has been normal.

In the first months of life *syphilis* can result in metaphyseal and periosteal lesions similar to those under discussion. However, the bone lesions of syphilis tend to be symmetrical and are usually accompanied by other stigmata of the disease. Serological tests should be obtained in questionable cases.

Osteogenesis imperfecta also has bony changes which may be confused with those due to trauma, but it too is a generalized disease, and evidence of the disorder should be present in the bones which are not involved in the disruptive-productive reaction. Even when skull fractures are present, the mosaic ossification pattern of the cranial vault, characteristic of osteogenesis imperfecta, is not seen in the battered-child syndrome. Fractures in osteogenesis imperfecta are commonly of the shafts; they usually occur in the metaphyseal regions in the battered-child syndrome. Blue sclerae, skeletal deformities, and a family history of similar abnormalities were absent in reported instances of children with unrecognized trauma.

Productive diaphyseal lesions may occur in *infantile cortical hyperostosis*, but the metaphyseal lesions of unrecognized trauma easily serve to differentiate the two conditions. The characteristic mandibular involvement of infantile cortical hyperostosis does not occur following trauma although obvious mandibular fracture may be produced.

Evidence that repetitive unrecognized trauma is the cause of the bony changes found in the battered-child syndrome is, in part, derived from the finding that similar roentgenographic findings are present in *paraplegic patients with sensory deficit* and in patients with *congenital indifference to pain;* in both of whom similar pathogenic mechanisms operate. In paraplegic children unappreciated injuries have resulted in radiologic pictures with irregular metaphyseal rarefactions, exaggerated subperiosteal new bone formation, and ultimate healing with residual external cortical thickening comparable to those in the battered-child syndrome. In paraplegic adults, excessive callus may form as a consequence of the lack of immobilization, and the lesion may be erroneously diagnosed as osteogenic sarcoma. In children with congenital indifference (or insensitivity) to pain, identical radiologic manifestations may be found.

To summarize, the radiologic manifestations of trauma are specific, and the metaphyseal lesions in particular occur in no other disease of which we are aware. The findings permit a radiologic diagnosis even when the clinical history seems to refute the possibility of trauma. Under such circumstances, the history must be reviewed, and the child's environment, carefully investigated.

MANAGEMENT

The principal concern of the physician should be to make the correct diagnosis so that he can institute proper therapy and make certain that a similar event will not occur again. He should report possible willful trauma to the police department or any special children's protective service that operates in his community. The report that he makes should be restricted to the objective findings which can be verified and, where possible, should be supported by photographs and roent-genograms. For hospitalized patients, the hospital director and the social service department should be notified. In many states the hospital is also required to report any case of possible unexplained injury to the proper authorities. The physician should acquaint himself with the facilities available in private and public agencies that provide protective services for children. These include children's humane societies, divisions of welfare departments, and societies for the prevention of cruelty to children. These, as well as the police department, maintain a close association with the juvenile court. Any of these agencies may be of assistance in bringing the case before the court which alone has the legal power to sustain a dependency petition for temporary or permanent separation of the child from the parents' custody. In addition to the legal investigation, it is usually helpful to have an evaluation of the psychological and social factors in the case; this should be started while the child is still in the hospital. If necessary, a court order should be obtained so that such investigation may be performed.

In many instances the prompt return of the child to the home is contraindicated because of the threat that additional trauma offers to the child's health and life. Temporary placement with relatives or in a well-supervised foster home is often indicated in order to prevent further tragic injury or death to a child who is returned too soon to the original dangerous environment. All too often, despite the apparent cooperativeness of the parents and their apparent desire to have the child with them, the child returns to his home only to be assaulted again and suffer permanent brain damage or death. Therefore, the bias should be in favor of the child's safety; everything should be done to prevent repeated trauma, and the physician should not be satisfied to return the child to an environment where even a moderate risk of repetition exists.

SUMMARY

The battered-child syndrome, a clinical condition in young children who have received serious physical abuse, is a frequent cause of permanent injury or death. Although the findings are quite variable, the syndrome should be considered in any child exhibiting evidence of possible trauma or neglect (fracture of any bone, subdural hematoma, multiple soft tissue injuries, poor skin hygiene, or malnutrition) or where there is a marked discrepancy between the clinical findings and the historical data as supplied by the parents. In cases where a history of specific injury is not available, or in any child who dies suddenly, roentgenograms of the entire skeleton should still be obtained in order to ascertain the presence of characteristic multiple bony lesions in various stages of healing.

Psychiatric factors are probably of prime importance in the pathogenesis of the disorder, but our knowledge of these factors is limited. Parents who inflict abuse on their children do not necessarily have psychopathic or sociopathic personalities or come from borderline socioeconomic groups, although most published cases have been in these categories. In most cases some defect in character structure is probably present; often parents may be repeating the type of child care practiced on them in their childhood.

Physicians, because of their own feelings and their difficulty in playing a role that they find hard to assume, may have great reluctance in believing that parents were guilty of abuse. They may also find it difficult to initiate proper investigation so as to assure adequate management of the case. Above all, the physician's duty and responsibility to the child requires a full evaluation of the problem and a guarantee that the expected repetition of trauma will not be permitted to occur.

REFERENCES

Snedecor, S. T., Knapp, R. E., and Wilson, H. B. "Traumatic ossifying periostitis of newborn." *Surg. Gynec. Obstet.* 61(1935):385–87.

Caffey, J. "Multiple fractures in long bones of infants suffering from chronic subdural hematoma." *Amer. J. Roentgenol.* 56(1946):163–73.

Snedecor, S. T., and Wilson, H. B. "Some obstetrical injuries to long bones." *J. Bone Joint Surg.* 31A(April 1949):378–84.

Smith, M. J. "Subdural hematoma with multiple fractures." *Amer. J. Roentgenol.* 63(March 1950):342–44.

Frauenberger, G. S., and Lis, E. F. "Multiple fractures associated with subdural hematoma in infancy." *Pediatrics* 6(Dec 1950):890–92.

Barmeyer, G. H., Alderson, L. R., and Cox, W. B. "Traumatic periostitis in young children." *J. Pediat.* 38(Feb 1951):184–90.

Silverman, F. "Roentgen manifestations of unrecognized skeletal trauma in infants." *Amer. J. Roentgenol.* 69(March 1953):413–26.

Woolley, P. V., Jr., and Evans, W. A., Jr. "Significance of skeletal lesions in infants resembling those of traumatic origin." *JAMA* 158(June 1955):539–43.

Bakwin, H. "Multiple skeletal lesions in young children due to trauma." *J. Pediat.* 49(July 1956):7–15.

Caffey, J. "Some traumatic lesions in growing bones other than fractures and dislocations: clinical and radiological features." *Brit. J. Radiol.* 30(May 1957):225–38.

Weston, W. J. "Metaphyseal fractures in infancy." *J. Bone Joint Surg. (Brit.)* (no. 4) 39B(Nov. 1957):694–700.

Fisher, S. H. "Skeletal manifestations of parent-induced trauma in infants and children." *Southern Med. J. 51(Aug 1958):956–60.*

Miller, D. S. "Fractures among children." *Minnesota Med.* 42(Sept 1959):1414–25 (Oct. 1959).

Silver, H. K., and Kempe, C. H. "Problem of parental criminal neglect and severe physical abuse of children." *J. Dis. Child.* 95(1959):528.

Altman, D. H., and Smith R. L. "Unrecognized trauma in infants and children." *J. Bone Joint Surg.(Amer.)* 42A(April 1960):407–13.

Elmer, E. "Abused young children seen in hospitals." *Soc. Work* (no. 4) 5(Oct. 1960):98–102.

Gwinn, J. L., Lewin, K. W., and Peterson, H. G., Jr. "Roentgenographic manifestations of unsuspected trauma in infancy." *JAMA* 176(June 1961):926–29.

Boardman, H. E. "Project to rescue children from inflicted injuries." *Soc. Work* (no. 1) 7(Jan. 1962):43.

CHAPTER 10

Child Abuse Prevention and Treatment Act, 1974*

5101. NATIONAL CENTER ON CHILD ABUSE AND NEGLECT

Establishment

(a) The Secretary of Health, Education, and Welfare (hereinafter referred to in this chapter as the "Secretary") shall establish an office to be known as the

---

*United States Code Annotated. Title 42, The Public Health and Welfare, pp. 199–205.

National Center on Child Abuse and Neglect (hereinafter referred to in this chapter as the "Center").

Functions

(b) The Secretary, through the Center, shall—

Annual Research Summary

(1) compile, analyze, and publish a summary annually of recently conducted and currently conducted research on child abuse and neglect;

Information Clearinghouse

(2) develop and maintain an information clearinghouse on all programs, including private programs, showing promise of success, for the prevention, identification, and treatment of child abuse and neglect;

Training Materials for Personnel

(3) compile and publish training materials for personnel who are engaged or intend to engage in the prevention, identification, and treatment of child abuse and neglect;

Technical Assistance

(4) provide technical assistance (directly or through grant or contract) to public and nonprofit private agencies and organizations to assist them in planning, improving, developing, and carrying out programs and activities relating to the prevention, identification, and treatment of child abuse and neglect;

Research into Causes, Prevention, Identification, and Treatment

(5) conduct research into the causes of child abuse and neglect, and into the prevention, identification, and treatment thereof; and

Study

(6) make a complete and full study and investigation of the national incidence of child abuse and neglect, including a determination of the extent to which incidents of child abuse and neglect are increasing in number or severity.

Grant and Contract Authority

(c) The Secretary may carry out his functions under subsection (b) of this section either directly or by way of grant or contract.

Pub.L. 93–247, § 2, Jan. 31, 1974, 88 Stat. 4; Pub.L. 93–644, § 8(d)(1), Jan. 4, 1975, 88 Stat. 2310.

Historical Note

1975 Amendment. Subsec. (c). Pub.L. 93–644 added subsec. (c).

Short Title. Section 1 of Pub.L. 93–247 provided: "That this Act [this chapter] may be cited as the 'Child Abuse Prevention and Treatment Act'."

Legislative History. For legislative history and purpose of Pub.L. 93–247, · see 1974 U.S. Code Cong. and Adm.News, p. 2763. See, also, Pub.L. 93–644, 1974 U.S. Code Cong. and Adm.News, p. 8043.

Library References

Infants § 13.   C.J.S. Infants § 11 et seq.

5102. DEFINITIONS

For purposes of this chapter the term "child abuse and neglect" means the physical or mental injury, sexual abuse, negligent treatment, or maltreatment of a child under the age of eighteen by a person who is responsible for the child's welfare under circumstances which indicate that the child's health or welfare is harmed or threatened thereby, as determined in accordance with regulations prescribed by the Secretary.

Pub.L. 93–247, § 3, Jan. 31, 1974, 88 Stat. 5.

Historical Note

Legislative History. For legislative history and purpose of Pub. L. 93–247, see 1974 U.S. Code Cong. and Adm.News, p. 2763.

5103. DEMONSTRATION PROGRAMS AND PROJECTS

Grants and Contracts; Scope of Activities; Funds for Fiscal Year

(a) The Secretary, through the Center, is authorized to make grants to, and enter into contracts with, public agencies or nonprofit private organizations (or combinations thereof) for demonstration programs and projects designed to prevent, identify, and treat child abuse and neglect. Grants or contracts under this subsection may be—

(1) for the development and establishment of training programs for professional and paraprofessional personnel in the fields of medicine, law, education, social work, and other relevant fields who are engaged in, or intend to work in, the field of the prevention, identification, and treatment of child abuse and neglect; and training programs for children, and for persons responsible for the welfare of children, in methods of protecting children from child abuse and neglect;

(2) for the establishment and maintenance of centers, serving defined geographic areas, staffed by multidisciplinary teams of personnel trained in the prevention, identification, and treatment of child abuse and neglect cases, to provide a broad range of services related to child abuse and neglect, including direct support and supervision of satellite centers and attention homes, as well as providing advice and consultation to individuals, agencies, and organizations which request such services;

(3) for furnishing services of teams of professional and paraprofessional personnel who are trained in the prevention, identification, and treatment of child abuse and neglect cases, on a consulting basis to small communities where such services are not available; and

(4) for such other innovative programs and projects, including programs and projects for parent self-help, and for prevention and treatment of drug-related child abuse and neglect, that show promise of successfully preventing or treating cases of child abuse and neglect as the Secretary may approve.

Not less that 50 per centum of the funds appropriated under this chapter for any fiscal year shall be used only for carrying out the provisions of this subsection.

Grants to States; Funds for Fiscal Year; Qualifications for Assistance; Compliance of Social Security Provisions with Certain Requirements

(b)(1) Of the sums appropriated under this chapter for any fiscal year, not less than 5 per centum and not more than 20 per centum may be used by the Secretary for making grants to the States for the payment of reasonable and necessary expenses for the purpose of assisting the States in developing, strengthening, and carrying out child abuse and neglect prevention and treatment programs.

(2) In order for a State to qualify for assistance under this subsection, such State shall—

(A) have in effect a State child abuse and neglect law which shall include provisions for immunity for persons reporting instances of child abuse and neglect from prosecution, under any State or local law, arising out of such reporting;

(B) provide for the reporting of known and suspected instances of child abuse and neglect;

(C) provide that upon receipt of a report of known or suspected instances of child abuse or neglect an investigation shall be initiated promptly to substantiate the accuracy of the report, and, upon a finding of abuse or neglect, immediate steps shall be taken to protect the health and welfare of the abused or neglected child, as well as that of any other child under the same care who may be in danger of abuse or neglect;

(D) demonstrate that there are in effect throughout the State, in connection with the enforcement of child abuse and neglect laws and with the reporting of suspected instances of child abuse and neglect, such administrative procedures, such personnel trained in child abuse and neglect prevention and treatment, such training procedures, such institutional and other facilities (public and private), and such related multidisciplinary programs and services as may be necessary or appropriate to assure that the State will deal effectively with child abuse and neglect cases in the State;

(E) provide for methods to preserve the confidentiality of all records in order to protect the rights of the child, his parents or guardians;

(F) provide for the cooperation of law enforcement officials, courts of competent jurisdiction, and appropriate State agencies providing human services;

(G) provide that in every case involving an abused or neglected child which results in a judicial proceeding a guardian ad litem shall be appointed to represent the child in such proceedings;

(H) provide that the aggregate of support for programs or projects related to child abuse and neglect assisted by State funds shall not be reduced below the level provided during fiscal year 1973, and set forth policies and procedures designed to assure that Federal funds made available under this chapter for any fiscal year will be so used as to supplement and, to the extent practicable, increase the level of State funds which would, in the absence of Federal funds, be available for such programs and projects;

(I) provide for dissemination of information to the general public with respect to the problem of child abuse and neglect and the facilities and prevention and treatment methods available to combat instances of child abuse and neglect; and

(J) to the extent feasible, insure that parental organizations combating child abuse and neglect receive preferential treatment.

(3) Programs or projects related to child abuse and neglect assisted under part A or B in title IV of the Social Security Act shall comply with the requirements set forth in clauses (B), (C), (E), and (F) of paragraph (2).

Prohibition of Assistance for Construction of Facilities; Lease or Rental and Alteration or Repair of Facilities

(c) Assistance provided pursuant to this section shall not be available for construction of facilities; however, the Secretary is authorized to supply such assistance for the lease or rental of facilities where adequate facilities are not otherwise available, and for repair or minor remodeling or alteration of existing facilities.

Criteria for Equitable Distribution of Assistance

(d) The Secretary shall establish criteria designed to achieve equitable distribution of assistance under this section among the States, among geographic areas of the Nation, and among rural and urban areas. To the extent possible, citizens of each State shall receive assistance from at least one project under this section.

Definition

(e) For the purpose of this section, the term "State" includes each of the several States, the District of Columbia, the Commonwealth of Puerto Rico, American Samoa, the Virgin Islands, Guam and the Trust Territories of the Pacific.

Pub.L. 93–247, § 4, Jan. 31, 1974, 88 Stat. 5; Pub.L. 93–644, § 8(d)(2), Jan. 4, 1975, 88 Stat. 2310.

Historical Note

References in Text. Part A and B of Title IV of Social Security Act, referred to in subsec. (b)(3), are classified to sections 601 et seq. and 620 et seq. of this title.

1975 Amendment. Subsec. (e). Pub.L. 93–644 added subsec. (e).

Legislative History. For legislative history and purpose of Pub.L. 93–247, see 1974 U.S. Code Cong. and Adm.News, p. 2763. See, also, Pub.L. 93–644, 1974 U.S. Code Cong. and Adm.News, p. 8043.

Code of Federal Regulations

Program policies and procedures, see 45 CFR 1340.1-1 et seq.

5104. AUTHORIZATION OF APPROPRIATIONS

There are hereby authorized to be appropriated for the purposes of this chapter $15,000,000 for the fiscal year ending June 30, 1974, $20,000,000 for the fiscal year ending June 30, 1975, and $25,000,000 for the fiscal year ending June 30, 1976, and for the succeeding fiscal year.

Pub.L. 93–247, § 5, Jan. 31, 1974, 88 Stat. 7.

Historical Note

Legislative History. For legislative history and purpose of Pub.L. 93–247, see 1974 U.S. Code Cong. and Adm.News, p. 2763.

5105. ADVISORY BOARD ON CHILD ABUSE AND NEGLECT

Appointment; Membership; Federal Agencies Represented; Functions

(a) The Secretary shall, within sixty days after January 31, 1974, appoint an Advisory Board on Child Abuse and Neglect (hereinafter referred to as the "Advisory Board"), which shall be composed of representatives from Federal agencies with responsibility for programs and activities related to child abuse and neglect, including the Office of Child Development, the Office of Education, the National Institute of Education, the National Institute of Mental Health, the National Institute of Child Health and Human Development, the Social and Rehabilitation Service, and the Health Services Administration. The Advisory Board shall assist the Secretary in coordinating programs and activities related to child abuse and neglect administered or assisted under this chapter with such programs and activities administered or assisted by the Federal agencies whose representatives are members of the Advisory Board. The Advisory Board shall also assist the Secretary in the development of Federal standards for child abuse and neglect prevention and treatment programs and projects.

Report to President and Congress

(b) The Advisory Board shall prepare and submit, within eighteen months after January 31, 1974, to the President and to the Congress a report on the programs assisted under this chapter and the programs, projects, and activities related to child abuse and neglect administered or assisted by the Federal agencies whose representatives are members of the Advisory Board. Such report shall include a study of the relationship between drug addiction and child abuse and neglect.

Report to President and Congress; Funds

(c) Of the funds appropriated under section 5104 of this title, onehalf of 1 per centum, or $1,000,000, whichever is the lesser, may be used by the Secretary only for purposes of the report under subsection (b) of this section.

Pub.L. 93–247, § 6, Jan. 31, 1974, 88 Stat. 7.

Historical Note

Legislative History. For legislative history and purpose of Pub.L. 93–247, see 1974 U.S. Code Cong. and Adm.News, p. 2763.

5106. COORDINATION OF FEDERAL PROGRAMS; REGULATIONS; ARRANGEMENTS

The Secretary shall promulgate regulations and make such arrangements as may be necessary or appropriate to ensure that there is effective coordination between programs related to child abuse and neglect under this chapter and other such programs which are assisted by Federal funds.
Pub.L. 93–247, § 7, Jan. 31, 1974, 88 Stat. 8.

Historical Note

Legislative History. For legislative history and purpose of Pub.L. 93–247, see 1974 U.S.Code Cong. and Adm.News, p. 2763.

PART III

Characteristics of Abusive Parents

The effects [of child abuse] may continue for several generations, a bitter confirmation of the biblical assertion that the iniquities of the fathers are visited upon the children even unto the third and fourth generation.

(Bakan, 1971, p. 107)

Editor's Introduction

Publication of *The Battered Child Syndrome* in 1962 (see Chapter 9) raised the consciousness of the *zeitgeist* to the existence of child abuse and gave impetus to examination of its medical and legal aspects (Helfer and Kempe 1968; McCoid 1965; Paulsen 1966, 1967; Silver, Dublin, and Lourie 1969; Simons and Downs 1968). In addition, a body of data was developing that belied romantic fictions of domestic bliss and unalloyed parental love for children and that helped to stimulate studies on the psychosocial aspects of child abuse.

Reports from the Federal Bureau of Investigation (1966) indicated that violence in the home was the major source of violence in the United States. Twenty-five percent of all homicides occurred in the family, half of these to a spouse and one-seventh to a child. The President's Commission on the Causes and Prevention of Violence reported that one-third of adult Americans had been hit frequently during childhood, and one-fifth of the males approved of slapping his wife's face. Physical assault against a spouse was found to be an important factor in divorce (Levinger 1966). Between 1960 and 1965, more policemen were killed responding to domestic disturbances than to any other calls. Clearly, the family that stayed together often slayed together.

Increasingly, inane myths and platitudes about home and family were inundated by data suggesting that a marriage license was often a beating license and home-sweet-home was often home-beat-home, especially at Christmas, when child abuse and conjugal violence are found to increase. Despite the ever burgeoning data on widespread violence in the American home, many professionals continued to show selective inattention to the facts. For example, not one article published in the *Journal of Marriage and the Family,* from its founding in 1939 through 1969, included the term "violence" in its title (O'Brien 1971). Nevertheless, the data did ultimately triumph over denial and sentimentality. The problem of domestic violence could no longer be minimized, and its psychosocial aspects received increasing professional attention.

It is understandable that the earliest and largest focus of psychosocial investigations was on the abusive parents. There was great perplexity about the personalities of parents who could bring themselves to batter their own children; and understanding them could contribute to early screening, protection of the children, and prevention of child abuse. Furthermore, many of the pioneers in child abuse were social workers and pediatricians to whom the informants were the parents as well as the client or patient. Appraisal of psychosocial characteristics of parents and the parent-child relationship is an integral part of family casework and the pediatric examination. Descriptions of abusive parents reported during the sixties and earlier were based primarily on these clinical observations made in the context of ongoing casework or medical examinations of the maltreated children. Reports of these observations generated hypotheses that continue to be tested in experimental investigations.

Perhaps because parental violence against children is so sensational, the large majority of studies has centered on actively abusive parents. Hardly any research has been directed toward understanding the passive abuser, the parent who fails to protect the child against abuse by the assaultive parent or who, by verbal or subtle encouragement, participates in the abuse of the child. Although estimates suggest that neglect may have a higher incidence and often harms children more than abuse, little is known about the psychosocial characteristics of neglectful parents. Polansky, De Saix, and Sharlin (1973) stated that abusive parents are more emotionally invested in their child than neglectful parents, yet Scott (1974) found no differences among her samples of actively abusive, passively abusive, and neglectful mothers.

Research findings and clinical observations indicate that actively abusing parents have in common certain psychosocial characteristics, but it must be emphasized that these are not sufficient and may not be necessary factors in producing the abuse. For example, a background of early maternal deprivation or inadequacy characterizes many abusive parents, yet some parents with this background do not abuse their children.

Despite his early background of abuse, neglect, and maternal deprivation, novelist Charles Dickens did not abuse any of his ten children. In fact, as Gardner points out in Chapter 34, Dickens transformed the memory of his childhood suffering into a commitment to child advocacy exemplified in his compassionate speech in behalf of sick children (Chapter 7). Psychotherapy with adults abused as children (Williams, unpublished data) indicates that some of them refrain entirely from physical punishment of their children because of their intense empathy with those in pain. Others, like Cameronchild (Chapter 3), are able to use their traumatic early experiences by contributing to the helping professions.

The factors that counteract the predisposition to abuse have hardly been investigated. Hunter (1978) found that a sample of nonabusive parents who had been abused as children had the following characteristics: involvement in social and religious groups, willingness to seek outside support and assistance including prenatal care, and spacing of the births of their children.

The complexity of causal factors in child abuse must be kept in mind in examining the characteristics of parents that predispose them to abuse and neglect of their children. As Spinetta indicates in Chapter 11, there is no single type of child abuser, and no one set of characteristics is sufficient to explain the abuse. The causes of child abuse and neglect are multiple and interacting.

Except for Chapter 12, the papers in this section deal with characteristics of actively abusive parents. In Chapter 11, Spinetta and Rigler review the literature on this topic for the decade following the publication in 1962 of the classical article on "the battered child syndrome" by Kempe and his associates (Chapter 9). The authors emphasize that studies indicating that child abuse is the result of low socioeconomic class reflect artifacts in reporting. Social agencies have much more access to the poor and are more likely to report the cases of child abuse than private physicians who serve middle- and upper-class parents. A consistent finding is that, regardless of socioeconomic class, many abusive parents have been abused, neglected, or maternally deprived in childhood.

In Chapter 12, Scott conceptualizes child abuse and neglect in terms of socialization and attachment theories. Her findings indicate that mothers of abused or neglected children differed from a control sample in their early attachment experiences and subsequent affiliative and parental behaviors.

Unwanted pregnancy is related to murder of the neonate, according to Resnick who, in Chapter 13, reviews the world literature on murder of neonates by their parents. In contrast with mothers who murder older children, mothers who commit neonaticide are not likely to be psychotic. Their motivation for the murder is that they do not want the child. These and other findings in the paper suggest that an increase in abortions would decrease the incidence of murder of the newborn.

In Chapter 14, Wright describes the manipulativeness and psychopathology of abusive parents in his sample, characteristics corroborated in the case studies reported in Chapter 15 by Money and Werlwas. These authors describe the pathological collusion between abusive parents of psychosocial dwarfs (a syndrome discussed in detail in Part VI). The final Chapter 16 in this section, by Meadow, deals with an unusual syndrome of abusive parents who, by fabricating their children's physical symptoms, needlessly expose them to harmful medical procedures.

G.J.W.

REFERENCES

Bakan, D. *Slaughter of the Innocents: A Study of the Battered Child Phenomenon*. San Francisco: Jossey-Bass, 1971.

Federal Bureau of Investigation. *Uniform Crime Reports, 1966*. Washington, D.C.: U.S. Government Printing Office, 1967.

Helfer, R. E., and Kempe, C. H. (eds). *The Battered Child*. Chicago: University of Chicago Press, 1968.

Hunter, R. Paper presented at the convention of the American Psychiatric Association, Atlanta: 1978.

Levinger, G. "Sources of marital satisfaction among applicants for divorce." *American Journal of Orthopsychiatry* 36(1966):804–806.

McCoid, A. H. "The battered child and other assaults upon the family." *Minnesota Law Review* 50(1965):1–58.

O'Brien, J. E. "Violence in divorce prone families." *Journal of Marriage and the Family* 33(1971):692–98.

Paulsen, M. G. "Legal protection against child abuse." *Children* 13(1966):43–48.

————. "Child abuse reporting laws: The shape of the legislation." *Columbia Law Review* 67(1967):1–49.

Polansky, N. A., DeSaix, C., and Sharlin, S. A. *Child Abuse and Neglect: Understanding and Reaching the Parent.* New York: Child Welfare League of America, 1973.

Scott, W. J. "Attachment and Child Abuse: A Study of Social History Indicators Among Mothers of Abused Children." Ph.D. dissertation, University of Minnesota, 1974.

Silver, L. B., Dublin, C. C., and Lourie, R. S. "Child abuse syndrome: The 'gray areas' in establishing a diagnosis." *Pediatrics* 44(1969):594–600.

Simons, B., and Downs, E. F. "Medical reporting of child abuse: Patterns, problems and accomplishments." *New York State Journal of Medicine* 68(1968):2324–30.

CHAPTER 11

The Child-Abusing Parent:
A Psychological Review

John J. Spinetta and David Rigler

Review of professional opinions in the literature reveals that (*a*) the abusing parent
was himself raised with some degree of deprivation; (*b*) the abusing parent brings to
his role as parent mistaken notions of child rearing; (*c*) there is present in the parent a
general defect in character structure allowing aggressive impulses to be expressed too
freely; and (*d*) while socioeconomic factors might sometimes place added stresses on
basic personality weakness, these stresses are not of themselves sufficient or necessary causes of abuse. A critique is made of a recent demographic survey in light of
the foregoing data.

Why does a parent physically abuse his or her own child? During the past ten
years, many attempts have been made to answer this question. An extensive
literature has emerged on the medical and legal aspects of the problem of child
abuse since the publication of an article by Kempe, Silverman, Steele,
Droegemueller, and Silver (1962) and the pursuit of child-protective laws in
California by Boardman (1962, 1963). Sociologists and social workers have
contributed their share of insights, and a few psychiatrists have published their
findings, but surprisingly little attention has been devoted to the problem of child
abuse by the psychologist. One seeks with little success for well-designed studies
of personality characteristics of abusing parents. What appears is a literature
composed of professional opinions on the subject.

The aim of this review is to bring together professional opinions of this
decade on the psychological characteristics of the abusing parent, in order to
determine from the most commonly held opinions what generalizations can be
induced and thus to lay the groundwork for systematic testing of hypotheses.

DEFINITION

What is child abuse? Kempe et al. (1962) limited their study to children who had
received serious physical injury, in circumstances which indicated that the injury

Reprinted with permission from the *Psychological Bulletin* 77(1972):296–304. Copyright 1972,
American Psychological Association.

The authors wish to thank James T. Kent, of the Division of Psychiatry, Children's Hospital of Los
Angeles, for his critical reading of earlier versions and for his helpful suggestions and support during
the research.

was caused willfully rather than by accident. They coined the term "battered child" to encompass their definition. Zalba (1966), after a brief review of definitions, likewise addressed himself primarily to those cases in which physical injury was willfully inflicted on a child by a parent or parent substitute.

Because of the difficulty of pinpointing what is emotional or psychological or social neglect and abuse, and because of the extent of the literature on physical abuse alone, this review, following Kempe's and Zalba's lead, limits the term "child abuse" to the concept of physical injury to the child, willfully inflicted. The review omits studies of parents who neglect their children—emotionally, socially, or psychologically—and adults who sexually molest them.

MEDICAL AND LEGAL HISTORY

Literature on the medical and legal aspects of the problem of child abuse is extensive. The edited volume of Helfer and Kempe (1968) contains a general overview, as do the articles by Paulson and Blake (1967), Silver (1968), and Zalba (1966). Legal aspects are delineated in De Francis (1970), McCoid (1965), and the various articles by Paulsen (1966a, 1966b, 1967, 1968a, 1968b). Simons and Downs (1968) gave an overview of patterns, problems, and accomplishments of the child abuse reporting laws. A thorough bibliography on child abuse was published by the United States Department of Health, Education and Welfare (1969).

This review is not concerned with the medical and legal aspects of the problem and refers only to those articles that gave more than a passing mention to the psychological and social determinants of parental abuse of children.

REVIEW OF THE LITERATURE

Most of the studies of child abuse are subject to the same general criticism. First, the studies that set out to test specific hypotheses are few. Many start and end as broad studies with relatively untested common-sense assumptions. Second, in most studies in this area, the researchers used samples easily available from ready-at-hand local populations, and thus the samples were not truly representative. We shall have to rely on the convergence of conclusions from various types of sampling to establish generalizations. Third, practically all of the research in child abuse is ex post facto. What is left unanswered and still to be tested is whether one can determine prior to the onset of abuse which parents are most likely to abuse their children, or whether high-risk groups can only be defined after at least one incident of abuse has occurred.

In spite of these criticisms, the studies of child abuse do give general data that can furnish hypotheses for more rigorous research design, and for a more differentiated approach to the question of why parents abuse their children.

Demographic Characteristics

In an attempt to discover whether or not various social or economic stresses make abuse more likely, many of the studies have described demographic characteristics of abusing families. Kempe et al. (1962) found in the abusing families a high incidence of divorce, separation, and unstable marriages, as well as of minor criminal offenses. The children who were abused were very young, often under one year of age. In many of the families, children were born in very close succession. Often one child would be singled out for injury, the child that was the victim of an unwanted pregnancy.

Various other studies enter figures from their own samples, generally repeating Kempe's findings (Birrell and Birrell 1968; Cameron, Johnson, and Camps 1966; Ebbin, Gollub, Stein, and Wilson 1969; Elmer and Gregg 1967; Gregg and Elmer 1969; Helfer and Pollock 1967; Johnson and Morse 1968; Nurse 1964; Schloesser 1964; Skinner and Castle 1969).

Elmer (1967) and Young (1964) add to Kempe's findings the factors of social and economic stress, lack of family roots in the community, lack of immediate support from extended families, social isolation, high mobility, and unemployment.

While pointing to the role that economic and social stresses play in bringing out underlying personality weaknesses, the majority of the foregoing authors caution that economic and social stresses alone are neither sufficient nor necessary causes for child abuse. They point out that, although in the socially and economically deprived segments of the population there is generally a higher degree of the kinds of stress factors found in abusing families, the great majority of deprived families do not abuse their children. Why is it that most deprived families do not engage in child abuse, though subject to the same economic and social stresses as those families who do abuse their children?

A study that sheds light on the fact that social and economic factors have been overstressed as etiological factors in cases of child abuse is that of Steele and Pollock (1968), whose sample of abusers consisted mainly of middle-class and upper-middle-class families. Though social and economic difficulties may have added stress to the lives of the parents, Steele and Pollock considered these stresses as only incidental intensifiers of personality-rooted etiological factors.

Simons, Downs, Hurster, and Archer (1966) conducted a thorough study delineating abusing families as multiproblem families in which, not the socioeconomic factors alone, but the interplay of mental, physical, and emotional stresses underlay the abuse.

Allowing that child abuse in many cases may well be the expression of family stress, Adelson (1961), Allen, Ten Bensel, and Raile (1969), Fontana (1968), Holter and Friedman (1968), and Kempe et al. (1962) considered psychological factors as of prime importance in the etiology of child abuse. There is a defect in character structure which, in the presence of added stresses, gives way to uncontrolled physical expression.

Paulson and Blake (1969) referred to the deceptiveness of upper- and middle-class abusers, and cautioned against viewing abuse and neglect as completely a function of educationally, occupationally, economically, or socially disadvantaged parents, or as due to physical or health impoverishment within a family.

If it is true that the majority of parents in the socially and economically deprived segments of the population do not batter their children, while some well-to-do parents engage in child abuse, then one must look for the causes of child abuse beyond socioeconomic stresses. One of the factors to which one may look is parental history.

Parental History

One basic factor in the etiology of child abuse draws unanimity: Abusing parents were themselves abused or neglected, physically or emotionally, as children. Steele and Pollock (1968) have shown a history of parents having been raised in the same style that they have recreated in the pattern of rearing their own children. As infants and children, all of the parents in the groups were deprived both of basic mothering and of the deep sense of being cared for and cared about from the beginning of their lives.

Fontana (1968) also viewed the parents as emotionally crippled because of unfortunate circumstances in their own childhood. The parents reacted to their children in keeping with their own personal experiential history of loneliness, lack of protection, and lack of love. Many authors corroborated the hypotheses of Steele and Pollock and of Fontana.

In a study surveying 32 men and 7 women imprisoned for cruelty to their children, Gibbins and Walker (1956) concluded that it was rejection, indifference, and hostility in their own childhood that produced the cruel parents.

Ten years later, Tuteur and Glotzer (1966) studied ten mothers who were hospitalized for murdering their children and found that all had grown up in an emotionally cold and often overtly rejecting family environment in which parental figures were either absent or offered little opportunity for wholesome identification when present.

Komisaruk (1966) found as the most striking statistic in his study of abusing families the emotional loss of a significant parental figure in the early life of the abusive parent.

Perhaps the most systematic and well-controlled study in the area of child abuse, that of Melnick and Hurley (1969), compared two small, socioeconomically and racially matched groups on eighteen personality variables. Melnick and Hurley found, among other things, a probable history of emotional deprivation in the mothers' own upbringing.

Further support for the hypothesis that the abusing parent was once an abused or neglected child is found in Bleiberg (1965), Blue (1965), Corbett (1964), Curtis (1963), Easson and Steinhilber (1961), Fairburn and Hunt (1964),

Fleming (1967), Green (1965), Harper (1963), Kempe et al. (1962), McHenry, Girdany, and Elmer (1963), Morris, Gould, and Matthews (1964), Nurse (1964), Paulson and Blake (1969), Silver, Dublin, and Lourie (1969b), and Wasserman (1967).

In a summary statement Gluckman (1968), repeating the findings of earlier observers, set up a 10-point differential diagnosis category. His main point, and the point of this section of the review, is that the child is the father of the man. The capacity to love is not inherent; it must be taught to the child. Character development depends on love, tolerance, and example. Many abusing parents were raised without this love and tolerance.

Parental Attitudes toward Child Rearing

In addition to concurring on the fact that many abusing parents were themselves raised with some degree of abuse or neglect, the authors agreed that the abusing parents share common misunderstandings with regard to the nature of child rearing, and look to the child for satisfaction of their own parental emotional needs.

Steele and Pollock (1968) found that the parents in their study group expected and demanded a great deal from their infants and children, and did so prematurely. The parents dealt with their children as if older than they really were. The parents felt insecure and unsure of being loved, and looked to their children as sources of reassurance, comfort, and loving response, as if the children were adults capable of providing grown-up comfort and love.

Melnick and Hurley (1969), in their well-controlled study of personality variables, also found in the mothers severely frustrated dependency needs, and an inability to empathize with their children.

Galdston (1965) concurred that abusing parents treated their children as adults, and he added that the parents were incapable of understanding the particular stages of development of their children.

Bain (1963), Gregg (1968), Helfer and Pollock (1967), Hiller (1969), Johnson and Morse (1968), Korsch, Christian, Gozzi, and Carlson (1965), and Morris and Gould (1963) also reported that abusing parents have a high expectation and demand for the infant's or child's performance, and a corresponding disregard for the infant's or child's own needs, limited abilities, and helplessness. Wasserman (1967) found that the parents not only considered punishment a proper disciplinary measure but strongly defended their right to use physical force.

In a 1969 study, Gregg and Elmer, comparing children accidentally injured with those abused, judged that the mother's ability to keep up the personal appearance of the child when well, and her ability to provide medical care when the child was moderately ill, sharply differentiated the abusive from the nonabusive mothers.

The authors seem to agree that abusing parents lack appropriate knowledge of child rearing, and that their attitudes, expectations, and child-rearing techniques set them apart from nonabusive parents. The abusing parents implement culturally accepted norms for raising children with an exaggerated intensity and at an inappropriately early age.

Presence of Severe Personality Disorders

There has been an evolution in thinking regarding the presence of a frank psychosis in the abusing parent. Woolley and Evans (1955) and Miller (1959) posited a high incidence of neurotic or psychotic behavior as a strong etiological factor in child abuse. Cochrane (1965), Greengard (1964), Platou, Lennox, and Beasley (1964) and Simpson (1967, 1968) concurred. Adelson (1961) and Kaufman (1962) considered only the most violent and abusive parents as having schizophrenic personalities. Kempe et al. (1962), allowing that direct murder of children betrayed a frank psychosis on the part of the parent, found that most of the abusing parents, though lacking in impulse control, were not severely psychotic. By the end of the decade, the literature seemed to support the view that only a few of the abusing parents showed severe psychotic tendencies (Fleming 1967; Laupus 1966; Steele and Pollock 1968; Wasserman 1967).

Motivational and Personality Variables: A Typology

A review of opinions on parental personality and motivational variables leads to a conglomerate picture. While the authors generally agree that there is a defect in the abusing parent's personality that allows aggressive impulses to be expressed too freely (Kempe et al. 1962; Steele and Pollock 1968; Wasserman 1967), disagreement comes in describing the source of the aggressive impulses.

Some authors claim that abuse is a final outburst at the end of a long period of tension (Nomura 1966; Ten Have 1965), or that abuse stems from an inability to face life's daily stresses (Heins 1969). Some claim that abuse stems from deep feelings of inadequacy or from parental inability to fulfill the roles expected of parenthood (Cohen, Raphling, and Green 1966; Court 1969; Fontana 1964; Johnson and Morse 1968; Komisaruk 1966; Silver 1968; Steele and Pollock 1968). Others described the parents as immature, self-centered, and impulse-ridden (Cochrane 1965; Delaney 1966; Jacobziner 1964; Ten Bensel 1963).

Some authors consider a role reversal between the spouses as a prime factor in the etiology of child abuse. A home in which the father is unemployed and the mother has taken over the financial responsibility of the family is considered a breeding ground for abuse (Galdston 1965; Greengard 1964; Nathan 1965; Nurse 1964).

Finally, there are those authors who considered low intelligence as a prime factor in the etiology of child abuse (Fisher 1958; Simpson 1967, 1968), although this point is disputed in the findings of Cameron et al. (1966), Holter and Friedman (1968), Kempe et al. (1962), and Ounsted (1968).

Is there a common motivational factor behind child abuse? Is there only one "type" of abusing parent? Realization that each of the above described characteristics was found to exist at least in some individual circumstances has led some authors to group together certain characteristics in clusters, and to evolve a psychodynamic within each cluster. The first major attempt at a typology was made by Merrill (1962). Because Merrill's typology is the most often quoted, it is summarized in some detail.

Merrill identified three distinct clusters of personality characteristics that he found to be true both of abusing mothers and fathers, and a fourth that he found true of the abusing fathers alone. The first group of parents seemed to Merrill to be beset with a continual and pervasive hostility and aggressiveness, sometimes focused, sometimes directed at the world in general. This was not a controlled anger, and was continually with the parents, with the only stimulation needed for direct expression being normal daily difficulties. This angry feeling stemmed from conflicts within the parents and was often rooted in their early childhood experiences.

The second group Merrill identified by personality characteristics of rigidity, compulsiveness, lack of warmth, lack of reasonableness, and lack of pliability in thinking and in belief. These parents defended their right to act as they had in abusing their child. Mothers in this group had marked child-rejection attitudes, evidenced by their primary concern with their own pleasures, inability to feel love and protectiveness toward their children, and in feelings that the children were responsible for much of the trouble being experienced by themselves as parents. These fathers and mothers were extremely compulsive in their behavior, demanding excessive cleanliness of their children. Many of these parents had great difficulty in relaxing, in expressing themselves verbally, and in exhibiting warmth and friendliness.

Merrill's third group of parents showed strong feelings of passivity and dependence. Many of these parents were people who were unassuming, reticent about expressing their feelings and desires, and very unaggressive. They were individuals who manifested strong needs to depend on others for decisions. These mothers and fathers often competed with their own children for the love and attention of their spouses. Generally depressed, moody, unresponsive, and unhappy, many of these parents showed considerable immaturity.

Merrill's fourth grouping or cluster of personality characteristics included a significant number of abusing fathers. These fathers were generally young, intelligent men with acquired skills who, because of some physical disability, were now fully or partially unable to support their families. In most of these situations, the mothers were working, and the fathers stayed at home, caring for the children. Their frustrations led to swift and severe punishment, to angry, rigid discipline.

Two further attempts at classification, Delsordo (1963) and Zalba (1967), with slight modifications, can be reduced to Merrill's categories.

The use of categories seems simple, unifying, and time saving. If further work can be done in refining the categories, validating them in field research, perhaps they or similar clusters shown to be empirically valid can be used as an aid in the determination of high-risk parents.

In this section, we have seen a conglomerate picture of parental motivational and personality variables, with one author's attempt to cluster the characteristics into a workable unity. One basic fact of agreement emerges from the studies in this section. The authors feel that a general defect in character—from whatever source— is present in the abusing parent allowing aggressive impulses to be expressed freely. During times of additional stress and tension, the impulses express themselves on the helpless child.

CRITIQUE OF A SURVEY

Of the studies surveying the demographic characteristics of families in which child abuse has occurred, the most extensive in scope was the national survey undertaken by Gil (1968*a*, and 1968*b*, 1969).[1] In 1969, Gil reported that the phenomenon of child abuse was highly concentrated among the socioeconomically deprived segments of the population. Concluding that "physical abuse is by and large not very serious as reflected by the data on the extent and types of injury suffered by the children in the study cohort [p. 862]," Gil placed his intervention strategy in the general betterment of society. For Gil, the cultural attitude permitting the use of physical force in child rearing is the common core of all physical abuse of children in American society. Since he found the socioeconomically deprived relying more heavily on physical force in rearing children, he recommended systematic educational efforts aimed at gradually changing this cultural attitude, and the establishment of clear-cut cultural prohibitions against the use of physical force as a means of rearing children. He viewed this educational effort as likely to produce the strongest possible reduction in the incidence and prevalence of physical abuse of children.

For Gil, child abuse is ultimately the result of chance environmental factors. While admitting to various forms of physical, social, intellectual, and emotional deviance and pathology in caretakers, and in the family units to which they belong, Gil stressed a global control of environmental factors as the solution to the problem of child abuse. He suggested: (*a*) the elimination of poverty from the midst of America's affluent society; (*b*) the availability in every community of resources aimed at the prevention and alleviation of deviance and pathology; (*c*) the availability of comprehensive family planning programs and liberalized legislation concerning medical abortions, to reduce the number of unwanted children; (*d*) family-life education and counseling programs for adolescents and adults in

[1]Gil's book reporting his national findings (*Violence against children: Physical child abuse in the United States*. Cambridge, Mass.: Harvard University Press, 1970) appeared after the present review was accepted for publication. Although the book offers greater detail, the findings and conclusions are identical to those in the cited references.

preparation for and after marriage, to be offered within the public school system; (*e*) a comprehensive, high-quality, neighborhood-based national health service, to promote and assure maximum feasible physical and mental health for every citizen; (*f*) a range of social services geared to the reduction of environmental stresses on family life; and (*g*) a community-based system of social services geared to assisting families and children who cannot live together because of severe relationship problems. Gil's ultimate objective is "the reduction of the general level of violence, and the raising of the general level of human well-being throughout our entire society [p. 863]."

While one must praise the efforts of the Gil study in data collection, and the ultimate objective of reducing the general level of violence and raising the general level of human well-being in our entire society, one cannot help but feel that Gil did not address himself to the question of child abuse. If there really does exist as strong a link as Gil suggests between poverty and physical abuse of children, why is it that all poor parents do not batter their children, while some well-to-do parents engage in child abuse? Eliminating environmental stress factors and bettering the level of society at all stages may reduce a myriad of social ills and may even prove effective, indirectly, in reducing the amount of child abuse. But there still remains the problem, insoluble at the demographic level, of why some parents abuse their children, while others under the same stress factors do not.

Other authors throughout the decade have allowed for the types of services outlined by Gil, but less globally and in a manner less disregarding of parental personality factors. That raising the general educational and financial level of families that are socioeconomically deprived is of long-range value in the lessening of the prevalence of child abuse is generally agreed upon, and finds support throughout the literature. However, most of the authors explicitly caution against considering abuse, as does Gil, as a function solely of educational, occupational, economic, or social stresses. This point is made by Adelson (1961), Allen et al. (1969), Elmer (1967), Fontana (1968), Helfer and Pollock (1967), Holter and Friedman (1968), Kempe (1968), Kempe et al. (1962), Paulson and Blake (1967), Silver et al. (1969a, 1969b), and Steele and Pollock (1968).

The great majority of the authors cited in this review have pointed to psychological factors within the parents themselves as of prime importance in the etiology of child abuse. They see abuse as stemming from a defect in character leading to a lack of inhibition in expressing frustration and other impulsive behavior. Socioeconomic factors sometimes place added stress on the basic weakness in personality structure, but these factors are not of themselves sufficient or necessary causes of abuse.

CONCLUSIONS

The purpose of this review has been to bring together the published professional opinions on the psychological characteristics of the abusing parent, in order to determine from the most commonly held opinions what generalizations can be induced, and thus to lay the groundwork for more systematic testing of hypotheses.

The psychologist, both as a specialist in the functioning of the human as an individual, and as a scientist trained in research methodology, is in a unique position to test the hypotheses raised by professionals in the fields of medicine and social work, in the study of the personality characteristics of the abusing parent.

Certainly, one would hope that research can eventually develop criteria to distinguish those inadequate parents who, with professional help, can meet the needs of their children, from those who cannot. We need eventually to be able to identify the high-risk families prior to the onset of abuse, but should be satisfied for the time being if we can help determine after the fact of abuse which families must receive the most attention to assure the further safety of their child.

REFERENCES

Adelson, L. Slaughter of the innocents: A study of forty-six homicides in which the victims were children. *New England Journal of Medicine,* 1961, 264, 1345–1349.

Allen, H. D., Ten Bensel, R. W., and Raile, R. B. The battered child syndrome. *Minnesota Medicine,* 1969, 52, 155–156.

Bain, K. Commentary: The physically abused child. *Pediatrics,* 1963, 31, 895–898.

Birrell, R. G., and Birrell, J. H. W. The maltreatment syndrome in children. *Medical Journal of Australia,* 1968, 2, 1023–1029.

Bleiberg, N. The neglected child and the child health conference. *New York State Journal of Medicine,* 1965, 65, 1880–1885.

Blue, M. T. The battered child syndrome from a social work viewpoint. *Canadian Journal of Public Health,* 1965, 56, 197–198.

Boardman, H. E. A project to rescue children from inflicted injuries. *Social Work,* 1962, 7, 43–51.

———. Who insures the child's right to health? *Child Welfare,* 1963, 42, 120–124.

Cameron, J. M., Johnson, H. R. M., and Camps, F. E. The battered child syndrome. *Medicine, Science, and the Law,* 1966, 6, 2–21.

Cochrane, W. The battered child syndrome. *Canadian Journal of Public Health,* 1965, 56, 193–196.

Cohen, M. I., Raphling, D. L., and Green, P. E. Psychologic aspects of the maltreatment syndrome of childhood. *Journal of Pediatrics,* 1966, 69, 279–284.

Corbett, J. T. A psychiatrist reviews the battered child syndrome and mandatory reporting legislation. *Northwest Medicine,* 1964, 63, 920–922.

Court, J. The battered child: Historical and diagnostic reflections, reflections on treatment. *Medical Social Work,* 1969, 22(1), 11–20.

Curtis, G. Violence breeds violence—perhaps. *American Journal of Psychiatry,* 1963, 120, 386–387.

De Francis, V. *Child abuse legislation in the 1970's.* Denver: American Humane Association, 1970.

Delaney, D. W. The physically abused child. *World Medical Journal,* 1966, 13, 145–147.

Delsordo, J. D. Protective casework for abused children. *Children,* 1963, 10, 213–218.

Easson, W. M., and Steinhilber, R. M. Murderous aggression by children and adolescents. *Archives of General Psychiatry,* 1961, 4, 1–10.

Ebbin, A. J., Gollub, M. H., Stein, A. M., and Wilson, M. G. Battered child syndrome at the Los Angeles County General Hospital. *American Journal of the Diseases of Children,* 1969, 118, 660–667.

Elmer, E. *Children in jeopardy: A study of abused minors and their families.* Pittsburgh: University of Pittsburgh Press, 1967.

Elmer, E., and Gregg, G. S. Developmental characteristics of abused children. *Pediatrics,* 1967, 40, 596–602.

Fairburn, A. C., and Hunt, A. C. Caffey's 'third syndrome': A critical evaluation. *Medicine, Science, and the Law,* 1964, 4, 123–126.

Fisher, S. H. Skeletal manifestations of parent-induced trauma in infants and children. *Southern Medical Journal,* 1958, 51, 956–960.

Fleming, G. M. Cruelty to children. *British Medical Journal,* 1967, 2, 421–422.

Fontana, V. J. *The maltreated child: The maltreatment syndrome in children.* Springfield, Ill.: Charles C Thomas, 1964.

———. Further reflections on maltreatment of children. *New York State Journal of Medicine,* 1968, 68, 2214–2215.

Galdston, R. Observations on children who have been physically abused and their parents. *American Journal of Psychiatry,* 1965, 122, 440–443.

Gibbins, T. C. N., and Walker, A. *Cruel parents.* London: Institute for the Study and Treatment of Delinquency, 1956.

Gil, D. G. California pilot study. In R. E. Helfer & C. H. Kempe (eds.), *The battered child.* Chicago: University of Chicago Press, 1968. (*a*)

———. Incidence of child abuse and demographic characteristics of persons involved. In R. E. Helfer & C. H. Kempe (eds.), *The battered child.* Chicago: University of Chicago Press, 1968. (*b*)

———. Physical abuse of children: Findings and implications of a nationwide survey. *Pediatrics,* 1969, 44(5, Supplement), 857–864.

Gluckman, L. K. Cruelty to children. *New Zealand Medical Journal,* 1968, 67, 155–159.

Green, K. Diagnosing the battered child syndrome. *Maryland State Medical Journal,* 1965, 14(9), 83–84.

Greengard, J. The battered-child syndrome. *American Journal of Nursing,* 1964, 64(6), 98–100.

Gregg, G. S. Physcans, child-abuse reporting laws, and injured child: Psychosocial anatomy of childhood trauma. *Clinical Pediatrics,* 1968, 7, 720–725.

Gregg, G. S., and Elmer, E. Infant injuries: Accident or abuse? *Pediatrics,* 1969, 44, 434–439.

Harper, F. V. The physician, the battered child, and the law. *Pediatrics,* 1963, 31, 899–902.

Heins, M. Child abuse: Analysis of a current epidemic. *Michigan Medicine,* 1969, 68, 887–891.

Helfer, R. E., and Kempe, C. H. (eds.). *The battered child.* Chicago: University of Chicago Press, 1968.

Helfer, R. E., and Pollock, C. B. The battered child syndrome. *Advances in Pediatrics,* 1967, 15, 9–27.

Hiller, R. B. The battered child: A health visitor's point of view. *Nursing Times*, 1969, 65, 1265-1266.

Holter, J. C., and Friedman, S. B. Principles of management in child abuse cases. *American Journal of Orthopsychiatry*, 1968, 38, 127-136.

Jacobziner, H. Rescuing the battered child. *American Journal of Nursing*, 1964, 64(6), 92-97.

Johnson, B., and Morse, H. A. Injured children and their parents. *Children*, 1968, 15, 147-152.

Kaufman, I. Psychiatric implications of physical abuse of children. In V. De Francis (ed.), *Protecting the battered child*. Denver: American Humane Association, 1962.

Kempe, C. H. Some problems encountered by welfare departments in the management of the battered child syndrome. In R. E. Helfer and C. H. Kempe (eds.), *The battered child*. Chicago: University of Chicago Press, 1968.

Kempe, C. H., Silverman, F. N., Steele, B. F., Droegemueller, W., and Silver, H. K. The battered-child syndrome. *Journal of the American Medical Association*, 1962, 181, 17-24.

Komisaruk, R. Clinical evaluation of child abuse: Scarred families, a preliminary report. *Juvenile Court Judges Journal* (Wayne County, Michigan), 1966, 17(2), 66-70.

Korsch, B. M., Christian, J. B., Gozzi, E. K., and Carlson, P. V. Infant care and punishment: A pilot study. *American Journal of Public Health*, 1965, 55, 1880-1888.

Laupus, W. E. Child abuse and the physician. *The Virginia Medical Monthly*, 1966, 93(1), 1-2.

McCoid, A. H. The battered child and other assaults upon the family. *Minnesota Law Review*, 1965, 50, 1-58.

McHenry, T., Girdany, B. R., and Elmer, E. Unsuspected trauma with multiple skeletal injuries during infancy and childhood. *Pediatrics*, 1963, 31, 903-908.

Melnick, B., and Hurley, J. R. Distinctive personality attributes of child-abusing mothers. *Journal of Consulting and Clinical Psychology*, 1969, 33, 746-749.

Merrill, E. J. Physical abuse of children: An agency study. In V. De Francis (ed.), *Protecting the battered child*. Denver: American Humane Association, 1962.

Miller, D. S. Fractures among children: Parental assault as causative agent. *Minnesota Medicine*, 1959, 42, 1209-1213.

Morris, M. G., and Gould, R. W. Role reversal: A concept in dealing with the neglected/battered child syndrome. In *The neglected battered-child syndrome: Role reversal in parents*. New York: Child Welfare League of America, 1963.

Morris, M. G., Gould, R. W., and Matthews, P. J. Toward prevention of child abuse. *Children*, 1964, 11, 55-60.

Nathan, H. Abused children. *American Journal of Psychiatry*, 1965, 122, 443.

Nomura, F. M. The battered child 'syndrome': A review. *Hawaii Medical Journal*, 1966, 25, 387-394.

Nurse, S. Familial patterns of parents who abuse their children. *Smith College Studies in Social Work*, 1964, 35, 11-25.

Ounsted, C. Review of K. Simpson, Battered baby syndrome. *Developmental Medicine and Child Neurology*, 1968, 10, 133-134.

Paulsen, M. G. Legal protection against child abuse. *Children*, 1966, 13, 43-48. (*a*)

————. The legal framework for child protection. *Columbia Law Review*, 1966, 66, 679-717. (*b*)

————. Child abuse reporting laws: The shape of the legislation. *Columbia Law Review,* 1967, 67, 1–49.

————. A summary of child-abuse legislation. In R. E. Helfer and C. H. Kempe (eds.), *The battered child.* Chicago: University of Chicago Press, 1968. (a)

————. The law and abused children. In R. E. Helfer and C. H. Kempe (eds.), *The battered child.* Chicago: University of Chicago Press, 1968. (b)

Paulson, M. J., and Blake, P. R. The abused, battered and maltreated child: A review. *Trauma,* 1967, 9(4), 3–136.

————. The physically abused child: A focus on prevention. *Child Welfare,* 1969, 48, 86–95.

Platou, R. V., Lennox, R., and Beasley, J. D. Battering. *Bulletin of the Tulane Medical Faculty,* 1964, 23, 157–165.

Schloesser, P. T. The abused child. *Bulletin of the Menninger Clinic,* 1964, 28, 260–268.

Silver, L. B. Child abuse syndrome: A review. *Medical Times,* 1968, 96, 803–820.

Silver, L. B., Dublin, C. C., and Lourie, R. S. Child abuse syndrome: The 'gray areas' in establishing a diagnosis. *Pediatrics,* 1969, 44, 594–600. (a)

————. Does violence breed violence? Contributions from a study of the child abuse syndrome. *American Journal of Psychiatry,* 1969, 126, 404–407. (b)

Simons, B., and Downs, E. F. Medical reporting of child abuse: Patterns, problems and accomplishments. *New York State Journal of Medicine,* 1968, 68, 2324–2330.

Simons, B., Downs, E. F., Hurster, M. M., and Archer, M. Child abuse: Epidemiologic study of medically reported cases. *New York State Journal of Medicine,* 1966, 66, 2783–2788.

Simpson, K. The battered baby problem. *Royal Society of Health Journal,* 1967, 87, 168–170.

————. The battered baby problem. *South African Medical Journal,* 1968, 42, 661–663.

Skinner, A. E., and Castle, R. L. *78 battered children: A retrospective study.* London: National Society for the Prevention of Cruelty to Children, 1969.

Steele, B. F., and Pollock, C. B. A psychiatric study of parents who abuse infants and small children. In R. E. Helfer & C. H. Kempe (eds.), *The battered child.* Chicago: University of Chicago Press, 1968.

Ten Bensel, R. W. The battered child syndrome. *Minnesota Medicine,* 1963, 46, 977–982.

Ten Have, R. A preventive approach to problems of child abuse and neglect. *Michigan Medicine,* 1965, 64, 645–649.

Tuteur, W., and Glotzer, J. Further observations on murdering mothers. *Journal of Forensic Sciences,* 1966, 11, 373–383.

United States Department of Health, Education, and Welfare. *Bibliography on the battered child.* Washington, D.C.: U.S. Government Printing Office, 1969.

Wasserman, S. The abused parent of the abused child. *Children,* 1967, 14, 175–179.

Woolley, P. V., and Evans, W. A. Significance of skeletal lesions in infants resembling those of traumatic origin. *Journal of the American Medical Association,* 1955, 158, 539–543.

Young, L. *Wednesday's children: A study of child neglect and abuse.* New York: McGraw-Hill, 1964.

Zalba, S. R. The abused child: A survey of the problem. *Social Work,* 1966, 11(4), 3–16.

————. The abused child: A typology for classification and treatment. *Social Work,* 1967, 12(1), 70–79.

CHAPTER 12

Attachment and Child Abuse: A Study of Social History Indicators among Mothers of Abused Children

Winifred J. Scott

INTRODUCTION

The occurrence of neglect or nonaccidental injury of children while in the care of their parents has increasingly been recognized as a serious social problem. Child abuse is a term that refers to serious neglect or inflicted injury of children by adults responsible for their care. Although precise incidence and prevalence rates are not available, it has been shown that large numbers of children are affected each year with deleterious consequences to their immediate and long-term health and development.

Speculation about causes of child abuse has focused on characteristics specific to the mother or infant or on interactional effects. In addition, environmental or situational stress has received a great deal of emphasis in the etiology of child abuse. A wide variety of personality types has been found among parents of abused children. However, in a thorough survey of the literature, Paulson and Blake (1969) were not able to draw conclusions about specific types, but rather stated the personality characteristics of abusive parents are all-inclusive.

Personality traits that have frequently been linked with disturbances of abusive parents include aggression and dependency.

One commonly recognized theory is that the adult who has unresolved dependency conflicts may tend to perceive his children as deliberately displeasing him and being as demanding or rejecting as his own parents were (Morris and Gould 1963; Steele and Pollock 1968; Galdston 1965; Terr 1970). Other investigators have suggested the abusive parent is aggressive as a result of more pervasive hostility and anger (Merrill 1962; Zalba 1967; Corbett 1964; Delsordo 1963).

Aggression toward the child has also been thought to be a result of displacement of hostility as a result of marital discord (Allen 1966; Bennie and Sclare 1969; Holter and Friedman 1968) or of the parent's attempt to get revenge on a spouse by hurting the child (Resnick 1969).

Though there is little consensus with regard to specific personality types that are thought to be associated with child abuse, the importance of unresolved childhood conflicts is a recurring theme among a number of investigators.

Unresolved childhood conflicts as a major contributing factor to child abuse have been reported by a number of investigators (Bennie and Sclare 1969; Brown and Daniels 1968; Corbett 1964; Feinstein et al. 1964; Boardman 1962; Laury and Meerloo 1967). Morris and Gould (1963) suggest that abusing parents feel that they were unsatisfactory to their own parents as children. Steele and Pollock (1968) found that abusing parents suffered a lack of mothering in their own childhoods. Spinetta and Rigler (1972) suggest that there is virtually unanimous agreement that a basic factor in the cause of child abuse is that abusing parents were physically or emotionally abused or neglected as children. Emphasizing the cyclical nature of child abuse and the notion that abusing parents were abused themselves as children, Gunn (1970) points out that today's abused children grow up to repeat the mistakes of their parents with their own children. Of these possible etiologic factors, the potential for abuse within the parent is of particular interest for this investigation.

This paper is an attempt to relate the problem of child abuse to existing socialization theories and to develop and test a hypothesis based on attachment theory.

Mothers of abused children, rather than abusers were selected for this study, since it is hypothesized that the mother plays a significant role in abuse, whether she injures or neglects the child herself or fails to protect him from another abuser.

Moreover, antecedents for the mothering function are, by inference and by commonly held opinion, to be found in the history of the mother's own childhood. Alluding to this notion Steele and Pollock (1968) have suggested that the pattern of mothering in adult life probably has its roots in early infancy, and have attributed the cause of child abuse to a derailment of the mothering function. Since the mother is thought to be a function of her history, she is viewed not only in her parental role, but as the child she once was and as the adolescent and adult that she became.

BACKGROUND

On the basis of the results of a preliminary study of mothers of abused children (Scott 1974), this study was undertaken in which mothers of abused children (experimental group) were compared with mothers of nonabused children (comparison group) on a number of social history indicators related to the following events:
1. events in infancy that are thought to reflect insufficient or distorted attachment relationship in their own childhoods;
2. events that reflect dysfunctional affiliative behavior during adolescence;
3. events that reflect dysfunctional affiliative behavior during adulthood;

4. events that reflect inadequate maternal or care-taking behavior during adulthood.

Derivation of the specific indicators used in this study was based on attachment theory and has been described elsewhere (Scott 1974). The complete list is to be found in Table I.

Table I. Description of variables used to test the discriminability of experimental and control groups

---

Childhood history
   Mother was abused by her mother
   Mother was abused by her father
   Mother was separated from her mother
   Mother was separated from her father
   Mother was separated from both parents
   Mother's mother abused alcohol
   Mother was brought up in several different homes
Adolescent history
   Mother left high school before graduation
   Mother left home prior to finishing school
   Mother was placed in a foster home or an institution
   Mother was on probation
Adult adjustment
   Mother gave birth to an illegitimate child
   Mother has made a suicide attempt
   Mother has been hospitalized on a psychiatric ward
   Mother has abused alcohol and/or drugs
   Mother has had problems with police
   Mother gets assaulted by a significant male
Parental experiences
   Mother has temporarily placed a child in a foster home or with relatives
   Mother has permanently placed a child for adoption or long-term care outside her home
   Mother has lost a child as a result of "crib death"

PURPOSE

The purpose of this study was to test the following null hypothesis: "There are no differences between a group of mothers of abused children and a group of mothers whose children have not been abused."

METHOD

Population

The population from which experimental subjects used in this study were drawn included 113 families in which one or more of the children were physically abused or severely neglected. In all cases, the families were referred to the Ramsey County Child Abuse Team between August 1, 1970 and January 1, 1974 for evaluation and coordination of services. Of the total sample, abuse was confirmed and the abuser was identified in 81 cases. Table II lists demographic characteristics of the abuse incidents.

Table II. Demographic characteristics of abuse incidents (N=81)

I. Reason for referral (%)

	Primary neglect	21
	Inflicted injury	79
	Total	100

II. Relationship of abuser to child (%)

	Mother	57
	Other female	1
	Father	19
	Stepfather	7
	Boyfriend	14
	Other male	2
		100

III. Age of child this incident

Months	(%)	Cum. (%)
Birth–3 mos.	10	10
4–6 mos.	15	25
7–9 mos.	3	28
10–15 mos.	6	34
16–18 mos.	8	41
19–24 mos.	12	54
25–36 mos.	7	61
37–48 mos.	17	78
49–60 mos	15	93
60 +	6	99

IV. Age of mother this incident

Age	(%)	Cum. (%)
16–17	1	1
18–19	12	13
20–21	20	33
22–23	17	50
24–25	14	64
26–35	23	87
35 +	6	93
Unknown	6	99

Other criteria for inclusion in the experimental group included:
1. The abused child must have been under the age of five at the time of referral to the Child Abuse Team.

2. Information about the mother of the abused child related to at least one of the
   areas of investigation (i.e., childhood history, adolescent history, adult adjustment, or parental behavior other than that related to care of the abused
   child) must be available either from public agency records or other sources.
It was necessary to include this latter criterion because in a few instances extremely limited information was available about the mother of the abused child.
Of the 81 cases, criteria for inclusion in this study were met by a total of 67
families.

The comparision group of 29 mothers was randomly selected from 856
families who received medical care from a large Children's Hospital Clinic.
Criteria for inclusion in the comparison group were as follows:

1. The family must reside in Ramsey County.
2. There must be at least one child in the family who reached the age of five on or
   after August 1, 1970.
3. The mother must agree to participate in the study and be available for an
   interview.
4. The family must not be currently receiving services from the Ramsey County
   Welfare Department, Child Protection Section.

Two of the mothers in the Children's Hospital Clinic population had been
referred to the Ramsey County Mental Health Center within the past year because
of possible neglect and abuse of their children. However, because they were not
known to Ramsey County Welfare Department, Child Protection Service (i.e.,
they met the stated criteria for inclusion), they were included in the control
group. Two others were known to be mothers of abused children on the basis of
previous referrals to the Ramsey County Welfare Department, Child Protection
Section, therefore these two mothers were excluded from the study.

Procedures

The first step in this study of differences between groups of mothers of
abused and nonabused children was to select a group of 30 mothers from the total
sample of 67 mothers of abused children to be used for comparison with the
control group. Following is a description of the way in which this sample was
selected.

In the preliminary study (Scott 1974) no differences were found among the
three types of mothers of abused children: 1) mothers who inflicted injuries;
2) mothers who neglected but did not injure their children; 3) mothers who had
failed to protect their children from injury by another person. However, as a
precautionary measure, the three types of mothers were equally represented in
the experimental sample. This was accomplished by randomly drawing ten cases
from the total number of each of the three types of mothers. Thus the experimental sample was comprised of ten mothers who abused their children, ten mothers
who had neglected but not abused their children, and ten mothers who had failed
to protect their children from another abuser.

The remaining group of 37 mothers of abused children was used for a cross-validation study that will be described later.

Data for the experimental group had been obtained previously from case records, as described in the discussion of the Preliminary Study (Scott 1974).

Data for the comparison group mothers were obtained through personal interviews. The mothers were first given an explanation of the project and were then asked if they would be willing to provide the needed information. If they agreed to participate in the study, an interview was arranged during which they were advised of the importance of reporting information accurately and assured of complete confidentiality and anonymity, and the relevant information was obtained.

Since the problem involved comparison of two groups on multiple indicators to establish concurrent validity, a test for differences between groups was needed. Application of chi square was used to compare differences of the "yes"-"no" responses between the experimental and comparison groups.

In addition to comparison of the groups according to item content, a comparison was made on the basis of the total number of significant or "yes" responses made by individual members of the groups. To obtain this comparison, total number of responses were tallied for each individual and recorded according to group membership.

Cross-Validation

The final step in the procedure involved selecting a second group of mothers of abused children to be used in a cross-validation study to establish predictive validity. This was accomplished by randomly selecting a second experimental group comprised of thirty different cases from the remaining subjects (N=37) of the original sample (N=67) of mothers of abused children.

In the cross-validation, the two experimental groups were compared by obtaining the expected and observed rates of responses to the indicators. Again, chi square was applied, since the situation involved finding discrepancies between observed and expected frequencies according to the patterns of response obtained during concurrent validation.

In order to obtain an estimate of the likelihood of membership in the experimental groups on the basis of a given response to particular item content, Bayes Theorem was applied. In order to apply Bayes Theorem in this way, it was necessary to estimate a population base rate of "yes" responses for each of the items.

Since the principle of insufficient reason states that when there is no way of knowing or logically estimating the actual population base rate of occurrence of the particular event, a chance occurrence must be assumed. The extent that this assumption is incorrect in the estimate of the probability of membership in the experimental group, given that a "no" response was obtained, is in error, but the error is in the conservative direction.

RESULTS

Comparison Study

On the basis of chi-square comparisons of responses to specific items the null hypothesis is rejected, and these results indicate that there are differences between mothers of abused children and control mothers in terms of the specified indicators.

Items are listed in Table III according to the order with which they discriminated differences between the two groups tested against an expected 50:50 split. It is to be noted that 14 of the 20 items discriminated between groups at a significant level of $p > .05$ or better.

Table III. Social history indicators listed according to power of discrimination between groups

Items that discriminated between groups at a significant level of
  $p > .05$ or greater

Mother was on probation as an adolescent	$p = .001$
Mother abused alcohol and/or drugs as an adult	$p = .001$
Mother has been assaulted by a significant male as an adult	$p = .001$
Mother was separated from her father as a child	$.001 > p > .01$
Mother was placed in a foster home or an institution as an adolescent	$.001 > p > .01$
Mother has previously given birth to an illegitimate child	$.001 > p > .01$
Mother has made a suicide attempt	$.01 > p > .02$
Mother has been hospitalized on a psychiatric ward as an adult	$.01 > p > .02$
Mother has previously placed a child for adoption or for permanent long-term care outside her home	$.01 > p > .02$
Mother has had problems with police as an adult	$.02 > p > .05$
Mother was abused by her father as a child	$.01 > p > .02$
Mother was separated from both parents as a child	$.02 > p > .05$
Mother was separated from her mother as a child	$.02 > p > .05$
Mother's mother abused alcohol	$.02 > p > .05$

Items that discriminated between groups at significance levels of
  .05 or less

Mother has previously lost a child as a result of "crib death"	$.05 > p > .10$
Mother was brought up in several different homes during her childhood	$.05 > p > .10$
Mother left high school before graduation	$.05 > p > .10$
Mother was abused by her mother as a child	$.10 > p > .20$
Mother voluntarily left home prior to finishing school	$.0 > p > .20$
Mother has previously placed child in a temporary foster home or with relatives	$p = .30$

Table IV. Differences between experimental
and control groups in total number of significant
responses

Experimental (N=30)		Control (N=29)	
0		0	XXXXXXXXXX
1	X	1	XXXXXXX
2	XX	2	XXXXX
3	XXX	3	XXXXX
4	XXXXX	4	
5	XXX	5	X
6	XXXXX	6	X
7	XXX	7	
8	X	8	
9	XXX	9	
10	X	10	
11	XX	11	
12		12	
13		13	
14	X	14	
15		15	

For many items, low base rates contributed heavily to relatively low levels of significance. According to McNemar (1963) the use of chi square is suspect if any one E is less than 5, and an allowance for discontinuity could be made by applying Yates's correction. The Yates's correction was not incorporated, since the items to which it should be applied were not significant and the correction would not improve the significance.

Three of the items were not useful for discriminating between the groups despite reasonably adequate base rates of occurrence.

Table IV shows the total number of significant or "yes" responses given by individual subjects in both the experimental and the control groups. It can be seen that six mothers in the experimental group gave three or fewer significant responses, whereas all but two of the control mothers gave three or fewer significant responses. Thus 80% of the mothers of abused children fall above a cutting line drawn to indicate a total of four or more "yes" responses, while only approximately 7% of the control mothers fall above that line.

Since the low-scoring experimental mothers are like the control mothers in terms of total number of significant responses, it would seem possible that this subset of experimental mothers might in some way be involved in less severe abuse situations or might tend to have more positive prognoses. Therefore, these low-scoring mothers of abused children were compared with each other on the basis of item content of significant responses, type of abuse, relationship of abuser to abused child, outcome or prognosis, and pertinent aspects of the abuse situation.

The six mothers responded significantly to ten of the twenty possible items, and there did not appear to be any particular pattern that would suggest communality in terms of response to item content by these low-scoring mothers.

In Table V, the low-scoring experimental group mothers are compared with each other on the basis of a number of indices. It is apparent from examination of Table V that circumstances related to these abuse incidents are widely variant in terms of type and severity of abuse, relationship of the abuser to the child, age of the abused child, previous abuse, and case outcome.

There is no evidence from this evaluation to suggest that low-scoring mothers might be in some way less culpable, less psychiatrically disabled, or

Table V. Comparison of low-scoring mothers of abused children (N=6) on basis of various indices of communality

Type of abuse	
Neglect	2
Minor bruising	2
Long bone fracture	1
Suffocation	1
Total	6
Relationship of abuser to child	
Mother	4
Father	1
Stepfather	1
Total	6
Age of abused child	
5 weeks	1
5 months	1
10 months	1
22 months	1
25 months	1
47 months	1
Total	6
Previous abuse of this child	
Not formally reported	2
Formally reported	1
None known	3
Total	6
Severity of physical injury to child	
Death	2
Very severe	1
Moderate	1
Mild	2
Total	6

Table VI. Expected and observed frequencies of occurrences of responses in a cross-validation

	Expected (N=30)	Observed (N=30)	Control (N=29)
Childhood history			
Abused by mother	2	7	0
Abused by father	6	5	0
Separated from mother	5	8	0
Separated from father	14	14	4
Separated from both parents	5	8	0
Mother abused alcohol	5	5	0
Brought up in a series of homes	3	3	0
Adolescent history			
Left high school before graduation	17	12	10
Left home before high school graduation	10	5	5
Placed in foster home or institution	11	8	2
On probation	13	12	2
Adult adjustment			
Gave birth to illegitimate child	21	18	9
Made previous suicide attempt	8	8	1
Hospitalized for psychiatric treatment	10	10	2
Alcohol/drug abuse	12	8	0
Problems with police	7	7	1
Assaulted by significant male	18	15	0
Parental experiences			
Previous short-term placement of abused child in foster home or with relatives	6	15	3
Previous loss of child through placement out of home or adoption	6	7	0
Previous "crib death"	3	2	0

more amenable to therapeutic or casework efforts to maintain or restore the family unit than high-scoring mothers, nor is there evidence of a significant degree of communality in any of the areas investigated.

Cross-Validation

A degree of predictive validity is also established by the cross-validation comparison of the original group of mothers of abused children according to expected and observed incidence of the various events (see Table VI). It can be seen that there is a high degree of consistency between expected and observed frequencies of the various indicators in this comparison of the two experimental groups.

It was not feasible to obtain a second control group for this part of the investigation, so observed frequencies for the original control group are listed for comparison with observed frequencies of the cross-validation group.

DISCUSSION

It is evident that there were a number of methodological problems in this study, particularly related to sample selection and methods of data collection.

In any case, the experimental group represents a subpopulation of mothers of abused children and the comparison group is representative of the larger population of the Children's Hospital Clinic patients. Every effort was made to obtain accurate and complete information for subjects in both groups. Missing information for the experimental group would have the effect of biasing the results against the hypothesis and therefore of strengthening the results of the study.

It was my impression that there was little if any dissimulating or falsification of information among comparison group subjects. To whatever extent this may have occurred, the results of the study would be less significant than they appear to be based on the information actually obtained.

The methodological problems discussed above do not seriously challenge the validity of the findings; rather they indicate a need for replication studies that may be used to further amplify and clarify interpretation of the data.

The results of this study confirm the hypothesis that mothers of abused children are different from mothers of nonabused children on the basis of certain social history indicators. The differences between the groups of mothers are indicated by chi-square analysis, responses to specific item content, total numbers of significant responses and cross-validation.

SUMMARY AND CONCLUSIONS

In this paper, child abuse was examined in the light of attachment theory and empirical investigation. Of the possible etiologic factors, the potential for abuse within the parent was the focus of investigation. Mothers of abused children, rather than abusers were selected for study, since it is hypothesized that the mother plays a significant role in abuse, whether she injures or neglects the child herself or fails to protect it from another abuser. Crucial to the mothering function is the history of the mother's own childhood.

It was hypothesized that mothers of abused children would be different from mothers of nonabused children in: (1) early childhood experiences related to the development of attachment; (2) subsequent affiliative behavior in adolescence and adulthood; (3) subsequent parental behavior.

To test this hypothesis, social history indicators were selected to reflect early attachment experiences and subsequent affiliative and parental behavior.

In this study, 30 mothers of abused children were compared with 29 mothers of nonabused children. Mothers of abused children were found to be different from mothers of nonabused children on 14 of the 20 indicators at the 0.05 level of significance or better. Two of the indicators were not useful for discrimination between groups. Significant social history indicators included: (1) separation from one or both parents or abuse in childhood; (2) delinquency or placement in a foster home or institution in adolescence; (3) psychiatric problems, drug or alcohol abuse, police involvement, illegitimate pregnancy, or assault by a significant male in adulthood; (4) temporary or long-term separation from one or more children prior to the abuse incident.

The consistent finding of differences between the experimental and control groups on the indicators used for this study tends to confirm the utility of this particular set of events for further study and supports the notion that attachment theory can fruitfully be used as a theoretical framework for increased understanding of child abuse and for designing further research.

This investigation has clearly shown that mothers of abused children have suffered a variety of adverse or traumatic experiences in their own childhoods. It is ominous that the abused children in our sample have suffered and continue to suffer the very experiences that were found to be significant in the lives of their parents. Extensive research into treatment alternatives, as well as assessment of their long-term results for abused children, is essential if we are to break the cycle through which abuse is perpetuated.

REFERENCES

Allen, A. F. "Maltreatment syndrome in children." *Canadian Nurse* 62 (1966):40–42.

Bennie, E. H., and Sclare, A. B. "The battered child syndrome." *American Journal of Psychiatry* 125 (1969):975–79.

Boardman, H. "A project to rescue children from inflicted injuries." *Social Work* 7 (1962):43–51.

Brown, J. A., and Daniels, R. "Some observations of abusive parents." *Child Welfare* 47 (1968):89–94.

Corbett, J. T. "A psychiatrist reviews the battered child syndrome and mandatory reporting legislation." *Northwest Medicine* 63 (1964):920–22.

Delsordo, J. "Protective casework for abused children." *Children* 10 (1963):213–318.

Feinstein, H., Paul, N., and Esimol, P. "Group therapy for mothers with infanticidal impulses." *American Journal of Psychiatry* 120 (1964):852–86.

Galdston, R. "Observations on children who have been physically abused and their parents." *American Journal of Psychiatry* 22 (1965):440–43.

Gunn, A. D. G. "The neglected child." *Nursing Times* 66 (1970):946–47.

Holter, J. C., and Friedman, S. B. "Principles of management in child abuse cases." *American Journal of Orthopsychiatry* 38 (1968):127–36.

Laury, G. V., and Meerloo, J. A. M. "Mental cruelty and child abuse." *Psychiatric Quarterly Supplement* 41 (1967):203–54.

Merrill, E. J. "Physical Abuse of Children: An Agency Study." In *Protecting the Battered Child*. Denver: Children's Division, The American Humane Association, 1962.

Morris, M. G., and Gould, R. W. "Role reversal: A necessary concept in dealing with the 'battered child syndrome.'" *American Journal of Orthopsychiatry* 33 (1963):298-99.

Paulson, M. J., and Blake, P. R. "The physically abused child: A focus on prevention." *Child Welfare* 48 (1969):86-95.

Resnick, P. J. "Child murder by parents: A psychiatric review of filicide." *American Journal of Psychiatry* 126 (1969):325-34.

Scott, W. J. "Attachment and Child Abuse: A Study of Social History Indicators Among Mothers of Abused Children." Ph.D. dissertation, University of Minnesota, 1974.

Spinetta, J. J., and Rigler, D. "The child-abusing parent: A psychological review." *Psychological Bulletin* 77 (1972):296-304.

Steele, B. F., and Pollock, C. B. "A Psychiatric Study of Parents Who Abuse Infants and Small Children." In R. G. Helfer and C. H. Kempe (eds.), *The Battered Child.* Chicago: University of Chicago Press, 1968.

Terr, L. C. "A family study of child abuse." *American Journal of Psychiatry* 127 (1970): 665-71.

Zalba, S. R. "The abused child: II. A typology for classification and treatment." *Social Work* 12 (1967):70-79.

CHAPTER 13

Murder of the Newborn:
A Psychiatric Review of Neonaticide

Phillip J. Resnick

A simple child.
That lightly draws its breath.
And feels its life in every limb.
What should it know of death?
                                    Wordsworth

There is no crime more difficult to comprehend than the murder of a child by his own parents. Nevertheless, the killing of children goes back as far as recorded history. Reasons have included population control, illegitimacy, inability of the mother to care for the child, greed for power or money, superstition, congenital defects, and ritual sacrifice (40). The practice of stabilizing buildings by enclosing children in their foundations is still symbolically represented by our foundation stones (47).

There was an ancient concept that those who create may destroy that which they have created. Roman law formalized this concept under *patria potestas,* which recognized a father's right to murder his children. Among Mohave Indians, half-breeds were killed at birth (9). A merciless environment forced Eskimos to kill infants with congenital anomalies as well as one of most sets of twins (12). The killing of female infants was common in many cultures. In China this practice was widespread as late as the 1800s. Daughters were sacrificed because they were unable to transmit the family name and imposed the burden on their parents of paying their marriage portion (29, 41). It is claimed that the widespread murder of children in ancient times was first stemmed by the influence of the Christian religion (43).

In the literature, all child murders by parents are usually lumped together under the term "infanticide." In the author's opinion, there are two distinct types of child murder, "Neonaticide" is defined as the killing of a neonate on the day of its birth. "Filicide" is operationally defined as the murder of a son or daughter older than 24 hours. The data for this paper were obtained by reviewing the world

Read at the 125th anniversary meeting of the American Psychiatric Association. Miami Beach, Fla. May 5-9, 1969.

Reprinted with permission from the *American Journal of Psychiatry* 126 (April 1970):1414-20. Copyright 1970, American Psychiatric Association.

literature on child murder from 1751 to 1968; relevant articles were found in 13 languages. From these papers and three cases treated by the author, 168 case reports were collected. A previous publication described the 131 cases that fell into the filicide category (42). This paper will discuss the 37 neonaticides (2, 3, 11, 20, 21, 23-30, 32, 33, 36, 44, 45, 48). The cases are reported in varying detail from mental hospitals, psychiatrists in practice, prison psychiatrists, and a coroner's office.

Since neonaticide is usually viewed in a sociologic context, it has received little attention in the psychiatric literature. The purpose of this paper is to draw together our psychiatric knowledge about this crime. Neonaticide will be shown to be a separate entity, differing from filicide in the diagnoses, motives, and disposition of the murderer. Legal considerations and the present status of neonaticide will be discussed.

METHODS OF NEONATICIDE

The methods of neonaticide listed in order of greatest frequency are suffocation, strangulation, head trauma, drowning, exposure, and stabbing (6, 7, 13, 17, 35). Less common methods include dismemberment, burning, acid, lye, throwing to pigs, and burying alive. The need to stifle the baby's first cry makes suffocation the method of choice for mothers attempting to avoid detection (38). The drownings are most often accomplished in toilets. Case reports of up to 48 stab wounds or decapitation may reflect the bitterness of the abandoned girl, who sees the child in her lover's image (34, 44). Some mothers use extreme cleverness to avoid discovery of their deed. In India these methods have included drowning in milk and poisoning by rubbing opium on the mother's nipples (31). Some midwives killed newborns by thrusting a needle under the eyelid or into the anterior fontanel (16, 22). A needle from one such unsuccessful attempt was found at autopsy in the brain of a 70-year-old man (22).

DESCRIPTION OF THE MURDERERS

The 37 neonaticides were committed by 34 mothers, 2 fathers, and in one case, both parents. In order to simplify the data, only the mothers who committed neonaticide will be compared to the mothers who committed filicide (42). The mothers in the neonaticide group (range 16 to 38 years) were significantly younger than the mothers in the filicide group (range 20 to 50 years). Whereas most (89 percent) of the neonaticide group were under 25 years old, the majority (77 percent) of the filicide group were over 25. While 88 percent of the filicide group were married, only 19 percent of the neonaticide group enjoyed that status.

Comparison of the diagnoses of the two groups suggests that neonaticide and filicide are committed by two different psychiatric populations. Only 17 percent of the women in the neonaticide group were psychotic, but psychosis was evident in two-thirds of the filicide group. A serious element of depression was found in only three of the neonaticide cases, compared to 71 percent of the filicide group. Finally, suicide attempts accompanied one-third of the filicides, but none occurred among the neonaticide cases.

MOTIVES

In order to provide a framework for viewing child murder, the killings are divided into five categories by apparent motive (Table 1). This classification is based on the explanation given by the murderer and is independent of diagnoses. The "unwanted child" murders are committed because the victim was not desired or is no longer wanted by his mother. The "acutely psychotic" murders are committed by mothers under the influence of hallucinations, epilepsy, or delirium. The "altruistic" murders are carried out to relieve the victim of real or imagined suffering, or in association with suicide. "Accidental" murders, lacking in homicidal intent, are often the result of a battered child syndrome. The "spouse revenge" murders result from deliberate attempts to make the spouse suffer.

It is apparent from Table 1 that the motives that cause a mother to kill her newborn are considerably different from those that drive a mother to murder an older offspring. Whereas the majority of filicides are undertaken for an "altruistic" motive, the great bulk of neonaticides are committed simply because the child is not wanted.

The most common reason for neonaticide among married women is extramarital paternity. One example (32) is a woman who became impregnated by her brother-in-law while her husband was in prison. After cool deliberation, she murdered her infant at birth to avoid suspicion of her affair. It is commonplace for fathers to show some jealousy of their newborn children. The one case (26) in which both the husband and wife were known to consciously plan the murder of their expected infant is an extreme example of this. The 28-year-old father and 17-year-old mother made no preparations for the birth of their baby except to dig

Table 1. Classification of child murder by apparent motive

Category	Maternal neonaticide		Maternal filicide	
	Number	Percent	Number	Percent
"Unwanted child" murder	29	83	10	11
"Acutely psychotic" murder	4	11	21	24
"Altruistic" murder	1	3	49	56
"Accidental" murder	1	3	6	7
"Spouse revenge" murder	0		2	2
Total	35	100	88	100

a grave in the cellar. Both parents had physical deformities and feelings of inferiority. They were deeply in love and could not bear the thought of a third party interfering in their relationship. The husband initially proposed the crime against the "annoying animal" that deformed his "beloved wife's virginal figure." He assisted in the delivery at home, strangled the infant, and buried it.

The stigma of having an illegitimate child is the primary reason for neonaticide in unmarried women today, as it has been through the centuries. In 1826 Scott wrote:

> A delicate female, knowing the value of a chaste reputation, and the infamy and disgrace attendant upon the loss of that indispensable character, and aware of the proverbial uncharitableness of her own sex, resolves in her distraction, rather than encounter the indifference of the world, and banishment from society, to sacrifice what on more fortunate occasions, it would have been her pride to cherish (46).

Hirschmann and Schmitz (23) divided women who killed their illegitimate infants into two major groups. The women in the first group are said to have "a primary weakness of the characterological superstructure." In the second group are women with strong instinctual drives and little ethical restraint. All but a small minority of our 35 cases fall into the former group. These women are usually young, immature primiparas. They submit to sexual relations rather than initiate them. They have no previous criminal record and rarely attempt abortion.

Gummersbach (19) points out that passivity is the single personality factor that most clearly separates women who commit neonaticide from those who obtain abortions. Women who seek abortions are activists who recognize reality early and promptly attack the danger. In contrast, women who commit neonaticide often deny that they are pregnant or assume that the child will be stillborn. No advance preparations are made either for the care or the killing of the infant. When reality is thrust upon them by the infant's first cry, they respond by permanently silencing the intruder.

The women in the second group—those with strong instinctual drives and little ethical restraint—are more callous, egoistic, and intelligent. They tend to be older, strong-willed, and often promiscuous. Their crime is usually premeditated and not out of keeping with their previous life style.

A prominent feature in several of the neonaticides was the inability of the unwed girl to reveal her pregnancy to her mother. This may be due to the girl's shame or to fear that her mother's response would be anger, punishment, or rejection. In addition, unresolved oedipal feelings may cause some of these girls to have the unconscious fantasy that their pregnancy is proof of incest. One case treated by the author will be presented as an example of this speculation.

CASE REPORT

Mrs. C. a 36-year-old married, childless secretary, committed neonaticide at age 17. However, she did not have her first psychiatric contact until she made a suicide attempt almost two decades later.

Four months before her suicide attempt, Mrs. C. found a letter indicating that her husband had been unfaithful. As with each previous adversity she had encountered, she felt that this was retribution for her killing. She became anorectic and lost 22 pounds over a four-month period. She developed insomnia, indecisiveness, and inability to concentrate on her work. She began to feel that others could read her mind and influence her through voodoo. She had frightening dreams and fantasies in which both she and her husband were beaten, murdered, and crucified. When she looked in the mirror she saw herself as a devil. She became totally preoccupied with how "evil" she was, especially because of her neonaticide. Feeling that she deserved to die, she drank a glass of corrosive liquid that caused esophageal stricture, eventually necessitating a colon-esophageal transplant.

The patient was the third of four sisters. Mrs. C. described her father as a jolly, outgoing, talkative laborer who brought home his paycheck weekly, but who was more like a roomer than a husband. He "ran around," and the patient had often heard her mother speak of the "other woman." Her mother was described as a strong-willed, decisive, brusque woman who often hurt the patient's feelings. Even the tone of her voice could make the patient feel as if she were being hit. Mrs. C. was constantly seeking her mother's approval but never felt that she received it. Her first memory occurred at age three. Her father had taken her out in a new dress and showed her off to some men. They kidded him by saying that she was too cute to be his. The patient had a recurrent dream from age eight to eleven in which a terrifying monster came at her from behind but never quite reached her. As far back as Mrs. C. could remember, her parents had slept in separate bedrooms. When she was fifteen her parents separated permanently. However, her father would come back and have the patient launder his shirts.

The patient dated the boy who impregnated her only a few times. She passively submitted to sexual relations to avoid his disapproval. She did not know what to do about her pregnancy, but she was quite certain she could never let her mother know. She corsetted herself and successfully concealed the pregnancy from her family. Fortuitously alone at home when she began labor, she gave birth in the bathroom to a male child. She strangled the infant with her hands and then hung it on a towel rack with a hanger until she had cleaned up. She wrapped the body in old clothes and put it in a dresser drawer overnight. The next day she put it in the rubbish, and her crime was never discovered. She was amazed at her own coolness. She claims she had no feeling of guilt at the time. "It was just something that had to be done."

However, since the killing she has tried to do good "to even things up." She felt it would be appropriate for her to die in childbirth as a final balancing of the scales. She had an extended affair with a narcotics addict that ended after he had served a prison sentence. She felt it was her "lot in life" to put up with this man even though he treated her badly. The man who subsequently became her husband was married when she met him. During their affair she was very conscious of being the "other woman" of whom she had so often heard her mother speak.

The final diagnosis was psychotic depression. The patient's psychotic thinking cleared early in her three-month hospital stay. After her discharge she was seen weekly for one year as an outpatient.

Whereas some neonaticides result from psychosis, this case may be looked upon as a psychosis resulting in part from a neonaticide. When Mrs. C. learned of her husband's infidelity she developed murderous impulses toward him. In view of her past murder in reality, it was difficult for her to experience these wishes at a conscious level. Instead they took the form of fears in her psychosis that both she and her husband would be murdered. It is noteworthy that as Mrs. C.'s neonaticide injured her infant's throat, so her method of suicide damaged her own throat.

Various elements in the patient's history suggest that unresolved oedipal feelings may have been instrumental in this neonaticide. Her first memory questions her blood relationship to her father. Throughout her childhood the patient was unable to feel close to her mother. During psychological testing her response to Rorschach Card IV was of particular interest. She appeared terrified, threw down the card, and cried for a long time. She said it was dreadful, like the monster in her repetitive dream. Several months later she admitted that her first thought upon seeing the card had been that of her mother in a fur coat. After her parents' separation Mrs. C. took over the rather intimate chore of doing her father's laundry. In spite of protesting, she proceeded to become the "other woman" in relation to her husband. The sum of these factors suggests that Mrs. C. may have failed to reveal her pregnancy to her mother because of the unconscious idea that it would be viewed as proof of incest.

Although there are no previous reports of neonaticide attributed to an oedipal issue, this phenomenon has been observed in other pathological mother-child interactions. There is one report in which a married woman had an abortion because she unconsciously felt that she was carrying her father's child (49). Zilboorg (51) recounts a case of depression in a mother in which the central theme was a wish to destroy her child because she viewed it as living testimony of her unconscious incestuous attitude toward her father.

PATERNAL NEONATICIDE

Although it is not uncommon for fathers to murder older children, it is rare for a father to kill a newborn infant. Fathers have neither the motive nor the opportunity of mothers. Only two case reports were found in which the father was the sole killer. One mentally deficient 32-year-old man poisoned his newborn child because he felt that his own poor health might result in his death, leaving no one to provide for his wife and child (20). The other father was a bright 26-year-old man who was forced into marriage by his wife's pregnancy (36). He saw the coming child as a bar to his ambition. On one occasion he put poison in his wife's soup in an attempt to cause the infant to be stillborn. He strangled the infant while delivering it himself. Although free of overt psychosis at the time, he developed a full-blown picture of schizophrenia three years later. Both fathers were sentenced to ten years in prison. Fathers appear to receive more severe sentences than mothers for neonaticide and for filicide (42).

DISPOSITION

Mothers who commit neonaticide are more likely to be sentenced to prison or probation, whereas mothers who commit filicide are more likely to be hospitalized. This difference is in keeping with the lesser number of psychoses in the neonaticide group. Victoroff (48) notes that there is some appreciation that a mother who destroys her own child constructs enough guilt in this act to punish her sufficiently for the crime. Juries often find that the woman accused of neonaticide does not correspond to their imagination of a murderess. For no other crime is there such a lack of convictions (19). Even those who are convicted often receive only probation or minimal prison sentences.

The likelihood of a woman's killing a second newborn child after standing trial for neonaticide is very slim. There are a few reports in which a mother did kill two (10, 11) or three (5, 14) successive newborns. However, in all but one case the previous neonaticides had been undiscovered and unpunished. There is a greater chance of recidivism if the crime is consistent with the life style of the mother.

LEGAL CONSIDERATIONS

To understand the current legal status of infant murder, it is instructive to review the English law regarding this crime. In the reign of James I, the law presumed an illegitimate newborn found dead to have been murdered by its mother unless she could prove by at least one witness that the child had been born dead (48). In 1803 the same rules of evidence and presumption became required as in other murders (15). Death sentences for this crime were almost invariably commuted (29). Juries hesitated to find a verdict of guilty and send the accused to the gallows. Abse states, "Those juries knew that at or about the time of birth, dogs, cats, and sows . . . sometimes killed their own young. They were not prepared to extend less compassion and concern to a mentally sick woman than they would to an excitable bitch" (1).

A desire to make the punishment more suitable to the crime led to the Infanticide Act of 1922. This act reduced the penalties to those of manslaughter for a woman who killed her newborn child while the "balance of her mind was disturbed from the effect of giving birth" (29). Critics of this law suggest that if a woman were insane at the time of the crime she should not be held responsible, rather than be convicted of a lesser crime (4).

Several European countries provide lesser penalties for neonaticide than for adult murder. These universally apply only to the mother; if a father kills a newborn child he is charged with murder (21, 38). In the United States there is no legal distinction between the murder of adults and the murder of newborn infants. Although it is a common occurrence to find dead newborn infants in sewers, alleys, and incinerators in any metropolitan community, convictions are rare because of the difficulty in proving the guilt of those responsible (2). Several states have passed laws against the more easily prosecuted offense of concealment of birth.

In order to convict an individual of neonaticide it must be proven that he killed the infant by a specific act of commission or omission (8). It must also be proven that the infant breathed and had a viable separate existence from the mother after being fully extruded from the birth canal. Proving live birth was made easier by Swammerdam's discovery in 1667 that fetal lungs would float on water if respiration had occurred (40). However, this test was found to be not infallible, and even careful microscopic examination of neonatal lungs today does not always reveal a definitive answer (2). The other vexing forensic problem is proving that the child was wholly born. It is theoretically possible for a woman to cut the throat of her half-born infant, report the incident to the authorities, and therefore escape prosecution for either murder or concealment. Such cases have been reported (7).

PRESENT STATUS OF NEONATICIDE

It is extremely difficult to get accurate figures on the incidence of neonaticide because so many cases are never discovered. Published figures do suggest a decline in the last century (7, 13, 17, 18, 37, 39). Several factors may have contributed to this. Effective birth control measures are now widely available. Since the advent of antibiotics, abortions are rarely life threatening. Homes for unwed mothers have become available as a shelter from the "scoff and scorn of a taunting world," and placement of unwanted children can often be arranged. Finally, welfare payments today have reduced a woman's prospect of being destitute. Yet in spite of these advances, hundreds and possibly thousands of neonaticides still occur in this country each year.

Psychiatric intervention to prevent neonaticide is extremely difficult. Unlike filicide, in which 40 percent of murdering mothers seek medical or psychiatric consultation shortly before their crime, it is rare for women who commit neonaticide to seek any type of prenatal care. One way to further reduce the incidence of neonaticide would be a liberalization of abortion laws. Although this approach is far from ideal, it would provide women a less cruel alternative than killing their newborn infant. Each neonaticide is tragic—not only for the infant but also for the continuing effect that the crime has on the life of the mother.

SUMMARY

This paper has attempted to show that the killing of a newborn infant is a separate entity from other filicides. Hence a new word, "neonaticide," is proposed for this phenomenon. When mothers who commit neonaticide are compared with mothers who kill older children, they are found to be younger, more often unmarried, and less frequently psychotic. Whereas the majority of filicides are committed for "altruistic" reasons, most neonaticides are carried out simply because the child is not wanted. Reasons for neonaticide include extramarital paternity, rape, and seeing the child as an obstacle to parental ambition. However, illegitimacy, with its social stigma, is the most common motive.

The unmarried murderesses fall into two groups. In the first group are young, immature, passive women who submit to, rather than initiate, sexual relations. They often deny their pregnancy, and premeditation is rare. The women in the second group have strong instinctual drives and little ethical restraint. They tend to be older, more callous, and often promiscuous.

It is speculated that unresolved oedipal feelings may contribute to some neonaticides that have previously been attributed to entirely sociologic factors.

REFERENCES

1. Abse, L. Infanticide and British Law, *Clin. Pediat.* 6:316–317, 1967.
2. Adelson, L. Some Medicolegal Observations on Infanticide, *J. Forensic Sci.* 4:60–72, 1959.
3. Baker, J. Female Criminal Lunatics: A Sketch, *J. Ment. Sci.* 48:13–25, 1902.
4. Bartholomew, A. A., and Bonnici, A. Infanticide: A Statutory Offence, *Med. J. Aust.* 2:1018–1021, 1965.
5. Buhtz, G. Totung von Drei Neugeborenen Kindern Durch Die Eigene Eheliche Mutter, *Arch. Kriminol.* 110:14–19, 1942.
6. Busatto, S. Infanticidio per Arma Bianca, *Arch. Antro. Crim.* 55:239–266, 1935.
7. Curganaven, J. B. Infanticide, Baby-farming and the Infant Life Protection Act, 1872. *Sanitary Record, London* 10:409; 461, 1888–1889, 11:4; 415, 1889–1890.
8. Deadman, W. J. Infanticide, *Canad. Med. Ass. J.* 91:558–560, 1964.
9. Devereux, G. Mohave Indian Infanticide, *Psychoanal. Rev.* 35:126–139, 1948.
10. Doerr, Fr. Doppel-Kindsmord, *Arch. Kriminol.* 65:148–149, 1916.
11. Drouinceau, G. Apropos d'un Infanticide. *La Revue, Philanthropique* 38:49–54, 1917.
12. Garber, C. M. Eskimo Infanticide, *Scient. Month.* 64:98–102, 1947.
13. Gilli, R. L'infanticidio Nella Provincia di Firenze nel Cinquantennio, *Minerva Medicoleg.* 72:135–138, 1952.
14. Glos. Eine Ruchfallige Kindsmorderin, *Arch. Kriminol.* 20:49–50, 1905.
15. Greaves, G. Observations on Some of the Causes of Infanticide, *Tr. Manchester Statist. Soc.* 1–24, 1862–1863.
16. Griffiths, W. H. Infanticide, *Lancet* 2:519–520, 1873.
17. Grzywo-Dabrowski, W. L'avortement et L'infanticide à Varsovie après la Guerre, *Ann. Med. Leg.* 8:545–552, 1928.
18. Guareschi, G. L'infanticidio Commesso su Gemelli, *Arch. Antrop. Crim.* 60:870–880, 1940.
19. Gummersbach, K. Die Kriminalpsychologische Persönlichkeit der Kindesmördernnen und ihre Wertung im Gerichtsmedizinischen Gutachten, *Wien. Med. Wschr.* 88:1151–1155, 1938.
20. Hackfield, A. W. Crimes of Unintelligible Motivation as Representing an Initial Symptom of an Insidiously Developing Schizophrenia; Study of Comparative Effects of Penitentiary vs. Hospital Regime on such Cases, *Amer. J. Psychiat.* 91:639–668, 1934.
21. Harder, T. The Psychopathology of Infanticide, *Acta Psychiat. Scand.* 43:196–245, 1967.

22. Haun, K. Beitrag zur Lehre vom Kindesmord, *Deutsch. Z. Ges. Gerichtl. Med.* 10:58–69, July 1927.
23. Hirschmann, V. J., and Schmitz, E. Structural Analysis of Female Infanticide, *Psychother.* 8:1–20, 1958.
24. Hulst, J. P. L. Kinderdoodslag, Poging tot Verbranden Grof Geweld en Worging, *Nederl. Geneesk.* 2:1610–1616, 1927.
25. Le Foyer, J. Un Cas de Fausse Enclitophilie, *Ann. Med. Leg.* 19:47–57, 1939.
26. Ley, A. Infanticide et Jalousie, *Revue Droit Penal et Criminologie* 40:30–49, 1940.
27. Lopez Bancalari, E., and Delpiano, J. Peturbación Mental de Origen Gravidico, Pericia, *Médicolegal, Prensa Med. Argent.* 24:1088–1090, 1937.
28. Mann, E. C. Psychological Aspects of Three Cases of Infanticide Considered in Their Relations to Forensic Medicine, *Alienist and Neurologist* 8:30–42, 1887.
29. Matheson, J. C. M. Infanticide, *Med. Age* 15:741–747, 1897.
30. McDermaid, G., and Winkler, E. G. Psychopathology of Infanticide, *J. Clin. Exper. Psychopath.* 16:22–41, 1955.
31. Mody, C. R. An Essay on Female Infanticide; to which the Prize Offered by the Bombay Government for the Second Best Essay Against Female Infanticide Among the Jodajas and other Rajpoot Tribes of Guzerat was Awarded. Bombay: Education Society's Press, 1849.
32. Niedenthal, R. Eine Verbrechersippe, *Oeff. Gesundheitsdienst III,* 24:966–973, 1938.
33. Ortiz Velasquez, J. Infanticidio. *An. Acad. Med. Medillín,* 2:68–72, 1946.
34. Paul, C. Infanticide Sadique, *Ann. Med. Leg.* 22:173–174, 1942.
35. Perotti, D. Infanticidio con Arma da Taglio, (Scannamento e Ferite Multiple), *Boll. Soc. Medicochir. Pavia,* 4:191–213, 1929.
36. Pfister-Ammende, M. Zwei Falle von Kindstotung in Psychiatrischev, Beurteilung, Schweiz, *Arch. Neurol. Psychiat.* 39:373–387, 1937.
37. Pinkham, J. G. Some Remarks Upon Infanticide, with Report of a Case of Infanticide by Drowning, *Boston Medical and Surgical Journal* 109:411–413, 1883.
38. Pollak, O. *The Criminality of Women.* Philadelphia: University of Pennsylvania Press, 1950.
39. Puppe, G. Zur Psychologie und Prophylaxe des Kindesmordes, *Deutsch. Med. Wschr.* 43:609–615, 1917.
40. Radbill, X. "History of Child Abuse and Infanticide," in Helfer, R. E., and Kempe, C. H. eds.: *The Battered Child.* Chicago: University of Chicago Press, 1968, pp. 3–17.
41. Relative Prevalence of Infanticide in Japan and China (discussion), *Tr. Sei-I-Kwai, Tokyo, Trans.* 47:(Suppl. 12) 137–141, 1885.
42. Resnick, P. J. Child Murder by Parents: A Psychiatric Review of Filicide, *Amer. J. Psychiat.* 126:325–334, 1969.
43. Ryan, W. B. Child Murder in Its Sanitary and Social Bearings, *Sanitary Review of London* 4:165–184, 1857.
44. Sarrat, J. De L'infanticide Dans Ses Rapports Avec Les Psychoses Transistoires des Femmes en Couches. Lyon: Faculté de Medecin et de Pharmacie de Lyon, 1911.
45. Saurbrey, J., and Wilcke, B. Mental Confusion Associated with Childbirth: 6 Case Reports, *Acta Med. Leg. Soc.* 9:237–245, 1956.
46. Scott, D. Case of Infanticide, *Edinburgh Medical and Surgical Journal* 26:62–73, 1826.

47. Stern, E. S. The Medea Complex: Mother's Homicidal Wishes to Her Child, *J. Ment. Sci.* 94:321–331, 1948.

48. Victoroff, V. M. A Case of Infanticide Related to Psychomotor Automatism: Psychodynamic, Physiological, Forensic and Sociological Considerations, *J. Clin. Exper. Psychopath.* 16:191–220, 1955.

49. Winnik, H. Z. Psychopathology of Infanticide, A Case Study, *Israel Ann. Psychiat.* 1:293–306, 1963.

50. Wordsworth, W. "We are Seven," in Stevenson, B. E.: *The Home Book of Verse,* vol. 1. New York: Holt, Rinehart and Winston, 1965, pp. 316–318.

51. Zilboorg, G. Sidelights on Parent-Child Antagonism, *Amer. J. Orthopsychiat.* 2:35–43, 1932.

CHAPTER 14

The "Sick but Slick" Syndrome as a Personality Component of Parents of Battered Children

Logan Wright

PROBLEM

The battered child represents a very important developmental and social as well as mental health problem and very appropriately has become the object of widespread interest by clinicians and researchers alike. Discovery of any existing personality profile, or description of any personality characteristics common to battering parents, is a prerequisite to identifying and treating suspected or potential child abusers. Researchers (1–4, 6, 9, 11, 12) have reported a variety of characteristics of battering parents. One is they are emotionally immature, poorly prepared for the problems of parenthood, and maintain unrealistic fantasies and expectations for their child's rate of development and his ability to take care of himself:

"Henry J., in speaking of his sixteen month old son, Johnny, said, "He knows what I mean and understands it when I say 'come here.' If he doesn't come immediately, I go and give him a gentle tug on the ear to remind him of what he's supposed to do. In the hospital it was found that Johnny's ear was lacerated and partially torn away from his head. (6, p. 110)"

These parents also seem to see their children as agents for providing emotional support to mother rather than *vice versa:* "I have never felt really loved all my life. When the baby was born, I thought he would love me; but when he cried all the time, it meant he didn't love me, so I hit him. Kenny, age three weeks, was hospitalized with bilateral subdural hematomas. (6, p. 110)" Many battering parents are found to have a history of deprivation of love and affection from their parents and often have been battered themselves. As a result, they are presumed to have many unmet dependency needs. Economic and social difficulties (such as having too many babies over a short period of time, inability to meet economic demands, or separation from supportive relatives) also are felt to contribute to battering.

Reprinted with permission from the *Journal of Clinical Psychology* 32 (1976):41–45.

Wright (13) has described a picture of battering parents as disturbed, but capable of presenting an outwardly convincing picture of being normal and highly unlikely to abuse their children. This cluster of traits was termed the "sick but slick syndrome." Similarly, Smith, Honigsberger, and Smith (10) and Lund (8) have stressed the combined schizoid and psychopathic nature of disturbance in parents of battered children. Also, Steele (12), as well as Isaacs (7), has described child abusers as normal-appearing and overly conscientious parents.

The logistics of research on child abuse sometimes can be overwhelming, and Ss may have valid reasons to be evasive and uncooperative. These problems, combined with the primitive level of theory and research in this area, have produced a body of literature comprised primarily of impressionistic articles rather than more vigorously conducted studies. With the exception of Melnick and Hurley (9) and Lund (8), the research cited above is based on clinical observations rather than quantifiable data that utilized control groups, *etc*. The purpose of the present study was to explore the personalities of battering parents by obtaining quantifiable data about them from standard personality measures. This was not an experimental study in the sense that an independent variable is manipulated, with the predicted effect on a dependent variable determined on an *ad hoc* basis. Rather, the investigation was an inductive search for any consistencies in the personalities of child abusers.

METHOD

Ss were 13 parents convicted in court, but not incarcerated, for battering their children (experimental group) and 13 nonbattering, control parents of children hospitalized with infections, bone fractures, *etc*. in which the parents were not felt to be negligent. Each was selected because he represented a matched pairs partner for a given experimental S on the basis of age, sex, race, number of children, marital and educational status, family income and the fact that his child had been hospitalized. Each group consisted of 5 males and 8 females. Age differences between the matched pairs did not exceed 1 year. Total family income differences between the matched pairs of each group were less than $1000 per year. Parents were matched on years of schooling to within 2 years, and differences in number of children did not exceed one. The Peabody Picture Vocabulary Test (PPVT) also was administered to both groups in an attempt to control for the effects of intelligence.

Each parent received a battery of personality tests between 2 and 6 months after the battering episode. The battery consisted of the Rorschach, Minnesota Multiphasic Personality Inventory (MMPI), and Rosenzweig Picture Frustration Study (PF). The 13 validity and clinical scales of the MMPI were selected to measure overall level of psychopathology as well as to indicate specifics with regard to affect, character and other symptoms. The Rosenzweig was employed because intropunitiveness, extrapunitiveness and impunitiveness seemed highly relevant to child abuse. Also, the group conformity rating supposedly is related to psychopathic tendencies. The Rorschach was used in order to balance the battery with a less structured, projective task. It was scored for overall psychopathology, negative affect, psychopathic deviancy and bizarre content. The latter rating was an attempt to assess "craziness" in an overt sense. All four variables on the Rorschach were scored by an experienced clinician who was naive with regard to which group, experimental or control, given Ss belonged.

RESULTS

Since *ad hoc* predictions were not made, two-tailed, match-pair *t*-tests were performed on each of the study variables between experimental and control Ss. These results are shown in Table 1. Battering parents received scores significantly lower than nonbattering parents on the Rorschach variable of bizarre content ($t = 2.35$, $df = 12$, $p < .05$). Battering parents obtained scores signifi-

Table 1. Performance of experimental and control parents on 25 study variables

Measure	$\bar{X}_E$	$\bar{X}_C$	df	t
Rorschach				
Level overall pathology	28.0	27.7	12	.11
Negative affect	30.0	28.5	12	.57
Psychopathic deviancy	30.5	26.9	12	1.11
Bizarre content	24.0	29.6	12	2.35*
Rosenzweig picture frustration				
Group conformity rating	64.3	57.3	12	2.41*
Extrapunitive	31.3	43.5	12	2.06
Intropunitive	35.6	25.0	12	3.17**
Impunitive	32.0	31.4	12	.14
MMPI				
L	54.7	46.7	12	2.86*
F	61.0	54.7	12	1.52
K	56.2	49.5	12	2.37*
Hs	56.5	54.9	12	.38
D	61.5	53.2	12	1.74
Hy	60.2	57.3	12	.81
Pd	67.6	57.5	12	2.10
Mf	52.2	54.9	12	1.05
Pa	60.2	55.8	12	1.35
Pt	61.3	52.5	12	1.84
Sc	64.2	56.9	12	1.10
Ma	57.9	59.1	12	.23
Si	55.2	53.7	12	.50
PPVT				
IQ	97.0	111.2	12	2.95*

*$p < .05$; **$p < .01$.

cantly higher than nonbattering parents on the Rosenzweig group conformity rating ($t = 2.41$, $df = 12$, $p < .05$), the Rosenzweig intropunitiveness scale ($t = 3.17$, $df = 12$, $p < .01$), the MMPI lie scale ($t = 2.86$, $df = 12$, $p < .05$), and the MMPI K scale ($t = 2.37$, $df = 12$, $p < .05$). Thus, statistically significant differences were found for 5 of the 21 variables, while fewer than 2 would be expected by chance if the variables are assumed to be uncorrelated. The difference between experimental and control Ss on the psychopathic deviancy (PD) scale of the MMPI approached significance ($t = 2.10$, $t .05 = 2.18$); battering parents appeared more psychopathic. Battering parents also scored significantly lower than nonbatterers on the intelligence control measure (PPVT) ($t = 2.95$, $df = 12$, $p < .05$).

DISCUSSION

The fact that battering parents differed from their control Ss on IQ is difficult to explain. It seems unlikely that this could be accounted for by an emotional disturbance that effected cognitive functioning on a simple task such as the PPVT. On the other hand, the possibility that true differences in IQ exist between two populations matched so closely on the number of years of education and income is hard to accept. One possible explanation is a characterological one, wherein the energies of psychopathic individuals tend to be vested in atypical or "divergent" thinking (5) rather than in typical or "convergent" tasks such as measured by IQ tests. Smith, *et al.* (10) previously have reported battering parents to be both psychopathic and of low intelligence. In any event, this variable was not controlled successfully in the selection of the two study groups. The obtained differences on personality measures, however, do not seem attributable to IQ.

This study was not structured in such a manner as to make its results definitive. The sample is small, the number of comparisons relatively large and the number of significant findings somewhat meager. By design, the data are interpreted on a *post hoc* rather than an *ad hoc* basis. Such studies are not so much of value to test hypotheses, but rather to generate them. Hopefully, such new hypotheses serve a heuristic function and are tested in future investigations. More importantly, it is hoped that they may be tried and tested in the clinical work of practitioners.

Within the framework of this inductive search for relevant data on battering parents, the study data are internally consistent. Their most interesting characteristic is that experimental parents appear significantly less like batterers on test items that are logically derived (low bizarre content on the Rorschach, high *intro*-punitiveness and group conformity on the Rosenzweig). They appeared *more* psychopathic on the L, K and PD scales of the MMPI, whose items were derived empirically. In other words, the battering parents were able to appear significantly healthier on those instruments based on content or face validity, in which the social desirability of each item is more obvious. However, for items based on concurrent or statistical validity, where the socially desirable response is more ambiguous, they appeared significantly more disturbed. This, combined with the fact that the nature of the revealed disturbance on the MMPI is a near-classic profile for psychopathy, suggests that battering parents do possess such tendencies, but will portray themselves inversely whenever possible. This latter tendency is apparently the manifestation of defense mechanisms such as compensation and/or reaction formation.

These data support a "slick but sick" (particularly "slick") component in the personality characteristics of parents of battered children. Yet the fact that these data do not portray battering parents as severely disturbed is more open to conjecture. Possibly *S*s are a biased sample due to the fact that only convicted parents were studied. More obviously disturbed parents might have been dealt with differently by physicians, the police or the courts and thus prevented from entering the study. On the other hand, most earlier conclusions, that battering parents are highly disturbed, are based on the clinical impressions of experienced psychodiagnosticians. Possibly their intuition was biased by the fact that they knew the parents had battered their children. Or, possibly the clinicians are right, and such parents *are* disturbed, in spite of the fact they can successfully appear healthy on psychometric items that possess rather obvious social desirability.

The psychopathic character of battering parents, which is suggested here, irrespective of the severity of any accompanying disturbance, carries implications for those who deal with suspected child abusers. One is that we should be careful not to be lulled or conned into underestimating the potential of certain reasonable-appearing adults for disturbance and violence. The "sick but slick" syndrome also suggests potential deterrents to success with traditional psychotherapeutic intervention, namely denial and misrepresentation of self.

SUMMARY

Thirteen parents convicted in court of battering their children and 13 matched controls were administered a battery of personality tests, with significant differences obtained on 5 of 21 study variables. Battering parents appeared healthier on those instruments based on content validity, where the social desirability of the items is more obvious. They appeared more disturbed (*i.e.*, psychopathic) on items based on concurrent or statistical validity. It was concluded that battering parents were psychopathically disturbed, but whenever possible presented a distorted picture of themselves as healthy and unlikely to abuse their children. This tendency has been labeled the "sick but slick syndrome."

REFERENCES

1. Bishop, F. I. Children at risk. *Med. J. Austral.*, 1971, 1, 623–628.
2. Buglass, R. Parents with emotional problems. *Nursing Times*, 1971, 67, 1000–1001.

 3. Callaghan, K. A., and Fotheringham, B. J. Practical management of the battered baby syndrome. *Med. H. Austral.,* 1970, 1, 1282 1284.
 4. Court, J., and Kerr, A. The battered child syndrome. 2. A preventable disease? *Nursing Times*, 1971, 67, 695–697.
 5. Guilford, J. Three faces of intellect. *Amer. Psychol.,* 1959, 14, 469–479.
 6. Helfer, R. E., and Kempe, C. H. *The Battered Child,* Chicago: University of Chicago Press, 1968.
 7. Issacs, S. Neglect, cruelty and battering. *Brit. Med. J.,* 1972, 3, 224–226.
 8. Lund, S. N. Personality and personal history factors in child abusing parents. Paper presented for preliminary oral examination, University of Minnesota, May 8, 1973.
 9. Melnick, G., and Hurley, J. R. Distinctive personality attributes of child-abusing mothers. *J. Consult. Clin. Psychol.,* 1969, 33, 746–749.
10. Smith, S. M., Honigsberger, L., and Smith, C. A. E.E.G. and personality factors in baby batterers. *Brit. Med. J.,* 1973, 3, 20–22.
11. Spinetta, J. J., and Rigler, D. The child-abusing parent: A psychological review. *Psychol. Bull.,* 1972, 77, 296–304.
12. Steele, B. F. Violence in our society. *Pharos Alpha Omega Alpha Honor Med. Soc.,* 1970, 33, 42–48.
13. Wright, L. Psychologic aspects of the battered child syndrome. *South. Med. Bull.,* 1970, 58, 14–18.

CHAPTER 15

Folie à Deux in the Parents of Psychosocial Dwarfs: Two Cases

John Money and June Werlwas

INTRODUCTION AND PURPOSE

Though the term *folie à deux* (Lasègue and Falret 1877; Gralnick 1942) is not common in current psychiatric usage, the phenomenon is recognized from time to time. In its strictest sense it means that two people manifest identically the same symptom, often an *ideé fixe,* or a shared delusion. There is no literature on *folie à deux* in connection with the syndrome of reversible hyposomatotropinism or psychosocial dwarfism (recently reviewed by Patton and Gardner 1975).

The purpose of the present report is to present evidence of pathological collusion which constitutes *folie à deux* in the parents of two separate families. Each family contains one psychosocial dwarf, a victim of child abuse. One parent initiates child abuse while the other condones it.

THE NATURE OF THE SYNDROME OF REVERSIBLE HYPOSOMATOTROPIC DWARFISM

The presenting complaints of the syndrome are: failure of statural growth, which may be so extreme that at age 4½ a child has the size of a 12-month-old baby; failure of mental growth with apparent mental retardation; and various bizarre forms of behavior associated with self-preservation.

In affected children, growth hormone secretion is deficient, but the deficiency is subject to reversal upon change of domicile as, for example, when the child is admitted to the hospital. This reversibility is the primary pathognomonic feature of the syndrome. It is accompanied by catch-up statural and mental growth, and by improvement in behavioral pathology.

The behavioral pathology of the syndrome, in addition to disorders of eating

Research has been supported by USPHS #HD-00325 and by The Grant Foundation, Inc.
Reprinted with permission from *The Bulletin of the American Academy of Psychiatry and the Law* 4 (1976):351–62. Copyright 1977, The American Academy of Psychiatry and The Law.

and drinking, includes disorders of sleeping; disorders of elimination; pain agnosia; elective mutism; accommodation to somatic trauma; short-lived though infrequent temper tantrums; roaming; impaired IQ; impaired motor development; social distancing; delayed puberty; and, during the recovery phase, compensatory hyperkinesis. Temper tantrums, if present, coexist with affection-seeking and social compliance, as does the social-distancing behavior. The compensatory hyperkinesis appears as limit testing and coexists, during the recovery phase, with an increase in both intellectual and statural growth.

The diagnosis of reversible hyposomatotropic dwarfism is definitively established not by laboratory or clinical findings alone, but by growth acceleration secondary to increased growth hormone secretion, following change of domicile. The syndrome evidences the clearest known example of a correlation between factors in the social and behavioral environment, on the one hand, and impairment of endocrine regulation of somatic growth as well as behavioral maturation, on the other.

Taxonomically, the syndrome of reversible hyposomatotropic dwarfism is known also as psychosocial dwarfism (Reinhart and Drash 1969). Reversible hyposomatotropinism is a more operational term, and one which does not imply spurious accuracy concerning etiology. In the past, the syndrome has been variously identified with failure to thrive (Barbero and Shaheen 1967; Pollitt, Eichler and Chan 1975), and maternal deprivation (Patton and Gardner 1969). It has also been known as deprivation dwarfism (Silver and Finkelstein 1967; Gardner 1972; Patton and Gardner 1975); and as emotional deprivation and growth retardation simulating idiopathic hypopituitarism (Powell, Brasel and Blizzard 1967; Powell, Brasel, Raiti and Blizzard 1967). Recently, the term abuse dwarfism (Money 1977)* has been used synonymously with psychosocial dwarfism.

THE SAMPLE

The two families of this study were selected from forty documented cases of the syndrome, not at random, but because of their diversity. They were similar and different as follows: (1) each family resides within commuting distance of The Johns Hopkins Hospital; (2) there exists sufficient evidence in both case histories to warrant further research into family dynamics, in that one family history clearly indicates psychopathology, whereas the other gives an overt appearance of stability with covert indications that surfaces may be deceiving; (3) one patient is female, one male; (4) the girl spent eight months away from home, the boy eight years; and (5) the girl is a child, the boy an adolescent.

The two children have been seen repeatedly by members of the pediatric endocrine clinic and its psychohormonal research unit at The Johns Hopkins Hospital from 1965 (Patient H.K.) and 1973 (Patient J.G.) until the present.

---

*The present paper is one of a series on psychosocial dwarfism produced by members of the psychohormonal research unit. See bibliography.

They were both referred primarily because of growth failure. Family members were included in interviews when they accompanied the child to a scheduled hospital appointment; or if they agreed to, or requested, individual interviews.

No known systematic bias exists with respect to selection of these two cases from among the other 38 patients with the same diagnosis. Probably the process which brings about referral of reversible dwarfism from the community at large is subject to bias, though to an unknown degree. The morbidity and mortality of the syndrome are unknown. Affected individuals may, or may not, survive without receiving professional attention.

PROCEDURES

Original and followup taped and transcribed interviews and notes were obtained from patients, parents, guardians, social workers, and nurses.

The interviews always began with open-ended inquiry prior to factual and true-false questioning. Direct observation of child and parental behavior in the hospital and during home visits provided additional information, as did school reports.

To provide contemporary followup and to fill any existing gaps in historical data, the two sets of parents of origin in this study were interviewed in their homes for approximately six (Patient J.G.) and eight (Patient H.K.) hours, respectively. The parents consented to the use of their information, including the tape-recorded portions, as data for a written report concerning families of children with the same diagnosis as their own growth-retarded child.

The proper names, including initials, used in this study for patients and family members are pseudonymous.

BACKGROUND DATA: THE KIRK FAMILY

The parents of 17-year-old Herbert Kirk married twenty years ago. This is the first marriage for the mother and the second for the father. They have always belonged to the blue-collar, white, lower-middle class socioeconomically. They have four living sons. The husband is seven years older than his wife.

Two successive miscarriages preceded their second child's birth. This child, Herbert, with a history of reversible hyposomatotropinism, was the product of an unexpected twin birth. The twin who died at four days of age reputedly had cystic fibrosis. The parents' suspicion that Herbert also had cystic fibrosis, because of his odor as a neonate, was not corroborated by medical records.

Herbert had six major hospital admissions during his first six years of life. Reasons for referral varied. Referrals were either initiated by physicians for further studies or initiated by the parents when they were dissatisfied with prior treatments or test results.

When first measured in The Johns Hopkins pediatric endocrine clinic at age

6 11/12 years, Herbert had the height of less than a three-year-old. Accelerated growth occurred during subsequent hospitalizations and five foster home placements. At present he has average height for age 17 years.

A son of the father's first marriage lived with Mr. and Mrs. Kirk for the first two years of their marriage. At approximately age 3 the son was admitted to a state hospital for severe mental retardation. At the present age of 22, he resides at this same hospital.

Mr. Kirk, in a recent interview, reported a suspicion that his first wife dropped the retarded son in early infancy, ostensibly causing brain injury and retardation. The reason Mr. Kirk gave for his speculation was that the first wife refused to take the baby to a physician at any time following the birth, which occurred at home. When asked why he didn't take the child to a physician himself, Mr. Kirk said that his first wife made the decisions and his role was "just going along with her like blowin' with the wind." A similar attitude characterizes his relationship with his second wife.

According to Mr. Kirk, he and his second wife made the following agreements concerning the retarded son:

—immediately after their marriage to assume full caretaking responsibility of their son;

—one year after the marriage, to hospitalize the son, who ostensibly became difficult for the second Mrs. Kirk to manage;

—before and after state hospitalization, to prevent, by legal means, the son's mother-of-birth from visiting him;

—during the past few years, never to visit, plan to visit or make contact with the son at all.

Mr. Kirk's siblings of origin are three brothers, one of whom is younger than he. After his father's death when Mr. Kirk was 17 years old, he helped his mother raise his younger brother. He recalled never "raising a hand" to the younger brother because discipline was his mother's job. His mother and brothers do not, at present, live within easy visiting distance.

By self-report, Mr. Kirk has been unemployed for the past twelve years owing to a "heart condition and nerves." Hospital records include suggestions by a cardiologist and two psychiatrists that Mr. Kirk return to work. As a former union laborer, he now receives unemployment disability payments sufficient to support his family. He spends his time building intricate wooden models, for example, of locomotives, and performing light housekeeping chores.

Mrs. Kirk is the second of four siblings and has two living brothers. She had an allegedly mentally retarded younger sister who died at age 19 at a state hospital, the day following the birth of Herbert and his deceased twin. Because her mother worked, Mrs. Kirk as a young girl had caretaking responsibility for the sister until her admission to the state hospital three weeks before her death. Mrs. Kirk adamantly refused to release the medical records of her sister. Nothing is known concerning the etiology of her mental retardation, or indeed of the authenticity of its diagnosis.

Mrs. Kirk has always lived within easy visiting distance of her parents and brothers. She has, during the past two years, attempted to work as a shop clerk from time to time. Family illness was, by her report, the reason for her inability to work steadily. Mrs. Kirk said that she "took care of," when they were ill, the following members of her immediate family: her sister; her husband's son; her second child, Herbert; her husband, who 12 years ago was briefly hospitalized for psychiatric reasons, and has recurring attacks of "nerves"; her aging parents; and her fourth son, 10-year-old Luther.

Luther was designated by his parents as the surrogate, or substitute patient, when Herbert left the Kirk family. His behavior, according to the parents, was similar to Herbert's behavior while living in their home (see Findings).

Mr. and Mrs. Kirk, within the past year, moved from their long-term residence in an apartment in the home of Mrs. Kirk's parents into a house of their own. They presently have two of their four children living in their three-bedroom home. Herbert arranged to have himself adopted by foster parents. Approximately two months after Luther's residential placement, Mr. Kirk became ill again, according to Mrs. Kirk. Luther is living at a residential school for emotionally handicapped children. The reasons for the move, according to Mrs. Kirk, were to prevent her mother's interfering with the firm discipline used by Mrs. Kirk in her attempt to control Luther's behavior, and to be closer in distance to Herbert's new home.

During recent husband-wife interviews in the Kirks' home, Mrs. Kirk was observed clearly to dominate the conversation while Mr. Kirk repeatedly nodded his head in agreement. Mr. Kirk did state that he loves his wife and sees her as a wonderful woman who can manage almost anything. The statement was repeated by Mr. Kirk at a later date during an individual interview.

BACKGROUND DATA: THE GRAY FAMILY

The parents of Joanne Gray were married eleven years ago. This is the only marriage for both parents, whose age difference is four years, the husband being older. Occupationally, the father has been able to upgrade his family's socioeconomic status so it is now blue-collar, managerial, black, middle class.

The parents have six children, five boys and one girl. The fifth child in birth order, Joanne, age 7, is diagnosed as having reversible hyposomatotropic dwarfism. The third child in birth order, 10-year-old Matthew, was the designated surrogate patient in this family; he exhibited symptoms similar to his sister's, such as growth failure and behavioral impairments. Matthew's diagnosis was not confirmed owing to his parents' failure to bring him to the hospital for outpatient appointments. His impairments of growth and behavior accelerated during the time Joanne's growth and behavior improved.

Home visits were conducted between two and three years after Joanne's diagnosis and treatment. During these visits, neither Joanne nor Matthew was observed to exhibit the behavioral characteristics typical of reversible hyposomatotropinism. However, the sixth child, age 5, was, by sibling and parental report, different from the others. His behavior, as observed by two interviewers, was hyperactive and included hitting, kicking and punching siblings; jumping, tumbling and running during a quiet recording session; and dumping the contents of a large drawer on the floor.

During this same home visit, Mr. Gray reported that no problems presently exist with respect to any of the children. Mrs. Gray agreed with him. Together they seemed oblivious to their sixth child's hyperactivity. They ignored it, much in the same way as they had ignored Joanne's and Matthew's former physical and behavioral impairments.

By Mrs. Gray's report and Mr. Gray's agreement, Joanne's birth was different from the births of the other five children in that Joanne "was taken from" the mother. According to hospital records, delivery, at about the expected due date, was accomplished by Caesarean section 1½ hours after admission. The diagnosis was placenta praevia. The newborn was normal and weighed six pounds two ounces.

On the surface, the family appears to give no evidence of psychopathology:
—Mr. Gray is successful in his work.
—Mrs. Gray tried working but prefers to be home with her children.
—The home, in a well-kept residential area, is itself well-kept but not scrupulously clean.
—Neither parent has received psychiatric treatment.
—The parents speak positively about all their children.
—Mr. Gray talks of pleasurable family outings, both past and planned.
—Both parents keep in contact with their own families of origin.
—Both parents have high ambitions for their children's success.

Mrs. Gray is the second child in a family of thirteen and the oldest living girl. Her parents are both living. She had, in her family of origin, caretaking responsibility of a retarded sibling. As observed in the clinic and at home, she appeared to be impaired in spontaneity and to experience some degree of constraint in emotional expression and responsiveness, though placid and pleasant. She was described by school personnel as cooperative and congenial. By contrast, a psychologist described her as quasi-catatonic.

Mr. Gray is personable, outgoing, and verbal. In interviews with hospital professionals he supplied most of the information concerning the development of the children. He is third in a family of four. He has an older sister and brother and a younger sister. Since the death of Mr. Gray's mother six years ago, his father lives alone and visits the family frequently.

During eight months in a recovery center, nearly three years ago, Joanne exhibited a remarkable reversal of growth and behavioral impairments. When first seen at The Johns Hopkins Hospital at age 4 3/12, she had the weight of a four-month-old, the height of a one-year-old and the bone age of a 15-month-old. While in the recovery center, she gained over 12 pounds and grew 6 inches in eight months. The growth rate was 10 inches a year and demonstrated the catchup growth spurt by which the diagnosis of reversible dwarfism was confirmed. After returning to the home of origin, her growth rate decreased to approximately three inches a year, a rate within the normal limits of yearly growth, but not sufficient for adequate catchup growth.

The parents did not agree to discharge from the recovery center to a foster home, but did consent to having their daughter stay with an aunt who lived near them and who had always shown a special degree of understanding for the child. Then they unilaterally decided to keep their daughter at home, without informing their doctors or other case workers of their action.

Both Mr. and Mrs. Gray presented to friends, relatives and professionals an image of their family life as intact and harmonious. There were, however, obvious discrepancies with this image which are included in the following sections.

EXAMPLES OF ABUSE: TWO FAMILIES

For the purposes of this paper, abuse is defined as documented noxious motor and/or vocal behavior of parents or guardians toward a child such that it injures or impairs either their somatic or behavioral and mental growth, or both, to such a degree that an impartial jury of peers in consultation with experts would call the child abused. Medical reports of the initial referrals of both Herbert Kirk and Joanne Gray to The Johns Hopkins Hospital document impairments of growth and behavior.

The existence of parental abuse was not recorded in the medical history at the time of the children's initial visits. It required followup interviews with both the Kirk and Gray families to ascertain the following forms of abuse: corporal punishment; deprivation of food, sleep, social contact and sensory stimulation.

Mrs. Kirk, in the presence of her husband, admitted that she had used the following disciplinary techniques with Herbert: whipping; locking him in a closet; tying him to his bed and also to a chair; restricting food and drink by constant watchfulness; and restricting social play.

The following disciplinary actions which occurred in his home-of-origin were reported by Herbert to his present adoptive mother: he was locked in a closet for several days without food; he was tied to his bed; he was given only mushy cereal to eat while siblings ate fresh cereal; he did not get enough to eat, whereas his siblings had plenty; often he was tied to a chair; and he had been made to lie naked on the floor next to his mother's bed while his mother stepped on him.

In the Gray family, the father disclosed that he regularly used his belt to discipline his daughter for soiling herself. He self-righteously used her age, four years, as his criterion for bowel control, ignoring the fact that she weighed only 13 pounds. The mother disclosed that she restricted Joanne's food and drink because of bad eating habits. She kept the child isolated in her crib away from other family members for most of the time she was awake, claiming she was happier when left alone. The child had a deep scar across the bridge of the nose, possibly from being trapped between the rungs of the crib.

FINDINGS

The parents in each of the two families maintained their role as child abusers in such a way that amounted, within their contriving, to psychopathological collusion. This was true whether the abuse was somatic or psychic.

Sometimes each parent reiterated the pathological idea of the other. Sometimes each endorsed the pathology of the other by way of silent consent instead of critical intervention. Their collusion was manifested in such a way that it was difficult for professional observers to differentiate beliefs from rationalizations, or *ideés fixes* from quasi-delusions.

COLLUSION: THE KIRK FAMILY DISCIPLINE

When both parents together were interviewed at home, the interviewer noted that the father agreed verbally and by head nodding that his wife's descriptions of past punitive actions with Herbert were necessary "for the good of the family." They gave the following examples of Herbert's behavior, each time failing to mention why he may have done it: (a) he constantly frustrated his mother and would not allow her to have any peace of mind; (b) he deliberately provoked other family members; (c) he roamed the house at night whenever he could get away with it; (d) he had to be watched constantly because he would eat anything he could get his hands on; (e) he made strange repetitious whining and moaning noises and talked and sang to himself; (f) he picked bedding and clothing to pieces and tried to hide the resulting lint; (g) he drank water from the toilet bowl; and (h) he sat in one position, without responding, once for as long as 47 minutes.

Subsequent investigations revealed that the parents, knowingly or unknowingly, instigated the behavior they deplored. For example, the child's bizarre eating and drinking habits and roaming at night appeared, in retrospect, as a response to being hungry and thirsty. His alleged provocation of family members was probably a response to documented physical abuse from siblings as well as parents. His perseverative sounds and activities were a response to discipline and to long periods of isolation.

Consistently in all their interviews over the years, both parents maintained that Herbert had created "a wall" between his mother and himself since birth. They cited this wall as the main reason for their use of harsh discipline. Both of them believed that the wall prevented Mrs. Kirk from communicating with Herbert in the same way she communicated with her other children.

It was the opinion of all the professionals concerned with the case that the mother was the primary initiator of abuse and the father, the secondary consentor.

PLACEMENTS

Mr. and Mrs. Kirk's collusion was unbroken when Herbert was away from their home in the hospital or a foster home. According to medical records, during each placement they pled for their child's return to the home. The last time he was returned home they became frustrated with his behavior, threatened to send him away, and again requested his removal from their home.

Interviews with present and past foster parents included the following examples of the Kirk parents' behavior during Herbert's placements: They would plead with him to visit them and then mistreat him with verbal and physical abuse; they would, for long periods of time, make no effort to contact him or return his phone calls; they seemed unable to treat the child as a human being; they would repeatedly break promises; they once responded to a phone call from Herbert, who said he'd be a little late for his expected Christmas visit to their home, with "Don't bother to come at all."

When Herbert at age 19 had himself legally adopted by his foster parents, both Mr. and Mrs. Kirk agreed that it was a shame. Mrs. Kirk said that one of the reasons (see Background Data) she wanted her family to move from their former residence was to be closer to Herbert. The adoptive mother said that she viewed the move as another attempt by Herbert's family to interfere with his progress. She cited that prior to the adoption, Herbert ceased his former practice of phoning the Kirks and/or requesting to visit them.

Because of his adoptive father's change of job, Herbert and his adoptive family recently moved out of state. The patient maintains contact with the psychohormonal research unit. He is doing well.

THE SURROGATE (SUBSTITUTE) PATIENT

In the Kirk family, the patient's youngest brother, Luther, has consistently been the surrogate, although his statural growth has not been retarded. His two admissions to a children's psychiatric ward were for treatment of school phobia and other behavioral symptoms. The first admission coincided with Herbert's possible permanent placement in a foster home, while the second corresponded with Herbert's legal adoption by a foster family.

Luther's problems were described by Mrs. Kirk, with Mr. Kirk in agreement, in the following manner: "Yes, he's picked up some of Herbert's way because Luther always watched everything he did. And true, he picked up his 'oohing' bit" (tic-like moans) "and his throwing a fit if he can't have his way. He knows, because he used to watch Herbert and all, and he has taken up at the same place Herbert left off. And I tell him to stop that. I'll tell him, I'll tell him too, 'You're acting just like Herbert.' " The parents described other undesirable behavior that Luther had copied from Herbert, classifiable as social distancing; temper tantrums; problems of eating, sleeping, playing; and pain agnosia. An example of pain agnosia, as well as abuse, was evidenced when Mrs. Kirk described Luther's standing outside in the cold in his bare feet and not feeling the cold. She reported that since Luther doesn't feel anything, she pulled him up the steps by the hair ("for that he feels") to get him out of the cold.

The Kirk parents did not allow Luther to join the Boy Scouts, as formerly they had prohibited Herbert from doing. The two other siblings were active in scouting. Luther, in the presence of an interviewer and both parents, said he wanted to join the Scouts. The mother, with the father verbally supporting her, said that Luther could not join because he would come running home on the first camping trip. As if they together followed the same script, both parents gave their son several reasons why he would come running home.

Luther presently lives in a residential institution. In the absence of both Luther and Herbert, Mr. Kirk is the member of the family who has developed psychiatric symptoms which, according to his wife, require her to stay home and care for him.

COLLUSION: THE GRAY FAMILY DISCIPLINE

Mr. Gray accepted his wife's absurd dietary ideas. During a home interview he actually verbalized agreement with her stated reasons for restricting Joanne's nutrition. Mrs. Gray said that Joanne had bad eating and drinking habits, which included gulping food and drink, eating too fast, eating garbage, chewing and swallowing poorly, and intermittently refusing to eat. These habits ostensibly caused the daughter to have a bloated stomach, to wheeze, and to be susceptible to germs. According to the mother, food restriction was a method of discipline to correct bad habits as well as to prevent physical illness.

Collusion with respect to discipline was further evidenced by Mrs. Gray's denial of any knowledge that her husband used his belt to beat the 13-pound child. Mr. Gray had reported spanking his daughter "maybe two or three times a week" for soiling her diapers. Mrs. Gray, in a separate interview, said, "I will spank her if she's really wrong but my husband, he won't spank her."

Joanne's isolation from family activities involved further parental collusion in defining the daughter's isolation from her brothers not as deprivation or punishment but as a form of protection. According to Mrs. Gray, the other children were not permitted to go upstairs near Joanne's crib because she caught colds and germs easily. Mr. Gray agreed with his wife's statement that Joanne "was always the type to stay to herself. She didn't want to be around nobody." The parents said that, rather than being with the other children, Joanne preferred being quiet most of the time; playing with her hands; staring; just sitting; and mumbling to herself.

PLACEMENTS

During Joanne's 8-month placement in the recovery center, her parents visited regularly. Mrs. Gray's actions during those visits were described by a hospital clinician as "removed and distant." She would, for example, sit and do needlework while watching Joanne play rather than attempt to talk or play with the child directly.

Though Mr. Gray did play with Joanne during these visits, he did not attempt to involve his wife in closer contact with her daughter.

During her 8-month stay at the recovery center, Joanne learned to walk, to control elimination, and to speak in three-word sentences. She grew rapidly in height and weight (see Background Data).

After the child's discharge from the recovery center, the parents missed the next three scheduled appointments at the pediatric endocrine clinic. The father brought the child for a check-up only after the family was informed that protective services would be notified if the patient missed further appointments.

The parents cited their prayers as an explanation for her growth during the recovery placement. Acknowledged with head-nodding by her husband, Mrs. Gray said, "All I know is we prayed every night, and by her being out there, our praying and the different climate she was surrounded by, I think it really caused her to start growing and walking and doing all the things she was supposed to be doing."

Mr. Gray gave his description of the recovery center as: "You know, that's the place where all the children go, out there, and they let them run wild and let them do anything they want to do." Mrs. Gray nodded in approval of his statement.

THE SURROGATE (SUBSTITUTE) PATIENT

In addition to Joanne, Matthew, who is two years older than his sister, has exhibited symptoms of lack of statural and behavioral maturation. As if on a see-saw, one child's health has been balanced by the other's illness.

Prior to Joanne's birth, Matthew was the growth-retarded patient of the family. At age 1½ he was hospitalized and diagnosed as failure to thrive. He allegedly ceased to have growth and behavior problems near the time of Joanne's first hospitalization at age two, when she was diagnosed as failure to thrive. The parents did not keep clinic appointments for Matthew during the three years that Joanne was the obvious, non-growing, nonmaturing patient in the family. Matthew returned for a medical check-up at a comprehensive clinic at the time of Joanne's return home from the recovery hospital. Mrs. Gray reported that Matthew overate, gulped his food, and had "milk poisoning" which caused his stomach to bloat. She forbade him to eat any food at school except what she gave him. When he returned home from school, she lifted his shirt to see if his abdomen was bloated. If so, that was her proof that he had illicitly eaten milk-containing food at school.

The family pediatrician suggested residential placement for Matthew, but the parents refused. Again, they did not keep scheduled appointments. When the family was threatened by protective services for missed appointments, both Joanne and Matthew improved in growth and behavior.

At present, the Gray parents have been keeping appointments at a comprehensive clinic for Joanne and Matthew. During a recent home visit the parents spoke with pride of their two children who formerly "were shy and didn't grow."

None of the Gray children appears shy or dwarfed at present. Their sixth child, however, a boy age 5, is regarded by parents and siblings as the "trouble causer." He shows classic signs of the hyperactive child. His activity rarely is shared with that of his siblings, and he is recognized in the family as being odd.

DISCUSSION

The present findings may relate to the findings of Spitz (1946) with respect to hospitalism and those of Bowlby (1969, 1973) with respect to separation and loss. Neither of these two authors, however, recorded measures of statural growth. Also, neither author construed the behavior of adults in the child's social environment in terms of psychopathological collusion.

It is fair to make the inference that, in the case of the institutions studied by Spitz, the hospital personnel accepted what today would be considered a pathological philosophy of caretaking which is a *de facto* form of collusion. Pathological collusion is not synonymous with voluntary malevolence. It can happen covertly and without planned intention; it can also be defended with self-righteous devotedness, as in the case of the parents presented in this paper. The same may well apply to the parents studied by Bowlby.

The findings of the present paper obviously relate to those of authors who have used the diagnostic terms "failure to thrive" (Barbero and Shaheen 1967), "maternal deprivation" (Patton and Gardner 1969; Rutter 1976), and "deprivation dwarfism" (Silver and Finkelstein 1967; and Gardner 1972). These authors were clearly aware of noxious events in the child's social environment as well as the failure of statural growth, though at the time of their observations, the pathological behavior of adults was recognized only in individual clinical observations. With respect to pathological parental collusion, these same authors, like Spitz and Bowlby, did not report it. There is no case study delineating the collusion between parents in which abuse masquerades as devoted parenthood.

Another point of discussion is with reference to infantile autism (Kanner, 1948), childhood schizophrenia (Bradley 1941; Bradley and Bowen 1941), and symbiotic psychosis (Finch 1960). In these conditions impaired statural growth is not a standard feature. However, the following behavioral symptoms are uncannily similar to those observed in psychosocial (abuse) dwarfism prior to the catch-up growth spurt: seclusiveness; bizarre eating habits; catatonic manifestations including posturing and grimacing; awkward gait; preoccupation; daydreaming; and physical inactivity.

There exists a great deal of documentation concerning covert collusion in the parents of children diagnosed as schizophrenic. In fact, it has been theoretically fashionable to point the etiological finger at parents, attributing pathology in the child to the parents' collusive pathological behavior.

Nowadays, however, there is greater willingness to accept the hypothesis that an infant may actually trigger some pathological behavior in the parents. The mechanism of this triggering may, by speculation, occur neonatally as an impairment of the infant's ability to react in such a way as to elicit parental caretaking responses, thus impeding the establishment of a parent-child pair-bond.

Failure of pair-bonding may very well be a common factor shared or manifested in the syndrome of childhood schizophrenia and the syndrome of abuse dwarfism, despite the differences in the ultimate phenomenology and prognosis of each syndrome. There may also be a difference in the etiological factors responsible for the failure to pair-bond in each syndrome.

In Spitz's and Bowlby's hospitalized infants, the etiology of the failure to pair-bond clearly lies in the institution's methods of caretaking. The etiology of the failure in abuse dwarfism or childhood schizophrenia remains unknown.

In addition to the syndromes of hospitalism, failure to thrive, and childhood schizophrenia, there is a fourth condition which has relevance to abuse dwarfism, namely Munchausen's syndrome. In its classic form, Munchausen's syndrome is a condition in which the etiology of symptoms appears completely hidden but, in fact, the symptoms are self-induced. There is a close parallel with the symptoms observed in abuse dwarfism except that the symptoms are parent-produced instead of self-induced. Whereas in Munchausen's syndrome the patient gives a false medical history, in abuse dwarfism the parents give the false history while the patient remains silent. That is to say, one has a case of Munchausen's syndrome by proxy.

The same condition of Munchausen's syndrome by proxy also occurs in cases of child abuse without dwarfism. There is not yet enough comparative information to permit a statement as to why some abused children become dwarfs whereas others are presented simply as victims of trauma.

There is also not yet enough comparative information to permit a statement concerning how specific is the relationship of reversible IQ impairment to the syndrome of abuse dwarfism. There is, however, one important study (Dennis 1973) concerning reversible IQ impairment secondary to institutional rearing. The institution was a foundling home in Beirut, Lebanon, in which children were subject to severe social deprivation. Dennis took advantage of a new law that in 1956 permitted legal adoption for the first time in the country. Before 1956, all foundlings lived in the home throughout childhood and adolescence. Among them, the average IQ was slightly above 50. After 1956, if adoption occurred before age 2, then the IQ distribution of the children was normal, the average IQ being 100. Children who lived in the institution for longer than two years lost six months of mental age for each year of residence in the institution. After adoption, when catch-up mental growth began, they were unable to catch up the 50% of deficient mental growth. Thus if a child of 12 would be adopted with a mental age of 6, the missing six years could not be regained in catch-up growth. The six years were lost forever, and represented a permanent IQ impairment. Though the evidence is still incomplete, it would appear that the same type of permanent IQ impairment occurs in abuse dwarfism, and is thus a by-product of parental collusion.

SUMMARY

The two families studied in this report, each with one child diagnosed as having reversible hyposomatotropinism, represent diverse as well as similar aspects of collusional psychopathology. Parental complementarity in these two families is, in part, *folie à deux* in that both sets of parents share a delusion of righteous parenthood. This self-righteousness permitted the parents to perpetrate or condone both covert and overt child abuse. Parental collusion does not, however, explain the phenomenological reversibility of growth failure and behavioral disorder. More familial and individual evidence is needed to determine what common factors preceded the final common pathway to reversible growth failure and reversible behavior disorder.

REFERENCES

Barbero, G. J., Shaheen, E: Environmental failure to thrive: A clinical view. *Journal of Pediatrics* 71:639–644 (1967).

Bowlby, J.: *Attachment and Loss,* Vol. 1. *Attachment,* New York, Basic Books, 1969.

Bowlby, J.: *Attachment and Loss,* Vol. 2. *Separation.* New York, Basic Books, 1973.

Bradley, C.: *Schizophrenia in Childhood.* New York, Macmillan, 1941.

Bradley, C., Bowen, M.: Behavior characteristics of schizophrenic children. *Psychiatric Quarterly* 15:296–315 (1941).

Dennis, W,: *Children of the Crèche.* New York, Appleton-Century-Crofts, Educational Division, Meredith Corporation, 1973.

Finch, S. M.: *Fundamentals of Child Psychiatry.* New York, Norton, 1960.

Gardner, L.: Deprivation dwarfism. *Scientific American* 227:76–83 (1972).

Gralnick, A.: *Folie à deux:* the psychosis of association: a review of 103 cases and the entire English literature. *Psychiatric Quarterly* 16:230–263 (1942).

Kanner, L.: *Child Psychiatry.* Springfield, Ill., Charles C Thomas, 1948.

Lasègue, C., Falret, J.: La folie à deux ou folie communiquée. *Annales Medico-Psychologiques,* 5s. 18:321–355 (1877).

Money, J.: The syndrome of abuse-dwarfism (psychosocial dwarfism or reversible hyposomatotropinism): behavioral data and case report. *American Journal of Diseases of Children.* 131:508–513 (1977).

Money, J., Annecillo, C.: IQ change following change of domicile in the syndrome of reversible hyposomatotropinism (psychosocial dwarfism). *Psychoneuroendocrinology* 1:427–429 (1976).

Money, J., Annecillo, C., Werlwas, J.: Hormonal and behavioral reversals in hyposomatotropic dwarfism. In *Hormones, Behavior and Psychopathology,* E. J. Sachar, ed., New York, Raven Press, 1976.

Money, J., Needleman, A.: Child abuse in the syndrome of reversible hyposomatotropic dwarfism (psychosocial dwarfism). *Journal of Pediatric Psychology* 1:20–23 (1976).

Money, J., Wolff, G.: Late puberty, retarded growth and reversible hyposomatotropinism (psychosocial dwarfism). *Adolescence* 9:121–134 (1974).

Money, J., Wolff, G., Annecillo, C.: Pain agnosia and self-injury in the syndrome of reversible somatotropin deficiency (psychosocial dwarfism). *Journal of Autism and Childhood Schizophrenia* 2:127–139 (1972).

Patton, R. G., Gardner, L. I.: Short stature associated with maternal deprivation syndrome: disordered family environment as cause of so-called idiopathic hypopituitarism. In *Endocrine and Genetic Diseases of Childhood,* L. I. Gardner, ed., Philadelphia, Saunders, 1969.

Patton, R. G., Gardner, L. I.: Deprivation dwarfism (psychosocial deprivation): Disordered family environment as cause of so-called idiopathic hypopituitarism. In *Endocrine and Genetic Diseases of Childhood,* 2. L. I. Gardner, ed., Philadelphia, Saunders, 1975.

Pollitt, E., Eichler, A., Chan, C.: Psychosocial development and behavior of mothers of failure-to-thrive children. *American Journal of Orthopsychiatry* 45:525–537 (1975).

Powell, G. F., Brasel, J. A., Blizzard, R. M.: Emotional deprivation and growth retardation simulating idiopathic hypopituitarism. I. Clinical evaluation of the syndrome. *New England Journal of Medicine* 267:1271–1278 (1967).

Powell, G. F., Brasel, J. A., Raiti, S., Blizzard, R. M.: Emotional deprivation and growth retardation simulating idiopathic hypopituitarism. II. Endocrinologic evaluation of the syndrome. *New England Journal of Medicine* 267:1279–1283 (1967).

Reinhart, J. B., Drash, A. L.: Psychosocial dwarfism: environmentally induced recovery. *Psychosomatic Medicine* 31:165–172 (1969).

Rutter, M.: *The Qualities of Mothering: Maternal Deprivation Reassessed.* New York, Aronson, 1974.

Silver, H. K., Finkelstein, J.: Deprivation dwarfism. *Journal of Pediatrics* 70:317–324 (1967).

Spitz, R. A.: Hospitalism. *Psychoanalytic Study of the Child* 2:113–117. New York, International Universities Press, 1946.

Werlwas, J.: Reversible hyposomatotropinism (psychosocial dwarfism): behavioral data in two cases and their families. Thesis for the Department of Psychiatry and Behavioral Sciences, The Johns Hopkins University School of Medicine, Phipps Library, 1975.

Wolff, G., Money, J.: Relationship between sleep and growth in patients with reversible somatotropin deficiency (psychosocial dwarfism). *Psychological Medicine* 3:18–27 (1973).

CHAPTER 16

Munchausen Syndrome by Proxy: The Hinterland of Child Abuse

Roy Meadow

INTRODUCTION

Doctors dealing with young children rely on the parents' recollection of the history. The doctor accepts that history, albeit sometimes with a pinch of salt, and it forms the cornerstone of subsequent investigation and management of the child.

A case is reported in which over a period of six years, the parents systematically provided fictitious information about their child's symptoms, tampered with the urine specimens to produce false results and interfered with hospital observations. This caused the girl innumerable investigations and anæsthetic, surgical, and radiological procedures in three different centres.

The case is compared with another child who was intermittently given toxic doses of salt which again led to massive investigation in three different centres, and ended in death. The behaviour of the parents of these two cases was similar in many ways. Although in each case the end result for the child was "non-accidental injury," the long-running saga of hospital care was reminiscent of the Munchausen syndrome, in these cases by proxy.

CASE-REPORTS

First Case

Kay was referred to the pædiatric nephrology clinic in Leeds at the age of 6 because of recurrent illnesses in which she passed foul-smelling, bloody urine. She had been investigated in two other centres without the cause being found.

In the child's infancy, her mother had noticed yellow pus on the nappies, and their doctor had first prescribed antibiotics for suspected urine infection when Kay was 8 months old. Since then, she had had periodic courses of antibiotics for presumed urine infection. Since the age of 3 she had been on continuous antibio-

Reprinted with permission from *Lancet* (August 13, 1977): 343–45.

tics which included co-trimoxazole, amoxycillin, nalidixic acid, nitrofurantoin, ampicillin, gentamicin, and uticillin. These treatments had themselves caused drug rashes, fever, and candidiasis, and she had continued to have intermittent bouts of lower abdominal pain associated with fever and foul-smelling, infected urine often containing frank blood. There was intermittent vulval soreness and discharge.

The parents were in their late 30s. Father who worked mainly in the evenings and at night, was healthy. The mother had had urinary-tract infections. The 3-year-old brother was healthy.

At the time of referral, she had already been investigated at a district general hospital and at a regional teaching hospital. Investigations had included two urograms, micturating cystourethrograms, two gynæcological examinations under anæsthetic, and two cystoscopies. The symptoms were unexplained and continued unabated. She was being given steadily more toxic chemotherapy. Bouts were recurring more often and everyone was mystified by the intermittent nature of her complaint and the way in which purulent, bloody urine specimens were followed by completely clear ones a few hours later. Similarly, foul discharges were apparent on her vulva at one moment, but later on the same day her vulva was normal.

On examination she was a healthy girl who was growing normally. The urine was bloodstained and foul. It was strongly positive for blood and albumin and contained a great many leucocytes and epithelial cells. It was heavily infected with *Escherichia coli*.

The findings strongly suggested an ectopic ureter or an infected cyst draining into the urethra or vagina. Yet previous investigations had not disclosed this. Ectopic ureters are notoriously difficult to detect, and, after consultation with colleagues at the combined pediatric/urology clinic, it was decided to investigate her immediately after she began to pass foul urine. No sooner was she admitted than the foul discharge stopped before cystoscopy could be done. More efficient arrangements were made for the urological surgeon concerned to be contacted immediately should she arrive in Leeds passing foul urine. This was done three times (including a bank holiday and a Sunday). No source of the discharge was found. On every occasion it cleared up fast. Efforts to localise the source included further radiology, vaginogram, urethrogram, barium enema, suprapubic aspiration, bladder catheterisation, urine cultures, and exfoliative cytology. During these investigations, the parents were most cooperative and Kay's mother always stayed in hospital with her (mainly because they lived a long way away). She was concerned and loving in her relationship with Kay, and yet sometimes not quite as worried about the possible cause of the illness as were the doctors. Many of the crises involved immediate admission and urgent anæsthetics for examinations or cystoscopy, and these tended to occur most at weekend holiday periods. On one bank holiday, five consultants came into the hospital specifically to see her.

The problem seemed insoluble and many of the facts did not make sense. The urinary pathogens came and went at a few minutes' notice; there would be one variety of *E. coli* early in the morning and then after a few normal specimens, an entirely different organism such as *Proteus* or *Streptococcus faecalis* in the evening. Moreover, there was something about the mother's temperament and behaviour that was reminiscent of the mother described in case 2, so we decided to work on the assumption that everything about the history and investigations were false. Close questioning revealed that most of the abnormal specimens were ones that at some stage or other had been left unsupervised in the mother's presence.

This theory was tested when Kay was admitted with her mother and all urine specimens were collected under strict supervision by a trained nurse who was told not to let the urine out of her sight from the moment it passed from Kay's urethra to it being tested on the ward by a doctor and then delivered to the laboratory. On the fourth day, supervision was deliberately relaxed slightly so that one or two specimens were either left for the mother to collect or collected by the nurse and then left in the mother's presence for a minute before being taken away. On the first 3 days, no urine specimen was abnormal. On the first occasion that the mother was left to collect the specimen (having been instructed exactly how to do so), she brought a heavily bloodstained specimen containing much debris and bacteria. A subsequent specimen collected by the nurse, was completely normal. This happened on many occasions during the next few days. During a 7-day period, Kay emptied her bladder 57 times, 45 specimens were normal, all of these being collected and supervised by a nurse; 12 were grossly abnormal, containing blood and different organisms, all these having been collected by the mother or left in her presence. All the specimens were meant to be collected in exactly the same way as complete specimens, and the mother was using the same sort of utensils as were the nurses. On one evening the pattern was as follows:

Time	Appearance	Collection
5.00 P.M.	Normal	By nurse
6.45 P.M.	Bloody	By mother
7.15 P.M.	Normal	By nurse
8.15 P.M.	Bloody	By mother
8.30 P.M.	Normal	By nurse

On that day the mother was persuaded to provide a specimen of urine from herself. She produced a very bloody specimen full of debris and bacteria which resembled the specimens she had been handing in as Kay's urine. The mother was menstruating. Kay was given xylose tablets so that we could identify which urine came from her. All the specimens handed in by the mother contained xylose which meant that each specimen contained some of Kay's urine. The help of the Yorkshire Police forensic laboratory was obtained. Kay and her mother had similar blood-groups, but erythrocyte acid phosphatase in the blood in the urine specimens was of group Ba which was similar to the mother's but not to Kay's.

At this stage, there was enough evidence to support the theory that the mother's story about her daughter was false, and that she had been adding either her own urine or menstrual discharge to specimens of her daughter's urine. Other abnormal findings could similarly be explained by the deliberate actions of the mother.

The consequences of these actions for the daughter had included 12 hospital admissions, 7 major X-ray procedures (including intravenous urograms, cystograms, barium enema, vaginogram, and urethrogram), 6 examinations under anæsthetic, 5 cystoscopies, unpleasant treatment with toxic drugs and eight antibiotics, catheterisations, vaginal pessaries, and bactericidal, fungicidal, and œstrogen creams; the laboratories had cultured her urine more than 150 times and had done many other tests; sixteen consultants had been involved in her care.

The various fabrications occupied a major part in the mother's life and arrangements were made for her to see a psychiatrist at a hospital near her home. At first, she denied interfering with the management of her daughter. However, during the period of psychiatric outpatient consultation, Kay's health remained good. The urinary problems did not recur and her parents said that they felt that "since going to Leeds, Kay had been much better and their prayers had been answered."

Later it emerged that the mother had a more extensive personal medical history than she had admitted and that during investigation of her own urinary tract she had been suspected of altering urine specimens, altering temperature charts, and heating a thermometer in a cup of tea. She was a caring and loving mother for her two children. Kay was a long-awaited baby (in the hope of which the mother had taken a fertility drug), but after the birth she sometimes felt that her husband was more interested in the child than in her.

Second Case

Charles had had recurrent illnesses associated with hypernatræmia since the age of 6 weeks. He was the third child of healthy parents. The attacks of vomiting and drowsiness came on suddenly, and on arrival in hospital he had plasma-sodium concentrations in the range 160–175 mmol/1. At these times his urine also contained a great excess of sodium. The attacks occurred as often as every month; between attacks he was healthy and developing normally. Extensive investigations took place in three different centres. He was subjected to radiological, biochemical, and other pathological procedures during several hospital admissions. These showed no abnormality between attacks, and his endocrine and renal systems were normal. When given a salt load, he excreted it efficiently. The attacks became more frequent and severe, and by the age of 14 months it became clear that they only happened at home. During a prolonged hospital stay in which the mother was deliberately excluded, they did not happen until the weekend when she was allowed to visit. Investigation proved that the illness must be caused by sodium administration, and the time relationship clearly incriminated the mother. We did not know how she persuaded her toddler to ingest such large quantities of salt (20 g of sodium chloride given with difficulty by us raised the serum-sodium to 147 mmol/1 only). The mother had been a nurse and was presumably experienced in the use of gastric feeding tubes and suppositories.

During the period in which the local pædiatrician, psychiatrist, and social-services department were planning arrangements for the child, he arrived at hospital one night, collapsed with extreme hypernatræmia, and died.

Necropsy disclosed mild gastric erosions "as if a chemical had been ingested". The mother wrote thanking the doctors for their care and then attempted suicide.

She too was a caring home-minded mother. She had an undemonstrative husband, a shift worker who did not seem as intelligent as she. As a student she had been labelled hysterical, and during one hospital admission had been thought to be interfering with the healing of a wound.

DISCUSSION

These two cases share common features. The mothers' stories were false, deliberately and consistently false. The main pathological findings were the result of the mothers' actions, and in both cases caused unpleasant and serious conse quences for the children. Both had unpleasant investigations and treatments, both developed illnesses as a result of the malpractice and the treatments, and the second child died.

Both mothers skilfully altered specimens and evaded close and experienced supervision. In case 1, a specimen of the child's urine collected under "close supervision" was abnormal, but it emerged that the mother had momentarily persuaded the nurse to leave the cubicle and leave the specimen unguarded for about a minute. Expressed breast milk collected from the mother of case 2 early in the course of the illness had a very high sodium content. It had been collected under supervision for chemical analysis, but when the supervisory nurse was instructed not to leave the specimen between its emergence from the mother's breast and its delivery to the laboratory, the next specimen was normal.

During the investigation of both these children, we came to know the mothers well. They were very pleasant people to deal with, cooperative, and appreciative of good medical care, which encouraged us to try all the harder. Some mothers who choose to stay in hospital with their child remain on the ward slightly uneasy, overtly bored, or aggressive. These two flourished there as if they belonged, and thrived on the attention that staff gave to them. It is ironic to conjecture that the cause of both these children's problems would have been discovered much sooner in the old days of restricted visiting hours and the absence of facilities for mothers to live in hospital with a sick child. It is also possible that, without the excellent facilities and the attentive and friendly staff, the repetitive admissions might not have happened. Both mothers had a history of falsifying their own medical records and treatment. Both had at times been labelled as hysterical personalities who also tended to be depressed. We recognise that parents sometimes exaggerate their child's symptoms, perhaps to obtain faster or more thorough medical care of their child. In these cases, it was as if the parents were using the children to get themselves into the sheltered environment of a children's ward surrounded by friendly staff. The mother of case 1 may have been projecting her worries about her own urinary-tract problems on to the child in order to escape from worries about herself. She seemed to project her own worries on to the child in many different ways, once informing another hospital that a specialist from Switzerland was coming to see her daughter in Leeds because she had an incurable kidney tumour which emptied into the vagina causing the discharge.

This sort of fabricated story is reminiscent of the Munchausen syndrome. The parents described, share some of the common features of that syndrome in which the persons have travelled widely for treatment, and the stories attributed to them are both dramatic and untruthful. But those with Munchausen syndrome have more fanciful stories, which are different at different hospitals. They tend to discharge themselves when the game is up. They cause physical suffering to themselves but not usually to their relatives. Munchausen syndrome has been described in children, the confabulations being made by the child.[1] Case 1 seems to be the first example of "Munchausen syndrome by proxy."

The repetitive poisoning of a child by a parent (case 2) has been described before. Rogers and colleagues[2] described six cases in 1976 and they suggested that such poisoning was "an extended form of child abuse." Larsky and Erikson[3] suggested marital conflict as a possible cause for such poisoning, one spouse harming a child who was considered to be unfairly favoured by the other. The resulting illness of the child tended to restore marital relations at the child's expense.

None can doubt that these two children were abused, but the acts of abuse were so different in quality, periodicity, and planning from the more usual nonaccidental injury of childhood that I am uneasy about classifying these sad cases as variants of nonaccidental injury.

Whatever label one chooses to describe them, these cases are a reminder that at times doctors must accept the parents' history and indeed the laboratory findings with more than usual scepticism. We may teach, and I believe should teach, that mothers are always right; but at the same time we must recognise that when mothers are wrong they can be terribly wrong.

Asher began his paper on Munchausen's syndrome[4] with the words "Here is described a common syndrome which most doctors have seen, but about which little has been written." The behaviour of Kay's mother has not been described in the medical literature. Is it because that degree of falsification is very rare or because it is unrecognised?

This paper is dedicated to the many caring and conscientious doctors who tried to help these families, and who, although deceived, will rightly continue to believe what most parents say about their children, most of the time.

REFERENCES

1. Sneed, R. C., Bell, R. F. *Pediatrics*, 1976, 58, 127.
2. Rogers, D., Tripp, J., Bentovin, A., Robinson, A., Berry, D., Goulding, R. *Br. Med. J.* 1976, i, 793.
3. Larsky, S. B., Erikson, H. M. *J. Am. Acad. Child Psychiat*. 1974, 13, 691.
4. Asher, R. *Lancet*, 1951, i, 339.

PART IV

Predisposing Characteristics of the Victims

Righteous Heaven, who hast permitted
All this woe: what fatal crime
Was by me, e'en at the time
Of my hapless birth, committed?

(Calderon, in Feuerbach, 1832)

Editor's Introduction

Once research on the psychosocial characteristics of abusive parents was underway, investigators began to focus their attention on the victims. Again, the focus was more on the predisposing characteristics of victims of abuse than of neglect.

Age was one of the first variables noted. Research consistently demonstrated that although children of all ages were abused, child abuse was more frequent among infants and young children. The higher incidence of nonaccidental injuries contrasted significantly with incidence rates for accidental injuries that were minimal among infants of nine months or younger.

In their review of the literature in Chapter 17, Friedrich and Boriskin describe characteristics of children that predispose them to abuse by their parents. These include mental retardation, physical handicaps, prematurity, and other vulnerabilities. The finding that abused children are characterized by special vulnerabilities invalidates the scientifically unfounded "blame the victim" hypothesis that abused children solicit abuse from their parents. The authors emphasize that the factor of "specialness" does not operate in isolation with respect to child abuse. Rather, various combinations and permutations of parent and child variables interact with other variables to elicit the abuse.

The complexity of this interaction is demonstrated by the research of Klein and Stern in Chapter 18. These investigators found that low birth weight was related to subsequent parental abuse. The incidence of low birth weight among abused children in their sample was 23.5% compared to that of the control sample which ranged from 7-9%. Low birth weight, however, was related to a number of adverse factors in these infants and their mothers, such as preexisting mental retardation, mother-infant separation during the neonatal period, and, as discussed in detail in Part III, a history of maternal and social deprivation among the abusive mothers.

In Chapter 19, Klaus and Kennell focus on the separation of neonates from their mothers, a factor which seems to play a significant role in later abuse of the child. The authors suggest that there is a maternal sensitive period during which separation of the mother from her neonate may interfere with her attachment to and subsequent care of the infant. Thus, the common hospital practice of separating mothers from their premature or sickly infants may be the crucial factor that puts them at risk for abuse.

These findings have been corroborated and discussed more fully by Kennell, Voos, and Klaus (1978) and Klaus and Kennell (1976). In Chapter 20, Money and Needleman discuss a variety of adverse conditions during the prenatal period and neonatorum among mothers who subsequently abused their children who later presented the syndrome of psychosocial dwarfism. The finding of adverse experiences during this period that seem to contribute to bonding failure between mother and child has also been corroborated in England by Lynch (1975). The abused infants and mothers in her sample were characterized by a higher number of adverse experiences compared to their nonabused siblings. These included illness in the mother and/or the infant during the infant's first year of life, neonatal and other early separation from the mother, and abnormal pregnancy, labor, and delivery.

In Chapter 21, Schwarzbeck views the mother-infant relationship as a single variable in his examination of the origins of child abuse and neglect. He posits a subtle interplay of asynchronous signals between mother and infant that sets the stage for abuse.

Research on the predisposing characteristics of the victims of abuse and the vicissitudes of the neonatorum adds a new dimension to the understanding of abuse. In the discussion of the predisposing characteristics of abusive parents in the Introduction to the papers in Part III, emphasis was placed on a causal model of child abuse that is multiple and interactive. The line of investigation cited in Part IV highlights even further the complexity and subtlety of the many processes that interact to create the abuse. Preexisting vulnerabilities in the infant, such as low birth weight and illness, are often compounded by enforced separation from the mother during the neonatal period. In addition to her exposure to these sources of interference with attachment to the infant, the mother herself is likely to have experienced a number of early adversities.

Helfer (1975) and Kempe and Kempe (1978) maintain that, in addition to predisposing characteristics of the parent and actual or perceived deviance in the child, other conditions must be present for abuse to occur. These include a crisis and the lack of a social support network for the family. Justice and Justice (1978) found that abusive parents had high scores on a measure of social change, the Social Readjustment Rating Scale (Holmes and Rahe 1967). They concluded that life crisis, a chronic bombardment of unpredictable changes, decreases the family's ability to adjust and increases the risk of violence toward the child. Justice and Duncan (1978) refer to such work-related problems as unemployment, job-related moves, and overwork as examples of life crises that predispose the family to abuse. Fontana (1971) suggests that alcohol plays "a lubricating role" in triggering abuse toward the child.

A woman from a maternally deprived background, for example, who has a premature child from whom she has been separated in the first few weeks of life, is likely to abuse the child after a series of continued life crises, such as her husband's work-related frequent absence from the home and the absence of friends in the community. A single predisposing characteristic or condition is insufficient to elicit violence toward the child. It is the combination of these predisposing vulnerabilities and adversities, however, that generates child abuse.

G.J.W.

REFERENCES

Calderon, L. "Life Is a Dream." In P. J. von Feuerbach, *Beispiel Eines Verbrechens am Seelenleben des Menschen*. Ansbach, 1832.

Fontana, V. J. "Which parents abuse children?" *Medical Insight* 16 (1971):18–21.

Helfer, R. E. *Child Abuse and Neglect: The Diagnostic Process and Treatment Programs*. Washington, D.C.: U.S. Department of Health, Education and Welfare, Publ. No. (OHD) 75–69, 1975.

Holmes, T. H., and Rahe, R. H. "The social readjustment rating scale." *Journal of Psychosomatic Research* 11 (1967):213–18.

Justice, B., and Duncan, D. F. "How do job-related problems contribute to child abuse?" *Occupational Health and Safety* (July–August 1978):42–45.

Justice, B., and Justice, R. *The Abusing Family*. New York: Human Sciences Press, 1976.

Kempe, R. S., and Kempe, C. H. *Child Abuse*. Cambridge, Mass.: Harvard University Press, 1978.

Kennell, J., Voos, D., and Klaus, M. "Parent-Infant Bonding." In *Child Abuse and Neglect: The Family and the Community*. Cambridge, Mass.: Ballinger Publishing Co., 1976, pp. 25–53.

Klaus, M. *Maternal-Infant Bonding*. St. Louis: Mosby Co., 1976.

Lynch, M. A. "Ill-health and child abuse." *Lancet* (August 16, 1976):317–19.

CHAPTER 17

The Role of the Child in Abuse: A Review of the Literature

William N. Friedrich and Jerry A. Boriskin

A number of current theories concerning the etiology of child abuse place heavy emphasis on the role of parental psychopathology. Spinetta and Rigler (43) concluded their review of the child-abusing parent by stating that ". . . the great majority of the authors cited . . . have pointed to psychological factors within the parents themselves as of prime importance in the etiology of child abuse. They see abuse as stemming from a defect in character." (p. 302) Socioeconomic factors were not felt to contribute significantly to abuse.

However, Kempe and Helfer (22) stated that only a small number (less than 10%) of the parents of abused children are seriously mentally ill. In addition, Steele and Pollock (44) maintained that psychopaths and sociopaths make up only a small portion of abusers, and that their sample of abusers would not seem much different than a random sample of people on a downtown street. More important to Steele and Pollock than severe psychopathology was the disruption of the "mothering function" in the development of children who later became abusers.

Increasingly, research on abused and neglected children suggests that the child plays more than a passive role in abuse. Gelles's (15) social-psychological model of the causes of child abuse, which admirably demonstrated the complexity and interrelatedness of the factors leading to abuse, assumes that a certain amount of child abuse is a function of child-produced stress. Helfer's psychodynamic model of abuse (20) holds that, for abuse to occur, three conditions are required: (1) a very special kind of child, (2) a crisis or series of crises, and (3) the potential (in the parent) for abuse. Although the potential may be composed of many characteristics the parent has acquired as he moves through his "world of abnormal rearing," (20) it is triggered by a "special" child, a crisis, or both. Helfer took great pains to state that the child is either viewed by the parent as being special, or actually is a special, different child. Green (17) offered a four-factor explanation of the etiology of child abuse, similar to

Reprinted with permission from the *American Journal of Orthopsychiatry* 46 (October 1976):580–90.

Helfer's, but adding as the fourth factor "a cultural tolerance for severe corporal punishment."

Sandgrund, Gaines, and Green (39) stated that child abuse appears to result from the interaction of three factors: immediate environmental stress, personality traits of the parents, and actual characteristics of the child that make him vulnerable to scapegoating. In this view, theories that focus on only the first two etiological factors would fail to present the complete picture.

An early theory on the role of the child in abuse was offered by Milowe and Lourie, (32) who suggested four possible causal factors of abuse, two of which dealt specifically with characteristics of the child. One category included those cases in which the precipitating factor was a defect in the child (especially a defect that contributed to a lack of responsiveness, resulting in parental frustration). The second category included physical damage resulting from parental neglect or mishandling. Their third category covered a little-researched area of abuse—abuse resulting from assaultive behavior by unsupervised siblings. The final category included abuse resulting from characteristics in the child's personality that served to invite others to hurt him. As far as can be determined, these categories are the result of clinical experience, not controlled empirical investigation.

It is uncomfortable to think that a child can play a role in his own abuse. Furthermore, ". . . despite the contributions which infants make toward the disappointments and burdens of their parents, they can hardly be used as an excuse or adequate cause for child abuse" (44) (p. 155). Nevertheless, the fact remains that the child is not always a benign stimulus to the parent. For example, although it is not necessarily the fault of the child or the mother that a birth is premature, this characteristic of the child has an effect on its caregiver.

This paper will survey evidence that particular types of children produce parental stress reactions, some of which might stimulate abuse. It will consider the following points, in turn: (1) prematurity and children at risk for abuse, (2) mental retardation and children at risk for abuse, (3) physically handicapped and sickly children at risk for abuse, (4) genetic contributions to the child at risk for abuse, and (5) parents' perceptions of the abused child as different.

PREMATURITY

Although one can only speculate as to cause and effect, the recently revealed association of child abuse and prematurity cannot be ignored. Elmer and Gregg (10), in a sample of 20 battered children in the Chicago area, found 33% to have been premature. Klein and Stern (24) studied 88 battered children at the Winnipeg Children's Hospital, of whom 11 (12.5%) were premature. In addition, Klein and Stern reviewed the records of 51 battered children in the Montreal area, and found 12 (23.5%) to have been low-birth-weight infants; the rate of premature birth in Montreal is between 9 and 10%. It was suggested that multiple factors (preexisting mental retardation, maternal deprivation, isolation from mother in the early post-partum period, etc.) may increase the risk for these infants. Conversely, it was suggested that certain social characteristics of the mother (poverty, lack of prenatal care) may result in the delivery of low-birth-weight infants.

In an unpublished retrospective study of 292 suspected abuse cases in England from 1970, referred to by Martin *et al* (31), it was noted that 14.5% of the children, or twice the national average, had had a low birth-weight. However, it was not specified whether the children were born prematurely or were of adequate gestation with poor prenatal growth.

Fomufod, Sinkford and Louy (12), in a retrospective analysis of child abuse in the District of Columbia, found 10 of 36 (27.8%) abused children to be of low-birth-weight; the incidence of low-birth-weight in the D.C. area is 13.2%. A larger scale prospective study is underway to compare low-birth-weight infants with and without prolonged maternal separation.

Martin *et al* (31), found that 11 (19%) of their sample of 58 abused children weighed less than 2500 grams at birth. This was in comparison to an incidence rate of only 9.2% of all babies born in 1971 in Colorado. They feel that the normal mean IQs of even their smallest prematurely born children do not support the hypothesis that mental retardation or brain damage stemming from prematurity elicits abuse by parents. In this study, Martin *et al.* took special pains to include children with soft tissue damage, in addition to those who had incurred fractures, so that their sample would be as typical as possible of abused children, since only a small proportion of abused children receive fractures.

Bishop (4) supports the view that premature babies are particularly vulnerable. It is suggested that some premature babies are hypersensitive to all stimuli, and may even object to gentle handling. What proportion of abused premature babies fit this hypersensitive handling pattern is still unknown. Mussen, Conger, and Kagan (35) also stated that the premature child is more likely to be restless, distractible, and difficult to care for than a full-term baby, especially during the first year of life. A reason for this is that prematures are more prone to anoxia and colic, and irritability in the newborn period can result from these conditions. In addition, Dreyfus-Brisac (7) has pointed out that disturbances in sleep organization are very common among premature infants. Ounsted, Oppenheimer and Lindsay (37) reported that the colicky child syndrome was a prominent feature during infancy of most of the abused children in their sample.

Maternal attitudes toward premature infants must certainly play a role. Elmer and Gregg (10) suggested that the mother may perceive a child as being abnormal simply because it is premature. Leiderman (28) has found significant differences in both attitudes and behavior between mothers of premature infants and mothers of full-term infants. He stated that the "... attenuated relationship of mothers of prematures with their infants is consistent with reports in the literature that premature infants are more likely the victims of battering by their parents and are more likely to have behavior problems as children" (p. 154). Klaus and Kennell (23) also raised the question of whether the battered child syndrome is in part related to hospital care practices that frequently separate mothers from their premature infants for prolonged periods of time.

Fanaroff, Kennell and Klaus (11) analyzed the frequency of visits of 146 mothers of low-birth-weight infants. Thirty-eight mothers visited their babies less than three times in a two week period. Follow-up data from 6 to 23 months after release show that, in the 11 cases of abuse or failure to thrive, 9 mothers were in the infrequent visiting group. Thus, problems may be identified early, simply by monitoring the frequency of visits to the premature child.

Pasamanick (38) noted a significant linear relationship between maternal tension and signs of brain dysfunction in a longitudinal study of premature infants. Mothers of neurologically normal premature infants were no more tense than were mothers of neurologically normal, full-term infants. "It was the neurologically abnormal child, whether full-term or premature, who had a significantly tense mother" (p. 550). Knobloch and Pasamanick (25) contended that these abnormal children are disorganized, unstable, and more sensitive to stress. Pasamanick (38) speculated that these abnormalities precipitate parental distress, thereby reinforcing abnormal behavior in the child, which may ultimately result in abuse.

Whereas maternal perceptions of abnormality, socioeconomic status, prenatal care, and hypersensitivity in the premature infant are interacting variables of as yet unknown significance, current data do indicate significant association of prematurity and child abuse. Unraveling the complex interactions involved has only begun, but the basic point to be noted is that premature infants should be considered "children at risk" within the battered child syndrome.

MENTAL RETARDATION

Several researchers have reported a high incidence of mental retardation among battered and neglected children. However, the complexity of the phenomenon and the large number of interacting variables make any position as to cause and effect most tenuous. Elmer (9) reported 55% of the children in her sample had an IQ of less than 80; Morse, Sahler and Friedman (34) found 43% of their sample of abused children were similarly classified—all but one of the nine retarded children in this study were thought to have been retarded prior to abuse.

Brandwein (5), noting the association of abuse and mental retardation, suggested that brain damage resulting from child abuse was the primary factor in the increased frequency of mental retardation. One cannot ignore socioeconomic factors, stress, prenatal care or lack of it, parental depravity, differences in learning and reinforcement contingencies, physical damage to the CNS from abuse, genetic variables, as well as the inherent flaw of intelligence measures in accounting for any of the above variables, when evaluating this relationship. Considering what is known to date, and the difficulties inherent in this area of research, the factors contributing the most weight to the disproportionate retardation associated with abuse will not be readily apparent for some time. But we should not now overlook the distinct possibility that the child born with mental deficiencies may be more "abuse prone"; his unfortunate state may make him highly vulnerable to scapegoating.

In a recent study by Sandgrund, Gaines and Green (39), children from the same socioeconomic level were divided into three groups: confirmed abuse, confirmed neglect, and nonabused controls; the neglected group was included to control for the impact of neglect upon the abused children. They found that 25% of the abused sample were classified as retarded, 20% of the neglected children were deemed retarded, and only 3% of the nonabused controls were categorized as retarded. Whereas the relative weights of neglect and abuse are indeterminable from this study, a more careful examination of these variables is warranted. It is in fact impossible to make any statements as to what factors differentiate a neglected and abused child. It is precisely this lack of clarity that highlights current methodological problems and investigational gaps. Sandgrund, Gaines, and Green excluded subjects known to have suffered any serious head trauma; on this basis, their findings seriously challenge Brandwein's (5) organic damage hypothesis.

Sandgrund, Gaines, and Green's (39) hypothesis is supported by Martin *et al's* (31) determination that 43% of a sample of 37 abused children with no history of head trauma manifested slight to severe neurologic dysfunctions. However, only 29% of their sample of 21 abused children with a history of skull fracture did not manifest any neurologic dysfunction.

Nichamin (36) presented some reasons why the child with neurologic dysfunction can be very difficult to tolerate. He mentioned that these babies appear to be unhappy throughout infancy, and are very difficult to appease. Their crying consists to a great extent of high-pitched, disagreeable screaming.

While the association of retardation and abuse is clear-cut, etiological factors remain muddled, and there is a dearth of experimental data. Whereas the parental depravity hypothesis is well known and widely accepted, further experimental and clinical attention should be given to the "abuse prone" hypothesis.

PHYSICAL HANDICAPS

Johnson and Morse (21) reported on a study the Denver Department of Welfare carried out with 97 abused children. Based on child welfare worker reports, it was noted that nearly 70% of the children exhibited either a mental or physical deviation prior to the reported abuse. In addition, 20% were considered unmanageable due to severe temper tantrums, 19% had retarded speech development, and 17% demonstrated either a learning disability or mental retardation. However, the data in this study do not thoroughly substantiate that these behaviors were congenital or had occurred prior to abuse. Friedman (13), on the basis of a retrospective study of 25 cases of abused children, hypothesized that some abused children are hyperactive or intellectually precocious. He reported several instances in which the inquisitive behavior of a child who was intellectually more capable than his parents caused the child to be more vulnerable to abuse.

Green (17) found that 23% of 70 school-age schizophrenic children had suffered abuse. It was suggested that because schizophrenic children are generally unrewarding to the parents and are emotionally deviant, there is an increased risk of physical abuse. However, not enough information was provided to choose between this hypothesis, or the alternate possibility that schizophrenic behavior may result *from* abuse.

Gil (16), from data garnered in a two-year nationwide study, discovered that 29% of the abused children in his sample of 12,000 children had demonstrated abnormal social interactions in the year preceding the abusive act. He also noted that approximately 22% were suffering from either a deviation in physical or intellectual function. Among those children of school age, approximately 13% were in special classes or were in grades below their age level; however, at least half of these children had incurred abuse prior to the study year.

Ounsted, Oppenheimer and Lindsay (37) cited the case of an abused child who was found to be blind. Upon hearing this, the parents broke down, the mother saying that "he cried and cried and he never looked at me" (p. 448).

Birrell and Birrell (3), in an analysis of 42 cases of abuse, found congenital physical abnormalities (cleft lip, fibrocystic disease, talipes, etc.) in 11 cases (approximately 25%). However, this finding has not been substantiated by other studies; in a study of 58 abused children (31), no children with major abnormalities, or with more than one or two minor abnormalities (clinodactyly, hermis, etc.), were found.

Baron, Bejar and Sheaff (1) presented the case of an infant with no signs of abuse but with a presenting problem very similar to organic brain disease. The child was treated for a number of months before it was noticed that she had been battered. When the child was admitted to the hospital, her symptoms of organic brain disease cleared up within a week. The point made is that only adequate follow-up can show how often seemingly congenital neurologic abnormalities are the result of physical abuse.

In unpublished material from the National Clearing House on Child Abuse and Neglect at the American Humane Association in Denver, Soeffing (42) reported on preliminary incidence data from 1974. Of 14,083 abused and neglected children, 1680 had one or more "special" characteristics. For example, 288 were classified as mentally retarded, 195 had been born prematurely, 250 had a chronic illness (*e.g.,* multiple sclerosis, diabetes), 234 were physically handicapped, 130 were either twins or triplets, 180 had a congenital defect, 669 were reported as being emotionally disturbed, and 267 had "other special characteristics." It was also noted that the number of reported handicaps could increase as social workers learned how to better diagnose a handicap.

Lynch (29) found a significantly greater frequency of serious illness in the first year of life among abused children. It has been suggested by Morris (33) that sickly infants and premature infants, by virtue of their extended hospital stay, make it difficult for "claiming behavior" on the part of the mother to occur, and if this "claiming behavior" (attachment) does not occur, the child is at greater risk for abuse.

GENETIC CONTRIBUTIONS

Although not as clearly related as are physical abnormalities, individual differences and behavioral styles present in infants from birth may also contribute to abuse. Thomas, Chess, and Birch (45), on the basis of data gathered in their New York Longitudinal Project, were able to demonstrate that, seemingly from birth, children display nine different temperament styles. These temperaments tend to be present in clearly defined clusters, giving rise to a minimum of three "types" of children. "Slow-to-warm-up" children have as a significant core of their pattern of activity quiet withdrawal from, and then slow adaptation to, the new. The "difficult" child shows irregularity in biological functions, nonadaptability, predominantly negative (withdrawal) responses to new stimuli, high intensity, and frequent negative mood expressions. At the opposite end of the temperament spectrum from the "difficult" child is the "easy" child, who exhibits regularity in biological functions, approach responses to new stimuli, easy adaptability to change, and predominately positive mood of mild or moderate intensity. In this study, roughly 70% of the "difficult" children developed behavior problems; although they comprised only 10% of the sample, these children accounted for 23% of the group of children who later developed behavior problems.

Milowe and Lourie (32) made reference to children who seem to fall into the category of "difficult" children. At first, the researchers thought the irritable characteristics of the abused children they came in contact with were a result of their being battered. But after nurses found it difficult to take some of these infants for an eight-hour tour of duty, the researchers began to have second thoughts. The nurses commented on the irritable cry, the difficulty in managing, and the unappealing nature of some of these children. In this study, reference was also made to two children who each received battering in two different homes, presumably because of their "difficult" natures. Silver (41) also cited a case of an abused child who was admitted to the hospital, was subsequently removed to a foster home, and was battered in the foster home.

In a vein similar to Thomas, Chess, and Birch's (45) temperament clusters, Schaffer and Emerson (40) isolated two groups of infants—those who actively resisted close physical contact under all conditions (noncuddlers), and those who accepted close physical contact under all conditions (cuddlers). It was determined that this behavior was not peculiar to the relationship of the child with the mother. Shaffer and Emerson felt that a noncuddling pattern is not clinically a bad sign. Only if the mother is too rigid to attempt alternate methods of relating to the child, or if she feels the noncuddling behavior is a sign of rejection, is there risk of a pathological mother-child relationship. Ounsted, Oppenheimer, and Lindsay (37) have pointed out the implications of this risk for abused children. In their study of 24 children, about two-thirds of the mothers complained that the child could not be cuddled, although it was not reported whether this feature of the child's interactional pattern was present from birth.

In the area of individual differences in infants, Korner (26) has found differences in crying patterns among infants, and differences in soothability once they begin to cry. She pointed out the implications this could have for a young and inexperienced mother with a difficult to soothe child. These differences can directly affect the mother's feelings of competence as a caregiver.

In addition, Benjamin (2) has suggested that infants with low sensory thresholds are very prone to develop colic during the first few postnatal weeks, thus aggravating a developing mother-child relationship.

Woolf (46) described seven normal infant states: regular sleep, irregular sleep, periodic sleep, drowsiness, alert inactivity, waking activity, and crying. Korner (27) has suggested a concept of state-immaturity, in which infants exhibit only a limited range of states (*e.g.* two or three). These children have been shown to be very difficult to care for and will often develop subsequent psychopathological symptoms. For example, Brazelton (6) described a case in which an infant, capable of only two extreme states, so demoralized his mother, a young professional woman, that she became totally ineffectual and depressed. From the start, the mother felt "rejected" by the child.

Korner (26) concluded her paper by saying "... the finding that infants differ significantly from each other right from the very start suggests that there is more than one way of providing good child care; ... the only way to do so is to respond flexibly to ... each and every child (p. 617). However, parents are trained in the "right" way to raise kids, rather than focusing on each child's particular needs. Consequently, mothers are prone to feel a lot of guilt over deviant behavior in their children (6). Some of this might be reflected in battered children.

PARENTS' PERCEPTIONS OF
THE CHILD AS DIFFERENT

A number of studies (8, 14, 16) have shown that generally, even in multi-child families, only one child is abused. This has given rise to suggestions that the abused child is selected as a scapegoat, either because he is truly different from his siblings, or for some other, inexplicable reason. For example, Lynch's (29) study of 25 abused children and their nonabused siblings reported the nonabused siblings "... to have been exceptionally healthy, and, where population figures are available, show a lower than expected incidence of adverse factors" (p. 319). However, Johnson and Morse (21) noted that, while 36% of the abused children were illegitimate, 40% of the nonabused siblings were also illegitimate. In addition, there were similarities among the siblings in terms of personality and intellectual performance.

Morse, Sahler, and Friedman (34) noted that the mothers of 6 abused children who were progressing normally at the time of follow-up saw the parent-child relationship as good. However, the mothers of 7 abused children who were quite disturbed at follow-up described the parent-child relationship as poor. Originally, of the 25 children observed in this study, 15 were considered different by their parents. Nine of the children were retarded, and 3 of these were thought by their parents to be sickly. Six others were thought by their parents to be bad, selfish, spoiled rotten, or defiant in comparison to siblings. This suggests that, in addition to the child's abnormalities, the parents' perception of the child can also be critical.

Bishop (4) cited four cases of young children overdosed with sedatives by disorganized and depressed mothers who had perceived their child as "damaged." Physical examinations of the children provided no support of this perceptual bias. Consequently, Bishop claimed that when the parental perception of a "damaged" child is counter to objective evidence, the risk may be even greater.

In a similar vein, Martin and Beezley (30) have hypothesized that it is the children with mild or borderline abnormalties who are at greatest risk, while severely handicapped children are at lower risk for abuse. The basis for this hypothesis is unclear. Perhaps it is the ambiguity that introduces the greatest stress to the parent. Whatever the case, more data on parental perception of abnormalities in their abused children is needed.

CONCLUSION

On the basis of the evidence presented, it would be fanciful to conclude that the special child is the sole contributor to abuse. But the opposite extreme, the all too prevalent notion that abuse is exclusively a function of a parental defect, seems equally specious. Abuse is the product of a complex set of interactions, and assigning weights to any of its components is premature. A conceivable expansion upon Green's (17) four-factor equation of the causes of abuse may help to illustrate the problem:

a) special child + special parent + crisis + cultural tolerance = abuse
b) special child + normal parent + crisis + cultural tolerance = abuse
c) special child + normal parent + cultural tolerance = abuse

Each equation is feasible and has been clinically demonstrated. While the factors making up the first have been noted by Green and others, the implications of the other two equations have all too often been ignored. Emphasis upon a single factor in abuse (psychopathology of the parent, environmental stresses, etc.) may obscure the importance of relevant variables, and lessen the effectiveness of therapeutic and prevention programs. Popular emphasis on the depraved-parent model of abuse may make other parents more reluctant to seek counseling (for fear of labeling). A broader dissemination of the fact that there are "difficult" children who can induce stress, and that relatively normal mothers can experience severe anxiety with respect to child rearing, could reduce this reluctance and the guilt attached to it.

Furthermore, it must be shown that it is not necessary for a special child to be present, but that the parent's perception of the child as different can be sufficient to instigate abuse.

Current research does demonstrate that prematurity, mental retardation, physical handicaps, congenital malformations, and similar conditions are over-represented in abused populations. Even Martin *et al.* (31), who stress the role of the parent and deemphasize the role of the child, stated that the proportion of premature infants in their population was significantly different from the norms.

Obviously, a great deal of research is required before the multifaceted aspects of the etiology of child abuse are determined. However, particularly within the realm of present knowledge, we must take into account a relatively consistent correlation—the special child is at greater risk for abuse. In planning prevention and treatment programs, those who deal with child abuse must keep this postulate in mind.

REFERENCES

1. Baron, M., Bejar, R., and Sheaff, P. 1970. Neurologic manifestations of the battered child syndrome. *Pediatrics* 45:1003–1007.
2. Benjamin, J. 1961. The innate and the experiential in development. In *Lectures on Experimental Psychiatry*, H. Brosin, ed. University of Pittsburgh Press, Pittsburgh.
3. Birrell, R., and Birrell, J. 1968. The maltreatment syndrome in children: a hospital survey. *Med. J. Austral.* 2:1023–1029.
4. Bishop, F. 1971. Children at risk. *Med. J. Austral.* 1:623–628.
5. Brandwein, H. 1973. The battered child: a definite and significant factor in mental retardation. *Ment. Retard.* 11:50–51.
6. Brazelton, T. 1961. Psychophysiologic reactions in the neonate: I. the value of observation of the neonate. *J. Pediat.* 58:508–512.
7. Dreyfus-Brisac, C. 1974. Organization of sleep in prematures: implications for caregiving. In *The Effect of the Infant on Its Caregiver*, M. Lewis and L. Rosenblum, eds. John Wiley, New York.
8. Ebbin, J. et al. 1969. Battered child syndrome at the Los Angeles County General Hospital. *Amer. J. Dis. Childhd.* 118:660–667.
9. Elmer, E. 1965. The fifty families study: summary of phase—I. neglected and abused children and their families. Children's Hospital of Pittsburgh, Pittsburgh.
10. Elmer, E., and Gregg, G. 1967. Developmental characteristics of abused children. *Pediatrics* 40:596–602.
11. Fanaroff, A., Kennell, J., and Klaus, M. 1972. Follow-up of low birth weight infants—the predictive value of maternal visiting patterns. *Pediatrics* 49:287–290.
12. Fomufod, A., Sinkford, S., and Louy, V. 1975. Mother-child separation at birth: a contributing factor in child abuse. *Lancet* 2:549–550.

13. Friedman, S. 1972. The need for intensive follow-up of abused children. In *Helping the Battered Child and His Family*. C. Kempe and R. Helfer, eds. Lippincott, Philadelphia.

14. Friedrich, W. 1975. A survey of reported physical child abuse in Harris County, Texas. Unpublished Master's thesis, University of Texas School of Public Health, Houston.

15. Gelles, R. 1973. Child abuse and psychopathology: a sociological critique and reformulation. *Amer. J. Orthopsychiat.* 43:611–621.

16. Gil, D. 1970. *Violence against Children: Physical Child Abuse in the United States.* Harvard University Press, Cambridge, Mass.

17. Green, A. 1968. Self-destruction in physically abused schizophrenic children: report of cases. *Arch. Gen. Psychiat.* 19:171–197.

18. Green, F. 1975. Child abuse and neglect: a priority problem for the private physician. *Pediat. Clin. N. A.* 22:329–339.

19. Helfer, R. 1973. The etiology of child abuse. *Pediatrics* 51:777–779.

20. Helfer, R. 1975. The diagnostic process and treatment programs. Office of Child Development, Washington, D.C.

21. Johnson, B., and Morse, H. 1968. Injured children and their parents. *Children* 15:147–152.

22. Kempe, C., and Helfer, R., eds. 1972. *Helping the Battered Child and His Family*. Lippincott, Philadelphia.

23. Klaus, M., and Kennell, J. 1970. Mothers separated from their newborn infants. *Pediat. Clin. N. A.* 17:1015–1037.

24. Klein, M., and Stern, L. 1971. Low birth weight and the battered child syndrome. *Amer. J. Dis. Childhd.* 122:15–18.

25. Knobloch, H., and Pasamanick, B. 1966. Prospective studies on the epidemiology of reproductive causality: methods, findings, and some implications. *Merrill-Palmer Quart.* 12:27–43.

26. Korner, A. 1971. Individual differences at birth: implications for early experience and later development. *Amer. J. Orthopsychiat.* 41:608–619.

27. Korner, A. 1974. Individual differences at birth: implications for child care practices. In *The Infant at Risk,* D. Bergsma, ed. Stratton Intercontinental, New York.

28. Leiderman, P. 1974. Mothers at risk: a potential consequence of the hospital care of the premature infant. In *The Child in His Family: Children at Psychiatric Risk,* E. Anthony and C. Koupernik, eds. John Wiley, New York.

29. Lynch, M. 1975. Ill-health and child abuse. *Lancet* 2:317–319.

30. Martin, H., and Beezley, P. 1974. Prevention and the consequences of child abuse. *J. Operational Psychiat.* 6:68–77.

31. Martin, H., et al. 1974. The development of abused children: a review of the literature and physical, neurologic, and intellectual findings. *Advances in Pediat.* 21:25–73.

32. Milowe, I., and Lourie, R. 1964. The child's role in the battered child syndrome. *J. Pediat.* 65:1079–1081.

33. Morris, M. Detection of High Risk Parents (unpublished).

34. Morse, C., Sahler, O., and Friedman, S. 1970. A three-year follow-up of abused and neglected children. *Amer. J. Dis. Childhd.* 120:439–446.

35. Mussen, P., Conger, J., and Kagan, J. 1974. *Child Development and Personality,* 4th ed. Harper and Row, New York.

36. Nichamin, S. 1973. Battered child syndrome and brain dysfunction. *JAMA* 223:1390.

37. Ounsted, C., Oppenheimer, R., and Lindsay, J. 1974. Aspects of bonding failure: the

psychopathology and psychotherapeutic treatment of families of battered children. *Developmental Med. Child Neurol.* 16:447–456.

38. Pasamanick, B. 1975. Ill-health and child abuse. *Lancet* 2:550.
39. Sandgrund, A., Gaines, R., and Green, A. 1974. Child abuse and mental retardation: a problem of cause and effect. *Amer. J. Ment. Defic.* 79:327–330.
40. Schaffer, H., and Emerson, P. 1964. Patterns of response to physical contact in early human development. *J. Child Psychol. Psychiat.* 5:1–13.
41. Silver, L. 1968. The psychological aspects of the battered child and his parents. *Clinical Proceedings of the Children's Hospital. Washington, D.C.* 24:355–364.
42. Soeffing, M. 1975. Abused children are exceptional children. *Exceptional Children* 42:126–133.
43. Spinetta, J., and Rigler, D. 1972. The child-abusing parent: a psychological review. *Psychol. Bull.* 77:296–304.
44. Steele, B., and Pollock, C. 1974. A psychiatric study of parents who abuse infants and small children. In *The Battered Child*, R. Helfer and C. Kempe, eds. University of Chicago Press, Chicago.
45. Thomas, A., Chess, S., and Birch, H. 1968. *Temperament and Behavior Disorders in Children*. New York University Press, New York.
46. Woolf, P. 1966. The causes, controls and organization of behavior in the neonate. *Psychol. Issues* 5 (monogr. 17).

CHAPTER 18

Low Birth Weight
and the Battered Child Syndrome

Michael Klein and Leo Stern

Fifty-one cases of battered child syndrome seen over a period of nine years at the Montreal Children's Hospital were reviewed to explore the possibility that low birth weight predisposes to this condition. Of these 51 infants, 12 (23.5%) were low birth weight infants; the expected low birth weight rate based on the Quebec perinatal figures is 7% to 8%. Associated with these instances of battering of former low birth weight infants was a high degree of isolation and separation of infant from the parents in the newborn period (mean hospital stay, 41.4 days) and a strong history of deprivation in the maternal history and in the child prior to battering. Suggestions are made for early detection and intervention.

The battered child syndrome is well known to readers of the pediatric literature. Much has been written recently about the characteristics of both the abusing parents (1) and the abused child (2-4). It has been suggested that abnormality in the child predisposes to battering. Because of the rapid growth in North America of centers devoted to the care of very small, extremely ill, premature infants, and particularly because these centers have the ability to increase the survival of hitherto unsalvagable infants, we examined the records of our hospital to determine if low birth weight was associated with an increased risk of battering.

METHODS

All charts signed out with the diagnosis of "battered child syndrome" for the years 1960 through 1969 were retrieved from the records of the Montreal Children's Hospital. All patients were in-patients because of both hospital policy requiring admission of suspected cases and the nature of the injuries. All related diagnoses are coded in the same category. The records of the hospital Social Service Department were studied, as well as those of the Radiology Department,

Reprinted with permission from *American Journal of Diseases of Children* 122(1971):15–18.

This study was supported in part by grant MT3037 from the Medical Research Council of Canada.

which keeps a separate registry of cases of "multiple unexplained skeletal trauma." With only one exception, the radiological classification coincided with the discharge diagnosis and social service records. With respect to cases of battering not associated with skeletal evidence, social service records and discharge diagnosis coincided.

Each chart was reviewed completely and categorized as to age at diagnosis, sex, birth weight, gestation, age of the mother, type of battering, newborn problems, evidence for maternal-child separation in the neonatal period, mental retardation, deprivation in the maternal background, and outcome. Infants were divided into normal birth weight and low birth weight (less than 2,500 gm [5 lb 8 oz]). Where the chart did not indicate the weight, an inquiry was sent to the Ministry of Health in Quebec City. The ministry responded with the birth weight and gestation in all but three cases. Though battering is regarded as the final point on a continuum from "failure to thrive" and breakdowns in the maternal-child relationship (5), cases called battered in this study were either frank unexplained skeletal trauma or severe bruising or both, or such neglect as to lead to severe medical illness or immediate threat to life. An illustrative case is presented below.

REPORT OF A CASE

A 1,050 gm (2 lb 5 oz) boy was born on Aug. 4, 1968, after a 27-week pregnancy, to a 17-year-old, gravida 2, para 1 mother and 19-year-old unemployed father. Both parents had come from backgrounds of extreme deprivation, married because of pregnancy, and were immature, disorganized, impulsive, and isolated. The mother was frankly depressed and possessed a dependent personality. (These social data were obtained a year after the birth of the child.)

At 6 hours of age, the patient was transferred to the Montreal Children's Hospital where he remained for 80 days. The baby had severe respiratory distress syndrome and was artificially ventilated from the third to the seventh day of life. Just prior to ventilation, the arterial hydrogen ion concentration was $159 \mu mEq/$ liter. This corresponds to an arterial pH of 6.80. Arterial carbon dioxide tension ($Paco_2$) was 20 mm Hg and oxygen tension (Pao_2) was 20 mm Hg. He had three exchange transfusions and a peak bilirubin level of 12.4 mg/100 ml. At 24 days of age, an electroencephalogram showed severe disturbances in cerebral activity with a diffuse epileptiform pattern. On several occasions anemia was severe enough to require transfusions. He was discharged after 80 days, weighing 2,509 gm (5 lb 9 oz), with a hemoglobin level of 7.9 gm/100 ml and a reticulocyte count of 6.2%.

At 3 months of age, when the child first visited the Newborn Follow-Up Clinic, he weighed 2.70 kg (6 lb) and was reported as "doing well."

At 4 months of age, the child weighed 3.73 kg (8 lb 4 oz) and the house officer examining the patient noted some questionable spasticity and "early psychomotor retardation."

The child was admitted for short stays at 7 and 9 months of age, each time without a diagnosis being established, coupled with rapid weight gain in the hospital. Possible breakdown in the maternal-child relationship was not identified and social service involvement was not sought.

The patient failed to appear for his 10-month check-up at the Newborn Clinic.

One day prior to his final admission at 12 months of age, the maternal grandmother called a local social service agency to report that she felt the child was being abused. She reported that she had seen bruises on the face and neck and had heard the mother express the desire to kill the baby. The agency called and made an appointment for the Newborn Follow-Up Clinic for three days hence. One day later the child was admitted to the Montreal Children's Hospital in shock with signs of peritonitis. At surgery, the child was found to have ruptured stomach and peritonitis; he died four days later. The chest roentgenogram taken prior to death showed multiple rib fractures in various stages of healing. Several old fractures of the long bones were noted postmortem. When questioned about the rib fractures, the parents stated that the child had fallen off a couch once. The case was handled through the criminal courts, and the parents have been indicted for manslaughter. The case is still pending.

RESULTS

In 51 cases the criteria of battering were met and records were obtainable. Of these, 39 infants (76%) were full-term and 12 (23.5%) were of low birth weight.

	No. of infants
Birth weight >2,500 gm	39
Birth weight <2,500 gm	12
Total battered babies in study	51

Of the 39 battered infants with birth weight 2,500 gm, 15 had significant medical illness (Table 1). We did not analyze for maternal-child separation and isolation in the newborn period for this group.

The analysis of the records of the 12 low birth weight infants is listed in Table 2. Of particular note is the presence of major neonatal problems in 9 of 12 cases and the length of stay (mean, 41.4 days) for these 9 infants. Six of the infants had definite psychomotor retardation prior to battering. Finally, social service records indicated that ten of the 12 infants came from deprived home environments in which the mother herself had usually suffered maternal and environmental deprivation in childhood. The life situation at the time of birth of

Table 1. Associated conditions of 15 of 39 battered infants with birth weight >2,500 gm

	No. of infants
Asphyxia neonatorum with normal mental development	2
Asphyxia neonatorum with mental retardation	2
Mental retardation without history of asphyxia	8
Cleft lip and palate, mild mental retardation, and hyperactivity	1
Cystic fibrosis	1
Hypospadias	1
Apparently normal	24
Total	39

the battered low birth weight infant included a high incidence of parental alcoholism, unemployment, extreme poverty, and social disorganization.

COMMENT AND IMPLICATIONS

Our investigation was subject to the usual problems of a retrospective study, i.e., incomplete information, possible changes in diagnostic criteria with time, etc. Because of the existence of a battered child committee monitoring this problem and because of similarity of classification in the Record Room, the Social Service Department, and the Radiology Department, we feel the data reflect the actual situation. Also, there is no reason to suspect that the Montreal Children's Hospital is selected as a place where parents bring former low birth weight infants.

In this review, 12 of 51 battered babies were found to be former low birth weight infants. This apparent association between low birth weight and the battered child syndrome was first cited by Elmer and Gregg in 1967 (7). In their series of 20 patients there were 13 white children, 5 of whom were premature (33%). This figure should be compared to prematurity rate of 7% among whites in Chicago (7). At the June 1970 meeting of the Canadian Medical Association, McRae reported that of 88 battered children studied at the Winnipeg Children's Hospital during the past 12 years, 11 were prematures (12.5%).

Our data suggest that multiple factors may be operating to select the low birth weight infant for battering, i.e., preexisting mental retardation, maternal deprivation, and isolation from mother in the newborn period. Not only may low birth weight predispose to battering but certain social characteristics of the mother may predispose to delivery of low weight infants. Specifically, the increased incidence of low birth weight infants among women from deprived backgrounds where prenatal care is either not available or not utilized is well known (8–10). Our data do not permit us to categorize our cases by precise social class or by prenatal care, but it can be assumed that the incidence of low birth weight infants among a group of women from deprived backgrounds (10 of our

Table 2. Analysis of the records of 12 low birth weight (<2,500 gm) battered infants

Case	Sex	Birth weight (gm)	Gestational age (weeks)	Age at diagnosis (mo)	Type of battering	Newborn problems	Newborn hospital stay (days)
1	M	1,980	32	30	Multiple fractures	2 exchange transfusions	60
2*	M	1,050	27	24	Multiple fractures, starvation, ruptured stomach	Multiple, severe fractures (case reported)	80
3	F	2,367	32	24	Multiple fractures, emotional deprivation	Prematurity only	14
4*	M	1,247	30	42	Starvation, fractures	Hyperbilirubinemia, 3 exchange transfusions, apnea, severe hyaline membrane disease	66
5	F	1,984	32	2	Multiple fractures	Pneumonia, Rh erythroblastosis, 4 exchange transfusions	35

	Sex						
6	F	1,205	31	7	Severe neglect	Hyaline membrane disease, asphyxia neonatorum cyanosis, severe	30
7*	F	2,268	?	48	Severe neglect	None	7†
8	M	1,814	35	12	Severe neglect, dehydration	Abruptio placenta microcephaly	30
9	F	1,616	34	30	Multiple bruises	Birth asphyxia, severe hyperbilirubinemia, 2 exchange transfusions	28
10	M	2,285	36	6	Multiple bruises, skull fracture	Birth asphyxia, microcephaly, seizures	30
11	F	1,928	36	30	Multiple fractures	None	7†
12	F	2,070	30	18	Multiple fractures	None	7†
Mean		1,783 (n=11)	32.2 (n=11)	22			41.4 (n=9)

*Indicates death from battering.

†Estimate: these three cases were excluded from calculation of the mean.

12 cases) might be higher than that for Quebec as a whole. On the other hand, Quebec data from 1967 indicate that low birth weight perinatal mortality was 130/1,000 live births or 34 times the rate for infants who weighed more than 2,500 gm (3.8/1,000) (6). The incidence of low birth weight among those who survive the newborn period, then, would operate in the opposite direction from social class and deprived maternal background. Using the 7% to 8% incidence figure for low birth weight in Quebec, P is < 0.001 that 12 of 51 infants would be of low birth weight by chance. Taking a hypothetical incidence figure of 10%, which takes into account the higher low birth weight rate for women of deprived background, significance is nevertheless achieved at the $P = 0.0014$ level using the binomial approximation. The rate of low birth weight for the hospitals on the Island of Montreal which serve almost exclusively the indigent population is reported as 9% to 10% (6). Since the factors which predispose to child abuse (poverty, deprivation, social class, alcoholism) tend to be associated with low birth weight, it is important to keep in mind that in Montreal the lowest socioeconomic class has only a slightly increased rate of low birth weight. The figure of 23.5% of former low birth weight children among abused children appears excessive even when the social factors are taken into consideration. Additionally, more than half the low birth weight infants were below 2,000 gm (4 lb. 6 oz). The incidence of infants in this weight group is again overrepresented and adds significance to the data.

The contribution of the usually accepted newborn intensive care practices should also be considered. Recently, Barnett et al. (11), explored the feasibility of bringing mothers into premature nurseries early and allowing them to touch their very sick infants. This would be expected to assist normal maternal-child bonding and lessen the usual isolation experienced by the mother of a small premature infant. It appears likely that the enforced separation so commonly practiced in premature units contributes to abnormal maternal-child relationships, including rejection, neglect, and finally, battering. The early entry of the mother into the nursery to handle her infant should also give the staff the opportunity to observe the mother with her child. Clues as to the mother's ability to care for and cope with what may be a difficult infant can be picked up and opportunity for early support and intervention taken.

To the extent that the infant may be damaged, it is necessary that he be followed closely after discharge. Since it is often impossible to state whether damage has taken place, one must have a high index of suspicion and awareness of the characteristics of the parents that would increase the risk to the infant. Many premature units have social workers who should be ideally suited for early detection of high risk situations.

The individual roles played by maternal deprivation, mental retardation or other medical conditions, and enforced maternal-child isolation cannot be separated from our data. It is possible that one or more of these factors may be more significant to battering than low birth weight itself. What can be said is that these factors tend to coincide in many low birth weight infants. It is hoped that their recognition will lead to the activation of preventive services.

REFERENCES

1. Steele, B. F.; Pollock, C. B.: A psychiatric study of parents who abuse infants and small children. In Helfer, R. E., Kempe, C. H. (eds): *The Battered Child*. Chicago, University of Chicago Press, 1968, pp. 103–145.
2. Courte, J.: The battered child: I. Historical and diagnostic reflections. *Med. Soc. Work* 22:11–20, 1969.
3. Morse, C. W.; Sahler, O. J. Z.; Friedman, S. B.: A three-year follow-up study of abused and neglected children. *Amer. J. Dis. Child.* 120:439–446, 1970.
4. Friedman, S. J.: The early detection of the battered child. In Helfer, R. E., Kempe, C. H. (eds): *Helping the Parents of the Battered Child*. Philadelphia, J. B. Lippincott Co. to be published.
5. Koel, B. S.: Failure to thrive and fetal injury as a continuum. *Amer. J. Dis. Child.* 118:565–567, 1969.
6. Quebec Perinatal Mortality Commission: *Annual Report, 1967*. Quebec City, Province of Quebec, Ministry of Health, 1967.
7. Elmer, E.; Gregg, G. D.: Developmental characteristics of abused children. *Pediatrics* 40:596–602, 1967.
8. Wallace, H. M.: Factors associated with perinatal mortality and morbidity. *Clin. Obstet. Gynec.* 13:13–43, 1970.
9. Rider, R. V.; Taback, M.; Knobloch, H.: Associations between premature birth and socioeconomic status. *Amer. J. Public Health* 45:1022–1028, 1955.
10. Aubry, R. H.; Nesbitt, E. L.: High-risk obstetrics: I. *Amer. J. Obstet. Gynec.* 105: 241–247, 1969.
11. Barnett, C. R.; Leiderman, H.; Grobstein, R. S. W.; Klaus, M.: Neonatal separation: The maternal side of interactional deprivation. *Pediatrics* 45:197–205, 1970.

CHAPTER 19

Mothers Separated
from Their Newborn Infants

Marshall H. Klaus and
John H. Kennell

Mothers separated from their young soon lost all interest in those
whom they were unable to nurse or cherish.

P. Budin

Multiple observations suggest that a human mother's care of her baby derives
from a complex mixture made up of her endowment or genetics, the way the
baby responds to her, a long history of interpersonal relations within her own
family, past experiences with this or previous pregnancies, and absorption of the
values and practices of her culture (5, 11, 13, 42, 67, 69). Recently, attention has
been directed toward another significant factor—the events of the early postpartum days. Behavioral studies in a large range of animal species as well as
preliminary studies of human maternal behavior suggest that what happens in the
period immediately following delivery may be critical to later maternal behavior
(4, 35, 57). Observations in humans have proceeded far enough to allow us to
infer that a woman's physical relationship with her infant in the early days and
months after delivery require thorough investigation.

This report will review these studies in animals and humans as well as a
number of situations noted in women following the birth of premature or high-
risk infants, and suggest their clinical relevance. To understand the human
mother's current position in the high-risk and newborn nurseries, it is necessary
for us to begin with a review of how she has been treated historically.

HISTORY

During the past ninety years, the role and responsibilities of the mother in the
hospital nursery have varied. In the American hospital of the 1880's, rooming-in
(still an accepted mode in Europe) was prevalent. The Johns Hopkins Hospital,
built without a separate nursery, continued rooming-in as standard procedure

This work is supported by the Grant Foundation and the Educational Foundation of America.
Reprinted with permission from *Pediatric Clinics of North America* 17 (1970):1015–37.
Copyright 1970, W. B. Saunders.

until 1890; the Nursery and Children's Hospital did so until after 1896, and the New York Hospital until after 1898 (47).

In the premature nurseries of Pierre Budin (14) (1895), the most famous of the early neonatologists, the mother's participation in the care of her baby was welcomed. Although most of the milk for the small premature babies was supplied by wet nurses, mothers were encouraged to breast feed their premature infants, because as Budin noted, "Unfortunately . . . a certain number of mothers abandon the babies whose needs they have not had to meet, and in whom they have lost all interest. The life of the little one has been saved, it is true, but at the cost of the mother." Because of the increased survival rate of infants who were discharged feeding from their mothers' breasts, Budin gave special instructions to keep up the milk supply and suggested that the mothers of small premature babies also nurse full-term infants to stimulate milk production.

The first change in the mother's role occurred as a result of Budin's desire to gain approval for his methods of premature infant care. A young Alsatian student, Martin Cooney, was sent to the Berlin Exposition of 1896 to display the survival of premature infants brought to his *Kinderbrutanstalt* ("child hatchery"). He became both a clinical and commercial success (44). Cooney subsequently traveled as an exhibitor to fairs in England and the United States. He finally settled on Coney Island where during the next thirty-nine years, he raised over 5000 premature infants. In most respects, Cooney's handling of the infants was similar to that of Budin; however, mothers did not participate in the care of the infants in the exhibits, but were allowed to attend with free passes. It is significant that Cooney sometimes had difficulty inducing parents to take the children back. Despite Cooney's commercialism, many of his methods were adopted in the first premature nurseries in hospitals in the United States.

By the early 1900s, the high mortality and morbidity of infants (usually resulting from epidemic diarrhea, respiratory infection, and inadequate equipment) (12, 17) led to stricter isolation techniques and to the development of separate wards for all patients who were free from infection. At this time, small premature infants were housed either in the regular nursery or on the infant ward. Hospitalization was avoided whenever possible; special rules were adopted to prohibit visiting by relatives and friends; handling of the infant was reduced to a minimum (21, 23, 48). Rigid measures to prevent infection, and the example set by Cooney's exhibits, thus completely removed the mother from the hospital nursery.

The first hospital premature infant center was started at the Sarah Morris Hospital in Chicago in 1923 by Hess. He also used wet nurses as a source of milk, although the infants in the hospital were not usually nursed at the breast. Like Budin, Hess made every attempt to continue breast milk feeding (29). He encouraged the mother to produce milk for her own infant and bring it to the hospital daily, and to continue breast feeding after discharge. As soon as the infant's condition warranted, the mother was instructed in his hospital care and was permitted to nurse him at the breast.

Premature units which developed after the Sarah Morris Nursery had similar rules and regulations: babies were kept in separate units of the hospital; careful and minimal handling by everyone, including physicians, was recommended; strict isolation techniques were used; mothers were categorically excluded, except in some nurseries when just before discharge they were permitted to nurse or bottle feed their infants; and early discharge was suggested to prevent infection.

Recommendations for the hospital care of full-term and premature infants written by Ethel Dunham and Marian Crane (18) for the Children's Bureau in 1943 outlined special measures to protect the infant from infection and specified that visitors should be excluded from the nursery, limiting the mother to viewing her premature infant through the glass windows. Standard textbooks on newborn care from 1945 to 1960 by Parmelee (56), Crosse (15), and Hess (30), as well as the newborn manual of the American Academy of Pediatrics, continued to recommend minimal handling, strict isolation, and the exclusion of all visitors from the nursery. It is significant that a survey of children's wards in 1954 revealed that for over 50 percent of the beds, visiting hours were limited to 1 to 2 hours once a week (43). About this time, renewed interest in rooming-in for the mother of a full-term infant was stimulated by the work of Edith Jackson (31).

During this later period, two other different approaches to premature care were begun. In Miller's studies of home nursing of premature babies at Newcastle-on-Tyne (49), mortality was, surprisingly, only moderately greater than in a comparable group of infants nursed in the hospital. Miller believed that care at home gave the infant a good start and "is far better than if he were taken away to hospital and returned a month or 6 weeks later, an unknown infant, feared and strange." Another system of care originated because of a shortage of skilled nurses. At the Baragwanath Hospital in Johannesburg, South Africa, Kahn arranged for mothers to remain in the hospital, and, with supervision, care for their premature infants (32, 33).

Mothers are still excluded from the majority of premature nurseries in the United States; however, at present several nurseries have begun to admit mothers on a trial basis (4, 35, 64).

ANIMAL STUDIES

As in other areas of neonatology, it has been useful to study mothers and infants of many species during the neonatal period. Although certain aspects of behavior differ from species to species, there are some over-all patterns and trends which can be discerned. Despite the reluctance of many investigators to accept the concept that these patterns may apply to humans, the possibility of their extension to the human should not be neglected when they are found in a large number of species.

First, in goats, sheep, and cattle, when a mother is separated from her young in the first hour or the first few hours after delivery and then the two are reunited, the mother will show disturbances of mothering behavior, such as failure to care for her young, butting her own offspring away, and feeding her own and other babies indiscriminately (27, 40, 50). In contrast, if the mother and infant are kept together for the first four days and are separated on the fifth day for an equal period of time, the mother quickly returns to the maternal behavior characteristic of her species when the pair is reunited. It thus appears that there is a sensitive period immediately after delivery; if the animal mother is separated from her young during this interval, deviant maternal behavior may result. (It is important to note that not all mothers are equally affected by these early separations and that the disturbed mothering performance can be modified by special handling.) Surprisingly, in spite of this sensitive period, adoptions can be arranged. Hersher, Richmond, and Moore induced sheep and goats to adopt strange lambs and kids—between as well as within species (28). This required delicate arrangements of timing to prevent the mother from destroying the strange infant. In other species, such as mice and rats, when mother and young are separated in the first few hours following delivery and then brought together again the rodent mother will care for the young, but not as skillfully (60). Thus the effects of early separation on later maternal behavior vary with the species. Harlow studied rhesus monkey mothers deprived of tactile contact but allowed to see and hear their infants (25). After two weeks without any tactile contact these mothers rapidly decreased the amount of time they spent viewing their infants. This indicated that viewing alone is not enough stimulus to maintain maternal interest. The results of similar studies in humans will be considered later.

Secondly, clear-cut species-specific maternal behavior patterns such as nesting, retrieving, grooming, and exploring have been observed in nonhuman mammalian mothers immediately after delivery. For example, in the cat during labor and just before delivery the mother licks the genital region; then, following delivery, the mother licks the kitten completely, eats the membranes and placenta, and remains in close, almost constant physical contact through the first three to four days. This perinatal behavior may be severely distorted if the mother herself has received abnormal care as an infant (8, 24), or if the normal sequence of behavior is altered, as shown in Birch's experiments with rats. Noting the increased amount of self-licking (especially in the anogenital region) in the pregnant rat and hypothesizing that this self-licking might extend to the pups after delivery, Birch fashioned high collars which were placed on the necks of pregnant rats to prevent self-licking (8). The collars were removed shortly before birth. These rats subsequently exhibited abnormal maternal behavior: waiting a long interval before initial licking of the pups, consuming them once licking began, and in the instance of pups surviving the licking period, refusing to allow them to suckle; no offspring survived the nursing period. Control mothers and mothers wearing collars similar to those described but notched to permit self-licking did not exhibit this aberrant behavior.

Thirdly, for some period after delivery, usually weeks or even months, animal mothers have characteristic patterns of behavior and orders of behavior. For example, the rhesus monkey mother grooms her infant more at 1 month than at other times. Initially she spends little time retrieving, whereas at 1½ months retrieving is maximum (25). Recurring patterns of maternal behavior within a species can be distinguished in a large number of animal species. Careful observations by Ainsworth in Uganda suggest that repeating sequences are also found in human mothers (1).

HUMAN MATERNAL BEHAVIOR IN OTHER CULTURES

Dr. Clifford Barnett (3), an anthropologist, has searched for variations in human maternal behavior following delivery in the Human Relations File which lists 220 cultures. He found that every society exhibited some regularized manner of dealing with the entry of a new member into that society. In most cultures, during the three to seven days while the navel heals the mother and infant are secluded together. The mother has little or no responsibilities other than the infant. This is true even in Israel, where infant houses separate from those of the parents have been established (in the socialistic communities known as kibbutzim). In the early days after delivery, the mother-infant pair are kept together part of the day; separation does not occur until after the fifth day and then usually for only part of each 24 hours (66). In Russia, mothers are not separated from their infants in the early weeks of life (45).

It is therefore of special interest that routine complete separation of mother and infant in the first days after delivery exists only in the high-risk and premature nurseries of the Western world.

MATERNAL BEHAVIOR OF THE HUMAN MOTHER

Preliminary data on the behavior of the human mother following separation from her infant have been brought together from a number of different sources: (1) long-term, extensive in-depth interviews of a small number of mothers, primarily by psychoanalysts; (2) clinical observations during medical care procedures; (3) naturalistic observations of mothering; (4) structured interviews or observations; and (5) preliminary results from a small number of controlled studies of the mothers of premature infants (5, 51, 52, 53).

From these diverse observations it is possible to begin to piece together how affectional bonds between human mothers and their infants are built, and to determine what alters or distorts this process temporarily or permanently. Because the human infant is wholly dependent upon his mother or caretaker for all his physical and emotional needs, the strength of these attachment ties may well determine whether he will survive and develop optimally. The actual process by which attachment bonds are formed between mother and child is unknown; however, the time-periods which are probably crucial in this process are listed in Table 1.

Table 1. Steps in attachment

Planning the pregnancy
Confirming the pregnancy
Fetal movement
Birth
Seeing the baby
Touching the baby
Caretaking

Pregnancy

Bibring (7), Deutsch (16), and Benedeck (6) have described in detail the behavioral changes that occur during pregnancy. Bibring outlines the first phase for a mother in the early weeks of pregnancy as the acceptance of the growing fetus as an ''integral part of herself.'' When fetal movement becomes perceptible the developing baby begins to be considered as a separate individual, and the woman gradually prepares psychologically for delivery and anatomic separation. Interview data covering this time-period often describes marked changes in attitude toward the unborn infant. Once fetal movement begins, infants who are unplanned and unwanted by the mother often become more accepted. Any medical problem which threatens the health or survival of the fetus or the mother during this period may delay the mother's planning for the infant and retard the process of bonding.

Delivery

Surprisingly, specific data for this period are scanty. Newton and Newton (54) noted that the mothers who were most likely to be accepting and pleased with their infants on first sight were those who stayed calm and relaxed in labor, cooperated with their attendants, received more solicitous care, and had good rapport with their attendants. These observations are in agreement with veterinary experience that dams and sows are more easily induced to accept their offspring if their surroundings during delivery are quiet, peaceful, and private. Although unconsciousness during delivery in certain animals results in the rejection of offspring, no such effects have been noted in humans (55). Using the degree of mourning as a measure of affectional bonding, Kennell, Slyter, and Klaus (36) noted affectional ties to be present after delivery even before tactile contact was made. In a study of 20 mothers they observed that clearly identifiable mourning was present in each woman whose infant had died. The mother grieved whether the infant lived for 1 hour or 12 days, whether he weighed 3000 gm. or a nonviable 580 gm., and whether or not the pregnancy was planned.

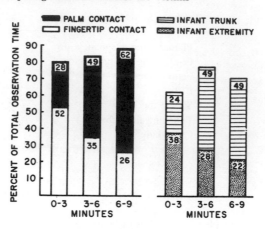

Figure 1. Fingertip-palm progression

First Weeks after Delivery

As in other animal species, the human mother demonstrates an orderly progression of behavior after she gives birth. Using filmed observations, Klaus, Kennell, Plumb, and Zuehlke (38) observed that when nude full-term infants were brought to their mothers shortly after birth the mothers started a routine pattern of behavior which began with fingertip touching of the infant's extremities and proceeded in 4 to 8 minutes to massaging and encompassing palm contact on the trunk (Fig. 1). In the first 3 minutes, the extent of fingertip contact was 52 percent, 28 percent being palm contact. In the last 3 minutes of observation, fingertip contact had markedly decreased. Rubin (62) observed a similar sequence but at a much slower rate (3 days). Mothers of normal premature infants who were permitted early contact followed a similar sequence of touching but at a slower rate. Perhaps this is an example of species-specific behavior.

Both groups of mothers expressed strong interest in eye-to-eye contact. Robson (58) suggests that eye-to-eye contact is one of the innate releasers of maternal caretaking responses. The mother's marked concentration on the eyes of the infant is of interest when considered in conjunction with the early functional development of the human infant's visual pathways. His ability to attend and follow, especially during the first hours, coincides with his mother's interest in his eyes.

Though the process of affectional bonding is well underway prior to delivery, the clinical observations of Rose (59), and Kennell and Rolnick (37) suggest that the affectional ties can be disturbed easily and may be altered permanently. Relatively minor illnesses in the immediate newborn period appeared to alter the relationship between mother and infant. Some of these minor problems included slight elevations of bilirubin, slow feeding, and the need for incubator care in the first 24 hours for mild respiratory distress secondary to meconium aspiration. Even though the infant's problem had been resolved completely prior to discharge, the behavior of his mother was often disturbed for the first year of his life or longer.

Support for the concept that close continual contact between mother and infant during the first days of life may facilitate mothering behavior came from observations in Duke Hospital when rooming-in was made compulsory. After this change was effected, McBryde (47) noted that the incidence of breast feeding rose from 35 to 58.5 percent, while phone calls from anxious mothers during the first weeks after discharge decreased by 90 percent.

Barnett et al. (4, 41) from Stanford and the authors from Case Western Reserve University (35, 36, 38) are engaged in a long-term study to evaluate the effects of the early mother-infant separation which is now a standard aspect of care in most premature nurseries. Mothers in one of the study groups are permitted to enter the nursery, place their hands in the isolettes, and even carry out simple caretaking tasks, beginning in the first five days after delivery and continuing throughout the hospitalization (Early Contact). Those in the second group have only visual contact with their infants in the glass-enclosed nursery and are unable to touch, smell, or hear them until after the first 20 days (Late Contact 1). In a third group, handling is delayed until the infants are 30 to 40 days of age (Late Contact 2). A control group of mothers of full-term infants from similar socioeconomic backgrounds is also being studied. The hypothesis is that if human mothers are affected by this period of separation, then one might expect to see altered maternal attachment during the first weeks or months of life, and, as a result, to find that differences in infant development were produced and would become evident as the infant grows. To date, these studies have shown no increase in infection when mothers and fathers are permitted to visit and no disruption in the care of the infant. (It has been a consistent observation that mothers wash their hands longer and more thoroughly than most physicians!)

Though both projects are still in progress, two separate studies of maternal behavior after different periods of separation have been reported.

The first study (41) compared two sets of mothers, Early Contact and Late Contact 2. Observations of the mother and infant were made on three occasions: (1) on the mother's fifth visit to her infant in the discharge nursery, (2) in the home one week after discharge, and (3) in the pediatric clinic one month after discharge. Mothers allowed early physical contact with their infants were more skillful in caretaking only during the first observation. Attachment behavior (looking at the infant, smiling at the infant, the closeness with which the infant is held, and caressing the infant) of the nonseparated mothers was greater than that of the separated mothers at each of the three observations; it was significantly greater only at the third observation.

In the second study (35) observations were recorded using time-lapse photography and were analyzed for the first 10 minutes of each feeding. The behavior of mothers who had been separated from their infants for 20 days (Late Contact 1) was studied at a feeding just before discharge and was compared with the discharge feeding of the group of mothers who were permitted physical contact within the first 5 days of life (Early Contact). Feeding was chosen as a

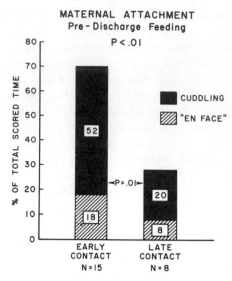

Figure 2. Percentage of en face and cuddling times in early and late contact mothers of premature infants

measure of maternal performance because of its universality and its central position in the mother-infant relationship (13). Twenty-five activities were recorded for each mother, including her caretaking skills (such as the position of the bottle and the presence of milk in the tip of the nipple) as well as measurements of maternal affection (such as the contact of the mother's chest or abdomen with the infant's trunk, which was termed "cuddling"). For example, a mother may look at her baby, while the baby feeds from a bottle, so that her eyes are focused on the baby in the "en face" position (defined as the mother's face in such a position that her eyes and those of the infant meet fully in the same vertical plane of rotation). Alternatively, the eyes may be focused on the baby, but not in the en face position. The mother's abdomen may touch the infant's trunk (cuddling) with the bottle held perpendicular to the baby's mouth with the milk in the tip of the nipple. Or, the mother may hold the baby without cuddling, and with the bottle not perpendicular and the milk not in the nipple. The differences in the amount of cuddling combined with en face in the two approaches during the predischarge feedings are shown in Figure 2. Cuddling was a universal component of infant-feeding before this century when almost all infants were breast-fed. When mothers in one group show an increased tendency to hold their babies away from their bodies during feeding, we can question whether this unusual behavior may reflect incomplete attachment or diminished maternal affection. In the monkey maternal affection appears to wane progressively as the frequency of close ventral contacts between mother and infant decreases (25).

One month after discharge, after almost 200 feedings at home, the mothers were filmed again during a feeding. The Late Contact mothers held their babies differently, changed position less, burped less, and were not as skillful in feeding as mothers in the Early Contact group. These differences in mothers are of interest when taken in light of the observations of Judith Rubenstein (61) who has shown that early maternal attentiveness facilitates later exploratory behavior in infants. Thus stimulation may have a decisive influence on the infant's later development.

DISCUSSION

If the procedures for the care of mother and baby in the hospital today were to be based on what is known of other cultures and what has been learned from studies and observations of both animal and human behavior, it would not be unreasonable to change many of our existing rules and regulations. However, no widespread change should take place until there is strong evidence that what we are doing today is damaging, and that a change would be desirable. In the past it has been the custom of the health professions to make major changes affecting behavior and environment in order to promote what appeared to be a beneficial innovation in medical care without prior critical study of all the side effects. In this century both birth and death, the two most important events in the life of the individual, have been moved into the hospital and away from the family and centuries of traditions and cultural patterns of behavior. Practices surrounding both events appear to have been almost wholly determined by the psychological needs, the convenience, the limited perspective, and the bias of the dominant members of the hospital culture (nurse, physician, and administrator).

With these historical perspectives in mind, we think it is important that the needs of the human mother be thoroughly investigated before radical changes are recommended. The experience with rooming-in provides one example. This naturalistic arrangement may be of immense value for the mother and child. Yet it has not been and never will be widely adopted in the Western world until more data clearly support its advantages.

It is our impression that massive alterations may be required once information about the behavioral requirements of mothers is collected. For example, if we adopt the standards or levels of deprivation suggested by Barnett (4) (Table 2) it is apparent that most normal deliveries in this country are associated with several days of deprivation for the mother (Table 3). The mother who delivers a premature suffers complete deprivation from the first day and severe deprivation from then until the eighth week (if she can only see her infant through a glass wall). Only mothers who deliver at home or room-in with their infants experience no deprivation.

Kaplan and Mason and others (34, 45, 65, 71) have viewed the maternal reactions to the birth of a premature as an acute emotional crisis and note four psychological tasks which the mother must complete: (1) prepare for possible loss (anticipatory grief); (2) acknowledge and face maternal failure to deliver a full-term infant; (3) resume the process of relating to the infant; and (4) learn how the premature differs from a full-term infant and understand his special

Table 2. Levels of interactional deprivation and component variables*

Levels of deprivation	Duration of deprivation	Sensory modalities of interaction	Caretaking nature of interaction
I. no deprivation	Full time	All senses	Complete
II. partial deprivation	Part time	All senses	Partial
III. moderate deprivation	Part time	All senses	None
IV. severe deprivation	Part time	Visual only	None
V. complete deprivation	None	None	None

*From Barnett, C., et al.: *Pediatrics,* 45:199, 1970. Reproduced by permission.

needs. These tasks may relate in part to what a physician says and to whether or not the mother and infant are separated.

The mothering behavior of each mother, her ability to tolerate adverse stresses, and her need for special attention differ greatly and depend on a multitude of factors. At the time the infant is born some of the determinants of the mothers mothering behavior are ingrained and unchangeable, such as the mother's own mothering, the practices of her culture, her endowment, and her relations with her family and husband. Other determinants can be altered: the attitudes, statements, and practices of the doctor in the hospital; whether or not there is separation from the infant in the first days of life; and the nature of the infant himself—his temperament as well as whether he is healthy, sick, or malformed. One of the most easily manipulated variables is the separation of an infant from his mother during the first hours and days after birth.

There are a series of disorders of mothering which range from mild (such as persisting concerns about a baby following a minor abnormality which has been completely resolved in the nursery) to the most severe manifestation, the battered child syndrome. It is our hypothesis that this entire range of problems may be, in part, the end result of separation in the early newborn period. This concept is supported by the high incidence of premature infants who return to the hospital because of failure to thrive. In studies of failure-to-thrive infants (2, 63), 15 to 30 percent had no organic disease; of this group, 25 to 41 percent were premature. In their report on the vulnerable child syndrome (children who are expected by their parents to die prematurely and who develop severe emotional disturbances), Green and Solnit (22) observed that 44 percent of these infants were either premature or severely ill and separated from their mothers in the first weeks of life.

It is the present custom in this country for adoptions to take place at three to six weeks of age or later. Would the behavioral problems of the adopted child be as great if adoptions occurred at 1 day or 1 hour of life? In many societies where there is a high maternal mortality rate, a substitute mother is close at hand and ready to take over immediately following the death of a mother.

The battered child syndrome provides the most dramatic evidence of a disor-

Table 3. Deprivation levels over time, related to birth situation*

Birth situation	Deprivation level, days and weeks postpartum					
	Day 0	Day 1	Day 3	Day 7	Week 8	Week 9
Home, full term	II, partial deprivation	I, no deprivation	I, no deprivation	I, no deprivation	I, no deprivation	I, no deprivation
Hospital, full term, rooming-in	III, moderate deprivation	I, no deprivation	I, no deprivation	I, no deprivation	I, no deprivation	I, no deprivation
Hospital, full term, regular care	III, moderate deprivation	II, partial deprivation	II, partial deprivation	I, no deprivation	I, no deprivation	I, no deprivation
Premature, mother allowed in nursery	V, complete deprivation	IV, severe deprivation	III, moderate deprivation	II, partial deprivation	II, partial deprivation (discharge nursery)	I, no deprivation
Premature regular care (separated)	V, complete deprivation	IV, severe deprivation	IV, severe deprivation	IV, severe deprivation	II, partial deprivation (discharge nursery)	I, no deprivation
Unwed mother, refuses contact	V, complete deprivation	V, complete deprivation	V, complete deprivation	V, complete deprivation	V, complete deprivation	V, complete deprivation

*From Barnett, C., et. al.: *Pediatrics*, 45:200, 1970. Reproduced by permission.

der of mothering. We have searched the literature to determine the incidence of separation following delivery in these mother-infant dyads, but the authors usually fail to record this information. The incidence of either prematurity or serious illness was 39 percent, combining two series (totaling 44 patients) reporting birth weight or gestational age (19, 70). During the period in which this project has been underway, the authors have been told about a number of clinical examples in which battering occurred after discharge of normal healthy premature infants who had been small and seriously ill shortly after birth so that they had been separated from their parents for prolonged periods (39). Although multiple factors contribute to this problem (such as the mother's own rearing), early separation may be a significant factor (26). The formation of close affectional ties may remain permanently incomplete if extended separation occurs and anticipatory grief becomes too far advanced.

* * * * *

CASE PROBLEMS

The clinical relevance of this subject can best be appreciated by the following case example and the questions it raises.

Mrs. H. was happily married, had had a previous miscarriage, and had planned on having a baby for the past three years. She delivered a 3 lb., 2 oz. male infant following a normal pregnancy. The infant cried immediately but then developed moderate respiratory distress, requiring arterial catheterization and a plastic hood over his head for administration of oxygen. At 36 hours of age in an environment of 70 percent oxygen the pH was 7.31, the Pco_2 60mm. Hg, and the Po_2 73 mm. Hg.

The following questions must be answered when caring for this mother-infant dyad:

1. Should the mother be permitted to go into the nursery?
2. Should she be in a separate room on the maternity division?
3. What is the best method of communicating with both parents?
4. How should advice be given when first discussing the situation with the parents? What should they be told about their infant and his chances for survival?
5. Can the nurses help the mother adapt to the premature infant?
6. Should the mother go home before the respiratory distress syndrome has subsided?
7. If the infant dies, how can the mother be helped and how long will she grieve?
8. If the infant survives, what problems will the mother face and how can she be helped?

Answers to these questions follow. We encourage the reader to think out his own answers first.

Answers to case problems. 1. The mother should be permitted to enter the nursery if she wants to. With current therapy the outlook for this baby is good.

There is no evidence that the mother will have an unduly upsetting reaction if he does die; on the contrary, having already had a miscarriage, she will probably be relieved to see for herself that the baby is well-formed.

2. The mother should be alone in a separate room on the maternity division if she so desires, and as far away as possible from the sights and sounds of normal babies and more fortunate mothers whose healthy infants *come to them* every four hours.

3. The best method of communicating with both parents is to have both sitting down together with you in a quiet, private room. You will be most effective if you can listen to the parents. Let them express their worries and feelings; then give simple, realistically optimistic explanations.

4. When first discussing the situation with the parents, advice should be given promptly, simply, and optimistically. As soon as possible after the birth, the mother can be told that the baby is small but well-formed, that you will be doing routine tests and giving the usual treatment for a premature infant, and that you will report back to her when you have had time to complete more tests and observations.

   When it is clear that the baby has respiratory distress and arterial catheterization is necessary, you can explain to the mother that the child has a common problem of premature infants ("breathing difficulty") owing to the complex adjustments he must make from life in utero to life outside. Further, it should be stated that because it is common you know how best to treat it; that this treatment will involve putting a tube in the blood vessel through which she fed the baby while he was inside her, and that you will use this tube to obtain tiny amounts of blood on frequent occasions to guide your therapy; that the baby will be transferred to a nursery for small babies; that prior to his transfer her husband can see the baby and the baby will be brought to her in a special transport incubator for her to see; that babies sometimes get worse before they improve, but the outlook is good for complete recovery after several days; that you will keep her and her husband posted on the baby's progress and will tell them if problems arise; that you would like them to call at other times if they have questions; and that you would like her to come to the nursery to visit and see the baby.

   At 36 hours you have a firmer basis for an optimistic report, which should be kept simple but should include an explanation of the hood, apnea monitor, and other visible aspects of therapy. You might say, for example, "I'm pleased with your son's progress. He has responded well to our treatment, and his outlook is excellent. If you haven't been over to see him yet, I'd like to encourage you to do this today, because you will be pleased with his progress."

5. The nurses can help the mother adapt to the premature infant by standing close to the mother and explaining about the equipment being used for him; by welcoming the mother by name and with personalized comments at each visit, and encouraging her to come back soon; by carefully considering the mother's concerns and feelings; by explaining to her that the baby will benefit from her

visits; and by showing her how she can gradually assume more of the baby's care and do the mothering better than the nurses. An example of the nurses' encouragement to mothers to continue visits later on in the patient's course is the type of note our nurses put on a baby's crib: "My mother is coming to feed me at 1:30. Boy! Will I be happy to see her! —David."

6. If mother is confident that the infant will live, she should go home before the respiratory distress has subsided. Staying in a maternity unit and only visiting her baby one or two times a day is not tolerated very long by many mothers unless they can actively care for their babies or provide breast milk. It is particularly difficult for a woman if she has young children at home. Most mothers can return daily to visit the baby from home.

   If she lives far away, is unlikely to return for many days, and is greatly concerned the baby will die, the mother should not go home before the respiratory distress syndrome has subsided. It is best to reach a point where both you and the mother are confident about the baby's survival.

7. If the baby dies, at the time of death it would be wise to tell the parents about the usual reactions to the loss of a newborn infant (crying, sadness, loss of appetite, inability to sleep, increased irritability, preoccupation with the lost infant, inability to return to normal activities and feelings of guilt about the early delivery, the illness, and death of the baby). It will be beneficial if you can indicate to the parents that it is best for them to talk freely with each other about their feelings. Many couples who have communicated well with each other prior to a loss will keep their feelings to themselves, and this lack of full communication will often intensify the distress of both. When you meet with them again one or two days after the death and go over the same suggestions, you will find that many of your suggestions have been missed or misunderstood owing to the emotional shock of the baby's death. Another interview is important three or four months after the death to inquire about their grief, to discuss the autopsy findings and to answer any further questions. These three discussions are of value to all parents who lose a child. The normal grief reaction will last approximately six months, with brief episodes of sadness on occasion after that time.

8. When the infant survives, in spite of all the steps that have been recommended this mother may have withdrawn some of her attachment to the baby through anticipatory grief. Under the best of circumstances she will have had much less contact with her baby than a normal mother. Therefore, affectional bonds will not be as well developed as with a healthy full-term infant and she will have done relatively little caretaking. The continuation of support to the mother, so that she will visit, touch, and provide increasing care for the baby (holding, feeding, bathing, and diapering) is important during the hospital period. Detailed preparation for the care of the baby at home, the availability of support by telephone during the hospital stay, and continuing support after the baby returns home are indicated, especially during the first months at home. Through the early years of the infant's life the pediatrician should be alert to evidence that the baby is being handled differently than other children

(delay in weaning, over-protection, excessive permissiveness, or excessively regimented management). A discussion at this time with the mother about her early experiences, and her feelings and worries about the baby may be advisable. When specific questions have been answered it may be best, if appropriate, to reassure the mother that the baby's early problems are over and will not recur, that the baby was small in the beginning but is now normal in size and development, and that for his ultimate well-being he should be handled as normally as possible.

SUMMARY

Changes in medical practices during the past fifty years have remarkably altered maternal care practices that have evolved over centuries.

Detailed observations of a wide range of mammalian mothers and babies have shown that each species exhibits recurring sequences of maternal behavior around the time of delivery and during the first days and months of life. Interference with these behavior patterns may result in undesirable, even catastrophic, effects on the young. The knowledge that there is a sensitive period shortly after birth during which brief periods of partial or complete separation may drastically distort a mother animal's feeding and care of her infant would lead a caretaker or naturalist to be extremely cautious about any intervention in the period after birth.

Observations in human mothers suggest that affectional bonds are forming before delivery, but that they are fragile and may be easily altered in the first days of life. A preliminary inspection of fragments of available data suggests that maternal behavior may be altered in some women by a period of separation, just as infant behavior is affected by isolation from the mother (10).

The studies of maternal behavior in animals, a survey of maternal practices in other cultures, and preliminary observations in human mothers after periods of early separation from their infants force a thorough review and evaluation of our present perinatal care practices. Before any major changes should be made again, the following unknowns must be answered:

1. Is there a critical or sensitive period in the human mother as there is in the animal mother?
2. What are the needs of most mothers with normal full-term infants in the first hours after delivery and during the first week?
3. Has the hospital culture, which has taken over both birth and death, produced disorders of mothering which last a lifetime?
4. Are the diseases of failure-to-thrive, the battered child syndrome, and the vulnerable child syndrome in part related to hospital care practices?
5. How should the minor problems as well as the major problems which the infant develops or is born with be handled with mothers of different backgrounds, cultures, and requirements?
6. Should the adopting mother receive her infant in the first hour of life? Are the

problems of the adopted child a result of adoption practices and early separation? What are the needs of the biological mother who gives the baby up for adoption?

REFERENCES

1. Ainsworth, M. *Infancy in Uganda*. Baltimore: Johns Hopkins Press, 1967.
2. Ambuel, J., and Harris, B. Failure to thrive: A study of failure to grow in height or weight. *Ohio Med. J.* 59:997, 1963.
3. Barnett, C.: Personal communication.
4. Barnett, C., Leiderman, P., Grobstein, R., and Klaus, M. Neonatal separation: the maternal side of interactional deprivation. *Pediatrics* 45:197, 1970.
5. Bell, R. A re-interpretation of the direction of effects in studies of socialization. *Psychol. Rev.* 75:81, 1968.
6. Benedek, T. *Studies in Psychosomatic Medicine: The Psycho-Sexual Function in Women*. New York. Ronald Press Co., 1952.
7. Bibring, G. Some considerations of the psychological processes in pregnancy. *Psychoanal. Study Child,* 14:113, 1959.
8. Birch, H. Sources of order in the maternal behavior of animals. *Amer. J. Orthopsychiat.* 26:279, 1956.
9. Blau, A., Slaff, B., Easton, K., Welkowitz, J., Springarn, J., and Cohen, J. The psychogenic etiology of premature births: a preliminary report. *Psychosomat. Med.* 25:201, 1963.
10. Bowlby, J., Ainsworth, M., Boston, M., and Rosenbluth, D. The effects of mother-child separation: a follow-up study. *Brit. J. Med. Psychol.* 29:211, 1956.
11. Bowlby, J. *Attachment and Loss*. New York, Basic Books, Vol. I, 1969.
12. Brenneman, J. The infant ward. *Amer. J. Dis. Child.* 43:577, 1932.
13. Brody, S. *Patterns of Mothering*. New York, International Universities Press, 1956.
14. Budin, P. *The Nursling*. London, Caxton Publishing Co., 1907.
15. Crosse, M. *The Premature Baby*. Boston, Little, Brown, 2nd ed., 1957.
16. Deutsch, H. *The Psychology of Women: A Psychoanalytic Interpretation*. Vol II, *Motherhood*. New York, Grune & Stratton, 1945.
17. Dunham, E., and McAlleney, P., Jr. Study of 244 prematurely-born infants. *J. Pediat.* 9:717, 1936.
18. Dunham, E., and Crane, M. Standards and Recommendations for Hospital Care of Newborn Infants, Full-Term and Premature. U.S. Children's Bureau, Washington, Bureau of Publications, No. 242, 1943.
19. Elmer, E., and Gregg, G. Developmental characteristics of abused children. *Pediatrics,* 40:596, 1967.
20. Fanaroff, A. Personal communication.
21. Gleich, M. The premature infant: Parts III and IV. *Arch. Pediat.* 59:157, 1942.
22. Green, M., and Solnit, A. Reactions to the threatened loss of a child: a vulnerable child syndrome. *Pediatrics* 34:58, 1964.
23. Gyllensward, C. Anticatarrhal vaccination in homes for children under school age. *Acta Paed.* 17(Suppl.):78, 1935.

24. Harlow, H., and Harlow, M. The effect of rearing conditions on behavior. *Bull. Menninger Clin.,* 26:213, 1962.
25. Harlow, H., Harlow, M., and Hansen, E. The maternal affectional system of rhesus monkeys. In Rheingold, H., ed., *Maternal Behavior in Mammals.* New York, John Wiley and Sons, 1963.
26. Helfer, R., and Kempe, C., eds. *The Battered Child.* Chicago, University of Chicago Press, 1968.
27. Hersher, L., Richmond, J., and Moore, A. Maternal behavior in sheep and goats. In Rheingold, H., ed., *Maternal Behavior in Mammals.* New York, John Wiley and Sons, 1963.
28. Hersher, L., Richmond, J., and Moore, A. Modifiability of the critical period for the development of maternal behavior in sheep and goats. *Behaviour* 20:311, 1963.
29. Hess, J., and Lundeen, E. Premature infants, a report of 761 consecutive cases. *Penn. Med. J.* 33:429, 1930.
30. Hess, J., and Lundeen, E. *The Premature Infant: Medical and Nursing Care.* Philadelphia, J. P. Lippincott Co., 2nd ed., 1949.
31. Jackson, E., Olmstead, R., Foord, A., Thomas, H., and Hyder, K. Hospital rooming-in unit for 4 newborn infants and their mothers: Descriptive account of background, development, and procedures with few preliminary observations. *Pediatrics* 1:28, 1948.
32. Kahn, E., Wayburne, S., and Fouche, M. The Baragwanath premature baby unit—an analysis of the case records of 1,000 consecutive admissions. *South African Med. J.* 28:453, 1954.
33. Kahn, E. Pediatrics in industrialized part of Africa. *J. Pediat.* 58:277, 1961.
34. Kaplan, D., and Mason, E. Maternal reactions to premature birth viewed as an acute emotional disorder. *Amer. J. Orthopsychiat.* 30:539, 1960.
35. Kennell, J., Gordon, D., and Klaus, M. The effects of early mother-infant separation on later maternal performance. *Ped. Res.* (accepted for publication, 1970).
36. Kennell, J., Slyter, H., and Klaus, M. The mourning response of parents to the death of a newborn. *New Eng. J. Med.* 283:344, 1970.
37. Kennell, J., and Rolnick, A. Discussing problems in newborn babies with their parents. *Pediatrics* 26:832, 1960.
38. Klaus, M., Kennell, J., Plumb, N., and Zuehlke, S. Human maternal behavior at the first contact with her young. *Pediatrics* 46:187, 1970.
39. Klein, M. Personal communication.
40. Klopfer, P., Adams, D., and Klopfer, M. Maternal "imprinting" in goats. *Proc. Nat. Acad. Sci.* 52:911, 1964.
41. Leifer, A., Leiderman, P., and Barnett, C. Mother-infant separation: Effects on later maternal behavior. *Child Develop.* 1970 (in press).
42. Levy, D. *Behavioral Analysis.* Springfield, Ill., Charles C Thomas, 1958.
43. Liberal Visiting Policies for Child in Hospital. Report by Citizens' Committee on Children of New York City. *J. Pediat.* 46:710, 1955.
44. Liebling, A. Profiles: Patron of the preemies. *New Yorker Magazine,* June 3, 1939, pp. 20–24.
45. Mason, E. A method of predicting crisis outcome for mothers of premature babies. *Public Health Report* 78:1031, 1963.
46. Maternal and Child Care. Report of the Medical Exchange Mission to the U.S.S.R. Department of Health, Education and Welfare, Publication No. 954, 1960.
47. McBryde, A. Compulsory rooming-in in the ward and private newborn service at Duke Hospital, *J.A.M.A.* 145:625, 1951.

48. McKhann, C., Steiger, A., and Long, A. Hospital infections. *Amer. J. Dis. Child.* 55:579, 1938.

49. Miller, F. Home nursing of premature babies in Newcastle-on-Tyne. *Lancet* 2:703, 1948.

50. Moore, A. Effects of modified care in the sheep and goat. In Newton, G., and Levine, S., eds., *Early Experience and Behavior*. Springfield, Ill., Charles C Thomas, 1968, pp. 481–529.

51. Morris, M. Psychological miscarriage: An end to mother love. *Trans-actions*, January 1966.

52. Moss, H. Methodological issues in studying mother-infant interaction. *Amer. J. Orthopsychiat.* 35:482, 1965.

53. Moss, H. Sex, age and state as determinants of mother-infant interaction. *Merrill-Palmer Quart. Behav. Develop.* 13:19, 1967.

54. Newton, N., and Newton, M. Mothers' reactions to their newborn babies. *J.A.M.A.* 181:206, 1962.

55. Newton, N., Peeler, D., and Rawlins, C. Effects of lactation on maternal behavior in mice with comparative data on humans. Lying-In: *J. Reproduc. Med.* 1:257, 1968.

56. Parmelee, A. *Management of the Newborn*. Chicago, Yearbook Publishers, 2nd ed., 1959.

57. Rheingold, H., ed. *Maternal Behavior in Mammals*. New York, John Wiley and Sons, 1963.

58. Robson, K. The role of eye-to-eye contact in maternal-infant attachment. *J. Child Psychol. Psychiat.* 8:13, 1967.

59. Rose, J., Boggs, T., Jr., Alderstein, A., et al. The evidence for a syndrome of "Mothering Disability" consequent to threats to the survival of neonates: A design for hypothesis testing including prevention in a prospective study. *Amer. J. Dis. Child,* 100:776, 1960.

60. Rosenblatt, J., and Lehrman, D. Maternal behavior of the laboratory rat. In Rheingold, H., ed., *Maternal Behavior in Mammals*. New York, John Wiley and Sons, 1963, pp. 8–57.

61. Rubenstein, J. Maternal attentiveness and subsequent exploratory behavior in the infant. *Child Develop.* 38:1089, 1967.

62. Rubin, R. Maternal touch. *Nurs. Outlook* 11:828, 1963.

63. Shaheen, E., Alexander, D., Truskowsky, M., and Barbero, G. Failure to thrive—a retrospective profile. *Clin. Pediat.* 7:255, 1968.

64. Smith, N., Schwartz, J., Mandell, W., Silberstein, R., Dalack, G., and Sacks, S. Mothers' psychological reactions to premature and full-size newborns. *Arch. Gen. Psychiat.* 21:177, 1969.

65. Solnit, A., and Stark, M. Mourning and the birth of a defective child. *Psychoanal. Study Child.* 16:523, 1961.

66. Spiro, M. *Children of the Kibbutz*. Cambridge, Mass., Harvard University Press, 1958.

67. Spitz, R. *The First Year of Life*. New York, International Universities Press, 1965.

68. Standards and Recommendations of Hospital Care of Newborn Infants. Committee on Fetus and Newborn. W. A. Silverman, Chairman, Evanston, Illinois. Amer. Acad. Pediatrics, 1964.

69. Steele, B., and Pollock, C. A psychiatric study of parents who abuse infants and small

children. In Helfer, R., and Kempe, C., eds., *The Battered Child*. Chicago: University of Chicago Press, 1968, pp. 103–147.

70. Weston, J. The pathology of child abuse. In Helfer, R., and Kempe, C., eds., *The Battered Child*. Chicago: University of Chicago Press, 1968, pp. 77–100.

71. Wortis, H. Review of Kaplan, D., and Mason, E. Maternal reactions to premature birth viewed as an acute emotional disorder. *Amer. J. Orthopsychiat*. 30:549, 1960.

CHAPTER 20

Impaired Mother-Infant Pair Bonding in the Syndrome of Abuse Dwarfism: Possible Prenatal, Perinatal, and Neonatal Antecedents

John Money and Andrea Needleman

INTRODUCTION AND PURPOSE

Newborn primates continuously deprived of the haptic experience of clinging and hugging eventually may die. If they survive, despite the prevention of haptically pair bonding with the mother or her substitute, the deprivation leads to permanent and severe behavioral pathology. A history of defective haptic pair bonding, usually designated as maternal deprivation, is retrospectively uncovered with great frequency, and may be universal in the biographies of children who subsequently develop the syndrome of abuse dwarfism.

In recent years, a history of defective mother-infant pair bonding has been implicated in other syndromes, namely, childhood schizophrenia, and child battering. Pollack and Woerner (1966) reviewed five studies of complications of pregnancy and delivery in the histories of childhood schizophrenics and found a greater than chance prevalence. Studies of the prevalence of birth and neonatal complications (Vorster 1960; Taft and Goldfarb 1964) revealed a similar increased association with subsequent childhood schizophrenia. With reference to the battered child (child abuse) syndrome, Lynch (1975) cited abnormal pregnancy, labor, or delivery, and neonatal separation or illness as significant factors in defective mother-child bonding.

The antecedents of defective mother-child bonding in abuse dwarfism have not been systematically documented. It is possible that another sibling will become a surrogate victim if the original victim is removed from the home. Otherwise, it is rare to find more than one victim in a family. Thus, there very well may be some prenatal, perinatal, or neonatal factor in the history of the victim that interferes with proper mother-infant bonding. It is the purpose of this paper

Supported by USPHS Grant #HD00325.

to present, from a survey of eight cases, the prenatal, perinatal, or neonatal phenomena, retrospectively ascertained, that might be implicated in a history of defective mother-infant bonding in abuse dwarfism.

From 1959 to 1976, 44 children with growth retardation were given the diagnosis of reversible hyposomatotropinism in the Pediatric Endocrine Clinic and its Psychohormonal Research Unit of The Johns Hopkins Hospital. The diagnosis was confirmed when, upon an approximate two-week hospital admission for evaluation, growth hormone levels began their rise to normal values, in the absence of endocrine treatment, and the resumption of statural growth ensued.

The sampling criteria for the present study pertained to the genealogical mothers in these 44 cases as follows: they lived within commuting distance of The Johns Hopkins Hospital; and they agreed to participate in a study concerning the pregnancy and neonatal histories of children with growth problems. Eight mothers qualified. Among the 36 nonqualifiers, 5 were adoptive or foster mothers; 13 were lost to follow-up; 5 were too distant; and 3 did not respond to the invitation to participate.

Relevant background data on the eight cases of the sample are given in Table 1. Four families were white; four black. Four children were boys and four girls. Three mothers had resumed rearing their child at home, and five had not.

PROCEDURE

Pertinent information was abstracted and tabulated from each patient's consolidated obstetric (if retrievable), pediatric, and psychoendocrine record on file in the Psychohormonal Research Unit. Additional obstetrical and neonatal data were obtained in an interview tape-recorded with the mother at home, and subsequently transcribed, abstracted, and tabulated. The interview followed a schedule of topics. For each topic, the inquiry began open-ended, so as to maximize spontaneous disclosure of the personal biography, and progressed to a more direct examination.

FINDINGS

Mother's Own Childhood

Three of the eight mothers in the sample claimed that in childhood they got along satisfactorily with their parents, and five did not. Three of the five said they were raised under very unsatisfactory conditions. One of the three was raised by maternal grandparents, having been deserted by her mother. The mother of another was hypochondriacal and addicted to drugs, and the father was

Table 1. Sample description

Identification	G.B.	R.B.	M.C.	S.C.	P.M.	N.S.	D.S.	B.T.
Race and sex	black male	black female	white male	black male	black female	white male	white female	white female
Approximate family annual income	<$5,000	$5,000-$10,000	$20,000-$30,000	<$5,000	<$5,000	<$5,000	$5,000-$10,000	$5,000-$10,000
Mother's age at patient's birth	22 yr.	19 yr.	32 yr.	24 yr.	20 yr.	22 yr.	19 yr.	23 yr.
Patient's date of birth	1.09.64	12.02.68	1.23.56	2.14.65	7.18.69	9.30.58	6.05.67	12.21.63
Patient's gestation	9 mo.	9 mo.	8 mo.	8 mo.	7 mo.	7 mo.	9 mo.	9 mo.
Patient's birth weight	2.0 kg.	2.8 kg.	2.3 kg.	1.4 kg.	1.4 kg.	1.4 kg.	3.4 kg.	4.1 kg.
Patient's birth length	?	49.5 cm.	48.3 cm.	?	41.9 cm.	48.3 cm.	47.0 cm.	48.3 cm.
Employment during pregnancy	no	until 5 mo.	no	no	no	no	no	no
Father's age at patient's birth	abandoned family	25 yr.	33 yr.	28 yr.	29 yr.	28 yr.	24 yr.	21 yr.
Marital status at patient's birth	single	married	married	single	single	married	single	married
Patient's birth order*	2	5	3	4	2	2	2	3
Reproductive loss prior to patient's birth	0	1	2	1	0	1	0	1

*Includes only live births.

tempestuous. The mother of the third was domineering and the father docile. In each of the eight cases, the mother recognized similarities between her treatment as a child and the treatment she gave her dwarfed child. The mother herself was not dwarfed, nor was the father.

Mother's Health during Pregnancy with Patient

As can be seen in Table 2, six of the eight mothers reported vaginal bleeding during their pregnancies with the patients. Six of the eight women also reported moderate to severe morning sickness. One of the two mothers who reported no morning sickness complained of a feeling of extreme lassitude during the pregnancy. The other experienced sharp stomach pains during the second month of gestation.

The one woman who was taking dilantin and phenobarbital for epilepsy did not do so regularly and had seizures during the pregnancy. Heavy dosages of progesterone were prescribed to the woman who had a history of several reproductive losses and extensive vaginal bleeding.

Mother's Psychological Response to Pregnancy with Patient

Two of the four unwed mothers in the sample stated that they felt calm when the pregnancy was confirmed. One unmarried mother was upset when the pregnancy was confirmed, but decided in her fourth or fifth month of gestation that "it would be okay to have the baby." She claimed to have been "doing crazy things" at the time of the pregnancy, including having suicidal thoughts. The fourth unmarried mother took the attitude of "what had to be, had to be." Two of the four married women described also a laissez faire reaction to the confirmed pregnancy. One married mother was apprehensive, owing to her previous history of reproductive losses. The fourth married mother was glad to be pregnant, although she was interested in remaining employed at her job.

Four mothers indicated that stressful events were apparent during their pregnancies with the patients. Two of these mothers were unwed and were subject to parental criticism; the third was unhappily married, and the fourth was separated from her husband for five days of each week because he was newly employed a considerable distance from his family. Her husband's commuting ended when their newly built house became habitable, at which time the baby was three weeks of age.

Four mothers claimed that they were not worried during their pregnancies with the patients. Two of the four worried mothers were concerned about finances; another about the baby's health; the fourth about reproductive losses. In reference to anticipatory preference for a boy or girl, three mothers showed no preference. Two patients were of the same sex as their mothers' preferences; three were not.

Table 2. Mothers' health during pregnancy with patient (N=8)

	Frequency
1. Morning sickness	
None	2
Moderate (6 mo., 5 mo., 1 mo.)	3
Severe (7 mo., 4 mo., 2 mo.)	3
2. Hemorrhaging	
None	1
Vaginal bleeding in 9th month	2
Vaginal bleeding in 8th month	1
Vaginal bleeding in 3rd month	1
Vaginal bleeding in 3rd and 4th months	1
Vaginal bleeding in 3rd, 7th, and 8th months	1
Spitting up blood throughout pregnancy	1
3. Drugs	
Cigarettes	3
Vitamins	5
Iron pills	2
Alcohol	1
Cold medicine	2
Medicine for nausea	1
Dilantin and phenobarbital	1
Progesterone	1

Antenatal Preparation

The initial medical visit for antenatal care was at one month's gestation for three of the mothers, at two months' gestation for two others, and in the fifth or sixth month for the remaining three. Only one mother read books on parturition and child care. None participated in a preparatory natural childbirth program.

Six of the mother's planned antenatally not to breast feed: one questioned her ability to breast feed because of the smallness of her breasts; one expected to resume working (but did not until the baby was two years old); two claimed modesty, supported by rationalizations such as not "running home to breast feed a baby," or not being able to "sit still long enough"; and two who had had sore nipples from breast feeding a former child wanted to avoid a repetition of the soreness. The two women who were not antenatally averse to breast feeding said they were advised against it by their doctors. Thus, all eight of the babies were bottle fed.

Labor and Delivery of Patient

Table 3 summarizes the data on labor pain. Four mothers felt that during the stages of labor, pain distracted them from entertaining thoughts about their babies. The one woman who delivered her child "ten minutes" after her seven-month check-up stated that she did not have the time to think about the baby during labor. The remaining three mothers were worried about their infants while they were in labor. One woman was concerned about her infant's premature status; she did not know what to anticipate. Another was afraid that the large clot she passed was a part of the baby; and the third feared her baby's suffocation because the placenta was presenting itself before the infant.

As can be seen in Table 3, five of the mothers experienced operative or instrumental deliveries; three deliveries were spontaneous. The majority of babies presented head first; two of these presentations were the first-born of a pair of twins. One Caesarian section was performed due to placenta previa; the other because of a previous history of Caesarian sectioning. None of the deliveries was unmedicated. Six women were medicated with both an analgesic and anesthetic. An analgesic alone was administered to one mother; anesthetic alone to another.

In no instance did the mother have the baby's father or other family member or friend accompany her beyond the hospital reception room to the labor or delivery room.

The two mothers who delivered by Caesarian section recognized the necessity of such a delivery, but preferred nonoperative delivery. One of these mothers

Table 3. Labor and delivery of baby (N=8)

	Frequency
1. Intensity of pain	
None	1
Moderate (7 hr., 5 hr., 4 hr., 3 hr.)	4
Severe (5 hr., 4½ hr., 2 hr.)	3
2. Nonmedical persons present	
None	7
Mother	1
3. Type of delivery	
Vaginal	3
Caesarian section	2
Forceps	3
4. Presentation	
Nonoperative	
Vertex	5
Breech	1
Operative (Caesarian section)	2
5. Medication	
None	0
Analgesia	7
Anesthesia	
General	6
Local	1

had experienced four normal deliveries, three at home and one in a hospital, prior to the Caesarian section. She spoke of having had the baby "taken from her" in an unnatural way that somehow stigmatized the baby.

The one woman who watched her vaginal delivery in a mirror thought it interesting but "gross"; at the time of the infant's birth she was concerned about the afterbirth. The remaining five mothers elected not to watch their deliveries. Of the five, two wondered about their infants' appearance; two characterized pain as primary in their thoughts at the time of delivery. The fifth mother who elected not to watch her delivery stated that she was concentrating on delivering the second infant of a set of twins. She claimed that she would have preferred being asleep and "wouldn't want to go through any more deliveries like that," and that after the birth of the first twin, "a nurse of 250 pounds lay across her in order to move the second twin to a lower position." She thought her back was breaking from the nurse's weight and wondered what was wrong with her premature twins.

Two of the eight mothers recalled adverse reactions to the medication. One woman complained of nausea; the second gave an elaborate account of her poor reaction to nitrous oxide. She described her reaction as follows: "It's like one word going over and over in your head rhyming . . . faster and faster. Then, everything goes real tight and it jerks you right out. I come out of it real hard." She also complained of bad dreams associated with inhaling the gas. After the baby's birth, she was given a second inhalation so that the obstetrician could investigate excessive vaginal bleeding.

Postpartum (0–3 Months) Data

Table 4 indicates that only four of the babies were seen by their mothers immediately, at birth. Three of these four mothers held their babies. The fourth had visual contact only, as the baby was immediately put in an incubator, and she did not hold it until one month later. Of the three mothers who had tactual contact with their babies immediately after delivery, only one expressed a feeling of joy associated with holding her newborn. The second woman felt it disgusting to hold her slimy, bloody baby. The third woman's newborn was placed on her abdomen; she felt too weak to try to hold it.

Four mothers did not have the opportunity to see their newly born babies. Each of these four mothers was anxious about her infant's smallness when initial contact was made. For three of the four women, initial holding and first sight of the infant coincided. One mother first saw her infant when it was one day old, but first held it when it was two months old. There were three instances of lengthy postpartum separations (Table 4). Six mothers manifested complications in their postpartum recovery.

Stress was especially evident in the postpartum stage of the two mothers who delivered twins. One mother claimed that after the delivery a nun told her not to get her hopes up because neither of the twins would live. In fact, the co-twin died

Table 4. Postpartum (0–3 months) data (N=8)

	Frequency
1. Patient's age when first seen by mother	
Newborn	4
One day old	2
Three days old	1
Two months old	1
2. Infant's discharge from hospital to home	
Coincident with mother's discharge	5
One month after mother's discharge	1
Two months after mother's discharge	1
Three months after mother's discharge	1
3. Complications in recovery from delivery	
Postdelivery blues (3 mo., 2 mo., 1½ mo., 2 days)	4
Heavy hemorrhaging (4 days)	1
Fever (1 week)	1
None	2

of cystic fibrosis three days later. Two days later still, the mother's younger retarded sister, whom she had virtually reared as an alter ego, unaccountably died. The mother became convinced that her surviving baby had the peculiar smell of cystic fibrosis, which the deceased baby had had, and would, therefore, develop the disease and die.

The co-twin born to the other mother of twins was released from the hospital at 2½ months of age; the index twin was discharged at 1 month of age. At 3 months of age, the co-twin died a crib death. The mother stated that she hated children when her infant died. Neighbors told her that the first twin would also die. She was afraid to be near the patient and adopted the belief that this first-born twin would also die unless the "safe" age of 6 years was reached.

In all eight cases, the mothers recalled retrospectively that they did not experience the desire to have another baby while the one under discussion was still an infant.

Mother-Infant Communication (3–6 Months)

Six of the eight mothers stated that their babies did not cry excessively during the first six months of life. Both mothers whose babies cried excessively expressed resentment toward them. Each mother claimed that her baby's feeding and sleeping schedules were self-regulated.

Seven of the eight mothers described a gap in or impairment of their relationships with their babies. The two mothers of twins disliked handling the index case as a baby, felt aversive to developing strong mother-infant ties, and feared the infant's death. The two mothers whose infants cried excessively found it difficult to relate to them. A fifth mother felt uncomfortable relating to a very slight, slowly-developing infant. The sixth woman, an epileptic, did not trust herself to be alone with her infant; she relinquished most of her maternal responsibilities to her mother. The seventh mother indicated that she felt close to her infant, but felt it wasn't close to her.

All mothers assumed the philosophy of "spare the rod and spoil the child." In addition, they limited the attention given the infants to avoid spoiling them.

Mother's Speculations about Source of Patient's Growth Failure

Two mothers attributed the child's growth failure to genetic constitution. Two hadn't any ideas about its cause. Two others felt that the distant nature of their relationships with the baby caused the growth failure. One mother postulated that her childbirth experience affected her interaction with, and the ensuing growth failure of, the baby. The remaining mother believed that an aspirin overdose caused her child's stunted growth.

Three women hadn't any advice for future mothers of children with growth failure. The advice of three mothers was for women to seek counseling in order to understand their feelings about their children. The remaining two mothers proposed the bestowal of maternal love and affection, regardless of one's fears, in order to preclude growth failure in future children.

DISCUSSION

It is pathognomonic in child abuse and neglect that it is extremely difficult and time-consuming to establish a relationship of trust and confidentiality with the parents: they are wary about incriminating themselves. In addition, the syndrome of abuse dwarfism is infrequently diagnosed, even though its prevalence may be much greater than ascertained cases would indicate. Until fifteen years ago, the very existence of the syndrome passed unnoticed, partly because it was mistakenly diagnosed, and partly because many cases are not brought to medical attention. Thus it is an achievement to have obtained as many as eight cases for the present study, even though by ordinary statistical standards eight is too small a sample, except for a pilot study which this, in fact, is.

A pilot study serves to indicate whether a hypothesis is worth pursuing further. The present evidence does indeed indicate that there may be some antecedent associated with the pregnancy, delivery, or, more especially, the neonatorum that interferes with effective mother-infant pair bonding which, in turn, facilitates maternal neglect and abuse of the child. There is no consistent antecedent that applies to all cases, however. Nor is there evidence of any particular antecedents that might be uniquely associated with the future development of abuse dwarfism in the baby. Thus in order to find antecedents to the mother's abuse and neglect of her baby, it is likely that one will have to look rather to the personal meaning she ascribes to the events and adversities of pregnancy, delivery, and the neonatorum, rather than to the meaning ascribed to them by others. The meaning ascribed by the mother may be in some way derived from her own childhood history, including her childhood conceptions and fantasies of pregnancy, delivery, and the mother-infant pair.

It may transpire that mothers of abused dwarfs are, as a group, in some way distinguishable from other comparison groups, such as mothers of babies with idiopathic hypopituitary dwarfism, mothers of nondwarfed abused or neglected children, mothers who deliver with their husbands trained to help as labor coaches in prepared childbirth, and so on. It will be valuable to have such comparison studies, if they can be financed. In addition, one needs normative data on a suitably large random sample concerning various antecedents and postcedents of impaired mother-infant bonding.

Pregnancy and delivery are not essential antecedents of the abuse and neglect associated with abuse dwarfism, for in some cases the baby is not reared by the mother of birth. Logically, the father may be implicated as the instigator of abuse and neglect. In cases of abuse dwarfism, the small amount of evidence presently available points to the mother as the primary agent, with the father subordinate, aquiescent, and collusional. He adopts his wife's self-righteous justifications of abuse and neglect in what amounts literally to *folie à deux* (Money and Werlwas, 1976).

SUMMARY

In abuse dwarfism the pathological mother-child pair bond characterized by abuse and neglect of the child is already manifested in early infancy. The findings in eight cases are compatible with the hypothesis that there may be even earlier antecedents associated with anomalies and adversities of pregnancy, delivery, and especially the neonatorum, according to the evidence of this study. Such antecedents are not syndrome-specific, nor are they consistently present, alone or in combination. Insofar as they are etiologically significant, it is presumably by reason of the meaning personally ascribed to them, notably by the mother rather than the father, whose role in child abuse and neglect in this syndrome appears to be one of collusion with his wife.

REFERENCES

Barbero, G. J., and Shaheen, E. "Environmental failure to thrive: A clinical view." *Journal of Pediatrics* 71(1967):639.
Graham, G. G., Cordano, A., Blizzard, R. M., and Cheek, D. B. "Infantile malnutrition: Changes in body composition during rehabilitation." *Pediatric Research* 3(1969):579.

Hadden, D. R. "Glucose, free fatty acid, and insulin interrelations in kwashiorkor and marasmus." *Lancet* 2(1967):589.

Harlow, H. F. "The Development of Affectional Patterns in Infant Monkeys." In *Determinants of Infant Behavior*, B. M. Foss, ed. London: Methuen, 1961.

――――. "Early Social Deprivation and Later Behavior in the Monkey." In *Unfinished Tasks in the Behavioral Sciences*, A. Abrams, H. Garner, and J. Toman, eds. Baltimore: Williams and Wilkins, 1964.

Harlow, H. F., and Suomi, S. J. "Induced psychopathology in monkeys." *Engineering and Science* 33(1970):8.

Kerr, G. R., Chamove, A. S., and Harlow, H. F. "Environmental deprivation: Its effect on the growth of infant monkeys." *Journal of Pediatrics* 75(1969):833.

Lynch, M. A. "Ill health and child abuse." *Lancet* 2(1975):127.

Marks, V., Howorth, N., and Greenwood, F. C. "Plasma growth-hormone levels in chronic starvation in man." *Nature* 208(1965):686.

Melzack, R. "Early experience: A neuropsychological approach to heredity-environment interactions." In *Early Experience and Behavior*, C. Newton and S. Levine, eds. Springfield, Ill.: Thomas, 1968.

Miller, R. E., Mirsky, I. A., Caul, W. F., and Sakata, T. "Hyperphagia and polydipsia in socially isolated rhesus monkeys." *Science* 165(1969):1027.

Money, J. "The syndrome of abuse dwarfism (psychosocial dwarfism or reversible hyposomatotropinism): Behavioral data and case report." *American Journal of Diseases of Children* 131(1977):508.

Money, J., Annecillo, C., and Werlwas, J. "Hormonal and Behavioral Reversals in Hyposomatotropic Dwarfism." In *Hormones, Behavior, and Psychopathology*, E. J. Sachar, ed. New York: Raven Press, 1976.

Money, J., and Werlwas, J. "*Folie à deux* in the parents of psychosocial dwarfs: Two cases." *Bulletin of the American Academy of Psychiatry and the Law* 4(1976):351.

Money, J., and Wolff, G. "Late puberty, retarded growth and reversible hyposomatotropinism (psychosocial dwarfism)." *Adolescence* 9(1974):121.

Money, J., Wolff, G., and Annecillo, C. "Pain agnosia and self-injury in the syndrome of reversible somatotropin deficiency (psychosocial dwarfism)." *Journal of Autism and Childhood Schizophrenia* 2(1972):127.

Patton, R. G., and Gardner, L. I. "Influence of family environment on growth: The syndrome of 'maternal deprivation.'" *Pediatrics* 30(1962):957.

――――. *Growth Failure in Maternal Deprivation*. Springfield, Ill.: Thomas, 1963.

――――. "Short Stature Associated with Maternal Deprivation Syndrome: Disordered Family Environment as Cause of So-called Idiopathic Hypopituitarism." In *Endocrine and Genetic Diseases of Childhood*, L. I. Gardner, ed. Philadelphia: Saunders, 1969.

Pimstone, B. L., Wittmann, W., Hansen, J. D. L., and Murray, P. "Growth hormone and kwashiorkor. Role of protein in growth-hormone homeostasis." *Lancet* 2(1966):779.

Pollack, M., and Woerner, M. "Pre- and perinatal complications and 'childhood schizophrenia': A comparison of five controlled studies." *Journal of Child Psychology and Psychiatry* 7(1966):235.

Powell, G. F., Brasel, J. A., and Blizzard, R. M. "Emotional deprivation and growth retardation simulating idiopathic hypopituitarism. I. Clinical evaluation of the syndrome." *New England Journal of Medicine* 276(1967a):1271.

Powell, G. F., Brasel, J. A., Raiti, S., and Blizzard, R. M. "Emotional deprivation and growth retardation simulating idiopathic hypopituitarism. II. Endocrinologic evaluation of the syndrome." *New England Journal of Medicine* 276(1967b):1279.

Reinhart, J. B., and Drash, A. L. "Psychosocial dwarfism: Environmentally induced recovery." *Psychosomatic Medicine* 31(1969):165.

Silver, H. K., and Finkelstein, M. "Deprivation dwarfism." *Journal of Pediatrics* 70(1967):317.

Taft, L., and Goldfarb, W. "Prenatal and perinatal factors in childhood schizophrenia." *Developmental Medicine and Child Neurology* 6(1964):32.

Thompson, W. R., and Melzack, R. "Early environment: How do environmental influences at the beginning of life shape the behavior of an animal?" *Scientific American* 194(1956):38.

Vorster, D. "An investigation of the part played by organic factors in childhood schizophrenia." *Journal of Mental Science* 106(1960):494.

Whitten, C. F., Pettit, M. G., and Fischhoff, J. "Evidence that growth failure from maternal deprivation is secondary to undereating." *Journal of American Medical Association* 209(1969):1675.

Wolff, G., and Money, J. "Relationship between sleep and growth in patients with reversible somatotropin deficiency (psychosocial dwarfism)." *Psychological Medicine* 3(1973):18.

CHAPTER 21

Identification of Infants at Risk for Child Abuse: Observations and Inferences in the Examination of the Mother-Infant Dyad

Charles Schwarzbeck III

Because of the growing realization of the high frequency of reports of infant abuse, many clinicians and researchers have focused their efforts on earlier screening and detection of abused children. In 1973, Task Forces IV and V of the Committee on Clinical Issues by the Joint Commission on Mental Health of Children stated that identification of "... personality and family relationship problems which are predictive of child battering need to be pursued actively to increase the possibility of intervening *before* the first battering even occurs" (p. 275). This paper outlines considerations that might predispose the *mother-infant dyad*—not the infant *or* the parent—to frustrating experiences for the mother and subsequently abusing practices. Not only is the quality of the abusing mother's relationship with her baby usually observed and described as "inconsistent," "unpredictable," and "unsmooth," but it is also likely that these qualities may have a causative influence. This paper attempts to answer the challenge of the 1973 Joint Commission by describing subtle interrelationships between constitutionally determined bases of behavior and the mother's and baby's capacities to achieve a synchronous relationship.

Efforts directed at predicting early child-abusing patterns have been varied. Helfer and Kempe (1) attempted to predict abuse measuring mothers' claiming—disclaiming behaviors in the delivery room. Walworth and Metz (2) used a Pediatric Multiphasic Examination that considered both parental dissatisfactions with the child's behavior and the child's family background in predicting parental mistreatment. Others (e.g., Fillipi and Rousey) (3) have delineated disposition to violence, possibly itself a developmental deviation, as a primary predictor of abusing patterns. Yet, what about the mother who "claims" and loves her neonate very much, but subsequently abuses it? What about infants who are very much wanted and have identical familial and socioeconomic

A more comprehensive form of this paper was presented at the conference "Child Abuse: Where do we go from here?" March 1977, Children's Hospital National Medical Center, Washington, D.C., and at the Hospital for Sick Children, Toronto, Canada, April 1977.

backgrounds—why does one become an abused infant and another does not? The 1973 Task Forces indicated that the battered child is often from large families with children closely spaced in age; why is it that often only one of several children born to a mother becomes an abused infant? I believe that one area that may provide answers to these questions is the examination of the *process* of the mother-infant interaction. Many of the vital clues to disturbances in the relationship between mother and child are apparent first in the course of observing them together. At these times the mother's anguish about misinterpretation of, or lack of responsiveness to, her baby's communication is vividly realized. In many cases, the investigator may have to throw away his plan to find what is deviant about the parent (and how he/she could be a better one), and instead investigate deviances in the interaction process. In some instances, a diagnostic study might consider what the infant is doing to prevent a "good" relationship with its mother!

It is not infrequent that mothers who are suspected of giving less than good care to their babies report that their child is rejecting them, or that it makes them feel stupid and inadequate. These complaints may be understood within the context of the failure of the infant to successfully cue its mother and/or the failure of the mother and infant to cyclically maintain brief (five to ten second) but intense interactions, in which they both experience characteristic rises, peakings, and falls in arousal levels. Additionally, a stimulus-response model must be rejected, because the inclusion of an organismic state in the observation-inference process makes any evaluation of the dyadic relationship a complicated process. Thus, we may often understand a well-meaning mother's complaints or behavior within the context of the interaction process, that is, *the quality of synchrony of arousal clusters within the framework of the organismic state*.

The observational and inferential components mentioned in this paper were empirically studied (4) and directly derived from split-screen observation techniques developed by Stern (5), Brazelton, et al. (6), and Tronick and Brazelton (7). Split-screen films with superimposed time displays have allowed investigators to simultaneously view the mother and infant, and examination inferences and techniques have been pursued later and less systematically once the "split-screen mental set" had been established. (It must be emphasized that an appreciation of this split-screen observation of affect and attention is usually required before salient aspects of the interactional system can be realized and applied by the examiner.)

With this methodological basis, the following considerations may be integrated into the examiner's observation and inference procedures. The factors below are not inclusive in any sense, nor are they in themselves diagnostic of clinical syndromes or predictive of infant abuse. Alternatively, various constellations of these factors may predispose the mother-infant *interaction* to more complexities than is usually the case in achieving mutual and synchronous interchanges. Given this possibility, the mother may experience distancing from a lack of communication with, and increasing frustration toward, her baby, as she concludes that failure to achieve rhythmical, smooth interaction is an indication of her inadequacy as a mother. (In the following paragraphs, however, it will be realized that many characteristics of the infant, rather than the mother, may dictate the quality of the mother's interchanges with her baby.)

CONSTITUTIONAL FACTORS

In my opinion constitutional factors unique for each infant lay the groundwork for the quality of that child's input into the reciprocal relationship. Evaluations of organismic state characteristics, motoric postures and levels of activity, alertness, capacity to receive and respond to cues, and habituation capabilities are repeated several times during a twenty to thirty minute period, as the examiner begins to consider the possibility of difficulty in achieving dyadic synchrony. Higher organizational functioning is more systematically studied using the Brazelton Neonatal Assessment Scale.

Examples of constitutionally determined developmental delays that may precede or parallel strained dyadic interactions are:

2-6 days: abnormal reflexes such as suck, Moro or pale dyanotic (score=1: Brazelton N.A.S.) skin color characteristics;

2-6 days: failure to habituate to light, sound, and pinprick stimuli after seven or more trials;

1-5 weeks: hypersensitivity to touch (discomfort with physical closeness) and noises (including human voices);

5-10 weeks: inability to sustain attention.

TEMPERAMENT

The infant's basic temperament, a constitutional factor that must be considered in its own right, and its state of consciousness, as it dictates and modifies the dyadic interaction, is the foundation of the behavioral system. (This factor is more comprehensively described in my earlier paper (4) and in the brilliant work of Thomas and Chess) (8). The infant's behavioral inputs are never to be considered direct responses to stimuli, but instead they are in many ways a function of the particular organismic state. The nature of initiation of the behavior *and* the quality and efficiency of the capacity to control reactions and shut down responsiveness to adverse or distracting stimuli are understood within the context of the infant's use of its ongoing organismic state. The organismic state characteristic lays the groundwork for the infant's over-all self-organizing capabilities.

The infant is also viewed relative to other infants whom the mother has come in contact with and relative to the mother's basic disposition. Infants may be relatively overactive vs. passive, or easily irritable vs. placid. Additionally, when either the infant or the mother are independently observed to have a depressed level of affective and/or attentional receptivity, the dyadic interaction may be considered at risk for arhythmic functioning (and not simply a slow down or withdrawal on the part of one member of the dyad).

MATCHED BEHAVIORS AND INTERACTIONAL VARIABLES

After state variables and habituation capacities have been taken into account, various dyadic considerations may be noted in determining the quality of the mother-infant process. Space limitations permit only brief descriptions of some selected factors here. It is most important to note that these are interaction characteristics not evaluative characteristics of the mother or infant. The emphasis here is on the *quality of the match* and the usefulness of some of the following factors in alerting the examiner to possible dissynchronics in the match.

EYE CONTACT

The visual-motor system is the young infant's main voluntary control mechanism in modulating the input of arousing stimuli in the first few months of life. Particularly important are the infant's and mother's gazes (used to initiate interactions and to accelerate arousal intensities) and gaze aversions (used to terminate interaction sequences and to lower arousal). Of at least equal importance is the fact that the signaling value of eye contact is unique for each mother-infant pair. What seems to be an identical eye contact interaction between two dyads (including a longitudinal observation of a mother with two of her infants—twins included) may in fact be quite different relative to exhibitory vs. inhibitory and initiating vs. averting mechanisms. Eye contact may be a signal to orient and to initiate a new interactive sequence, while the same eye contact interaction may cue a mother to alter her body proximity or to change the quality of her vocalizations. Many specific considerations are important, including development of the social smile, coordination of gazes with other behavioral systems, "isolated smiles," abilities on the part of the mother and infant to tolerate eye contact, and forced or intrusive contact that results in abruptly increasing arousal and stimulus overload. (Space limitations do not permit descriptions of these and other phenomena.)

What is important for the purposes of this paper is recognition of complex eye contact sequences as some times indicative of qualities of the dyadic interaction. Again, this most important interaction variable is considered within the framework of the organismic state model. Clearly, when a mother and her baby are unable to use eye contact effectively in the communication process—e.g., in reciprocally modulating arousal levels in each other—both may have frustrating experiences.

MOLDING

Molding concerns the positions of the mother's and the infant's bodies during face-to-face interactions both when they are separated and when the infant is held (usually chest-to-chest) by the mother. I have chosen to include this variable in this list of selected phenomena because it is a prime example of a truly *integrated* part of the reciprocal mother-infant interaction; it clusters specific system arousal levels as it interacts primarily with gaze and vocalization variables. By the twentieth week of life, the infant is often seen to alternately mold itself into the contour of its mother's body, stiffen, and then struggle against the contour, only to return to a contented molded posture. This phenomenon, like other matched occurrences, is dictated by state characteristics at the times of observation.

The molding variable not only serves as an integrator of other interaction behaviors, but mothers may often use it as an indicator of the quality of their interactions. In my experience, it has not been infrequent that the whole tenor of a mother's description of her baby has changed when I asked her about or observed her holding her child. Mothers' senses of their match with their babies are not intellectualized thoughts, and they often will share their own experience as well as their experience of their baby when conversations progress to "what he/she feels like when you hold him/her."

The technique that the mother employs may closely interact with the infant's state characteristics to dictate significant aspects of the developing relationship. Infants are sometimes held by their mothers in a way that avoids chest-to-chest contact. As the mother carries the infant with it's back placed against her chest, the infant is often rendered powerless to visually cue its mother. Additionally, these dyads do not take part in the facial-cuddling behavior frequently seen. This method of carrying the child thus parallels a unique quality of gaze interactions and may result in abrupt changes in arousal levels. Often these interactions seem mechanical, and the mother may describe her baby as "unpredictable" or even "cold." Thus, while this example of a holding-molding pattern is truly a characteristic of the *interaction process,* the mother may regard it as insignificant, or a sign that her baby is not interested in her, and the observer may see it as something the mother is doing wrong. Pieces of the interaction may *not* be applied as evaluative of one member of the dyad; they are instead indicators of the quality of the reciprocal relationship, and eventually they may be used to understand sequences on an affective/attentional basis.

At this point we have been able to identify several other matched behaviors that aid the examiner in beginning to understand the quality of mother-infant interchanges. Mention is made elsewhere (4) of factors including vocalizations, separations, the importance of unique interactions with fathers as well as his presence or absence. While it may be possible to identify deviant aspects within these variables, it is often the case that the "fit" is a good one, and no pathological syndrome develops. Similarly, emotional distress may be evident in the infant, even though the infant and mother are able to behave normally within individual criteria. It is with these cases that the notion of coordination of systems as the salient factor becomes even more evident. The inference principles described in this paper, considered independently, are artificial at best. All of the "parts" of the reciprocal process are obviously not known, but even if they were, the total reciprocal interaction is certainly greater than the sum of its parts.

OVERVIEW AND POSSIBLE APPLICATIONS

Mothers sometimes sense that their infant is intentionally rejecting them or that it is "making me feel like I'm doing something wrong." Caring for the child may become the unemotional execution of a mechanized schedule. We, as concerned professionals, may perceive the mother as behaving inadequately when, in fact, it may be more a case of the inability of both the infant and mother to "empathize" with each other (to use a rather inappropriate adult construct). We may understand the mother as frustrated and angry as the infant becomes actively distressed and good intentions turn into a futile effort.

While much infant mistreatment involves unwanted children, emotionally disturbed parents, or gross incompetence, I believe that there are abused infants for whom none of this is true. The well-intentioned and even experienced mother may become frustrated and unresponsive to her baby because she simply misreads her child's communications. When the relationship is characterized by asynchrony and abrupt changes in arousal levels (particularly on the part of the infant), there is an accompanying incapacity of each to detect the other's intentions: the infant is unable to coordinate its intentions with those of the mother. The partners quickly realize their inability to formulate and maintain the rules of their interaction, and the frustrating consequence may be uncontrollable deceleration and "turning-off." The mother may then sense that she is causing this, that she is inadequate, and subsequently blame her baby for making her feel "bad" and miserable.

While the process of the mother-infant interaction is clearly a complex matter, it is evident that a significant proportion of mistreated babies come into the world with constitutionally determined factors (temperament, clear-cut but clinically nonsignificant developmental delays, etc.) that may predispose them for a rather poor "fit" with their mothers. The combination of the mother's constitutional make-up, her expectations, and the organismic state characteristics of her baby can determine much of the course of the developing interaction—in many ways beyond the best intentions of the parent.

So, where do we go from here? In my opinion it is of great importance to help the distraught mother to understand that the neonate is a significant personality before delivery. The idea of the infant playing an active, even an initiating role, in the mother-infant interaction is often a particularly difficult concept for parents to grasp. Yet, such an idea may permit a sense of relief, even though there may be disappointment that much may be beyond the control of the parent.

I am not suggesting that fancy, intellectual explanations be offered to mothers. In fact, my experience has been that when mothers view split-screen films of interchanges with their babies, they are unable to verbalize what they see (and sometimes discover). Helping the parents to see that their baby has a personality of sorts and that, almost at birth, it mobilizes unique modes of signaling and playing with its mother can often be extremely helpful. (I frequently approach this matter with parents from the point of view of what the infant does that seems "fun.") We will not be able to change the mother-infant interaction, nor would we want to. With this population of mother-infant pairs potentially at risk for mistreatment, however, we may be able to understand why the mother feels deprived, possibly help her to see the *unique* and *active* role of her baby, and give the two of them a second chance at realizing an exciting and gratifying relationship.

REFERENCES

1. R. E. Helfer, and C. H. Kempe, eds. *The Battered Child*. Chicago: University of Chicago Press, 1968.
2. Walworth, J. and Metz, J. R. Unpublished presentation to The Joint Commission on Mental Health of Children, 1969.
3. Fillipi, R. and Rousey, C. L. Positive carriers of violence among children: Detection by speech deviation. *Mental Hygiene,* 55 (1971):157–161.
4. Charles Schwarzbeck, "Observations and inferences in the examination of the mother-infant dyad." Unpublished Proceedings of The Hampstead Child Therapy Clinic, 1978.
5. D. N. Stern, "A micro-analysis of mother-infant interaction." *J. American Acad. Child Psychiatry* 10 (1971):501–17.
6. T. B. Brazelton, B. Koskowski, and M. Main, "The Origins of Reciprocity: The Early Mother-Infant Interaction." In *The Effect of the Infant on Its Caretaker,* Vol. 1, M. Lewis and L. Rosenbaum, eds. New York: Wiley, 1974.
7. E. Tronick and T. B. Brazelton, personal communication, 1975.
8. A. Thomas and S. Chess, *Temperament and Development,* New York: Bruner-Mazel, 1977.

PART V

Psychobiological Responses to Parental Abuse and Neglect of Children

Abuse is not an isolated physical trauma, but a syndrome of altered and abnormal parent-child interactions that causes devastating damage to the victim—the abused child.

(Martin and Beezley, 1974, p. 76)

Editor's Introduction

Studies on the effects of child abuse and neglect began with naturalistic observations of children reared under conditions of extreme social isolation or grossly atypical early environments. As far back as the eighteenth century, Carl Linnaeus, the originator of plant and animal classification, categorized persons who had been reared away from civilization as *homo ferus,* or feral man. A detailed description of the "wild boy of Aveyron" was published by Itard in 1801. In 1832, a report on Kaspar Hauser was published in German by Feuerbach and translated into English the following year under the subtitle: *An Account of an Individual Kept in a Dungeon, Separated from All Communication with the World, from Early Childhood to About the Age of Seventeen.* One hundred and ten years later, the diary of Singh (Singh and Zingg 1942) describing the "wolf children" was published posthumously in a book that also described other known cases of persons reared in extreme isolation. This volume, which contained forewords by Gesell, Davis, and other distinguished scholars, reported the deleterious effects of early isolation on perception, motility, speech, social relationships, and other psychosocial processes.

In the forties, a number of investigators (Ribble 1943; Goldfarb 1945; Spitz 1945; Spitz and Wolf 1946; Bakwin 1949) studied children reared in institutions or otherwise deprived of maternal care. The effects of these early experiences included severe intellectual impairment, anaclitic depression, failure to thrive, and death. The consequences of institutionalization were so harmful that Bowlby, in an influential monograph published in 1951, contended that even an inadequate home in which the mother was present was better for children than an institution.

In his monograph, Bowlby referred to the usefulness of animal studies for the understanding of the effects of early experiences on the later behavior of the human infant. Research in the sixties on subhuman primates (Harlow and Harlow 1962, 1965; Harlow, Harlow, Dodsworth, and Arling 1966) was especially influential in later conceptualizations on the effects of abuse and neglect on children. Steele and Pollock (1968) referred to the observations by the Harlows on monkeys in 1962 as appearing "to show striking analogies to the phenomena seen in abusing and neglecting human parents" (p. 116).

It was not until the sixties that most of the studies specifically focusing on the effects of parental abuse of children began to be published. Initially, attention was paid primarily to the manifold physical effects of abuse, such as fractures, neurological damage, orthopedic and sensory handicaps, gastrointestinal and other medical problems. Investigations on the psychological effects of child abuse have been undertaken relatively recently, in contrast with the studies on the effects of social isolation and maternal deprivation that addressed psychological effects from their inception.

One effect of child abuse and neglect is death. More children under five years of age die from injuries and illnesses inflicted by their parents than from the combined effects of tuberculosis, whooping cough, polio, measles, diabetes, rheumatic fever, and appendicitis (Leavitt 1974). The average age at death is slightly under three years (Mitchell 1977). The reported number of deaths from child abuse and neglect is 6,000 annually, but Roberts (1974) estimates that the actual number of deaths attributable to child abuse and neglect is 50,000 a year.

The U.S. Department of Health, Education and Welfare (HEW 1976) indicates that heavy case loads, inconsistencies in criteria, and other technical factors contribute to the unreliability of statistics on death rates of abused and neglected children, which are probably greatly underreported. For example, HEW reported that the official causes of death in the following cases were listed as "undetermined" and "natural," respectively. In the first case, a five-week-old infant was found with a four-inch ring around his throat that the parents stated had been there since birth; the bassinet pillow was stained with blood. In the second case, a sixteen-months-old baby was extremely undernourished at the time of death, had been treated for anemia one month earlier, and had been treated for burns on both legs at four months of age.

Child abuse and neglect are not one-time occurrences. Abused and neglected children have been exposed to continued trauma. Abuse and neglect are pathological patterns of child rearing that have profound effects on the developmental and psychosocial processes of children. The more prolonged the maltreatment, the less likely the damaging effects will be reversible.

The first group of papers in this section deals with the manifold psychological effects of abuse and neglect on children.

One of the most ignored topics in the study of child abuse and neglect has been their effects on personality and emotional behavior. Martin, a pioneer in this area, and Rodeheffer describe in Chapter 22 the traumatic interpersonal environments to which abused children are forced to adapt and the effects on their personality development and emotional behavior. Reidy's research, reported in Chapter 23, gives empirical support to the view that violence breeds violence, for he found significantly greater hyperaggressiveness among abused children compared to nonabused and neglected children.

The authors of Chapter 24 used "natural experiments" as a basis for theorizing about the effects of grossly atypical rearing during infancy and the conditions of their possible reversibility. Freedman and Brown theorize about three sets of children: two who were studied directly after having been reared in almost total isolation by their psychotic mothers; the "wolf children" as described in published accounts; and a group of children, including Kaspar Hauser, who experienced extreme deprivation since later infancy (Chapter 6).

The authors attribute the poor progress of the first two children to the near absence of coenesthetic stimulation. Spitz (1965) used the neglected term, coenesthetic, to refer to primitive, nonlocalized, nonverbal signals such as equilibrium, vibration, tension, skin contact, rhythm, pitch, and other forms of diffuse stimulation assumed to be experienced during earliest infancy. Freedman and Brown view the "wolf children," not as deprived, but rather as having been exposed to intense though distorted coenesthetic stimulation. Their greater ego development is attributed to the presence of such stimulation during infancy. The reversibility of the effects of extreme sensory deprivation in the third group of children is attributed to their early coenesthetic stimulation prior to their experience of deprivation.

The research of Reidy, Anderegg, Tracy, and Cotler in Chapter 25 and Kent in Chapter 26 demonstrates the presence of both intellectual and psychosocial impairment in abused and neglected children. In Kent's sample, these effects were partially reversible following foster-home placement; furthermore, a trend toward lesser impairment among younger children suggests the importance of early intervention.

In Chapter 27, Applebaum reports developmental delays in cognitive, motor, social, and language areas in abused infants as young as 2 to 39 months. Inasmuch as infants with severe head trauma were excluded from the research, the early impairment appears to reflect inadequate parent-infant bonding and other deficits in parenting.

In Chapter 28, Buchanan and Oliver describe a group of children whose abuse- and neglect-induced brain damage and consequent intellectual retardation was so profound that institutionalization was required.

The next group of papers refers to the variables associated with reversibility of psychobiological impairment induced by abuse and neglect.

Chapters 29 and 30 by Koluchová describe the remarkable development of twins who suffered extreme deprivation and abuse until they were rescued at seven years of age. As in Weinberg's longitudinal study in Chapter 45, a poor prognosis would seem to have been appropriate. Yet their rather unconventional placement in the stable, nurturing home of two middle-aged sisters, in addition to special educational arrangements, resulted in significant advances in all psychobiological spheres. Follow-up when the twins were fifteen years old revealed average intelligence, as compared to severe intellectual retardation when rescued. There was also an absence of psychopathology. In commenting on Koluchová's first report, Clarke (1972) emphasized that the "results underline the inadequacy of theories stressing the over-riding importance of early experiences for later growth" (p. 106). He further states:

> The relatively late age of rescue (7 years) from 5½ years of almost unprecedentedly bad conditions, as well as the responsiveness to remediation, underlines the resilience of these children, and has a bearing on such concepts as critical periods of development. Where studies stress the permanency of the effects of early deprivation, one should examine carefully the new situation in which the child finds himself

and ask whether it continues to reinforce earlier experiences. Indeed, the pessimism with which the whole area has been surrounded may have itself contributed to a passivity in the subsequent treatment of deprived children (p. 106).

The need to revise theories of early childhood development is also suggested by the fact that the twins had been reared in an institution for the first eighteen months of life prior to the onset of the prolonged abuse and neglect.

Dennis's chapter (31) describes a group of institutionalized children who were deprived of psychological stimulation during infancy and early childhood. Those adopted after the age of two years showed irreversible intellectual impairment, in many cases as much as 50 percent for each year of deprivation. Those who were adopted before two years of age, however, overcame their early retardation and showed subsequent average intelligence.

Money and Annecillo report, in Chapter 32, that progressive IQ elevation by as much as 55 to 60 points may follow placement of psychosocial (abuse) dwarfs in a domicile away from the abusive parents. These changes were accompanied by increases in statural growth. Such studies indicate that the whole quality of life in the domicile to which abused and neglected children are transferred, rather than the separation from parents per se, is the crucial therapeutic factor.

G. J. W.

REFERENCES

Bakwin, H. "Emotional deprivation in infants." *Journal of Pediatrics* 35 (1949):512-21.
Bowlby, J. "Maternal Care and Mental Health." Monograph Series No. 3. Geneva: World Health Organization, 1951, 355-533.
Clarke, A. D. B. "Commentary on Koluchová's 'Severe deprivation in twins: A case study.'" *Journal of Psychology and Psychiatry* 13 (1972):103-106.
Goldfarb, W. "Effects of psychological deprivation in infancy and subsequent stimulation." *American Journal of Psychiatry* 102 (1945):18-33.
Harlow, H. F., and Harlow, M. K. "The effect of rearing conditions on behavior." *Bulletin of the Menninger Clinic* 26 (1962):213-24.
Harlow, H. F., and Harlow, M. K. "The Affectional Systems." In A. Schrier, H. F. Harlow, and F. Stollnitz, eds., *Behavior of Non-Human Primates,* Vol. 2, New York: Academic Press, 1965.
Harlow, H. F., Harlow, M. K., Dodsworth, R. O., and Arling, G. L. "Maternal behavior in rhesus monkeys deprived of mothering and peer associations in infancy." *Proceedings of the American Philosophical Society* 110 (1966):58-66.
Levitt, J. E. *The Battered Child.* Morristown, N.J.: General Learning Press, 1974.
Martin, H. P., and Beezley, P. "Prevention and the consequences of child abuse." *Journal of Operational Psychiatry* 6 (1974): 68-77.
Mitchell, R. G. *Child Health in the Community: A Handbook of Social and Community Paediatrics.* Edinburgh: Churchill Livingstone, 1977.
Ribble, M. *Rights of Infants: Early Psychological Needs and Their Satisfaction.* New York: Columbia University Press, 1943.

Roberts, A. R. *Childhood Deprivation*. Springfield, Ill.: Charles C Thomas, 1974.

Singh, J. A. L., and Zingg, R. M. *Wolf Children and Feral Man*. Denver: University of Denver, 1942 (reprinted by Archon Books, 1966).

Spitz, R. A. "Hospitalism: An Inquiry into the Genesis of Psychiatric Conditions in Early Childhood." In *The Psychoanalytic Study of the Child,* Vol. I: 53–74. New York: International Universities Press, 1945.

———. *The First Year of Life: A Psychoanalytic Study of Normal and Deviant Development of Object Relations*. New York: International Universities Press, 1965.

Spitz, R. A., and Wolf, L. M. "Anaclitic Depression: An Inquiry into the Genesis of Psychiatric Conditions in Early Childhood." In *The Psychoanalytic Study of the Child,* Vol. 2: 323–42. New York: International Universities Press, 1946.

Steele, B. F., and Pollock, C. B. "A Psychiatric Study of Parents Who Abuse Infants and Small Children." In R. E. Helfer and C. H. Kempe, eds., *The Battered Child,* pp. 103–47. Chicago: University of Chicago Press, 1968.

U.S. Department of Health, Education and Welfare. *Child Abuse and Neglect: The Roles and Responsibilities of Professionals,* Vol. 2. Washington, D.C.: National Center on Child Abuse and Neglect. DHEW Publ. No. (OHD) 75-30074, 1976.

von Feuerbach, P. J. *Beispiel Eines Verbrechens Am Seelenleben Des Menschen*. Ansbach: 1832.

CHAPTER 22

The Psychological Impact of Abuse on Children

Harold P. Martin and Martha A. Rodeheffer

The consequences of being assaulted by one's parents are pervasive and long term. The physical attack and injury are of significance, in and of themselves, but it is the particular environment in which the attack occurred that will determine the psychological scars that result. The impact of inflicted injury upon the development of the child must be evaluated in light of the nature of the parent-child bond. It is important to clarify that the psychic damage is not due just to the dramatic physical attack that bursts into public view at the time of a reported abuse incident. Rather, physical abuse emerges from pervasive dysfunction in the family. Physical abuse is part of a persistent pattern of parent-child interaction rather than being an isolated incident. This is corroborated by research data suggesting that at least 60% of children reported have histories of being previously abused; that over 25% of these children have siblings who were also previously abused; and that over 30% of the mothers and 40% of the fathers reported for physically attacking a child have been perpetrators of abuse in the past (1). While physical attack upon children is perhaps the most dramatic, it is still only one of many signs of the pathological interactions taking place in the family. Both the physical abuse and the home environment in which it is embedded take their toll on children. As will be pointed out below, the current methods of treatment of child abuse take their own toll on the child's psychic development as well.

EFFECTS OF TRADITIONAL TREATMENT

The distinction between the physical attack per se and the abusive child-rearing environment that spawns the attack, has become important inasmuch as many professional teams attempting to intervene in child abuse continue to focus exclusively upon the physical effects of trauma inflicted upon children. Insufficient attention is focused on the psychological consequences of such attack, on the psychological consequences of being reared in an abusive environment, and on

Reprinted with permission from the *Journal of Pediatric Psychology* 1 (1976):12–15.

the additional psychic trauma introduced for the child as a result of the reporting of the abuse.

The traditional and most common approach to intervening in serious cases of child abuse is to take the child into protective custody in order to protect him or her from further physical trauma. The only treatment offered to the child is medical care of injuries and provision of a place of physical safety. Some form of treatment is offered to the parent as a preventative measure geared to minimize the chance that physical trauma to the child will recur. Reunion of parent and child is made contingent upon the parents convincing authorities of their willingness to change their parenting behavior and to utilize therapeutic services; e.g., casework, lay therapy, public health nursing, or homemaker services, or possibly even psychotherapy. Such a treatment paradigm must be based on an assumption that the child's problems are entirely physical, caused by the physical attack which needs to be eliminated from the parenting repertory. A second assumption appears to be that if social and psychological intervention is provided for the parents, the parent-child relationship will be positively affected and that the benefits of these interventions will "spill over" to the child. In our experience, the first assumption is invalid and the second is doubtful at best.

The abused child has psychological and developmental wounds which need attention. Prescribed separation from the parents adds to the emotional problems already present in the abused child and introduces yet another complicating factor into an already tenuous parent-child relationship. For the child, the usual course of events set in motion by the reporting of abuse may be quite devastating. Consider for the moment the effect upon the young child of first being attacked and of then being suddenly separated from the parent at the very point of having incurred such extreme parental wrath toward oneself. The police may come and whisk the child away from angry, distressed parents. He may be placed in a hospital, or he may be placed in a receiving home with a new and frighteningly strange family, only to be removed a short time later and placed with a foster family. With the many delays and cumbersome legal machinery of our system, the child may remain in foster care for months or years before a final determination is reached as to parental rights. It is not unusual for the child to experience several changes in foster care homes before that final disposition is reached. Loss after loss of parental figures is suffered while the child is in the midst of legal and social storms. While in foster care, which is an inadequate environment at best (2), social agencies may severely restrict contact with the biological parents, the child's primary love objects.

The treatment procedures with the parents may result in conflict resolution and reduction of familial stress and still have little impact on the parent's feelings, perceptions, and/or behaviors toward the child. When the child is returned home, which is usually the case, the abnormal parenting behaviors may remain basically unchanged and pose psychological and possibly physical danger for the child. This is obvious from the high recidivism rate reflected in the re-abuse of young children.

As alarming data regarding developmental delays and emotional-social dis-

turbance become increasingly available on abused children who have continued
to be raised in abusive environments (3), it becomes imperative that our approaches to treating abusive families be reassessed in terms of how to best meet
the problems and needs of the abused child. The following exploration of the
psychological and developmental sequellae of abuse and of living in an abusive
environment seems timely.

EFFECTS OF INFLICTED PHYSICAL TRAUMA

Before turning to the abusive environment, a few comments concerning the
impact of physical assault per se are in order. Physical abuse may result in a
number of biological consequences, including death, brain damage, mental retardation, cerebral palsy, learning disorders and sensory deficits. The neurological handicaps of physical abuse are of particular interest because of their chronicity and significance to the long range functioning of the individual. It is estimated
that between 25 and 30% of abused children who survive the attack have brain
damage or neurological dysfunction resulting directly from physical trauma
about the head (4).

All too often the psychological effects of the physical assault and the
psychological overlay of the resultant brain damage are overlooked. A physical
assault from the very person to whom the child looks for love, nurturance, and
protection is in and of itself a psychic trauma of major proportions. Parental
attack results in interpersonal ambivalence and a hypervigilant preoccupation
with the behavior of others. The child's constant mobilization of his defenses in
anticipation of impending danger is reinforced by intermittent sudden attacks by
the parent.

There are psychological consequences to brain damage which occur even
when the damage to the central nervous system is attributable to causes other than
parental infliction of injury (5). The inability to adequately perceive and act on
the environment in pursuit of mastery, the inability to keep up with peers, and the
inability to meet expectations of those around him creates much frustration.
Given the lack of opportunity for even normal childhood dependency in the
home, the abused child with brain damage may be poorly defended against
psychological stress. The brain-damaged child may be in particularly grave risk
of re-abuse due to the inability to meet parental expectations so crucially related
to abuse.

EFFECTS OF THE ABUSIVE ENVIRONMENT

Apart from the mortality and medical consequences of abuse and the abusive-
neglectful environment, there are serious psychological consequences of being
reared in an abusive environment. It has been noted that the abuse of a child is

only one of many signs of an inadequate and distorted parent-child relationship. In the majority of instances, the environment of the abusive home also contains some elements of deprivation, neglect, psychological disturbance in parents, sexual abuse, undernutrition, or other forms of unstable family function. Any one of these is known to have a deleterious effect on the child's development. A review of the literature on each of these malevolent factors as it applies to abused children is available to the reader (6).

There is a remarkable paucity of research into the psychological effects of the abusive environment. The authors and their colleagues have recently documented a number of specific behaviors and personality characteristics of abused children (7). In the present discussion, we have chosen to highlight three important aspects of the abusive environment which impact upon the child and give rise to many of his psychological problems.

Abused Children Must Adapt to a Dangerous and Hostile Environment

The child is in a family where verbal and physical aggression, hostility, and disparagement are frequently but unpredictably directed toward him. Rarely is physical abuse to the child an isolated incident in which an otherwise normal parent experiences sudden loss of impulse control. Rather, the attacks are reflections of a pattern of child rearing that makes extensive use of physical threat and force toward children for management and disciplinary purposes. The child must somehow adapt to this dangerous and often unpredictable world. There are a number of ways in which he may enhance his survival by accommodating his behavior to the needs of the aggressors in his environment. The abused child constantly checks out the safety of his moment-by-moment existence. He may develop extremely precocious skills in initiating social contact with adults. There is, however, a quality of defensiveness about his social contacts that precludes real empathy and enjoyment of social intercourse. The abused child is basically an asocial, lonely, joyless being.

A common form of this survival adaptation is hypervigilance. In an attempt to stay out of harm's way the child becomes a "watcher," an observer acutely sensitive to adults and to any sudden change in the environment that is inexplicable to him. This behavior is particularly noticeable in situations such as during developmental testing. The child appears stressed by the close observation of the examiner and frequently announces what he is going to do before acting so as to "test the waters" of the unknown adult. Noises outside the room or sudden movements of the examiner (such as picking up a pencil to score a test item) draw the child's attention and interfere with play or test performance. This hypersensitivity extends to remarkable acuity for perceiving the mood of adults in his surroundings. Slight changes in facial composure are noted and often commented on by the child.

The abused child develops a rather "chameleon nature," learning to change and shift his own behavior in accordance to nuances of the erratic and inconsistent interpersonal environment in which he lives. This reactive life stance has many ramifications for the developing personality.

Another form of this adaptation to the abusive nature of the environment is a restriction of various autonomous ego functions, a defense mechanism first described in the classic work of Anna Freud (8). To try a task and fail may be more dangerous than not to try at all. To be silent may be safer than talking and exposing oneself to ridicule or punishment for saying the wrong thing. To inhibit one's activity may avoid the adult antagonism that is elicited by moving freely about and exploring the environment. Inhibition, denial of one's own drives and impulses, and withdrawal and avoidance are defensive maneuvers that have an adaptive function when living in a physically abusive family.

The abused child attempts to maintain some self-integrity without openly challenging the authority of adult caretakers. Seldom does the young abused child make a direct verbal refusal to perform as requested by the parent. The normal phase of two-year-old oppositional independence and practicing of saying, "no" are ominously absent in children who have been physically abused. This is not to say that the child does what is requested, but only that he does not blatantly elicit abuse by being openly oppositional. The abused child becomes an expert at passive resistance, of appearing to do without doing. He makes cooperative gestures and noises, even saying "yes" and stating that he is doing what is requested while he is doing quite the opposite. Here we see the beginnings of denial and distortion of his own behaviors. He often feigns incompetence or lack of understanding.

The Abused Child Lives in an Environment Where Love and Nurturance Are Not Readily Available

The abused child is valued or appreciated only when he is meeting the expectations of the parent. This may be when the child is obeying; when the child is staying out of the way; when the child is taking care of the adult, etc. The child is not seen or valued as a person with rights, feelings, drives, and interests of his own. He is an extension of the parents. He is truly a need-satisfying object for the parent. The child must learn to exist in this atmosphere. The implications of this dynamic between parent and child are apparent in the abused child's problems with development of object relations, a sense of self, autonomy, initiative, and superego structures.

One of the most frequent adaptations to this aspect of the abusive environment is seen in the child with precocious islands of ego development as first described by Malone (9). The abused child is often seen to be taking care of his parents, physically and emotionally. The preschool child may do the family wash, fix breakfast, baby-sit an infant sibling. More striking is the emotional support of the parent, a behavior described by Morris and Gould (10) as a role-reversal which occurs between the abused child and the parent. These behaviors not only keep the child safe from verbal or physical attack, but are also ways by which the child has learned to obtain attention and approval from his parents.

This dynamic is frequently more complex and convoluted. The abusive parent who needs a scapegoat for expression of his or her own unacceptable impulses will encourage and reinforce behavior in the child which is then alternately and erratically punished and denigrated. This is a very schizophrenogenic world for the child to negotiate. The child may play out the "misbehavior" and alternately receive punishment and/or approval. The abused child may cope with the chaos of such a situation by withdrawal or oppositional provocativeness or rage.

Clearly the child in such a family has little sense of self as he only exists to meet the needs and expectations of the parent. He can have little self-respect. Even if adequately cared for, he is truly a deprived child. He grows up without experiencing his parents' joy and delight in his own autonomous behavior.

Developmental Delays, Distortions, and Arrests Are the *Sine Qua Non* of the Abused Child

We have spoken of the restrictions of autonomous ego functions as an adaptation to a dangerous punitive environment. This inhibition of autonomous functioning also results in the development of the delays seen in abused children at play, in school, and in the developmental testing situation. The abused child often appears less competent than he truly is. In a study of abused preschoolers at the National Center for Prevention of Child Abuse and Neglect in Denver, deficits in gross motor development, speech, and language were noted with striking frequency (11). Lack of experience and stimulation account for many of these delays. Restriction of the child, physically and emotionally, does not allow the abused child to explore and investigate his world even as an infant. Age-appropriate modeling and stimulation are not available to help the child master his world. The abusive parent has little patience with the child. Approximations to mastery of a task are not appreciated and reinforced but are criticized as imperfect failures.

An energy model of psychic functioning is also helpful in understanding many of the delays of the abused child. Consider the hypervigilant environmentally-cued child described earlier. He has little energy left over to spend on exploring or enjoying his world as his psychic antennae are constantly attuned to the adults about him. He is slow to get into dramatic play and easily distracted from active manipulation of play materials even when they are available to him. The child's anxieties, fears, and fantasy life preempt his attention.

A number of psychological developmental stages are also delayed or distorted. The sense of trust described by Erickson (12) can hardly be negotiated when the parent is not providing a predictable, safe, secure world for the infant. Object permanence and object constancy can hardly be accomplished satisfactorily when the parents themselves have such distortions of normal object relationships. Mahler's (13) concept of the establishment of object constancy (14) stipulates that the child learns to appreciate important people (primarily the mothering figure) in other than need-satisfying ways. The parent is valued and loved even when she is not meeting the child's needs, even when the parent is absent. The love object is no longer split into "bad mother" and "good mother" but an integration is achieved wherein the young child is able to value and love the mother whether she is being loving or disapproving. This stage requires a successful negotiation of separation-individuation, a developmental sequence which the abusive parent neither supports nor tolerates.

The process by which the gradual internalization of controls normally takes place is also disrupted for the abused child. The child is identifying with an inconsistent, disturbed adult who models aggressive behavior but restricts expression of aggression in the child. The fragility of the abused child's developing self-control is obvious in the breakdown of the extreme inhibition and sudden volatile aggressive assaults upon siblings and other children when the supervision of an adult is not readily available. It is also seen in his tendency to snatch and hoard food and possessions. These children are identifying with parents who have not learned to have friends, or to use people and activities for fun and sustenance. It is no wonder that so many abused children grow up to be abusing parents.

SUMMARY

The abused child has psychological wounds as incapacitating and chronic as his physical wounds. We have pointed out that some of the unusual behaviors of the abused child are important adaptations with survival value within the abusive environment. On the other hand, those very adaptations play an active role in the etiology of developmental delays so frequently observed in abused children. There are a number of other psychological manifestations of the abusive environment which space does not allow us to detail here. Neither have we spoken to our experiences encountered in the variety of treatment regimes for these children. We have highlighted the chameleon nature of the abused child in order to explain why his behavior in any particular setting is less validly predictive of his behavior in other settings than is the case with other children. We have alluded to the fact that his overt behavior is less accurately a reflection of his inner psychic state than with less guarded and less fearful children. This knowledge requires of the professional attempting to assess the development of the abused child, a larger sampling of behavior. It also requires a more concerted effort to elicit unconscious material from the child, for his play and fantasy life will be more guarded and less available for our clinical understanding.

The primary purpose of this paper is to promote interest in the psychological status of abused children. It is hoped that from such understanding it will be possible to consider and provide the necessary treatment for the psychological wounds of abused children.

REFERENCES

1. Gil, D. G., *Violence against Children: Physical Child Abuse in the United States,* Cambridge, Mass: Harvard University Press, 1970; and, Glazier, A. E., *Child Abuse: A Community Challenge,* New York: Henry Stewart, 1971.
2. Wolins, M., *Selecting Foster Parents: The Ideal and the Reality,* New York: Columbia University Press, 1963; and, Goldstein, J., Freud, A., and Solnit, A. J., *Beyond the Best Interests of the Child,* New York: Free Press, 1973.
3. Martin, H. P., "The Child and His Development," in Kempe, C. H. and Helfer, R. E. (eds), *Helping the Battered Child and His Family,* Philadelphia: J. B. Lippincott Co., 1972, 93-114; and Martin, H. P., Beezley, P., Conway, E. F., and Kempe, C. H., "The Development of Abused Children," *Advances in Pediatrics,* 1974, 21:25-73.
4. Elmer, E., and Gregg, G. S., "Developmental Characteristics of Abused Children," *Pediatrics,* 1967, 40:596-602; Gregg, C. S., and Elmer, E., "Infant Injuries: Accident or Abuse," *Pediatrics,* 1969; 44:434-439; Martin, H. P., "The Child and His Development," in Kempe, C. H. and Helfer, R. E. (eds), *Helping the Battered Child and His Family,* Philadelphia: J. B. Lippincott Co., 1972, 93-114; and, Martin, H. P., Beezley, P., Conway, E. F., and Kempe, C. H., "The Development of Abused Children," *Advances in Pediatrics,* 1974, 21:25-73.
5. Rutter, M., et al., *A Neuropsychiatric Study in Childhood,* Philadelphia: J. B. Lippincott Co., 1970.
6. Martin, H. P., Beezley, P., Conway, E. F., and Kempe, C. H., "The Development of Abused Children," *Advances in Pediatrics,* 1974, 21:25-73.
7. Martin, H. P., (ed), *The Abused Child: A Multidisciplinary Approach to Developmental Issues and Treatment,* Boston: Ballinger Publications, 1976.
8. Freud, A., *The Ego and the Mechanisms of Defense,* New York: International Universities Press, 1966.
9. Malone, C. A., "Safety First: Comments on the Influence of External Danger in the Lives of Children of Disorganized Families," *American Journal of Orthopsychiatry,* January 1966, 36:6-12.
10. Morris, M. G., and Gould, R. W., "Role Reversal: A Necessary Concept in Dealing with the 'Battered Child Syndrome'," *American Journal of Orthopsychiatry,* 1963, 33:298-299.
11. Martin, H. P., (ed), *The Abused Child: A Multidisciplinary Approach to Developmental Issues and Treatment,* Boston: Ballinger Publications, Chapter VI, 1976.
12. Erikson, E. H., *Childhood and Society,* New York: Norton, 1963.
13. Mahler, M. S., Pine, F., and Bergman, A., *The Psychological Birth of the Infant: Symbiosis and Individuation,* New York: Basic Books, 1975.
14. Fraiberg, S., "Libinal Object Constancy and Mental Representation," *Psychoanalysis St. Child,* 1969, 24:9-47; and, Burgner, M., and Edgcumbe, P., "Some Problems in the Conceptualization of Early Object Relationships, Part II: The Concept of Object Constancy," *Psychoanal. St. Child,* 1972, 27:315-333.

CHAPTER 23

The Aggressive Characteristics
of Abused and Neglected Children

Thomas J. Reidy

ABSTRACT

Awareness of child abuse as a serious social problem has risen sharply in recent years, yet there has been only limited and inadequate research on the abused child's growth and development. This study investigated the aggressive characteristics of young abused children with those of nonabused, neglected, and normal children, a comparison not previously made. Results indicated that abused children exhibited significantly more aggression than the nonabused, neglected, and normal children on TAT stories and in a free play environment. Both the abused and nonabused neglected groups demonstrated significantly more aggression in a school setting than normals. The findings lend empirical verification to previous descriptions of abused children as overly aggressive and support the social learning formulation that children exposed to aggressive parental models will demonstrate aggressive characteristics outside the home. The data are also consistent with prior research linking physical punishment in the home with hyperaggressiveness in children. The need for early identification and treatment of abused children is discussed.

During the past few years, child abuse has become a topic of increasing concern. Especially since the reported incidence of child abuse has risen as a result of more enlightened laws and more stringent reporting procedures, awareness of the child abuse problem has intensified. One reflection of this increased awareness is the increase in research related to this topic. As Spinetta and Rigler (1972) point out in their review, however, most of these studies focus primarily on demographic and causal factors rather than on the abused child himself. This lack of attention to the relationship between abuse and the abused child's growth and development is unfortunate, since the few observations that have been made suggest that physical abuse has serious psychological consequences. Specifically, abused children have been described as aggressive and full of hatred (Fontana 1973); uncontrollable, negativistic, and subject to severe temper tantrums (Johnson and Morse 1968); lacking in impulse control (Elmer 1967); emotionally disturbed, with behavior problems at home and at school (Morse,

Reprinted with permission from the *Journal of Clinical Psychology* 33 (1977):1140–45.

Sahler, and Friedman 1970); withdrawn and inhibited (Rolston 1971). In addition, cognitive and neurological deficits have been noted (McRae, Ferguson, and Lederman 1973; Morse et al. 1970; Martin 1972; Martin, Beezley, Conway, and Kempe 1974; Sandgrund, Gaines, and Green 1974).

The problems of the abused child apparently do not disappear with adulthood. Most disturbing is the frequent finding that abused children become abusive parents when they themselves have children (Spinetta and Rigler 1972). It seems then that abused children need help to alleviate their current problems and to prevent further problems from developing in adulthood. If intervention is to be successful, however, it needs to rest on a firm knowledge of the abused child's development. Unfortunately, the present research focusing on the abused child is difficult to interpret due to serious methodological problems, including different definitions of abuse, inadequate descriptions of subjects, uncontrolled procedures, imprecise reports of results, and lack of matched control subjects. The purpose of the present research was, therefore, to consider in an adequately controlled study one aspect of the abused child's behavior that is relevant both to his present problems and to his potential as an abusive parent: the abused child's level of aggression.

The expectation that abused children would differ from other children in their level of aggression was based on past research with nonabused, normal children, as well as on clinical observations of abused children. Past investigators of normal child development have reported a significant positive relationship between children's aggressiveness and the use of severe physical punishment in the home (Sears et al. 1957). Similarly, mothers who used physical and verbal aggression were found to have children who displayed such tactics in peer relationships (Hoffman 1960). This evidence is consistent with the social learning formulation that children can acquire aggressive behavior by observing aggressive parental models, particularly in the context of disciplinary activities (Bandura 1973). In addition, Ulrich (1967) indicates that physical pain, discomfort, or the blocking of positive reinforcement can lead to aggression in children. Since abused children have experienced extreme punishment at the hands of aggressive parental models, it was hypothesized that young, abused children would exhibit more aggressive characteristics than their nonabused counterparts.

To test this hypothesis, both the aggressive fantasies and the overt aggressive behavior of young abused children were compared with two groups of matched controls: nonabused, neglected children and normal children. Aggressive fantasy was measured with the Thematic Apperception Test (TAT) (Murray 1943), while two measures of overt aggressiveness were utilized: observers' ratings during free play and teachers' ratings on the Behavior Problem Checklist (BPC) (Quay and Peterson 1967).

The nonabused neglected group was included to provide a control for any potential effects produced by inadequate physical care and attention common among abused children, as well as to help clarify the potential effects of child neglect. The normal group provided a reference point from which to demonstrate effects attributable to abuse or neglect. To the author's knowledge, no prior study has included a statistical comparison of abused with neglected and normal children on the variables used in this study.

METHOD

Subjects

Three groups of children were used in this study, which was part of a larger investigation: physically abused (N=20), nonabused neglected (N=16), and normal (N=22). The abused and neglected children were referred from the Illinois Department of Children and Family Services (IDCFS) and the Bowen Center for Abused and Neglected Children. Normal children were referred from neighborhood day-care centers serving low- and middle-income families.

An abused child was defined as a child who had suffered either bone fractures, contusions, abrasions, cuts or burns inflicted by a parental caretaker on more than one occasion. A neglected child was a child whose parents had failed to provide food, clothing, supervision, medical care, or sanitary living conditions, and for whom there was no evidence of physical abuse. Both the abused and neglected children had no known evidence of neurological impairment from abuse, neglect, or any other source. The criteria for abuse and neglect were validated for each child by IDCFS caseworkers.

At the time the study was conducted, twelve abused children were living in foster care, and eight in their natural homes. The neglected group consisted of twelve children in the natural homes and four in foster homes. Table 1 provides a summary of the demographic information gathered and indicates that the three groups were adequately equated on age, sex, SES, and race.

Table 1. Demographic characteristics

	Age	Race		Annual parental income		Sex	
	Months	Black	White	0–3000	4–8000	Male	Female
Abused							
Mean	77.8	11	9	10	10	16	4
SD	12.4						
Neglected							
Mean	82.8	9	7	5	11	7	9
SD	13.6						
Normal							
Mean	78.1	13	9	10	12	16	6
SD	12.0						

Note: The groups did not differ in terms of age $F(2,55)=.81$, $p>.05$; race $\chi^2(2)=.075$, $p>.05$; parental income $\chi^2(2)=1.35$, $p>.05$; sex $\chi^2(2)=5.79$, $p>.05$.

Procedure

All children were brought by the examiner to a playroom at the De Paul University Mental Health Center. Each child was administered cards 13B, 7GF, 3GF, 10, 6GF, and 13MF from the TAT as a measure of aggressive imagery. The stories were rated by judges for aggressive content by the Hafner and Kaplan (1960) aggression scoring system. Interjudge reliability for this method was determined to be 0.91.

Immediately following the test situation each child was brought into a playroom in which age- and sex-appropriate toys were present. The following instructions were given: "In this playroom there are many different types of toys. See them all. You may play with any toy, but you must tell me a story or put on a show for me with each toy you play with." The examiner remained in the room with the child for twenty minutes. Two observers situated behind a one-way mirror rated the occurrence of aggressive behavior, which was defined as any hostile action on the part of the child toward the toys or examiner, (e.g., throwing or hitting toys against the table or the examiner). Aggressive responses were rated by using a precise-time sampling procedure in which the twenty-minute observation period was divided into fifteen-second intervals by an electric interval timer. During the first ten seconds of each interval the observer counted the number of aggressive responses made by the child, and in the subsequent five-second interval the observer recorded the behaviors occurring in the preceding ten seconds. Any aggression occurring during this five-second period was not recorded. Inter-rater reliability of 0.89 was established for this observation procedure.

The BPC was mailed to each child's teacher, who rated the child on the aggression scale, providing a measure of such behavior as fighting, temper tantrums, uncooperativeness, anger, and destructiveness. The total score for each child was the sum of aggressive behavior checked by the teacher.

RESULTS

Analysis of variance for the TAT aggression scores, using the Hafner and Kaplan (1960) scoring system, revealed a statistically significant main effect for groups, $F(2,55)=3.94$, $p < .05$. Additional comparisons demonstrated that the abused children expressed significantly more fantasy aggression in responding to the TAT when compared to both the neglected children, $t(34)=1.98$, $p < .05$, and the normal children, $t(40)=2.62$, $p < .01$. The neglected children did not differ significantly from the normal children. Table 2 provides the mean and standard deviations for each group.

Since the data for aggression shown in the free play setting did not meet the requirement of homogeneity of variance necessary to perform an analysis of variance, an extension of the median test (Ferguson 1966) was used for statistical purposes. Results demonstrated that there was a significant difference among

Table 2. Means and standard deviations for TAT aggression, free play aggression, and teacher ratings of aggression

	TAT aggression	Free play aggression	Teacher ratings of aggression
Abused			
Mean	12.05	6.20	8.89
SD	6.56	9.42	4.68
Neglected			
Mean	7.94	.13	8.69
SD	5.67	.34	5.82
Normal			
Mean	6.82	.32	3.77
SD	6.37	1.09	4.65

the medians, X^2 (2)=5.44, $p<.05$. It is apparent (Table 2) that abused children used aggressive behavior with much greater frequency in this setting than either neglected or normal children, whose mean frequency of aggression was less than one.

Behavior Problem Checklist ratings of aggression by teachers were analyzed by one-way analysis of variance. Results indicated a significant difference among groups on this measure, F (2,53)=6.70, $p<.001$. Abused children were judged significantly more aggressive than normals, t (38) = 3.45, $p<.01$, as were the neglected children, t (36)=2.89, $p<.01$. No significant difference was found between abused and neglected children. The means and standard deviations for teacher ratings are listed in Table 2.

Finally, abused children who were living in their natural homes were compared with abused children in foster care (N=12) to see if aggressiveness varied with place of residence. Although these two groups did not differ in amount of overt aggression as measured by the teachers ratings on the BPC or by the amount of aggression displayed during free play, t-tests revealed that abused children in their natural homes expressed significantly more fantasy aggression than abused children in foster homes, $t(16)=2.19$, $p<.05$. However, a large number of t-tests were performed within the context of the larger study and very few significant differences were found. This suggests that the significant difference in fantasy aggression between abused children in foster care and abused children in their natural homes might result from Type I error alone. Since fantasy aggression was the only variable on which the two groups differed, a tentative interpretation could be that, in general, abused children living in foster care do not differ significantly from those living in their natural homes.

DISCUSSION

The purpose of the present study was to determine if child abuse influences aggression in young children. The results clearly indicate that abused children are significantly more aggressive than nonabused, normal children in three distinct areas: fantasy, free play environment, and school environment. Abused children expressed significantly more fantasies containing themes of aggression and violence than did normal children. In addition, abused children showed more overt aggression during free play and were reported by their teachers to have more behavior problems at school than control subjects.

These findings support previous observations by others (Elmer 1967; Fontana 1973; Johnson and Morse 1968; Morse et al. 1970) that abused children exhibit overly hostile and aggressive characteristics. Results also lend additional support to previous research linking physical punishment in the home and hyperaggressiveness in children (Hoffman 1960; Sears et al. 1957). Finally, the data from this investigation are consistent with the social learning theory formulation that children exposed to extremely aggressive parental models will demonstrate aggressive characteristics in situations outside the home.

Given the tendency of abused children to become abusive parents in adulthood, and the tendency of level of aggression to remain stable over time (Bloom 1964; Kagan and Moss 1962), it seems likely that the aggressiveness of abused children is frequently an enduring pattern of behavior perpetuated into adolescence and adulthood. This study thus strongly suggests that intervention should be initiated as soon as a child is identified as abused, rather than waiting until his problems increase in severity.

The results relating to differences between abused children who are in foster care and abused children in their natural homes also have implications regarding the treatment of these children. It may be recalled that abused children in foster care expressed significantly less hostile fantasies than those in their natural homes, but showed as much overt aggression as abused children who remained in their natural homes. If there is little difference between children in foster care and those in their natural homes, at least in relation to direct expression of aggression, then simply removing a child from the abusive environment is inadequate to reduce his level of aggression and problems in school. This suggests that foster care placement alone is not an adequate remedy for the psychological damage suffered by abused children, but needs to be supplemented by treatment for the child and/or support for the foster parents. The impact of foster care placement on the characteristics of abused children is clearly an important area for further research, which ought to take into account relevant factors (such as the age at which abuse occurred, length of time in foster care, etc.) to see under what conditions foster homes are most effective in remediating the problems of the children placed in them.

The fact that neglected children were similar to abused children in terms of aggression at school, but resembled normals on fantasy and free play aggressiveness, implies that neglect does influence aggressive behavior problems, but not to the same degree as child abuse. One interpretation for these findings is that neglectful parents, being non-nurturant, may subject their children to more punishment and verbal abuse than normals, but may not punish with the same aggressive intensity or frequency as abusive parents. Thus, neglected children may normally be nonaggressive in unstructured environments, such as fantasy or free play situations, but may have failed to learn the skills necessary to cope nonaggressively with the provocations and frustrations inherent in more structured environments, such as the school. Part of the difficulty in interpreting differences between neglected and abused children is the lack of research focusing on the characteristics of neglected children and the tendency of some authors to lump abused and neglected children together. The present study suggests that these two groups do differ and that further research is necessary to understand the neglected child and the school behavior problems that he appears to have.

REFERENCES

Bandura, A. *Aggression: A Social Learning Analyses*. Englewood Cliffs, N.J.: Prentice-Hall, 1973.

Bloom, B. S. *Stability and Change in Human Characteristics*. New York: John Wiley & Sons, 1964.

Elmer, E. *Children in Jeopardy*. Pittsburgh: University of Pittsburgh Press, 1967.

Evans, I., Dubanoski, R., Higuchi, A. "Behavior therapy with child abusing parents: Initial concepts underlying predictive, preventive and analogue studies." Paper presented at the Eighth Annual Convention of the Association for the Advancement of Behavior Therapy, Chicago, November 1974.

Ferguson, G. A. *Statistical Analysis in Psychology and Education*. New York: McGraw-Hill, 1966.

Fontana, V. J. *Somewhere a Child Is Crying*. New York: MacMillan & Co., 1973.

Hoffman, M. "Power assertion by the parent and its impact on the child." *Child Development* 31 (1960):129-43.

Hafner, A. J., and Kaplan, A. M. "Hostility content analysis of the Rorschach and TAT." *Journal of Projective Techniques* 24 (1960):134-43.

Johnson, B., and Morse, H. "Injured children and their parents." *Children* 15 (1968):147-52.

Martin, H. "The Child and His Development." In R. E. Helfer and C. H. Kempe, eds. *Helping the Battered Child and His Family*. Philadelphia: J. B. Lippincott Co., 1972.

Martin, H., Beezley, P., Conway, E., and Kempe, C. H. "The development of abused children." *Advances in Pediatrics* 21 (1974):25-73.

McRae, K., Ferguson, C., and Lederman, R. "The battered child syndrome." *Canadian Medical Association Journal* 108 (1973):859-66.

Morse, C. W., Sahler, O. J. Z., and Friedman, S. B. "A follow-up study of abused and neglected children." *American Journal of Diseases of Children* 120 (1970):439-46.

Quay, H. C., Peterson, D. R. *Manual for the Behavior Problem Checklist*. Champaign: University of Illinois, Children's Research Center, 1967.

Rolston, R. "The effect of prior physical abuse on the expression of overt and fantasy aggressive behavior in children." Doctoral dissertation, Lousiana State University, 1971. *Dissertation Abstracts International* 32 (1971):2453B-3086B. (University Microfilms No. 71-29, 389).

Sandgrund, A., Gaines, R. U., and Green, A. H. "Child abuse and mental retardation: A problem of cause and effect." *American Journal of Mental Deficiency* 79 (1974):327–29.

Sears, R. R., Maccoby, E. E., and Levin, H. *Patterns of Child Rearing*. Evanston, Ill.: Row, Peterson, 1957.

Spinetta, J. J., and Rigler, D. "The child abusing parent: A psychological review." *Psychological Bulletin* 77 (1972):296–304.

Ulrich, R. *The Experimental Analysis of Aggression*. (Office of Naval Research, Group Psychology Branch, Contract Number N00014-67-A-0421-0001, N R 171–807). Kalamazoo: Western Michigan University, Department of Psychology, 1967.

CHAPTER 24

On the Role of Coenesthetic Stimulation in the Development of Psychic Structure[1]

David A. Freedman and Stuart L. Brown

I

Over the past twenty months we have had the opportunity to observe two young-sters who were reared by their psychotic mother in virtually total isolation from one another as well as the rest of the world. The data appear both to supplement and complement that obtained from the study of infants reared in institutions (1, 2, 3, 5, 7, 8, 15, 21, 22, 27, 29) and observations made on congenitally blind youngsters (10, 14, 20). Similar cases in the literature tend to be considered together with another distinct, albeit related, set of problems—that of the so-called feral or wolf child. Common to both groups are experiences in the mother-infant dyad which, to say the least, are outside the range of the average and expectable. It seems to us that consideration of the striking qualitative differences in their respective experiences in conjunction with the subsequent life histories of the individuals is of theoretical interest.

II

Case One

Anne is the second child of parents of Eastern European stock who reside in a semirural community. There is no known history of inheritable physical or

This study was supported by grants from the Medical Research Fund of Texas and U.S.P.H.S., HD02763.02.

Reprinted with permission from the *Psychoanalytic Quarterly* 37 (1968):418–38.

[1]According to Spitz (24, 25), during the first six months of life and, to some extent beyond this period, sensory experience is in the coenesthetic mode. Unlike diacritic sensation which predominates later, this is poorly localized and diffuse rather than discrete. The signs and signals to which the infant responds belong to the following categories: equilibrium, tension (muscular or otherwise), posture, temperature, vibration, skin and body contact, rhythm, tempo, duration, pitch, tone, resonance, clang, and probably a number of others of which the adult is hardly aware.

mental illness in either of the large extended families from which the parents derive. They are of average stature and physical development. We have no evidence of significant behavioral disturbance in either of them prior to marriage. Both completed high school. After their marriage they are said to have withdrawn from contact with family and friends, although the father continued to be gainfully employed.

During her first pregnancy the mother expressed the conviction that her baby would be born defective. However, the delusion did not affect her handling of the child to the extent that it did his siblings when it reappeared in her subsequent pregnancies: Anne's older brother has negotiated the usual developmental stages more or less adequately and is now in the third grade of school. Because after Anne's birth the mother continued to be convinced that this baby was defective, she felt it necessary to keep her isolated. Aside from occasional visits to a physician, Anne was confined to home and was out of sight to all visitors until she was six years old. At that time, a relative who refused to be put off any longer by the excuse that Anne and her younger brother were asleep, managed to see them. What she saw led her to initiate the legal proceedings which ultimately brought the children to our attention.

Social workers who investigated the situation found that Anne, then age six, shared a room with her older brother. While he was able to come and go pretty much as he pleased and was attending school, she was confined to the room. He had a bed but she slept on a straw pallet on the floor. She was unable to feed herself or talk meaningfully, although she did repeat some words and sentences in echolalic fashion. She displayed no affective reaction to either her mother or the strangers who came to investigate. Subsequently when she was removed from the home she showed no response either to leaving or to the new environment and handling. The social worker commented that when Anne was picked up she offered no resistance. Her body, however, remained unresponsive in that she did not mold in response to the worker's handling.

On admission to a hospital her height was noted to be forty-two and a half inches and her weight thirty pounds. By both criteria she ranked below the third percentile in physical development. She was incontinent of urine and feces and indifferent to the overtures of the staff. Much of her time she spent sitting in bed rocking. She was able to stand and walk without assistance. During the relatively brief hospitalization of eight weeks, she is said to have become continent, learned to feed herself, learned to call some objects by name, and at times seemed to display affectional responses to members of the staff. She was returned to her family for another nine months before the slowly moving legal process eventuated in placement in a foster home.

The description from the foster mother indicates that the gains made during her hospitalization were short-lived. Although she was able to pass objects from hand to hand and to her mouth, this seven-year-old child could neither handle eating utensils nor feed herself by hand. At home her only food is said to have been a moderately thick gruel served in a nursing bottle. She was described as extremely obedient and it was noted that when told she would sit literally for hours in one position. She exhibited no interest in either her environment or her body. At no time was she observed to engage in masturbatory activity. On the Vineland Social Maturity Scale, she scored at the ten-month level.

Anne and her younger brother were in foster care for eighteen months. The foster family, of the same religious and economic background as the parents, included five children. It provided a warm, well-structured environment, with a judicious balance between permissive indulgence and expectation.

By the criteria of the intelligence tests and social conformity Anne developed over this period into a child in many respects similar to a four-year-old; she is now eight. In height she continues close to the third percentile for her age. She has, however, gained considerably in weight during the past six months. Although growth and development have been continuous, they have not been adequate to narrow the gap which was noted at the time of her hospitalization. She gives the appearance of a robust youngster, but one roughly half her chronological age. She very quickly learned such basic skills as eating and toileting. Unlike her younger brother she has consistently shown evidence of awareness of and concern for the response of adults in her immediate environment. Her foster parents describe her as timid, because she never takes food or water or plays with objects without obtaining permission. We assume that this characteristic must reflect her long experience of confinement with her older brother, whose spontaneous coming and going she could watch but was not permitted to emulate.

She now responds more or less in kind to the affectionate overtures of adults. The quality of her response is, however, distinctive. She continues unable to mold her body to another person. In this respect, as she is held, one is reminded of Mahler's characterization of the autistic as opposed to the symbiotic child (16). To the casual observer she appears to be a friendly, affectionate little girl. On closer inspection, however, her outgoing qualities prove more apparent than real. She makes no discriminations among people and goes willingly to anyone, friend or stranger. Five months after she came to foster care she and her brother were presented to a large conference. One of the authors who, at the time, had only seen them through a one-way screen picked up the children and carried them into the room. Not only were they unaffected by his handling of them, but also they showed no concern during the demonstration. Their response to their teachers who were present was not noticeably different from their response to the total strangers.

Anne continues to show this lack of concern. She will go without question or hesitation to and with anyone who wishes to take her. She shows nothing to suggest that her awareness of, or attachment to, any one person, place, or object is sufficient to have led her to concern herself with the strange as opposed to the familiar, or the dangerous as opposed to the safe and secure. Recently, the children have been adopted; neither Anne nor her brother, who will be described below, has shown any evidence of concern over this change in their circumstances. Despite some eighteen months in a warm and loving environment they showed no signs of grief or loss, and have made no inquiry concerning the foster family. The adoptive parents, who at once became 'mother' and 'daddy,' have elected to change the children's given names. The new names have been accepted as though the old ones never existed.

When Anne is engaged in play these characteristics persist. The examiners are of little interest to her. She is most concerned with part objects such as pieces of anatomy like nose, mouth, ear, etc., or articles of dress. It is not possible to involve her in games which require spontaneity and mutual interchange.

Anne's speech has progressed from the monotonous repetition of a few words to a considerable vocabulary. She now uses some abstract concepts. However, she continues to articulate poorly and much echolalia persists. Her responses to verbal stimuli seem best described as reflexive in character. Thus to the question, 'What do we say at the table?', she replies, 'Don't talk with food in your mouth'. When the question is restated and emphasis placed on sitting down, she makes the sign of the cross and rattles off grace. She began to use the first person pronoun only in the last six to eight months.

Nearly two years after coming into foster care her differentiation of herself from the environment is incomplete. The following episode is illustrative. She was asked to show the ear of a doll which she was holding. At once, she reached for her own ear, hesitated, and then touched the doll's. The question, 'Where is the other ear?', evoked reaching again for the same ear. Further questions made it clear that the concept of 'other', as well as of 'two', like the image of the ear as something both she and the doll possess, remains extremely tenuous in the eight-year-old girl. A psychological report from roughly the same time noted it was frequently difficult to determine whether she was referring to the examiner or herself.

Motor coördination has improved remarkably since our observation began. Her attempts to perform relatively skilled acts, however, remain rudimentary. Her use of a pencil continues at the two-year level.

Case Two

Albert, unlike Anne, was isolated virtually *in toto*. We do not have certain information but he very probably was kept from birth up to age four in a room approximately eight by ten feet in size. When he was first seen by the public officials he was confined to a crib. The only other furniture in the room was a chamber pot. The wall next to the crib was marred by deep grooves evidently made by his fingers. The only window was covered by burlap sacking. Scraps of paper and the remnants of a doll were the only evidence of playthings.

Like Anne, he was fed exclusively by bottle. His diet also consisted of a thin gruel which would pass through an enlarged nipple hole. We have reason to believe that his mother only entered the room to feed and diaper him. In his later years we know that it was her wont to place him on the potty where he would, on command, sit for long hours. But he never learned the intended connection between the potty and excretion.

When he was hospitalized at age four he was thirty-seven inches in height and weighed twenty-three pounds. Like his sister, he was well below the third percentile in both height and weight. He walked with a peculiar waddling gait and was incapable of even the most elementary use of his hands. Neither the manipulation of objects nor hand-to-mouth activity was present; he was unable to masticate, was incontinent of urine and feces, and totally devoid of articulate speech. He made some grunting sounds and at times he screamed. The latter were interpreted by the nurses in attendance as a fear response. During the hospitalization locomotion improved and he became able to hold his cup and to clutch toys. He was never observed to play with objects or people. The nurses' notes indicate that he showed glee while smearing feces.

Nine months later, when admitted to foster care, he had lost most of these paltry advances. As was true of his sister, he would sit long hours almost immobile. He was unable to handle objects or to feed himself. Head banging and rocking were chronic. The latter, a side-to-side motion, with arms extended before him, had originally occupied all his time in bed. As he improved in foster care this decreased progressively in amount. At this writing, it occurs only when he is asleep; nightly, both the foster and adoptive mothers have found him engaged in this movement.

A striking observation, the credibility of which is much enhanced by similar observations by both Itard (13) and Zingg (30), was a total lack of pain sensibility when he was first observed. The foster mother offered the information that during the first several months he would fall and cut or bruise himself, get up, and continue what he was doing. Only after some evidence of affectional attachment to her had developed did he also show evidence, in the forms of tears and the seeking of comfort from her, that he had been hurt. As was the case with his sister, for many months after placement he showed no concern with his perineum. More recently there has been some evidence of genital interest. We surmise that visceral sensation also was defective from the fact that for the first year in the foster home he would eat anything he was offered, and as much as he could reach. The only effective method of restricting his food intake was to remove him bodily from the source of supply.

Albert's physical development has continued, as has his sister's, but at a pace which leaves him in the retarded range. Intellectual development also has continued at a constant but retarded pace. While skills have improved considerably, his gait is not out of keeping with what would be expected of a child of his size and apparent age—i.e., between two and three years. He is markedly hyperkinetic and tends to engage in relatively violent activity which often results in the destruction of the object he is using.

His speech has progressed from guttural noises to the use of jargon comprehensible only to his sister, to the use of single words in a discriminating fashion. Four months after placement he was echolalic. Three months later he was first heard to use 'I', and in the next three months he began to make queries and to speak in short sentences. Four months after placement, when he was five and a half, he understood well enough that he was in the office of a doctor who had previously given him an injection and he began to cry. He was first noted to laugh and to exhibit anger two months after coming to foster care. About this time he also evoked and reciprocated in affectional behavior with the foster mother.

At the present time he continues to show the same indifference concerning strangers as does his sister. While he seems able to handle objects more efficiently than she, his awareness of the environment is even less well developed. It is not possible for him, for example, to engage even in the limited kind of give and take which allowed us to infer the uncertainty of Anne's body ego boundaries.

III

Zingg (30) has noted that reports of so-called feral man generally include two distinct groups of cases, those who have suffered severe maternal deprivation and those who have had highly distorted experiences in their early maternal relations. Our subjects and Kingsley Davis' (7, 8) patient belong to the group that experienced extreme isolation and virtually total lack of maternal care. These youngsters, like those reared in institutions and those congenitally blind individuals who become deviant, have suffered a degree of neglect which jeopardized even the possibility of survival (I).

Furthermore, the neglect began so shortly after birth that there has been a massive lack of experience in that period of life when the coenesthetic mode of perception predominates. The consequence has been, in Spitz's terms (26), that their sensoria as well as external objects were never cathected and the primordial stimulus barrier has, to a large extent, remained intact. We have already indicated there is no evidence that our patients ever differentiated the presumptive mothering figure let alone developed affectional attachments to her. On the contrary, we know that they displayed absolutely no concern when at ages four and six and again at ages five and seven they were abruptly separated from their mother and the milieu in which they had spent their entire lives. Even after spending a year and a half in an environment which provided ample supplies of affectionate concern and attention, they accepted both a new home and new names with a degree of insouciance that indicated a total lack of prior libidinal attachments.

We feel that their poorly differentiated ego boundaries, their inability to maintain a sustained interest in either people or objects, their tendency to be involved with easily encompassed parts of objects, and their propensity for undelayed motor discharge must be associated with their inability to form primary affectional attachments. While they have acquired considerable vocabularies they continue to be predominately echolalic and to use their verbal resources otherwise only in a highly concrete fashion. It is impossible, for instance, to engage these children in any form of verbal play. They are incapable of comprehending even the simplest stories. Their motor skills remain fragmented and 'out of context', in the sense that they engage in little purposeful activity.

IV

It is with some trepidation that we now turn to a consideration of the published accounts of wolf children. Even if our data were not second hand, the possibility that such children might exist would seem very remote. Yet, Linnaeus was sufficiently persuaded of the authenticity of the reports he heard to establish the category of feral man in the tenth edition of the *Systema Naturae* (1758), and to ascribe to it the characteristics of mutism, four-footedness, and hirsutism. In the intervening years there has been a sufficient number of accounts by reliable reporters (11, 23, 28, 30) to make it seem probable that human infants have been reared by wolves—more accurately by night-roaming animals more akin to the jackal than the North American timber wolf—as well as by other mammals.[2]

The best documented cases have been reported from India. Linnaeus' cases, whose verisimilitude is admittedly much enhanced by the more nearly contemporaneous and better documented Indian cases, were described during the seventeenth and eighteenth century and even earlier from Central Europe (23). Poland in particular was the source of many accounts. Of his three criteria, two, mutism and four-footedness, have characterized all the recent cases. We will now summarize the available data concerning the best known wolf children, Kamala and Amala.

The Reverend Singh, an Anglo-Indian priest who was present at the 'rescue' of these children, had them under observation until their deaths one and a half and seven years later. From external evidences (e.g., dentition) their ages when they were encountered were estimated to be eighteen months and eight years. How long they had lived with the wolves could not be determined. Apparently, however, in the region of India around Midnapore it is not at all uncommon for wolves to carry off neonates. It happens occasionally that a lactating female will adopt such a youngster and rear it with her own cubs.

Singh was one of a group that sought to track down two human 'ghosts' which had been seen in the neighborhood of a remote village. They were traced to an abandoned termite nest in the jungle. When this was uncapped it proved to

---

[2]The conclusion that wolf children may exist is by no means universally held. Bettelheim (4), for instance, considers the reported children to be autistic—a conclusion which at best begs the question but at the same time does not seem to fit the clinical description of two children, Kamala and Amala, reported by the Reverend J. A. L. Singh (23). Ogburn (18, 19), in his search for evidence from eye witnesses, seems to have regarded as creditable those individuals who offered alternative explanations concerning the children's early rearing. He has no doubt that the children as described were observed, but prefers to believe some other explanation must account for their behavior. Another possible explanation has been offered by Dr. C. V. Ramana who, in a personal communication, tells us that youngsters abandoned in very early childhood often join the troops of monkeys which live in the neighborhood of temples in the northeastern section of India. These children take on many of the behavioral characteristics of the monkey, including quadrupedal locomotion.

be occupied by an adult female wolf and a huddled mass of cubs. As these latter took flight they were found to include, in addition to three immature wolves, the two human children. They were brought to the orphanage of which he was the director. His observations fall naturally into three temporal divisions: (1) the period from capture up to Amala's death; (2) Kamala's period of mourning; and (3) the subsequent seven-year period.

1. When they were first observed, the children were huddled together with their cubmates. In the mass exodus from the invaded den they ran on all fours— i.e., the palms of their hands and soles of their feet—and this remained their principle mode of locomotion. They were described as extremely agile and able to outrun a human adult. They were unable to extend fully either their hip or knee joints. Some hyperextensibility of their jaws, so that maxilla and mandible appeared to separate completely when they chewed, was observed. While they used their hands to some extent as prehensile organs, they ate crouched over their dishes like dogs. They drank by lapping with their tongues. Like our case, Albert, they would eat voraciously. Unlike him, they had very definite preferences and would refuse food they disliked. They sought out and ate carrion but never hunted to kill.

Their vision was noted to be poor during the daylight hours but excellent in the dusk and dark when, it was also observed, 'their eyes glowed'. The senses of smell, hearing, and touch (at least touch by other individuals in the institution) were extremely acute. On the other hand, they seemed to be indifferent to extremes of temperature and would remain in the same naked state whatever the season. No comment is made concerning pain.

In the confines of the orphanage, they would spend long hours—as many as four or five at a stretch—huddled together facing a corner. They ignored, brushed aside, or responded with bared teeth to all human efforts to make contact with them. However, when they could escape into the field, they ran about agilely and played with the animals kept at the orphanage. There was no evidence of concern with perineal function. They were incontinent and seemed indifferent to both the excretory process and its products. They displayed no interest in their genitalia.

To quote the Reverend Singh, 'Kamala had a smiling face but the emotion of joy was far from it'. Their pleasures were, as he put it, 'animal pleasures'—i.e., eating and running. When they were excited their ears would change color and tremble, their nostrils would dilate, and their lips would tremble. They would insist on being together at night and always slept curled up around one another.

When they were first observed, the children would on two or three occasions each night emit loud howling noises. Amala would also occasionally make a sound approximately like 'bhoa-bhoa'. These vocalizations aside, they were mute. Communication came only in association with eating and followed a pattern strongly reminiscent of Helen Keller's recollection of her efforts to express wishes during the period prior to her contact with Miss Sullivan (6). That is, they would behave in a manner which suggested they were hallucinating gratification. When hungry they would go to the place where they were usually fed and sniff. If they were not fed, they would leave and then come back. This routine would be repeated until they received food. When Kamala was thirsty, she would lick her lips until she was given water. Some four months after their capture they began to come to Mrs. Singh, the person who gave them food, and remain beside her until fed. In other words, they apparently shifted from the site of the feeding to the feeding person as the object associated with their wishes.

Food was the first medium through which attempts were made to approach them. After ten months, they would take crackers from Mrs. Singh's hand. Otherwise, they remained on the periphery of the group of children. It was noted, however, that they showed evidence of interest when the word 'cracker' was mentioned as in the course of story telling.

2. This state of affairs continued unchanged until eighteen months after their capture, when Amala died. The Reverend Singh reported Kamala's reaction as follows:

> . . . she watched Amala for some time and thought she was sleeping; she came to Amala several times and tried to wake her up by touching her hand and even trying to drag her out of bed. She touched her face, opened the lids of her eyes and parted her lips . . When Kamala found Amala did not get up and did not even move, she left her side and moved away to her own bed. This she repeated the whole day till Amala was removed for burial. . . . She stuck to the place where the dead body was until Amala was placed in her coffin. Two tear drops were observed to fall from her eyes.

For approximately seven days after Amala's death, Kamala remained by herself in a corner. Subsequently, she would come for food but did so much less frequently than she had previously. About three weeks later, she was found smelling the places Amala used to frequent. She roamed about and cried out constantly in a peculiar voice and seemed to be returning to her 'old ferocious ways'. About a month later she began again to play with some kids which were kept at the orphanage. She would pass her hands over them lovingly and prattle like a baby to them. Over the next several months her interest gradually extended to include other animals—cats and a hyena cub. During this period, she avoided all humans including Mrs. Singh.

In addition to attempting to engage the children through feeding, Mrs. Singh, shortly before Amala's fatal illness, had attempted to establish contact with them through increasing body contact. To this end she instituted a regular program of body massage. During what we refer to as Kamala's period of mourning she redoubled her efforts in this regard. Approximately two months after Amala's death when Mrs. Singh approached her bed, Kamala moved over slightly to make room for her. This was the first overt indication of a libidinal tie. What progress she made in the next six years in developing human qualities followed this event.

3. To summarize her achievements briefly: She coöperated actively in a series of exercises and games which eventuated in her learning to stand and to walk erect. Affectional relations with other children in the orphanage were developed and included, in addition to pleasure in somesthetic stimulation, ability

to play with and be protective toward younger children. She became concerned with receiving marks of approval first from Mrs. Singh and subsequently from the Reverend Singh; no doubt as a result of this she became concerned with body exposure and insisted on wearing a dress at all times. Before Amala died, loincloths literally had to be sewn on the children and they tore off all other clothes. Kamala learned to turn to the parent surrogates in times of stress— including occasions when she seemed to have felt unjustly treated by other children. A vocabulary was gradually acquired and at the time of her death she had forty-five words she was able to use in short sentences.

V

It seems clear that the wolf children did not suffer deprivations similar to those experienced by our subjects. We suggest that the difference is most succinctly stated in terms of minimal experience and its sequelae as opposed to highly distorted experience and its sequelae. For both groups atypical conditions began in earliest infancy and continued through what in usual circumstances would be the entire preœdipal period. The evidence indicates, however, that the feral children were provided with a rich supply of somesthetic, labyrinthine, oral, and visual nutriment—i.e., of the nonspecific coenesthetic stimulation characteristics of the primal cavity (24, 26).

That this was from sources remote from that which is average and expectable for humans goes without saying and provides the basis for their consideration in the present report. For, however distorted their experiences may have been in terms of what is normative, these feral children were provided with an experiential substrate which enabled them to differentiate self from environment, to cathect and introject external objects and to form strong libidinal attachments. Ego apparatuses effective in handling the environment in which they lived were evolved. When we compare them with our patients we can say that the latter failed to differentiate more than the rudiments of psychic structure whereas the feral children developed structures which were highly distorted as to content but in which nonetheless both drive organization and ego elements can be distinguished.

Whether we can also attribute to them anything analogous to the primary superego functions is an open question. Certainly it is difficult to detect behavioral evidence of what we can call superego or its precursors in Kamala's and Amala's early days in the orphanage. Yet, the extent to which the processes of identification and introjection may have led to the development of regulators of behavior analagous to the primordial superego could not be assessed in the context of the change in their living circumstances once they came into human care.

Particularly impressive from the standpoint of this thesis is the description of Kamala's response to Amala's death. As would be anticipated from a youngster with a more typical early life, she passed through a period characterized by evidence of profound grief and desolation. This was then followed by the seeking out of new objects. Only after Kamala, in the course of this search, cathected Mrs. Singh did she become concerned with acquiring qualities which we can consider human. In this regard we would underscore the use of body massage by Mrs. Singh in her effort to establish an affectional relation with the child. This nonspecific coenesthetic mode of stimulation appears to have been the medium through which their attachment to one another was evolved. It is no doubt more than happenstance that one hundred years earlier, the nurse whom Itard provided for Victor, the Wild Boy of Aveyron (13), hit upon precisely the same device in her efforts to establish an affectional relation with him. The progress this child made seems also to have followed the establishment through this medium of what we propose to call a coenesthetic bond.

Another extraordinary case in the psychological literature seems to underscore the importance of adequate nonspecific coenesthetic experience for subsequent structural development. In 1942, Mason reported her experience with a girl born illegitimately to an aphasic mother (17). The mother was totally uneducated; she could neither read nor write and communicated with her family by gestures. From the time the pregnancy was discovered she, and subsequently her child, was kept in a locked room behind drawn shades. Six and a half years later, carrying her child, the mother made her escape and the child came to the attention of public authorities. Mason saw the child when she was admitted to a children's hospital. The first two days the child spent in tears. Mason's overtures were greeted by a gesture of repulsion from, to quote her, 'the wan-looking child whose face bore marks of grief and fear'. Sensing that no direct approach was possible, Mason attempted to involve her by playing dolls with another little girl while ostensibly ignoring her. By this method, one which would have been entirely inapplicable to either the apathetic children we report or the aggressively negative wolf children, she was able to engage the child's interest and establish a mutual relation with her. Within a year and a half she had acquired a vocabulary of between fifteen hundred and two thousand words, could count to one hundred, identify coins, and perform arithmetic computations to ten. Mason describes her at eight and a half as having an excellent sense of humor, being an inveterate tease, and an imaginative, affectionate, and loving child. In less than two years she made the transition from a world of silence, fear, and isolation to an excellent adjustment in the average expectable social world of childhood.

As we attempt to account for the striking difference between her response and that of our own cases, Kingsley Davis' patient, and the wolf children, one overriding fact emerges: this child was isolated with her mother. Despite the paucity of all other modes of stimulation we can infer that she received ample nutriment in the coenesthetic mode as well as other nonverbal communication.

We know of two other instances in which an analogous set of circumstances has been recorded—i.e., one in which a child has had considerable and gratifying experience in the coenesthetic mode either accompanied or followed by marked sensory deprivation. Helen Keller, whose history has been studied from a psychoanalytic standpoint by Dahl (6), is one. She was a healthy active eighteen-month-old when she was stricken by meningitis. That she was able ultimately to respond to the efforts of her teacher, Miss Sullivan, may well have been contingent on this earlier experience. Still another case in point is that of the legendary Kaspar Hauser (9). This young man, apparently the heir to the duchy of Baden, was a victim of post-Napoleonic dynastic intrigues. He was kidnaped in early infancy and left in the care of a nursemaid until he was three. From his third to his seventeenth year he was confined to a narrow dungeon. During this period he was never allowed to see or communicate verbally with another human being. When he appeared in Nuremberg in 1828 he could hardly walk and his vocabulary was limited to a few stereotyped incomprehensible repetitive phrases. His demeanor is described as in keeping with that of a child of scarcely two or three years. During the two and a half years between his appearance and his assassination he became a somewhat limited but warm, friendly, articulate young man. Indeed, it was widely believed at the time that concern over what he might reveal, having learned to talk, led to his murder.

While the anecdotal nature of these latter cases cannot be discounted, neither, we feel, can the trend of the material they contain. From the standpoint of early exposure in the coenesthetic mode, the cases we have reviewed may be characterized as follows: The wolf children had had rich but highly distorted experiences. For them, or rather Kamala, to develop ego apparatuses compatible with the demands of the average expectable human environment, it was necessary to go through a process of decathexis, of unlearning. It is impressive that she was able to do this only after Amala's death and a period of mourning. During the critical early period, our patients had a bare minimum of experience in this sphere. These youngsters came to foster care virtually devoid of evidence of structural differentiation. Nearly two years later they have made considerable advances in development, yet they continue to show very poorly differentiated ego boundaries and little or no capacity to enter into mutual affectional relations with another person. Finally, there are individuals like the three last described who, having had adequate experience in the coenesthetic experience mode, were able very rapidly, later in life, to make up for marked deprivation.

On the basis of this conceptualization it may be possible to account for certain discrepancies in the literature concerning the prognosis of individuals who have suffered significant maternal deprivation. Most authors have agreed with Spitz (27) that the consequences of hospitalism are irreversible. Certainly much of Harlow's experimental work with primates also points to this conclusion. Yet, Harlow has expressed the opinion that many of the deleterious effects of maternal deprivation in monkeys are avoided if the infant animal is provided with sensory nutriment from a sibling instead of an adult (12). Beres and Obers (3) have also provided evidence to indicate that the dismal outcome we associate with this syndrome is not inevitable. They studied a group of thirty-eight adolescents who had been institutionalized at various ages from two weeks to twenty-one months. The children remained in the institution for varying periods up to four years. Nine of their group (twenty-three per cent) were found in adolescence to be either satisfactorily adjusted or to have evolved sufficient psychic structure to present a neurotic conflict. The brief clinical vignettes these authors present, as well as their discussion, indicate that the remaining twenty-nine showed many of the characteristics of our patients—e.g., inability to tolerate frustration, a demand for immediate instinctual gratification, absence of evidence of shame or guilt, and inability to form more than transient object relations. These characteristics seem to have persisted even in youngsters who made considerable intellectual advances. They cite, for example, one girl whose IQ at age five was 59 and at age eighteen was 105, but who showed nonetheless all the evidences of ego deficiency we enumerate.

The observations of Beres and Ober, and the data we present, suggest the importance of differentiating those factors in early experience that are central to the differentiation of self from those which are relevant to the development of such specialized ego apparatuses as intellectual capacity. Thus, a strong well-defined ego structure such as characterized the wolf children may actually interfere with the possibility of making significant intellectual achievements. Our patients and some of the patients reported by Beres and Obers may in this sense be considered to have an advantage. They have little or nothing to unlearn. What they acquire, however, seems to remain unstructured, inchoate, and without the evidences of relation to a central unifying concept of self. This unifying concept of self, we propose, has as a prerequisite for its development adequate nutriment in the coenesthetic sphere.[3]

REFERENCES

1. Bakwin, Harry. *Emotional Deprivation in Infants.* J. Pediatrics, 35 (1949):512–21.
2. Bender, Lauretta. *Infants Reared in Institutions—Permanently Handicapped.* Bulletin of the Child Welfare League of America 24 (1945):1–4.
3. Beres, David, and Obers, Samuel J. "The Effects of Extreme Deprivation in Infancy on Psychic Structure in Adolescence." In *The Psychoanalytic Study of the Child, Vol. V.* New York: International Universities Press, 1950, pp. 212–35.
4. Bettelheim, Bruno. *Feral Children and Autistic Children.* Amer. J. Sociology 44 (1959):455–67.
5. Coleman, Rose, and Provence, Sally. *Environmental Retardation (Hospitalism) in Infants Living in Families.* J. Pediatrics 19 (1959):285–92.

[3]Since this manuscript was completed, the authors have learned of two, as yet unpublished, studies which they feel provide significant support to their central thesis. Gouin-Decarie in a study of the mental and emotional development of the thalidomide child observes that there is no direct correlation between the severity of the skeletal abnormalities and the affective and cognitive development of her twenty-two subjects. The presence or absence of 'normal behavior' patterns seemed to be dependent on the quality of the human attachments the subjects were able to achieve. In a recent report to the Society for Research on Child Development, W. A. Mason reported that it is possible to prevent the development of Harlow's maternal deprivation syndrome in monkeys by having the surrogate mother on which his animals are reared so suspended that it moves freely and unpredictably in space. In addition to providing labyrinthine stimulation, this preparation demanded of the infant monkey that it be constantly aware of the whereabouts of the surrogate.

6. Dahl, Hartvig: *Observations on a 'Natural Experiment': Helen Keller*. J. Amer. Psa. Assn. 13 (1965):533–50.

7. Davis, Kingsley. *Extreme Isolation of a Child*. Amer. J. Sociology 45 (1940):554–65.

8. _____. *Final Note on a Case of Extreme Isolation*. Amer. J. Sociology 52 (1946):432–37.

9. V. Feuerbach, A. *Caspar Hauser*. London: Simpkin and Marshall, 1833.

10. Fraiberg, Selma, and Freedman, David A. "Observations on the Development of a Congenitally Blind Child." In *The Psychoanalytic Study of the Child, Vol. XIX*. New York: International Universities Press, 1964, pp. 113–69.

11. Gesell, Arnold. *Wolf Child and Human Child*. New York: Harper & Brothers, 1940.

12. Harlow, Harry F., and Margaret K. *Learning to Love*. American Scientist 54 (1966):244–72.

13. Itard, J. M. G. *The Wild Boy of Aveyron*. Trans. by George and Muriel Humphrey. New York: New World Century Co., 1952.

14. Klein, George W. "Blindness and Isolation." In *The Psychoanalytic Study of the Child, Vol. XVII*. New York: International Universities Press, 1962, pp. 82–93.

15. Levine, Seymour. "The Effects of Infantile Experience on Adult Behavior." In *Experimental Foundations of Clinical Psychology*, Arthur J. Bachrach, ed. New York: Basic Books, 1952.

16. Mahler, Margaret S. *Autism and Symbiosis. Two Extreme Disturbances of Identity*. Int. J. Psa. 39 (1958):77–83.

17. Mason, Marie K. *Learning to Speak After Six and One Half Years of Silence*. J. Speech Disorders 7 (1942):295–304.

18. Ogburn, William F. *On the Trail of the Wolf Children*. Genetic Psychol. Monographs 40 (1959):117–96.

19. _____. *The Wolf Boy of Agra*. Amer. J. Sociology 44 (1959):449–54.

20. Omwake, Eveline, B., and Solnit, Albert J. " 'It Isn't Fair', The Treatment of a Blind Child." In *The Psychoanalytic Study of the Child, Vol. XVI*. New York: International Universities Press, 1961, pp. 352–404.

21. Patton, R. G., and Gardner, L. I. *Influence of Family Environment on Growth: The Syndrome of Maternal Deprivation*. Pediatrics 30 (1962):956–62.

22. Provence, Sally, and Lipton, Rose C. *Infants in Institutions*. New York: International Universities Press, 1962.

23. Singh, J. A. L., and Zingg, R. M. *Wolf Children and Feral Man*. New York: Harper & Brothers, 1942.

24. Spitz, René A. *Diacritic and Coenesthetic Organizations; The Psychiatric Significance of a Functional Division of the Nervous System into a Sensory and Emotive Part*. Psa. Rev. 32 (1945):146–62.

25. _____. *The First Year of Life*. New York: International Universities Press, 1965.

26. _____. "The Primal Cavity: A Contribution to the Genesis of Perception and Its Role in Psychoanalytic Theory." In *The Psychoanalytic Study of the Child, Vol. X*. New York: International Universities Press, 1955, pp. 215–40.

27. _____. "Hospitalism." In *The Psychoanalytic Study of the Child, Vols. I and II*. New York: International Universities Press, 1945, 1946.

28. Squires, Paul I. *Wolf Children of India*. Amer. J. Psychol. 38 (1927):313–15.

29. Yarrow, Leon J. *Maternal Deprivation*. Psychol. Bulletin 58 (1961):459–90.

30. Zingg, Robert M. *Feral Man and Extreme Cases of Isolation*. Amer. J. Psychol. 53 (1940):487–517.

CHAPTER 25

Abused and Neglected Children: The Cognitive, Social, and Behavioral Correlates

Thomas J. Reidy, Thomas R. Anderegg,
Robert J. Tracy, and Sheldon Cotler

ABSTRACT

The purpose of this study was to lend empirical verification to reports of psychological damage sustained by abused children. In order to clearly demonstrate the effects of child abuse, two comparison groups were used: a nonabused, neglected group and a normal control group. Abused and neglected children had significantly lower IQ scores than normal children as well as significantly more behavior problems in school. Abused children also rated themselves significantly lower in self-esteem than neglected or normal children. These findings document the cognitive, social, and behavioral impairments noted in subjective observations of abused and neglected children.

Child abuse and neglect represent critical social problems and primary concerns to legislators, clinicians, and researchers. Since it is children who must ultimately suffer the sequelae of mistreatment, it is incumbent on social scientists to identify the social and developmental effects of such trauma. Recent reports (e.g., Reidy 1975) have called attention to the effects of abuse or neglect on aggressiveness. Unfortunately, the relationship of mistreatment to the abused child's cognitive and social growth is unclear.

A review of the literature yields little substantial data on the effects of this trauma on later development. Experimental studies using control groups with adequate methodology are almost nonexistent; descriptive studies frequently are vague concerning what tests or measures have been employed. Especially unfortunate is the tendency of authors to discuss abused and neglected children as a single group, making it impossible to identify any potential between-group differences.

This article is based on a dissertation submitted to the Department of Psychology, De Paul University, by the first author under the direction of the third and fourth authors. The second author was instrumental in data collection and analysis. The authors gratefully acknowledge Toni D. Bernotas for her assistance in editing and preparation of the manuscript. Appreciation is extended to the Illinois Department of Children and Family Services for their cooperation with respect to providing the abused and neglected sample.

Despite the paucity of empirically derived studies, there is some evidence to suggest that physical abuse or neglect has serious psychological consequences for the child. Green, Gaines, and Sandgrund (note 1), comparing children between the ages of five and thirteen, reported both abused and neglected children to be more disturbed than normal with respect to "ego pathology" and "cognitive intactness." Similarly, Rolston (note 2) reported abused children in foster homes to be significantly more inhibited and depressed than nonabused children in foster homes.

Other less rigorous studies have reported a variety of psychological problems associated with abuse and neglect, i.e., school failure, truancy, fighting (Young 1964), and poor peer relations with behavior problems at home and school (Morse, Sahler, and Friedman 1970). In addition, Martin, Beezley, Conway, and Kempe (1974) report a negative correlation between IQ scores of abused and neglected children and family instability, parent unemployment, geographic, mobility, and the length of time the child has remained in a punitive home environment. Still other abused children have been categorized as emotionally disturbed, with poor impulse control (Elmer 1967) and as immature and anxious (Morse et al. 1970).

The evidence suggests an association between physical abuse or neglect sustained by children early in life and psychological damage reflected in the children's mental functioning, self-evaluations, and interpersonal behavior. The purpose of the present study, therefore, was to provide quantifiable data in support of these hypotheses. In addition, it seemed important to more clearly distinguish abuse from neglect. Since these two factors have been frequently combined in previous studies, a separate nonabused, neglected group was added to this study.

Specifically, it was predicted that: (a) abused or neglected children would receive lower IQ scores than normal; (b) abused or neglected children would rate themselves as lower in self-esteem than normal; and (c) abused or neglected children would be rated by teachers as more behaviorally impaired than normal.

METHOD

Subjects

Twenty physically abused, sixteen neglected, and twenty normal children served as subjects in this study, which was part of a more extensive investigation of child abuse (Reidy, note 3). The abused and neglected children were referred from the Illinois Department of Children and Family Services (IDCFS). Normal children were referred from local day-care centers serving low- and middle-income families.

For purposes of this study, an abused child was defined as a child who had suffered physical trauma inflicted by a caretaker (e.g., bone fractures, contusions, abrasions, cuts, or burns). A neglected child was one whose parents had

Table 1. Demographic characteristics

	Age	Race		Annual parental income		Sex	
	Months	Black	White	0–3000	4–8000	Male	Female
Abused							
Mean	77.8	11	9	10	10	16	4
SD	12.4						
Neglected							
Mean	82.8	9	7	5	11	7	9
SD	13.6						
Normal							
Mean	78.1	13	9	10	12	16	6
SD	12.0						

failed to provide proper nutrition, clothing, supervision, medical care, or sanitary living conditions and for whom there was no known evidence of physical abuse. Abused and neglected children with known neurological impairments or mental retardation were excluded from the study. These criteria were validated by IDCFS caseworker reports. At the time the study was conducted, twelve abused children were living in foster care, and eight in their natural homes. The neglected group consisted of twelve children in their natural home and four in foster homes.[1] The children were equated as closely as possible for age, race, sex, and parental income (Table 1). There were no statistically significant differences between groups on any variable.

Procedure

All children were brought by the examiner to a playroom at the De Paul University Mental Health Center, where a battery of psychological tests was administered. The Peabody Picture Vocabulary Test (Form B), the measure of cognitive functioning, was the first test administered to all children. Following that, the California Test of Personality (CTP) subscales of Self-Reliance, Sense of Personal Worth, Sense of Personal Freedom, Feelings of Belonging, and Withdrawing Tendencies were administered. This test was presented verbally to each child to control for possible differences in reading ability. Finally, each child's teacher was contacted and asked to complete the Behavior Problem Checklist (Quay & Peterson 1967) to obtain a measure for behavior in a natural setting.

---

[1]Although the place of residence for these children is an important variable theoretically, the variable was not systematically controlled. However, post hoc analysis did not yield effects beyond chance levels.

RESULTS

The IQ scores from the Peabody Picture Vocabulary Test were analyzed by a one-way analysis of variance (see Table 2 for means and standard deviations). Results indicated a significant main effect for groups, F (2, 55) = 8.84, p < .001. Follow-up analysis revealed that abused and neglected children did not differ significantly from each other. However, abused children did differ significantly from normals, t (40) = 4.06, p < .001, as did neglected children, t (36) = 3.01, p < .01.

Significant differences among groups were found for the California Test of Personality subscales of Self-Reliance, F (2, 55) = 3.23, p < .05, and Feelings of Belonging, F (2,55) = 3.25, p < .05. Additional post hoc comparisons demonstrated that abused children rated themselves lower than normal children on Self-Reliance, t (40) = 2.65, p < .01, and Feelings of Belonging, t (40) = 2.93, p < .01. The neglected children did not differ significantly from either abused or normal children on any measure. The means and standard deviations for each CTP scale across groups are presented in Table 2.

Results from the Behavior Problem Checklist (BPC) yielded a significant main effect for groups on the subscales of Aggression, F (2, 53) = 6.70, p < .001, and Inadequacy-Immaturity, F (2, 53) = 3.83, p < .05. Further comparisons involving these subscales revealed that abused children received significantly higher ratings than normal children on Aggression, t (38) = 3.45, p < .01 and Inadequacy-Immaturity, t (38) = 2.49, p < .01. The aggression scores of neglected children also were higher than those of normal children, t (36) = 2.89, p < .01, as were their Inadequacy-Immaturity scores t (36) = 2.37, p < .05. The abused and neglected groups did not differ significantly on any BPC measure. Table 3 provides the mean teacher ratings for all groups on each BPC scale.

Table 2. Intellectual and social measures

Group	PPVT		California Test of Personality			
	IQ	Self-reliance	Personal worth	Personal freedom	Feeling of belonging	Withdrawing tendencies
Abused						
M	82.30	3.95	4.85	4.95	4.50	2.80
SD	14.64	1.50	1.57	1.67	1.32	2.14
Neglected						
M	85.75	4.81	5.75	5.00	5.19	4.12
SD	15.64	1.38	1.44	1.41	1.22	2.42
Normal						
M	100.46	5.10	5.54	5.45	5.73	4.00
SD	14.32	1.57	1.22	1.44	1.93	2.47

Table 3. Teacher rating on the Behavior Problem Checklist

Group	Aggression	Anxious-withdrawn	Inadequacy-immaturity	Delinquency
Abused				
M	8.89	5.39	3.22	.78
SD	4.68	2.46	2.46	1.35
Neglected				
M	8.69	4.44	2.88	.75
SD	5.82	1.67	1.67	.93
Normal				
M	3.77	3.15	1.64	.50
SD	4.65	1.53	1.53	.80

DISCUSSION

The belief that abuse and neglect have serious consequences for the child is widely held, yet there are scant data from controlled studies to substantiate clinical observations. Therefore, the most important features of the present study lie in the quantifiable nature of the results, the use of matched comparison groups, and the distinctions between abused and neglected children. In general, the empirical results are consistent with earlier observations that abused and neglected children exhibit impaired psychological development (Elmer 1967; Green et al. note 1; Morse et al. 1970; Sandgrund et al. 1974).

In the realm of cognitive functioning, both the abused and neglected groups received significantly lower IQ scores than normals, obtaining scores 18 and 15 points below the normal sample, respectively. These results support previous findings (Sandgrund et al. 1974) which suggest that abused children have not developed the necessary cognitive skills for success in school. A home environment that is traumatically abusive, rejecting, and harsh may not foster a positive atmosphere for learning. Parents, by active modeling, cognitive stimulation, and interest, provide the foundation and framework that teaches and encourages children to organize and process information, problem solve and make judgments. If the parents are themselves deficient in these skills and overwhelmed by their own life stresses, they will provide little intellectual stimulation for their children.

Self-esteem scores for the abused group were significantly lower than those of the normal children for the subscales of Self-Reliance and Feelings of Belonging. The neglected children's self-esteem scores did not differ significantly from either the abused or the normal samples. A child's positive attitude toward himself develops within the context of strong family support that provides guidance, consistent behavior models, and discipline in an atmosphere of respect. As Coopersmith (1967) points out, a child subjected to disinterested parents who emphasize punishment and not reward is not likely to develop a favorable self concept. This view is consistent within the data for the abused but not for the neglected sample, although scores from the latter group were generally in the expected direction.

Behaviorally, both the abused and neglected children were rated by teachers as significantly more aggressive and inadequate-immature than normal children in the school setting. These children seem to lack the prosocial behavior necessary to establish successful relationships and cope with the demands of a school setting. The lack of self-esteem shown by the abused children is possibly reflected in teacher perceptions of inept, immature behavior. The children's aggressiveness may be related to inadequate socialization resulting in poor impulse control and immaturity. The contributive roles of modeling and anger-induced emotional arousal (Rule and Neodale 1976) to observed aggression must also be included as potential explanations.

On all measures investigated (except Sense of Personal Worth) it was found that nonabused, neglected children exhibited symptoms of disturbance at a level between those of the abused and normal samples. Perhaps one explanation for these data is that neglect is a more passive form of maltreatment than abuse; i.e., neglecting parents do not punish with the same hostility, intensity, or frequency as abusive parents. This lends support to Fontana's contention (1973) that child abuse represents one end of a continuum of maltreatment, with other less obvious or defined forms of mistreatment (e.g., neglect) having similar but less ominous consequences.

In summary, while it must be noted that causal inferences about the above findings are limited, it has nevertheless been demonstrated that those children identified as abused and neglected do demonstrate certain important deficits. The cognitive, social, and behavioral impairments evident in these very young children will certainly affect every aspect of their growth and development. It is essential for future investigators to provide empirically based studies of this very high-risk population so that contributing causal factors can be better understood and adequate treatment programs can be established.

NOTES

1. Green, A. H., Gaines, R. H., Sandgrund, A., and Haberfeld, H. *Psychological Sequelae of Child Abuse and Neglect.* Unpublished manuscript, 1974 (available from Division of Child and Adolescent Psychiatry, Downstate Medical Center, Brooklyn, New York).
2. Rolston, R. "The effect of prior physical abuse on the expression of overt and fantasy aggressive behavior in children." Doctoral dissertation, Louisiana State University, 1971, *Dissertation Abstracts International* 32 (1971):2453B–3086B. (University Microfilms no. 71-29, 389).
3. Reidy, T. J. "The Social, Emotional and Cognitive Functioning of Physically Abused and Neglected Children." Doctoral dissertation, De Paul University, 1975.

REFERENCES

Coopersmith, S. *The Antecedents of Self-Esteem*. San Francisco: Freeman, 1967.

Elmer, E. *Children in Jeopardy*. Pittsburgh: University of Pittsburgh Press, 1967.

Fontana, U. J. *Somewhere a Child Is Crying*. New York: MacMillan and Co., 1973.

Martin, J., Beezley, P., Conway, E., and Kempe, C. "The development of abused children." *Advances in Pediatrics* 21 (1974):25–73.

Morse, C. W., Sahler, O. J. Z., and Friedman, S. J. "A follow-up study of abused and neglected children." *American Journal of Diseases of Children* 120 (1970):439–46.

Quay, H. C., and Peterson, D. R. *Manual for the Behavior Problem Checklist*. Champaign: University of Illinois, Children's Research Center, 1967.

Reidy, T. J. "The aggressive characteristics of abused and neglected children." *Journal of Clinical Psychology*, in press.

Rule, B. G., and Neodale, A. R. "Emotional arousal and aggressive behavior." *Psychological Bulletin* 83 (1976):851–63.

Sandgrund, A., Gaines, R. U., and Green, A. H. "Child abuse and retardation: A problem of cause and effect." *American Journal of Mental Deficiency* 79 (1974):327–29.

Young, L. R. *Wednesday's Children: A Study of Child Neglect and Abuse*. New York: McGraw–Hill, 1964.

CHAPTER 26

A Follow-up Study of Abused Children

James T. Kent

This paper will present some of the findings of a retrospective follow-up of abused children. All children in the study were under the jurisdiction of the Juvenile Court in Los Angeles at the time of follow-up. The findings to be reported here were part of a larger survey conducted jointly by Children's Hospital of Los Angeles and the County Department of Public Social Services which attempted to learn more about the characteristics of abusing families, the children, and their course after legal intervention. This paper is concerned only with the children. It is about them that we know least.

Considerable data have been collected over the last fifteen years on the characteristics of abusive parents and their environments. Much of these data have been collected in an attempt to find distinguishing characteristics of the parents that would permit inferences about the psycho-social etiology of abusive behavior. It is assumed that such information would help in the prevention and treatment of abuse. It is a common and reasonable assumption in clinical research.

What is unusual about the clinical research in child abuse is that it says little about just what it is we are intervening to prevent or remedy, apart from the obvious reinjury. No one would maintain that the most significant effects of an abusive environment on the development of a child could be measured by the extent of his physical injuries. There are four published follow-up studies of abused children. A fifth, still unpublished, has recently been completed. Two others are known to the author by personal communication.

The first study was by Elmer (1) who followed up 31 children suspected from hospital x-rays to be victims of physical abuse. Most of these children displayed marked intellectual and/or physical deficits on follow-up. Thirteen other children from the original sample couldn't be followed up because they were institutionalized (five) or had died (eight).

Other studies showed similar effects of abuse. Morse (2) found that 15 of 21 children had a significant intellectual or emotional deficit three years after a hospital admission for abuse. Silver (3) found that physical abuse may be a factor

This paper was prepared in part with assistance from NIMH grant Number MH 24741-01.
Reprinted with permission from the *Journal of Pediatric Psychology* 1 (1976):25–31.

in juvenile delinquency. Unpublished reports by Howell (4) and Steele (5) also indicate that abuse is associated with delinquency.

Howell followed up a group of children who had first come to the attention of authorities during a one-year period in Los Angeles because they were abused and found that subsequently about half of them had criminal records as adults. Steele interviewed 100 consecutive juvenile offenders in a detention facility and found that most had experienced an incident of physical abuse a week or two prior to the offense.

Martin (6), in a longitudinal follow-up of 58 children who were physically abused, found them to manifest a high incidence of growth and neurological problems (about 30% and 50% respectively) and impaired emotional functioning, as evidenced by problems in behavior and relationships.

All of these studies indicate that abused children are at risk for deviant development. There is, however, a problem in establishing a connection between the abuse and child outcome. With one possible exception, the children studied were almost exclusively from low socio-economic status (SES) families. (Martin does not report SES data for his families). This is clarifying with respect to the etiology of abuse but obscuring with respect to its sequelae.

The finding is clarifying in that it suggests that socio-economic factors play an important role in the incidence of child abuse. This suggestion is made with full knowledge that there are probably significant reporting biases in the known incidence of child abuse. Families which experience socioeconomic distress are more likely to be in contact with the major reporting agencies (public welfare, police, and hospital emergency and ambulatory services) for a number of reasons other than those connected with child abuse. Those families are thus more liable to discovery and more likely to be reported than families which are economically self-contained and can afford private medical care (7). At the same time, it is plausible to assume that increasing stress on parents through socio-economic deprivation and decreasing the possibility of adequate respite care (for the same socioeconomic reasons) will serve to aggravate parent-child tensions and increase the possibility of abusive behavior.

The low SES status of abusive families which have been followed up is an obscuring factor in that it confounds the effects of physical abuse with the effects of a depriving environment. Such environments are more likely to manifest higher levels of family disorganization; substandard housing, nutrition and health care and less opportunity for good educational and socialization experiences. Thus, there is the problem of partialing out the effects of physical abuse from the more pervasive effects of a deficit environment. Elmer (8) in a recent study of abused children that utilized two control groups (abuse vs. accident vs. nonaccident) concluded that "the effects of abuse on child development are insignificant compared to membership in the lower (SES) classes."

In addition to the problems of confounding the effects of low SES with the effects of abuse, there is another difficulty in the available research data. That difficulty is a lack of data demonstrating that intervention accomplishes more than reducing the incidence of abuse in a family—if indeed it always does that. In

Silver's (9) study, abuse continued in about one-third of the families even after intervention. The concern here is for evidence that intervention makes an important difference in the psychosocial functioning of the children.

That will seem like an absurd concern to those who work with the problem clinically. We know that we can help many families. In any case, there is no rational alternative for a person when confronted with an abused child except to respond with every available resource, whatever prognosis the statistics indicate. From that point of view, data collection on the effects of intervention would be an irrelevant process. The problem speaks for itself. Money spent in data collection is money diverted from clinical services. It employs researchers and statisticians at the expense of the children they study.

On the other hand, it is also clear that if we know what it is we are intervening to prevent (apart from the obvious reinjury) then we can do a better job of allocating scarce resources. There is, however, an even more immediate problem. Much of the stimulus for recently improved intervention services has been provided by the Federal Child Abuse Prevention Act. Most of the funds provided by that Act are obligated or have been spent. The Act terminates in 1977. State and local agencies have been slow to acknowledge the need to provide continuing financial support for these expanded services or to initiate others. If we are to argue for the continuing support of these services beyond the usual intervention (i.e., medical treatment, legal remedy and protective services case work), we are going to have to demonstrate that social intervention does make a difference.

The present study is concerned with these two issues: (1) providing data about the effects of intervention on the subsequent development of abused children, and (2) providing data about the possible effects of abuse independent of the effects of low SES. Evidence for these two issues will be provided by survey level data from a retrospective follow-up of abused children.

METHOD

The particular intervention mostly employed for these children was removal from the abusive environment to a foster home. This form of intervention is radical, costly, and carries with it many problems of its own (some of these will be discussed later). It is not being proposed as a "model." It was simply found to be the most commonly employed intervention in Los Angeles County at the time of the study.

For the purposes of this study, foster homes had the advantages of providing a relatively standard intervention and a recovery environment which, generally, was not physically abusive (corporal punishment of foster children is not sanctioned in California). The methods of selecting homes which qualify to provide foster care in Los Angeles County would not systematically ensure exceptional parenting. Standards for selection have more to do with the availability of adult supervision and the size of the house. These services are well compensated by the County, and there is no shortage of foster homes. Thus the recovery environments were assumed to represent a fair cross section of family environments in Los Angeles—some good, some bad, most just average.

The problem in disentangling the effects of abuse from the effects of SES arises because of the reporting bias discussed earlier. There is not an identified high SES abuse group available for comparison. It was not felt that simply matching an abuse group with a low SES non-abuse group would provide a fair comparison. Socioeconomic status is a broad-gauged indicator that obscures many differences in family function that are independent of SES but relevant to the psycho-social development of children. To cope with this problem, it was decided to compare two different kinds of abuse groups, then compare both abuse groups to another low SES group that also manifested severe family dysfunction but without overt abuse.

The first step in this strategy was to differentiate inflicted injury, or "nonaccidental trauma" (NAT) from gross neglect (NEG). While both are often referred to generally as "physical abuse," it seemed likely that they had different etiologies and surely had different effects on a developing child. At the same time, both were more likely to be reported from lower SES groups and represented cases of severe family dysfunction. Thus differences between the two groups at the time of intake would permit some inferences to be drawn about the effects of specific kinds of abuse.

The second step in the strategy was to locate a nonabuse group which also manifested evidence of severe family dysfunction in a low SES environment. The group was recruited from families for which specialized children's services had been requested from the County Department of Public Social Services (DPSS). The reasons for requesting such services in Los Angeles County include, in part, suspicion of child abuse but are concerned mostly with a broad range of factors which constitute an abuse-prone environment. That is, while physical abuse to the person of the child was not grossly evident, the environment was one in which healthy growth and development were likely to be severely compromised. The referral reasons in this group are described in the next section.

The three groups included in this study then are nonaccidental trauma (NAT), gross neglect (NEG), and protective services (PS). Follow-up data were not available for the protective service families. Nevertheless, a comparison of differences among the three groups at intake would provide evidence about the effects of specific kinds of abuse independent of SES. Differences between the intake and follow-up status of the two abuse groups would provide evidence about the effectiveness of intervention.

SAMPLE

The sample for the two abuse groups was drawn from children under court dependency in Los Angeles County during November 1971. In that month there were 7,069 such children. Children who had been court dependent for less than six months were omitted because there was not enough cumulative information on them. Of the 5,500 cases remaining, 1,235 had been subjected to one of the two forms of abuse (NAT or NEG) as adjudicated by the Juvenile Court. Cases in which both kinds of abuse were part of the Juvenile Court allegation were deleted. Finally, cases were deleted so that no DPSS worker would have more than three study families in her caseload. The final NEG sample was manipulated to ensure that every child who had been diagnosed as "failure to thrive" was included (53 children). NAT cases were simply deleted by case numbers. The final sample consisted of 219 NAT cases (24% of the original sample) and 159 NEG cases (48% of the original sample).

The protective services families were selected from a sampling of every tenth call to DPSS for specialized services for one month. Most (76%) of the calls were for protective services. There were 185 families in that group; all of them were used. This group was formed and data collected approximately 12 months later than for the two abuse groups.

The "protective services" or "nonabuse" group contains a small percentage (12%) of cases where the call concerned allegations of abuse. Since, at the point these data were collected, none of the allegations has been adjudicated in court these cases were retained in the sample. It is clear from an inspection of the reasons for referral that this group is likely to include a large percentage of high-risk environments.

DATA COLLECTION

For the two abuse groups, a precoded survey questionnaire was distributed to each of the Department of Public Social Service dependency workers who had a study family in her caseload. No worker had more than three study children in his/her caseload. The questionnaires were completed by the social worker, using DPSS records of contacts with the children and families, hospital records, reports of police investigation (mandatory for every court adjudicated case), reports from foster homes, and a standard report submitted by the schools for every child of school age. If the information requested in the questionnaire was not available in these records, the worker was requested to contact the appropriate person or agency to get the information.

This questionnaire, with some modification, was then used for the "protective services" group. It was completed by the services social worker who investigated the call. The modifications were required by the somewhat different circumstances of the protective services cases and the needs of DPSS for information other than that collected on the abuse groups.

RESULTS

The results to be reported here are concerned mainly with differences between the intake and follow-up status of the children. Before these results are given, family structure and SES characteristics will be described. There are several differences in family structure among groups. The PS families tend to be smaller, are more often headed by a single parent, and the parents tend to be older. The NAT family is younger and more often has two parents in the home. The NEG family stands out as being both relatively young and very large. It is not clear what implications these differences have for the purposes of this study. The data are offered simply to provide a context for the discussions that follow.

Three variables were selected to reflect SES: parent education, parent employment, and a ratio of net family income per month to number of family members. The findings indicate that, with respect to education and employment, the NAT and PS mothers are comparable. The PS fathers tend to be somewhat better educated than NAT fathers, 16% more of them having at least some college education, but this difference is not reflected in their respective employment rates. The NEG parents are clearly more depressed in terms of education and employment than either the NAT or PS parents.

The average monthly support per family member indicates a larger difference between the NAT and PS families in favor of the PS families. This difference cannot be translated directly into SES differences, however, because more PS families depended on public financial aid (67%) than did NAT families (54%). The NEG families, again, appear as the most impoverished and also as more likely to depend on public aid (72% of all NEG families.)

The conclusion is that there may be a slight SES difference between the NAT and PS families, depending upon how much weight is given to welfare status vs. actual dollar support available. The NEG families appear as more depressed on all indicators. Overall, it is clear that in terms of employment and families receiving public aid, we are dealing with three groups that are all SES depressed.

Regarding the children's characteristics, in general, only data which were available for all three groups will be described. The major exception concerns ratings of developmental lags. These were not available for the PS group; however, differences between the NAT and NEG groups were considered interesting enough in themselves to be presented. Outcome data for the PS group were not available.

It is clear from the findings that the PS children tended to be older than either the NAT or NEG children. The NEG children tended to be the youngest. This is

Table 1. Height of children at intake and follow-up

Height in percentiles	Intake		Follow-up	
	Nat	Neg	Nat	Neg
Below 3rd percentile	30%	40%	6%	7%
3rd–25th percentile	25	26	14	23
26th–50th percentile	15	13	21	18
Over 50th percentile	30	21	59	52

Table 2. Weight of children at intake and follow-up

	Intake		Follow-up	
Weight in percentiles	Nat	Neg	Nat	Neg
Below 3rd percentile	17%	44%	11%	15%
3rd–25th percentile	33	20	23	26
26th–50th percentile	19	11	18	23
Over 50th percentile	31	25	48	36

probably due in part to the forced inclusion of all "failure to thrive" children in the NEG group. These children are more likely to be diagnosed during infancy because of their malnourished status.

Intake and follow-up characteristics of the children in the three groups will be presented. Three kinds of data are presented. The first kind concerns the physical growth of the abused children (not available for the PS group). The second kind concerns social worker ratings of certain behavioral characteristics based on direct observation and reports from parents, foster parents, or health professionals. No attempt was made to standardize the basis of the ratings. It was assumed that individual differences among workers in making these ratings would be normally distributed and thus not affect the magnitude of observed differences among groups.

A check on a possible tendency of the social workers to maximize improvement in their ratings is provided by the third kind of data to be presented. These data are based on the school performance of older children. These ratings are made by teachers for all children under court jurisdiction on a form provided by the DPSS. The ratings are made prospectively and, in the cases to be presented here, the intake ratings and outcome ratings were generally made by different teachers.

At the time of follow-up for the two abuse groups, most (90%) of the children had been under court jurisdiction for at least 12 months. As a matter of fact, nearly half (40%) had been under jurisdiction for three years or more. About 80% of the children were still placed out of home at the time of follow-up, most of them in foster care (65%), some to relatives (28%), and the rest in institutions.

Tables 1 and 2 display the changes in height and weight, respectively, of the two abuse groups from intake to follow-up.

It is clear that the abused children grew better after intervention. Most encouraging are the relative gains in height for both groups. This is a better indicator of nutritional adequacy than weight gains.

Table 3 displays ratings of certain behavioral characteristics of the children at intake and follow-up. An additional section of the table describes outcome rating of children judged as too young to rate at intake.

Table 3. Behavioral and developmental characteristics of children rated as "present" at intake and follow-up

Behavioral characteristic	Intake			Follow-up		Follow-up— too young at intake	
	Nat	Neg	PS	Nat	Neg	Nat	Neg
1. Excessive disobedience[1]	44%	29%	18%	34%	30%	12%	9%
2. Severe tantrums[1]	31	29	10	22	25	20	14
3. Emotional withdrawal	51	59	*	34	29	30	18
4. Aggression toward adults and peers[1]	44	34	21	35	37	19	9
5. Poor peer relationship[2]	54	42	20	45	34	15	21
Developmental characteristic							
6. Delay in motor development	25	64	*	23	40	18	24
7. Delay in language development	39	72	*	30	49	29	38
8. Delay in ADL development[3]	34	79	*	18	37	17	25

*Ratings not available.
[1] Excludes children less than 3 years old.
[2] Excludes children less than 4 years old.
[3] ADL is "activities of daily living," e.g., feeding, dressing, hygiene, toileting.

Several interesting differences emerge from this table. The following are noted especially:

1. Both abuse groups are rated as manifesting a higher incidence of the problem behaviors than the PS group on intake. This suggests that abusive environments do increase the incidence of certain problem behaviors independent of low SES or general family dysfunction.

2. Within the abuse groups, the NAT group is rated as more aggressive, more disobedient, and as having more problems in peer relationships than the NEG group on intake. This suggests that one sequela of physical assault on children is an increase in problems in managing their own aggression.

3. On follow-up, the NAT group appears to have improved more with respect to the management of aggression (variables 1, 2, and 4) and resembled the NEG group. The NEG group changes very little on follow-up (in fact, there is a slight increase in behavior in two of the three variables). This further suggests that the increased incidence of these behaviors for the NAT group at intake was specific to the kind of abuse.

4. Both NAT and NEG groups were improved on nearly all the problem behaviors, especially the incidence of emotional withdrawal, on follow-up. This suggests that intervention in the form of removal of the child from the abusive environment had beneficial results.

5. In the ratings of development, the NEG group is rated as substantially

more delayed at intake. They improved markedly on follow-up but continued to manifest a higher incidence of delay than the NAT group. This suggests that the delays were specific to the neglecting family environment, that intervention was beneficial, and possibly that this group (NEG) continues at risk for developmental delay even after intervention.

6. Both the NEG and NAT groups manifest greater developmental delays in language on follow-up than in the other two areas. The studies by Elmer (10) and Martin (11) also noted a higher incidence of language delays in their abused children.

7. The follow-up incidence of problem behaviors or developmental delays in children rated "too young" at intake was substantially less than for the older children at intake, with the magnitude of the difference decreasing on follow-up. This argues for early intervention and also supports the other indications that intervention is beneficial.

8. The direction of differences between the NAT and NEG groups on each variable except one is the same in the "too young at intake" sample as in the older sample. This gives us some confidence about the findings of differences between the two abuse groups.

The last set of tables displays ratings of the three groups by school teachers. These ratings are routinely requested of teachers for all children under court jurisdiction. In general the intake and follow-up ratings are made by a different teacher for each child. The instruction to the DPSS workers was to use the first and last set of school ratings available in the case records.

Two variables were selected from the school rating form as being most sensitive to psychological status: academic performance and peer relationships. Tested intelligence was added as a third variable to help interpret academic performance. (At the time of this study, school children in Los Angeles were routinely given group intelligence tests about every two years.)

Again, the tables separately display follow-up information for a sub-group of children who could not be rated at intake because of age (i.e., they were not yet enrolled in school).

The findings in the school ratings depicted in Tables 4 and 5 are entirely

Table 4. Average academic performance of children at intake and follow-up

Academic level	Intake			Follow-up		Follow-up—too young at intake	
	Nat	Neg	PS	Nat	Neg	Nat	Neg
Above average	10%	0	9%	14%	15%	9%	14%
Average	37	18	63	58	48	62	54
Below average	34	53	20	25	37	28	32
Failing	19	29	8	3	0	2	0

Table 5. School peer relationships of children at intake and follow-up

Rating	Intake			Follow-up		Follow-up—too young at intake	
	Nat	Neg	PS	Nat	Neg	Nat	Neg
Satisfactory	33%	40%	77%	62%	65%	70%	62%
Unsatisfactory	67	60	23	38	35	30	38

consistent with the DPSS social worker ratings in that they showed marked improvement of the NAT and NEG groups in functioning after intervention. The IQ findings depicted in Table 6 still show a somewhat truncated distribution, which Martin (12) also found, but there was a definite shift toward a more normal distribution. The NAT group shows an advantage over the NEG group in tested IQ which again raises a serious question about permanent residuals of gross neglect. It is interesting to note, however, that this difference in IQ is not reflected as strongly in the academic performance ratings on follow-up. The ratings of peer relationships are in every way comparable to those made by the social workers.

These findings also show that the PS group is functioning better than the two abuse groups at the time of intake. Follow-up results show that in academic performance the two abuse groups resemble the PS groups at intake but continue to lag in peer relationships. That trend was also noted in the social worker ratings.

The follow-up findings of children too young to be in school at the time of the intake in the NEG group do not show a pronounced difference from the findings of the older children at follow-up except in IQ. The same is generally true for the NAT, although the "too young" children there have somewhat better peer relationship ratings.

Table 6. Tested intelligence of children at intake and follow-up

IQ score	Intake		Follow-up		Followup—too young at intake	
	Nat	Neg	Nat	Neg	Nat	Neg
Below 70	24%	39%	13%	28%	12%	17%
70–89	20	39	28	23	32	22
90–110	51	23	46	49	28	61
111–130	6	0	13	0	24	0
Over 130	0	0	1	0	4	0

[1] Ratings not available for PS children.

DISCUSSION

The results of the study are regarded as demonstrating that intervention improved the emotional and cognitive functioning of the abused children. Retrospective and prospective ratings from two sources are consistent with each other and both sets of ratings support the value of intervention.

With respect to the specific effects of abuse, it is suggested that NAT children tend to have more problems in managing aggressive behavior and more problems in establishing peer adult relationships. NEG children manifest more problems in developmental delay. That is not surprising in that the NEG sample was manipulated to include all "failure to thrive" children. Both abuse groups show higher rates of problem behavior and developmental delay (both at intake and follow-up) than a control group of PS children.

The improvement in the psychosocial functioning of the abused children after removal from the home of the parents also supports the conclusion that the abusive environments have specific effects. This finding, however, is somewhat confounded by the fact that the foster homes (the usual recovery environment) would on the average represent a higher SES environment than the parents' homes. It is possible that low SES children from non-abusive families would show similar changes. The fact that the two abuse groups changed at different rates in two areas (problem behavior and developmental delay) is suggestive that the intake characteristics were in part specific to abuse and not just low SES, but in itself this finding is not conclusive. In conjunction with the findings of marked differences between the two abuse groups and the PS group at intake, it is possible to infer that the differences were specific in part to abuse.

Overall, the findings are regarded as indicating that (1) abusive environments do put children seriously at risk for problems other than physical injury independent of SES, and (2) an intervention which alters that environment will reduce the risk. Such conclusions are not likely to contradict anyone's clinical experience. In mathematics, it might be called a "trivial result," i.e., an unnecessary proof of the obvious. The fact remains that despite the virtual explosion of literature on child abuse in the last few years, there is still virtually no quantitative data to demonstrate that we know how to intervene in ways which make a significant long term difference. This brings us to a consideration of the intervention that formed the basis for this study.

The paper began by suggesting that it would be necessary to demonstrate the effectiveness of intervention programs beyond the usual medical-legal-casework interventions in order to encourage support of more comprehensive services. The study described here demonstrates that one kind of radical intervention does improve the follow-up status of the children. However, this form of intervention has problems of its own, and despite the improvement of the affected children on the follow-up, incidence of continuing problems is alarmingly high.

Some problems of out-of-home placement as an intervention method are these: (1) it leaves unresolved the safety and psychosocial health of the children remaining in the home; (2) even if all the children are removed, the parents are young, still in prime child-bearing years, and can be expected to have more children; (3) most of the children are going to eventually return home anyway and there is no evidence that we know how to help parents deal effectively with abusive tendencies when the potential target is totally removed from their care; (4) prolonged separation would tend to weaken a parent-child bonding which is already highly conflicted; and (5) there is evidence (not cited) from the study presented here that length of time in foster care is negatively correlated with child follow-up status. The correlation with outcome and number of foster placements is significantly negative, and multiple placements were experienced by the majority of the children. The magnitude of these correlations is small (less than .20) but the direction is of concern.

In addition to these problems, there is the problem of a relatively high incidence of deficit behaviors continuing in the abused children even after foster care intervention. The absolute magnitude of the incidence is not certain, given the methods of the study. But it is likely that social workers who were responsible for supervising the children in dependency would be more prone to under-report than over-report difficulties on follow-up. Nevertheless, follow-up results indicate that a large percentage of the abused children continue to manifest problems in psychosocial functioning. The conclusion is that, while the follow-up results are encouraging with respect to the potential for altering the effects of abuse on children, they are by no means comforting with respect to the problems that continue.

These remarks should in no way be construed as an indictment of the usefulness of foster homes or the capabilities of foster parents. What is suggested is that foster care placement cannot alone be expected to resolve the problems of the abused child. It can help some problems, but it just defers others (e.g., helping the parents to cope more effectively with the child), and if overused, it can create problems of its own. One could also raise questions about the upside-down social priorities that will provide two or three times more money to support a child in foster care than to support that same child at home. However, it was not the purpose of this paper to debate the relative value of different strategies for intervention.

The major point to be made here is that abusive environments tend to produce highly troubled children. This process can be interrupted, at least in part. This point needs to be reinforced with solid data about the effects of intervention if we are to influence social policy and priorities to benefit abused children in any sustained way. In short, we are going to have to develop a data base that consists of more than shocking photographs and newspaper stories. Those attract attention but not for long. We have developed a short attention span for atrocity. The greater need now is for evidence that we can intervene effectively in abusive situations. Such evidence would help shape the policies that control our capabilities for intervention.

CONCLUSION

It was the purpose of this study to investigate the specific effects of abusive environments on the psychosocial development of children and the possible reversibility of these effects with intervention through foster home placement. It was concluded that abusive environments do have specific effects independent of low SES and general family dysfunction. It was also concluded that these effects are in part reversible. Reservations about the intervention method that was predominant in the study were discussed.

REFERENCES

1. Elmer, Elizabeth. *Children in Jeopardy*. Pittsburgh: University of Pittsburgh Press, 1967.
2. Morse, Carol, et al. "A Three-Year Follow-Up Study of Abused and Neglected Children." *American Journal of the Diseases of Childhood* 120 (1970):439-48.
3. Silver, Larry, et al. "Does Violence Breed Violence? Contributions from a Study of the Child Abuse Syndrome." *American Journal of Psychiatry* 126 (1969):404-407.
4. Howell, Jacqueline. Child Abuse Unit, Los Angeles Police Department, personal communication, 1974.
5. Steele, Brandt. University of Colorado Medical Center, personal communication, 1975.
6. Martin, Harold, et al. "The Development of Abused Children." In Schulman, Irving (ed.), *Advances in Pediatrics*. Chicago: Year Book Medical Publishing, 1974.
7. The percentage of cases of child abuse reported here from the private medical sector is extremely low, averaging about 1% nationally and in Los Angeles County, the site of the present study. This may be due in part to a reluctance of the private physician to become involved in a painful social and legal process which has questionable benefits to his patients, but it may also reflect a "low index of suspicion" for child abuse when the physician has known the family as patients for several years. Whatever the cause, it is clear that the more impersonal circumstances of a hospital's emergency and ambulatory services are more conducive to reporting.
8. Elmer, Elizabeth. *Children in Jeopardy*. Pittsburgh: University of Pittsburgh Press, 1967.
9. Silver, Larry, et al. "Does Violence Breed Violence? Contributions from a Study of the Child Abuse Syndrome." *American Journal of Psychiatry* 126 (1969):404-407.
10. Elmer, Elizabeth. *Children in Jeopardy*. Pittsburgh: University of Pittsburgh Press, 1967.
11. Martin, Harold, et al. "The Development of Abused Children." In Schulman, Irving (ed.), *Advances in Pediatrics*. Chicago: Year Book Medical Publishing, 1974.
12. Martin, Harold, et al. "The Development of Abused Children." In Schulman, Irving (ed.), *Advances in Pediatrics*. Chicago: Year Book Medical Publishing, 1974.

CHAPTER 27

Developmental Retardation in Infants As a Concomitant of Physical Child Abuse

Alan S. Appelbaum

ABSTRACT

The impact of child abuse on the developmental functioning of infants was investigated. Thirty verified cases of physically abused children were compared to a reference group of thirty nonabused children matched for age, sex, race, and socioeconomic status. Abused children scored significantly lower in terms of cognitive and motor development as measured by the Bayley Scales of Infant Development. Developmental delay on three of the four sectors of the Denver Developmental Screening Test, personal-social, language, and gross motor, were also found in the abused children. There were, however, relatively few item differences between the two groups on the thirty more general behavioral variables comprising the Bayley Infant Behavior Record. Results appear to confirm clinical observation of abused children as developmentally retarded, with specific delays in the language and gross motor areas. Although methodologically complex, longitudinal studies are clearly indicated to assess the stability and/or reversibility of the present findings.

The primary focus of the literature in the area of child abuse has been the adults involved: their demographic characteristics, psychological functioning, and treatment approaches aimed at modifying their abusive behaviors. Consequently, our present knowledge of the abused child is limited mostly to clinical observations and theorizing. Specifically, little is known of the immediate or long-range consequences of abuse as they are manifest in the child's behavior.

While several authors have suggested that one of the consequences of abuse may be impaired cognitive development and retarded intellectual functioning, few studies have directly attempted to investigate this relationship (Brandwein 1973). Some retrospective studies (e.g., Morse, Sahler, and Friedman 1970) have reported a high incidence of retarded functioning among abused children

The author is indebted to John E. Overall for statistical analysis of the data, and to Drs. Joan Hebeler, Margaret McNeese, Manon Brenner, and Sally Robinson for their invaluable assistance in obtaining children for this study and to the M.D. Anderson Foundation for its support of this project.

upon follow-up. These studies, however, suffer from the methodological problems of high attrition rates and lack of inclusion of control samples. In the only well-controlled study available, Sandgrund, Gaines, and Green (1974), employing a matched control group found significantly lower intellectual functioning in abused and neglected 8½-year-olds. They also found a higher percentage of retardation in the abused and neglected groups as defined by Wechsler IQs below 70.

Since a number of studies summarized by Helfer and Kempe (1974) indicate that the majority of abused children are under 3 years of age, the present study is an attempt to investigate the impact of child abuse on developmental functioning in the young child. The specific hypothesis to be tested is that abused children under 2½ years of age will be developmentally retarded in comparison to their nonabused peers, while the hypothesis to be disproved would be that the two groups do not differ in level of developmental attainment.

METHOD

Subjects

Sixty children, thirty abused and thirty nonabused controls matched for age, sex, race, and socioeconomic status were evaluated. All abused children were current cases actively being followed by the Child and Family Protective Services Treatment Program, University of Texas Medical Branch, Galveston. The diagnosis of abuse was made by this agency. The nonabused control children were obtained from the Pediatric Outpatient Clinic.

Criteria for classifying children as abused were a diagnosis of significant nonaccidental trauma by the examining pediatrician, as well as confirmation by investigation of the relevant child welfare agency. While several children were diagnosed as having multiple injury, the modal injury was bruises followed by fractures, burns, and lacerations. Children known to have suffered severe head trauma were excluded from the sample. Also, children whose injury was secondary to the parents' failure to provide adequate care or supervision (neglect) were excluded, as were children who were diagnosed as "nonorganic failure to thrive."

All children were between the ages of 2 mos. and 29.83 mos., with an average age of 14.66 mos. The mean age of the experimental group children and the control group children was 15.78 mos. ($SD = 8.81$) and 13.55 mos. ($SD = 8.49$), respectively. This difference was not statistically significant, $t(58) = 1.00$. The two groups were composed of an equal number of males and females. Five (16%) of the abused children and seven (23%) of the control children were black. Both groups consisted of an equal number of children above and below 12 mos. of age.

All children studied came from homes where the head of the household met Hollinghead's (note 1) criteria for categories IV and V of the two-factor index of social position. Mean total years of education for the abused and nonabused groups were 11.13 (*SD* = 2.30) and 10.05 (*SD* = 2.21), respectively, with 20 being the highest ranking possible; average occupational rankings were 6.0 (*SD* = 0.95) and 5.47 (*SD* = 1.31), respectively, with 7 being the lowest ranking possible. The mean age of the mothers and number of children under 18 in the family were 22.35 yrs. (*SD* = 3.18) and 2.04 (*SD* = 1.04) for the abused and 24.80 yrs. (*SD* = 4.64) and 2.00 (*SD* = 0.96) for the nonabused groups, respectively. All mean differences between groups were nonsignificant.

Materials and Procedure

The Bayley Scales of Infant Development (Bayley 1969) and the Revised Denver Developmental Screening Test (Frankenburg, Dodds, and Fandal 1970) were administered to each child in a counterbalanced order, so that half of the infants received the Bayley Scales first and the other half received the Denver first. All sixty children were evaluated by the same experienced examiner, who performed the evaluation in a "blind" fashion with no information as to the child's history available. Both the Bayley Mental and Psychomotor Scales were administered. Also, the Bayley Infant Behavior Record (Bayley 1969), based only upon behaviors observed during testing, was completed by the examiner immediately after each evaluation.

All measures were administered and scored as instructed in the respective test manuals (Bayley 1969; Frankenburg, Dodds, and Fandal 1970). In addition, Denver mental age scores were calculated for each of the four sectors (personal-social, fine motor-adaptive, language, and gross motor) using the 50% pass method (Frankenburg, Camp, and Van Natta 1971). The four sectors were also averaged to obtain a mental age score for the total Denver and developmental quotients derived by the formula of mental age/chronological age × 100 were computed (Frankenburg, Camp, Van Natta, Demersseman, and Voorhees 1971).

RESULTS AND DISCUSSION

The data were analyzed by means of a three-way factorial multivariate analysis of variance with abuse, sex, and race as between groups factors and age partialed out as a linear covariate (Overall and Klett 1972). Since the two groups were not precisely matched on age, the covariance analysis was employed to control for the effects of this variable. Main effects of race and sex and the interactions of these factors with each other and with abuse were all negligible. The main effects of abuse revealed significant differences for eight of the nine dependent measures; all interactions involving abuse and other variables were nonsignificant. Table 1 presents means and standard deviations for the two groups of children studied.

Table 1. Means and standard deviations for abused and nonabused children on nine dependent measures

Measure	Abused children			Nonabused children		
	Mean		SD	Mean		SD
Bayley						
Mental Development Index	75.07	(74.68)*	18.92	106.00	(104.56)	18.94
Age equivalent	12.03	(10.54)	7.26	13.48	(14.26)	7.89
Psychomotor Development Index	85.53	(83.70)	23.60	125.93	(125.86)	15.15
Age equivalent	13.19	(11.28)	7.66	16.14	(17.58)	9.76
Denver Mental Ages						
personal, social	13.14	(12.69)	8.93	13.69	(14.75)	8.63
fine motor-adaptive	11.19	(10.79)	5.67	10.85	(11.45)	5.85
language	9.13	(8.90)	6.99	10.91	(11.84)	6.43
gross motor	11.80	(11.12)	7.98	13.21	(14.22)	8.16
Denver Developmental Quotient	72.29	(77.11)	14.74	93.03	(92.02)	11.05

*Covariate adjusted means.

Bayley

On the Bayley Mental Scale the difference in the magnitude of the scores between the two groups was highly significant, $F(1, 51) = 29.19$, $p < .001$, with the abused children attaining a mean Mental Development Index significantly below that attained by the nonabused control children. The same disparity in functioning was reflected in the Mental Scale Age Equivalent scores, $F(1, 51) = 20.39$, $p < .001$, with the abused children performing on the average approximately four months below the nonabused controls. Similar results were obtained with reference to the Bayley Motor Scale (see Table 1), with the abused children yielding scores significantly smaller in magnitude than the nonabused controls, $F(1, 51) = 46.06$, $p < .001$. Again, the same difference is reflected in the Motor Scale Age Equivalent scores, $F(1, 51) = 37.71$, $p < .001$, with the abused children performing on the average five to six months below the nonabused controls.

The nonabused control children obtained Bayley Mental Scale scores generally consistent with but somewhat higher than normative expectations (mean Mental Development Index = 106.00), while the same children obtained Bayley Motor Scale scores that were significantly above normative expectations (mean Psychomotor Development Index = 125.86). The present results on the basis of the Mental Development Index parallel other findings on similar populations at this age level (King and Seegmiller 1973). Although mental test performance generally has not been shown to be related to socioeconomic status before fifteen months of age, psychomotor test performance has been shown to be related to this variable. Several authors (e.g., Bayley 1965) have reported a "generalized motoric precocity" in lower socioeconomic status black infants that tends to diminish with increasing age. Since the present findings are based on a primarily white sample and the main effects of race were negligible, the data would seem to imply that the observed motor precocity may be a function of socioeconomic status rather than racial variables. This conclusion is consistent with the findings of Williams and Scott (1953).

Denver

The performance of the two groups of children on the Revised Denver Developmental Screening Test generally parallels their performance on the Bayley. In terms of Denver nominal classification, all of the nonabused children were classified as "normal," while 53%, 30%, and 17% of the abused children were classified as "normal," "questionable," and "abnormal," respectively. Mental age levels obtained by the abused children (see Table 1) were significantly lower in magnitude in three of the four Denver sectors, personal-social, $F(1, 51) = 4.87, p < .05$; language, $F(1, 51) = 6.60, p < .05$; and gross motor, $F(1, 51) = 11.04, p < .001$. Mental age levels were not significantly different between the two groups in the fine motor-adaptive sector, $F(1, 51) = 1.25$, n.s. As would be expected from the sector mental age levels, developmental quotients were significantly different in magnitude between the two groups, $F(1, 51) = 15.91, p < .001$. It is noteworthy that of the four sectors, gross motor yielded the most discrepant mental age levels and was also one of the Bayley Infant Behavior Record items (see below) that was rated as significantly lower in the abused children. These findings would seem to confirm the observation (note 2) that along with language, delayed or retarded gross motor development is one of the most consistently mentioned characteristics of abused children, on the basis of clinical observation.

Infant Behavior Record

The findings with reference to more general behavioral variables as assessed by the Infant Behavior Record are less decisive than for either the Bayley Mental and Motor Scales or the Denver. There were relatively few item differences between the two groups on the thirty variables comprising this measure. Abused children showed more persistent object attachment, $F(1, 51) = 7.01, p < .05$, a behavior generally associated with younger children. Abused children also showed less endurance in terms of behavior constancy in adequacy of response to the demands of the tests, $F(1, 51) = 4.12, p < .05$, and during testing they demonstrated poorer gross motor coordination than the controls, $F(1, 51) = 7.35, p < .01$. In addition, general evaluation of abused children was less favorable, with many more being classified as exceptional, $F(1, 51) = 23.68$, $p < .001$.

Conclusions

These data appear to indicate that differences in the developmental functioning of abused children can be detected as early as four months of age. The youngest group of physically abused children differ from their nonabused peers on several measures of cognitive and psychomotor development. They were generally not, however, judged as otherwise behaviorally deviant. The implication of the present findings for clinical management seems clear. Specifically, assessment of the child's total developmental progress is always relevant because inflicted injuries may be only one component of the child's situation.

It has been suggested (Brandwein 1973; Martin, Beezley, Conway, and Kempe 1974) that the observed relationship between physical abuse and retarded intellectual functioning may be secondary to head trauma. While such an etiological relationship may be valid in certain situations, it does not appear to be a very plausible explanation for the present results. Children known to have suffered severe head trauma were excluded from study. Also, while the possibility of preexisting significant developmental abnormalities cannot be ruled out, this may be the case only infrequently (Martin and Beezley 1974). Parenting behavior may be a more plausible explanation. This would include both the frequently described lack of bonding and limited child-rearing skills of many abusing parents (Ounsted, Oppenheimer, and Lindsay 1974; Pollock and Steele 1972), as well as the aspect of general neglect often felt to accompany physical abuse (Sandgrund et al. 1974).

While the longitudinal stability of the present findings is difficult to assess, retrospective studies of older abused children tend to corroborate the present results. Although there are many methodological problems, longitudinal studies are clearly indicated. Above all, perhaps the most important issue concerns the reversibility of the observed developmental deviancy in abused children. Effectiveness of parental treatment and consequent changes in child-rearing practices and attitudinal patterns, the availability of alternate living environments, and remedial educational/stimulation experiences would all be meaningful variables for study in conjunction with longitudinal study of the child.

NOTES

1. Hollingshead, A. B. "Two-factor index of social position." Unpublished manuscript, 1957. (Available from 1965 Yale Station, New Haven, Connecticut).
2. Kempe, R. S. "Treatment of children." Paper delivered at the Seventh Annual Symposium on the Battered Child, 1975, Denver, Colorado.

REFERENCES

Bayley, N. "Comparisons of mental and motor test scores for ages 1–15 months by sex, birth order, race, geographical location, and education of parents." *Child Development* 36 (1965):379–411.

————. *Manual for the Bayley Scales of Infant Development*. New York: Psychological Corporation, 1969.

Brandwein, H. "The battered child: A definite and significant factor in mental retardation." *Mental Retardation* 11 (1973):50–51.

Frankenburg, W. K., Camp, B. W., and Van Natta, P. A. "Validity of the Denver Developmental Screening Test." *Child Development* 42 (1971):475–85.

Frankenburg, W. K., Camp, B. W., Van Natta, P. A., Demersseman, J. A., and Voorhees, S. F. "Reliability and stability of the Denver Developmental Screening Test." *Child Development* 42 (1971):1315–25.

Frankenburg, W. K., Dodds, J. B., and Fandal, A. *Manual for the Revised Denver Developmental Screening Test*. Denver: University of Colorado Press, 1970.

Helfer, R. E., and Kempe, C. H. (eds.). *The Battered Child*, 2nd ed. Chicago: University of Chicago Press, 1974.

King, W. L., and Seegmiller, B. "Performance of 14- to 22-month-old Black firstborn male infants on two tests of cognitive development: The Bayley Scales and the Infant Psychological Development Scale." *Developmental Psychology* 8 (1973):317–26.

Martin, H. P., and Beezley, P. "Prevention and the consequences of child abuse." *Journal of Operational Psychiatry* 4 (1974):68–77.

Martin, H. P., Beezley, P., Conway, E. F., and Kempe, C. H. "The development of abused children." *Advances in Pediatrics* 21 (1974):25–73.

Matheny, A. P., Dolan, A. B., and Wilson, R. S. "Bayley's Infant Behavior Record: Relations between behaviors and mental test scores." *Developmental Psychology* 10 (1974):696–702.

Morse, W., Sahler, O. J., and Friedman, S. B. A three-year follow-up study of abused and neglected children." *American Journal of Diseases of Children* 120 (1970): 439–46.

Ounsted, C., Oppenheimer, R., and Lindsay, J. "Aspects of bonding failure: the psychopathology and psychotherapeutic treatment of families of battered children." *Developmental Medicine and Child Neurology* 16 (1974):447–56.

Overall, J. E., and Klett, C. J. *Applied Multivariate Analysis*. New York: McGraw–Hill, 1972.

Pollock, C. B., and Steele, B. F. "A Therapeutic Approach to the Parents." In C. H. Kempe and R. E. Helfer, eds., *Helping the Battered Child and His Family*. Philadelphia: J. B. Lippincott Co., 1972.

Sandgrund, A., Gaines, R. W., and Green, A. H. "Child abuse and mental retardation: a problem of cause and effect." *American Journal of Mental Deficiency* 79 (1974):327–30.

Williams, J., and Scott, R. "Growth and development of Negro infants. IV: Motor development and its relationship to child rearing practices in two groups of Negro infants." *Child Development* 24 (1953):103–21.

CHAPTER 28

Abuse and Neglect as a Cause of Mental Retardation: A Study of 140 Children Admitted to Subnormality Hospitals in Wiltshire

By Ann Buchanan and J. E. Oliver

The survey of 140 children under 16 in two subnormality hospitals showed that 3 percent of the children had definitely been rendered mentally handicapped as a consequence of violent abuse, and that a possible maximum total of 11 percent might have been thus rendered mentally handicapped. In 24 percent of the children, neglect was considered to be a contributory factor in reducing intellectual potential.

Impairment of intellect from abuse and neglect, especially in those with 'vulnerable' brains due to pre-existing abnormality, may be much commoner in children than is generally realized.

INTRODUCTION

A survey of severely ill-treated young children in North-East Wiltshire (Oliver *et al*, 1974) found that, out of thirty severely ill-treated children, eight had been rendered intellectually impaired. At least three of these eight suffered severe or profound mental handicap due to massive, obvious brain damage associated with abuse. Their cases were described in a further paper "Microcephaly following baby battering and shaking" (Oliver *et al*. 1975a).

During the last five years several authors have drawn attention to the consequences of child abuse in relation to brain damage and mental function (Guthkelch 1971; Martin 1972; Martin *et al*. 1974; Caffey 1974; Sarsfield 1974; Smith and Hanson 1974; MacKeith 1975; Jones 1976). The British Paediatric Association Survey reported to the Parliamentary Select Committee on Violence in the Family that 92 out of 869 'Non-Accidental Injury' cases reported by paediatricians in the United Kingdom were left with brain damage and 48 with visual defects (BPA, June 1976). The Royal College of Psychiatrists, reporting

Reprinted with permission from the *British Journal of Psychiatry* 131 (1977):458 67.

to the same Committee, estimated that "... if 75 young children per million of total population are severely attacked each year, then 18–19 per million could suffer intellectual impairment each year, often of a profound degree" (R. C. Psych., June 1976). Baldwin, projecting from the N. E. Wilts data, gives a crude minimum estimate of 240 new cases of severe subnormality (IQ below 50) in England and Wales per year resulting directly from parental assaults on babies and toddlers (Baldwin 1976).

Closely related to the effects of abuse on mental function are the effects of neglect and deprivation on intellectual development. Psychosocial deprivation as a cause of mental handicap is, of course, recognized by all the international classification systems (for instance, General Register Office 1968; Grossman 1973). Different aspects of this important field of research, in particular the effects of underfeeding and under stimulation on the brains and intellects of young children are considered by the following: Stott 1962; Bullard 1968; Birch and Gussow 1970; Hertzig *et al.* 1972; Pilling 1973; Chase *et al.* 1974; Dobbing 1974; Lewin 1974; Blackie *et al.* 1975; Forrest 1975; Watts 1976.

However, we are not aware of any systematic survey planned to assess the number of children in subnormality hospitals in Britain whose handicap might be related to abuse or neglect. We therefore set out to discover, in children in NHS subnormality hospitals in Wilts:

i) What proportion had been victims of neglect and abuse.

ii) What proportion had been *definitely* rendered mentally handicapped as a direct result of assaults.

iii) What proportion with previously healthy brains had *possibly* been rendered mentally handicapped as a result of abuse.

iv) What part neglect and deprivation had played in reducing intellectual potential, with resultant admission to hospital.

THE CHILDREN

The 140 children admitted to the two Wiltshire subnormality hospitals during 1972 and 1973 (under 16 years old in the year of their admission) constituted the basis for the survey.

These 140 children came from 137 families. Three families had two children each in hospital. Seventy-seven of the cases in the survey were short-term or programmed admissions only; the remainder were long-term or had become so by 1975. Twenty children (of the 140) were admitted only to the unit in one of the hospitals which specializes in emotionally disturbed and/or psychotic children. Table I gives the diagnostic groupings. For most children there were ostensible medical, psychiatric or education-training reasons for admission but for three-quarters of the survey social pressures were often the most forceful arguments used to get the child into hospital. Pressure to admit children of parents in the armed services (from families transiently in the locality) on a

Table I. Medical diagnoses under ICD system

ICD code, together with the appropriate (broad) category description	Number children
Causation of mental handicap	
.0 Mental handicap following infections and intoxications	16
.1 Mental handicap following trauma or physical agents (including birth anoxia, etc)	24
.2 Mental handicap associated with disorders of metabolism, growth or nutrition	1
.3 Mental handicap associated with gross brain disease	6
.4 Mental handicap associated with diseases and conditions due to (unknown) prenatal influence	28
.5 Mental handicap with chromosomal abnormalities	9
.6 Mental handicap associated with prematurity	2
.7 Mental handicap following major psychiatric disorder	13
.8 Mental handicap associated with psychosocial (environmental) deprivation	12
.9 Mental handicap—other and unspecified	25
Children admitted to hospital who were not mentally handicapped	4
Total children	140
Degree of mental handicap	
313–314 Severe and profound mental retardation (IQ under 35)	77
312 Moderate mental retardation (IQ 36–51)	36
311–310 Mild and borderline mental retardation (IQ 52–85)	23
Not mentally handicapped	4
Total children	140

permanent basis has always been resisted—not always successfully. Neither hospital was viewed as a special refuge for maltreated children. Despite these factors, we felt that the children admitted to the two hospitals were fairly typical of children admitted to other subnormality hospitals in Britain.

Most children in the survey had had fairly extensive investigations for their mental handicap before admission to our hospitals. Seventy-two children (51 percent) had been investigated or treated at specialist centers outside our districts (at neurological units, pediatric hospitals, pediatric departments of Teaching Hospitals). Of these 72, 18 had been seen at Great Ormond Street. Ninety-two children (66 percent) had been investigated at the pediatric departments of local District General Hospitals (some had also been investigated at specialist units elsewhere). Only 19 children (14 percent) had had no detailed investigations outside our two hospitals. Of these, 10 children had been given a clear-cut diagnosis at, or very soon after, birth (9 children of Down's syndrome); 5 were mentally handicapped but came to hospital through the Child Guidance Departments comparatively late in development; and the remaining 4 were not mentally handicapped.

METHODS OF STUDY

Efforts were made to obtain *all* medical and social records of the 140 children, to link these with family records, and to relate them to current clinical findings. This entailed searches of records from at least 25 different types of medical or social agencies concerned with child welfare.

Starting with our own hospital file on each patient, possible sources of records were followed-up. Scanning checks were made in all areas of the child's and sibs' residence, with vigilance exercised over the frequent occurrence of alternative names and addresses.

Our work did not just depend on retrospective collated data. All the children and many of the families were known to one of us (Oliver) during or before their admission to hospital. Ongoing information was obtained from Oliver's clinical work in the field of mental handicap, child guidance and child abuse; and also from the three paediatric and two other psychiatric consultants who had clinical responsibilities within the hospital. Some of the children and some relatives had been studied in the previous survey "Severely Ill-treated Young Children in N.E. Wilts" (Oliver *et al.* 1974).

In most cases it was possible to obtain original data relating to the child's birth and to plot the child's development through paediatric and health visitor notes and specialist investigations. These findings could then be linked to corresponding events in the social history of the family and related to current clinical findings.

The huge amount of previously uncollated material collected is indicative of the help and cooperation from the medical and social agencies approached.

Diagnoses

Diagnoses and codings under the International Classification of Diseases (General Register Office 1968) were made by three consultants (in the combined subspecialties of Child Psychiatry and Mental Handicap) and three pediatricians, as part of their routine clinical commitment. These diagnoses were based predominantly on the investigations and opinions of paediatricians. Where our research elicited new medical information which might be relevant to diagnosis, aspects of this information were discussed with the appropriate specialist. In many cases, specialists in other areas discussed their findings with us.

Definitions

For this survey, the following definitions were used:

VIH* (Violence-induced Handicap): Mental handicap following brain damage caused by assault(s). Assaults included fierce or repetitive shaking and/or throwing of a baby or young toddler—more dangerous practices than simple fist blows.

Abuse: Independent professional evidence that, before admission to hospital, the child had been a victim of physical assault(s) inappropriate to its age or development, and to an extent which warranted concern and/or intervention on the child's behalf.

Neglect: Independent professional evidence that the child was suffering as a result of inadequate parental care, which warranted concern and/or intervention on the child's behalf (see Table IV for instances).

Ascertainment of Violence-Induced Handicap (VIH Cases)

Minimum Figure. In this survey, to ascertain *definite* VIH cases, the following four methods of substantiation were used (in the cases reported under Results, we were in fact able to substantiate each case under three or four of the headings. In other localities, only strong suspicions may be possible).

1) Paediatric evidence at the time of the assault(s) or soon afterwards. Microcephaly following assaults can also be confirmed by serial head measurements (Oliver 1975*a*).

2) Statements by parent(s) or persons responsible.

3) Direct observations by relatives and others.

4) Consensus on diagnosis amongst all professionals concerned with the family.

Maximum Figure. Because it was felt that the *Minimum* figure for VIH cases gave no indication of the likely size of the problem, a further screening procedure was undertaken to produce a possible *Maximum VIH* figure. The aim was to find out how many additional children with seemingly healthy brains in early infancy *might* have been damaged as a result of concealed abuse, for instance secret shaking of crying or troublesome babies.

It was recognized that this screening procedure might miss some children who, because they had preexisting abnormalities, might be particularly at risk of abuse (Lynch 1975). Furthermore, it might include other children who had preexisting 'biological' abnormalities which had not been recognized by doctors.

---

*VIH is not so difficult to confirm where a child has previously been entirely normal and healthy. Nevertheless, abnormal children may be most at risk. This definition, therefore, includes doubtfully healthy or abnormal children, whose intellect was *unequivocally further impaired* following assaults affecting the brain. In this latter instance, the VIH must usually have been severe.

The following screening procedure was undertaken:

1) Inclusion only of children who had been passed as normal neonatally and up to three months old (sometimes for much longer).

2) Inclusion only of children whose families showed factors and behaviour generally associated with child abuse at the critical period when the child ceased to develop normally. Assaults on sibs, violence between marital partners, mental or physical illness in parent, multiagency involvement, severe social/domestic stress especially 'diffuse' social problems (Lynch 1976a) and situations leading to bonding failure (Lynch 1975, 1976b).

3) Inclusion only of children for whom there had been professional concern that the child in question had been at risk of abuse and/or evidence that the child had actually been the victim of assaults in his first three years, during the period of maximum (postnatal) brain growth spurt.

4) Inclusion only of children for whom there were no indications that birth trauma or factors in pregnancy had caused mental handicap.

5) Exclusion of children with clear-cut diagnoses (related to biological causes) under the ICD system—for instance, all children with Down's syndrome (000.5).

6) Exclusion of children from families where there were indications that mental handicap or still-births, involving parents and/or sibs, were part of a family inheritance; and exclusion of children with congenital stigmata associated with mental handicap.

Ascertainment of Neglect and Deprivation As a Contributory Factor in Reducing Intellectual Potential

It was recognized that there would be no easy means of incriminating neglect as a *sole* cause of mental handicap (*B.M.J.*, 1975a, b). The medical diagnosis under the ICD 000.8 (mental retardation associated with psychosocial environmental deprivation) does not allow for the interactions of other factors in the causation of mental handicap. Nevertheless it was felt important to ascertain those children for whom neglect had been a contributory factor in reducing intellectual potential.

All children, therefore, for whom there was evidence of neglect, in particular at the critical period of postnatal brain growth spurt (Dobbing 1974), were reassessed in detail. Diagnoses, early paediatric evidence (especially episodes of 'failure to thrive' for nonmedical reasons), and social evidence (NSPCC records of neglect) were considered, and the children were assigned to the following categories:

1) Neglect—*a predominating cause* of mental handicap in the absence of other important identifiable features which could contribute to the reduced intelligence.

2) Neglect—*a major contributory factor*, with no other clear-cut causes of mental handicap.

3) Neglect—*an important contributory factor* but in the presence of other identifiable causes of mental handicap. All the children in this group appeared to have multiple causes for their mental handicap rather than one clear-cut cause—thus no children with Down's syndrome appear here.

RESULTS

I. Abused Children

There was independent professional evidence that 31 children had been victims of physical assaults inappropriate to their age or development, before admission to hospital, which had warranted concern and/or intervention on the child's behalf. This was 22 percent of the total survey cases. For three-quarters of the assaulted children, the physical abuse was not an isolated incident but a habitual rearing pattern.

Table II gives details of injuries and the age at which these were sustained. There were a number of fractures occurring in children under the age of 2, some

Table II. Abused children—type of, and age at, abuse among 140 children

Type of abuse	Under 2 years	2–5	6+	Total
Abused children with head injuries	6	5	1	12
Fractures associated with physical abuse:				
A Numbers of children with skull fractures	2	1	—	3
(Number of rib fractures)*	(4)	(1)	—	(5)
B Numbers of children with rib fractures	3	1	—	4
(Number of other fractures)	(4–7)	(1)	—	(5 8)
C Numbers of children with other fractures	3	2	—	5
(Number of other fractures)	(4)	(2)	—	
D Total number of children with fractures associated with physical abuse	6	3	—	9
(Total number of fractures)*	(12–15)	(4)	—	(16–19)
Children receiving beatings, or bruisings and other surface injuries associated with abuse	14	11	2	27
Child victims of killing attempts	2	—	—	2
Total number of children with evidence of abuse	15	14	2	31

*Sometimes old fractures were uncertain on x-ray. Where there are two figures in brackets, these represent the maximum and minimum numbers of fractures.

of which might have been overlooked or unsuspected if the x-ray investigations had not been carried out at critical times in relation to the assaults and the child's development.

In addition to the abused children, there was evidence of recorded professional concern that the child was *at risk* of assault in a further 10 per cent of the cases. Furthermore, thirteen children had been threatened with injury or death by their parents.

II. Violence-Induced Handicap (VIH): Minimum Confirmed Figure

At least four children (3 percent) had *definitely* suffered assaults as babies which caused brain damage, rendering them severely or profoundly mentally handicapped. These children were ascertained by the methods already described.

Three of the children had been mentally and biologically normal before suffering the assaults which caused very severe and obvious brain damage. These three children were twelve months old or under at the time of the assault. They all had evidence of retinal hemorrhages and intracranial bleeding; but only two of them had skull fractures. Today they are all severely mentally handicapped, spastic, and with small heads (Oliver 1975*a*). A fourth child had suffered assaults at a year old. He had suffered severe bruising to the head and face. When found, he was partially asphyxiated; his throat had been forcibly obstructed by materials. Fits, cyanosis, and coma ensued, with subsequent slow and partial recovery. This child had evidence of neurofibromatosis, but was reported by his father, the family doctor and hospital doctors to have been developing normally before the catastrophe. The assault episode and/or its complications were seen to have been the main cause of the severe mental handicap. Fits and neurological features were conspicuous in the period following the assaults. At 4 years he still had not reached again some of his achievements at the age of one. The fits diminished as he grew older, but he now has an IQ of less than 30.

III. Violence-Induced Handicap (VIH): Maximum (Possible) Figure

A maximum of 16 children (11 percent of the total survey) *could have been* rendered mentally handicapped as a result of abuse. This figure includes the four children *definitely* rendered mentally handicapped as a result of abuse.

Eleven children were ascertained by the screening procedure for the Maximum VIH figure previously described. A further child is included in the maximum VIH figure because, although he was not ascertained by the screening procedure, it is highly probable that repeated trauma to the head, which was well documented, was responsible for brain damage and a subsequent impairment of intellectual ability. This child, from a mobile chaotic family, had more than ten episodes of (mostly severe) head injury, from assaults, before the age of 5, the main known episodes being at 4 months, 2½ years, and 3 years. He had been

Table III. Incidence of certain clinical features seen in the 16 children who comprised the maximum (possible) figure for violence-induced handicap

Clinical feature present	Number of children out of possible 16 children with feature
1. Gross and persistent CNS damage associated with spasticity, sensory defects and severe or profound mental retardation	5
2. Spasticity reported (usually by pediatrician) at some stage in the life of child	8
3. As for (2) above, but also including children with a variety of 'softer CNS signs,' often with mention of organic psychosis or organic brain damage	14
4. Epileptic fits	10
5. Rages or frenzies a prominent feature of the child's behavior— excluding (1) above	10*
6. Abnormal EEG, often with indications of 'multiple patchy areas of damage' of 'multifocal cerebral damage,' etc—excluding (1) above	10*

*Out of 11.

described as a 'bright' baby and toddler, but subsequently became a severely mentally and emotionally disturbed boy who required admission to the special unit within the subnormality hospital. He is now, after much special care, in the range of borderline subnormal intelligence, with a clearly abnormal EEG and clinical features suggesting brain damage. It seems probable, but not certain, that repeated trauma to the head was responsible for brain damage and subsequent impairment of intellectual ability.

This case illustrates the weaknesses of our screening procedure, and is typical of three or four others in the survey. These extra 3–4 cases are not included in the Maximum (possible) VIH figure because the assault episodes are less well documented.

Table III details the clinical features seen in the 16 children included in the Maximum VIH figure. None of these features were part of the original screening procedure. No child had less than two of the features. Four of the children were profoundly mentally retarded, 7 were severely mentally retarded, 1 was moderately retarded and 4 had mild or borderline mental retardation, but with severe behavior disorders.

Special mention must be made of one of the 11 children derived by the screening process. There was well-documented evidence that the child had suffered suffocatory episodes by being held under water at the age of 2. Although the child was already mentally handicapped at the time of the documented incidents, there were strong indications that he suffered frequent or severe suffocatory episodes at a much earlier age. A recent Australian paper suggests that this in itself can be a cause of mental handicap (Nixon and Pearn 1977).

VIH Children in the Wessex Region. Seven part-time or full-time consultants in mental subnormality, the entire membership of the Wessex Regional Consultants in Subnormality Group, gave individual independent estimates of the numbers of children in institutions for which they had responsibility, who *might* have been brain damaged as a consequence of battering. The *mean* estimate was 2.5 percent. This broad, partly guessed, clinical estimate compares well with the actual Minimum VIH figure given in this survey of 2.8 percent. Two of the consultants stressed that severe shaking causes greater damage to the brains of babies than fist blows or other 'battering'.

IV. Neglected Children

For 67 out of the 140 children (48 percent of the total) there was recorded evidence in the notes by independent professionals that the child was suffering as a result of inadequate parental care. For 57 of these children (41 percent) this represented a habitual pattern of rearing. In most cases, the first evidence of inadequate parental care was initially recorded for children under the age of 2 (Table IV).

V. Neglect As a Contributory Factor in Reducing Intellectual Potential

In 34 children (24 percent of the survey) neglect was felt to be a contributory factor in reducing intellectual potential. In 2 of these, with mild or borderline mental handicap, neglect appeared to be *the predominating cause* of mental handicap in the absence of other important identifiable features which could contribute to the reduced intelligence. In another 15, neglect was *a major contributory factor,* with no other clear-cut causes of mental handicap. In the remaining 17 children, neglect and deprivation were considered to be *important contributory factors,* but in the presence of other identifiable causes of mental handicap. In all 17 children there were multiple adverse factors in the history of the child's birth and development.

Out of the total 34 children, 20 had been known to the NSPCC, primarily for neglect. For 9 children there were detailed records of 'failure to thrive' for nonmedical reasons. Twelve of these 34 children had been diagnosed as mental retardation associated with psychosocial (environmental) deprivation.

VI. Children Who Suffered Abuse and Neglect

In the case of 29 children (21 percent of the survey) there was evidence of both abuse and neglect. There was no clear-cut cause for the handicap in 22 out of the 29, so it appears possible that the combination of abuse and neglect *could*

Table IV. Neglected children—type of neglect among 140 children

Type of neglect	Total children
1. General low standards of care or neglect specified	33
2. General low standards of care or neglect specified, with consequential multi-agency involvement	28
3. Inadequate feeding specified	16
4. Experiential (psychosocial) deprivation	33
5. Failure to seek essential medical care, or cooperate in treatment of child	13
6. Child exposed to unnecessary hazards	5
7. Child exposed to cold with inadequate clothing	5
8. Sexual abuse	2
9. Professional intervention necessary as child was unattended for long periods	6
10. Other forms of neglect or unspecified	12
Habitual pattern of rearing	57
Isolated incident	10
Total children suffering as a result of inadequate parental care	67

have contributed in an important way to impairment of the intellects of these 22 children.

DISCUSSION

1. VIH should be recognized as a major cause of mental handicap.

Children rendered mentally handicapped as a result of abuse may account for many more cases than phenylketonuria. The consequences are frequently more severe than those of Down's syndrome.

2. Difficulty of recognition of VIH.

In this survey we were fortunate in having the time and facilities for investigation which would not normally be available to other specialists. An awareness of the following difficulties, which we experienced in our investigations, may help the recognition of VIH:

a) Evidence for VIH, if not realized, investigated and documented soon after an assault, may not be available at a later date. In brain damage resulting from shaking, the retinal hemorrhages (which may also signify punctate hemorrhages within the brain substance) may be unnoticed or may have resolved by the time a child is admitted to a subnormality hospital. Similar considerations may apply to rib, skull or other fractures.

b) Before 1973, standard medical files seldom included details of, or even any reference to, the NSPCC, the Social Services, the Probation Department or other agencies concerned with the welfare of the child in question, *or with his sibs*. These agencies, in turn, may have been unaware of the crucially important medical considerations of leaving children under two at risk. This may still be the case in many localities, even now.

c) Identification of abused children is at all times difficult. It is especially so in the case of mentally handicapped children. The caring professions are usually sympathetic to the difficulties of a family with a mentally handicapped child, and tend not to record evidence derogatory to the parents.

d) It is much easier to incriminate tangible factors in the causation of mental handicap—toxaemia of pregnancy, damaged placenta, difficult birth—than emotionally charged medicosocial factors—cruelty or neglect in rearing. Parents assist in the distortion of emphasis by concealing more than they reveal to the trusting doctor or social worker.

e) The method of diagnostic coding used by the main subnormality hospitals in Wiltshire follows the International Classification of Diseases system (General Register Office 1968; Spencer 1974, 1975, 1976). The insistence of a primary (single) diagnosis can rule out the probability of interactions. In particular, it is unsatisfactory to code neglect/deprivation (000.8) as an all-or-nothing effect in isolation from other possible aetiological factors (including abuse).

3. Combinations of neglect and abuse.

These may be a handicapping factor for much larger numbers of children than is generally recognized, especially for those children with already 'vulnerable' brains. Some of the neglected children had adverse genetic inheritance, or had suffered damage in the prenatal or perinatal period. Such children seemed particularly vulnerable to aspects of inadequate care which might not have so adversely affected the brains of children from healthier backgrounds. One case of a child with a potentially preventable brain damage was not recognized until too late because the mother refused to see health visitors or take her child to the clinic. This clear-cut case was nevertheless the exception. The effects of underfeeding, maternal rejection and psychosocial deprivation most often seemed to exaggerate the impaired development of a child already in precarious health. This was so in 32 out of those 34 neglected children whose intellectual potential appeared to have suffered as a consequence of inadequate rearing.

4. Need for recognition of the extent of VIH and the role of neglect.

There is not a sufficient awareness among the general public of the vulnerability of young brains and their susceptibility to stress, especially during the period of maximum brain growth spurt (up to 2 years). In particular, the dangers of shaking a young child could be emphasized. A suffocatory act (for instance, holding a young child under water) may also induce mental handicap (Nixon and Pearn 1977) and this is more widespread than is generally recognized (Oliver *et al.* 1974).

5. The high incidence of maltreatment in children admitted to Subnormality Hospitals.

The rate for children who suffered abuse and/or neglect in our survey is approximately twelve times greater than that found in a comparable survey of children in the general population in N.E. Wilts (Oliver 1975*b*). This survey used identical definitions and covered a similar area.

6. Inadequate families.

A proportion of children admitted to subnormality hospitals must inevitably come from families who have been unable to care for their mentally handicapped offspring adequately. Nevertheless, we would like to stress that, for nearly half the children in the survey, there was evidence of at least adequate, and in some instances, exceptionally devoted parental care before the child's admission to hospital.

The authors would like to express their appreciation to their colleagues and to the many other professionals who cooperated in this survey, and to Dr. J. A. Baldwin who helped in the design of the study.

REFERENCES

Baldwin, J. A. (1976) Personal communication.

Birch, H. G., and Gussow, J. D. 1970. *Disadvantaged Children.* New York: Grune & Stratton.

Blackie, J., Forrest, A., and Witcher, G. 1975. Subcultural mental handicap. *British Journal of Psychiatry,* 127, 535–9.

British Paediatric Association. 1976. Evidence presented to the Select Committee on Violence in the Family, 8 June 1976.

Bullard, D. M., Glaser, H. H., Heagarty, M. C., and Pivchik, E. C. 1968. Failure to thrive in the 'neglected' child. *Annual Progress in Child Psychiatry and Child Development,* chapter 32, pp. 540–54. New York: Brunner-Mazel.

Caffey, J. 1974. The whiplash shaken infant syndrome. *Paediatrics,* 54, no. 4, 396–403.

Chase, H. P., Canosa, C. A., Dabiere, C. S., Welch, N. N., and O'Brien, D. 1974.

Postnatal undernutrition and human brain development. *Journal of Mental Deficiency Research,* 18, 355–66.

Dobbing, J. 1974. The later development of the brain and its vulnerability. Chapter 32 in *Scientific Foundations of Paediatrics,* eds., J. A. Davis and J. Dobbing. London: Heinemann.

Editorial. 1976*a*. The ultimate cost of malnutrition. *British Medical Journal, ii,* 1158–9.

Editorial. 1976*b*. Koluchová's twins. *British Medical Journal, ii,* 897–8.

Forrest, A. D. 1975. Mental handicap and syndromes of brain damage in children. *British Medical Journal, ii,* 71–3.

General Register Office. Studies on Medical and Population Subjects (1968, amended 1973). *A Glossary of Mental Disorders, No. 22.* HMSO.

Grossman, H. J. 1973. *Manual on Terminology and Classification in Mental Retardation.* American Association on Mental Deficiency, Special Publication No. 2. Washington.

Guthkelch, A. N. 1971. Infantile subdural haematoma and its relationship to whiplash injuries. *British Medical Journal, ii,* 430–1.

Hertzig, M. E., Birch, H. G., Richardson, S. H., and Tizard, J. 1972. Intellectual levels of school-children severely malnourished during the first two years of life. *Paediatrics,* 49(6), 814–24.

Jones, C. 1976. The fate of abused children. Presented at the *Symposium on Child Abuse,* held at The Royal Society of Medicine 2–4 June 1976, London. Proceedings to be published in 1977 in a book edited by A. W. Franklin.

Lewin, J. 1974. Malnutrition and the human brain. *World Medicine,* 10(5), 19–21.

Lynch, M. A. 1975. Ill-health and child abuse. *Lancet, ii,* 317–19.

————. Roberts, J., and Gordon, M. 1976*a*. Early warning of child abuse in the maternity hospital. *Developmental Medicine and Child Neurology,* 18, 759–66.

————. 1976*b*. Child abuse—the critical path. *Journal of Maternal and Child Health,* July, 25–9.

Mackeith, R. 1975. Speculation on some possible long-term effects of child abuse. Chapter 8 in *Concerning Child Abuse* (ed. A. W. Franklin). London: Churchill Livingstone.

Martin, H. P. 1972. The child and his development. Chapter 7 in *Helping the Battered Child and His Family,* eds., C. H. Kempe and R. E. Helfer. Philadelphia: J. B. Lippincott and Co.

———— *et al.* 1974. The development of abused children. In *Advances in Pediatrics,* 21, 25–73. Chicago: Year Book Medical Publishers.

Nixon, J., and Pearn, J. 1977. Non-accidental immersion in bath-water: another aspect of child abuse. *British Medical Journal, i,* 271–2.

Oliver, J. E., Cox, J., Taylor, A., and Baldwin, J. A. 1974. *Severely Ill-Treated Young Children in North-East Wiltshire.* Oxford University Unit of Clinical Epidemiology, Oxford Record Linkage Study, Research Report No. 4.

————. 1975*a*. Microcephaly following baby battering and shaking. *British Medical Journal, iii,* 262–4.

————. 1975*b*. Child abuse. Chapter in *Social Crises in Service Communities. Proceedings of Triservice Multidisciplinary Conference,* pp 73–136 (taken from Symposium held at Amport House, Hants, 30 September 1975).

Pilling, D. 1973. *The Handicapped Child:* Research Review, Vol III. From Studies in Child Development, Longman Press (in association with the National Children's Bureau).

Royal College of Psychiatrists. 1976. Evidence presented to the Select Committee on Violence in the Family, 8 June 1976.

Sarsfield, J. K. 1974. The neurological sequelae of non-accidental injury. *Developmental Medicine and Child Neurology,* 16, 826–7.

Smith, S. M., and Hanson, R. 1974. 134 Battered children: a medical and psychological study. *British Medical Journal, iii,* 660–70.

Spencer, D. A. 1974. The use of the WHO International Classification of Disease (Mental Retardation) in a hospital for the mentally handicapped. *British Journal of Psychiatry,* 125, 333–5.

————. 1975. Use of 1974 AAMD classification in hospitals for the mentally handicapped. *British Journal of Psychiatry,* 126, 298.

————. 1976. New long-stay patients in a hospital for mental handicap. *British Journal of Psychiatry,* 128, 467–70.

Stott, D. H. 1962. Abnormal mothering as a cause of mental subnormality. *Journal of Child Psychology and Psychiatry,* 3, 79–91 and 133–48.

Watts, G. 1976. Malnutrition in context. *World Medicine,* 11(10), 57–60.

CHAPTER 29

Severe Deprivation In Twins:
A Case Study

Jarmila Koluchová

CASE HISTORY

The Background of Deprivation

This is a case record of monozygotic twins, two boys *P.M.* and *J.M.*, born on 4 September 1960. Their mother died shortly after giving birth to them and for 11 months they lived in a children's home. According to the records their physical and mental development was normal at that stage. Their father then applied to take them into the care of his sister, but soon afterwards he remarried and the boys were again placed in a children's home until the new household could be established. This new family included 2 natural elder sisters of the twins, and 2 children (a boy and a girl) of the stepmother—6 children altogether, the oldest being 9-yr-old. The married couple *M.* bought a house in the suburbs of a small town where nobody knew them. All the subsequent events concerning the twins could only be reconstructed after their discovery in the autumn of 1967.

For 5½ yr the twins lived in this family under most abnormal conditions. Some of the neighbours had no idea of their existence, others guessed there were some little children in the family although they had never seen them. It is surprising that this could happen in a quiet street of family houses where the environment and social relations are very like those in a village. During the trial, however, the people next door testified that they had often heard queer, inhuman shrieks which resembled howling, and which came from a cellar leading to the back court. The father was once seen beating the children with a rubber hose until they lay flat on the ground unable to move. The neighbors, however, did not interfere in any way because they did not want to risk conflict with the children's stepmother, who was known to be a selfish, aggressive woman, unwilling to admit anyone into her house.

Reprinted with permission from *Journal of Child Psychology & Psychiatry* 13 (1972):107–14. Copyright 1972, Pergamon Press Ltd.

Acknowledgements—In the presentation of this paper, the assistance of Professor A. D. B. Clarke, University of Hull, and Geoffrey A. Dell, principal psychologist at the Child Guidance Clinic, Glasgow, is gratefully acknowledged.

In spite of very good and extensive child welfare services in the country, the true situation of these children was somehow undetected by the authorities concerned. The children had never been medically examined either routinely or because of illness. They were not registered for school attendance at the appropriate age. The relatives of the natural mother of the twins complained that the children were very poorly cared for, but their complaints were never properly investigated by a personal visit to the family from a social welfare officer. It was a quite exceptional case which, because of its severity, was scrutinized very closely by the jury when the matter came to light.

The central figure in the family, and in the tragedy involving the twins, was the stepmother. All the investigations, and especially the trial at the district and regional court, showed that she was a person of average intelligence, but egocentric, remarkably lacking in feeling, possessing psychopathic character traits and a distorted system of values. The father was a person of below average intellect, passive, and inarticulate; the stepmother dominated the family. Her own two children (the first of them illegitimate and the second the product of a disturbed marriage which ended in divorce) were reared in early childhood by their maternal grandmother. The stepmother therefore had little experience with small children and showed no interest in them. When the twins joined the family she fed them, but the other aspects of their care were left to their father. This disinterest developed into active hostility toward the twins, and she induced a similar attitude toward them in other members of the family. The other children were forbidden to talk to the twins or to play with them. The father, who worked on the railways, was often away from home and took little interest in the boys. He probably realized that they were not receiving proper care but he was incapable of changing the situation. The twins therefore grew up lacking emotional relationships and stimulation, and were totally excluded from the family. Relationships between the other members of the family were also unnaturally cool due to the mother's abnormal personality. The elder children were well dressed, their homework was supervised and so on, but these measures seemed to have been motivated by the mother's ambitions. She accepted the two stepdaughters into the family though she preferred her own children, but with none of the children did she have a genuine maternal relationship.

The boys grew up in almost total isolation, separated from the outside world; they were never allowed out of the house or into the main living rooms in the flat, which were tidy and well furnished. They lived in a small, unheated closet, and were often locked up for long periods in the cellar. They slept on the floor on a polythene sheet and were cruelly chastised. They used to sit at a small table in an otherwise empty room, with a few building bricks which were their only toys. When one of their natural sisters was later examined for another reason, she depicted this scene in a drawing entitled "At Home".

The twins also suffered physically from lack of adequate food, fresh air, sunshine, and exercise. At the end of August 1967 the father brought one of the boys to a pediatrician, asking for a certificate that his son was unfit to enter primary school. Because the boy looked as if he were 3-yr-old rather than 6, hardly walked, and was at first sight severely mentally retarded, the doctor agreed to postpone school entry, but insisted that the twins should be placed in a kindergarten, and that the family situation should be investigated by a social worker and a district nurse. The stepmother objected to these visits, criticized everybody concerned, and stressed that she was overworked at home. Probably anticipating further intervention by the welfare authorities, she tried to remove traces of the way in which the twins had been living.

Gradually it became clear that this was a case of criminal neglect. In December 1967 the twins were removed from the family and placed in a home for preschool children, while legal proceedings were taken against the parents. Several days after their admission to the home it was found that the twins suffered from acute rickets, a disease which has been practically eliminated in modern Czechoslovakia. The children were admitted to an orthopedic clinic and at the same time examined by a multidisciplinary team.

PSYCHOLOGICAL FINDINGS

On admission to hospital attempts were made to assess the mental status of the twins. It was clear that the improvement in their living conditions during the three months prior to hospital admission had allowed some progress to take place. For example, on admission to the kindergarten the twins did not join in any activities but were timid and mistrustful. They had to be brought to the kindergarten in a wheelchair, because they could barely walk, and when given shoes could not walk at all. During their last three months with the family they were not locked in the cellar and their little room was better equipped, but at the same time the stepmother's negative attitude towards them became even more acute, because she saw in them the cause of the unwelcome interference from outside.

While in hospital, the children were psychologically examined. They were encouraged to become familiar with the testing room and adapted to it very well. At first it was impossible to use a diagnostic tool which required their direct cooperation, and the preliminary step in assessment was the observation of their spontaneous behavior, and in particular of their free and controlled play. Later it was possible to establish direct contact and to move on to more formal testing in which the author used Gesell's scale and the Terman-Merrill test.

The boys' restricted social experience and very poor general information was most strikingly shown in their reactions of surprise and horror to objects and activities normally very familiar to children of their age—e.g., moving mechanical toys, a TV set, children doing gymnastic exercises, traffic in the street, etc.

However, their inquisitiveness gradually prevailed, the reactions of terror disappeared, and they began to explore their environment, although often they were easily distracted. Their shyness with people was reduced during their stay in the children's home, and in the hospital ward they were the centre of interest. They related to adults positively and indiscriminately, in a way that is typical of deprived children. Their relations with other children were at an immature and uncontrolled level for their age.

The spontaneous speech of the boys was extremely poor. In order to communicate with each other they used gestures more characteristic of younger children. They tried to imitate adult speech, but could repeat only two or three words at a time with poor articulation. They could not answer questions, even if it was evident from their reactions that they had understood them. It was obvious that they were not used to speech as a means of communication.

Their spontaneous play was very primitive, and predominantly at first it was only the manipulation of objects, but imitative play soon developed. As they became familiar with the toys and with their surroundings in the clinic their play gradually reached more mature levels, but they continued to need adult intervention to initiate and develop a play activity and were unable to join in the play of other children.

A remarkable finding was that the boys could not understand the meaning or function of pictures. It was impossible therefore to measure the extent of their vocabulary by means of pictures, because they had never learned to perceive and understand them. We started therefore with pictures which were of the same size and color as the real objects which they represented. After repeated comparisons of picture and object, understanding of the relationship emerged and extended to a constantly widening range of phenomena.

The author felt that to express the boys' intellectual level in terms of an IQ would be quite inadequate. Their IQs at that stage would have been within the range of imbecility, but qualitative analysis of their responses, their total behavior, and their considerably accelerated development since they had been taken away from their family, all unambiguously suggested that this was a case not of a primary defect in the sense of oligophrenia, but of severe deprivation. It seemed more appropriate therefore to consider their mental ages, which in December 1967 varied for both boys around the 3-yr level, with a range of ±1 yr for separate component items. At this time their chronological age was 7 yr 3 months.

After the period of hospitalization the children returned to the children's home, where they made good progress. They began to participate with the children there; this was made easier for them by the fact that the other children in the home were some two to three years younger. Relationships with adults and children improved and they acquired much of the knowledge and many of the skills appropriate to preschool children. As their health improved so their motor abilities developed; they learned to walk, to run, to jump, to ride a scooter. Similar progress was also noted in their fine motor coordination.

After six months' stay in the children's home the boys were readmitted to the clinic for a short time to enable pediatric, audiological, and psychological examinations to be made. Their mental age was by this time approximately 4 yr, with a narrower range of passes on the component items than on the previous examination. There was evidence of considerable progress in habit formation, experience, and the development of knowledge.

THE FORENSIC PROBLEM

During the first period of hospitalization the investigating authorities requested a report from a forensic pediatrician, who in turn asked for a consultant psychologist's report. However, the problem of assessment seemed too complex to be handled on the basis of one or more consulting examinations. We therefore asked the investigating authorities to assign an expert psychologist to the case, who would have both the support of the court and the right of a forensic expert as well. The panel of forensic specialists followed the progress of the boys for a period of six months while they were in the children's home and undertook careful control examinations during the second period of hospitalization. The problem for the panel was to assess the total developmental picture presented by the children and to decide whether their disabilities were likely to have been congenital or acquired. The psychologist, moreover, had also to try to answer the question as to whether the twins were likely to grow up to become mentally and emotionally normal people.

The psychologist's report was of considerable importance in this case. It was necessary to disprove the statement of the defendant that the children had been defective from birth and to prove that their disabilities were caused by severe neglect and lack of stimulation. For this reason a lengthy period of six months' observation was necessary, although it was apparent much earlier that the children were developing more quickly in the environment of the children's home than they ever had in their family home. During the trial, too, we had to refute the statement of the defendant and her husband that the children had had experience of picture material and play opportunities at home.

It was more difficult to answer the question about the future development of the twins. There was no evidence from the literature on deprivation, and because the case was so exceptional we had no personal experience to guide us. We could therefore only outline a probable prognosis and assume that in a good environment the children would develop in every respect, that their developmental deficits would show a tendency to be reduced, but that it was necessary to take into account the possible consequences of such severe deprivation on the development of personality. We pointed out to the judges some of the handicapping effects of this deprivation: entry to school delayed by three years, the probable necessity for the boys to attend a school for mentally retarded children, the effects on employment prospects, and the possibility of other difficulties in their social and intellectual development. We recommended that the children be placed as soon as possible in a compensating foster home, on the grounds that even the best children's home could not be the optimal solution in the long term.

The main trial at the district court lasted for three days, all the forensic specialists being present. The defendant did not admit to having damaged the twins in any way. She denied that anything unusual had happened and maintained that they had been handicapped since infancy and that she had done her best for them by cooking and cleaning. She poured out her own troubles and expressed again her sense of being overworked. The court sentenced her to four years' deprivation of liberty and both father and stepmother also lost their parental rights.

In his final speech the public prosecutor and the chairman of the senate of judges, in confirming the verdict, emphasized the importance of the experts' reports in their evaluation of the defendant's guilt.

THE FURTHER DEVELOPMENT OF THE CHILDREN

In the school year 1968-69 the boys remained in the preschool children's home. Their mental development was better than the original prognosis had suggested. Whereas some experts were doubtful about their educability, a psychologist's assessments showed that the retardation was diminishing and that the boys had reached a level of readiness for school. Because of their retarded speech, and relatively poor fine motor coordination and powers of concentration, we thought that a school for mentally retarded children was indicated as an initial step, since there were greater possibilities of individual teaching and a slower pace of learning.

Simultaneously with their starting school we tried to solve the problem of their foster-home placement. A number of families were willing to take the children, but we had to assess the motivation of the applicants very carefully, considering the personalities of the potential substitute parents and existing family structures. Finally, in July 1969, the boys were placed with a family who have been able to accept them as natural and loved children. After two years of observation we still consider this to be the optimal placement, although in the conventional sense the family is not a complete family at all. It consists of two unmarried middle-aged sisters, both intelligent, with wide interests, living in a pleasant flat, and capable of forming very good relationships with the children. One of these sisters had already adopted a baby girl some years before, and this child is now an intelligent well-educated 13-year-old. The second sister became the foster mother of the twins. Our observations, and information from many sources, show that deep emotional bonds have been formed between the children and their foster family, and many of the consequences of deprivation—e.g., a narrow outlook, a small range of emotional expression, etc.—which had remained during their stay in the children's home, are gradually diminishing. The boys have recollections of their original home, and though the foster family tries to avoid reviving the past, the boys themselves will sometimes begin to talk about it; we also have touched on this during our psychological examinations. Until recently the boys did not have sufficient language ability to describe even in outline their life in their original family. If we compare their story now with the facts established during and before the trial, it is evident that their account is reliable. They have a completely negative attitude to their stepmother, and refer to her as "that lady," or "that unkind lady." They remember the names of their brother and sisters, and they recollect how they used to be hungry and thirsty, how they were beaten about the head (their scalps are badly scarred), and how

Table 1. Wechsler Intelligence Test scores (WISC)

Twin *P.* IQ		Twin *J.* IQ	
8 yr 4 months			
Verbal	80	Verbal	69
Performance	83	Performance	80
Full scale	80	Full scale	72
9 yr			
Verbal	84	Verbal	75
Performance	83	Performance	76
Full scale	82	Full scale	73
10 yr			
Verbal	97	Verbal	94
Performance	85	Performance	86
Full scale	91	Full scale	89
11 yr			
Verbal	97	Verbal	96
Performance	93	Performance	90
Full scale	95	Full scale	93

they used to sit at the small table. The stepmother often carried them into the cellar, thrashed them with a wooden kitchen spoon until it broke, and put a feather-bed over their heads so that no-one would hear their screaming.

For a long time they had a dread of darkness. They appreciated the physical warmth of their new home, the good food they received, and the fact that they were no longer beaten. During our first visit to them in the foster home we had to reassure them that we would not take them away from their foster mother.

In September 1969 they were admitted to the first class in a school for mentally retarded children. On the basis of our observations of the children in class, the teacher's records, and our further examinations, we found the boys soon adapted themselves to the school environment and began to excel their classmates. Their writing, drawing, and ability to concentrate improved remarkably in the second term, and it became clear that this type of school would not extend them sufficiently. Accepting that there was a risk involved, we recommended a transfer to the second class of a normal school from the beginning of the next school year. In spite of the difference in curriculum and teaching methods, they proved to be capable of mastering the subject matter of the normal school, and did well enough to suggest that they have the ability to complete successfully the basic 9-yr school course which, however, they would finish at the age of 18 instead of the normal age of 15. Their schoolmates are three years younger, and it remains to be seen how relations between them and the twins develop, particularly as they enter puberty; the effects on the self-confidence and personality of the twins may be considerable, but only extended observation will give us the answer to this.

A summary of the psychological test findings shows that in the fifteen months from June 1968 to September 1969 the mental age of the twins increased by three years; this was an immense acceleration of development, indicating how the change of living conditions provided a rapidly effective compensation for the consequences of earlier deprivation.

At first the children were assessed using Gesell's Developmental Scale and later the Terman-Merrill Scale in which their verbal level was markedly below nonverbal test items. Since the age of 8 yr and 4 months the boys have been examined by means of the Wechsler Intelligence Scale (WISC). The test scores are presented in Table 1 and indicate the low-level verbal response initially, especially in the Twin *J*, and the subsequent improvement over three years. Both children now seem to be functioning almost at an average level for their age.

CONCLUSIONS

This is a very exceptional case of deprivation, first because of the lengthy period of isolation, and second because of the unusual family situation which by outward appearances was a relatively normal and orderly one.

The children suffered from a lack of stimulation and opportunity for psychomotor development. The most severe deprivation, however, was probably their poverty of emotional relationships and their social isolation. The stepmother did not even partially satisfy their need for maternal nurturance. She was on the contrary, as the dominating person in the family, the instigator of hostile attitudes toward the children and an active agent in their physical and mental torment. The influence of the father was confined to occasional repressive actions. The stimulating influence of brothers and sisters was also lacking. Thus we may speak of a combination of outer and inner causes of deprivation, the inner or psychological ones being primary.

We have not found in the literature a similar case of such severe and protracted deprivation in a family. Following Langmeier and Matejcek (1968), we can define the situation of the twins as one of extreme social isolation, where the children are still fed by people, but are almost completely isolated from human society. Cases in the literature differ from ours both in recording a shorter period of social isolation, and in showing more severe consequences of deprivation than we have so far found. We assume, therefore, that the twins were able to bear the onerous situation better than any single child would have done.

Almost four years of observation of the twins have shown that in comparison with analogous cases in the literature their mental and social development has been very good. It is, however, difficult to foresee how their intelligence will develop, what the course of their development will be, how their personalities will be formed, and what residual effects of the deprivation will remain. The comparison between these monozygotic twins, living in essentially the same environment, will also be of interest.

SUMMARY

The author reports an unusual case of deprivation. Monozygotic twin boys were reared from age 18 months to 7 years in social isolation by a psychopathic stepmother and an inadequate father. On discovery, their mental age level was three years, but after treatment, a period in a children's home and approximately two years in a good foster home, they had made remarkable progress and now appear about average for their age. Forensic aspects of the case are discussed, as are features of the foster home placement, and the significance of twinship in the recovery. Residual effects of deprivation will be studied by an extended follow-up.

Because of the criminal behavior of the stepmother the children were exposed to living conditions which resembled those of an experimental situation. From the human standpoint, of course, it was an extremely cruel and unrepeatable experiment. From the scientific point of view, however, it was also a very valuable one. It will be important, therefore, to follow up the case over a long period, in the hope of contributing to a solution of some of the problems associated with mental deprivation.

REFERENCES

Langmeier, J., and Matejček, Z. (1968). *Psychická deprivace v detství*. Praha, SZDN.

Pelikán, K., Mores, A., Koluchová, J., Siroky, J., and Fárková, H. (1969). Tezký deprivační syndrom u dvojčat po dlouhodobé sociálni izolaci. *Cs. Pediat.* 24, 980–83.

CHAPTER 30

The Further Development of Twins after Severe and Prolonged Deprivation: A Second Report

Jarmila Koluchová

This paper follows up a previous study of severe and prolonged deprivation of twin boys born in 1960 (Koluchová 1972). From age 18 months until 7 years they had been isolated and cruelly treated, such that on discovery they could barely walk, suffered from rickets, and were frightened of normally familiar objects, and failed to understand the meaning or function of pictures. Their IQs were in the forties. Although their subsequent development had been surprisingly good even at the time of the first report, and it was possible to exclude gross damage of their intellect and personality, a number of problems remained which could only be solved in a long-term study. The importance of observing the case over a long period was emphasized also in Clarke's (1972) commentary. Having observed the twins until now, the author wishes to record their further development, to mention similar cases and to arrive at some more general conclusions concerning the diagnosis and remediation of severe deprivation.

In the school year 1971–72, the twins, then aged between 11 and 12, attended the third class. Their speech was entirely adequate for their age, both in form and content. As the predictions of speech pathologists and pediatricians concerning the development of speech had been rather pessimistic, an attempt will be made to explain the fact that their speech is at a good level and allows full social integration.

Until the eleventh month of their age the children had lived in an infants' home, then—for a shorter period of time—in a family of their relatives and later, in a home for toddlers. According to the available records of the infants' home, the children had been developing adequately for their age. It is possible to assume that at that time, which is often regarded as a preparatory period for speech, and during which a mainly passive knowledge of a language is developed, the children had mastered actively several words and had com-

Reprinted with permission from the *Journal of Child Psychology and Psychiatry* 17 (1976):181–88. Copyright 1976, Pergamon Press Ltd.

The author would like to express her gratitude to Professor A. D. B. Clarke for his interest in her work.

prehended the communicative function of speech. They had probably retained those abilities during the whole period of deprivation, mostly in a latent form only, because the small amount of speech they had been used to hear between 18 months and 7 years, had not had a communicative character for them. The basic prerequisite for the development of speech had also been missing, i.e., the individual contact of an adult with a child and the resulting positive stimulating relationship. But, although the period until their third year, which is often considered the terminal limit for generating the ability to speak, had been missed, the twins' speech started to develop, in spite of the fact that they had scarcely spoken at all until the age of 7. The development was quickest after their ninth year when they came to their foster family, which provided them with all the prerequisites both for the development of speech and for the whole personality. At school, and in a collective of children, the boys were agile, gay, and popular; there were no signs of eccentricity or troubles in the social sphere. Until the fourth class of their school attendance their results were very good—they used to have a grade two in the Czech language only (mother tongue). They were the best pupils of the class in arithmetic (grade 1), which arose, first, by a quick compensation of the retardation in the sphere of intellectual functions, and second, by their being two to three years older than their fellow pupils.

Gradually, they began to feel older in comparison with their schoolmates and began to be aware of their late start at school, both these being due to the acceleration of their growth and a rather delayed commencement of prepuberty. Both the teachers and the foster mother supported their natural ambition to master, during the fourth class, the subject matter of the fifth class. They succeeded in their effort and after the holidays passed the examinations of the fifth class; then they were moved up from the fourth, directly to the sixth class. Thus, they found themselves among children of more approximate age and their self-confidence was reinforced. Their results fell to the average, but the situation has been gradually improving since then. Both of them like attending school and, naturally, some subjects are favorite and others less attractive for them. They love reading, ride bicycles, can swim and ski, they play the piano well and they have both creative and technical talent. It is interesting that musical ability started to develop only at about the age of 10, but it is now at a good level. In the present school year (1974–75) the boys attend the seventh class; their schoolmates are, on the average, one and a half years younger. As their adolescence began about a year late in comparison with the average of our population, the whole status of their development and interests now corresponds approximately with the standard of their present schoolmates. After finishing basic education (9 classes) they would like to study at a secondary vocational school, for which they show sufficient aptitudes.

The development of the twins' intellectual level has been observed continually by means of several methods; to compare previous scores with more recent findings the author presents in Table 1 the boys' IQ obtained by means of the WISC.

It will be recalled that shortly after their discovery (age 7), IQs were proba-

Table 1. Wechsler Intelligence Test scores
(WISC)

Age (yr)	Twin P. IQ	Twin J. IQ
8	80	72
9	82	73
10	91	89
11	95	93
12	95	104
13	98	100
14	100	101

bly in the forties, rapidly rising by 30 to 40 points. After this spurt, the next most rapid development occurred between the ninth and tenth years, namely, the first year of their stay in the foster family and the first year of their school attendance. According to the past trend, it is possible that their intelligence scores may continue to show a slight increase. In the nonverbal scale of the WISC and in Raven's Matrices test, the achieved scores are a little higher than in the verbal, which may be explained by the fact that the verbal score is to a certain extent dependent on education, which is still slightly retarded (1 year) according to their age. In spite of initial differences in their development, their general standard has now come to be equal; however, some features of their character have continued to differ. J. is a little slower in comparison with his brother, but he is in general of calmer disposition. P. perceives more quickly, he reacts more promptly, but his attention is rather labile, he is a little preoccupied and shows symptoms of autonomic lability.

In the development and forming of the personalities of the boys no psychological symptoms or eccentricities appear at present. It is possible to say that there are no consequences of the deprivation remaining which would cause retardation or damage to their development. It does not mean, however, that five years of hardship and ill-treatment by their cruel stepmother have not left any traces at all. The dread of darkness, which persisted for a long time, has already faded, but under oppressive or unusual conditions the boys sometimes show the feeling of fear and their reaction is neurotic. For example, once they happened to come to a cellar similar to the one in which they had often been imprisoned, which frightened and upset them and again called up the recollections of past suffering. In the cheerful environment of their new family, and with the help of their foster mother, who is always ready to understand, the boys will calm down quite easily and revert to their normal mood.

The twins hate recalling the conditions of their deprivation, and are even unlikely to speak about it with each other. However, by occasional remarks and the reactions mentioned above, it is evident that some recollections have remained and will probably be retained forever. The boys' foster mother mentions that they will tell her something about their cheerless childhood now and then, but always each of them separately in an intimate talk. Comparing their previous and present recollections, it is apparent that there is no tendency to distort or exaggerate their experiences; their evidence conforms with the data stated in the judicial trial of their stepmother. The boys' recollections of the past are no longer associated with fear of possible recurrence of such living conditions and of losing their new family.

The awareness of the relationship with the family is profound and makes the boys feel safe and assured. Natural emotional bonds with all members of the family have arisen; apparently the relationship with their foster mother, who is in a dominant position in the family, is emotionally deepest. Her sister is an aunt for them. As mentioned in the 1972 paper, the latter had adopted a girl—now 16 years old and besides her there is another 10-year-old girl (staying with the family during the last four years), whose brief history will follow. Thus, there are two foster mothers and their four children, who have very nice brother and sister relations with each other, although they of course know they are not consanguineous relatives. There is a happy atmosphere in the whole family, full of mutual understanding. Undoubtedly, it is possible to object to such a family without a father, whom the boys would need just at present in the period of their puberty. The boys' foster mother is aware of this and is trying to compensate for the lack of a man in the process of bringing up the boys by their frequent meeting with her brother and other relatives and friends, who have close relations with the boys.

The fact that has intensified their awareness of firm relationships in this family, and has helped to establish the feeling of safety and assurance, was the agreed change of surname to that of their foster mother. Even before the change was completed, the boys had been using this surname; they have never uttered their original surname, as it has evidently raised negative emotions in them.

As the most important factor in the conditions of deprivation of the twins from 18 months until 7 years of age was almost total social isolation and hostile relations with the members of that family, especially with their stepmother, the question arises—how it has been reflected in their social relations and behavior?

In the 1972 report, relations of the twins with each other, with other children and also with adults were described. The situation has been developing as follows: immediately after they had been removed from the family and placed in the children's home, a strong emotional bond with each other was evident. Apparently, it had developed because it had been the only positive emotion that could have been built up and, moreover, it had helped them to bear the difficult living conditions. The outer demonstration of their relations, however, corresponded with a much lower age: they used to make themselves understood like toddlers, using mostly mimicry and gestures. Their original shyness with people and reactions of terror had disappeared rather quickly and the children reacted positively both to adults and children in a way that is more characteristic of younger children. Mainly, they showed a lesser differentiation of emotional relations and a prevailing interest in adults.

The children's gradual socialization was facilitated by the fact that they had lived for a longer period of time among children approximately three years younger, which corresponded with their developmental deficit. Starting to attend a school for mentally retarded children at the age of 9, they had access, for the first time, to a larger, well-organized group of children, in which they joined successfully; undoubtedly, the individual attention of their teacher, who had been informed of their history, helped a lot. There were no striking features in their social contacts, they did not show any symptoms of timidity, shyness or any other abnormality and they never behaved aggressively either at the school for mentally retarded children or at the normal school later on. The boys have always had close relations with each other—an emotional bond much firmer than is usual with brothers of their age. But, of course, common teasing or petty conflicts are present, as is usual with children in normal families.

Making the boys acquainted with their suffering during the early and pre-school age appears to be a relatively difficult educational and psychotherapeutic problem. They can remember that period of time only in fragments without being able to comprehend the essentials of the whole event, its circumstances and causes. We consider it advisable to make them acquainted with the main facts concerning their parentage, family, the trial, and further events until their coming to this family, from the point of view of realization of the continuity of their personalities, self-evaluation, and also as a precaution against possible trauma caused by incidental information or experience in later life. It is necessary to respect the long-standing aversion to reverting to the past, but at the same time their pubescent inquisitiveness and their efforts to know and to evaluate themselves should be employed. The foster mother is aware of the gravity of this task and she appears to manage it well. The author wants to focus her attention on those problems, too, in her talks with the twins within the framework of their psychological observation, naturally, in close cooperation with their foster mother.

Appreciating the children's general development as highly successful—in contradiction with the original prediction of doctors—it is also necessary to evaluate the therapeutic factors that have contributed to this. As already stated in the 1972 report, the children had been treated at an orthopedic and pediatric clinic after their withdrawal from the family and after their rickets had been overcome. At the same time they had been examined in psychiatric and ophthalmological clinics and in a phoniatric ward. Their somatic condition having improved, they were placed in a children's home. Also there, exceptional individual care was bestowed upon them and their future was discussed and planned carefully. The most important factor for solving that problem was a good prediction consequent to psychological examinations. The present foster family was selected from several families interested. Having been placed in this family, the children started to attend speech training and they were also practicing their pronunciation intensively at home. Consequently they managed to inhibit their nasal speech and in general to modify their poor articulation. The children have also been carefully looked after by a district pediatrician, who knows everything about the family and the children themselves. Another important curative factor is the attitude of their teachers, which is individual and full of sympathy, although they expect the boys to meet reasonable scholastic demands without any preference or special tolerance.

Continuing care, carried out during the whole period by the same psychologist (the author), has proved to be fortunate. Besides the experimental direction, she also acts as an advisor and passes psychological reports to the school and to other institutions. In the author's opinion, the main advantage of such procedure lies in her detailed knowledge of the whole history, including court reports. Moreover, the twins trust her, which has enabled her to observe the dynamism of their development over seven years.

Even if all the above-mentioned curative factors are by no means significant, it is necessary to emphasize that the most effective and integrative curative factor is their foster mother and the whole environment of their family. Although the lady is employed, she devotes all her leisure time to the children with a lot of self-sacrifice; her solicitude for them is the content and purpose of her life, without spoiling the children or adopting uncritical attitudes.

The specialists, who had not believed in any possibility of remedying the severe deprivation damage in the twins, later referred to their quick development as an exception to the rule which states that severe deprivational damage at an early age is irremediable. According to the author's experience, however, there are a number of similar cases, but they are not usually correctly diagnosed, professionally observed and described.

As an example of the importance of a correct diagnosis and the difficulty of remedying severe deprivation, we want to outline a brief history of a girl L. H., born in 1965, living now in the same family as the twins. This girl was withdrawn legally from her own family at the age of four as a consequence of almost total social isolation and cruel treatment by her psychopathic mother. The child had been hated by her mother; tormented by hunger, she had been constantly kept alone in an unfurnished room, had slept on a straw mattress, and had not acquired the basic habits of body hygiene. All of her mother's seven elder children had earlier been withdrawn from her legally. This girl was placed in a children's home, where she behaved anxiously, agitatedly, even aggressively; her language ability was almost totally undeveloped and she was still incontinent. The schoolmasters in the home considered her ineducable and it was decided that she should be placed in a mental home. For diagnostic and therapeutic reasons the child was admitted to a psychiatric hospital and dismissed after a month with the diagnosis of severe mental handicap.

The family in which the twins live happened to hear about this girl. Encouraged by the good development of the twin boys, they decided to adopt the girl into the family as a foster daughter in spite of the fact that the prediction of her development was rather pessimistic, being based on a supposition that she had been primarily an intellectually defective child. Even though the child was difficult to care for in the family during the first weeks, due to her agitation and anxiety, soon both the ladies understood that she had been damaged by cruelty and isolation and that she had a good intellectual capacity. During our first examination of the child soon after her arrival in the family we were able to eliminate mental subnormality even if her retardation was considerable and deprivation symptoms conspicuous. The child started learning to speak rather quickly, she was bright, and she began to attend a kindergarten.

On the whole, however, this child has always been an incomparably greater educational problem than the twins. She attends a school for normal children, she can read and write well and she has an outstanding talent for music, but her attention is very labile, she is not able to take adequate pains while learning and she shows some shortcomings in the functions of her memory, which might be due to her having suffered meningitis, caused probably by frequent, uncured otitis media, from which she still suffers. She has continued to have some problems in the social sphere, though, thanks to kind-hearted and consistent upbringing, there has been some improvement and rectification even here, which could not have been achieved in a children's home. The girl joins in with other children or the collective of pupils in her class with great difficulty; sometimes she is aggressive and intolerant with her contemporaries, while she is gentle and kind with younger children.

It is interesting to compare the girl with the twins. The deprivational history of the three children is rather similar; they live in the same family now and are given the same attention. Their different development in the social sphere can be explained by distinct congenital dispositions, but mainly by the fact that the twins had mutually reduced their isolation and terrible living conditions. The girl's mother is a severely psychopathic person with disorders in character and the social sphere. There are no valid data about her father. On the other hand, the twins' mother was quite normal in intelligence and personality structure. The father of the twins was already characterized in the 1972 report as passive and of below-average intellect. According to preserved photographs and to reliable reports, the twins seem to possess their mother's features, both in the somatic and psychological sphere. But their better development in the social sphere should be explained in the first place by the fact that they could build up emotional relations with each other, they could stimulate each other to some extent and thus they did not experience the tormenting feeling of loneliness as intensely and destructively as would a child totally isolated.

We have recorded more cases similar to the twins and the above-mentioned girl, but their detailed history has not yet been obtained and they have been observed only for a shorter period. The author could often confirm, in her work as a clinical psychologist, that children who suffered severe and prolonged deprivation, coming either from inadequate families, often chastised and socially isolated, or living for a long time in a children's home environment, are misdiagnosed as mentally subnormal by pediatricians, child psychiatrists and psychologists. The clinical picture of severe deprivation and mental subnormality is similar in certain symptoms, which can lead to a confusion of the two diagnoses when the subjects are only routinely examined, when the test methods are mechanically used or are misinterpreted and when the history is not known in detail. Both the cases are typical of general retardation of development and speech, social immaturity and a lowered ability to learn. Especially, the development of children up to the third year of age may be so profoundly affected as a consequence of all the external and internal conditions of a children's home environment lacking stimulation, that it is rather difficult to differentiate such cases from mental subnormality.

As these children are usually socially forlorn, i.e., their parents cannot or do not want to look after them, it is necessary to solve the problems of their future and therefore a correct diagnosis is of immense value. The author thinks that, while performing a difficult, consequential differentially-diagnostic consideration, the psychological findings should always be respected. Only psychological examination can reveal subtle differences between severely deprived and mentally subnormal children. However, cursory, nonresidential examination will not do; it is absolutely necessary to carry out a detailed repeated examination by means of both psychometric and nontest methods, aimed at the structure and dynamics of their developmental deficit. Such an examination enables a skilled psychologist to differentiate deprivation from subnormality and to determine the prognosis for its development. Here the psychological diagnosis is not only a theoretical problem, but above all a basis for educational, juridical, and therapeutic actions.

In cases of severe deprivation originating at an early age, the therapeutic prognosis has usually been considered poor. But the above-mentioned cases of deprived children, together with others that are still being observed, prove that even gross damage, previously considered to be irreversible, can be remedied. Our experience with the development of speech, too, contradicts the traditional view concerning the critical period for the development of speech. In the twins, as well as in other cases, successful development of speech was observed three to six years after their passing to a stimulating environment, sometimes even later. Thus, the prediction for the retarded development of speech in deprived children seems to be more optimistic if the defect is not organically or genetically conditioned, and when the child is given sufficient professional care and above all, placed in a kind-hearted family environment.

The view that the effects of severe deprivation were irreparable arose from the fact that for severely deprived children there is difficulty in finding suitable foster care. According to our experience, the environment of a family, stimulating and full of understanding, giving them a feeling of safety and firm relationships, is the only effective therapy, although very exacting and time-consuming. This conclusion, together with the fact that the family is considered to be the most important educational factor, led to several arrangements for the care of children living outside their own families in our country, which are designed to prevent deprivation or remedy existing deprivation. There has been a general effort to assimilate a children's home environment to a family environment, e.g., to integrate a number of children of different ages into so-called "family groups" with unchanging tutors.

Besides the standard children's homes, there have arisen new forms of substitute family care—so-called "children's villages" in which foster mothers with eight to ten children live in separate houses; then, there are so-called "big families," where a married couple looks after a similar number of children. Those "big families" are not concentrated in "villages," but they live in normal houses, both in towns and in the country. "The father" is employed somewhere like the father of a normal family and "the mother" looks after the children and is paid by the state on the same basis as "mothers" in "children's villages." There are also cases of paid foster parentage in natural families. Both such families and the people interested in the work either in "children's villages" or in "big families" are carefully selected, including by psychological examination; all the forms of substitute family care are paid and methodically guided by the state authorities and advisory boards, in which psychologists also work. A special advisory service has also been established with psychologists and pediatricians, and, if necessary, other experts can be summoned, for example, child psychiatrists.

Several years' experience with these forms of care indicate the great therapeutic prospects offered by a stimulating family environment. To observe and evaluate them is a task for long-term studies, which might be a valuable contribution to the diagnosis and remediation of deprivation.

SUMMARY

A previous (1972) report on the good development of twins after severe and prolonged deprivation is followed up, and progress over three further years is described. Intelligence is now average. No psychopathological features or eccentricities, either in behavior or social relations, can be identified. The boys are sociable, happy, and have firm emotional bonds with their foster family; they attend a school for normal children, with good results. A case of a 10 year old girl with a similar background now living in the same foster family is also described.

The psychological diagnosis of severe deprivation and its remediation are also discussed.

REFERENCES

Clarke, A. D. B. Commentary on Koluchová's "Severe deprivation in twins: A case study." *J. Child Psychol. Psychiat.*, 13 (1972):103–106.

Koluchová, J. "Severe deprivation in twins: A case study." *J. Child Psychol. Psychiat.*, 13 (1972):107–114.

Langmeier, J., and Matejcek, Z. *Psychicka Deprivace v Dětstvi*. Prague: Avicenum, 1974.

CHAPTER 31

Children of the Crèche:
Findings and Implications

Wayne Dennis

A BRIEF REVIEW OF FINDINGS

Our study of the role of environment in the development of human behavior took advantage of a "natural experiment" brought about by cultural change. This "experiment" was performed by the Crèche, a Lebanese social agency devoted to the care of foundlings which had for years institutionalized its charges from birth to 16 years. In 1956 it began to substitute for this practice the placement of foundlings in adoptive homes, and within a few years adoption became a matter of general policy. This report summarizes the results of this change upon the IQ of the foundlings and other aspects of their behavior.

Before adoption was introduced, all foundlings received by the Crèche were kept in that institution until they were about 6 years of age. In this period there was no significant difference between the mean DQs and IQs of boys and girls: The mean in both sexes after the first year was slightly above 50.

After their transfer to another institution (Zouk), the mental growth of the girls continued at the same rate. The average foundling girl at 16 years (and later) had a mean IQ of approximately 50. Most of the scores were between 30 and 60; none reached 100.

The boys, who were sent to a separate institution (Brumana) fared better, because the institutional program was better. They attained in the institution a mean IQ of about 80.

Soon after adoption was introduced by the Crèche, all the foundlings, except a few physically handicapped cases, were made available for adoption. Thus in the early years of adoption the ages of the children who were adopted ranged from birth to 6 years. A few were older than 6 years when they left the Crèche. After the policy of placing all foundlings in adoptive homes had been in effect for

Reprinted from *Children of the Crèche* by Wayne Dennis. The Century Psychology Series, K. MacCorquodale, G. Lindzey, and K. E. Clark, eds. New York, Appleton-Century-Crofts, 1973; Doswell, Va., Margaret Dennis, 1978.

Abbreviations used in this chapter. IQ: intelligence quotient. DQ: developmental quotient. MA: mental age. RMD: rate of mental development. S-B: Stanford-Binet (IQ).

a few years, no older foundling remained in the Crèche, and only foundlings between birth and two years were available for adoption.

It was found that, as a group, children adopted from the Crèche within the first two years of life overcame their initial retardation and soon reached a mean IQ of approximately 100, which was maintained. In other words, children adopted prior to age 2, who, if they had remained in institutions as had their predecessors would have had very low IQs, in adoptive homes reached normality.

It was found that, on the average, the children who were adopted after the age of 2 years developed intellectually at a normal rate; that is, typically in one chronological year they gained one year of MA. But unlike those who were adopted at 2 years or under, they did not overcome their preadoption retardation. Those adopted at 4 years of age who were retarded to the extent of two years in mean MA, when tested subsequently at ages 10 or 14, were found, as a group, still to be retarded by two years, although during the adoptive period they underwent gains in years of MA equivalent numerically to the years of adoption.

During adoption they increased in IQ, because their fixed amount of retardation in MA became smaller and smaller in relation to chronological age as time passed. Because of their residual retardation no subgroup of foundlings adopted after age 2 attained a mean IQ of 100. Furthermore, the greater the age at adoption, the lower the eventual mean IQ attained. For example, cases adopted at age 6 were retarded approximately three years at age 16.

In addition to these findings on the comparative intellectual development of foundlings during periods of institutionalization and periods of adoption, other findings of the present research include the intelligence of groups of children who were family-reared in Lebanon and tested at various ages. In general, their mean scores approximated those of comparable American groups.

While the test scores have received the greatest emphasis in this report, the data, fewer in quantity, on school progress, social, marital, and vocational adjustment, and psychiatric referrals are probably of equal importance. It has been shown that the two kinds of data are closely related. Those who were in experientially deprived institutions throughout childhood were not only of low intelligence but also evinced more signs of social maladjustment and personality disorder than did the adoptees.

THE GENETIC POTENTIAL INTELLIGENCE OF ADOPTED CHILDREN

We have proposed that the mean genetic potential of Crèche foundlings for intellectual development in a modern middle-class environment was approximately 100. We base this estimate upon the fact that those adopted from the Crèche within the first 2 years of age reached a mean IQ of only slightly less than 100 after only a few years of adoption, and can be assumed to have reached a mean of 100 sometime later.

That children available for adoption at an early age are potentially normal in intelligence is not a new finding, as we shall now show. In our review of several earlier investigations, which follows, we shall deal only with the point at issue, ignoring other voluminous data which these studies have supplied.

A series of investigations dealing with the intelligence of adopted children began to be published in 1928. Two were published in that year, one by Burks and one by Freeman, Holzinger, and Mitchell. These were followed by Leahy's report (1935) and by studies by Skodak and Skeels and their associates published between 1935 and 1966. These varied and extensive reports form the core of our knowledge of the effects of heredity and environment upon intelligence at the present time. They have been reviewed and interpreted many times and are fundamental to the recent discussions by Jensen (1969) and his adversaries. Since the planners of these studies wished to study the development of adopted children who had been reared in normal environments from an early age, they chose for study primarily children who had been placed in adoptive homes before they were 2 years of age, in many cases before they were 6 months of age. Selection on this basis served to rule out most adoptions occasioned by the mother's or father's illness and death. The adoptees in these investigations, as in the present one, were in the main children of unwed mothers who, when the babies were born, turned them over to the care of others.

Burks (1928) reported on the intelligence of 214 children adopted at the mean age of 3 months (none was over 1 year when adopted) and on 105 "own" children who were matched with the controls in age, sex, and the locality in which they lived. In addition, the foster fathers of the adoptees and the fathers of the controls were matched in occupational level. Intelligence tests were administered at various times between the ages of 5 and 14 years. The mean IQ of the adopted children was 107, that of the "own" children 115. While the own children tested higher than the adopted ones, the mean of the latter was above the norm of 100..

In the Freeman, Holzinger, and Mitchell report (1928) the subgroup, which closely resembles the early-adopted foundlings of the present study, consisted of 111 illegitimate children who were placed in foster homes before they were 2 years of age. When tested several years after adoption, their mean IQ was 106. Classified according to the rated excellence of their foster homes, those placed in "good" homes averaged 112, those in average homes 105, those in poor homes 96.

The Leahy study (1935) was similar to that of Burks. The 194 adoptees were in all cases illegitimate and were adopted at 6 months or earlier. An equal number of "own" children chosen for comparison were matched with the foster children, so that the two sets of homes were approximately equal in several respects. There was evidence which indicated that in both groups of subjects the parents and the homes were somewhat above average. The members of each matched pair were tested at about the same age. The testing occurred between 5 and 14 years of age; the mean IQ of each group was 110.

The studies by Skodak, Skeels, and their associates at the State University of

Iowa constitute a complex series of investigations which it is not feasible to review in detail. We shall refer only to those studies which contain data concerning the intelligence of adopted children.

We shall mention first a study which was reported by Skodak in 1939, again by Skeels in 1940, and summarized by Skeels in 1942. This investigation dealt with 154 children, 140 of whom were illegitimate, who were adopted under 6 months of age. Their average age when they were first tested was 2 years 7 months. They were retested at the average age of 4 years 4 months. In this study, the Kuhlman test was used for those under 3½ years; the S–B was administered to older subjects. The mean IQ on Test I was 116; on Test II it was 112. Twenty-eight of the cases were tested at age 5 years or later and averaged 111.

Additional follow-up studies of 100 of these children when they were between the ages of 11 and 17 years were reported in 1945 and 1949 by Skodak and Skeels. These studies involved additional administrations of the S–B, which yielded essentially the same results as had earlier tests; that is, a mean level of intelligence of above 100 was maintained at later age levels.

The studies just reviewed are in agreement with our findings that, if children, most of them illegitimate, are adopted before the age of 2 years, their mean IQ is usually 100 or above. In other words, as a group, the children who soon after birth become available for adoption, and are adopted, have the genetic capabilities for becoming normal in intelligence. That some groups of adopted children have mean IQs several points above 100 may be due to their having been placed in better-than-average homes, or it may be that children of superior genetic potential were chosen for adoption.

CAUSES OF THE RETARDATION OF CRÈCHE FOUNDLINGS

We believe that it has now been established that the *potential mean IQ* of foundlings who entered the Crèche, including those who later entered the institutions at Zouk and Brumana prior to 1956 and those adopted after 1956, was in the neighborhood of 100. But the *functional mean IQ* obtained from 50 foundlings in the Crèche between ages 1–0 and 7–1 was 53. For 35 older foundlings tested at Zouk or elsewhere at ages beyond 12–0 the mean IQ was 54. The mean of foundling boys at Brumana was 81.

It is our conviction that the difference between these means and the post-adoptive mean of about 100 of those who were adopted within their first 2 years of age was due to the deprivation of cognitive experiences in the institutional environments.

What are the alternative hypotheses? Some sort of selection of the "best" cases for adoption and the retention by the institutions of the "worst" cases is the obvious possibility. But on what basis could the "best" have been chosen for adoption in the first 2 years of life? No test or other measure of behavior made in the first 2 years of life has been shown to have more than a slight relationship to later IQs. There *is* a relationship between later intelligence of the child and the intelligence of the biological parents, but we doubt that the adoptive parents were given any information about the biological mother, and we doubt that the nuns knew who, or what kind of man, was the biological father. But if the natural parents had been known by the nuns, how could selection on the basis of potential intelligence have occurred? Most of the older Zouk girls and Brumana boys who became our subjects left the Crèche before the practice of adoption began. And at the time that they left, *all* foundlings, with the exception of a few physical defectives and some children reclaimed by relatives, were being sent to Zouk and Brumana. In contrast, in the years during which our *adopted* subjects left the Crèche nearly *all* foundings were being adopted. How could massive selection have occurred?

An additional problem is the following: How could a nun, or a prospective foster parent, even given omniscience, select from a population in which no scores of 100 occur a group of adoptees whose mean is 100? Even if some slight selection on the basis of someone's knowledge of parentage had taken place, it could have taken place only within a period of two or three years, when only some of the foundlings were being adopted. Only a small proportion of our subjects left the Crèche during that period.

We have examined every possibility of which we can conceive which might explain an eventual mean IQ of roughly 50 for Crèche foundling girls who were tested in the Crèche and at Zouk, of 81 at Brumana, and an eventual mean of approximately 100 for foundling girls and boys who were adopted from the Crèche during the first 2 years of life. The only explanation possible appears to be that the institutionally reared girls were environmentally deprived to a great extent in respect to cognitive experience, the Brumana boys to a lesser extent, and that both the boys and the girls after adoption in the first 2 years received normal childhood experiences in a family situation similar to the experiences of those on whom test norms are based. Furthermore, it appears that experiential deprivation which occurs before the age of 2-0 does not have lasting intellectual consequences if followed by normal everyday cognitive experience.

RESIDUAL RETARDATION AND
RATE OF MENTAL DEVELOPMENT

It is scarcely necessary to remind the reader that the adoptees and the Brumana boys improved in IQ after leaving the Crèche. But this improvement, within the upper limits of the ages covered by our investigations, did not enable them to attain a mean IQ of 100. The evidence indicates that, after being placed in an ameliorative environment at ages beyond 2-0, despite IQ gains, a deficit in MA remained and was probably permanent.

Evidence has been adduced to show that if the intellectual deficit of Crèche foundlings is stated in terms of retardation in MA, the mean deficit after leaving the Crèche and being placed in Brumana or being adopted remained the same as it was on their departure. It has also been shown that these two groups of subjects, after leaving the Crèche and entering other environments, had a mean RMD of 100. It does not seem possible to propose a sensible cause for the improvement in the intellectual progress of these two groups of subjects except to attribute it to the enrichment of cognitive experience provided by their new environments. Yet these subjects appeared to have an intellectual limitation which prevented their mean initial retardation from being reduced by more than a few months of MA and their mean RMD from rising but slightly above 100.

We should like to propose here that the RMD which occurs in experientially handicapped children when they are placed in a normal environment is comparable to the IQ which would have been characteristic of them if they had been in an intellectually favorable environment from birth. In other words, for those who suffer experiential deprivation which lasts beyond age 2 and who are later placed in an ameliorative environment, the RMD in the ameliorative environment may be an indicator of genetic potential intelligence. To put it another way, the way to measure the genetic potential of a child intellectually handicapped by his environment is to put him in a cognitively normal environment and measure his RMD. The index of his potential is not his earlier IQ, or even his improved IQ, but his RMD in his new situation. At this time, we are unable to suggest how additional tests of this hypothesis can be made, but it is likely that they will be forthcoming.

The corollary arising from this view is that if the RMD in a "good" environment is to quite an extent limited by genes, a complete recovery from the effects of earlier environmental handicap which has extended beyond the age of 2–0 will not occur, unless a method of remediation more effective than normal family life can be developed. It is our belief that, for a child who has been mentally retarded by experiential deprivation, no more effective and dependable program of remediation is available today than placement in a home with two adoptive parents, concerned, intelligent, and educated, who will spend several hours a day in cognitive interaction with him, in addition to providing him with classroom schooling and child contacts. It remains to be seen whether or not a better scheme can be devised.

Our own data on the RMD of foundlings at Brumana may be cited as refuting the opinion we have just espoused, because at Brumana an RMD of 100 prevailed. Our answer is that the families which adopt foundlings are not, in the main, extraordinary families, and are not difficult to find. On the other hand, the cognitive possibilities available to Brumana boys were unusual, and the presence of a Mother Superior who could take full advantage of them was even more extraordinary. One cannot expect that many parochial institutions, government projects, or volunteer agencies will equal the record of the institution at Brumana, just as not many hungry animals can count upon being fed by St. Francis. Only a very unusual institution can equal an adoptive family, and probably few exist which provide advantages *superior* to adoption.

THE IMPLICATIONS OF OUR FINDINGS
FOR INSTITUTIONS AND FOR ADOPTION

The implications of our findings for those persons connected with institutions and for those playing a role in adoptions may be obvious, but nevertheless we have an obligation to express our conception of them.

We have visited a considerable number of institutions other than those on which we have reported here. We believe it possible for an institution to be "good." We are able to cite Brumana as a case in point, and we could cite a few others in which we believe cognitive growth and personality development are not harmed. Institutionalization, and it sometimes is necessary, *can* produce normal development; that is, institutionalization can be made acceptable—but it seldom is. There seem to be few if any reasons why children should be retained in an institution if they can be adopted. Unfortunately, even today some institutions refuse to offer their children for adoption, even though many people want them. Some of these institutions are transforming children who are potentially normal in intelligence into adults of permanent feeblemindedness.

In our opinion it would be a reasonable requirement that each institution which receives abandoned or neglected children be required to submit to its governing board, annually, for each child the result of a mental test given by a qualified person. Such reports could well be the basis for remedial action with respect to the institutional regime and should serve to show whether or not adoption at an early age rather than retention in an institution should be introduced, at least on a trial basis.

If children are placed in an institution while awaiting adoption, it appears from our data, that unless the institution can show itself to be as favorable for mental development as are adoptive families, the children, if possible, should be placed in adoptive homes before they are 2 years of age. This is the current policy of enlightened placement agencies.

THE PREVALENCE OF EXPERIENTIAL DEPRIVATION

This report has been concerned almost entirely with the development of institutional children, adoptees, and their comparison groups. But our concern would be very restricted if it were limited to such groups. They serve to demonstrate that experiential deprivation can have severe and enduring consequences, but social and developmental impairment occurs not only in institutions but in much larger populations which will be affected but slightly if at all by a wider acceptance of adoption. We would be remiss if we ended an account of the effects of the poverty of experience which occur within institutions without indicating the extent to which they occur in much more populous settings.

In recent decades, child psychiatrists and psychologists have focused much of their attention upon early childhood with a stress upon the consequences of maternal deprivation and other kinds of restriction or neglect in infancy (Spitz 1945*a* and 1945*b*; Bowlby 1952; Goldfarb 1955; Casler 1961; and Ainsworth 1962*a* and 1962*b*). Among these consequences are sometimes low IQs.

However, these publications have usually failed to mention that other inves-tigators have shown that many groups of children, all of whom were living with their mothers and fathers, have also been found to have low IQs and that en-vironmental depression of intelligence is not limited to early childhood. To provide a wider perspective for the present study, we present a brief review of some of these other studies, most of which were conducted in the 1920s and 1930s.

An early and famous report of low intelligence among underprivileged chil-dren who remained with their parents was that concerning English canalboat children and gypsy children by Gordon (1923). The parents of both groups were not only poor and illiterate, but they were also itinerants who almost continually moved about, the gypsies by land and the boatmen by canals. As a consequence, the children remained in a given school only a short time and often were not in school at all. Their total days of formal schooling in a year were few. The intellectual background of their parents provided only the limited requirements of their occupations, which did not include reading, writing, or extensive vo-cabularies.

Gordon, one of His Majesty's inspectors of schools, conducted a remarkably good study. He was one of the first in England to use the Stanford 1916 revision of the Binet-Simon Tests in a research study. His original monograph is difficult to find, but excerpts from it have been reprinted by Al-Issa and Dennis (1970) and by Dennis (1972).

Gordon found among the canal-boat children a correlation of $-.76$ between age and IQ, that is, the older the child the lower the IQ. The average IQ at about 6 years of age was 87; at about age 12 it was 60, which is nearly as low as that of the Zouk girls. Apparently the cognitive environment of the canal-boat homes was almost adequate for normal development at the 6 year level but not for 12-year-olds.

The gypsies were more in contact with the English communities among whom they moved than were the canal-boat people. Their children attended school more frequently, were not as low in IQ as the canal-boat children, but showed the same downward trend in IQ with age. The numbers at various age levels are not sufficient to yield reliable averages at each age, but the mean for the gypsies at ages 5 and 6 was about 95 and at ages 11 and 12 about 75.

The situation of the Virginia mountain children studied by Sherman and Key (1932) was similar to that of Gordon's subjects except that the mountain children were not mobile. The social, cultural, and educational isolation of the mountain children was due to geography rather than to the transient residence of their parents. The isolation of the mountain families at that time was attributable largely to the sparseness and scattered nature of the population and the absence or bad condition of roads. These two conditions made it impossible to provide transportation to schools (in some communities all transportation was by foot only). Isolation also prevented or reduced outside employment in and social and cultural contacts with the nearby towns and cities.

The mountain homes provided little cognitive stimulation. Since parents could not read, the homes contained no printed matter. In 1929–30, radios were not present in mountain homes. The book of reminiscences by Pollock (1960) provides a much fuller picture of primitive life in the isolated portions of the Blue Ridge mountains in 1930–32 than does the article by Sherman and Key and the subsequent book by Sherman and Henry (1933).

Sherman and Key obtained S–B scores on 32 children in four mountain valleys. These scores are not reported by age. The mean IQ was 72. The Pintner-Cunningham test, the National Intelligence test, the Draw-a-Man test, and a Performance Scale were given to a larger number of mountain subjects. Among the 12 or 13 subjects at ages 6 to 8, the mean IQs in the various tests ranged from 80 to 91. At ages 12 to 16, the total number of subjects given each test ranged from 15 to 27. The means were much lower than those for the younger children, the mid-average being 68. The corresponding averages for the nearby town of Briarsville were somewhat higher but also declined with age on each test. For example, the average on the Draw-a-Man test declined from 93 at ages 6 to 8 to 70 at ages 14 to 16.

Skeels and Fillmore (1937) studied the IQs upon admission to an orphanage of children who had previously been in underprivileged homes. Those entering at ages 2 to 4 years had a mean IQ of 93. Those entering later had progressively lower IQs on admission, reaching the low mean of 80 for those admitted at ages 13 and 14. Similar reports for the low IQs of underprivileged children have been reported by Asher (1935), Edwards and Jones (1938), and Wheeler (1932 and 1942).

While the studies of U.S. groups just reviewed do not tend to show early retardation, low mean IQs do occur in many groups before the age of 6 years. We have reported (Dennis 1966) results obtained from forty groups of children to whom the Goodenough Draw-a-Man test was administered at about 6 years of age; the Draw-a-Man test was employed because it does not require verbal responses and is acceptable to almost any group. The mean scores among these groups ranged from a top mean of 125 to a low mean of 53. The two lowest means were obtained from children of two illiterate groups, one consisting of Bedouins in Syria and one of Shilluk Negroes in Sudan. Neither attended school. The respective means were 56 and 53. The means of six other groups, three of them in the United States, were below 80.

No concerted effort has been made by anyone to estimate the number of persons below specified levels of intelligence among various groups, including groups in nonmodernized countries. Our own efforts in that direction have consisted in finding the means, below which 50 percent lie, in a miscellany of groups on the Draw-a-Man test. Results have been obtained in approximately sixty communities but are not as yet ready for presentation. We may say, however, that the information at hand warrants the prediction that there are millions of children with Draw-a-Man IQs below 70, and that the low values of these scores are due, in the main, to experiential deprivation. The moral, if one may call it a moral, is that many homes and communities in the world today are as intellectually vacuous as the life space of the foundlings of the Crèche and of Zouk.

The areas of lowest intelligence are those not as yet transformed by modern civilization. In these areas there are no tractors and trucks, in some regions not even mules. Man is the beast of burden, and the only source of power is human muscle. Under such conditions, the need for food and shelter and escape from disease are uppermost in the mind, and there is little concern for learning, schooling, reading, or interchange of information, even with regard to the immediate environment.

For these millions of children, adoption cannot provide the solution which it has provided to the children of the Crèche. Only the promotion of massive social changes, such as have occurred in "modern countries," can do it. Modernization is required to transform genetic potential into functional adequacy. Until this happens, children and adults in uncounted numbers around the world, be it Appalachia, India, Brazil, or elsewhere, living in stultifying and intellectually depressing environments, will have a mentality not much above that of the foundlings at Zouk.

REFERENCES

Ainsworth, M. D. "The effects of maternal deprivation. A review of findings and controversy in the context of research strategy." *Public Health Papers.* New York: World Health Organization 14 (1962*a*):97–165.

———. "Reversible and Irreversible Effects of Maternal Deprivation on Intellectual Development." In *Maternal Deprivation.* New York: Child Welfare League of America, 1962*b*, pp. 42–62.

Al-Issa, I., and Dennis, W. *Cross-Cultural Studies of Behavior.* New York: Holt, Rinehart and Winston, 1970.

Asher, E. J. "The inadequacy of current intelligence tests for testing Kentucky mountain children." *J. Genet. Psychol.* 46 (1935):480–86.

Bowlby, J. "Maternal Care and Mental Health," 2nd ed. Geneva: World Health Organization; Monog. Series 8, 1952.

Burks, B. S. "The relative influence of nature and nurture upon mental development; a comparative study of foster-parent-foster-child resemblance and true-parent-true-child resemblance." *27th Yearbook Nat. Soc. Stud. Educ.* 1 (1928):219–316.

Casler, L. "Maternal Deprivation: A Critical Review of the Literature." Monog. Soc. Res. Child Develop., No. 26, 1961.

Dennis, W. "Goodenough scores, art experience and modernization." *J. Soc. Psychol.* 68 (1966):211–28.

———. *Historical Readings in Developmental Psychology.* New York: Appleton-Century-Crofts, 1972.

Edwards, A. S., and Jones, L. "An experimental and field study of North Georgia mountaineers." *J. Soc. Psychol.* 9 (1938):317–33.

Freeman, F. N., Holzinger, K. J., and Mitchell, B. C. "The influence of environment on the intelligence, school achievement and conduct of foster children." *27th Yearbook Nat. Soc. Stud. Educ.* 1 (1928):101–217.

Goldfarb, E. "Emotional and Intellectual Consequences of Psychological Deprivation in Infancy: A Revaluation." In P. H. Hock and J. Zubin, eds., *Psychopathology of Childhood*. New York: Grune & Stratton, 1955, pp. 105–19.

Gordon, H. "Mental and Scholastic Tests among Retarded Children." Educ. Pamphlet 44. London: Board of Education, 1923.

Jensen, A. R. "How much can we boost IQ and scholastic achievement?" *Harvard Educ. Rev.* 39 (1969):1–123.

Leahy, A. M. "Nature-nurture and intelligence." *Genet. Psychol. Monog.* 17 (1935):235–308.

Pollock, G. F. *Skyland.* Berryville, Va., Chesapeake Book Co., 1960.

Sherman, M., and Henry, T. R. *Hollow Folk.* New York: Thomas Y. Crowell & Co., 1933.

Sherman, M., and Key, C. B. "The intelligence scores of isolated mountain children." *Child Develop.* 3 (1932):279–90.

Skeels, H. M. "Some Iowa Studies of the Mental Growth of Children in Relation to Differentials of the Environment: A Summary." In *Intelligence: Its Nature and Nurture.* 39th Yearbook Nat. Soc. Stud. Educ. (1940), II:281–308.

————. "A study of the effects of differential stimulation on mentally retarded children: A follow-up report." *Amer. J. Mental Def.* 46 (1942):340–50.

Skeels, H. M., and Filmore, E. A. "The mental development of children from underprivileged homes." *J. Genet. Psychol.* 50 (1937):427–39.

Skodak, M. "Children in Foster Homes." *Univ. Iowa Stud. Child. Welf.* 16 (1939), No. 1.

————. "A final follow-up study of one hundred adopted children." *J. Genet. Psychol.* 75 (1949):85–125.

Skodak, M., and Skeels, H. M. "A follow-up study of children in adoptive homes." *J. Genet. Psychol.* 66 (1945):21–58.

Spitz, R. A. "Hospitalism: An inquiry into the genesis of psychiatric conditions in early childhood." *Psychoanal. Study Child.* 1 (1945*a*):55–74.

————. "Hospitalism: A follow-up report." *Psychoanal. Study Child.* 1 (1945*b*):113–17.

Wheeler, L. R. "The intelligence of East Tennessee mountain children." *J. Educ. Psychol.* 23 (1932):351–71.

————. "A comparative study of the intelligence of East Tennessee mountain children." *J. Educ. Psychol.* 30 (1942):321–34.

CHAPTER 32

IQ Change Following Change of Domicile in the Syndrome of Reversible Hyposomatotropinism (Psychosocial Dwarfism): Pilot Investigation

John Money and Charles Annecillo

INTRODUCTION

In the syndrome of dwarfism characterized by reversible hyposomatotropinism occurring along with suspected or proved child abuse, an IQ increase by as many as 55 points has been documented (see below). The increase is a sequel to change of domicile and is paralleled by catch-up growth in stature. There has not yet been a systematic investigation of this phenomenon of IQ change, but there are some preliminary data, and it is the purpose of this report to present them.

SAMPLE SELECTION AND PROCEDURES

Initially it was not known that catch-up somatic growth in the syndrome of reversible hyposomatotropic dwarfism, with suspected or proven child abuse, might be associated with catch-up intellectual growth. Once this parallelism was suspected, we instituted a program of before-and-after testing for IQ. There are now sixteen patients, selected without known sampling bias, who satisfy two criteria: (1) There exists an IQ while height was severely dwarfed (tested from 8 months before to 6 months after change of domicile); (2) There exists at least one subsequent IQ obtained 2.5–8.25 yr later, after the onset of catch-up growth in stature. These sixteen patients are the subjects of this report. They are heterogeneous in that some had been away from their domicile of retarded growth much longer than others. Also, the relocation domicile had been more favorably growth-promoting for some than for others. A few had been relocated in a foster home from which removal was necessitated as a result of a recurrence

Reprinted with permission from *Psychoneuroendocrinology* 1 (1976):427–29. Copyright (1976), Pergamon Press Ltd.

of growth failure and associated neglect or child abuse. Eventually it will be possible to subclassify individuals according to age, duration of domiciliary change, type of domicile, and presence or absence of catch-up growth, but for this preliminary report subclassification was not feasible.

The procedure was to take before-and-after IQ data from the patients' files. Because some had a longer duration of follow-up than others, they had more follow-up tests for IQ. For present purposes, the most recent follow-up IQ was used.

RESULTS

Twelve of the sixteen patients manifested an IQ increase. Eight increased between 2 and 14 points; four increased between 29 and 55 points; one remained unchanged; three decreased between 1 and 12 points. The four with the largest increase all had a long interval (4.5–7.75 yr) between pre- and post-test. They also showed a complete remission of symptoms of impaired growth and behavior. Their new home environments were adjudged stable and beneficent. In contrast, the three patients with an IQ decrease showed persistence of varied symptoms such as bedwetting, temper tantrums, hyperkinesis, and atypical food and fluid intake, despite a test period in which catch-up growth had been proved possible. In one of these cases, there was evidence of a resumption of child abuse at the time the follow-up IQ was obtained, at which time he had been returned to his home of origin. The home environment for the second patient was quite unsatisfactory, and while there the boy manifested a decline in rate of catch-up growth. The third patient had an adequate home environment, according to the records available, and showed continuing improved statural growth. However, there was a persistence of symptoms usually associated with an unsatisfactory domestic life, namely bedwetting and hyperactivity. In the seven cases of moderate IQ elevation, the patients had, according to the evidence available, adequate living environments at the time of retest. The one patient without IQ change was living in a state mental institution at the time of retest.

Table I. IQ change and duration of change of domicile in 16 cases of reversible hyposomatotropinism (psychosocial dwarfism)

Group	Duration	Mean	IQ change range	Median
A n = 8	1 month—3 yr 7 months	8.8	−12 to +37	+5.5
B n = 8	4 yr 3 months—7 yr 6 months	17.5	−1 to +55	+10.5
Total	1 month—7 yr 6 months	13.1	−12 to +55	+6.5

The foregoing expansion of the findings, for all their incompleteness as preliminary data, support the hypothesis of a correlation between improved living environment and IQ elevation in the syndrome of child abuse and dwarfism with reversible hyposomatotropinism.

Further support for the hypothesis is evident in Table I which demonstrated a trend in the amount of IQ elevation that correlated with the amount of time a child had spent away from the noxious environment of the domicile of origin.

DISCUSSION

It is a platitude to say that both genetics and environment are responsible for intelligence. Environment has even more influence on the intelligence quotient as compared with the conceptual abstraction, intelligence. This is so because the very environment and process of testing for IQ can influence the result. The pendulum of fashion has swayed to favor either genetics or environment at different times and in different contexts. It is fashionable today to maximise genetics as a determinant of IQ differences. The present study draws attention to the living environment as an extraordinarily powerful determinant of IQ and its changes, namely, in the context of the syndrome of growth failure of dwarfism in association with reversible pituitary (growth-hormone) failure, occurring along with child abuse and neglect, either proved or suspected. Other syndromes may have more to teach us about environmental adversity and low IQ. One of them is the syndrome of cognitive neglect described by Wayne Dennis (1973).

REFERENCE

Dennis, W. *Children of the Crèche*. New York: Appleton-Century-Crofts, 1973.

PART VI

Dwarfism and Growth Responses

"Secretion of pituitary growth hormone in abuse dwarfism is deficient but can be reversed. The formula for reversal is simply to change the domicile from an abusing to a non-abusing one. . . . Pragmatically, the only effective form of intervention may be a change of domicile for the abused child so that s/he can grow in stature, intelligence, and behavior."

(Money and Needleman, 1976)

Editor's Introduction

The group of papers in Part VI focuses more intensively on the symptoms of this as yet insufficiently understood syndrome. In addition to impaired statural growth and failure of growth hormone secretion, adrenocorticotropin (ACTH) secretion may also fail, and if the child remains in the abusive environment after puberty, gonadotropin secretion also may fail, with the result that puberty is delayed.

The psychological effects accompanying the impaired endocrinological functioning in psychosocial dwarfs include retarded intellectual and motor development, pain agnosia, impaired aggression, and unusual eating and drinking behavior, as Chapters 33 through 36 show. As elaborated in Chapter 32, the syndrome is reversed after removal of the child from the abusive home and placement in a growth-promoting foster home or other domicile.

J.M.

REFERENCE

Money, J., and Needleman, A. "Child abuse in the syndrome of reversible hyposomatotropic dwarfism: Psychosocial dwarfism," *Pediatric Psychology* 1 (1976):20–23.

CHAPTER 33

The Syndrome of Abuse Dwarfism (Psychosocial Dwarfism or Reversible Hyposomatotropinism): Behavioral Data and Case Report

John Money

In abuse dwarfism the behavioral signs include some or all of the following: (1) a history of unusual eating and drinking behavior, reversible on change of domicile, such as eating from a garbage can and drinking from a toilet bowl, stealing food, alleged picky eating and rejecting food at the table, polydipsia and polyphagia, possibly alternating with vomiting and possibly also with self-starvation; (2) a history of such behavioral symptoms as enuresis, encopresis, social apathy or inertia, defiant aggressiveness, sudden tantrums, crying spasms, insomnia, eccentric sleeping and waking schedule, pain agnosia, and self-injury, all occurring only in the growth-retarding environment; (3) retarded motor development, with improvement on removal of the child from the domicile of abuse; (4) retarded intellectual growth, reversible on change of domicile by as much as 30 to 55 IQ points; and (5) a history of pathologic family relationships, including unusual cruelty and neglect, either somatic or psychic or both.

The nature of the syndrome of reversible hyposomatotropinism, otherwise known as psychosocial dwarfism, is delineated elsewhere (1–10). The purpose of this article is to show the relationship between reversible growth failure (reversible hyposomatotropinism with dwarfism) and child abuse, with particular attention to behavior, as illustrated by a well-documented and authenticated case.* The case is unusual because of the duration and severity of abuse, which continued long enough to inhibit the normal onset of puberty (9).

BACKGROUND DATA

The patient is now 21 years old. He first came to public attention at the age of 2½ months, when he was hospitalized with fever and malnutrition. During his childhood, neighbors and relatives sporadically complained of his maltreatment, but

Reprinted with permission from the *American Journal of Diseases of Children* 131 (1977):508–13. Copyright 1977, American Medical Association.
*See also Chapter 36.

no effective action was taken, and he was not seen again in the hospital until he was 16 years old. At that time he was brought to the hospital as a sequel to legal intervention initiated by the complaint of an older half-sister. This sister, aware of the history of child abuse, had recently married and was at last in a position of personal safety from which to take action on her brother's behalf. Four years earlier, acting on a relative's complaint, the police had found the boy nailed up naked, in a closet, with his own excrement. They took pictures and warned the parents, but did nothing further. At the age of 14, the boy had never attended school. Despite their repeated resistance, the parents finally were forced to release him to the Division of Special Education for a day of testing. The history of abuse was recorded, but no effective measures were undertaken on his behalf. He returned home, where he suffered another 1½ years of brutality and confinement. When he was finally liberated he went to live with a stepaunt for six weeks prior to hospitalization, and then was placed in a recovery center and eventually in a church-sponsored institutional community for the handicapped and retarded.

The parents (stepmother and legal father who disowned paternity) eventually came to trial and served two years in jail. They consistently refused to come to the hospital, and avoided all medical and social service contacts. The chief informant in the hospital, other than the patient himself, was his stepaunt. This woman identified herself as a half-sister of the patient's stepmother. A secret in the genealogy proved to be a key to the psychodynamic understanding of the boy's mistreatment: the father of the stepmother was, in fact, her mother's own father, the husband of the stepmother's grandmother. This incestuous fact of her genealogy was first revealed to her at the age of 15 or 16. Severely burned when her robe caught on fire, she was hospitalized at the time. In order to prepare her for the possibility of extreme unction, her grandmother disclosed to the girl the truth of her parentage. The girl recovered but underwent a change of personality, apparently in response to the trauma of learning of her origin. Her behavior became more "wild" and delinquent. In her late teens she had an illegitimate daughter. Then she married a man who later proved to be a bigamist. There were three more children by this union. When their father disappeared, and before she married again, the mother gave all three children out to adoption and did not see them again. At that time, she became depressed and was evaluated for psychiatric treatment, but did not follow through. On remarriage, she became the stepmother of four children. Her new husband disclaimed paternity of the youngest of these four, a boy of 3 years, the patient of this report. When this boy was 3 months old, both his mother and her boyfriend, the patient's father, had been killed in an automobile accident.

FORMULA OF CHILD ABUSE

In a manner typical in cases of child abuse, this case fits the formula of a child forced to suffer punishment by way of atonement for a parent's own shortcomings and transgressions. In the present instance, the stepmother, illegitimate herself and the mother of an illegitimate daughter (the only one of her first four children whom she did not put out to adoption), abused only one child, an illegitimate stepson. The other three stepchildren escaped, as did their three half-siblings by the second marriage. One may conjecture that the stepmother was, by proxy, pathologically destroying in the boy an image of what she could not tolerate in herself. In this respect the boy resembled a victim of the Inquisition, tortured so that the soul might be saved from eternal damnation. But he was not tortured until dead, for in child abuse it is usually more important to have a living victim than a dead one—a living symbol of continuous atonement. Hence one encounters such inconsistencies in child abuse as parental contrivance to allow a child to steal or otherwise obtain enough food to keep alive, but not to grow properly; to sleep, but not to get enough sleep; and to be injured but, when the injury becomes life-threatening, to be taken to a doctor. In the manner of Munchausen syndrome, the parents deceive the doctor regarding their personal responsibility for inflicting the injury.

As long as the stepmother acted out her pathologically cruel fantasy in what might be termed a character psychosis, she achieved a convincing semblance of social sanity. The customers at the local tavern where she worked thought highly of her, for example, and did not suspect her of child abuse. Her own rationale for the condition of her stepson was that he behaved like a freak and an "animal" whom most stepmothers would have had institutionalized, because he was born mentally defective. Her husband knew better, of course. In a *folie à deux* of acquiescence and collusion, typical in fathers of abused children, he shared responsibility for the boy's plight. In addition, he added his own abuse by beating and kicking the boy. In court, a relative reported this man, whom the boy called father, to have forced his son to bend, touching his toes, for as long as six hours at a time, kicking him brutally if he stopped.

BIOGRAPHY OF ABUSE

By the time the boy was rescued at age 16, there was some plausibility in the parents' claim that he was mentally retarded, a freak, and an animal, but only because they had, in effect, engineered it so. They required, for example, that if he were allowed any food at the time the rest of the family were at the meal table, he would like an animal be restricted to scraps from the others' plates, fed to him only if he were on all fours on the floor. They prevented him, as when they locked him in the closet, from having access to the bathroom and the toilet, so that he had no option but to soil himself, for which he was whipped. They gave him no chance to play and develop motor coordination and skills. They restricted his chance to hear language and use it; his speech was so defective and his vocabulary so impoverished that at age 16, when he was freed, he could scarcely be understood when he tried to communicate. Occasionally he had been allowed the stimulation of looking at television, but even this recreation was an ordeal, for his parents obliged him to stand motionless in a corner of the room. If he was seen moving, he was required to stand on his head for up to two hours. There were some occasions when he was removed from the house and taken with the family to the shore. While the other children played and swam, he was forced to sit in the blazing sun, forbidden to move to a shady place. If an adult relative took pity on him and defied his stepmother's order not to feed him or give him fluids, she threatened that person with physical assault with a knife. Any attempt at intervention on the boy's behalf met with such a threat.

Approximately once a week, he was tied to the newel post of the staircase in order to receive a beating with a stick, bat, or board. All of his siblings were required to beat him in turn. Otherwise their mother would beat them for disobedience. At the time of his rescue, the boy had permanent scars on his scalp as a result of his beatings. He was marked by dog bites as a result of having had the family's German shepherd set on him. Roentgenographically it was shown that his right elbow had been fractured and had healed without having been set. The boy said, and his stepaunt confirmed, that it was his stepmother who had broken his elbow. She then had refused to take him to a doctor.

SLEEP

As far as can be inferred in retrospect, the boy did not sleep regularly or soundly during the years of abuse, for his parents contrived to prevent proper sleep. They did so by confining him in too small a place to permit an ordinary, full-length sleeping position. He had no mattress, only bare boards. At different periods of his life his sleeping place was a wooden box, a locked closet, an unventilated attic in midsummer when the outside temperature was over 32 C (90 F), and an outside dog kennel when the frosts of early winter had arrived. Usually he had no blankets and, even though shivering, might be required to shed his usual dirty, ragged clothes and spend the night naked. A few months before his rescue, the boy demolished the lock of his prison closet. As punishment, his parents handcuffed him to the post of their bed and at night required him to sleep naked on the bare floor. As he told the story, recalling it with utmost reluctance when he was 19, they also padlocked the bedroom door at night and dragged their bed across it. The father pinned the padlock key to his undershorts in which he slept. Starving and thirsty, the boy used the night not to sleep but to free himself to forage for food and water, hiding whatever he could on an outside window ledge, or in a secret hole in the ceiling of his prison-closet. He got free by using a bobby pin, which he kept hidden in the crack between two floor boards, to open his handcuffs. While his father slept, he then unpinned the key to the padlock on the door, and moved the bed enough to be able to open the door and go to the kitchen in search of food, collecting scraps from the garbage if nothing else was available. Before he broke the lock on his closet, he had no way of getting food and water at night, and so he had to make the best of daytime opportunities to take food surreptitiously and hide it.

Not only hunger and thirst, but also fear of punishment, by day or night, interfered with the boy's ability to sleep. When he was locked away, he was not always able to distinguish day from night. Except by sounds, he could not predict the safe times when, with the rest of the household sleeping, he might sleep too. For self-preservation, he needed to be constantly vigilant.

The fact that there is a correlation between good sleep and good growth, and poor sleep and impaired growth in the syndrome of reversible hyposomato-tropinism is demonstrated in the report of Wolff and Money (8). The mechanism responsible for this correlation has not yet been discovered.

EATING

It is already apparent from the foregoing sleep history that the boy's food intake was highly abnormal. It was almost certainly deficient also, but to what extent cannot be ascertained. In view of the prevarication and deceit typical in child abusers, it probably never will be ascertained. For the same reason, one cannot be sure about the nutritional balance achieved in the amount of food the child did ingest. He did not appear clinically to be suffering from specific nutritional deficit when first brought in for medical evaluation at age 16. Nor did he have the emaciated appearance of starvation. Typically for the syndrome, his bodily system's response to lack of food was to inhibit or shut off growth, rather than to become emaciated. The mechanism of the shutoff, which may be related to sleep impairment, remains to be discovered.

SELF-DISCLOSURE AND MARTYRDOM

Much of the foregoing biographical data, and some that follows, was given first by a relative, in either the legal or the medical record, and later confirmed by the patient himself. It was difficult for him to talk about the rigors of his life, however, and he was explicit in saying that he did not want to be reminded of the past by talking about it. With the passage of time, he felt more secure and was able to supply more details of what had actually happened to him.

In this respect, this patient was typical of abused children. Usually they are so tight-lipped that it seems as though there must be some complicity between abuser and abused. The cover-up continues for quite some time after removal to a safe environment, so that it is not simply a precaution against immediate reprisals. Perhaps the only way to comprehend it is to recognize that the abused child is an involuntary martyr and that martyrdom becomes a deeply imbedded trait in his personality, imperative to survival. For him abuse is as inevitable a part of life as ice is an inevitable part of life to an Eskimo. It is pointless for an Eskimo to complain about ice, snow, and subzero weather, for they constitute the only environment he knows. Likewise, it is pointless for an abused child to complain about his forms of abuse, because they constitute the only environment he knows. Here, perhaps lies a key to the appealing and appeasing ways of many children with the syndrome of abuse dwarfism. Like the kicked and beaten cur that repeatedly returns to the farmer begging for affection and kindness, so abused children relentlessly try to meet their abusers' demands, as if trying finally to win love and appreciation.

It was only by a slow process of disillusionment that the patient finally gave up trying to contact his relatives in order to establish some sort of family membership for himself. They all failed him, as did society at large by not succeeding in providing him with the surrogate, foster family he so greatly needed.

It is very difficult indeed for abusive parents as well as their abused child to change. They are more likely to succeed if separated for a while, with the child taking a "rest cure." The professional time and cost involved is enormous, and usually there is not enough of either for proper treatment and rehabilitation of the parents, since nothing short of entire, long-term family therapy is sufficient. For the child's welfare, if not his very survival, the only humane procedure, therefore, may be separation and long-term placement in a new environment.

GROWTH STATISTICS

When released from domestic confinement, the boy's chronological age was 16 years and 10 days. His height was 129.5 cm, which represents a height age of 8 years, and his weight was 27.5 kg (a weight age of 7 years 11 months). He had his first medical examination six weeks later, at which time his height was unchanged. His bone age was recorded as 11½ years. He had gained 4.5 kg (a weight age of 9 years 2 months) during the previous six weeks, at which time he had been living in the home of his stepaunt. This change of habitation was of sufficient duration for pituitary dysfunction to have corrected itself spontaneously. Thus the opportunity for laboratory confirmation of reversible hyposomatotropinism was lost. Table 1 shows his growth progress for the next five years. Though the amount of catch-up growth is remarkable, it is highly probable that the patient is shorter than he would have been had every year of childhood growth been normal.

Apart from findings, physical and mental, related to the history of abuse and of growth impairment and catch-up growth, there was nothing otherwise remarkable in the medical work-up and subsequent medical history.

IQ STATISTICS

The kind of deprivation to which the boy was subjected produced a de facto mental incompetence that was reversed to a remarkable degree after he was rescued.

By reason of the fact that the boy was tested in the Division of Special Education eighteen months before his escape from abuse, there is a before and after record of his IQ and its changes. The figures showing a progressive increase

Table 1. Growth progress

Months from date of admission	Domicile	Chronological age	Height, cm	Height age	Weight, kg	Weight age	Pubertal development
−1½	Home	16 yr	129.5	8 yr	27.5	7 yr 11 mo	Nil
0	Step-aunt's house	16 yr 1.5 mo	129.5	8 yr	32.8	9 yr 2 mo	Nil
10	Children's recovery center	16 yr 11 mo	139.5	9 yr 10 mo	35.8	10 yr 3 mo	Penis lengthened 1 cm; scrotal skin darker
20	Capstone*	17 yr 9 mo	145.5	10 yr 11 mo	39.9	11 yr 3 mo	Early signs of progressing
30	Capstone	18 yr 7 mo	152.5	12 yr 2 mo	40.8	11 yr 6 mo	Pubertal
34	Capstone	18 yr 11 mo	158.0	13 yr	35.4	12 yr 6 mo	Adult scrotum; adult axillary and pubic hair; mild acne; thin moustache
46	Group home†	19 yr 11 mo	159.0	13 yr 2 mo	47.2	12 yr 11 mo	Postpubertal
62	Group home	21 yr 3 mo	162.5	13 yr 8 mo	46.7	12 yr 4 mo	Postpubertal

*Capstone: church-sponsored institution for the handicapped and retarded.
†Group home: a subsidiary of Capstone, a type of halfway house for graduates from Capstone. It was organized in the manner of a family, and supervised by surrogate parents.

Table 2. IQ statistics

Site of testing	Date	Test*	Full IQ	Verbal IQ	Performance IQ
Board of education	11/67	WISC	51	60	50
Juvenile court	7/69	WAIS	59	64	58
Moore Clinic	12/69	WAIS	77	70	72
Psychohormonal research unit	5/72	WAIS	80	82	80
Psychohormonal research unit	8/74	WAIS	79	81	80

*Wechsler Adult Intelligence Scale, WAIS; Wechsler Intelligence Scale for Children, WISC.

of 29 points in full IQ, from 51 to 79–80, over the period of seven years are listed in Table 2. Even if further intellectual catch-up growth in the two years since the last testing is demonstrated, if and when follow-up costs can be subsidized, it is highly probable that, as in the case of statural growth, the ultimate attainment will be less than if each annual increment of intellectual growth had been normal throughout childhood.

Completely convincing evidence of a permanent and severe impairment of IQ by as much as 50%, as a result of infantile and early childhood developmental deprivation, is found in Wayne Dennis's *Children of the Crèche* (11). Data on IQ improvement in abuse dwarfism are reported by Money and Annecillo (12).

SPEECH

During the first months of his freedom, the boy's speech was extremely difficult to understand. In articulation, it was imperfect and cluttered. The sound *l* was wrongly pronounced. Vocabulary was impoverished. Syntax was idiosyncratic. On first impression, one observer reported that he mistook the child's language as not being English. In 1969, when the patient was 16 and newly released from his home of abuse, the secretary who transcribed a taped interview noted that, in many places, her transcription was only an approximation, and that many utterances were unintelligible. By 1972, such problems were gone. In the meantime, there had been some schooling and a brief program of speech therapy, while the patient was living in the institutional community for the handicapped and retarded. The following two samples illustrate the difference.

Oct. 19, 1969—Therapist: "What did you get yesterday evening for supper?" Patient: "That's what I'm thinking about. Let me see" (unintelligible). "Oh, chicken and one potato." Therapist: "And did you like that?" Patient: "Yeah." Therapist: "And how much did you eat?" Patient: "And string beans." Therapist: "String beans also," Patient: "And then we had peaches" (child has to repeat several times before making himself understood).

May 11, 1972—Therapist: "Was there any other problem you discussed with him?" Patient: "Like um, how much money I get a week and that I don't think it's fair only getting $2 a week." Therapist: "uh huh." Patient: "And he don't think so neither. He said I should be getting $5, like one of the girls. She only works three hours a day up at the club. She's getting $5. I'm only getting $2. Something is wrong with that."

KINESIS

Kinesis is a suitable term to encompass hypokinetic and hyperkinetic behavior. Hypokinesis is manifested as lack of motion or activity, slowness, apathy, and inertia. It is associated with compliance, uncomplaining martyrdom, complicity with the abuser, and denial of maltreatment in dwarfed, abused children, while they are not growing. Hyperkinesis is manifested as too much motion or activity, including talk, much of it agitated, poorly coordinated, and without consistency of purpose. It is commonly characteristic of the rehabilitation phase through which the abused dwarfs pass after separation from the agents of their abuse. For a while, their hyperkinesis may simulate hypomania. It may be punctuated by a relapse or reversion to an episode of apathetic or depressive hypokinesis, which is equivalent to an episode of homesickness. Finally, with rehabilitative success, normokinesis ensues and is permanently maintained.

In the present instance, the boy went through a "honeymoon phase" of happy, extroverted behavior when first released from parental abuse to the home of his stepaunt. Even so, he failed, according to his stepaunt, to be able to show genuine and appreciative affection, in the manner of her own children, for what she was doing on his behalf. This stepaunt, a working woman without a husband, could not take permanent responsibility for him. So following a brief hospital admission for diagnostic study, he went to a children's recovery center. While there he went through a phase of homesickness and despair. By picking on other children and being disobedient, he virtually invited more assault and injury of the type he had received at home—to the consternation and incomprehension of most of the staff. He claimed he did not want to live any more. He made attempts at self-strangulation, once with a belt and once with a wire coat hanger. He was accused of suicidal intent when once he took medications from the nurses' tray. One night, missing from his bed, he was found hiding outside among bushes, crying. For three days he was placed in a psychiatric hospital. Later he said his suicidal threats had not been serious in intent.

It is possible to interpret this phase of his recovery as part of a "readjustment syndrome" in which the boy was testing to the limits the authenticity and stability of his new, benign environment—even to the extent of proving that it would not allow him to die. Perhaps, also, there was an element of needing something even more than it could offer, namely, surrogate parents and a good family life. Subsequently, the boy has explicitly voiced his intense desire for a foster home, but the agencies responsible for his care have failed to oblige. The boy himself tried very actively to find a relative or friend who would accept him, but in vain. Eventually he did settle into the church-sponsored institution where he was placed, and eventually graduated to its "group home," a type of halfway house. His activity level, by then, was normokinetic. His social rehabilitation thenceforth was progressively positive, but slow. It is still not complete.

ACADEMIC AND WORK ACHIEVEMENT

Formal schooling began in the fall, three months after the boy's rescue from home. The academic establishment had no place for him as a beginner at age 16. He became academically classified as a mental retardate. Ideally, he should have been given personalized tutoring, while living in a private home with foster parents, as he so desperately longed to do. Economics and the inertia of the establishment forbade the realization of this ideal.

Lacking personalized tutoring, the boy's catch-up learning was unnecessarily incomplete. For example, in the group home he was chastised for running up a long-distance telephone bill when, in fact, he had not yet learned that long-distance calls cost more. He had made the call to an uncle. It was part of his desperate search to find new parents who would adopt him and treat him kindly. In a similar fashion, he was chastised for endangering himself by playing with an electrical outlet, whereas in fact, like a very young child, he had been investigating how it worked, before he knew of the danger of electricity. At this same stage of development, at chronological age 19, his achievement in reading, spelling, and arithmetic was at about the second grade level. His interest and achievement were higher in nonverbal than verbal skills, which might possibly be related to the nonverbal ingenuity without which, during the days of his maltreatment, he would have died from thirst and starvation.

By age 21, he was sufficiently skilled in photography to be able to develop his own pictures, selling some to the local newspaper. He worked full time as a helper in a restaurant. His formal education had been discontinued at age 19—probably before he had achieved his full academic potential.

PAIN AGNOSIA

In other cases of child abuse with dwarfism it has been possible to gather suggestive evidence of relative pain agnosia during the time when they were abused (7). For example, a child may be calmly indifferent to painful procedures when first brought to the hospital, saying that they don't hurt, while later complaining that they do hurt. In the present instance, there was no cut-and-dried evidence retrievable retrospectively to suggest insensitivity to pain, though it appeared that the boy was relatively stoic during the years when he was beaten and injured.

PSYCHOSEXUAL DEVELOPMENT

Data on the onset of puberty are included in Table 1. Like statural growth, pubertal maturation was suppressed in the abusive environment. Thereafter, the onset of puberty was rapid. At age 21, however, the patient still looked younger than his years. He had well-developed pubic and axillary hair and a thin, unshaven moustache. He easily could have passed for 15. He had the bone age of a 19-year-old (the upper limit of the scale), but the height age of a 13- to 14-year-old, which means that he has the appearance of being very short as an adult male.

When he was 16 there was an estimated discrepancy of at least five or six years between chronological age and social age. For academic age, the discrepancy was much larger. Devoid of experience with children of his own age, the boy shared few of their interests and little of their behavior. Other boys with different syndromes of dwarfism and pubertal failure have been mortified that their deficiency prevented their being accepted on equal status with peers socially and recreationally—dating and boy-girl relationships included. This boy was indifferent to romance and mixed-sex socializing.

He was not ignorant of sexual intercourse. He told of how he had been able to see through the keyhole when he was locked in the closet in his parents' bedroom and watch their copulatory and oral sexual activities. He claimed also that, on at least one occasion, his parents had actually required him to watch them. He had no knowledge of the relationship of coitus to pregnancy, and no other knowledge of reproduction.

Notes made during the week of hospitalization and the next four months of recovery center care indicate that the boy was occasionally observed to masturbate, apparently without ejaculation. In the recovery center, he talked jokingly and confidentially with a male occupational therapist about sex, and on at least one occasion shared his own knowledge of oral sex with other boys. He claimed having been required to try to have sex with the family's German shepherd, but there was an element of playfulness in his talk that precluded the separation of fact from fiction. Once he joked with an aide, saying she should get into bed with him. Her response was that he had his teddy bear, to which he replied that he couldn't do anything with that.

His first ejaculation may well have been the one at age 18, which occurred when a retarded adolescent boy living in the same church-sponsored community engaged him in mutual masturbation. "Well, this one boy was playing around," he reported, "and he was playing around with me, and I didn't know nothing about that. And then I got yelled at by the boss, because he told me." He described his first ejaculation as "being in another world."

In the church-sponsored community where he lived, he picked up the usual taboos against heterosexual activity. Though his opportunities for a girl-friend relationship were limited, he seemed at age 21 to be socially retarded in romantic and erotic maturation. His greatest longing was not to find a lover with whom to set up a home, but to first find surrogate parents who would provide him with the home life he had never known. He had a good fund of sexual knowledge, most of it gained from his hospital interviews. Overall, he showed common sense and good judgment regarding the sexual aspects of his life, and indeed of life in general, with a remarkable absence of self-pity, rancor, bitterness, or blaming others for what he had been through.

COMMENT

There is a syndrome of dwarfism associated with child abuse. It has been called deprivation dwarfism, psychosocial dwarfism, and reversible hyposomatotropinism. The latter term reflects the laboratory findings that, concomitant with growth impairment, pituitary growth hormone (somatotropin) secretion is suppressed. Both deficits are reversed on change of domicile. Proof of abuse in the domicile of origin is often extremely difficult to establish because abused children euphemize and cover up their plight. The adults in charge of them are, in the manner of Munchausen syndrome, mendacious and deceitful, and expert at hoodwinking professionals, playing them off against one another. For example, they enlist the sympathy of an unwary caseworker so as to sabotage the work of the physician.

Uncovering the correct biography of abuse, as in the case herein used illustratively, is facilitated by the use of auxilliary informants; home visits; precision interviewing of the parents for hour-by-hour daily and weekly happenings; and by long-term study until the child loosens up and talks.

This investigation was supported by US Public Health Service grant HD00325 and by the Grant Foundation Inc. New York.

REFERENCES

1. Patton, R. G., Gardner, L. I.: Influence of family environment on growth: The syndrome of "maternal deprivation." *Pediatrics* 30:957–962, 1962.
2. Patton, R. G., Gardner, L. I.: *Growth Failure in Maternal Deprivation.* Springfield, Ill., Charles C Thomas, 1963.
3. Patton, R. G., Gardner, L. I.: Deprivation dwarfism (psychosocial deprivation): Disordered family environment as cause of so-called idiopathic hypopituitarism, in

Gardner, L. I. (ed): *Endocrine and Genetic Diseases of Childhood and Adolescence,* ed 2. Philadelphia, W. B. Saunders, 1975.

4. Silver, H. K., Finkelstein, M.: Deprivation dwarfism. *Pediatrics* 70:317–324, 1967.
5. Powell, G. F., Brasel, J. A., Blizzard, R.: Emotional deprivation and growth retardation simulating idiopathic hypopituitarism: I. Clinical evaluation of the syndrome. *N Engl J Med* 276:1271–1278, 1967.
6. Powell, G. F., Brasel, J. A., Raiti, S. et al: Emotional deprivation and growth retardation simulating idiopathic hypopituitarism: II. Endocrinologic evaluation of the syndrome. *N Eng J Med* 276:1279–1283, 1967.
7. Money, J., Wolff, G., Annecillo, C.: Pain agnosia and self-injury in the syndrome of reversible somatotropin deficiency (psychosocial dwarfism). *J Autism Child Schizo* 2:127–139, 1972.
8. Wolff, G., Money, J.: Relationship between sleep and growth in patients with reversible somatotropin deficiency (pyschosocial dwarfism). *Psychol Med* 3:18–27, 1973.
9. Money, J., Wolff, G.: Late puberty, retarded growth and reversible hyposomatotropinism (psychosocial dwarfism). *Adolescence* 9:121–134, 1974.
10. Brown, G. M.: Endocrine aspects of psychosocial dwarfism, in Sachar, E. J. (ed): *Hormones, Behavior and Psychopathology.* New York, Raven Press, 1976.
11. Dennis, W.: *Children of the Crèche.* New York, Appleton-Century-Crofts, 1973.
12. Money, J., Annecillo, C.: IQ change following change of domicile in the syndrome of reversible hyposomatotropinism (psychosocial dwarfism): Pilot investigation. *Psychoneuroendocrinology* 1:427–429, 1976.

CHAPTER 34

The Endocrinology of Abuse Dwarfism:
With a Note on Charles Dickens
as Child Advocate

Lytt I. Gardner

When I first read John Money's remarkable description of abuse dwarfism, in which the abuse persisted long enough probably to have inhibited the normal onset of puberty, there lingered in my mind connotations of Charles Dickens. At first I thought this was due to Money's use of the King's English in his article; on further reflection it came to me that it was probably due to the Dickensian content of the report. It conveys the dark atmosphere of a nineteenth-century novel. There is the night terror quality of *Oliver Twist* or *The Old Curiosity Shop* or of Charlotte Brontë's *Jane Eyre*. That the latter two authors would come to mind is not exactly a coincidence, since both experienced abuse and maternal deprivation as children: Dickens being sent away to a workhouse (1); Brontë by the death of her mother followed by a harsh boarding school where two of her sisters died as a result of its hardships (2). Thus, both in their writings were especially attuned to the need for improved child protection, and the nature of their literary art often was a reflection of this.

In the present report by John Money, the author suggests that the stepmother was destroying in the boy, by proxy, an image of what she could not tolerate in herself, that he resembled a victim of the Inquisition—tortured so that the soul may be saved from eternal damnation, but not tortured until dead. These convoluted thoughts do indeed resemble plots from the "Gothic" novels of the last century, plots that one would not ordinarily associate with real life. But Money's patient is from real life, and living in the last quarter of the twentieth century.

Is there a thread that passes through the works of Dickens and Brontë and those of the pioneers in child protection such as Théophile Roussel, Abraham Jacobi, and Henry Dwight Chapin, and finally to the contemporary era beginning with Bakwin, Ribble, and Spitz in the 1940s? I believe there is. As is so often the case, the artist presages the scientist; the novelist spins out his or her story, and in so doing incorporates aspects of conscious or unconscious attitudes. He is followed by the scientist who examines the nature and mechanism of the pathological social or medical process and eventually by the public health worker and social activist. To a certain extent, Dickens inhabited both worlds. At age 12 he had been sent away from his family to live alone and work in a warehouse in an industrial section of London (1). His father was in and out of debtor's prison at the time. Dickens never got over the deprivation and humiliation of being sent away from his home at this time, especially when he wanted to go to school. He was bitter that his mother strongly favored his leaving home. As he wrote in the short autobiographical fragment that he left: "I do not write resentfully or angrily; for I know how all these things have worked together to make me what I am; but I never afterward forgot, I never shall forget, I never can forget, that my mother was warm for my being sent back" (3).

Dickens thus had suffered maternal deprivation in its most direct form, the realization at age 12 that his own mother had tried to turn him out of his home again, sentenced to child-labor, to sleep in a garret and work in a filthy warehouse swarming with rats. Later he included many personal experiences in his strongly autobiographical novel *Oliver Twist,* which portrayed the emotional crises, insecurities and fears of his life. Begged Oliver of Mr. Brownlow (chapter 14): "Don't turn me out of doors to wander in the streets again!"

Oliver Twist, published in 1838, was Dickens' first novel of social protest and his first novel of nightmarish genre. It had been a mere four years since the enactment of the Poor Law of 1834, which created the hated workhouse for the unemployed and their families, splitting up the family so that the children suffered most, deprived of schooling and forced into sweatshop labor at a tender age (1). Thus, it is not so surprising that *Oliver Twist* and Dickens' subsequent writings are peopled with abandoned, abused, crippled, dying, or dead children. In *The Old Curiosity Shop,* two children died: a nameless youth in chapter 25 and the famous Little Nell in chapter 71; in *A Christmas Carol,* Tiny Tim was crippled; in chapter 8 of *Dombey and Son,* a dying boy (Paul) is again deprived of a mother (". . . he pined and wasted after the dismissal of his nurse, and for a long time seemed but to wait his opportunity of gliding through their hands, and seeking his lost mother").

Dickens' works reached every nook and cranny of an America just poised for the industrial revolution. Inexpensive pirated editions were available everywhere. My mother was a young girl in rural North Carolina in the 1880s; she said that the literary fare in their home was mostly the Bible and Charles Dickens. There is little doubt that Dickens' artistry hastened social reforms. His literary works are held in the highest esteem in the Eastern countries, much as we view the work of Tolstoi or Golgol. One only need observe his powers of description in this passage from chapter 45 of *The Old Curiosity Shop* concerning what the then new industrial revolution was doing to humanity and environment in a British town. The picture is reminiscent of Dante's *Inferno:*

> Advancing more and more into the shadow of this mournful place, its dark depressing influence stole upon their spirits, and filled them with a dismal gloom. On every side, and as far as the eye could see in the heavy distance, tall chimneys crowding on each other, and presenting that endless repetition of the same dull, ugly, form which

is the horror of oppressive dreams, poured out their plague of smoke, obscured the light, and made foul the melancholy air. On mounds of ashes by the wayside, sheltered only by a few rough boards, or rotten penthouse roofs, strange engines spun and writhed like tortured creatures; clanking their iron chains, shrieking in their rapid whirl from time to time as though in torment unendurable, and making the ground tremble with their agonies. . . . Men, women, children, wan in their looks and ragged in attire, tended the engines, fed their tributary fire, begged upon the road, or scowled half-naked from the doorless houses. Then came more of the wrathful monsters, screeching and turning round and round again . . . never ceasing in their black vomit, blasting all things living or inanimate, shutting out the face of day, and closing in on all these horrors with a dense, dark cloud.

But night-time in this dreadful spot!—night, when the smoke was changed to fire; when every chimney spurted up its flame; and places that had been dark vaults all day now shone red-hot, with figures moving to and fro within their blazing jaws . . . night—who shall tell the terrors of the night to the young wandering child!

Dickens gave more overt assistance to child protection in 1858 when he, at age 46, gave a speech urging support for the Great Ormond Street Hospital for Sick Children in London. The speech is recorded in a thin pamphlet. Dr. James L. Gamble, Sr., quoted extensively from the pamphlet in a talk in which he compared the origins of The Hospital for Sick Children, Great Ormond Street, London, and The Children's Hospital in Boston. Dickens pulled out all the stops of pathos in his address when he described a dying child he had encountered in the Edinburgh slums, and ended his remarks with a fund-raising plea: "This is the pathetic case which I have put to you; not only on behalf of the thousands of children who annually die in this great city London, but also on behalf of the thousands of children who live half-developed, racked with preventible pain, shorn of their natural capacity for health and enjoyment. If these innocent creatures cannot move you for themselves, how can I possibly hope to move you in their name?" (4)

Now let us turn our attention again to Money's patient. Here we are, 119 years after Dickens' eloquent plea, still struggling with the manifold problems of psychosocial deprivation, neglect, and abuse in children. The accumulated knowledge of twentieth-century psychiatry and endocrinology permits Money to peer into the intrafamilial dynamics surrounding his patient in a manner that would have been impossible in earlier times, and in so doing to provide new insights into the behavioral and endocrine patterns of this modern "wolf child" who came into being in the midst of our supposedly developed society.

The patient described by Money fits well into the category of psychosocial deprivation with dwarfism. These patients classically show inadequate response to serum growth hormone after insulin or arginine stimulation while still in the growth-inhibiting environment (5, 6). Money's patient had escaped to the home of a relative when first seen and was already showing catch-up growth; hence, the chance to obtain laboratory confirmation of reversible hyposomatotropinism was missed.

As is now well documented, psychosocial deprivation with dwarfism has been shown to be associated with lack of adrenocorticotropic hormone (ACTH) reserve, and with the following growth hormone abnormalities: high fasting levels of growth hormone and inadequate levels after stimulation with insulin, arginine, beef broth (Bovril), exercise, and slow-wave sleep (5-8). All these findings revert to normal in a growth-promoting environment. Imura et al. (9) found that the impaired growth hormone response to insulin in a boy with psychosocial deprivation could be made normal by treatment with propranolol, a β-adrenergic blocker. Parra (10) also observed that propranolol plus epinephrine restored a normal response in five such patients who had defective growth hormone responses to insulin and arginine. It would thus appear that defective growth hormone release is the major mechanism leading to growth failure.

That there may be a connection with a neurotransmitter mechanism is suggested by the study of Imura et al. (9) and that of Parra (10). Brown (8) has pointed out in this regard that a profitable area for future investigations would be the examination of neurotransmitter regulation of growth hormone in patients with psychosocial dwarfism to determine whether dopamine or norepinephrine mechanisms are impaired. He also suggests an investigation of propranolol as a possible therapeutic agent.

The case presented by Money is especially noteworthy because the abuse suffered by the boy was so prolonged and severe that it may have interfered with normal pubertal development. He was 17 years old before earliest adolescent changes were noted; when this took place, he had been away from the growth-inhibiting environment for a year. It does not require a great stretch of the imagination to envision that an environment capable of inhibiting growth hormone release by the pituitary gland might not also under extreme circumstances inhibit pituitary gonadotropin release.

There is a clinical state that bears at least some superficial endocrine similarities to the patient under discussion, and that is the development of amenorrhea in the adolescent girl with anorexia nervosa. It has long been known that adolescent girls with anorexia nervosa develop clinical and laboratory evidence of gonadotropin lack (11), as well as lack of growth hormone response when stimulated (12). The defect appears to be in the release of gonadotropin from the pituitary, since the administration of luteinizing hormone-releasing hormone (LH-RH) to girls with anorexia nervosa is associated with a normal release of gonadotropins (13). Indeed the circadian secretory pattern of plasma luteinizing hormone (LH) becomes comparable to that of the prepuberal female (14). In remission the pattern reverts to the LH pattern of the normal postpuberal female.

In anorexia nervosa the initiating event, probably psychiatric, is followed by a host of endocrine events that appears to result in a new "not very steady" state, which persists until the patient goes into remission. These endocrine changes in anorexia nervosa include the gonadotropin abnormality mentioned above, as well as the following events: readjustment to a higher plasma level of the cortisol circadian rhythm, decrease in metabolic clearance rate of cortisol, prolongation of cortisol half-life, elevation of tetrahydrocortisol/tetrahydrocorticosterone ratio, and low plasma triiodothyronine level (15).

If the gonadotropin metabolism of Money's patient with the extreme degree of abuse dwarfism and delay in puberty could have been studied with the elegant endocrine techniques that have been applied to cases of anorexia nervosa, one would anticipate another array of interesting and important findings. But, as he points out, logistically it has been impossible to get into the home to make such observations, and bringing the patient into the hospital for study changes the environment. Nevertheless, studies of circulating gonadotropins, and the influence of releasing and inhibiting hormones on them, should be performed immediately if such a patient is hospitalized in the future. The same would hold true for the studies suggested by Brown (8) on neurotransmitter regulation of growth hormone and a therapeutic trial of propranolol, as well as additional documentation of the ACTH abnormality.

In conclusion, we have come a long way since young Charles Dickens was cast out of his home to do child labor and since the Brontë sisters wasted away and died in the orphan asylum. Much has been learned of the psychiatric and biochemical intricacies of psychosocial deprivation and related forms of child abuse. The next stage must be the perfection of techniques for the detection of families at risk and for the prevention of child abuse before it happens (16–19).

Professor Edmund Kerpel-Fronius provided helpful discussion.

REFERENCES

1. Shefter, H. Miller, W. J., Percefull, A.: Reader's supplement to *Oliver Twist*, in Dickens, C.. *Oliver Twist*. New York, Simon & Schuster, 1975, pp. 2–48.
2. Threapleton, M. M.: Introduction, in Brontë, C.: *Jane Eyre*. New York, Airmont, 1963, pp. 1–5.
3. Dickens, C.: Autobiography, in Finley, J. H. (ed): *The University Library*. New York, Doubleday Doran & Co., 1936, vol. 3, pp. 114–123.
4. Gamble, J. L.: The Hospital for Sick Children, Great Ormond Street, London and The Children's Hospital in Boston. *Harvard Med. Alumni Bull.* 1954, pp. 9–13.
5. Powell, G. F., Brasel, J. A., Raiti, S. et al.: Emotional deprivation and growth retardation simulating idiopathic hypopituitarism: II. Endocrinologic evaluation of the syndrome. *N. Eng. J. Med.* 276:1279–1283, 1967.
6. Brasel, J. A.: Review of findings in patients with emotional deprivation, in Gardner, L. I., Amacher, P. (eds): *Endocrine Aspects of Malnutrition—Marasmus, Kwashiorkor and Psychosocial Deprivation*. Santa Ynez, Calif., Kroc Foundation, 1973, pp. 115–127.
7. Powell, G. F., Hopwood, N. J., Barratt, E. S.: Growth hormone studies before and during catch-up growth in a child with emotional deprivation and short stature. *J. Clin. Endocrinol.* 37:674–679, 1973.

8. Brown, G. M.: Endocrine aspects of psychosocial dwarfism, in Sachar, E. J. (ed):*Hormones, Behavior and Psychopathology*. New York, Raven Press, 1976, pp. 253–262.

9. Imura, H., Yoshimi, T., Ikekubo, K.: Growth hormone secretion in a patient with deprivation dwarfism. *Endocrinol. Jap.* 18:301–304, 1971.

10. Parra, A.: Discussion of psychosocial deprivation, in Gardner, L. I., Amacher, P. (eds): *Endocrine Aspects of Malnutrition—Marasmus, Kwashiorkor and Psychosocial Deprivation*. Santa Ynez, Calif., Kroc Foundation, 1973, p. 155.

11. Russel, G. F. M., Loraine, J. A., Bell, E. T., et al: Gonadotropin and estrogen excretion in patients with anorexia nervosa. *J. Psychosom. Res.* 9:79–85, 1965.

12. Landon, J., Greenwood, F. C., Stamp, T. C. B. et al: The plasma sugar, free fatty acid, cortisol, and growth hormone response to insulin, and the comparison of this procedure with other tests of pituitary and adrenal function: II. In patients with hypothalamic or pituitary dysfunction or anorexia nervosa. *J. Clin. Invest.* 45:437–449, 1966.

13. Weigelmann, W., Solbach, H. G.: Effects of LH-RH on plasma levels of LH and FSH in anorexia nervosa. *Horm. Metab. Res.* 4:404, 1972.

14. Boyar, R. M., Katz, J., Finklestein, J. W. et al: Anorexia nervosa: Immaturity of the 24-hour luteinizing hormone secretory pattern. *N. Engl. J. Med.* 291:861–865, 1974.

15. Boyar, R. M., Hellman, L. D., Roffwarg, H. et al: Cortisol secretion and metabolism in anorexia nervosa. *N. Engl. J. Med.* 296:190–193, 1977.

16. Kempe, C. H.: Approaches to preventing child abuse. *Am. J. Dis. Child.* 130:941–950, 1976.

17. Metz, J. R.,Allen, C. M., Barr, G. et al: A pediatric screening examination for psychosocial problems. *Pediatrics* 58:595–606, 1976.

18. Fontana, V. J., Robison, E.: A multidisciplinary approach to the treatment of child abuse. *Pediatrics* 57:760–764, 1976.

19. McAnarney, E.: The older abused child. *Pediatrics* 55:298–299, 1975.

CHAPTER 35

Relationship between Sleep and Growth in Patients with Reversible Somatotropin Deficiency (Psychosocial Dwarfism)

Georg Wolff and John Money

SYNOPSIS

In a partly retrospective, partly follow-up study, 27 patients aged 1 year 10 months to 16 years 2 months with reversible somatotropin deficiency, showed a relationship between the rate of statural growth and sleep, graded as good, poor, or mixed. During periods of good sleep the overall growth rate averaged 1.04 cm per month, and during periods of poor sleep it averaged 0.34 cm per month ($t=8.46$, df$=32$, P $<$ 0.001). Presumably, good growth, good sleep, and optimal nocturnal somatotropin release intercorrelate in this syndrome of dwarfism, but the data with regard to nocturnal somatotropin release remain to be demonstrated empirically.

The sleeping behavior of patients with the syndrome of reversible somatotropin deficiency, so-called psychosocial dwarfism, has not yet been subject to systematic investigation. Powell, Brasel, and Blizzard (1967a), Silver and Finkelstein (1967), Drash, Greenberg, and Moncy (1968), as well as Capitanio and Kirkpatrick (1969), mentioned that a number of such dwarfed patients were reported to have had a history of sleeping disorders before hospitalization. The patients were said to get up at night, to search for food and water, or to roam about the house. One patient was even reported to run out into the street frequently at night (Powell *et al.* 1967a).

The purpose of this paper is to present data that point to a relationship between sleep and physical growth—namely, that patients with reversible somatotropin deficiency show poor and disturbed sleep at times of subnormal statural growth rates, whereas they exhibit normal sleeping behavior at times of

Supported by grants from the Erickson Education Foundation, the Stiles E. Tuttle Fund, and Mrs. Marion Tuttle Colwill, and by USPHS grants HD 18635, HD 00325, HD 01852, and MH 20855.

Reprinted with permission from *Psychological Medicine* 3 (1973):18–27. Copyright 1973, Cambridge University Press.

normal or catch-up statural growth rates. It is not part of the purpose of this paper to correlate sleep and growth rate with measured levels of growth hormone secretion, this being a task for a prospective, not a retrospective, study. It is sufficient for present purposes to note that growth hormone levels were below normal when measured during periods of inhibited growth, and that they were within normal range once catch-up growth began, following change of domicile from a noxious to an ameliorative environment.

METHODS

From 1959 to 1970, 27 growth-retarded children were given an authenticated diagnosis of reversible somatotropin deficiency in the pediatric endocrine clinic at The Johns Hopkins Hospital. The diagnostic criteria for this condition are presented by Patton and Gardner (1962; 1963; 1969), Powell *et al.* (1967*a, b*), Silver and Finkelstein (1967), and Capitanio and Kirkpatrick (1969). In brief, the most common diagnostic signs are:

1. History of significant slow-down in statural growth and skeletal maturation after the first months of life, resulting typically in a physical height below the third percentile for a given age, reversible if the child is transferred to the hospital or elsewhere from the domicile of growth failure.
2. Laboratory findings indicative of hypopituitarism before or upon admission to the hospital, but not after the change to the hospital or other ameliorative environment.
3. History of broken or disrupted relationship between parents or parent surrogates, and child.
4. History of unusual and bizarre behavioral symptoms, reversible upon change of domicile, such as eating from garbage cans; polydipsia and polyphagia possibly alternating with vomiting, and possibly alternating also with self-starvation; enuresis and encopresis; and social apathy or inertia, with or without aggressiveness and sudden tantrums.
5. Retarded motor development, with improvement upon removal of the child from the domicile of growth failure.
6. Retarded intellectual growth, reversible, with elevation by as much as 55 IQ points, upon removal from the environment of growth failure.

   All 27 patients of this sample were seen routinely in the psychohormonal research unit of the pediatric endocrine clinic. The sample consists of 20 boys and 7 girls, 22 whites and 5 blacks, and includes two pairs of brothers (E.B., M.B., and Rb.H., Rn.H., Table 3). Table 1 lists further descriptive-data regarding age upon admission, duration of follow-up, and number of height measurements.

   Upon admission to the hospital 10 patients were overweight (0.5 to 9.1 kg), compared with the expected weight for their height, and 17 patients were underweight (0.75 to 4.5 kg), compared with the expected weight for their height. None gave the appearance of emaciated exogenous starvation. Though parental

Table 1. Descriptive data for the 27 patients

	Range (yr)	Mean (yr)	SD (yr)
Age at first hospitalization for short stature	$1\frac{10}{12}$ to $16\frac{2}{12}$	$6\frac{3}{12}$	$3\frac{8}{12}$
Duration of total follow-up	$\frac{4}{12}$ to $9\frac{3}{12}$	$3\frac{2}{12}$	$2\frac{4}{12}$
Number of height measurements during total follow-ups	3 to 24	11.1	4.8

prevarication could not be ruled out with respect to a patient's home diet, so far as could be ascertained patients had not been fed differently from their siblings, who typically did not suffer from growth failure. The patients did not manifest diagnostic signs of specific nutritional deficits. Some had a history, reported from the home, of overeating and vomiting, while others had a history of partial self-starvation through failure to eat at mealtimes.

With only a few exceptions (Table 6), the patients were referred from the homes into which they were born. Typically, they were admitted to the pediatric clinical research unit at The Johns Hopkins Hospital for two to four weeks for clinical evaluation. They were then transferred to the Happy Hills Hospital, for between three and seven months, for further observation of their statural growth and behavior in a changed environment. Thereafter, they were placed in permanent residence, usually a foster home.

Systematic investigation regarding sleep, specifically for this study, was carried out from May 1969 through January 1970. In the majority of cases, information was obtained from interviews with parents, guardians, social workers, nurses, or other close observers of the patients, or with the patients themselves, if they were old enough. In addition, seven patients were observed at first hand while sleeping. Three lived at the Happy Hills Hospital, where they were observed for ten nights. Four were observed while admitted to The Johns Hopkins Hospital, as a supplement to routine nursing observation.

Interviews conducted in the hospital were recorded and transcribed. Outside the hospital, on home visits or elsewhere, written notes had to suffice. Inquiry regarding sleep was initiated with open-ended questions, to allow the informant to give maximum information spontaneously, before being questioned more directly.

Additional information for the years before 1969 was obtained retrospectively from interview transcripts already in the patients' records, from nightly sleep reports recorded by the night nurses during admissions at The Johns Hopkins Hospital (18 patients), and from weekly sleep reports recorded at other residential institutions (23 patients).

From all the accumulated information, subject to no known bias, three categories of data were extracted verbatim and tabulated for each patient:

Table 2. Criteria for good and poor sleep

Good sleep	Poor sleep
1. Sleep report: good, well, calm, restful	1. Sleep report: restless, disturbed, irritable, cries frequently at night
2. Falls asleep quickly (< 30 min)	2. Can't fall asleep quickly (> 30 min)
3. Sleeps soundly all night	3. Often awake at night
4. Seldom gets up at night	4. Gets up often at night: —to get something to eat or to drink —to roam the house —to play —to engage in destructive behavior —to go out into the street —to disturb other family members' sleep
5. Easily falls asleep after waking	5. Can't fall asleep after waking
6. Duration of sleep appropriate for age	6. Duration of sleep shorter than appropriate for age
7. Wakes up to start the day at regular times, predictably	7. Wakes up too early at unpredictable times to start the day
8. Naps during the day in infancy and sleeps soundly	8. Doesn't nap during the day and is either hyperactive or apathetic

1. Height measurements and where and when they were taken.
2. Information to reconstruct the sequence of domiciles in which the patients lived.
3. Information pertaining to sleep, in relation to age and location.

Height measurements were, in almost all instances, obtained according to standard anthropometric methods. The physicians who took the height measurements had no awareness of a possible relationship between statural growth and sleep, for the hypothesis then had not so much as been proposed, this being a retrospective study.

All of the work of extraction, rating, and reduction of data on sleep was done only once, though systematically spot-checked for three randomly selected cases by a graduate student assistant. The spotchecking included the calculation of the growth rates (see below).

The data on sleep were classified according to the eight criteria of Table 2. Then for each given period the sleep was assigned the rating of good, poor, or mixed. A rating of good sleep or poor sleep was given when all of the extracted information for a given time period qualified according to the criteria of column 1 or column 2, respectively, in Table 2. In cases where nights of good sleep and poor sleep both were reported for a given time period, the rating was mixed sleep, even if the nights of poor sleep qualified as such only by one criterion for poor sleep.

RESULTS

Sleep and Growth

Figures 1 and 2 are examples of the growth charts constructed for each patient on the basis of the foregoing procedures and ratings. Figures 3 and 4 show an actual patient. From each of the 27 charts, it was possible to calculate the growth rate, in centimeters per month, for periods of good, poor, and mixed sleep. When, over an individual patient's follow-up time, there was more than one time period of good, poor, or mixed sleep, respectively, a mean growth rate was calculated for the summated good, poor, or mixed sleep periods, severally.

Table 3 shows that only two of the 27 patients had no period of reported good sleep. During periods of good sleep in the other 25 patients (Table 4), the mean growth rate was 1.04 cm/month (SD, 0.38).

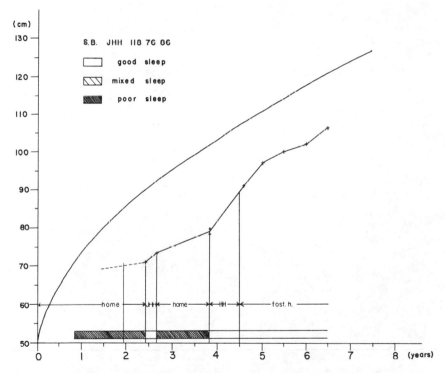

Figure 1. Growth chart of patient S.B. Vertical lines indicate at which time the patient was transferred from one domicile to another. Intervals between vertical lines indicate length of time the patient lived in the respective domicile. The dotted line before the first hospital referral and accurately recorded height measurement represents an estimate of the growth rate between the age of 1 year, the usual age of onset of growth retardation, and the age when the dwarfed stature was first measured. Home—home of origin; JHH=The Johns Hopkins Hospital; IIII=Happy Hills Hospital; fost.h.=foster home.

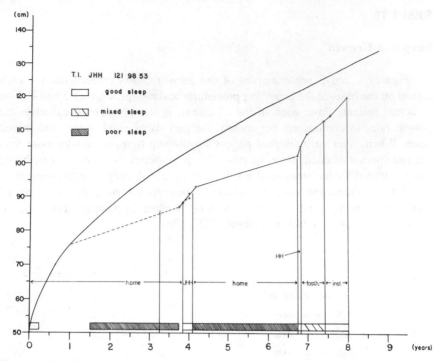

Figure 2. Growth chart of patient T.I. Home=home of origin; JHH=The Johns Hopkins Hospital; HH=Happy Hills Hospital; fost.h.=foster home; inst.=residential institution (see also legend to Fig. 1).

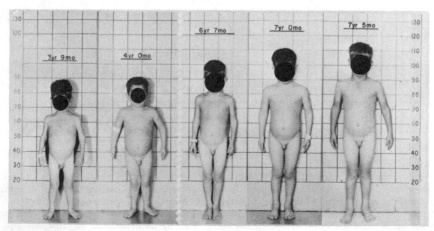

Figure 3. Composite of sequentially taken front views of patient T.I. The lines above the patient's head indicate the expected height (50th percentile) for the age at which each picture was taken.

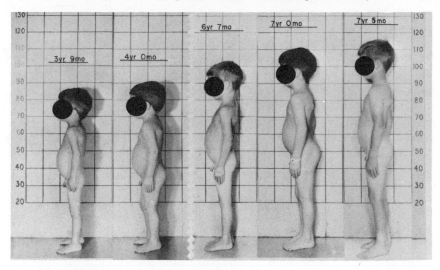

Figure 4. Composite of sequentially taken side views of the same patient as in Fig. 3.

Table 3 shows also that 11 of the 27 patients had no reported period of poor sleep for which a growth rate could be calculated. For the 16 patients with an authenticated record of poor sleep plus growth information (Table 4), the mean growth rate was 0.34 cm/month (SD, 0.13).

The difference between the growth rates under conditions of good and poor sleep is statistically significant at the level of $P < 0.001$ ($t=8.46$, df=32).

The data on mixed sleep in Table 3 are too few to be statistically useful. They are, however, concordant with the data on good and poor sleep: the mean growth rate falls between that for good and poor sleep (Table 4), and in no individual instance does the growth rate for mixed sleep fall below that for poor sleep.

In Table 3, there are 15 cases in which periods of both good and poor sleep were recorded, thus permitting each patient to be his own control. In each case, the change of sleep style concurred with change of domicile (see below). Table 5 shows the comparison. The mean rate of growth was 0.66 cm/month greater under conditions of good sleep, the improvement being statistically significant at beyond the 0.001 level ($t=5.06$, df=14). The predictive value of this association between sleep and growth in these 15 patients is high, as documented by an estimate (see Hays 1963, pp. 327–29) of the proportional reduction in error of 43.2% (estimated $\omega^2=0.432$). This means in the case of the 15 patients that the probability of making a correct prediction of a patient's growth rate (high or low) from knowing how the patient sleeps (good or poor respectively) increases from 50% chance to 71.5%.

A scattergram (not herewith reproduced) of the patients' growth rates at times of good, poor, and/or mixed sleep versus their respective age revealed that

Table 3. Growth rates during good, poor, and mixed sleep*

Patient	Total number of months observed	Good sleep		Poor sleep		Mixed sleep	
		Number of months observed	Growth rate (cm/mth)	Number of months observed	Growth rate (cm/mth)	Number of months observed	Growth rate (cm/mth)
S.A.	17	17	0·97	—	—	—	—
E.B.	4	4	1·25	—	—	—	—
M.B.	2	—	—	—	—	2	0·00
S.B.	55	35	0·86	20	0·30	—	—
R.C.	12	4	1·25	8	0·64	—	—
M.D.	15	15	1·32	—	—	—	—
J.D.	16	10	0·46	6	0·33	—	—
W.G.	45	26	0·51	19	0·54	—	—
Rb.H.	17	17	0·63	—	—	—	—
Rn.H.	10	10	1·42	—	—	—	—
R.H.	19	19	1·04	—	—	—	—
G.H.	31	25	0·62	6	0·38	—	—
T.I.	54	12	1·28	37	0·31	5	1·08

F.J.	25	7	0·47	12	0·33	6	0·75
J.K.	8	8	0·89	—	—	—	—
B.K.	29	9	1·91	20	0·15	—	—
G.M.	47	38	0·89	9	0·38	37	0·54
S.N.	55	18	0·90	—	—	—	—
C.N.	5	5	1·56	—	—	—	—
M.P.	10	4	0·98	6	0·33	—	—
A.R.	42	32	1·09	6	0·30	4	2·00
R.S.	51	4	1·23	40	0·15	7	0·49
S.S.	60	54	0·64	6	0·43	—	—
S.T.	13	7	1·26	6	0·35	—	—
C.W.	23	4	1·68	19	0·21	—	—
V.W.	21	21	0·88	—	—	—	—
B.Y.	23	—	—	17	0·38	6	0·83

*The greater the number of months with good sleep the s ower the growth rate (Spearman's rank correlation coefficients $r_s = -0.52$, $P < 0.01$). This inverse correlation reflects the fact that patients with reversible somatotropin deficiency usually show, upon removal from the domicile where the syndrome originated, a high catch-up growth rate at first, which then levels off to a more normal, age appropriate growth rate. The pattern of growth rate in these patients during and after their first hospitalization needs further investigation in a prospective study in which the patients' statural height is systematically measured at three-month intervals.

Table 4. Mean growth rates at times of good, poor, and mixed sleep

	N	Growth rate (cm/mth)	
		Mean	SD
Good sleep	25	1·04	0·38
Poor sleep	16	0·34	0·13
Mixed sleep	7	0·81	0·43

t(good vs poor)$=8·46$, df$=32$, P$<0·001$.

there was no correlation between growth rate and age that could have had an undue influence on the calculated mean growth rate (Table 4) during good, poor, or mixed sleep, respectively.

DOMICILE AND SLEEP

In Table 6 are listed the domiciles in which growth failure occurred and from which the children were referred to the pediatric endocrine clinic. For the most part, the children were living in their homes of origin when their growth failure and associated symptoms began, though not invariably so. Table 7 shows the distribution of good, poor, and mixed sleep, according to where the child was located at the time. The Table does not lend itself to statistical evaluation: the numbers are small, the duration of the period varies widely, and a child rated as having mixed sleep initially over a given period may actually have settled down into good sleep, subsequently. Despite such limitations, Table 7 nonetheless shows a quite clear trend for the quality of sleep to be related to the place of

Table 5. Comparison of growth rates in relation to good and poor sleep in 15 patients, each acting as his own control

	N	Growth rate (cm/mth)	
		Mean	SD
Good sleep	15	1·00	0·44
Poor sleep	15	0·34	0·13

$=5·06$, df$=14$, P$<0·001$, $\omega^2=0·432$.

Table 6. Pre-referral domicile in which growth failure occurred

	N
Domicile	(27)
Parental home	
Both parents present·	20
Step-parent's home	
Own mother present.	2
Own father present.	1
Foster home:	4

sleeping. More of the children slept poorly in the domicile of prereferral origin than in the hospital or other postreferral places of residence. This same rule applied where children, upon discharge from the hospital or other ameliorative environment, had no place to go except to return to the domicile of prereferral origin. In these cases poor sleep was again the rule as it had been before hospitalization and it remained so until and if it was possible to transfer the patients again to new living quarters, usually a foster home.

In four instances, growth failure began or was perpetuated in a foster home. Therefore, the parents of origin cannot always be implicated. As much as we have searched, we have not yet been able to implicate any factor or factors that invariably accompany the induction of poor sleep relative to domicile. Each child's insomnia might well be the end-product of different precipitating factors.

In the case of one of the four children whose growth failure occurred in a foster home, sleep and growth were impaired again when she returned to the same foster home, but not while she stayed at The Johns Hopkins Hospital or at Happy Hills. Since foster home replacement at the time was not feasible, it was decided to treat her insomnia for a trial period of medication with Seconal, 3/4 gr every night over a period of five months.[2] As compared with an 11-month period before the treatment (poor sleep, growth rate 0.43 cm/month) this girl's sleep improved greatly and the growth rate increased to 0.67 cm/month. The patient was reported to sleep 9 to 10 hours per night restfully and soundly. She was noticed to snore for the first time and did not get up at night. Before and during the treatment period, the girl lived in the same foster home, from which she originally had been referred to the hospital for psychosocial dwarfism. It remains, of course, speculative, on the basis of one single case study, whether the increased growth rate was actually a sequela to the improved sleep or to some associated change in the interaction between the family members, or in the child herself.

---

[2]The medication was prescribed and the treatment supervised by Dr. Robert M. Blizzard.

Table 7. Distribution of good, poor, and mixed sleep periods according to change of domicile*

		Good sleep	Poor sleep	Mixed sleep	No information
1. *Pre-referral domicile:* (home of parents, step-parents and foster home)	(N=27)	—	18	—	9
2. *Pre-referral domicile:* (same as 1; patients were returned after hospitalization and/or foster placement)					
a. First return	(N=19)	1	8	—	10
b. Second return	(N=8)	2	1	1	4
c. Third return	(N=2)	—	—	—	2
3. *Referral domiciles:*					
a. First JHH placement	(N=25)	16	—	—	9
b. Second JHH placement	(N=8)	3	—	—	5
c. First HH placement	(N=22)	14	—	4	4
d. Second HH placement	(N=1)	1	—	—	—
e. First residential institution placement	(N=6)	5	—	—	1
f. Second residential institution placement	(N=1)	1	—	—	—
g. Third residential institution placement	(N=1)	1	—	—	—
h. First foster home placement	(N=14)	10	1	1	2
i. Second foster home placement	(N=8)	6	—	1	1
k. Third foster home placement	(N=1)	—	1	—	—
l. Fourth foster home placement	(N=1)	1	—	—	—

Key: JHH=The Johns Hopkins Hospital; HH=Happy Hills Hospital.
*The placement periods range from at least two weeks to 41 months. Two patients were admitted to The Johns Hopkins Hospital for less than two weeks. Return of a patient to the same foster home was counted as a second placement, only if the interim placement elsewhere lasted at least four weeks.

DISCUSSION

The reported findings show that the patients grew better at times of good sleep than poor sleep. Moreover, the change in type of sleep and correlated rate of growth was reversible, sometimes rapidly so. This reversibility gives presumptive evidence against the possibility of a chronic brain lesion adversely affecting both sleep and growth.

Insofar as the brain is involved, it is obviously on a functional basis. The most likely function to be implicated is that of the relationship between the sleeping brain and the release of the growth hormone from the pituitary gland. Takahashi, Kipnis, and Daughaday (1968), Honda, Takahashi, Takahashi, Azumi, Irie, Sakuma, Tsushima, and Shizume (1969), and Sassin, Parker, Mace, Gotlin, Johnson, and Rossman (1969), observed in their sleep EEG studies that marked elevated secretion of plasma human growth hormone (HGH) is consistently related to slow wave, synchronized sleep stages (EEG stages 3 and 4). This finding pertains to normal healthy adult subjects, comparable sleep EEG studies in children having not yet been reported. However, total HGH secretion during the night, irrespective of EEG sleep stages, was shown by Hunter and Rigal (1965) to be many times greater than that for the same subjects during the day. Their subjects were children, aged 8 to 15 years, free of known growth disorder or other endocrinopathy.

Honda and coworkers (1969) conclude "that nocturnal sleep is a potent stimulator for the secretion of growth hormone, and that the secretion pattern of HGH is closely correlated with the depth and course of sleep." HGH secretion reaches its peak always soon after the sleeper passes the EEG stages 3 and 4, regardless of the hour he went to sleep. Inability to go to sleep and insomnia during the night may have an adverse effect on HGH release (H. P. Roffwarg, personal communication). Hypothetically, it is possible that patients with reversible somatotropin deficiency might, during periods when they sleep poorly, have a subnormal proportion of EEG stages 3 and 4. They might therefore also be deprived of considerable amounts of growth hormone, which deprivation in turn might be one reason for subnormal growth rates. The crucial sleep EEG studies to test this hypothesis remain to be done.

Our findings suggest a correlative, though not a causal relationship between high and low rate of statural growth and good and poor sleep, respectively. There is no virtue in proposing a cause and effect relationship so long as there are other covariant symptoms found in the syndrome of reversible somatotropin deficiency. For example, body weight, and behavioral anomalies, including apathy, may be symptoms that covary with changes in sleep and rate of statural height increase.

The matter of weight is of particular pertinence, since some investigators—for example, Kerr, Chamove, and Harlow (1969), and Whitten, Pettit, and Fischhoff (1969)—have proposed a hypothesis to the effect that malnutrition is etiologically responsible for the growth failure in patients with the syndrome of reversible somatotropin deficiency. The issue here is the familiar one of the cart and the horse: it is quite possible that the patients who lose weight, do so in response to self-starvation, despite episodes of polyphagia. There is a certain resemblance here to self-starvation in anorexia nervosa, which, coincidentally, has also been found to have sleeplessness as a covariant (Linn 1967; Fenton and Elphicke 1969).

Even if self-starvation could be ruled out, and weight deficiency when manifested could be explained on the basis of exogenous food deprivation, one still has to explain the association of the reversible somatic defect in height and weight with reversible behavior pathology, with reversible insomnia, and with reversible inhibition of somatotropin secretion.[3]

In brief, sleeplessness in the syndrome of reversible somatotropin deficiency is best interpreted as a symptom rather than a cause, and a symptom which may covary with other symptoms of the syndrome, including statural growth itself.

The primary etiology of periodic and reversible sleep disorder in children with the syndrome of reversible somatotropin deficiency ultimately remains a riddle. It could be that the children are in some way sleep impaired from birth onward. If so, their behavior as neonates could elicit an adverse reaction in the mother (or the mother surrogate), which in turn would have an adverse effect on the child. In this way a negative, reverberating behavioral feedback circuit would be established between the two of them. Alternatively, it might be the mother whose behavior could initiate the child's poor sleep pattern, leading to the same feedback effect as above.

When this cause and effect riddle is solved, then the traditionally accepted name of the syndrome, psychosocial dwarfism, may well be replaced by a more accurate one, like reversible somatotropin deficiency.

The clinical diagnosis and management of the patients of this sample were under the supervision of Dr Robert M. Blizzard in the pediatric endocrine clinic. His clinical cooperation and the availability of the medical files is gratefully acknowledged. We wish to thank Dr Rachel Steinhauser, post-doctoral fellow at the genetics clinic (Director, Dr Victor A. McKusick), for the referral of one patient. Robert Athanasiou and Heino Meyer-Bahlburg assisted with the statistical reduction of the data. Richard Clopper did the spot-checking of data extraction and processing. The personnel of the Happy Hills Hospital in Baltimore gave splendid cooperation during the sleep observation studies performed at this institution.

REFERENCES

Capitanio, M. A., and Kirkpatrick, J. A. 1969. Widening of the cranial sutures. A roentgen observation during periods of accelerated growth in patients treated for deprivation dwarfism. *Radiology,* 92, 53–59.

[3]By contrast with the syndrome of reversible somatotropin deficiency, somatotropin levels are actually elevated in syndromes of malnutrition (Graham, Cordano, Blizzard, and Cheek, 1969), including kwashiorkor (Pimstone, Wittmann, Hansen, and Murray 1966), marasmus (Hadden 1967), and anorexia nervosa (Marks, Howorth, and Greenwood 1965).

Drash, P. W., Greenberg, N. E., and Money, J. 1968. Intelligence and personality in four syndromes of dwarfism. In *Human Growth: Body Composition, Cell Growth, Energy, and Intelligence,* pp. 568–581. Edited by D. B. Cheek. Lea and Febiger: Philadelphia.

Fenton, G. W., and Elphicke, T. M. 1969. Sleep patterns in malnutrition: a longitudinal study of anorexic patients. (Abstract.) *Electroencephalography and Clinical Neurophysiology,* 27, 681.

Graham, G. G., Cordano, A., Blizzard, R. M., and Cheek, D. B. 1969. Infantile malnutrition: changes in body composition during rehabilitation. *Pediatric Research,* 3, 579–589.

Hadden, D. R. 1967. Glucose, free fatty acid, and insulin interrelations in kwashiorkor and marasmus. *Lancet,* 2, 589–593.

Hays, W. L. 1963. *Statistics for Psychologists.* Holt: New York.

Honda, Y., Takahashi, K., Takahashi, S., Azumi, K., Irie, M., Sakuma, M., Tshushima, T., and Shizume, K. 1969. Growth hormone secretion during nocturnal sleep in normal subjects. *Journal of Clinical Endocrinology and Metabolism,* 29, 20–29.

Hunter, W. M., and Rigal, W. M. 1965. Plasma growth hormone in children at night and following a glucose load. (Abstract.) *Acta Endocrinologica,* Suppl. 100, 121.

Kerr, G. R., Chamove, A. S., and Harlow, H. F. 1969. Environmental deprivation: its effect on the growth of infant monkeys. *Journal of Pediatrics,* 75, 833–837.

Linn, L. 1967. Clinical manifestations of psychiatric disorders. In *Comprehensive Textbook of Psychiatry,* pp. 546–577. Edited by A. M. Freedman and H. I. Kaplan. Williams and Wilkins: Baltimore.

Marks, V., Howorth, N., and Greenwood, F. C. 1965. Plasma growth-hormone levels in chronic starvation in man. *Nature,* 208, 686–687.

Patton, R. G., and Gardner, L. I. 1962. Influence of family environment on growth: the syndrome of 'maternal deprivation'. *Pediatrics,* 30, 957–962.

Patton, R. G., and Gardner, L. I. 1963. *Growth Failure in Maternal Deprivation.* Thomas: Springfield, Ill.

Patton, R. G., and Gardner, L. I. 1969. Short stature associated with maternal deprivation syndrome: disordered family environment as cause of so-called idiopathic hypopituitarism. In *Endocrine and Genetic Diseases of Childhood,* pp. 77–89. Edited by L. I. Gardner. Saunders: Philadelphia.

Pimstone, B. L., Wittmann, W., Hansen, J. D. L., and Murray, P. 1966. Growth hormone and kwashiorkor. Role of protein in growth-hormone homoeostasis. *Lancet,* 2, 779–780.

Powell, G. F., Brasel, J. A., and Blizzard, R. M. 1967a. Emotional deprivation and growth retardation simulating idiopathic hypopituitarism. I. Clinical evaluation of the syndrome. *New England Journal of Medicine,* 276, 1271–1278.

Powell, G. F., Brasel, J. A., Raiti, S., and Blizzard, R. M. 1967b. Emotional deprivation and growth retardation simulating idiopathic hypopituitarism. II. Endocrinologic evaluation of the syndrome. *New England Journal of Medicine,* 276, 1279–1283.

Sassin, J. F., Parker, D. C., Mace, J. W., Gotlin, R. W., Johnson, L. C., and Rossman, L. G. 1969. Human growth hormone release: relation to slow-wave sleep and sleep-waking cycles. *Science,* 165, 513–515.

Silver, H. K., and Finkelstein, M. 1967. Deprivation dwarfism. *Journal of Pediatrics,* 70, 317–324.

Takahashi, Y., Kipnis, D. M., and Daughaday, W. H. 1968. Growth hormone secretion during sleep. *Journal of Clinical Investigation,* 47, 2079–2090.

Whitten, C. F., Pettit, M. G., and Fischhoff, J. 1969. Evidence that growth failure from maternal deprivation is secondary to undereating. *Journal of American Medical Association,* 209, 1675–1682.

CHAPTER 36

Late Puberty, Retarded Growth, and Reversible Hyposomatotropinism (Psychosocial Dwarfism)

John Money and Georg Wolff

INTRODUCTION

Three years ago we had the opportunity to see a sixteen-year-old boy in the psychohormonal research unit of the pediatric endocrine clinic in The Johns Hopkins Hospital whose case warranted the triple diagnosis of battered child syndrome, reversible hyposomatotropic dwarfism, and delayed puberty.[1] He had the physique of an 8½-year-old boy, with a bone age of 11½. For all of his life, he had been imprisoned at home, often locked for hours in a closet, and otherwise severely traumatized somatically and psychically by his parents (see Case Report, below).

This boy's case fitted very well into two long-term studies in the psychohormonal research unit, one on the types and psychology of retarded puberty, and one on the psychology of so-called psychosocial dwarfism (better defined operationally as reversible hyposomatotropic dwarfism). He was kept in follow-up, despite the limitations of a long-distance foster placement. Along with other children being followed with a diagnosis of reversible hyposomatotropic dwarfism—some of whom had, and some whom had not been transferred from the home where they did not grow to one where catch-up growth began—this boy raised the issue of a possible relationship between an adverse living environment, on the one hand, and delayed puberty associated with statural growth retardation, on the other.

Reprinted with permission from *Adolescence* 9 (1974):121–34. Copyright 1974, Libra Publishers, Inc.

[1]See also Chapter 33.

Supported by USPHS Grants HD-18635, HD-00325, HD-01852 and RR-00035, and by a grant from the Erickson Educational foundation.

Robert M. Blizzard, M.D., and members of the pediatric endocrine clinic did the physical examinations and willingly cooperated to make copies of their records available. Other medical records for the case report were supplied by the courtesy of Dr. Rachel Steinhauser in the Moore Clinic (Dr. V. A. McKusick, director).

PURPOSE

One purpose of this paper is to present a case report on the above-mentioned patient (N.H.), to illustrate the temporal relationship between retardation of statural growth and puberty in an adverse home and family environment versus acceleration of both after transfer to a benign environment. Another purpose is to present evidence from eleven other cases of reversible hyposomatotropic dwarfism in support of the hypothesis that late onset of puberty may, in such cases, be a manifestation of generalized delay in growth and maturation during childhood which occurs only in the growth-retarding environment of the home and family of ascertainment, and not upon transfer to another growth-promoting environment—the definitive characteristics of either the growth-retarding or growth-promoting (for instance, the hospital) environment, constituting a puzzle still not fully solved.

DESCRIPTION OF THE SAMPLE

The sample constitutes a census of the 12 oldest patients, 10 boys and 2 girls, in a group of 32, being followed in the psychohormonal research unit of the pediatric endocrine clinic, with an established diagnosis of dwarfism with reversible inhibition of pituitary somatotropin release (reversible hyposmatotropic dwarfism, or psychosocial dwarfism). Eight had been transferred from their original domiciles where growth retardation had manifested itself and had remained in the new environment up to and beyond the onset of puberty. The other 4 either had not, at the time of pubertal onset, left the home where growth retardation manifested itself, or else had returned there after a period away in another environment where catchup growth had demonstrated itself.

The criteria for diagnosis of growth retardation with reversible hyposomatotropinism are variously discussed in Patton and Gardner (1962; 1963; 1969), Silver and Finkelstein (1967), Powell, Brasel and Blizzard (1967), Powell, Brasel, Raiti, and Blizzard (1967), Wolff and Money (1973), and Money, Wolff, and Annecillo (1972). Briefly stated, the main diagnostic signs are: history of significant slow-down in statural growth and skeletal maturation after the first months of life, resulting typically in a physical height below the third percentile for a given age, reversible if the child is transferred to the hospital or elsewhere from the domicile of growth failure.

Laboratory findings indicative of hypopituitarism before or upon admission to the hospital, but not after transfer from the growth-retarding home environment to the hospital or other growth-promoting environment. The change is as rapid as within two weeks.

Typically, if not universally, a history of a broken or disrupted relationship between the child and one or both parents or parent surrogates, including unusual cruelty and neglect, either somatic or psychic or both.

PROCEDURE

Information concerning the onset of puberty was taken from the patients' endocrine clinic records, using the criteria of Tanner (1969). By these criteria puberty in boys begins with enlargement of the testes and scrotum. About a year later, enlargement of the penis begins and pubic hair growth, though sparse and short is clearly in evidence. Because of its visibility, pubic hair, corresponding to Tanner's Stage 2 of pubic hair growth, was used as the criterion of pubertal onset in boys of the present study. The same criterion was used for girls. By the time of pubic hair Stage 2, budding of the breasts is also usually visibly evident, as the onset of breast development normally coincides with or antedates the beginning growth of pubic hair.

Two brothers joined their parents in adamantly refusing further hospital visits, but the necessary pubertal information, at age sixteen in each case, was obtained through the court appointed probation officer in charge of their cases when a physical examination was court ordered.

Information pertaining to pubertal adolescent psychosexual development was abstracted and tabulated from the patients' psychohormonal unit records. A current followup study was achieved by means of a hospital visit and interview when cooperation was forthcoming, otherwise by a home visit, except for four boys and one girl who became dropouts from followup earlier during adolescence. Interviews conducted in the hospital were tape-recorded and transcribed. The schedule of inquiry was systematic, but the sequence flexible, so as to prevent stiltedness.

FINDINGS: PUBERTAL ONSET

Table 1 presents a summary of data pertinent to pubertal onset, and Figure 1 presents the data graphically. The data show, as compared with Tanner's norms, a quite clear trend toward later puberty. The more advanced the age of the child before leaving the growth-retarding environment, or while remaining in it, the later the onset of puberty. In the four extreme cases, the delay of pubertal onset is beyond the upper limit of the normal age range, namely age 14 in girls and 15 in boys.

There is only one case, that of the boy, F.J., that deviates from the trend. This boy is the only one in the sample whose growth in early life had been at a normal rate. Growth retardation began after he was transferred to a foster home at age $7^3/12$. The early period of good growth may conceivably have had a long-term influence on the timing of pubertal onset, or there may be some other, unknown, explanation for the fact that puberty was not delayed. Apart from this boy, the three boys who lived constantly in the growth inhibiting environment were the three whose pubertal onset was most delayed—until the seventeenth year.

Table 1. Patients' age, weight, and height at the onset of puberty (N=13)

Name code, color, and sex	Date of birth	Age at last follow-up (years)	Age at leaving growth-retarding home or staying there until puberty (years)	Age at growth of pubic hair (years)	Weight at onset of puberty (pounds)	Height at onset of puberty (inches)	Deviation of weight from expected weight for height (pounds)
N.H. w m	6/ 6/53	18 11/12	16 0/12	16 11/12	79	55	+ 3.9
Rb.H. w m	12/22/54	17 6/12	16 3/12[1]	16 3/12	85.5	60.5	− 13.2
Rn.H. w m	11/16/55	16 7/12	16 1/12[1]	16 1/12	104.0[2]	63.25	− 3.0[2]
A.R. w m	12/13/53	15 2/12	11 6/12	13 6/12	91.9	54.75	+17.9
F.J. w m	7/10/55	14 10/12	13 2/12[1]	13 2/12	61.0	53.5	− 8.1
R.S. w m	9/30/58	13 3/12	12 9/12	13 2/12	61.0	52.75	− 5.5
G.M. w m	12/10/57	12 8/12	7 0/12	12 8/12	92.8	59.0	0.0
G.H. w m	3/11/54	13 9/12	7 10/12	12 6/12	95.0	60.0	− 2.0
W.G. w m	1/ 5/60	12 4/12	3 10/12	11 3/12	75.3	54.25	+ 3.4
S.A. w f	3/ 1/52	17 2/12	15 4/12	15 6/12	100.1	55.1	+25.0
V.W. b f	9/ 3/58	13 0/12	13 0/12[1]	13 0/12	73.7	54.9	− 2.3
S.N. b f	3/25/61	10 7/12	3 11/12	10 7/12	56.3	52.3	− 3.7

[1] These four children were still living in the growth-retarding environment or had returned there prior to the time of pubertal onset Rb.H. and Rn.H. did not leave their family for any significant length of time in boyhood. F.J. lived in a foster home from age $7\frac{3}{12}$ to $13\frac{9}{12}$ years during which his growth was retarded. V.W. lived in an orphanage from age $7\frac{3}{12}$ to $9\frac{9}{12}$ where she grew at a satisfactory rate and then returned to her parents' home where growth again became retarded.

[2] These height and weight measurements, the only ones available, were taken 6 months after pubertal onset. His mother reported that he had grown rapidly during these 6 months, but without atypical gain or loss of weight.

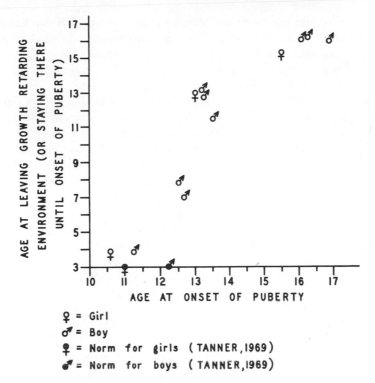

Figure 1. Relationship between age at onset of puberty and age at leaving the growth-retarding environment (or staying there until onset of puberty). N:12.

Among the girls, the case that needs special mention is that of V.W. who lived in a growth promoting environment from age $7^{3}/_{12}$ to $9^{9}/_{12}$, at which time she was returned to her parents (a return she had always wanted, as had most children in this sample, irrespective of neglect or maltreatment at home). Left in the growth promoting environment, she may well have gone into puberty earlier than at age 13 years, as happened in the case of S.N. at age $10^{7}/_{12}$ years.

Table 1 presents also data on height and weight at the onset of puberty. These figures show an absence of a unitary trend in either height, weight, or the ratio between them. They show that no patient was grossly underweight for height. The range of weights does not permit the hypothesis of Frisch and Revelle (1970) to apply to the present group of children. Based on normal sampling of girls, their hypothesis is that a critical body weight (M=68 lb. in girls) may trigger the onset of puberty.

FINDINGS: PSYCHOSEXUAL

There are no firm adolescent psychosexual data, only preliminary impressions to give at this time, owing to the fact that four boys and one girl could not be contacted for current psychosexual followup interviews (though two had given good sex-history interviews earlier); that the two brothers, visited at home, refused a return appointment; and that four of the five remaining were reticent to disclose too much. Therefore, the information available is more in the nature of what did not happen than what did.

Among these children and teenagers living in a growth-retarding environment, sexual behavior, including masturbation, was not prominent among symptoms of pathological or unacceptable behavior, either before or after puberty. There was no obsessive, ruminative preoccupation with sex, and no special proneness to gender-identity disorders, nor to paraphilias. Paralleling late onset of somatic puberty, there was some slowness and diffidence in establishing romantic relationships, but the cases are too few to know whether this slowness was primary, or secondary to a history of peer rejection because of short stature and deviant behavior, and to a history of a deficiency of unqualified affectionate relationships in infancy and childhood. There is a possibility that, as a group, these children might be classified as postpubertally hyposexual, and erotically somewhat apathetic or inert, at least to some degree.

CASE REPORT

The boy (N.H.) whose case instigated this paper first came to public attention on a few occasions during childhood when neighbors complained of his maltreatment. Once the police found the boy nailed-up, naked, in a closet. They took pictures and warned the parents, but nothing else was done. At age fourteen, he had never attended school. Despite strong parental resistance, he was transported to the Division of Special Education for testing, but no effective measures were taken on his behalf. He returned home to two more years of brutality and confinement. The extremity of his plight was finally acted upon when he was sixteen after his half-sister, from the safety of being newly married, reported his case. Thereupon, he went to live with a stepaunt for six weeks prior to hospitalization, followed by placement in a foster home and eventually in an institutional home.

The boy's mother had been killed in an auto accident when he was three months old. Her husband disclaimed paternity of this, the youngest child of four. He remarried when the boy was three. The new wife already had four children by two other men. The three of them by her former husband were given out to adoption. To the new husband's original four children, three more were added from the second marriage.

In the manner typical for victims of the battered child syndrome, this particular boy fits the formula of being forced to suffer punishment by way of atonement for his parent's own shortcomings and transgressions. In particular, the stepmother may have been pathologically destroying in him, by proxy, an image of what she could not tolerate in herself, namely, her own illegitimacy. This fact had traumatized her when her grandmother revealed it to her at age fifteen. She was hospitalized at the time, having been badly burned when her robe caught on fire. By rumor she learned also that her father was her mother's father. When she became a stepmother, her alibi for singling out one child, the ostensibly illegitimate one, for exceptional and pathological treatment was that he was mentally defective and "a freak." The father, subordinate to his wife, acquiesced.

Information about the boy's life comes from self-report, from his older sister, and from his aunt. The parents were not available to be interviewed.

While others sat at the table, the boy was required to eat scraps of food from the floor. He did not get enough to eat, so that he sometimes stole food and rummaged through garbage. He had no bed on which to sleep only the floor. At various times in his life, as when the family changed places of residence, he was required to sleep in a woodshed where he got frostbitten in winter; in a suffocating attic in summer; in a closet where he could only squat, with no provisions for excretion; or at his parents' bed, chained to the bed post, where there was no alternative except to go to sleep standing up. This latter happened after he had wrecked the imprisoning bolt on the closet door.

Whenever he was permitted to look at television, he had to stand in the corner alone, not moving. As a punishment for moving, he had to stand on his head. When the family went for a trip to the seashore, he was not permitted to join with others on the beach, but had to sit alone, and was punished if he moved. Sometimes he was tied to a decorative architectural pillar in the house and beaten. The other six children were forced to beat him, or else be beaten themselves. He still carries the x-ray evidence of a broken arm, untreated and imperfectly healed.

When given a medical examination six weeks after his sixteenth birthday, this boy had already spent six weeks living with his stepaunt. During this time, he was said to have gained 10 lb. in weight. Upon physical examination, he weighed 70 lb., 9.3 lb. more than expected for his statural height of 51 inches (height age, 8½ years; bone age 11½ years).

The delay between release from confinement and complete medical evaluation eliminated the possibility of a before and after hormonal evaluation. Such are the exigencies of clinical research that this invaluable information could not be obtained. There were no clinical signs of puberty at the initial evaluation at age 16 yr. 1 mo. Ten months later, at a height of 55 inches and a weight of 79 lb., the first growth of a few pubic hairs was in evidence. The scrotal skin had darkened, and the testes, described as formerly almost atrophied, had become easily palpable. The shaft of the penis had increased 1 cm in length. During this same period, statural growth had increased by 4 inches (10 cm).

During the first sixteen years of his life, this boy had received no schooling whatsoever. Despite his confinement, he did acquire some language, but his speech was cluttered in articulation and extremely difficult to understand. Vocabulary was limited, syntax was imperfect and, above all, conceptual understanding was impoverished and grossly retarded in development. All these aspects have, in the three ensuing years, improved dramatically, and continue to do so, as does also the once mentally defective IQ (from 51 to 81).

Sex education during the first sixteen years was limited to watching his parents' copulatory and oral sexual activities through the keyhole of the closet in which he was confined. He had no other knowledge of reproduction, and no knowledge of the relationship of these activities to reproduction when the first inquiries were made in an interview at age 16½ years.

Notes made while the boy was in the hospital or in convalescent care from age 16 yrs. 2 mos. to 16 yrs. 6 mos. indicate that he was occasionally observed to masturbate, apparently without ejaculation. In the convalescent hospital, he exchanged some confidential talk on sex with a male occupational therapist and shared his knowledge of oral sex with other boys. He claimed having been required to try and have sex with the family's German shepherd, but there was an element of playfulness in his talk that prevented the separation of history from fiction. Once he joked with an aide, saying she should get into bed with him. She replied that he had his teddy bear to which he replied that he couldn't do anything with that. A few weeks earlier, his aunt had expressed disappointment that he seemed not to be able to express gratitude or affection, as her own children could, despite her efforts on his behalf. But six months later he reported having had two girlfriends, with each of whom he had exchanged perfunctory kisses.

At the time of the most recent interview, the boy was one month short of his nineteenth birthday. He had the appearance of being two to three years postpubertal and could have passed as a fifteen-year-old. His height was 62¼ inches and his weight 100 lb. The height age was 13½ and the bone age 15½ years. He had well-developed pubic and axillary hair and a thin moustache, but did not yet need to shave. He was appealing and friendly in manner, with none of the hyperkinesis and hypomanic tendency formerly evident.

As one talked with him, there were many occasions when he seemed to be a living Rip van Winkle. For example, he once got into trouble over the cost of an attempted long-distance telephone call to an uncle, yet he did not in fact know that long-distance calls do not cost the same as local ones.

In a similar vein, he did not know that social attitudes to homosexuality are negative. In the institution where he was living, a retarded adolescent boy had engaged him in mutual masturbation. "Well, this one boy was playing around," he said, "and he was playing around with me, and I didn't know nothing about that. And then I got yelled at by the boss, because he told me." The experience resulted in what may have been his first ejaculation, at age 18.

By contrast, the boy had picked up the usual taboos in an institutional environment toward heterosexual activities. For lack of a family placement, he had been living in a church-sponsored, institutional community designed primarily for the rehabilitation of the handicapped and retarded, where the sexes were segregated. He had recently graduated to a newly established group home or halfway house and had a part-time job. His opportunities for a girl-friend relationship were limited, but he seemed also not to be socially too far matured into the girl-friend and dating stage. He had a good fund of basic sexual knowledge and concepts, much of it supplied in his hospital interviews. On the whole, he

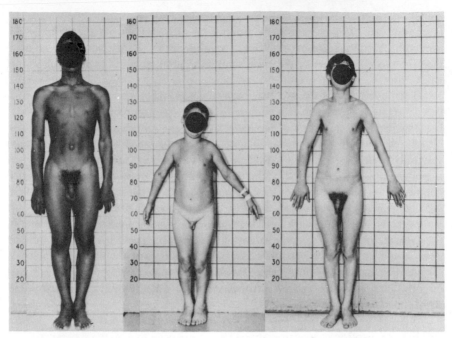

Figure 2. Left, youth aged 16 years, with normal growth history. Center, patient with history of growth inhibition, aged 16 years 1 month, one month after release from the growth-inhibiting environment. Right, the same patient at age 18 years 11 months, showing the effects of catchup growth and pubertal maturation after 2 years 10 months in growth-promoting environments.

showed a quite remarkable degree of common sense and good judgment regarding the sexual and other aspects of his life. His greatest longing was to find a home, either with relatives who would accept him, or with foster parents who would adopt him, neither of which seemed likely.

This case represents an extreme of neglect, deprivation and cruelty in childhood. It is instructive because, as an extreme, it throws light on other cases of reversible hyposomatotropic dwarfism where poor nutrition, sleep impairment and psychic assault are more subtle and may even be difficult to identify. Theoretically, it would be easier to understand this puzzling condition with its concomitant pubertal delay, if all cases were as dramatic as that of N.H.

DISCUSSION

Twelve cases constitute a remarkably small number on which to base a paper. Yet, when one is dealing with the statistics of extremes, twelve also is a crowd, and here one is, indeed, dealing with extremes. Dwarfism with reversible hyposomatotropinism is not commonly diagnosed, even though its incidence may be greater than suspected. The condition is less commonly diagnosed at or after the expected age of puberty than earlier. Early diagnosis leads to therapy, namely transfer of the child from the growth-delaying environment to a growth-promoting one. When the transfer cannot be effectuated, and the child is retrieved back into the growth-retarding environment by the parents or guardians, then these people, aided by the child's collusion, effectively repudiate follow-up study.

The importance of the present group of cases is that they draw attention to a type of retarded puberty in which there exists a relationship between the growth-environment and the timing of the onset of puberty—a relationship that has not hitherto been fully recognized. Diagnostically, the condition has, no doubt, generally been overlooked or misdiagnosed as a form of "constitutional delay" in pubertal onset. Now that the relationship is known to exist, it may eventually be possible to track down the primary variable responsible for later puberty in a growth retarding environment, and for earlier puberty in a growth-promoting environment. One will want to pay attention to, among others, the variable of food intake, and also to sleep. It seems highly probably that chronically disturbed sleep could account for growth retardation by interfering with the pituitary's release of somatotropin during sleep (Wolff and Money, 1973). Indirectly, if not directly, there might be a sleep effect on pubertal gonadotropin release from the pituitary.

Knowledge of the mechanism that delays puberty in prolonged, but reversible hyposomatotropic dwarfism may make it possible to achieve a better understanding of what is responsible for the constant lowering of the age of pubertal onset in the secular trend so convincingly identified by Tanner (1962) in the European and American population over the last century and a half.

SUMMARY

In twelve children with a diagnosis of retarded statural growth associated with reversible somatotropic deficiency (psychosocial dwarfism) the age of pubertal onset showed a positive correlation with the age of leaving the growth-retarding home environment (or of staying there until the onset of puberty). The more a child's age advanced in the growth retarding environment, the later the onset of puberty. Psychosexual development showed a parallel trend.

REFERENCES

Frisch, R. E., and Revelle, R. "Height and weight at menarche and a hypothesis of critical body weight and adolescent events." *Science* 169 (1970):397–99.

Money, J., Wolff, G., and Annecillo, C. "Pain agnosia and self-injury in the syndrome of reversible somatotropin deficiency (psychosocial dwarfism)." *Journal of Autism and Childhood Schizophrenia* 2 (1972):127–39.

Patton, R. G., and Gardner, L. I. "Influence of family environment on growth: The syndrome of 'maternal deprivation'." *Pediatrics* 30 (1962):957-62.

_____. *Growth Failure in Maternal Deprivation.* Springfield, Ill.: Charles C Thomas, 1963.

_____. "Short Stature Associated with Maternal Deprivation Syndrome: Disordered Family Environment as Cause of So-called Idiopathic Hypopituitarism," In *Endocrine and Genetic Diseases of Childhood,* L. I. Gardner, ed. Philadelphia: Saunders, 1969.

Powell, G. F., Brasel, J. A., and Blizzard, R. M. "Emotional deprivation and growth retardation simulating idiopathic hypopituitarism. I. Clinical evaluation of the syndrome." *New England Journal of Medicine* 276 (1967):1271-78.

Powell, G. F., Brasel, J. A., Raiti, S., and Blizzard, R. M. "Emotional deprivation and growth retardation simulating idiopathic hypopituitarism. II. Endocrinologic evaluation of the syndrome." *New England Journal of Medicine* 276 (1967):1279-83.

Reinhart, J. B., and Drash, A. L. "Psychosocial dwarfism: Environmentally induced recovery." *Psychosomatic Medicine* 31 (1969):165-72.

Silver, H. K., and Finkelstein, M. "Deprivation dwarfism." *Pediatrics* 70 (1967): 317-24.

Tanner, J. M. *Growth at Adolescence.* Oxford: Blackwell Scientific Publications, 1962.

_____. "Growth and Endocrinology of the Adolescent," In *Endocrine and Genetic Diseases of Childhood,* L. I. Gardner, ed. Philadelphia: Saunders, 1969.

Wolff, G., and Money, J. "Relationship between sleep and growth in patients with reversible somatotropin deficiency (psychosocial dwarfism)." *Psychological Medicine* 3 (1973):18-27.

PART VII

Responses to Abusive Incest

"The frequency of sexual abuse . . . is . . . just as common
as physical abuse and the failure-to-thrive syndrome."

(Kempe, 1978)

Editor's Introduction

Sexual abuse, especially incestuous sex at home, is subject to a response of such intense moral outrage that it is difficult to approach it with scientific impartiality. The ideological norm is negative, and it infects even investigators of child abuse, enabling them in their interventionist zeal, all too easily to adopt an overinclusive antisexualism.

In its strictest version, the sexual code we live by prescribes avoidance and neglect of sexuality in childhood. No matter how benign, any adult-child interaction that may be construed as even remotely sexual qualifies, a priori, as traumatic and abusive, regardless of empirical evidence. A synonym for masturbation is self-abuse. When an adult masturbates a fretful child to pacify it, as is the custom among other peoples, it is not defined as genital fondling but as criminal abuse.

The code of avoidance is most stringent with respect to age discrepancy. Strictly applied in the home, it proscribes parents from letting their children see or hear anything about adult sex. In many families, it is still true that knowledge about reproduction must be picked up, catch-as-catch-can, in the field and on the street from children of one's own age. In schools that profess to give sex education, the code of avoidance maintains itself, alive and well, in those jurisdictions in which it is forbidden to teach anything about either copulation or contraception.

Logically, the avoidance code has as its underpinning two propositions. One is that childhood is a period of innate sexual innocence at the end of which a normal sex instinct emerges, crocus-like in the snow, from the hormones of puberty. The other is that children are born in original sin and are, therefore, readily recruitable to sinful ways. Therefore, their exposure to sinful ways must be subject to rigorous avoidance.

To illustrate, the antihomosexual campaign led by Anita Bryant is based on this faulty proposition of original sin. Juveniles and adolescents, Bryant says, become homosexual because they are recruited by older homosexuals. Voters endorse this erroneous logic, despite the fact that there is no empirical evidence to support such a simple formulation of the cause of homosexuality.

Many parents still apply the code of avoidance to their own nudity in the presence of their children, but parental nudity, per se, does not qualify legally as sexual child abuse. Parental exposure of children to live coitus, or even to pictures and movies of it, is another matter. Psychiatry endorses the avoidance code by defining coitus, when witnessed by the child, as the primal scene, and writing prophetically rather than empirically about its dangers in relationship to the Oedipus complex. It is not difficult to envisage a court decision that would define exposure to coitus as sexual abuse, especially in this day and age when new laws on "kiddie porn" have been so loosely written that it is legally possible for a parent to be imprisoned for taking a photograph of his infant naked at the backyard poolside.

There is no doubt that the visual image of sex lies at the very heart of our society's sexual taboo, so that what parents let their children see of sex makes them more vulnerable to an accusation of sexual abuse than does what they tell them or let them read. Over and beyond seeing, hearing, and reading about sex, however, the norm of avoidance proscribes sexual touching of children at home. The incest taboo, of great antiquity and widespread distribution, all but universalizes the proscription of sexual contact between people who live together as a family, except for the licensed breeding couples. When limited to the home, the concept of the sexual abuse of the child means almost exclusively incest. Yet there is no clear-cut definition of incest. The mother who has an orgasm from suckling, while her infant at the breast has an erection could be accused of incest. So could the grandparent who shares a bed with a grandchild, the both of them snuggling very close in body contact. Oral and manual sex may also qualify as incest, irrespective of whether the partners are of the same or opposite sex, or of the same or different age.

It is penile-vaginal sex, however, that primarily qualifies as incest, and that constitutes the primary definition of child abuse at home. Since the taboo on incest is absolute, its occurrence is automatically defined as abuse of the younger by the older person. Legally, no differentiation is made between somatically or psychologically traumatic and nontraumatic incest. Clinically, however, biographical follow-up reports indicate that the experience of incest may be either traumatic or nontraumatic in outcome. There are no prevalence statistics for either outcome. It is highly probable that sibling incest is both more prevalent and more prevalently benign than is parent-child incest. For the young participant in incest, it may very well be that the burden of secrecy and deceit takes a heavier toll than does the sexual-erotic experience itself. When the genuine pair-bonding of erotic love has existed between the two partners in incest, then the discovery and disbanding of their partnership, not the partnership itself, may be the source of trauma. Such a psychologic reality, however, bears no weight with the law. The incest taboo is so strong that those who break it must be either secretive or boastful as deviants. Being a sexual deviant is like being a religious deviant in a one-religion society. It is too difficult for most young people to cope with. Add to this the fact that the partnership in incest may be not reciprocally balanced, but authoritative-submissive, and the difficulty of coping is compounded.

Abuse as an act committed is counterbalanced in the sexual context, as in other contexts, by neglect as an act omitted. At the present moment in history, the ideology of avoidance as it applies to sex is so powerful and universal that it is unheard of that parents should be accused and tried for neglecting their children's sexual and psychosexual development and education. Yet such neglect does occur and is very prevalent. There is cumulative clinical and experimental evidence to indicate that neglect of children's developmental sexuality paves the way, by default, for the development, in large degree, if not in toto, of the paraphilic psychosexual disorders (the so-called perversions) of adolescence and adulthood; and also for a major proportion of the sexual hypofunctions of adulthood, among which are erotic apathy, impotence and lubricatory failure, premature ejaculation and vaginismus, anorgasmia, erotic pain, and erotic anesthesia. In all of the scientific and medical literature, there is not yet a single article on the subject of sexual neglect to counterbalance the articles on sexual abuse.

Parental neglect of psychosexual development in childhood readily yields to abusive punishment. This happens when children manifest the species-specific sexual rehearsal play of childhood. Here follows a nineteenth-century example, quoted from *Time* magazine's February 28, 1977, review of Mary S. Hartman's *Victorian Murderesses*.

> Celestine Doudet was tried in Paris in 1855 for beating five young girls, sisters—one to death. The children's father, a fashionable English physician named James Marsden, had put them in the Frenchwoman's charge so that she might cure them of masturbation—a practice that Victorians believed caused epilepsy, asthma, paralysis and madness. Doudet's qualifications for this task were obscure; she had previously been employed as a wardrobe mistress to Queen Victoria, who gave her a warm testimonial. Once installed in a Paris apartment, Doudet began her course of treatment. She tied the children's wrists and ankles to the bedposts—a common method approved by their father. She also kept them on a starvation diet and subjected them to nasty tortures. On a rare visit to Paris, Marsden attributed his daughters' rickety, emaciated appearance to their persistence in the "secret vice" and ordered up some "preventive belts." Another physician who called upon the girls made a similar diagnosis. Women neighbors, seeing and hearing of the children's plight, managed to start a police investigation. Still Doudet persisted in brutalizing her charges, and one died of skull fracture. Even after this tragedy, Marsden was reluctant to press charges against Doudet, fearing that exposure of the girls' vice would stain the family honor. When the trial finally took place, it seemed as if the four surviving girls were charged rather than their tormentor. If masturbation was proved, Doudet's lawyer argued, then there was no need to invent mistreatment to explain the dreadful physical condition of the girls. The issue of whether the sisters did or did not masturbate was never resolved. Doudet claimed that the dead girl had been suicidal because of her uncontrollable masturbation and had hit her head against the wall. Acquitted of causing the child's death, the Queen's ex-wardrobe mistress got five years for child abuse.

In light of the sexual neglect of children, it is understandable that the sexual abuse of children, especially in the home, is a topic which until very recently was largely ignored by professionals. The group of papers in this section deals with this still taboo topic.

In Chapter 37, Renshaw and Renshaw examine the establishment of the incest taboo from biological, psychological, sociological, moral, and legal perspectives, discuss factors that contribute to its violation, and describe the effects on the family. In his review of the literature Henderson in Chapter 38 presents epidemiological and anthropological data on incest and examines its psychodynamics. Kaufman, Peck, and Tagiuri, in Chapter 39, describe the similarities in psychopathology and family dynamics of a group of girls who had been involved in incestuous relationships with their fathers, stepfathers, or other male relatives. The two case studies presented by Yorukoglu and Kemph in Chapter 40 describe mother-son and father-daughter incest. The authors discuss factors that protected the children from serious and permanent psychopathology.

A special approach to the treatment of father-daughter incest is described in Chapter 41. Contrary to simplistic explanations, sexual abuse of a child by a parent has its origin in highly complex dysfunctioning in the family. Giarretto's treatment focuses on all family members and, at different phases of treatment, includes individual, marital, father-daughter, mother-daughter, family and group counseling. In addition, some families participate in Parents United and Daughters United, self-help groups for families in which incest has occurred. The author reports that 95 percent of these families were reunited and that no recidivism occurred in families receiving at least ten months of treatment.

These findings contrast markedly with those of Kempe (1978) who reported that between 20–30% of the families in his sample in which incest had occurred were reunited. He states that "reuniting families should not be the overriding goal . . . [that] the best interests of the child should be served" (p. 387). Clearly, these differing viewpoints reflect the inchoate state of knowledge about the causes and treatment of incest. Both Giarretto and Kempe worked with families that came to the attention of the court. Hardly any ground has been broken with families in which incest is practiced but who are unknown to legal authorities.

J.M.

REFERENCE

Kempe, C. H. "Sexual Abuse, Another Hidden Pediatric Problem" *Pediatrics* 62 (1978):382–89.

CHAPTER 37

Incest

Domeena C. Renshaw and Robert H. Renshaw

Cleopatra, Queen of the Nile in ancient Egypt, married her brother. She herself was the product of a series of incestuous royal marriages. Historically, incest seemed to have occurred within rich and powerful families, who considered themselves to have special powers and privileges which were to be thus conserved and perpetuated. Most modern religions have special laws that prohibit incest, with special dispensation required for intermarriage. A few primitive cultures existing today still allow and regulate incest. In the hills of Kentucky, incest is not uncommon, even in this decade.

The term incest is defined as "unclean, unchaste" by Webster's. By common usage, it is taken to mean actual sexual intercourse between two people of the same kinship. In spite of the exceptions mentioned, incest is an almost universal taboo or prohibition by both religion and law. It is so grave a taboo that few persons can comfortably discuss the topic in depth and detail; as a result, investigation and understanding have been fraught with difficulty.

Lacking clear knowledge, we have not developed a treatment system, nor have we begun to plan for prevention in high-risk groups. Priests, ministers, and family physicians are usually the first professionals to whom the problem presents, unless a horrified observing neighbor rushes to the police first. It is possible, however, to review what data have accumulated and attempt to begin dialogue toward working out a therapeutic approach toward incest.

There is a hierarchy in the incest taboo; the most unacceptable being mother-son (witness the most extreme curse in all languages), then father-daughter, then brother-sister incest. Other kinships then follow: cousins, uncles, etc. *Step*-kinships are not included, although certain legal reforms are now attempting to include the step-kinship in United States civil law, to protect dependent children within the many remarriages resulting from the soaring numbers of divorces.

The incest taboo has shaped human society since the beginning of recorded history. It has been considered by some sociologists to be "the most extreme form of deviant behavior—the universal crime" (S. K. Weinberg) (8).

Reprinted with permission from the *Journal of Sex-Education and Therapy* 3 (1977):3-7.

Textbooks recurrently comment that "statistically, the occurrence of incest is negligible, and because of this infrequency, the extent of its disruptive effect on human group life is minor" (quoted as 7 per million in the U.S., i.e., coitus, not sex play). Yet, in clinical medical and psychiatric practice, we know this is simply *not true*. Incest is more widespread than reported to surveyors. As a presenting complaint, "incest" comes to a psychiatric clinic in about 2 per 1,000 cases, but turns up incidentally in psychiatric history in at least 5%; not as full intercourse, but fondling and masturbation. The grave concern, the powerful group condemnation, the reactive aversion, and the antipathy toward incest reported by anthropologists in a great majority of cultures, point to an intuitive recognition that powerful social sanctions are needed to curb powerful sexual drives (1, 10).

Psychosexual development occurs (for better or worse) within the intimacy of family life, often with crowded quarters, common beds, and relaxation of dress codes. Privacy must be taught; also there must be an opportunity to learn that society disapproves of and condemns incest. Weich has pointed out that the terms "mother" and "father" are used as a defense against incest, for parents are the only ones within the family unit who are allowed free sexual expression with each other (7). Others must learn to seek their partners outside of the family, with or without parental approval. The inputs are constant: "When you grow up, you will choose a wife or be chosen by a husband." There may be different customs or semantic variations for primitives or sophisticates, yet equally strong and repeated is this teaching of young and adult alike, that marriage will occur with someone outside of the immediate nuclear family.

Human sexual feelings and fantasies are a powerful part of daily functioning. They are easily aroused by a wide variety of stimuli, including visual or physical stimuli from family members. Conscious control can be and is applied to such stray fantasies of incest as arise, so that restraint may prevent their culmination in sex play, the usual prelude to intercourse. Toward this end, powerful and persistent messages are given to the developing child that parents and siblings are objects of family love and loyalty, but they are forbidden objects of sexual love.

Sexual exploration of self and other available persons (usually siblings and peers) is part of normal, prepubertal development, and occurs in all cultures (6). In primates, such sex play in the young is essential for adult mating. In humans, constant cultural inputs teach children respect for privacy, restraint, and appropriateness, so that limits are learned for sexual as well as for other social expressions. There is a distinct difference between sex exploration and incest, taken to mean regularly occurring full heterosexual intercourse.

Two important questions that must be raised are these:
1. How are such strong, *almost* universal, incest taboos built?
2. What causes the breakdown of powerful incest taboos?

I doubt whether the first question has as yet been really satisfactorily answered, or that it *can* be. Speculations and theories abound from five perspectives—biological, psychological, sociological, moral, and legal. In outline, theoretical factors in promoting taboos against incest are:

I. Biological:
   A. Once popular, today scientifically refuted, is the theory of inherited biological barriers to incest which allegedly restrain the human species uniquely (in contrast to oestrusbound animals, where incest is freely practiced). In the science of animal breeding, man has avoided close inbreeding to "lessen degenerate genetic consequences"; but both superior offspring, as well as perpetuation of genetic abnormalities, have been noted in both pedigreed animals and man, as many a physician knows, who has delivered and followed an infant of an incestuous union. This same result was reported of the Incas and the royal families of Hawaii and Egypt in the past. Today the people of the mountains of Kentucky also show both ends of the spectrum; increased incidence of mental retardation and epilepsy, but also offspring of incest who are far above average physically and intellectually.
   B. An "instinct" for incest-avoidance has been ruled out as having no demonstrable basis whatever.
II. Psychological:
   Humans show a strong affective affinity for the parents of both sexes. For the parent of the opposite sex, warm feelings quite naturally lead to sexual arousal. In the presence of strong sanctions, these sexual feelings are viewed pejoratively with no clear statement of *why* they are condemned. Are they bad per se, or in a particular context (toward father/ brother/ sister/ mother)? Ambivalence results. Coexisting opposite emotions (sexual attraction with guilt or anxiety) toward father/ brother/ mother cause confusion and discomfort. To defend against such discomfort, defenses must be built, namely, massive denial of the incestuous feelings, as well as of the ambivalence and the anxiety. This denial *is* the incest taboo, the basis of Freud's controversial Oedipus complex. He rocked the Victorian world by openly saying that little girls wanted to marry Daddy and little boys wanted to have sex with Mother. Still today the very mention of Oedipus complex causes attack. Last year I told a protesting medical student class, "I didn't invent the Oedipus complex, nor do you have to believe in it. Just *know* it and be alert when it appears clinically, personally, or as an examination question."
III. Sociological:
   Theories for the incest taboo abound among social scientists:
   A. Incest represents disintegration of family roles due to sexual rivalry (Malinowski) (1). This was disproved by a study in 1963 of a family where 15–40 members maintained incestuous relationships for almost 30 years with no breakdown of roles (Wilson) (11).
   B. Incest binds the individual too closely to the family, impeding broadened social relations.
   C. A better economy and therefore greater financial security is assured by outside marriages, which enlarge and extend the family (White) (10). However, royalty and aristocracy have historically consolidated property

and wealth by close kinship marriages, e.g., the Inca and Ptolemy dynasties.

D. Incest taboo maintains the generation gap; immaturity of the young is prolonged and the authority of parents is strengthened.

E. Forcing the adolescents out of the nest for their own sake shortens the child-rearing responsibilities of parents.

F. Parsons, a British sociologist, emphasized that control of erotic impulses is an indispensable element in *socialization,* that strong force which makes the developing individual accept the rules that have been laid down (2). If there is both religious and legal support, then the socializing force is strengthened. Sexual impulses must be frustrated and thrust outside the family, which thus protects itself by having new families formed.

G. Cultures or families which do not forbid incest tend to be socially isolated.

H. Post-incest adaptation to or by an errant incestuous spouse in marriage is difficult, due to confusion, shame, and guilt, and also due to resentment if exposure and penalties have occurred (4).

IV. Moral:

Is incest a moral absolute, or is it only relative to certain circumstances? Killing is also a strong taboo, but not a moral absolute, since church, society, and its legal system recognize times when killing is appropriate, as in self-defense or war. Is incest ever appropriate? Certain cultures and religions have ordained incest acceptable for some members in exceptional circumstances and have adapted adequately in that framework: kinship marriages, royalty, and ritualized tribal customs. However, no recorded culture has regarded incest as a "normal" practice for *all* its members. These are indeed difficult unresolved moral questions, but the taboo has through the ages invited avoidance.

V. Legal:

There are numerous extensive studies on incest cases (most common being father-daughter type) brought to trial in Germany, Sweden, and the United States (9). The majority of reported cases were of father-daughter incest in a family where the mother was a weak person and often aware that her daughter was sexually substituting for her; the fathers were described as domestic tyrants, over 40; some were of subnormal intelligence (most were not); violence or threat of violence was used on the "victim" in a third of the cases studied. In some cases there was absence of the mother and provocation from the daughter to her father for sexual approach. What causes the breakdown of powerful incest taboos?

A. Personal:

A great deal of material exists in the psychoanalytic literature which explores at length the psychodynamics of parent/child or brother/sister involved in incest (3). There is usually low self-esteem and also other personal problems, including poor impulse control and job difficulties.

These cases do not allow one to generalize, since presenting individuals will be unique and each requires in-depth exploration. In the cases that came to trial, excess use of alcohol was commonly reported. It is a drug that lowers controls and defenses; but in excess, alcohol causes impo tence (5). So this raises the probability of alcohol being merely an alibi ("I wouldn't if I was sober") rather than truly having caused a confused sensorium ("I thought my daughter was my wife"). It would be impor- tant for the evaluating professional to ask both father and daughter (if both are available) about erections and penetration. This may assist both in dealing with what actually transpired.

Also, psychosis, particularly the manic phase of manic-depression, should be excluded. In mania, characteristically, there is an undif- ferentiated sexual *urgency,* almost insatiable and with minimal erotic components. It is eminently treatable today, and lithium carbonate would constitute optimal medical management, with some supportive and edu- cational psychotherapy for the whole family to prevent recurrence.

B. Social:

Taking a clinical or legal approach and examining only the violators of incest taboo, fails to see the act in its true context—the social setting of the family in which it developed, its natural pathological framework. The whole family should be seen together. Failure to maintain the incest taboo prevailing in Western culture often has, for an incestuous family, these common features:

—family disorganization or disintegration;
—family relations and roles are abnormal or disorganized;
—absence of family discipline;
—isolation or retreat of the family from outside social relations;
—crowding;
—low value on privacy;
—unusual helplessness of family members.

EFFECTS OF INCEST ON THE FAMILY

Incest creates role distortions—father becomes "lover," or son, "husband," or sister, "mistress," and brother, "husband or lover." Confusion and conflict may occur when one participant was unaware that it was *not* a paternal preroga- tive to have intercourse with his daughter, as was the case with a 19-year-old girl from rural Illinois whose mother died when she was 12. She became housekeeper and regular sexual partner to her father and three older brothers. All of the men drank heavily, none had gone beyond sixth grade. She completed high school, got a job, and attended courses at a junior college, where she discovered that her sexual behavior was incest. She presented at an emergency room with an acute anxiety reaction. She made a good adjustment with minimal intervention, reas- surance, and some discussion to help her gain perspective and understand the shared responsibility for the acts, particularly of her father and also of her brothers. She soon moved out and later married.

Sometimes this discovery is quite incidental; at other times it is dramatic, with marked social disapproval and legal action, as when a neighbor or other person becomes aware of the incestuous relationship. Before detection of the incest, involved members of the family unit must have at some level accepted the incest in order to have stayed together. It is noteworthy that for a neglected young child, the warmth and sex play with an uncle or brother may be not upsetting but pleasant. A greater trauma may be if an angry battle should occur between father, mother, and uncle when the incest behavior is discovered. All members in such a family, however much they may fight within the home, usually still determinedly protect themselves from outside intervention.

After incest is detected, there is often intense social pressure by helping professionals to change the family structure. Sending father to jail does not solve the longstanding antecedent family problems, and conflicts may indeed be aggravated. Members blaming each other may take on destructive proportions, and the whole family may fragment by separate placements of minor children. One incestuous family I saw at first remained together by coalescing around blaming the absent, jailed father. There was great fear of retribution and violence when he got out, so the involved daughter had been fostered out to another family. Mother, on her husband's release, resumed the wife role by re-allying with him and "believing" his current denial (although he had previously admitted to the incest). Reintegration of the residual family then occurred around *not* discussing the incest affair, since that could threaten the fragile reunion. They were lost to follow-up.

Many individuals who have been subject to incestuous relations can and do, with or without professional help, obtain perspective and make a satisfactory life adaptation (4). They usually marry someone else later and usually share their guilty secret with their spouse, often before marriage. Acceptance by the partner is most enhancing to her/his own self-acceptance and self-esteem. Those who have strength and stability make a good marital adjustment. Others do not. They may be preoccupied with guilt, shame, and self-blame, and develop anxiety or depression. Those women who have *not* shared the secret of the incest with their husbands may be insecure and fear rejection and horror if the secret is told. They may need professional help to explore their feelings and the need to tell him now (is she inviting rejection?), and what purpose could be so served (could the trust and honesty actually *enhance* their relationship?). In an accepting partner, sharing an incest secret may draw the couple closer, but it is hard to predict.

Sometimes a victim of incest has hostility toward an unprotecting mother, plus a vindictive and destructive need to punish mother by telling her about the past secret after father has died. This hostile impulse could be better served by writing a letter, "as if" she could really mail it to her mother and get all of the resentment off her chest onto paper. As such, it is a valuable and relieving exercise and can then be productively discussed.

Incestuous offspring provide great tensions for the family due to their dual roles; mother-sister, father-grandfather, etc. This complicates effective rearing within that same family system and within the local community. Yet it is often the task of a family doctor, minister, or social worker to support the "stable (often secret) maladjustment" of the family in the best interest of the child and all members, while acting as guardian against recurrence by threat of legal action. Family physicians in rural or poverty areas have much to tell in the line of such experience.

In summary, many perspectives on incest have been explored. The anthropologist, sociologist, lawyer, social worker, doctor, psychiatrist, minister of religion, all see a separate segment of a highly complex and still poorly understood aspect of human sexual behavior. A natural sex act directed toward one who is strictly forbidden by law, due to close kinship ties, becomes by social convention a taboo and a crime. Superficially, it would seem that the incest taboo prevents isolation of the family from the community, which, if widespread, could splinter societal cohesion. Present evidence is that there are *no* reliable innate defenses against primary incest; each society must dynamically design and maintain its own taboos in the face of social changes, such as high divorce rates and remarriages. Up to now, the incest taboo has, for Western culture, stabilized the two-parent, two-sexes, two-generation family as an ideal unit for social cohesion (law and order) and nurturance of the young.

What is the role of the professional? As with all other presenting material, it is to be an *informed* listener—to evaluate the situation, to take *time* to take a detailed history. Of all sexual histories, this will be the most difficult, due to the discomfort of all concerned, including the professional. It is not easy in these circumstances to be nonjudgmental. Acceptance of the *patient* does not mean acceptance of the act. As an authority, the professional carries the values of the larger culture and the patient may need a check-out of these values. A simple statement that such behavior is unacceptable in this society, together with the consequential realities, is in order: "You will need a pregnancy/V.D. test, or a psychiatric evaluation for court," etc. Concern and plans for support and rehabilitation should be stated and implemented early, such as referral to a social worker or psychiatrist for family therapy, if this is acceptable to the family. If a minor is involved and treatment is refused, child protection laws will have to be invoked.

What of prevention? Perhaps the best we can do at present is to realize with humility the great need for more scientific study of this important, but complex, socially defined problem. Incest will *not* go away, even if we bury the word in the sand.

BIBLIOGRAPHY

1. Malinowski, B. *Sex and Repression in Savage Society.* New York: Harcourt, Brace and World, 1927.

2. Parsons, T. "The Incest Taboo in Relation to Social Structure and the Socialization of the Child," *British Journal of Sociology.* Vol. 2:101, 1954.
3. Poznanski, E. and Blos, P. "Incest," *Medical Aspects of Human Sexuality.* October, 1975, p. 46-76.
4. Renshaw, Domeena C. "Healing the Incest Wound," accepted for publication, *Medical Tribune.*
5. Renshaw, Domeena C. "Sexual Problems of Alcoholics," *Chicago Medicine.* Vol. 78, No. 10, May 17, 1975, p. 433-436.
6. Renshaw, Domeena C. "Sexuality in Children," *Medical Aspects of Human Sexuality.* October, 1971.
7. Weich, M. J. "The Terms 'Mother' and 'Father' as a Defense against Incest," *Journal of the American Psychoanalytic Association.* Vol. 16:4, 1958.
8. Weinberg, S. K. *Incest Behavior.* New York: Citadel Press, 1955.
9. Weiner, I. B. "On Incest—a Survey," *Excerpta Criminologica.* Vol. 4:607, 1962.
10. White, L. A. "The Definition and Prohibition of Incest," *American Anthropologist.* Vol. 50:416, 1948.
11. Wilson, P. J. "Incest: a Case Study," *Social and Economic Studies.* Vol. 12:200, 1963.

CHAPTER 38

Incest: A Synthesis of Data

D. James Henderson

A process like the removal of the primal father by the band of brothers must have left ineradicable traces in the history of mankind and must have expressed itself the more frequently in numerous substitutive formations the less it itself was to be remembered.

*Totem and Taboo** (1913)
Sigmund Freud

The subject of incest occupies a crucial position in psychoanalytic theory and psychiatric practice. While the occurrence of overt incest is not particularly common, there has scarcely been a culture or civilization where the social threat of incestuous behavior has not been tacitly acknowledged in an interlocking complex of institutions whose major function is to minimize this threat. For example, the incest taboo is perhaps the most binding moral constraint known to man.

The incest theme is pervasive in the literature and folklore of most civilizations, further reflecting the curious paradox of this forbidden matter—undeniable evidence asserts that incest is a universal preoccupation of the human condition, yet there is little frank and open discussion of it outside professional circles. Even among psychiatrists and throughout the psychiatric literature the attention devoted to this subject falls vastly short of its relative impact as the kingpin of psychodynamic formulation, and indeed of its very importance as a clinical phenomenon.

EPIDEMIOLOGICAL DATA

Despite the pervasiveness of the incest taboo, incest has been reported in almost all civilized countries, but reliable estimates of its incidence are not available. The vigor of the taboo and the crippling shame and guilt associated with overt incest have thus far proved insurmountable obstacles to full reporting. Different-

Presented at Canadian Psychiatric Association Meeting, Halifax, 1971.
Reprinted with permission from the *Canadian Psychiatric Association Journal* 17 (1972):299–313.
*Standard Edition, *Vol. 13*, London, Hogarth Press.

ial reporting according to social class further distorts the data, as incest occurring in families of lower socioeconomic status and among persons with a history of social deviance is more likely to be detected and reported than is incest in prosperous, 'respectable' families.

However, it is interesting to consider some representative statistics. In Sweden, where every incest offender receives a two-month pretrial psychiatric study, Weinberg (43) estimated the yearly incidence at 0.73 cases per million population. The comparable figures for the United States are: 1.2 cases per million (1910); 1.9 cases per million (1920); 1.1 cases per million (1930). Estimates of incest offences as a percentage of total sex offences vary from 2.4 percent to 6.3 percent.

Father-daughter incest has received more attention than other incestuous relationships. Weinberg, studying 203 cases in Illinois, reports 159 cases of father-daughter incest (78 percent), 37 cases of brother-sister incest (18 percent), 2 cases of mother-son incest (1 percent), and 5 cases of multiple incestuous relationships (3 percent).

Weinberg differentiates three groups of incestuous fathers: the first, where incest is part of a pattern of indiscriminate promiscuity; the second, where an intense craving for young children (pedophilia) includes the daughter as a sexual object; and the third, true endogamic incest, where the perpetrator chooses a daughter or a sister because he does not cultivate nor crave sexual contact outside his own family.

The influence of socioeconomic variables upon the occurrence of incest is disputed. Sonden (39) noted a rural preponderance of incest cases in Sweden, and stresses poor housing and geographic isolation as factors which promoted the seeking of emotional and social satisfactions within the family. The work of Riemer (36), Guttmacher (15), and Flugel (10) supports an inverse relationship between the occurrence of incest and socioeconomic status, and suggests that incest is commoner in poorer working-class and rural groups where poverty, inadequate housing, crowding and poor sanitary facilities lead to an enforced physical proximity in the absence of good opportunities for emotional investment outside the family. Lutier (23) emphasizes isolation as the major demographic variable associated with crimes of incest, and suggests that the archaic and regressive rural milieu recapitulates the conditions found in some 'primitive' societies where certain forms of incest were occasionally tolerated. Rhinehart (35) associates incest with socioeconomic disadvantage accompanied by social disorganization, where moral restrictions are a matter of relative indifference. Riemer postulates that fathers who are barred from sexual relations with their partner in a setting of personal, social, and economic decline institute an incestuous relationship with a daughter. Weinberg in the United States notes the disproportionate incidence of Polish peasant background in foreign-born incest offenders and feels this reflects a certain tolerance for incest in the Polish peasant community.

However, such data about socioeconomic variables related to incest are heavily biased by the unfortunate sampling procedures incorporated in the study designs. For example, studies drawn from criminal and court records reflect the generally higher conviction rates for all personal crimes among the lower social classes. The majority of persons appearing in criminal courts are of lower social position, borderline economic means and have crowded living quarters, so that a sample of incest cases drawn from such a population would reflect this bias— Szabo (40) reports that of his 96 cases, most fathers were of working or lower-class background, with a heavy incidence of alcoholism.

However, there is little firm evidence that poverty, overcrowding, and social isolation are of more than secondary etiologic importance—the cases reported by Weiner (44,45) and Cavallin (5) were drawn from middle-class backgrounds. Weinberg reports that rates of incest in the United States and England have not paralleled population growth, population density, or fluctuations of the business cycle. In general, the socioeconomic variables associated with incest in a given study appear to be those characterizing the population from which the study sample is drawn.

CONTRIBUTIONS FROM LITERATURE

Incest is an ever-recurring theme of the mythologies of diverse civilizations. Among the Greeks, Zeus is alleged to have murdered his father, Uranos, to have married his mother, Hera, and begotten by her a family of lesser gods.

The two outstanding biblical examples of father-daughter incest are those of the daughters of Lot (where liaison occurs after the loss of the girls' mother); and of Salome, whose incestuous stepfather was also her uncle. In the Book of *Leviticus* an entire chapter surveys the rulings for God's people regarding sexual relations *vis-à-vis* the integrity of family life.

Sophocles' *Oedipus Rex* (9) recounts superbly the tragic marriage of Oedipus to his mother, Jocasta. It is interesting in view of Freud's subsequent theory of the primal father that Sophocles invokes the concept of 'original curse,' which in Greek legend closely parallels the more familiar doctrine of 'original sin,' wherein succeeding generations pay a never-ending penalty for ancestral crime. In the story of Oedipus, the House of Labdacus labored under the curse of the Delphic Oracle, who prophesied to the royal family, Laius and Jocasta, that their son would slay his father and wed his mother. Hoping to evade Apollo's decree, they give their first-born son to a shepherd who is to let the infant die of exposure on a mountain. However, young Oedipus was adopted by King Polybus of Corinth. Learning of the Oracle's prophesy, Oedipus later fled Corinth, believing that the prophesy referred to his Corinthian foster parents. On the way to Delphi, he became involved in an altercation with a stranger, whom he slew, not realizing that the stranger was none other than his true father, Laius. Oedipus then continued to Thebes, and saved the city by guessing the Sphinx's riddle, was hailed by the Thebans as a savior and was offered Laius' throne and the queen, Jocasta. Through a complex series of disclosures, superbly related with dramatic irony by the master, Sophocles, Oedipus learns that Jocasta is his mother. Jocasta suicides and Œdipus gouges out his eyes, symbolically punishing his eyes for failing to perceive the grim lie he had perpetrated. His guilt lay not so much in marrying Jocasta, for he was ignorant then of her true identity, but in the willful and headstrong quest for power which secured his dubiously enviable immortality.

Electra (9) incites her brother, Orestes, to avenge the murder of their father, Agamemnon, by their mother, Clytemnestra. In the tragedies by Euripides and Sophocles, Electra is almost delusional in her hatred of Clytemnestra and, according to Euripides, she becomes deranged with guilt after her brother, Orestes, has slain her mother and the latter's paramour.

In his account of the 'Phaedra Complex', Messer (29) relates the account of the Phaedra legend in Euripides' play *Hippolytus*. Theseus, King of Athens, returns with his new bride Phaedra to the village where his son by Antiope has grown to be a strong and handsome young man. Phaedra falls in love with her step-son, Hippolytus, and, spurned by him, commits suicide, leaving a note for Theseus, falsely accusing the young boy of violating her. Hippolytus meets a violent death when a sea monster frightens his horse and wrecks his chariot. Theseus learns too late of his son's innocence and the King's violent death completes the tragedy. Drawing on Euripides' play, Messer uses the term 'Phaedra Complex' to refer to any physical attraction between step-parent and step-child.

ANTHROPOLOGICAL DATA

Kardiner (17) analyses data from several cultural groups, endeavoring to delineate the interaction of personality and culture, and notes that the Œdipus conflict took different forms, according to the nature of certain fundamental social institutions specific to a given culture. The nature and rigidity of the incest taboo varied from culture to culture, and only mother-son incest was found to be prohibited universally.

In ancient Egyptian civilization, marriage between sister and brother was not uncommon. According to Lutier (23), incest was not recognized as such between a brother and sister of the same father, but it was not permitted between offspring of the same mother. Some groups allow marriage between first cousins; others between second cousins and still others only with very distant nonblood relatives. Wolf (46) describes Chinese families who adopt and raise young girls, who are thus socialized into the same family unit into which they later marry. Aging parents are thus assured of their daughters-in-law's unending loyalty.

Devereux (7), regarding myths as a form of collective daydreaming, traces the ramifications of incest in all phases of Mohave Indian culture. Wherever Devereux found sexual relations between members of the narrow biological family, one or both participants were shamans, possessing evil powers. While the Mohave are sometimes lenient toward social deviance, people who practise witchcraft and incest are regarded as a menace to the entire tribe. It is a moot point whether the Mohave's own repressed incest wishes motivate such a condemnatory attitude. Devereux feels that incest characterizes the unsocialized Mohave, who fails to achieve the wide distribution of libido, characteristic of his culture, and invests it instead on his next of kin (the unresolved Oedipus complex). The shaman fulfils these criteria, and such an observation may possibly be related to the known association of incest and schizophrenia in our own culture.

THEORETICAL BASIS: THE INCEST TABOO

Gardner Lindzey (21) cautions that the incest taboo is an appealing area of theorizing, which has lent itself unduly to what Gordon Allport designates as "simple and sovereign" formulations. However, the incest taboo is multidetermined by a variety of instigating and sustaining factors. Needless conflict might be avoided were the theorists of different disciplines to entertain the possibility that there are a variety of theoretical avenues toward a common truth.

Freud (13) posed the question well in asking, "What is the ultimate source of the horror of incest which must be recognized as the root of exogamy?" "To explain it by the existence of an instinctive dislike of sexual intercourse with blood-relatives—that is to say, by an appeal to the fact that there is horror of incest —is clearly unsatisfactory; for social experience shows that in spite of this supposed instinct, incest is no uncommon event even in our present-day society, and history tells us of cases in which incestuous marriage between privileged persons was actually the rule." Drawing heavily on Charles Darwin's theory of the primal horde, Freud recalls Atkinson's hypothesis that in such a primal horde the younger men inevitably banded together and murdered the paternal tyrant who had jealously kept the women of the tribe to himself. There ensued rivalry and quarrelling among the young 'brothers', leading to ruinous disruption of the social organization, and to prevent such rivalry and social disintegration the incest prohibition was erected. Recognizing the shortcomings of this hypothesis, Freud goes on to speak of the "... inheritance of psychic dispositions which, however, need certain incentives in the individual's life to become effective.... We may safely assume that no generation is able to conceal its more important mental processes from its successor."

In the oedipal situation the child senses the jealousy and the prohibitive demeanor of his father and reacts with guilt and castration anxiety. The child recognizes his exclusion from the passionate love between his parents and feels hostile and destructive toward them. The dreaded retaliation of his father revives anxieties stemming from an earlier period when the more basic fear was not that of being castrated but of being unloved. Thus, pregenital experiences shapes castration anxiety arising in the phallic phase.

Dubreuil (8), speaking from an anthropological viewpoint, postulates that incest was rare and sporadic in primitive society by the very nature of social existence; it was necessarily infrequent and, like other exceptional acts, was at the same time an offense among the low, and a privilege and liberty among the exceptional. Just as unrestricted homicide would endanger the very structure of society, so incest would be socially isolating and therefore destructive. Both incest and homicide, however, are institutionalized and legitimate when they appear to benefit the social interest.

Dubreuil postulates instrumentalism applied to man in a sociocultural setting. Man operates on three levels: as an individual who uses others for security and power; as one who sees others in a reciprocal relationship with himself; and also as one at the service of his culture. The incestuous man fails to progress beyond the first level and sees demands for reciprocal relationships as an attack on his autonomy. He reconstructs his family on the model of a kingdom where his authority is total.

Considering biological explanations of the incest taboo (incest being detrimental to the race), Dubreuil observes that tribal society had little knowledge or fear of the physical degeneracy which modern science has shown to result from inbreeding. However, Lindzey argues convincingly for a biological basis to the incest taboo. A human group practising incest is selectively disadvantaged by the lesser fitness resulting from inbreeding *vis-à-vis* outbreeding human groups. From the 'random variation' in patterns of mating from society to society the human groups which insist on 'outbreeding' are favored and preserved by the process of 'survival of the fittest'. Lindzey argues that such a formulation does not imply that the groups involved understood the consequences of inbreeding (natural selection is not mediated by conscious awareness on the part of the individual organism), but he notes it is feasible that primitive man may indeed have noted a connection between incest and physical abnormality. Lindzey cites convincing data to support the lesser fitness of human and subhuman groups practising inbreeding.

Freud invoked the concept of the 'primal horde'. Anthropologists view the incest taboo as culturally determined and varying from culture to culture, while sociologists such as Talcott-Parsons (41) have pointed out the role of the incest taboo in facilitating socialization and role learning, forcing members of a nuclear family to choose love objects outside their group. Lindzey explains the incest taboo on the basis of a decrease in fitness as a biological consequence of inbreeding. Fox (11) and Wolf refer to developmental immunization, and Slater (37) invokes arguments based on demographic and ecological factors. Lindzey regards these latter mechanisms as significant in the maintenance rather than in the origin of the incest taboo, which like the occurrence of overt incest is multidetermined.

FACTORS PROMOTING THE BREAKDOWN OF THE INCEST BARRIER

Most authors agree that the father is aided and abetted in his incestuous liaison by a collusive wife, as a result of the latter's hostility toward her daughter. She forces a heavy burden of responsibility on to her daughter by causing her to assume the role of wife and lover with her own father and absolving the mother of this unwanted role.

Viewing incest in a transactional framework, Lustig (22) and his associates propose that it is a transaction which serves to protect and maintain the family in which it occurs. Incest, as a noninstitutionalized role relationship, reduces family tension by preventing confrontation with underlying sources of anxiety. Such a defensive maneuver is satisfactory so long as each member is able to maintain a façade of role competence. More specifically, father-daughter incest serves as a partial alleviation of the parents' pregenital dependency needs, as a defence against feelings of sexual insufficiency, as a mechanism for the daughter's revenge against the non-nurturing mother, as a device for reducing separation anxiety and as an aid to the maintenance of a façade of role competence for all protagonists. The role reversal between mother and daughter is an idiosyncratic solution to the tensions of such a dysfunctional family which is too 'sick' to employ culturally approved patterns of interaction. Both parents appear to define the daughter as a maternal object, with projection onto her of their respective maternal and sexual fantasies. In two of Lustig's cases, the latently homosexual father was able to vicariously gratify his female introjects through identification with his daughter-partner. If the father is simultaneously serving as the vehicle for the mother's unconscious homosexual impulses, a similar mechanism on her part would enable her to vicariously enjoy the father's role in the incestuous relation. It is clear that a capacity for regressive ego states among all parties is a condition of such a phenomenon.

Lustig defines five conditions of a 'dysfunctional' family which foster the breakdown of the incest barrier: (1) the emergence of the daughter as the central female figure of the household in place of mother; (2) the relative sexual incompatibility between the parents, leading to unrelieved sexual tension in the father; (3) the unwillingness of the father to seek a partner outside the nuclear family because of his need to maintain the public façade of a stable and competent patriarch; (4) the shared fears of family disintegration and abandonment, such that the family is desperately seeking an alternative to disintegration; (5) the unconscious sanction by the nonparticipant mother, who condones or fosters the assumption by the daughter of a sexual and affectional role *vis-à-vis* the father.

The contemporary pattern of small, highly mobile, vertical family units and the loss of the extended family may foster incestuous relationships. Within such compact families, each individual's need for affection and physical intimacy must be satisfied largely from within the nuclear unit. Further among the sociological factors predisposing toward overt incest are the prolonged absence of the father from the home, with his subsequent return to find an aging wife and a young, attractive and tempting daughter; the loss of the wife by divorce, separation, or death, leaving the father alone with an adolescent daughter; gross overcrowding, physical proximity, and alcoholism and also extreme poverty and geographic isolation, such that extra-familial social and emotional contacts are effectively impossible.

The age of family members is an important variable. Generally, the father is in his late thirties or early forties, and it is during this period that marital stress is most likely to develop and that death, separation, and divorce are more prone to appear upon the marital scene. When a father is confronted with an increasingly frustrating marriage and an increasingly attractive adolescent daughter, overt incest may occur.

Abraham defined 'neurotic endogamy' as a term which describes individuals who are unable to establish object relationships outside the kinship group and therefore tend to marry cousins or other relatives. Incest in the nuclear family may be related to an extension of such a neurotic developmental process.

According to some studies major mental illness is a factor in incestuous behavior. Magal (25) and his associates describe five incestuous families with major mental illness occurring in four of the five. He described a paranoid mother, a 'borderline' father, a paranoid psychotic father, and in one family both the father and mother psychotically depressed and suicidal. Commenting on the faulty resolution of incestuous drives in the families of schizophrenic patients, Lidz (20) and his group note serious deficiencies of the family structure, poorly-filled parental roles, and a parent-child interaction such that infantile erotic attachments between parents and children are maintained. The dissolution of the generation boundary in one family progressed to the point of role reversal between mothers and daughters, with daughters assuming the role of sexual gratification toward their fathers. In this family described by Kaufman (19) and his associates, an underlying fear of desertion seemed prominent in mothers, daughters and fathers alike.

Conceivably, intellectual deficiency and constitutional inferiority may also play a part in some cases of overt incest.

PSYCHODYNAMICS OF INCEST

For the purposes of the present discussion, both the Oedipus complex and Electra complex may be said to be universal, and as such the psychodynamics of incest are universal in their applicability. The incestuous fantasy inherent in the œdipal situation is now considered to have extensive roots in the pre-œdipal period.

Surveying cross-cultural evidence, Malinowski (26,27) attributes the phenomenon of sexual 'latency' in children of European civilization to environmental and social forces rather than to an inherent tendency. In India, for example, infantile marriage has been customary for centuries, and Bender notes that the 1921 census of India lists 2 million wives and 100,000 widows under the age of ten years. The *Memoirs of Casanova* and the *Confessions of La Marquise de Brincilliers* attest to the sexual precocity of certain 'children'. Malinowski states that in Melanesia girls may begin to have intercourse between the age of six and eight, and boys from the age of ten to twelve. Within our own culture such factors as constitutional intolerance of denial of satisfaction, unusually charming and attractive personalities, mental deficiency, emotional deprivation, and abnormal stimulation of children's urges by adults are factors listed by Bender as facilitating the retention of overt sex interest into the latency period.

Kaufman weaves a complicated but fascinating three-generational pattern surrounding cases of father-daughter incest. In his series of eleven cases all the fathers (or stepfathers) 'deserted' the children at some time, either through divorce, living away from home, alcoholism or desertion. Similarly the maternal grandfathers had deserted their families, and the mothers of the children included in this study deserted their husbands, leaving the daughter to assume the mother role. Desertion anxiety was thus pervasive, and the maternal grandmothers were consistently stern, demanding, cold, and hostile, and reacted to the desertion of their husbands by singling out one daughter whom they compared to the maternal grandfather and upon whom they lavished their displaced feelings of hostility and resentment. These daughters, who became the mothers of the daughters of the study, were hard, infantile, and dependent, and they married men who were similarly dependent and infantile. The mothers regarded themselves as worthless, yet were tied to the maternal grandmother in the futile hope of receiving the love and encouragement they never felt. These mothers single out one daughter to over-indulge and to develop into a replica of the maternal grandmother; then they displace onto these chosen daughters the hostility arising in their own unresolved oedipal conflict. Deserting their husbands sexually, and forcing their daughters to assume the role of sexual gratification toward their husbands, these mothers use the mechanism of denial to bind themselves to the incestuous liaison. Incest usually has its onset when the father and daughter feel abandoned owing to the mother giving birth to a new sibling, turning to the maternal grandmother, or developing some outside interest. These girls, lonely and fearful, then accept their fathers' sexual advances as an expression of affection, acquiescing in the tacit encouragement they receive from their mothers. Although the father-daughter liaison is genital, the meaning is pregenital, and indeed the reactions to sexuality in these girls take such pregenital forms as promiscuity, asceticism, and homosexuality.

Machotka (24) emphasizes the crucial role of the 'nonparticipating' member (mothers in cases of father-daughter incest) and points out the diversity of motives for that member's collusion. Denial exercised by the colluding member freezes the role relations and preserves them from change. He also suggests that among other things therapy must approach the denial and inappropriate role assignments so crucial to the faulty homeostasis.

Cavallin, describing incestuous fathers, notes the widespread occurrence of paranoid traits and unconscious homosexual strivings. This paranoid component is related to strong unconscious hostility toward the paternal grandmother and this hostility was subsequently transferred to the wife and daughter. Cavallin states that these patients' incestuous behavior reflected not only a displaced positive oedipal striving toward their mothers but also severe pregenital and genital conflicts, notably the fusion of oral aggression and positive sexual strivings. Accordingly, incest among fathers is an expression of unconscious hostility fused with primitve genital impulses discharged toward the daughter, a hypothesis supported clinically in the almost universal preoccupation among these fathers with having hurt their daughters and their fear of subsequent retaliation. Cavallin adds that the discharge of the incestuous impulse in the face of the incest taboo is facilitated by perception of the daughter as being incapable of retaliation, the tendency of the father to act out the aggression that he suffered passively as an infant, and seductiveness on the part of the daughter. Rascovsky and Rascovsky (31), employing a Kleinian theoretical framework, provide a detailed analysis of a young girl who had been a party to father-daughter incest. They postulate an extreme frustration in relation to the girl's mother and attempts at restoration from the basic depressive position leading to a precocious transition to the oral search for a father. In a situation dominated by extreme anxiety, there occurs an over-evaluation of the father's penis. The aggressive component against the partial object seeks satisfaction in the form of an urge to castrate. The incorporation of the penis as a substitute for the primary relation with the mother's breast leads her to a masculine identification with the penis, and there follows the choice of a feminine object disguised as a womanly man. The nymphomania results from anxiety over failure to obtain an orgasm, and the ego develops a greater capacity for sublimation favored by the real satisfaction afforded by incest.

Reich (34), commenting on heterosexual incest material presented during an analysis, points out that "... deeply repressed impulses are temporarily used for the purpose of warding off other contents." Marmor, in his discussion of orality in the hysterical personality, notes that much of the manifestly incestuous material of the hysteric may conceal deeper pregenital wishes of an oral character. He also notes that the incestuous dream of the hysteric may reflect not so much the symbolic wish to cohabit with the parent, but rather a deeper pregenital wish to be loved and protected by the mother, to the exclusion of the world. The sexuality of the hysteric is accordingly not a genital wish, but a pregenital oral-receptive one. The hysteric is approached as a woman but wishes to be taken as a child. "These oral fixations give the subsequent Oedipus complex of the hysteric a strongly pregenital cast" (28). It may happen that a woman who is apparently heterosexual uses a man not as an object *per se,* but rather as a weapon in a pre-Oedipal combat with mother. Freud, describing these cases, says "... the hostile attitude to the mother is not a consequence of the rivalry implicit in the Oedipus complex, but rather originates in the preceding phase and has simply found in the Oedipus situation reinforcement and an opportunity for asserting itself." Lillian Gordon (14) describes a case where clear and undisguised acting out of the œdipal situation reflects incestuous activity as an elaboration of a masochistic attachment to the mother during the oral phase. Activity with the father or a father substitute satisfies revenge wishes against the mother for pre-œdipal frustrations. Bergler describes the child as escaping from her mother as the formidable 'giantess of the nursery' to a less dangerous œdipal relationship.

Weich (42) proposes that one of the functions of the terms 'mother' and 'father' relates to a verbal taboo such that these terms function to minimize incestuous conflicts. Referring to parents through the use of such labels rather than by proper names is a way of describing a part of the individual (a function) and avoiding consideration of the total being—his feelings, sexuality, desires, and so on. This verbal institution maintains and supports the incest taboo. Weich notes a transient stage beginning at age two and a half, when children do refer to their parents by first names; however this phase generally does not persist beyond the age of six, being repressed under the influence of œdipal anxiety. The use of parental first names may again appear in early adolescence, this time by a taunting, mischievous adolescent. The parents' anger at such 'disrespect' may reflect their discomfort as the unconscious incestuous conflict is brought nearer to consciousness.

THE FATHERS IN CASES OF FATHER-DAUGHTER INCEST

Weinberg lists three categories of incestuous fathers: the first, an introversive personality leading to an extreme endogamic orientation with a disproportionate investment in the nuclear family; the second, a psychopathic personality characterized by indiscriminate promiscuity; the third, a psychosexually immature father with pedophiliac craving extending to sexual involvement with his own daughter. A period of absence of the father from the home frequently seems to be a precipitating factor, and there is almost always sexual estrangement between the incestuous father and his usual sexual partner. Frequently, the onset of the incestuous liaison is precipitated by a clear-cut rejection on the part of the father's wife; once initiated, the incestuous activity continues for a substantial period of time.

Incestuous fathers typically begin the liaison about the age of forty, commencing with the oldest daughter, and, in some instances, subsequently initiating incest with her younger sisters. These are the years when his marriage becomes increasingly frustrating, when death, separation, and divorce occasionally provide a real basis for desertion anxiety, and when his daughters are most likely to be reaching puberty and becoming sexually attractive.

In general, incestuous fathers have made poor sexual adjustments. Weinberg reports that the wives of these men describe their marital relations as relatively devoid of affection, and state that their husbands appeared to derive an exclusively physical satisfaction from intercourse. For some, a pseudoheterosexuality appears to mask latent homosexual urges. The difficulty these men have in achieving a stable heterosexual orientation may be reflected in a variety of coping mechanisms—sexual withdrawal, hypersexuality, flagrant promiscuity, and virtual abstinence.

Weiner notes that each of five incestuous fathers had a disturbed relationship with a harsh and authoritarian father, whom they ambivalently hated but admired, and ensuring passive homosexual longings promote a process whereby these fathers obtain a fantasied affection from their own fathers through an incestuous liaison with a daughter.

Raphling (30) and his associates note that the adults involved in incest may suffer from some degree of guilt and depression during their incestuous activity, but most often become remorseful and repentant after the incest has been disclosed. The incest taboo is a stringent one and incestuous fathers demonstrate a variety of defense mechanisms to cope with their pervasive sense of guilt. Such rationalization as 'parental duty', a necessity to teach the 'facts of life', and 'pacification' of an angry daughter seem insufficient to cope with the massive guilt ensuing from the violation of the incest taboo. Weiner, however, suggests that the guilt may arise not so much from the incestuous behavior, but from the disgrace and embarrassment rendered to their families.

Incestuous fathers seem to come from backgrounds of social deprivation in the form of parental conflict, marginal economic circumstances, poor education and occupational instability; however, population sample biases may account for some of these preponderances. Weiner, however, considering the criminal disposition of the incestuous father, concludes that the disposition toward incestuous behavior is largely independent of broader criminal tendencies.

There is little consensus as to the severity of emotional disturbance among incestuous fathers; reports vary from the finding of not much psychological abnormality to a heavy preponderance of psychotic disorder. Incest is probably one aspect of family dysfunction, and Cormier *et al.* (6) note the frequency with which public disclosure leads to the disruption of the family. The equilibrium is seldom regained and recidivism in incest cases is unusual.

THE WIVES OF INCESTUOUS FATHERS

The wives of incestuous fathers promote the occurrence of father-daughter incest by frustrating their husbands sexually or by symbolically deserting them, and by promoting a dysfunctional role allocation wherein their daughters are encouraged to assume a sexual role *vis-à-vis* their fathers. Kaufman (19) notes that incest usually has its onset when both father and daughter realize that the mother has abandoned them. The mothers (wives) in general are found to be dependent and infantile, pathologically attached to their own mothers and prone to panic in the face of responsibility, and they appear to push their daughters prematurely into the mothering role, including a sexual relation with the father.

These wives (mothers) uncommonly report the incest. As a rule they tolerate the incestuous activity with little protest, or they exercise such massive denial that the incest continues apparently unbeknown to them. Conceivably such wives identify with their daughters and fulfil in fantasy their childhood incestuous attachments to their own fathers. When these wives report the incestuous liaison it is not so much because they object to the incestuous act, but rather because they are angry over some other matter. As a rule they are too guilty over their own collusion or too fond of their husbands to report the offense.

THE DAUGHTERS IN CASES OF FATHER-DAUGHTER INCEST

As a general rule it is the eldest daughter whom the father selects for his incestuous involvement, proceeding afterward toward activity with her younger sisters.

The daughters apparently collude in most incestuous relations. Bender asserts that these girls play an active and initiating role in establishing the pattern and she adds that the incestuous activity continues until it is discovered, and the girls do not act as though they were injured. Kaufman similarly holds that frightened and lonely girls welcome their father's sexual advances as expressions of love.

Incestuous daughters are apparently unlikely to report the liaison or to protest about it. When they do it is generally because they are angry at their fathers for some other reason or jealous of their father's relation with another woman. Oedipal guilt may play a role in this reluctance to accuse their fathers. When accusation is made it is generally the result of jealousy and a desire for revenge, evoked by a perceived withdrawal of the father's attention. Some girls may avoid guilt feelings through a denial of pleasure and by assuming a consistently passive role in the relationship.

Noting that daughters who regret the incest seek forgiveness from their mothers (though the latter did not condemn them), Sloane *et al.* (38) suggest that the daughters' guilt stems not from violation of the incest taboo but rather from hostile impulses toward the mother. Psychodynamic hypotheses generally suggest a frustrated relationship with the mother, a compensatory penis envy and a subsequent incestuous involvement, reflecting a wish for a penis and revenge against an unloving mother.

Heims *et al.* (16) believe incestuous daughters to be precocious in learning, reality-mastery and motility, but they observed disturbed object relations and impaired feminine identification and adolescent ego development. Such girls tend to develop character disorders rather than neuroses or psychoses, and regression following the interruption of incest leads to learning disabilities, depression and homosexuality.

PSYCHOLOGICAL TESTING OF THE DAUGHTERS

Kaufman and his associates report psychological testing data for the daughters of seven out of eleven cases of father-daughter incest which were studied. The battery includes a Stanford-Binet or Wechsler-Bellevue Intelligence Test, a Rorschach, a Thematic Apperception Test (TAT) and the Goodenough Draw-a-Man Test.

Performance scores are generally higher than verbal. The Rorschach reveals depression, anxiety, confusion over sexual identification, fear of sexuality, oral depravation and oral sadism. Denial, repression and sometimes projection are the chief defense mechanisms revealed by the Rorschach and TAT. In the TAT, mother figures are seen as cruel and depriving and father figures as nurturant, weak and ineffectual or as frightening.

EFFECTS OF INCESTUOUS LIAISONS ON THE PARTICIPANTS

Generally, if the adults involved in incestuous relations harbor little anxiety or guilt concerning the affair the daughter will do likewise. Raphling *et al.* note that this is particularly true if the nonparticipating adult is permissive and allows the incestuous behavior to be expressed in an open and forthright fashion. Bender notes that incestuous daughters are found to be generally free of guilt feelings until they are exposed to censure from parents or authorities. However, their sample is generally preadolescent and, as noted by Cormier, when incest occurs prior to adolescence, anxiety and guilt are not pervasive.

In Sloane's cases the degree of guilt experienced by each of the girls sooner or later causes them to give up the incestuous relationship of their own accord despite the sexual laxity of the segment of the community of which they were a part. In three or four of Sloane's five cases the girls turn to promiscuous sexual relations with other men after giving up the incest. The promiscuity is reckless and compulsive and the acting out appears to take the place of neurotic symptom formation which is minimal.

According to Kaufman, most of the daughters appear surprisingly mature and capable and in some instances do well in school and are skilled and capable of assuming responsibility. However, during therapy this was shown to be a façade. These girls related to older women in a hostile dependent way and were prone to make impossible demands, acting out seriously when their demands were frustrated.

There is little consensus as to the role of incest in promoting pervasive subsequent psychopathology in the daughters. One view is that a parent who uses a child sexually produces conflict between the stimulated adult genital sexuality and the more appropriate social tendency for sublimation of sexuality in school and play, fostering lasting confusion and ambivalence in attitudes toward family relationships. However, Bender notes that the incestuous relations do not always seem to have a traumatic effect. These liaisons satisfy instinctual drives in a setting where mutual alliance with an omnipotent adult condones the transgression, and, further, the act offers an opportunity to test in reality an infantile fantasy whose consequences are found to be gratifying and pleasurable. Rascovsky and Rascovsky even suggest that the ego's capacity for sublimation is favored by the pleasure afforded by incest, and they state that incestuous acts diminish the person's chance of psychosis and allow for a better adjustment to the external world. Bender cites Rassmussen's (32) evidence that there is little deleterious influence on the subsequent personality of the incestuous daughter. Of Rassmussen's fifty-four follow-up cases, forty-six were none the worse from the experience. Many were married and had children and several were commendable pillars of their communities.

Bender (2) states that some of the daughters showed immediate harmful effects in the form of prolongation of the infantile stage, with sacrifice of the stage of latency, and in some instances mental retardation, anxiety states, and in prepubertal girls a premature development of adolescent interests and independence. A preoccupation with fantasies and a withdrawal from childhood activities may lead to the appearance of stupidity or a schizoid personality.

Kaufman, studying eleven girls between the ages of ten and seventeen, notes that following the disclosure of incest they all manifest depression and guilt. Generally, the guilt seems connected to the disruption of the home rather than the act of incest. Some girls are suicidal, others showed mood swings and most have the somatic complaints of a depression—fatigue, loss of appetite, generalized aches and pains, inability to concentrate, and sleep disturbances. Several girls exhibited learning difficulties, several are sexually promiscuous, and many experience somatic symptoms referable to the abdomen and accompanied by fantasies of pregnancy. They display a variety of methods of coping with their symptoms, including a search for punishment, seeking forgiveness from their mother, resorting to delinquency and sexual promiscuity. They appear well-integrated while permitted to act out, but become depressed when confined. Kaufman also notes that the sexuality of these girls has led to the arrest and incarceration of their fathers and to the disruption of their homes. The experience of seeing their destructive omnipotent fantasies realized has a particularly damaging effect upon the ego structure of these girls.

Anthropological literature quotes abundant instances of a disruptive and harmful effect of incest among its participants and of the dread with which it is viewed by 'primitive' cultures. Devereux, for example, reports a Mohave shaman, who commits incest with a married daughter who later felt she had been bewitched and became ill with a fatal mental illness. Her mother and sister subsequently became psychotic and died.

The divergent findings as to the harmfulness of incestuous activity may be age-related. Sloane *et al.* feel that the potential for psychological damage is greater with an older daughter and less when the girl is preadolescent. He also contends that the difference relates directly to the increased strength of inhibiting forces in the postpubertal years, so that while younger children react to incest no differently than to other forms of sexual activity, adolescents consider it to be socially reprehensible. When the incestuous liaison occurs in childhood the recollection is usually repressed, perhaps to reappear in later life in the form of neurotic conflicts.

TREATMENT

The prevention and treatment of incest are complicated by the multidetermined etiology of the condition, by the difficulty in ascertaining what weight to assign to each of the various etiologic factors and by the resistance of many of these factors to therapeutic change.

In Messer's review, some specific preventive measures are mentioned. Legal adoption of step-children may strengthen the step-parent's role in a family and thus strengthen the incest taboo. Also step-parent and step-child relations are generally strengthened when the new family relinquishes financial support of the child provided by an absent father.

The use of names is of importance—Weich notes that the terms 'mother' and 'father' serve to buttress the incest taboo, and children should be discouraged from referring to their parents by first names.

In any marriage, the couple need to reinvigorate their relationship periodically by reasserting 'exclusive possession' away from their children. Messer encourages 'second honeymoons' to help strengthen the marital bond, and he feels that this may diminish any need for either partner to seek 'romantic gratification' from a child.

In reconstituted families, open discussion of the fact that remarriage involves no disloyalty to the deceased or departed spouse helps foster a healthy family relationship. Parents who are openly affectionate with one another give a child a firm model on which to develop a healthy heterosexual role identification.

Perhaps there is a greater need to recognize the normalcy of family romance, even to the point of 'institutionalizing' the phenomena to render it a greater part of each family's awareness. It is not abnormal to see or fantasize a child or parent in a potential sexual role, a fact which is frequently recognized in smiles or gestures, or as a reaction formation by avoidance. A healthy awareness of this phenomenon is to be encouraged.

Bender mentions the following approaches to treatment: open discussion of sex; substitution of alternative modes of expression in play and social interaction and healthy affection from other adults in the environment. In certain cases, prolonged institutionalization appears to be a necessary part of the treatment approach.

Cormier maintains that incest is an extreme symptom of family maladjustment and that family therapy is the appropriate therapeutic modality.

Machotka, reviewing the dynamics of incest, advocates therapy focusing on the pervasive use of denial as a defense mechanism, stressing not only the denial of the incestuous liaison but also of the pervasive dysfunctional relationships within the family and the disordered role allocations. Each family member could be helped to recognize his own participation in the act, leading to a more healthy role allocation within the family.

SUMMARY

The incest taboo is a moral imperative; its force reflects a cross-cultural preoccupation with the incest theme. The importance of this subject in psychiatric theory and practice justifies a concerted effort to synthesize the available data into a coherent overview, drawing on the findings of a variety of relevant disciplines.

Epidemiologists have shown that almost all civilizations recognize incest, but that it is universally uncommon. The influence of sociocultural and socioeconomic variables upon the occurrence of incest is disputed, partly because of the contamination of data due to unfortunate study designs. A glance at the classical literature shows that incest is an ever-recurring theme of mythologies of many civilizations. Anthropologists have pointed out cross-cultural variations in the nature of the incest taboo but have generally substantiated its universal presence in some form.

The incest theme is an appealing area for theorists. The incest taboo is multidetermined. Freud spoke of the need to prevent the destruction of society by a band of brothers who would murder the tyrannical father, then mutilate the social order through a chain of 'fraternal' wars. However, a variety of biological, psychological and social theories have been carefully and thoughtfully articulated to explain the incest taboo and man's pervasive preoccupation with this theme.

The occurrence of overt incest is usually in the setting of a dysfunctional family and is accompanied by drastic role shifts so far-reaching as to constitute a virtual re-programming of the familial unit. Sociocultural, socioeconomic, and purely psychiatric factors may play a further part in the breakdown of the incest barrier in these situations. The psychodynamics of incest can best be conceptualized within the framework of a three-generational schema, with desertion anxiety being a recurrent theme. For example, in father daughter incest the mother deals with desertion anxiety stemming from the maternal grandmother by casting an older daughter in the role of homemaker and sexual partner to her husband. Overt incest is but the top of the proverbial 'ice-berg'. Incestuous behavior appears deeply rooted in the pre-œdipal period.

Incestuous fathers have usually been rejected recently by their usual sexual partners, and they deal with the guilt arising from incestuous behavior with flagrant and sometimes naive rationalizations. Their backgrounds are usually marginal. The wives of incestuous men collude with the incestuous liaison by rejecting their husbands sexually and by subtly encouraging their daughters to become the 'woman of the home'. Incestuous daughters are generally felt to encourage their fathers' sexual advances or at least to refrain from resisting them. Incestuous behavior in daughters is at least in part a function of hostile impulses toward the mother and a penis envy hypertrophied by the wish for revenge against the pre-œdipal mother.

In father-daughter incest, youth in the daughter and a relative absence of anxiety and guilt in the incestuous father or colluding mother are factors leading to a favorable prognosis, and the converse is also true.

Prevention of overt incest rests on measures to enhance the definitions of the social role and generational boundaries within the family and upon devices which serve to buttress the incest taboo. Insight psychotherapy may play a part in the treatment of discovered cases and family therapy with the aim of promoting a healthier role allocation in the dysfunctional family has proven helpful.

REFERENCES

1. Barry, Maurice J., and Johnson, Adelaide M. The incest barrier. *Psychoanal. Quart.* 27, p. 485, 1958.
2. Bender, Lauretta, and Blau, Abram. The reaction of children to sexual relations with adults. *Amer. J. Orthopsychiat.* 7, p. 500, 1937.
3. Bergler, E. *The Basic Neurosis.* New York: Grune and Stratton, 1949.
4. Berne, E. *Transactional Analysis in Psychotherapy.* New York: Evergreen Press, 1961.
5. Cavallin, Hector. Incestuous fathers: A clinical report. *Amer. J. Psychiat.* 122, No. 10, p. 1132, 1966.
6. Cormier, Bruno M., Kennedy, Miriam, and Sangowicz, Jadwiga. Psychodynamics of father-daughter incest. *Canad. Psychiat. Ass. J.* 7, No. 5, p. 203, 1962.
7. Devereux, George. The social and cultural implications of incest among the Mohave Indians. *Psychoanal. Quart.* 8, p. 510, 1939.
8. Dubreuil, Guy. Les bases psycho-culturel-les du tabou de l'inceste. *Canad. Psychiat. Ass. J.* 7, No. 5, p. 218, 1962.
9. *Encyclopaedia Britannica; v. 8 and v. 16,* William Benton, University of Chicago, 1962.
10. Flugel, J. C. *The Psychoanalytic Study of the Family.* London: L. and V. Woolf, 1926.
11. Fox, J. R. Sibling incest. *Brit. J. Sociol.* 13, p. 128, 1962.
12. Freud, Sigmund. "Female Sexuality" (1931); in Strachey, J. (ed.), *Standard Edition of the Complete Psychological Works of Sigmund Freud, v. 5,* London: The Hogarth Press, 1955.
13. Freud, Sigmund. Totem and Taboo (1912–13); in Strachey, J. (ed.), *Standard Edition of the Complete Psychological Works of Sigmund Freud, v. 13.* London: The Hogarth Press, 1955.
14. Gordon, Lillian. Incest as revenge against the pre-œdipal mother. *Psychoanal. Rev.* 42, p. 284, 1955.
15. Guttmacher, M. S. *Sex Offences.* New York: W. W. Norton and Co., 1951.
16. Heims, Lora W., and Kaufman, I. Variations on a theme of incest. *Amer. J. Orthopsychiat.* 33, p. 311, 1963.
17. Kardiner, Abram. *The Individual and His Society. The Psychodynamics of Primitive Social Organizations.* New York: Columbia University Press, 1939.
18. Karpman, B. *The Sexual Offender and His Offences.* New York: Julian Press, 1954.
19. Kaufman, Irving, Peck, Alice L., and Tagiuri, Consuelo, K. The family constellation and overt incestuous relations between father and daughter. *Amer. J. Orthopsychiat.* 24, p. 266, 1954.
20. Lidz, T., Cornelison, A. R., Fleck, S., and Terry, D. The intrafamilial environment of schizophrenic patients—marital schism and skew. *Amer. J. Orthopsychiat.* 114, p. 241, 1957.
21. Lindzey, Gardner. Some remarks concerning incest, the incest taboo, and psychoanalytic theory. *Amer. J. Psychol.* 22, p. 1051, 1967.
22. Lustig, Noel, Dresser, John W., Spellman, Seth W., and Murray, Thomas B. Incest: a family group survival pattern. *Arch. Gen. Psychiat.* 14, p. 31, 1966.
23. Lutier, J. Rôle des facteurs culturels et psycho-sociaux dans les délits incestueux en milieu rural. *Ann. Med. Leg.* 41, p. 80, 1961.

24. Machotka, Pavel, Pittman, Frank S., and Flomenhaft, Kalman. Incest as a family affair. *Family Process* 6, p. 98.
25. Magal, V., and Winnik, H. Z. Role of incest in family structure. *Israel Ann. Psychiat.* 5, No. 2, p. 173, 1968.
26. Malinowski, B. *Sex and Repression in Savage Society.* London: Routledge, Kegan Paul, 1927.
27. Malinowski, B. *The Sexual Life of Savages in Northwestern Melanesia.* London: George Routledge and Sons, 1929.
28. Marmor, Judd. Orality in the hysterical personality. *J. Amer. Psychoanal. Ass.* 1, p. 656, 1955.
29. Messer, Alfred, A. The 'Phaedra complex'. *Arch. Gen. Psychiat.* 21, p. 213, 1969.
30. Raphling, David L., Carpenter, Bob L., and Davis, Allan. Incest: A genealogical study. *Arch. Gen. Psychiat.* 16, p. 505, 1967.
31. Rascovsky, Matilde W., and Rascovsky, A. On consummated incest. *Int. J. Psychoanal.* 31, p. 42, 1950.
32. Rasmussen, A. Die Bedeutung Sexueller Attentate Auf Kinder Unter 14 Jahren Fur die Entwicklung von Geisteskrankheiten und Charakteranomalien. *Acta Psychiat. et Neurol.* 9, p. 351, 1934.
33. Raybin, James B. Homosexual incest. *J. Nerv. Ment. Dis.* 148, No. 2, p. 105, 1969.
34. Reich, Wilhelm. *Character Analysis.* New York: Orgone Institute Press, 1949.
35. Rhinehart, John W. Genesis of overt incest. *Compr. Psychiat.* 2, p. 338, 1961.
36. Riemer, S. Research notes on incest. *Amer. J. Sociol.* 7, p. 566, 1940.
37. Slater, M. Ecological factors in the origin of incest. *Amer. Anthropol.* 61, p. 1042, 1959.
38. Sloane, Paul, and Karpinski, Eva. Effect of incest on the participants. *Amer. J. Orthopsychiat.* 12, p. 666, 1942.
39. Sonden, T. Die Inzestverbrechen in Schweden und Ihre Ursachen. *Acta Psychiat. et Neurol.* 11, p. 379, 1936.
40. Szabo, Denis. Problèmes de socialisation et d'intégration socio-culturelles: contribution à l'étiologie de l'inceste. *Canad. Psychiat. Ass. J.* 7, No. 5, p. 235, 1962.
41. Talcott-Parsons, T. The incest taboo in relation to social structure and the socialization of the child. *Brit. J. Sociol.* 5, p. 101, 1954.
42. Weich, Martin J. The terms 'Mother' and 'Father' as a defence against incest. *J. Amer. Psychoanal. Ass.* 16, No. 4, p. 783, 1968.
43. Weinberg, S. K. *Incest Behaviour.* New York: Citadel Press, 1955.
44. Weiner, Irving B. Father-daughter incest: a clinical report. *Psychiat. Quart.* 36, p. 607, 1962.
45. Weiner, Irving B. On incest: a survey. *Excerpta Criminologica* 4, p. 137, 1964.
46. Wolf, A. P. Adopt a daughter-in-law, marry a sister: a Chinese solution to the problem of the incest taboo. *Amer. Anthropologist* 70, p. 864, 1968.

CHAPTER 39

The Family Constellation and Overt Incestuous Relations between Father and Daughter

Irving Kaufman, Alice L. Peck, and Consuelo K. Tagiuri

We are presenting a preliminary report of our study of family relations and character formation in cases where girls have been involved in incestuous relationships with either father, stepfather, grandfather, foster father or brother.[1] We plan a continued investigation and a more detailed report in the future.

Eleven girls, ranging in age from ten to seventeen, were referred to the Judge Baker Guidance Center for treatment. A protective agency referred seven patients and the court referred two. A family agency and a psychiatric clinic each referred one.

The age at which incest began ranged from six to fourteen years. The sexual relationship was a prolonged one, lasting a year or more in most cases, and in one instance as long as six years. Despite the long duration of the incestuous relationship, in only two cases did the mother report it to the authorities. The remainder of the cases came to the attention of the authorities through some external event, such as a neighbor's reporting neglect of children.

The period of contact with these cases ranged from five interviews to two years of continuous treatment.

Table 1 shows the statistics relative to the study, including the age at referral and the source, specific "fathers" involved, presenting symptoms, and psychological test results.

Only five of the eleven girls had sexual relations with their own fathers. There was a question as to two other girls.

We cannot detect from our material any apparent difference in the psychopathology of the participants regardless of whether the girl had relations with her father or with a father substitute.

Depression and guilt were universal as clinical findings in these girls. Other findings were as follows: learning difficulties in three girls, bossiness in two,

Reprinted with permission from the *American Journal of Orthopsychiatry* 24 (1954):266-79.
[1]Hereafter when we refer to the male figure involved we will call him "father."

sexual promiscuity in one, running away in one, and somatic complaints in four. Loss of appetite and abdominal distress were the most frequent somatic complaints. These abdominal symptoms appeared to be related to pregnancy fantasies in some of the girls.

Although learning difficulty was a presenting symptom in three cases, and one of these girls had had difficulties with schoolwork prior to the detection of the incest, it became apparent during the course of treatment that following its detection all but one experienced specific or general learning disabilities. Learning became so painful in two cases that the girls left school.

Although only one girl was referred for promiscuity, it became apparent during treatment that at least two others were promiscuous. Stealing, present in three cases, never reached major proportions or caused legal action.

Because of length of contact or special disposition of the case it was possible to test only 7 of the 11 girls. They were given a battery of psychological tests including either the Stanford-Binet (Form L) or the Wechsler-Bellevue (Form I) intelligence tests, the Rorschach, the Thematic Apperception Test and the Goodenough Draw-a-Man test. One girl was also given vocational guidance tests, and another girl had a group intelligence test at school.

It was the examiner's opinion that all the girls tended to perform below their ability. Performance scores were in general higher than verbal scores. The difference in one case between verbal and performance scores was 31 points; in another 16.

The main trends which showed up in the Rorschach were depression, anxiety, confusion over sexual identification, fear of sexuality, oral deprivation and oral sadism. The chief mechanisms of defense were denial, repression, and sometimes projection. These findings were substantiated by the TAT. The girls uniformly saw the mother figures in the latter test as cruel, unjust and depriving. Father figures were sometimes described as nurturant, sometimes as weak and ineffectual, sometimes as frightening. The Draw-a-Man test further demonstrated the confused sexual identifications of these girls.

When we studied the parents, we found similar factors present in the background of both the mothers and the fathers.

Although most of our information came from the mothers,[2] we learned that all of the "fathers" came from backgrounds characterized by poverty, alcoholism, little education, inadequate housing, and little warmth or understanding from the paternal grandparents. Cases where we had more information about these men showed that they left home and school at an early age, as did the mothers of this study, to find work and to escape from their unpleasant environments.

The occupational history of these men indicated general irresponsibility. Some had been continually unemployed.

---

[2]We had no contact with the "fathers" for the following reasons: The older brothers and foster fathers involved were out of the state. The paternal grandfather was dead. Five of the remaining men had been imprisoned by the time the cases were referred. The rest were unavailable for a variety of reasons, such as residence in another state or disappearance from home with whereabouts unknown.

Table 1. Summary of cases of consummated incest between daughter and father or father substitute

Case no.	Age at referral	Referral source	Age incest began	Duration of incest	Incestuous relations with	Presenting symptoms	Intelligence test results
1	16	Protective agency	11 or 12	4 yrs.	Stepfather Paternal grandfather (in latency)	Depression Feeding and sleeping disturbance	Superior
2	10	Psychiatric clinic	6	4 yrs.	Father	Learning difficulty Maladjustment	Borderline
3	14	Juvenile court	?12	?1 yr.	?Stepfather	Depression Running away	Superior
4	11	Protective agency	10	1 yr.	Father	Depression Psychotic-like rages Somatic complaints	Average
5	13	Protective agency	?13	?	?Father	Eating disturbance	Dull normal
6	15	Protective agency	14	1 yr.	Stepfather	Depression Somatic complaints	Not tested
7	17	Protective agency	11	6 yrs.	Father	Pregnancy	Not tested
8	10	Family agency	9	1 yr.	Father	Anxiety Hyperactivity Poor schoolwork	Dull normal (group test)
9	15	Juvenile court	12	3 yrs.	Father	Promiscuity	Bright normal
10	14	Protective agency	13	1 yr.	?Father Brother Foster father	Poor schoolwork Immaturity	Not tested
11	14	Protective agency	14	3 mos.	Brother Foster father ?Stepfather	Withdrawn behavior	Superior

444

All the fathers and stepfathers deserted their children at some time. This came about either as a result of divorce, living away from home, or just being away most of the time because of extreme alcoholism. At least eight of the men, and probably more, were alcoholic.

Just as the fathers and stepfathers deserted their families, so had the maternal grandfathers deserted their families, and so too did the mothers of the children included in this study in some way desert their husbands, leaving the daughters to assume the mother role. For example, one of the mothers in our study went upstairs to the maternal grandmother every night and left the children with the father and oldest daughter.

Generally, then, we see desertion and the reactions to this as being the prime common source of anxiety motivating all the individuals involved in the incest situation. When we studied the psychodynamics of the mothers, we were struck not only by the fact of desertion on the part of the maternal grandfathers, but by the striking similarity in the personality structure of the maternal grandmothers. They were stern, demanding, controlling, cold and extremely hostile women, who rejected their daughters and pampered their sons. They reacted to the desertion of their husbands by singling out one daughter whom they would describe as being like the maternal grandfather, and on whom they would displace their feelings of hostility and hurt at having been deserted by the maternal grandfather. These maternal grandmothers began the process of selecting one daughter to be the recipient of their resentments against the deserting maternal grandfather very early by continually pointing out how much of a tomboy the chosen daughter was, to the point where she would be denied pretty clothes and many of the normal feminine activities and interests.

The maternal grandmothers were generally employed as domestics, waitresses, etc., always in basically menial types of occupation. They were hard workers and masculine in character. As a rule they assumed most of the responsibility for the support of their families and gave their children good physical care but little real warmth and understanding.

The mothers of this study like the fathers and stepfathers left home and school at an early age to marry or seek employment. When first seen for interviews, they were described as hard, careless in dress and personal appearance, infantile, extremely dependent, and intellectually dull. Most of them were poor housekeepers, panicky in the face of responsibility, and seemed on the surface to be satisfied to live in disorder and poverty. However, on closer study they emerged as brighter than average with a potential of achievement far beyond their actual performance. They married men who were also dependent and infantile. If they married a second time, the second partner was even more irresponsible and unsuccessful than the first. This was a repetition of the pattern set by the maternal grandmothers.

These mothers had described their unhappy marital experiences as "throwing myself away," a pattern wherein they acted out what they felt was expected of them by the maternal grandmothers, who had rejected, destroyed, and thrown them away.

The maternal grandmothers acted as though these mothers were no good. The mothers' reaction to this attitude was on the one hand to act and feel as though they were worthless, and on the other hand to hope to receive some denial of this poor opinion of themselves. This pathologic interaction was one of the reasons it was difficult to work with these mothers. They were tied to the maternal grandmothers—literally and psychologically unable to move away from them. Despite the misery and futility of their relationship, these mothers kept trying to return to the maternal grandmothers in constant hope they would receive the love and encouragement they never felt. These attempts to win the maternal grandmother's approval always failed. For example, whenever they achieved any success, they were immediately deflated by the maternal grandmothers who were unable to tolerate any signs of progress or independence in them.

These mothers went to any lengths to satisfy their need for affection, attention and support and to deny their feelings of worthlessness. Because of their personality orientation they chose masochistic methods in their attempts to fulfill their needs. At least half of them attempted to satisfy these needs by promiscuity. Others neglected their health, hoping that someone would care enough to stop them. Some deliberately got into situations where they could have been injured physically.

The whole insidious process continued in the relationship between the mothers of this study and their daughters. The mothers singled out one daughter whom they treated in a special fashion. This daughter was given excellent physical care, was often overindulged materially, was encouraged to assume responsibility beyond her years, and gradually developed into a replica of the maternal grandmother. These mothers then displaced onto this chosen daughter all the hostility really felt for the maternal grandmother. They forced this daughter to become their confidante, helper with the other children, and adviser. They relinquished their responsibilities as parents so that they, in effect, became daughters again, and the daughter a mother. However, they became angry when the daughter became too directive, independent and hostile. It seemed that the mothers acted out in this way because they had not resolved their anxiety over their oedipal conflict. This resulted from the trauma of having been deserted by the maternal grandfathers. They dealt with this anxiety in other ways too, as we have mentioned, by choosing men who would desert them, and by deserting their husbands sexually. The mothers perpetuated their own experiences in these ways and finally created situations where they deserted the fathers, who then became involved in the incestuous relationship with the daughters. The mothers used the mechanism of denial to blind themselves to the incest, and when confronted with the evidence, they were more hostile toward the daughters than the husbands. This seemed to be because they projected onto the daughters the bad part of themselves which wanted to act out the oedipal relationship.

We have found too that the mothers not only displaced the hostility felt toward maternal grandmothers onto the daughters, but also onto numerous older women with whom they invariably became involved. They tended to become very dependent upon these women to the point where they began to feel smothered and threatened. Then their hostility and consequent anxiety reached a panic state. On one level, this seemed to represent a homosexual panic; fundamentally, it appeared to be a manifestation of their extreme hostile dependence.

All the family members appeared to be searching for a mother figure. Their frustration tolerance to the anxiety of desertion was minimal and something in the unconscious of the family members and their effect on each other caused them to handle their anxiety primarily by acting out.

Other cases known to us showed only one marriage partner with the personality structure we described as a prerequisite for the acting out of the incest, while the other partner showed some different personality structure. With this different family constellation, the father and daughter did not act out the incest but dealt with the oedipal conflict in some other way.

One of the typical cases in our study was June Smith. She was 11 years, 2 months old at the time of her referral. The family group consisted of the mother, 38; the father, 42; a brother, 17; the patient; a brother, 8; a sister, 7; and baby sister, 4. There had been a stillborn child between the older brother and the patient.

They lived in a two-family house in a working class neighborhood. The house was owned by the maternal grandmother who lived upstairs. They had moved there three years before referral to the clinic. Trouble between Mr. and Mrs. Smith began when they moved to this house. When they quarreled Mrs. Smith went upstairs to sleep with the maternal grandmother, leaving the children with Mr. Smith who often was drunk at these times. When Mrs. Smith deserted in this fashion, Mr. Smith began to have relations with June.

Two weeks before their incestuous relationship was discovered Mr. Smith found June talking to some boys on a street corner. He became angry and dragged the patient home to her mother. The patient then became angry at her father and told her mother that her father had had sexual relations with her. Mrs. Smith used this evidence to obtain a divorce. Mr. Smith readily admitted the charge and was sent to prison for five years.

June was sent to camp the following summer and did well for the first three weeks. Then she had a severe attack of abdominal pain simulating appendicitis. This was diagnosed as hysteria.

When June returned home in the fall there were frequent quarrels with her mother which often culminated in physical battles; the two fought like children. June ran away several times but never went more than a few blocks from home. The tension and conflict became so difficult by November that June was moved to a protective group placement. Arrangements were made at this time for her to come to the Judge Baker Guidance Center for treatment.

Throughout the clinic contact (eight interviews), Mrs. Smith, a nice-looking woman, very plainly dressed, never showed evidence of any attempt to look attractive. Her appearance and attitude were martyrlike. She was stiff and expressionless at first. She was more than willing to leave everything concerning June in the hands of others. She said June needed more attention but that this should come from others. She had no idea of anything she could do about it.

June had always seemed older than her years to Mrs. Smith. She said that June seemed more like her mother than her daughter. Although she felt that June's ideas were those of an older girl, she couldn't describe what she meant. She added briefly that June menstruated at eleven. Mrs. Smith commented that June could be very good when she wanted, taking over much of the care and responsibility of the home and children. Mrs. Smith said that she could only love little children and she hated to see them grow up.

Mrs. Smith's handling of June at home vacillated. At times she severely restricted the girl, locking her in her room and once even tying her hands and feet with a belt. At other times she gave her complete freedom, which she described as putting her on her own.

Mrs. Smith expressed the fear and the hope that June would run away. This preceded a runaway episode. Mrs. Smith had earlier expressed a similar wish about Mr. Smith. She wanted him out of the home, since this would leave her free with the maternal grandmother and the younger children whom she could love; the older boy was going into the service very shortly.

Mrs. Smith never mentioned her own father. She described the maternal grandmother as a strict woman who lacked understanding. She said she was never allowed and never dared to "run around." The maternal grandmother nagged mother and blamed her for June's behavior. Mrs. Smith, however, was aware of her great dependence on the maternal grandmother.

Mrs. Smith did not give much information concerning her attitude toward Mr. Smith. She expressed fears of his hostility toward the older boy and was concerned that he would kill this son. However, Mrs. Smith indicated that before moving to the maternal grandmother's home, she was very dependent on Mr. Smith. This attitude changed on Mrs. Smith's part when she turned her dependency back to the maternal grandmother.

The developmental history revealed nothing unusual. Mrs. Smith stated that the pregnancy was normal and full term. There were no problems associated with the birth or the puerperium. The child was bottle-fed, but there was no feeding problem at any time. She walked and talked at the average age.

The girl's psychological tests revealed an IQ of 100—not considered optimum. The projective tests demonstrated a severe depression lying close to the surface. The patient was busy constantly in an effort to blot out traumatic memories. This spread into a general fear of retention of any type of knowledge. There was tremendous expenditure of energy involved in warding off thoughts which threatened to destroy her ego identity. There was guilt over the consequences of her incestuous relationship and feelings of worthlessness, of being irreparably damaged, and of depression over the inevitable abandonment by her parents.

June had never been a school problem. Her grades were above average, especially in arithmetic. The teachers described her as a very likeable, conscientious child who might well have come from a superior home. She was well liked by her classmates and often chosen by them as a leader.

June, a very tall, attractive eleven-year-old, looked more like thirteen or fourteen. She was slender and secondary sex characteristics were precociously developed. She spoke freely and seemed to want to be friendly and make a good impression.

June described her life as a happy one until her parents moved in with the maternal grandmother. She said that the maternal grandmother tried to come between her mother and father. Mrs. Smith never had her own opinions; she always consulted the maternal grandmother. June often told her mother that she wasn't grown-up. June had to take care of the little ones and made her father's lunch. All the trouble was her mother's fault. If her mother hadn't quarreled with her father and gone upstairs to sleep with the maternal grandmother, there would not have been any trouble. Her father drank sometimes and it was when he was drinking that he made sexual advances to June.

She said that she had wanted to do what was best for her father, but she was very sorry now that she had told anyone about it. She didn't know that he would be put in prison for five years. Everyone told her nothing would happen to him; even the judge had lied to her. She was always her father's favorite and felt she could talk to him and never to her mother. She hated her eight-year-old sister, but loved the baby girl. She wanted to live with her father and the baby because this baby seemed like her own child.

She added that she wanted to be everything to her father because he had no one. Her mother was getting help and so was she, but nobody was doing anything to help her father. She felt terrible over putting him in prison. Everyone was against her because no one allowed her to see him. They didn't even give her the letters he wrote to her. Sometimes she became so angry that her stomach felt as if it was burning up. She was tired all the time and had no appetite.

During June's stay at the protective group placement she showed wide extremes of mood and behavior. She was hyperactive at times, and she assumed much responsibility, especially in the care of younger children. The workers there commented that at such times it was difficult for them to remember that June was only eleven, and that they often gave her responsibilities they would ordinarily give a fourteen- or fifteen-year-old. They were greatly puzzled and dismayed when she suddenly became a demanding, whining small child, sometimes seeming almost out of contact, curling up in a ball and crying, "I want my mummy," in a three-year-old's tone of voice. Such periods of infantile regression alternated with or culminated in severe rage reactions, during which June screamed and threw herself around, stiffened up rigidly, and hit out at anyone who came near her. As she gradually became worse, the director of the group placement asked for her removal and she was sent home to her mother until further plans could be made.

Her schoolwork during the above period deteriorated rapidly as well as her social adjustment with other children. She complained of their treatment of her, saying that they called her names and swore at her. She felt that wherever she was she spoiled things. She said that if she was not around, others had a good time. She said that when she was alone she thought that all the terrible things that happened were her fault.

June's behavior showed no essential change at home and she was placed in another group placement. Shortly afterward she ran away from there and was picked up by the police after having spent the night with several sailors who believed she was eighteen. She was sent to the training school for girls. When she was seen just before this episode, she continued to express the feeling that she was damaged, worthless, bad, and needed to be put in jail like her father. She begged to be allowed to see her father in prison and hated everyone for putting him there.

June represented a typical case which demonstrated many of the features characteristic of all these patients. When we reviewed all of the cases, certain facts stood out which we will present along with our conclusions and impressions.

The girls in this study were referred to the Judge Baker Guidance Center after the relationship with the father or stepfather had been detected and legal action had been taken. There was a disruption of the home and five of these girls were actually out of the home.

All of these girls were depressed and guilty. Their verbalized guilt, as far as our clinical material demonstrated, was in connection with the disruption of the home and not over the incest itself. The depression showed itself in many forms. Some of the girls verbalized their grief even to the extent of suicide threats; others demonstrated mood swings. Almost all had the somatic complaints characteristic of a depression. These included fatigue, loss of appetite, generalized aches and pains, inability to concentrate and sleep disturbances. Their physical symptoms were often of such severity as to cause considerable concern for their health.

The patients demonstrated various methods of dealing with their anxiety, guilt, and depression. Searching for punishment was one method. Some of the girls achieved this through somatic media such as submitting to painful medical procedures. Others verbalized this need; and others, by their provocative behavior, drew down upon themselves various forms of punishment. For example, June repeatedly said she wished she were imprisoned like her father and finally accomplished this through her delinquent behavior.

Another method of dealing with this anxiety was to seek forgiveness from the mother or mother figure. Some girls expressed this need by extensive gift giving to the mother. Others searched for forgiveness by turning to religion.

Some of these girls became delinquent. This was another method of coping with their anxiety. The purpose of the sexual promiscuity seemed to be to relive the experiences with the father and, hence, through the mechanism of the repetition compulsion, to work through their anxiety and at the same time achieve a restitution of the lost parent.

Although these girls during such a period of acting out seemed well integrated (almost expressing a hypomanic denial), they became depressed when they were confined and unable to act out. Their delinquency included several special problems. Since the sexuality of these girls led to the arrest and incarceration of the father and a disruption of the home, they had the experience of seeing their destructive omnipotent fantasies come true. This had a particularly damaging effect on their ego structure, which was intensified when further sexual activity led to the arrest of other men.

The resulting defect in the reality-testing function of the ego was overdetermined. Another factor was their disturbed object relationship. We see that these girls tended to act out rather than repress. This could be traced directly to their experiences with parents who did not help them to cope more adequately with their instinctual impulses.

Most of these girls at first appeared surprisingly mature and capable. Although many of them did well in school and were quite skilled and able in taking responsibility, it became clear during therapy that this was a façade.

Although these girls felt abandoned by both parents, they verbalized most of their hostility against the mother. They often idealized the father or father substitute and absolved him of guilt.

Incest usually began when the father and daughter felt the mother had abandoned them, either by giving birth to a new sibling, turning to the maternal grandmother, or developing some new interest outside the home. These girls in their loneliness and fear accepted the father's sexual advances as an expression of affection.

When the incest was associated with the birth of a new sibling, the girls often fantasied the child as theirs and father's. They then often expressed the wish to set up a new home with father and child and to push the mother out. They felt free to return the father's affection sexually because the mother had unconsciously given them permission. The mother did this not only by being absent, but more actively by setting up a situation where this could occur. An example of this was one mother who felt very guilty over the incest, but when asked to discuss the circumstances said she could not tolerate her husband's snoring and went to sleep in another room. Then out of concern that he would be lonely she put the daughter in her place in bed with the husband. As a result of this parental acting out, these girls felt guilty not for the incest itself, which seemed to be condoned by both parents, but for the disruption of the home.

These girls had long felt abandoned by the mother as a protective adult. This was their basic anxiety. One way they dealt with this anxiety was to search for a mother figure who would care for and protect them. Their reality sense was sufficiently disturbed for them to continue to pursue this search in spite of repeated disappointments. However, reality-testing was sufficiently adequate for the patients to realize their dissatisfaction and frustration in not achieving their wishes. Because of their painful experiences with their real mothers, they were never sure of gratification from any new mother figure. New relationships then held both the promise of fulfillment and the familiar fear of disappointment. Thus, as new relationships were formed in an effort to satisfy the need for a mother and to work through this anxiety, various complications ensued.

When many of these patients were placed in foster homes, the resultant dependent position caused them to regress and reveal their hostile demanding orality in the most primitive form. The regression which occurred in many of these girls approached psychotic states, such as prolonged confusional and stuporous periods or rage reactions.

These girls related to older women in a hostile dependent way and repeatedly made impossible demands, and if these could not be met they became furious. Because of the sexualization of their object relationships to both men and women, the search for the mother often appeared in a homosexual form. Also, the trauma associated with the heterosexual experience with the father caused future heterosexual experiences to be a source of anxiety and so further motivated the turn to homosexuality.

These girls had difficulty working out their feelings toward both male and female figures since they had experienced hostility from mother and the pathologic relationship with father caused the breaking up of the home. This pathology then in their identification figures and the conflicting ambiguous roles they assumed led to further complications in resolving their bisexual wishes. When some of these girls talked of their desire to be male, they expressed the wish and the fear both verbally and by various symptoms. For example, one adolescent who wet her bed tied this in with her fantasy that wetting represented male sexual activity.

The reactions to sexuality in these girls took various pregenital forms and ranged from promiscuity to asceticism and included homosexuality. Although the original sexual experience with the father was at a genital level, the meaning of the sexual act was pregenital and seemed to have the purpose of receiving some sort of parental interest.

The underlying craving for an adequate parent, then, dominated the lives of these girls.

SUMMARY

Incest occurred in families of a similar psychopathology which was peculiarly conducive to the acting out of this oedipal wish. The personality structure of the mother or of the father considered independently would not be sufficient to produce the acting out. The girls reacted to their mothers' unconscious desire to put them in the maternal role. They at the same time received gratification from the fathers as the parents who loved them in this pathologic way. However, they received no help in reality testing and super-ego development from either parent.

These girls showed a pseudo maturity, but this façade crumbled when they were placed in a dependent position and some experienced psychotic-like states.

When the incest was detected, these girls showed extreme guilt and anxiety over the disruption of the home, although they did not seem guilty over the incest which both parents condoned.

Some of these girls were extremely masochistic, searching for punishment in many ways. Some attempted to win their mothers' forgiveness. Others, by a repetition compulsion, attempted through promiscuity to bring back the lost father. They all tried by these and other ways to work through their depression, guilt, and anxiety.

DISCUSSION

ELEANOR PAVENSTEDT, M.D.:* I should like first of all to express my gratitude to the authors for this stimulating paper and to congratulate them on their courage in breaking through the incest barrier—a subject that has received relatively little attention in the literature on delinquency.

Most of us have trained ourselves to skepticism toward the claims of young girls who maintain that they have been seduced by their fathers, since we recognize the strength and reality value such fantasies can assume particularly in adolescence. The authors unfortunately say little about the evidence on which they base their impression that incest actually occurred. The fact that only five of the eleven girls had relations with their own fathers needs emphasis, for relations with grandfathers, stepfathers, foster fathers, and brothers do not have the same rigid taboo. We do not hereby imply disagreement with the authors, who are, we feel, justified in assuming that the psychological conditions are the same whether the incest occurs with fathers or father surrogates. We must ask ourselves whether our tendency to disbelief is not in part at least based on denial. The incest barrier is perhaps the strongest support of our cultural family structure, and we may well shrink from the thought of its being threatened.

In the cases just presented—unfortunately in a very condensed form owing to lack of time—the usual family structure of our society had disintegrated. The immaturity of the fathers and mothers alike was described: The fathers were anything but patriarchs and the mothers failed to guard their position with the fathers. In many unstable, immature families who barely maintain themselves in slum areas we see oedipal fantasies overtly displayed, with mothers and daughters involved in vituperative quarrels for the attention of the father. Here, however, the mothers do not maintain even this infantile rivalry with their daughters but actually manipulate their daughters into changing places with them. Neither parent upholds the incest barrier and the responsibility for the relationship is shifted by the incestuous pair onto the mother. Under these circumstances the relationship can continue for many months—and even years—without any marked psychological disequilibrium manifested by overt symptoms. We are again in full agreement with the authors that behind a façade of adequacy these girls hide an immature deprived personality.

A close scrutiny of the factors which lead to the discovery of the relationship should yield considerable insight into its elements and show at what point it finally begins to break down. Something must set in motion the vigilant forces of

*Boston University School of Medicine; Children's Psychiatric Clinic, Massachusetts Memorial Hospitals; James Jackson Putnam Children's Center, Boston.

society, even though the intervention appears to come from outside. Which member of the family first becomes uneasy? Is age a factor? What role does the mother play? And later—what motivates the daugher to accuse her father?

The evolution which the authors have sought to establish through three generations leading to the constellation responsible for the incestuous relationship is most thought-provoking. We feel unable to evaluate their hypotheses at present in the absence of more complete clinical data.

Various methods are described by means of which the girls attempted to deal with their guilt feelings, depression and anxiety following discovery. The authors attribute a number of psychotic-like breaks to the girls' finally finding a person upon whom they could become completely dependent. We wonder whether this relationship of hostile demanding dependency is not the result of an internal rather than external change (i.e., foster home placement); may it not be the last step in a regressive process? The incestuous relationship itself is a regressive phenomenon. The subsequent remorse over betrayal of the father, grief over his loss, the rude awakening to their actual status in the family and hence in society, and their heightened hostility toward the mother, who again has failed them, would constitute a sufficient burden to cause far stronger personalities to regress.

We would like to suggest that placement in a good training school might be preferable to a foster home situation. For one thing the girl does not have to adapt to a setup so reminiscent of the one in which she only recently reigned and was dethroned. Repetition compulsion operates very powerfully in these girls, and attempts to seduce the foster father are trying for everyone, even when maturely handled. The personnel of such an institution are educated to and have had long experience in dealing with the intense dependent demands of these girls. The staff have learned to divide the burden among a number of people, to deal with the insatiable nature of these demands with patience and kindliness while consistently utilizing their relationships with the girls toward slowly increasing tolerance for mild frustrations. Inclusion in a group of their own age lessens the intensity of the demands on adults although rivalry at times makes them flare up to a high pitch. Such a school would also be able to provide psychiatric care and facilities.

In closing I should like to stress that studies of family constellations which foster specific pathology such as the present one being undertaken by Drs. Kaufman and Tagiuri and Miss Peck are sorely needed. At a time when interest in the public health aspects of mental and emotional maladjustments is growing, our awareness of danger zones and of the specific danger involved can alone lead to adequate preventive measures.

CHAPTER 40

Children Not Severely Damaged
by Incest with a Parent

Atalay Yorukoglu and John P. Kemph

Often referrals to child guidance clinics are made by courts when they suspect that a child has been subjected to incest by a parent; in most cases it has been found that the children were seriously affected by incestual relations with either parent. More often than not these children show defects in their ego functioning. Apparently, in our culture the incest taboo is so strong that when parent-child incest occurs, it is psychologically traumatic to the child involved in the act; therefore, it is not surprising to find that either boys or girls may become psychotic after they have had incestual relations. A study by Fleck et al. (1959) on the intrafamilial environment of the schizophrenic patient provides evidence that parent-child incestual acts and fantasies play a much greater role in the development of schizophrenia than had hitherto been assumed. Rascovsky and Rascovsky (1950) reported that it was common to find family disorganization, alcoholism, depression, and sexual maladjustment between parents in the families where incest was consummated between father and daughter. Usually the child escaped into homosexuality as a characteristic outcome of incestuous relations. In cases of father-daughter incest, the psychopathology of the daughters ranged from severe personality disorder and sexual maladjustment to manifest psychosis.

In the cases of mother-son incest, the sons, according to various reports, were found to be seriously emotionally disturbed. Wahl (1960) and Guttmacher (1962) each reported a case of incest in which the son developed psychotic episodes following incestuous sexual relations with his mother. In another family studied by Brown (1963) murder occurred as a result of incestual relations. Since most cases of incest come to the attention of courts and psychiatrists as a result of family disintegration or severe emotional disturbance rather than because of the act itself, it may be assumed that there are many cases of incest that are undiscovered either due to lack of family disorganization, lack of recognized psychiatric illness, or due to the fear of scandal. In order to avoid scandal many families keep the parent-child incest a secret as long as possible. Furthermore, it seems to

Reprinted with permission from the *Journal of the American Academy of Child Psychiatry* 5 (1966):111–24. Copyright 1966, International Universities Press.

be the consensus of opinion (Masters 1963) that incest between brothers and sisters occurs more frequently and produces less psychic damage than incest involving a parent.

We here studied two children with apparently healthy ego functioning who had incestuous relations with a parent; we sought to determine why they were relatively unaffected by the incest. The two cases which are reported in this paper involve children who have had prolonged sexual contact with the parent without being at least manifestly seriously disturbed emotionally. In one of these, mother-son incest took place and in the other father-daughter incest occurred. Only pertinent material will be extracted from these case studies.

CASE A

Jim, a thirteen-and-a-half-year-old, tall, good-looking boy with mild manners appeared older than his chronological age. When he was twelve years old, his mother was arrested for gross indecency related to acts of homosexuality with another woman. At this time it became known that his mother had been having sexual relations with him and with his sister, two years his junior, as well as with many suitors, both male and female. His mother was sentenced to one to five years in a house of correction on these charges, and her children were taken into court's custody. Jim and his sister were placed in a receiving home. There Jim upset other youngsters, stole some pigeons, brought fire in a can into the kitchen, broke a number of windows, ran away, etc. His behavior with girls was at first aggressive; if the girl tended to become aggressive with him, he would run away. Jim had participated in mutual masturbation with different boys when they would get together in bed. He was said to have exhibited himself to younger boys and to have formed a strong attachment to a boy two years his senior who was also in the receiving home. He was described as manipulative and smooth. He became sulky and unpleasant if he felt he was not being well treated. From the description of Jim's sister's behavior in the receiving home, it would seem that she also had difficulty controlling her impulses. On numerous occasions she became involved in sexual activity with younger girls in an exploratory way. She was described as a very aggressive girl in this area, though compliant in most other areas.

Jim was finally transferred to the detention home because of his unmanageable behavior. In an interview with the psychiatrist at that time he referred to himself as having been a "bad boy" and he expressed dissatisfaction with his current situation. He felt that he was responsible for his incestuous actions which he had "confessed" to the police when they had questioned him. He seemed to be well aware that he and his sister were placed in the receiving home as a result of his mother's "fight with a lady" (who had told the police about the mother's incestual behavior), but he had no knowledge of her homosexual activities. At this time psychological testing revealed some degree of depression and self-destructive tendencies. For example, he replied in sentence completion tests, "Sometimes I feel I might kill myself." He drew a picture of a family which consisted of three figures, all shown with their hands crossing over the lower region of the trunk. This passive self-protective stance was interpreted as indicating his guilt over sexual impulses and his fear of castration. In response to direct questioning, he indicated that the boy in the drawing was most afraid of girls, while he hoped to marry a nice young lady. Asked to make three wishes, Jim spoke of returning to his mother and then wished for another little kid, a child to adopt from the orphanage. He told psychiatrists and psychologists, as well as others, that he would prefer to go back to his mother, if she would stop doing what she did with him.

While waiting to be admitted to the University of Michigan Children's Psychiatric Hospital, he remained in the detention home where his behavior improved markedly. He no longer got into major difficulties. He showed no homosexual tendencies, but continued to be interested in girls. Jim, upon admission for inpatient treatment, assured his therapist that he would cause no trouble here because he did not want to go back to the juvenile home. When asked why he was brought to this hospital, he stated that he would be helped to get off his mind things that had happened between him and his mother.

He told his therapist that the sex acts between him and his mother had occurred for about two years, almost always after she had been drinking. Returning home late at night from work his mother woke him up by getting into his bed. She played with his penis and instructed him to use his mouth on her genitalia. She also placed his hand on her genitalia while he was sucking on her breasts. Some time later Jim's sister took part in their sexual activities. There had been episodes in which the boy would suck on one breast and the girl on the other. On one occasion Jim's mother used a vibrator on her genitalia while the two children were sucking. He claimed that his sister engaged in these sexual orgies only on a couple of occasions; when he and his mother had sexual intercourse, they were always alone. He felt all along that there was something terribly wrong with the whole affair, but he was curious about these sexual activities and after awhile he did not resist his mother's invitations. At times he thought since his mother saw nothing wrong in this, it must have been right to do these things. At other times he felt he was bad to sleep with her and said to himself and to his mother that she was doing this because she was drinking heavily and didn't know what she was doing. He claimed that his mother had always been a good mother to them; when she was sober she always treated them alike. She didn't seem to change in any way toward Jim after they began to have sexual relationships. He professed aggressively that he wanted to have nothing to do with drinking, it was a waste of money, that you could die from it, it could become a habit, and it could make you do things you have never done before. He added that when he last saw his mother at the police station she acted as though she didn't know what it was all about because his mother didn't know what she was doing under the influence of alcohol. When asked if he felt he could have avoided these activities, he commented, "I don't know, I was too scared, I don't know. I just didn't want to do it with her. First I didn't know what this was all about." He repeatedly wanted the therapist's assurance that no one would discuss this with his sister.

During the stay in our hospital Jim handled himself very well. He cooperated fully, and participated in all activities. He verbalized his satisfaction with the hospital program, saying that the kids enjoyed much freedom here. The hospital had turned out to be a better place than he thought. He showed a good sense of humor. His school performance was average. His peer relationships were appropriate. He carefully avoided getting into trouble or participating in any gang activities, but in a subtle way he tried to establish pal-to-pal relationships. No bizarreness or any impulsiveness were noticed.

He showed some degree of embarrassment in psychotherapeutic interviews when the therapist brought up the subject of the incestuous aspect of his relationship with his mother. It was a great relief to him that the therapist did not take a critical, punishing attitude toward him. Although he was not evasive, he showed some significant memory gaps, blocked on many details of his unacceptable sexual behavior. He manifested no thinking disturbance or any neurotic symptoms.

Psychotherapy consisted of a supportive and ego-building type of approach, since he seemed to have put up adequate defenses against his guilt feelings and incestual impulses. An uncovering type of therapy was avoided since this might have stirred up a great deal of anxiety. For the same reason hospitalization was kept to a short time.

During the interviews with his therapist, Jim maintained a strong loyalty to his mother. The only fault he could find with her was her drinking. Psychological testing revealed that his mother's psychological impact seemed to present a Dr. Jekyll and Mr. Hyde riddle to him. He condemned her for her physical seduction of him, but he also liked her as a friend. He was still trying not to hurt his mother in any way by talking against her. It was also apparent that he had warm feelings toward her. He had apparently been able to split his perception of her; seeing her as a proper mother when she was herself and as a frightening seducer when she was not herself. He missed the type of relationship he had with her before the sexual contact began. He thought that if he had a father figure in the home this earlier relationship could be resumed; her sexual aggressiveness toward him could be deflected by an adult man. Jim still experienced fear that something awful might happen to him. Each new day brought with it the possibility of calamity. He thought that sometimes terrible things happen; for instance, an innocent bystander is hit by a flying rock. Although neurotic intrapsychic mechanisms are obvious here, still no manifest neurotic symptoms were noted.

Jim's superego, while punitive in some areas, was strangely pragmatic in other aspects. Although he had not been able to repress the memory of the sexual involvement with his mother, he had been successful in using repression and denial to disown the pleasure of the affect associated with it, remembering only his fear, puzzlement, and a sense of being helpless. He was anxious to reunite with his sister who was sent to a home for children following brief hospitalization in a different institution.

The mother's history was obtained from her after her release from prison. She was the seventh of nine children. There was a wide gap in age between her and her next oldest sibling. She was the fourth daughter. She described her father as "a hell fire and damnation preacher." He was so concerned about church activities and "saving souls" that he neglected his own family, but at the same time ruled with an iron hand. She reported that neither her mother nor her father ever had time to talk with her or her sisters. Her sisters made hasty marriages and left the home to end the control of the punitive father. An older sister was forced into marriage and herein lay, according to Jim's mother, the beginning of her own problems. She told that at the age of twelve, she was raped by this brother-in-law. All of the family knew of this, and because of their position in the community, nothing was done about it. This was followed with what appears to have been a stormy adolescence finally culminating in submission to the father's demands for Bible reading and no heterosexual contact. She reported being whipped repeatedly for breaking the rules set by her father, and on one occasion the father made her read a passage from the Bible dealing with the whoremongers. It is interesting to note that she harbored more resentment, however, against her mother than she felt against her father because her mother did not intervene for her.

At the age of seventeen she began to date and became fond of a boy who was a member of a church of another denomination. Since this was not acceptable to the parents, she stopped dating him. On the rebound she turned to Jim's father, an army lieutenant, who was five years her senior and belonged to the same church. She married him three months later. She indicated that this was an attempt to escape from her home. There followed a very unsuccessful five years of marriage in which she and her husband were separated forty-three times. The husband was unfaithful, drank excessively, and was continuously in difficulty with the police. She left him after he had severely beaten her. She said that he had been very brutal during sexual intercourse, which she never enjoyed. She had continuously supported the children by her earnings without help from her husband following their separation. She told her children that their father was dead.

She stated that she had never trusted anyone and felt inadequate in her relationships with adults. She was married a second time for approximately one year to a professional man whom she described as a "mama's boy, a weakling." During the interview it became obvious that Mrs. A. had been under great stress during and after her second marriage. She underwent a hysterectomy during her second marriage, and then she increased drinking and became sexually promiscuous. In the three years following the breakup of this marriage, Mrs. A. consistently increased her pattern of drinking which had begun during this second marriage. According to her report, "I was two people—one at work in a bar [as a bartender] and a different one at home. I wanted to break away from the business, but it offered me a good living and I knew of no other way to support myself and the children." There was continued guilt about her way of living, growing out of her earlier training. She said she worried constantly about her work, finances, and baby sitters. She said that she was drunk when she married for the third time. She didn't realize she was married until she sobered up several days later and immediately separated from this man.

In spite of this background history, Mrs. A. was a well-dressed, attractive woman with poise and good manners. She had a good vocabulary. She seemed to be eager to talk and make a good impression with her polished and well-rehearsed life story. She related her traumatic past experiences and sufferings, and stressed her sacrifices to be a good mother to Jim and his sister. She stated that it was extremely hard to lead two lives. This she had not realized until now. She felt that she had recently awakened from a daze in which she had been for years. She claimed that she had done a lot of growing up in the past few years. She described her early experiences, giving detailed accounts of the rigid upbringing and the incident of rape. She pictured herself as a helpless little girl who was the victim of circumstances.

One had the feeling that by discussing the early events she was avoiding the exploration of the most recent events and the more painful happenings in the incestual relationship with her children. She did not deny her homosexual relationship. Without showing any feelings she gave different versions of some of the events. She thought she was framed by a girl's lover who became jealous of their homosexual relationship. She neither denied nor confirmed her incestual relationship with Jim and Jim's sister, saying that it must be true since Jim never lied. When it was pointed out that on three occasions she contradicted herself and had given a different story earlier, she sheepishly stated that at the time she made up things because she was angry at one particular female interviewer. She added that she had no faith in women anyway. It was different with the psychiatrist because he was a man! She also denied that she told her children that their father was dead, showing mock surprise. Speaking of her parents she said that recently they had begged for her forgiveness for the wrongs they had done to her; she forgave them and now they are her best friends. She painted a rosy picture of the future and said she was looking forward to having her children with her.

Mrs. A. had a hysterical personality. Typically she sexualized everything, including motherhood. She was a very intelligent, but an emotionally immature and narcissistic woman who used very poor judgment in her interpersonal relationships. She had poor impulse control. She had made genuine attempts to change her way of life. She stopped drinking, gave up a job that paid well, and joined a new church in order to regain a new identity. She was obviously using denial to a great extent when she painted a rosy picture of her future in a conscious attempt to get her children back.

In her case one cannot help but think of the revenge nature of her sexual involvement aimed against her parents. Mainly on an unconscious level she tried to get even with her parents who denied her the most innocent pleasures but maintained a shameful silence when she was raped. It is interesting to note that she repeatedly stated that she forgave them for the wrongs they had done to her and that now they were her best friends.

Discussion

In this case of mother-son incest there was genital sexuality between the parent and the child, and at the same time mutual warm feelings. There seemed to be an absence of sadistic elements in this relationship, in contrast to the typical father-daughter incest cases, in which frequently the child is threatened by the parent.

Jim, in the absence of a father figure, was given an adult role in the family. This is clearly seen in Jim's attitude toward and his statements about his mother. He regarded her as a dependent little girl in need of protection against herself and against others. He formed an alliance with his mother against a hostile world. The family structure was similar to that described by Weinberg (1955) with the mother dominant, the father absent, and the mother the aggressor in the incest relationship. Although his sexual contact with the mother was probably pleasurable at times, at least to the extent that he maintained an erection, yet he was not able to achieve an orgasm. Thus his premature introduction to adult sexuality was not entirely gratifying. He felt that most of the time he was fulfilling his mother's desire by participating in these acts in which he was a passive partner. It is interesting that he came to realize the full gravity of his involvement in these sexual activities only after he was separated from his mother. As long as he was doing what his mother told him, there seemed to be no strong superego pressure. One might speculate that as long as he lived with her his guilt feelings stemming from oedipal conflicts were not overwhelming. He felt the full impact when society condemned their relationship. There was insufficient evidence to substantiate any particular psychodynamic formulation, such as superego lacunae or well-defended guilt. Possibly his passive feminine orientation and homosexual activities following his mother's arrest were aimed at denying his active role in this forbidden relationship. During the two-year period of incestuous relationship, Jim had no adjustment problem nor any scholastic difficulties. This would suggest that he was not severely disturbed during that period. Several factors may partially explain his ability to tolerate the incest. Clinical material in general suggests that forbidden fantasies may be as disturbing as the real trauma. Jim could recall no sexual fantasies toward his seductive and promiscuous mother. Since she had forced him into having sexual relations, he may have felt little responsibility for the incestual behavior. We have also some reason to believe that he had relatively good mothering prior to his mother's second marriage, which took place when Jim was about five years old. Before that time, despite serious marital difficulties, Jim's mother had been a full-time mother to her children and, as she stated, she had nothing but those children. Until her second marriage she had not been promiscuous, nor had she begun to drink. This may account in part for Jim's ego strength. The reports that we have received a year after his discharge from the hospital indicate that he continues to do well in his academic work, and his adjustment was described as excellent.

CASE B

Jean, a beautiful seventeen-year-old girl, was referred for an evaluation after it became known to the court that she had been having incestual relations with her father for a prolonged period of time. She recalled that the father began to show her more attention than usual when she was thirteen years of age and in the seventh grade in school. Both her mother and father had been in the habit of coming into her and her brothers' rooms at bedtime to kiss them good-night. Her mother would come first and her father would follow. As she began to develop into womanhood, her father would stay longer, and he began to feel different parts of her body. This practice became more and more prolonged each night until she began to sense that there was something wrong. She knew nothing about sex at the time because her mother had never given her any information about the difference between men and women or how babies were born as a result of sexual relations. She had picked up some information by hearing other girls talk at school, but she did not have a clear-cut idea as to what motivated people to have sexual relations. She sensed that her father was doing something that he shouldn't, but she felt also that she should do as he asked or she would be considered disobedient. He would occasionally lie down beside her in bed and this she felt was certainly wrong because she had heard that sleeping with men could get girls into trouble. Therefore, she began to reject her father's attentions and would not allow him to get in bed with her. Nevertheless, he persisted in trying to do this and continued to force his attentions upon her.

When Jean was in the eighth grade, she decided that her father's behavior was very much wrong and tried to escape his attentions; she told her mother who spoke to him about it. This only caused her father to become infuriated, to get drunk, be more vicious with her mother, her brother who was four years younger than she, and with herself. For the sake of the family, as well as her own self, she found it easier to allow him to have his way as briefly as possible. She was forced to lie in bed beside her father who would hold her close, feel her for long periods of time, and eventually would have intercourse until he would reach orgasm. Additionally, he would sometimes use his fingers in her vagina. He was never brutal. Whenever her mother was in another room, he would take the liberty of feeling her body.

For the first few years that her father showed Jean this attention she found sex very repulsive and felt that her father was some kind of sexual pervert with too much interest in it. Although she told her mother several times about his behavior, her mother spoke to the father about it, but nothing was ever done. As a matter of fact, her mother realized even before Jean told her that there was something of this kind going on between father and daughter.

For several months prior to the court referral her father's attention began to be pleasurable to Jean. She stated that she would occasionally become excited when her father would have intercourse with her. She felt at the time that it was probably a natural reaction, that after all, she was human, and even though she didn't want to experience any pleasure, it happened anyway. She then began to have severe anxiety and insisted that her mother do something more drastic to prevent her father from having sexual contact with her. She wanted her mother to stay with her more of the time. When the mother refused, the child went to the school psychologist and told him. The school psychologist suggested that she contact the juvenile court. One of the court workers brought the case before the judge who placed the father in a state hospital and referred the child and mother for psychiatric evaluation. The child indicated that she felt much more comfortable after the father was out of the home, but even so she felt guilty about her part in placing him in the state hospital.

The father was found to have chronic undifferentiated schizophrenia and was given a course of electroshock therapy with little or no change in his behavior. He tried to get his wife and daughter to lie for him to get him out of the hospital. The child, having found that the father did not change, stated that she felt a sick feeling in her stomach just as she used to when he would come into her bedroom and force his attentions on her. She had decided that she would do anything to evade his attentions because she felt she would go crazy if this continued. For the past year she had been going steady with a boy in school. She stated that she had never had intercourse with him even though she intended to marry this boy as soon as she graduated from high school.

The mother was a beautiful woman with considerable narcissism and hysteria in her psychopathology. She had never experienced sexual pleasure with her husband or any other man, although she behaved in a seductive manner with most men. She actually appreciated those times when her husband did not insist on having relations with her. Both the mother and the daughter agreed that the mother had never understood her husband and that the daughter seemed to be able not only to understand, but to help her father over acute aggressive outbursts merely by talking with him. The mother had unconsciously encouraged the daughter's becoming the sexual mate to her husband. The daughter enjoyed being able to help her father whenever he was agitated, but preferred that she keep her role in this category. She recognized that she saw her father more as a sick child than as a father.

Psychological testing indicated that this child had a superior intellectual capacity with an almost compulsive drive for achievement. She displayed considerable conscious control of impulsivity, although there appeared at times to be some weakening of this control in the Rorschach examination. She saw herself personally involved in many anxiety-arousing situations, yet she had a well-developed set of defenses which helped her to overcome this anxiety. She would often resort to escapist fantasies effectively during unfavorable impact with reality. However, her contact with reality was excellent.

Discussion

There are some common factors in these children which set them apart from others who have had incestual relationships with a parent. Both of them had the ability to see realistically the parent as a seriously disturbed person; often both assumed parental roles. They were obedient to the parent, mechanically performing a procedure as directed by the parent. Although they knew that the act was wrong, they were able to utilize sufficiently strong defenses to prevent themselves from consciously becoming aware of their own gratification from these relationships. Furthermore, they were able to prevent the development of, or defend themselves against, any intense superego pressure. Possibly the reason they were not seriously affected is that they had developed adequate ego functioning including defensive functions along with the resolution of early conflicts and adequate psychosexual development prior to their having the incestual relations.

They did not consciously strive for sexual contact, and actual sexual fantasies involving the parent were not remembered. Perhaps their having successfully resolved their oedipal conflicts in early childhood allowed them, paradoxically, to be involved in an incestual relationship without experiencing the anxiety which ordinarily results from the unresolved oedipus complex.

It is well known that even oedipal fantasies may produce serious conflict and developmental arrest. However, incest did not seem to produce long-lasting psychic symptoms in the children reported in this paper. Therefore, one might speculate that oedipal fantasies may be even more harmful than the actual physical consummation of either mother-son or father-daughter incest in cases where the child is merely performing the mechanical act of intercourse at the parent's request without fully experiencing the significance of this act. This explanation assumes that these children had resolved their oedipal conflicts successfully prior to their incestual experiences. The only basis for this assumption is the lack of evidence for psychopathology on psychological examinations, and in psychotherapeutic interviews and the historical information indicating that there were no symptoms or deviant behavior. In a personal communication, Dr. Irene Josselyn has proposed the possibility that there was a regression to (or fixation at) the prestructured superego of obedience to parents. Since there is inadequate evidence to support either of these explanations, they must be considered purely speculative.

Although both Jim and Jean are now functioning well with little evidence of intrapsychic conflict, it is possible that they may develop difficulty in later phases of development. For example, in marriage they may be unable to accept their roles as parents or as partners in heterosexual relations.

SUMMARY

In two cases of parent-child incest, one mother-son and the other father-daughter, the children were not seriously or permanently impaired psychologically. It was thought that their ability to withstand this trauma resulted from their having developed healthy ego functioning prior to the incestuous experience.

REFERENCES

Brown, W. 1963. Murder Rooted in Incest. In: *The Patterns of Incest,* ed. R. E. L. Masters. New York: Julian Press.

Fleck, S., Lidz, T., Cornelison, A., and Terry, D. 1959. The Intrafamilial Environment of the Schizophrenic Patient. In: *Individual and Familial Dynamics,* ed. J. H. Masserman. New York: Grune and Stratton, pp. 132-39.

Guttmacher, M. S. 1962. *Sex Offenses: The Problem, Causes and Prevention.* New York: Norton.

Masters, R. E. L., ed. 1963. *The Patterns of Incest.* New York: Julian Press.

Rascovsky, M. W., and Rascovsky, A. 1950. On consummated incest. *Int. J. Psycho-Anal.* 31:42-47.

Wahl, W. C. 1960. The psychodynamics of consummated maternal incest. *Arch. Gen. Psychiat.,* 3:188-93.

Weinberg, K. S. 1955. *Incest Behavior.* New York: Citadel Press.

CHAPTER 41

The Treatment
of Father/Daughter Incest:
A Psycho-Social Approach

Henry Giarretto

The prohibition of incest is an ancient taboo and rules regarding incest remain the most sternly enforced regulations for sexual relations and marriage throughout the world. But just as social systems differ, so do incest rules. To this day, laws governing the prohibition and punishment of incest are inconsistent, varying markedly among nations and among states in the United States

FATHER-DAUGHTER INCEST

Father-daughter incest is potentially the most damaging form of incest to the child and family. Certainly, it is the form most frequently prosecuted by the courts. The following discussion of a composite case history of such incest is based on our experiences with the middle-class families referred to the Child Sexual Abuse Treatment Program in Santa Clara County, California.

A typical father-daughter incestuous relationship imposes severe stresses on the structure of the family. The roles of father, mother, and daughter become blurred, leading to conflict and confusion among family members. The most bewildered member is the daughter, who is usually at an age when her budding sexuality requires clear and reassuring guidance. But the familiar father has suddenly put on the strange mask of lover and his daughter never knows which role he will play at any given time. Her mother, too, becomes unpredictable. At one moment she is the usual caring parent, at another she sends subtle, suspicious messages that can come only from a rival. The girl's relationships with her siblings are also affected adversely, as they become aware that she has a special hold on their father.

The average victim of incest is ten years old when her father begins his sexual advances. She has always been close to her Dad. When he tentatively begins to fondle her, she finds the experience strange but pleasurable. Slowly the

Reprinted from *Children Today* 5 (1976)2–5.

sex play becomes more sophisticated as it progresses to mutual oral copulation and, at puberty, to intercourse. Their meetings, which at first were excitingly secretive, now become furtive and anxiety-ridden. She is about to enter the difficult teenage years when the mounting tension within her becomes unbearable. Her father is now interfering unduly with her peer relations and she senses that his fatherly concern over boys who are paying her attention is tainted by jealousy. She can no longer tolerate body contact with him and tries to resist, but he refuses to stop. Ashamed to confess the affair to her mother, she turns desperately to an adult friend or teacher, who immediately calls the police.

Although the policeman tries to be kind, his probing questions are excruciatingly embarrassing to the young girl, who is frightened by the power and authority he represents. But an odd feeling of relief intermingled with exhilaration comes over her as she realizes that her secret has now been exposed and her father's power over her broken.

Her anxiety returns when she is brought to a Children's Shelter. Despite friendly attempts by attendants to make her stay pleasant, she feels alone and threatened. This is the first time she has been forcefully separated from the family. Overwhelmed by mixed emotions of fear, guilt, and anger, she is convinced she will never be able to rejoin her family or face her friends and relatives. If there is suspicion on the part of child protective services of inadequate protection by her mother, a foster home is found for her. However, she will not adjust to the new family, since the placement confirms her fear that she has been banished from her own family. Though often told that she is the victim in the incestuous relationship she believes she is the one who is being punished. As a result, she often enters a period of self-abusive behavior that is manifested variously through hostility, truancy, drug abuse, and promiscuity.

The father is usually convicted on a felony charge and given a jail sentence of one to five years. What savings he may have are wiped out by the lawyer's fee of several thousand dollars. He finds imprisonment extremely painful. From a respected position in society he has fallen to the lowest social stratum. His fellow inmates call him a "baby-raper." No one is more despicable. He is segregated and often subjected to indignities and violence. However, the loathing he directs toward himself is more intense than that of his fellow inmates. Gradually, he finds some relief in the fervent resolution that, given the chance, he will more than make it up to his child, wife, and family. A well-behaved inmate, he is released from jail in nine months. He has lost his job and after weeks of job-hunting, settles for a lower position. He faces an uncertain future with his wife and family.

The explosive reaction of the criminal justice system leaves the wife in shock and terror. She is certain that her family has been destroyed. In the questioning by police and even others she once regarded as friends, she senses subtle hints that she may have condoned the incestuous affair. She has failed both as wife and mother. Her feelings toward her daughter alternate between jealousy and motherly concern. Her emotional state vis-à-vis her mate is also ambivalent. At first she is blinded with disgust and hate at the cruel blow he has dealt her and vows to divorce him. Her friends and relatives insist this is her only recourse. But the rest of the children begin to miss him immediately and she realizes that on the whole he has been a good father. She is also sharply reminded that he has been a dependable provider as she faces the shameful task of applying for welfare. Nagging questions, however, continue to plague her. If she takes him back, what assurance does she have that he will not repeat the sexual offenses with her other daughters? Will her relatives and friends assume that she has deserted her daughter if she allows him to return home? Will the authorities ever permit her daughter and husband to live in the same home again? Is there any hope for their marriage?

It is evident from this composite case history that typical community intervention in incest cases, rather than being constructive, has the effect of a knockout blow to a family already weakened by serious internal stresses.

THE CHILD SEXUAL ABUSE TREATMENT PROGRAM (CSATP)

In 1971, cases similar to that described above aroused the concern of Eunice Peterson, a supervisor of the Juvenile Probation Department in San Jose, California. She conferred with Robert Spitzer, who was then the department's consulting psychiatrist. Dr. Spitzer believed that family therapy would be a good first step toward constructive case-management of sexually abusive families. I was invited to undertake a pilot effort limited to ten hours of counseling per week for a ten-week period. The initial criteria of the Child Sexual Abuse Treatment Program were:
* The clients would be counseled on-site at the Juvenile Probation Department.
* The therapeutic approach would follow a "growth" model predicated on humanistic psychology.
* Conjoint family therapy as developed by Virginia Satir would be emphasized.[1]

As the program got underway, I soon discovered that conjoint family therapy alone was inadequate and, moreover, could not be usefully applied during the early stages of the family's crisis. We did not discount the fundamental aim of family therapy, which is to facilitate a harmonious familial system. But, because incestuous families are badly fragmented as a result of the original dysfunctional family dynamics—which are further exacerbated by disclosure of incest to civil authorities—the child, mother, and father must be treated separately before family therapy becomes productive. Consequently, the treatment procedure included, in this order: (a) individual counseling for the child, mother and father; (b) mother-daughter counseling; (c) marital counseling, which becomes a key treatment if the family wishes to be reunited; (d) father-daughter counseling; (e) family counseling; and (f) group counseling. The treatments are not listed in order of importance; usually all are required for family reconstitution.

[1]Satir, Virginia. *Conjoint Family Therapy,* Palo Alto, Calif.: Science and Behavior Books, 1967.

Another important finding during the early phases of the program was that counselor-client therapy, although important, was not sufficient. The reconstructive approach would be enhanced, I learned, if the family was assisted in locating community resources for such pressing needs as housing, financial and legal aid, jobs, etc. This required close collaboration between myself and the juvenile probation officer assigned to the case.

Still another development that added immeasurably to program productivity was the formation, in 1972, of the self-help group now known as Parents United. The insight that led to this step came when a mother of one of the first families treated was asked to make a telephone call to a mother caught in the early throes of her family crisis. The ensuing conversation went on for over three hours and had a markedly calming effect on the new client. A week later, three of the more advanced mother clients met face-to-face for the first time and, after a few meetings, to which several other women were invited, Parents United was formally designated and launched.

Members of Parents United meet weekly and, after a brief conference to discuss progress in growth and effectiveness, they form various groups, i.e., a couple's group, an intense couple's group limited to five couples, a men's group, a women's group and a mixed group. A separate organization, Daughters United, composed of teenaged girls, meets earlier in the evening.

INCIDENCE OF INCEST

The consensus of students of the family and of modern society is that incest is destructive to both the family and the social system of which it is a part. There is less agreement, however, on the severity of the problem. Is incest a rare phenomenon or, conversely, is it widespread enough to warrant the special concern of the community and social scientists?

Until a decade or so ago, researchers seemed to agree that the annual number of detected cases in Western countries average from one to ten per million inhabitants. Most of the reports agreed that the methods of detection were inefficient and that the figures represented just "the tip of the iceberg." The findings of our Child Sexual Abuse Treatment Program (CSATP) indicate that the one-in-a-million statistic is wrong by a factor of at least 180.

The CSATP serves Santa Clara County, which had a population in December 1973 of 1,159,500. In 1971, 35 cases were referred to the program. The annual referral rate increased slowly over the subsequent two years, but accelerated sharply over fiscal years 1974 and 1975. In 1975, 180 cases were referred. During the first quarter of this year, 102 referrals were received. This burgeoning rate can only be attributed to increased public awareness and confidence in the program. Nonetheless, even the change from one to about 200 cases per million inhabitants does not reflect the true prevalence of incest in Santa Clara County or throughout the nation.

I think it is important to emphasize here that the average family treated by the CSAT Program is not at all like the incestuous family described in most studies. In *Incest Behavior,* S. K. Weinberg, for example, reported that 67 percent of the families he investigated were in the low socioeconomic bracket and that 64 percent of the incestuous fathers tested were below normal intelligence. He also noted that there was a disproportionate number of blacks in his sample.[2]

The 400 families which have been referred to the program constitute a cross-section of Santa Clara County. They are representative of the racial composition of the county, which is 76.8 percent white, 17.5 percent Mexican-American, 3.0 percent Oriental, and 1.7 percent black. The make-up of the work force leans toward the professional, semi-professional and skilled blue-collar groups. Average income is $13,413 per household, while the median educational level is 12.6 years.

PROGRAM OPERATION

The CSATP is now firmly established and supported by revenue sharing funds and by a grant from the Rosenberg Foundation. The staff includes the writer, three half-time assistants and ten part-time volunteers. The productivity of this relatively small staff is high because of the generous assistance it receives from both private and public community resources.

The current objectives of the program are:

• To provide immediate counseling and practical assistance to sexually abused children and their families, in particular to victims of father-daughter incest. We also provide counseling to children who abuse younger children, and to women who were sexually abused as children and are now suffering from sexual dysfunction which is handicapping their marriage and family life. An important part of the women's therapy is to help newly referred abused children in the program.

• To hasten the process of reconstitution of the family, and of the marriage, if possible, since children prosper best in normally functioning families headed by the biological parents.

• To marshal and coordinate the services of all responsible for helping the sexually abused child and the family, and to enlist other community resources to ensure comprehensive case management.

• To employ a treatment model that fosters self-managed growth of individuals capable of positive contributions to society, rather than a medical model based on the vagaries of mental disease.

• To facilitate expansion and autonomy of the two self-help groups initiated by the program—Parents United and Daughters United—and to provide guidance to their members by offering training in co-counseling, self-management, and

---

[2]Weinburg, S. K. *Incest Behavior,* New York: Citadel Press, 1955.

intra-family communication and by helping to locate medical, legal, financial, educational, and other resources in the community.

• To inform the public at large and professional agencies about the existence and supportive approach of the program and to encourage sexually-abusive families to seek its services themselves.

• To develop informational and training materials to help other communities organize similar programs or adopt the CSATP model.

• To develop demographic data recording forms for future analysis.

TREATMENT MODEL

The therapeutic approach of the CSATP is based on the theory and methods of Humanistic Psychology, in particular the relatively new incorporation by the field of the discipline known as psychosynthesis, founded by Roberto Assagioli.[3] Other seminal writers of importance to the CSATP are Carl Rogers, Abraham H. Maslow, Virginia Satir, Frederick Perls, Haridas Chaudhuri, and Eric Berne.

Assagioli agrees that many similarities exist between psychosynthesis and existentialist/humanistic views. Principal similarities include the concept of personal growth, the importance of the meaning which a person makes of his life, the key notions of responsibility and ability to decide among alternatives, the emphasis on the present and future, rather than on regrets or yearnings for the past, and the recognition of the uniqueness of each individual. In addition, Assagioli stresses the concepts of the will as an essential function of self, a positive, optimistic view of the human condition and systematic use of didactic and experiential techniques which follow an individuated plan for psychosynthesis, the harmonious blending of mind, body and spirit around the unifying essence, the Self.[3]

A central notion in the treatment model is the building of social responsibility, the realization that each of us is an important element of society. We must, then, actively participate in the development of social attitudes and laws or be helplessly controlled by them. Chaudhuri gives firm emphasis to this imperative: "Since psyche and society are essentially inseparable, one has to take into account the demands of society. . . . One may criticize society or try to remold it. But one cannot ignore society or discard it."[4]

The philosophy and objectives of the treatment model may sound over-ambitious and even grandiose. However, the essential purpose is not to extinguish or modify dysfunctional behavior by external devices. Rather, we hope to help each client develop the practice of self-awareness that leads to self-esteem and the ability to direct his or her own behavior and lifestyle (self-management).

[3]Assagioli, Roberto. *Psychosynthesis,* New York: Hobbs, Norman & Co. 1965.
[4]Chadhuri, Haridas. *Integral Yoga,* San Francisco: California Institute of Asian Studies, 1970.

PRELIMINARY RESULTS AND MILESTONES

No recidivism has been reported among the more than 300 families who have received a minimum of ten hours of treatment and whose cases have been formally terminated. Compared to the situations encountered before we started our program, the approach used indicates that:

• The children are returned to their families sooner—90 percent within the first month and 95 percent eventually.

• The self-abusive behavior of the victimized children, usually amplified after exposure of the incestual situation, has been reduced both in intensity and duration.

• More marriages have been saved—about 90 percent. Many families have said that their relationships are better than they were before the crisis.

• The offender's rehabilitation is accelerated, since the counseling program is started soon after his arrest and continues during and after incarceration. Before the program started, any individual counseling and marriage counseling that occurred took place after the offender was released from jail.

• In father-daughter incest, the difficult problem of reestablishing a normal relationship is resolved more often and usually in less time. A critical first step in attaining this end is for the father to state clearly to his daughter that he was entirely responsible for the incestuous relations.

• Parents United has grown from three mother-members to about sixty members, of which half are father offenders. Daughters United has also grown substantially. Both groups are becoming increasingly self-sufficient and several of the older members of both groups now act as group co-leaders.

In addition to the benefits members of Parents United receive in helping themselves during their family crisis, they are also discovering that they can become a strong voice in the community, a significant realization to those members who tend to regard themselves as pawns of civil authorities.

• Offenders, who formerly would have received long jail or prison sentences, are now given suspended sentences or shorter terms due to increasing recognition of our program by the judiciary as an effective alternative to incarceration.

• The difficult goal of mobilizing typically disjointed and often competitive services into cooperative efforts is gradually being reached.

• Due to efforts in public education, the referral rate has increased markedly. About 60 percent of the referrals now come from agencies other than the police or Juvenile Probation Departments, or directly from people heretofore fearful of reporting the problem.

• The CSATP is receiving nationwide coverage by the media. Staff members and, more important, members of Parents United have appeared on several TV and radio programs and our program has been the subject of numerous newspaper and magazine articles. Hundreds of informational packets have been sent to requestors throughout the country and several presentations and training seminars are conducted each year for professional groups by the writer and staff members. The presentations now include those mothers, daughters and fathers of families treated who are willing to answer questions from the audience—a major breakthrough.

• The CSATP is also involving many volunteers and graduate students who are making valuable contributions while being trained.

Possibly the most encouraging recognition and constructive endorsement of the CSATP was accorded recently through a bill introduced to the 1975–76 session of the California Legislature by Assemblyman John Vasconcellos, Santa Clara County. Under the bill (AB 2288), funds are to be provided for establishing a demonstration center for California based on the CSATP approach. Members of Parents United as well as a number of civic-minded professionals went to Sacramento to lobby for the bill. Approved by a vote of 68 to 1 by the Assembly and unanimously by the Senate, the bill was signed into law by Governor Brown at the close of the session.

DISCUSSION

Current attitudes and laws regarding incest are myth-ridden and ineffective. The penalties for incest in the United States range from a $500 fine and/or twelve months in prison in Virginia to a prison term of 1–50 years in California. The impact of criminal justice on incestuous families, particularly those in which the father is the offender, usually adds up to either rejection of the child victim's plea for help, if the evidence is not court-proof, or disruptive punishment of the entire family if the offender confesses.

I do not mean to imply by these observations that criminal laws in support of the incest taboo should be abolished and that offenders should be dealt with exclusively by mental health workers. Reliance on the weekly therapeutic hour alone has not proven effective in the histories of several CSATP families.

For example, in these families the mother had often become aware that the husband was sexually exploiting their daughter and threatened to break up the marriage if he did not seek psychiatric treatment. Although the offender complied, he stopped going to the therapist after a few sessions and, a month or two later, resumed the sexual abuse of his daughter. And in two instances the fathers continued their offenses while undergoing treatment. Therapeutic control could not be established or maintained.

In five other cases, in which punishment alone was employed, the deterrent effect hoped for proved equally inadequate. The five men came to the attention of the CSATP for repeating the offense with other daughters or step-daughters.

The CSATP works closely with the criminal justice system of Santa Clara and other local counties. We do not delude ourselves into thinking that the promising results which are coming to light would have occurred without the cooperation of the police, probation officers and the courts. The Police and Probation Departments are major referral sources. A distraught victim, mother or friend will usually turn to the Police Department for immediate help since members are available 24 hours a day. It is now a common practice for officers who investigate the cases to refer offenders and their families to the CSATP.

For the offender, the implication is that involvement in the CSATP is likely to be strongly considered by the judge and prosecuting attorney during court proceedings. His own lawyer will also urge him to join the CSATP. Though all offenders hope that the penalty will be softened by participation in the CSATP, many find it equally compelling to do so for the aid the program gives to their families. Also, each man soon realizes that the program will help him understand his misconduct and re-establish relationships with his wife, the daughter he victimized and his other children.

In all cases the authority of the criminal justice system and the court process the offender must undergo seems absolutely necessary in order to satisfy what may be termed an expiatory factor in the treatment of the offender and his family. It appears that the offender needs to know unequivocally that the community will not condone his incestuous behavior and that it will exact a punishment. Victims and their mothers have also admitted to deriving comfort from knowledge of the community's clear stand on incest. All family members, however, will do their best to frustrate the system if they anticipate that the punishment will be so severe that the family will be destroyed and that they, in turn including the child victim herself, will become "victims" of the criminal justice system.

No matter what the reasons may be for admission of an incestuous family into the CSATP, it is our responsibility to help the family reconstitute itself as quickly as possible, hopefully around the original nuclear pair. Even if the offender comes to the CSATP only for the purpose of saving his skin it is up to us to show him that he can reap more substantial benefits for himself and his family by honest participation in the program.

Of course, the CSATP is not equally effective with all clients. About 10 percent of referrals will elude our efforts. They will not come in for the initial interview or they will drop out soon after treatment has begun. Four couples were dismissed from the program because the father and/or his wife would not admit culpability and placed the blame entirely on the child victim and her seductive behavior. In these instances extraordinary effort was required in the treatment of the deserted child. Three of the girls, after many attempts, successfully adjusted to foster homes. They are now married and apparently content.

The CSATP is a growing community resource. Some of its objectives have been only partly achieved, others will be added, dropped or modified. But here is at least the beginning of a response to Vincent de Francis' clarion call to the American community to protect the sexually molested child.[5]

By working with the Criminal Justice System the CSATP shows promise of developing into a model for other American communities. Each community must be given the opportunity to treat incestuous families in a manner that is neither permissive nor cruelly punitive. A national position must be taken on the incest

[5]DeFrancis, Vincent. "Protecting the child victim of sex crimes commited by adults." *Federal Probation,* September 1971.

taboo and laws that are effective and consistent must be enacted. The community must publicize these statutes and the penalties for violating them.

Finally, comprehensive procedures, similar to those employed by the CSATP, must be established in each community to treat sexually abused children and their families, to enhance each family's chance for reconstitution and to prevent future violations.

PART VIII

Management, Treatment, and Prevention of Child Abuse and Neglect at Home

Bitter are the tears of a child:
    Sweeten them.
Deep are the thoughts of a child:
    Quiet them.
Sharp is the grief of a child:
    Take it from him.
Soft is the heart of a child:
    Do not harden it.

        (Pamela Glenconner)

Editor's Introduction

After extensive hearings before the Subcommittee on Children and Youth (1973) chaired by then Senator Walter F. Mondale, the Child Abuse Prevention and Treatment Act (Chapter 10) became law in 1974. The act gave great impetus to work on the management, treatment, and prevention of child abuse and neglect in the home. As Chapter 10 indicates, the act established the National Center on Child Abuse and Neglect, which conducts research on the incidence, causes, identification, treatment, and prevention of child abuse and neglect, publishes training materials for personnel in this field, and gives technical assistance to agencies and grants to states to expand and improve child protective services.

As Williams indicates in Chapter 42, treatment has lagged behind management, which refers to a number of practical arrangements and actions including identification, reporting, diagnosis, and crisis intervention. Guided by the goal of keeping the family together, treatment planners have focused major attention on the abusive and neglectful parents who receive psychotherapy, lay therapy, casework, homemaker services, and other remedial interventions. Early reports on federally funded demonstration projects suggest high recidivism rates among parents receiving such multidisciplinary services. Psychological treatment, though sorely needed by abused and neglected children, is infrequently applied. Thus far, remedial interventions for the children have focused on psychoeducational and cognitive development, medical treatment, and, occasionally, on removal from the home.

The next group of papers in this section refers to family-oriented treatment. The chapter by Ounsted, Oppenheimer, and Lindsay describes the management and treatment of abuse and neglect in Great Britain. The authors describe the seeming paradox of the maturation of the abusive parents during their placement in a regression-enhancing environment in which they were cared for as if infants. The formerly suspicious parents formed a "liberating bond" with the hospital and its personnel. The children, too, were provided with an accepting, safe, predictable, interpersonal environment that promoted trust and maturation.

Controlled regression of abusive parents is also a primary feature of the treatment described by Paulson and Chaleff in Chapter 44. They demonstrate that interaction with empathic, nonjudgmental male and female cotherapists in group therapy not only increases the sense of trust and closeness of abusive parents, but fosters identification with, and modeling of, these parent surrogates.

Chapter 45 is a rare example of a well-documented study of the psychopathology and treatment of a family through four generations. Physical and emotional abuse and neglect gradually lessened in successive generations. Although the manifold problems of this family indicated a poor prognosis, continued skilled psychotherapy and casework over the years led to a lessening of psychopathology and unpredicted improvements in functioning.

All too often, child abuse and neglect cases are bungled so badly by agencies and courts that additional stresses are placed on already maltreated children. In Chapter 46, Terr and Watson report on their intensive examination during a two-year period of the handling of ten cases by physicians, social agencies, and the courts. They describe a number of management and treatment problems that worsen the plight of abused and neglected children and suggest ways of improving services, namely, multiagency coordination, involvement of a variety of professionals, and back-up by the court.

Morrison and Brubakken, in Chapter 47, describe an effective treatment program for a severely neglected young child who exhibited autistic behavior that differed from classical autism in that improvement was shown in response to treatment. The child was provided with an intensive, multidisciplinary, psycho-educational program, including parent training, which was aimed at behavioral management and psychosocial development. Treatment resulted in significant decreases in aversive behavior and increases in expressive language, academic skills, visual perception, and social, motor, and cognitive development. Little improvement occurred, however, in attachment behavior and other affective responses. Another important example of effective treatment of abused children is found in Chapters 29 and 30.

In Chapter 48, Flanzraich and Steiner describe a treatment approach specifically geared to the level of ego development of abused and neglected children. They describe the unique characteristics of each behavioral phase, beginning with the most infantile, the depressive phase, through the negativistic, to the aggressive phase. These ego dysfunctions are viewed by the authors as precursors to the characterological problems that would predispose these children to abusing and neglecting their own children. They suggest that the correction of these ego distortions can lead to reducing the generational cycle of child abuse and neglect.

The final two papers deal with the prevention of abuse and neglect of children at home, the least investigated topic in the field. In Chapter 49, Kempe describes an early warning system for the detection of parental potential for child abuse and neglect. He presents signs of high risk for abuse that can be observed during the prenatal, perinatal, and postnatal periods and describes a program of active intervention for high-risk parents that resulted in the prevention of child abuse and neglect, a program that has been elaborated on in other publications (Gray, Cutler, Dean, and Kempe 1976; Kempe 1978a; Kempe and Kempe 1978; Schneider, Hoffmeister, and Helfer 1976). Inasmuch as many potentially abusive parents do not bring their children in for medical check-ups, a universal health visitor system, somewhat similar to that used for years in the United Kingdom (Justice and Justice 1976), but more extensive and imaginative, is proposed. In addition, Kempe, emphasizes the crucial need for authentic support of children's rights and for greater financial support of child-abuse prevention.

In the final chapter, Williams describes the unpopular but necessary trans-formations in programs, practices, and financial priorities that must take place if child abuse and neglect at home are ever to be eradicated. The high frequency of recidivism among abusive and neglectful parents who received extensive mul-tidisciplinary services in federally funded programs raises questions about the guideline of removing the child from the parents, except as a last resort. She examines evidence indicating that this guideline is a misapplication of the work of Bowlby (1951). Kempe (1971) describes one of the sacred slogans that inter-feres with the protection of children from abusive and neglectful parents:

> The . . . saying, "be it ever so humble, there is no place like home," is one that is in a sense rediscovered by those in the field of psychiatry and child care who are appalled at the spectre of babies raised in residential nurseries without a firmly identifiable mother figure. It is clear that many social workers have simply misread the message which has come from workers, such as Bowlby. It does not have to be the biological mother who mothers the baby, though there has to be a mothering person for every child (p. 36).

Another transformation that must take place is the provision of contraceptive and abortion counseling within programs that purport to prevent and treat child abuse and neglect, in addition to accessibility of such services to the general population. Public campaigns against sexist and pronatalist child-rearing, as well as the substitution of nonviolent alternatives to corporal punishment at home and school are other significant changes that can contribute to the eradication of child abuse and neglect. Finally, a reordering of financial priorities is urgently needed, so that adequate funding for children's programs is insured.

A number of ethical issues arise in connection with the changes required to eradicate child abuse and neglect at home. For example, should the community intervene because of the probability that a child will be maltreated by parents? Should nonviolent child-rearing be imposed on those who believe in harsh physi-cal punishment of children? Increasingly, such thorny ethical problems are being considered by scholars in the humanities, and by politicians as well as profes-sionals in the child care fields (Brody and Gais 1976; Duryea, Fontana, and Alfaro 1978; Wilson 1976).

G.J.W.

REFERENCES

Bowlby, J. *Maternal Care and Mental Health*. Geneva: World Health Organization, 1951.

Brody, H., and Gaiss, B. "Commentary on Ethical Issues." In R. E. Helfer and C. H. Kempe, eds., *Child Abuse and Neglect: The Family and the Community*. Cam-bridge, Mass.: Ballinger, 1976.

Duryea, P., Fontana, V. J., and Alfaro, J. D. "Child Maltreatment: A new approach in educational programs." *Children Today* 7 (1978):13–16.

Gray, J., Cutler, C., Dean, J., and Kempe, C. H. "Perinatal Assessment of Mother-Baby Interaction." In R. E. Helfer and C. H. Kempe, eds., *Child Abuse and Neglect: The Family and the Community*. Cambridge, Mass.: Ballinger, 1976.

Hearings before the Subcommittee on Children and Youth of the Committee on Labor and Public Welfare, United States Senate, 93rd Congress. First session on S. 1191 on the Child Abuse Prevention Act. Washington, D.C.: U.S. Government Printing Office, 1973.

Justice, B., and Justice, R. *The Abusing Family*. New York: Human Sciences Press, 1976.

Kempe, C. H. "Paediatric implications of the battered baby syndrome." *Archives of Disease in Childhood* 46 (1971):28–37.

————. "Child abuse—The pediatrician's role in child advocacy and preventive pediatrics." *American Journal of Diseases of Children* 132 (1978*a*):255–60.

————. "Sexual abuse, another hidden pediatric problem: The 1977 C. Anderson Aldrich Lecture." *Pediatrics* 62 (1978*b*):382–89.

Kempe, R. S., and Kempe, C. H. *Child Abuse*. Cambridge, Mass.: Harvard University Press, 1978.

Schneider, C., Hoffmeister, J., and Helfer, R. E. "A Predictive Questionnaire for Potential Problems in Mother-Child Interaction." In R. E. Helfer and C. H. Kempe, eds., *Child Abuse and Neglect: The Family and the Community*. Cambridge, Mass.: Ballinger, 1976.

Wilson, A. "Commentary." In R. E. Helfer and C. H. Kempe, eds., *Child Abuse and Neglect: The Family and the Community*. Cambridge, Mass.: Ballinger, 1976.

CHAPTER 42

Management and Treatment
of Parental Abuse and Neglect of Children:
An Overview

Gertrude J. Williams

ABSTRACT

Inasmuch as child abuse and neglect are not simple medical or social conditions, but complicated, multifaceted, psychosocial-medical-legal programs, no one discipline merits a special authoritative role in their management and treatment. Investigators consistently agree on the necessity of multidisciplinary coordination and cooperation among well-trained members of the child abuse and neglect team during the diagnosis and crisis intervention phases of management. Questions are raised, however, regarding the value and feasibility of multidisciplinary review teams in the long-term treatment of families in which child abuse and neglect have occurred.

The major goal of current programs is keeping the family intact, a focus that has precluded development and research on new strategies directed toward development of alternatives to keeping the child at home and based on the goals of the protection and enhancement of the child's well-being. The major treatment focus has been on the parents and on the improvement of the home. Such treatment includes group and individual therapy and homemaker services, parent aides, crisis nurseries, telephone hotlines, and parent education. The founding of Parents Anonymous has generated the development of self-help groups throughout the nation that are useful adjuncts to professional services. They lack models of good parenting, however, and despite wide media coverage and the apparent gratification with such programs by abusive parents, their effectiveness in stopping child abuse has not been demonstrated. Early findings from research on the effects of multidisciplinary treatment indicate that only 40–50 percent of treated parents stop the physical and emotional abuse and neglect of their children.

Psychological treatment, specifically geared to the emotional needs of abused and neglected children, is in a primitive stage of development. Thus far, treatment of the child has focused on psychoeducational and cognitive development in addition to medical attention. Intensely needed therapy directed toward ameliorating the effects of maltreatment on the child's personality is rare. In many instances, removal from the abusive home and placement in another domicile has been shown to have therapeutic effects on abused and neglected children.

Some portions of this chapter have been exerpted with permission from "Child Abuse," Chapter 7. *Psychological Management of Pediatric Problems,* vol. 2, pp. 253–91, P. R. Magrab (ed.), Baltimore: University Park Press, 1978.

The management and treatment of child abuse and neglect present a multitude of special difficulties not encountered in the remediation of other problems of childhood. Although damage to the child may be life-threatening, abuse and neglect are not medical diseases with specific etiology, symptomatology, course, management procedures, and treatment. In contrast with other pediatric conditions, the parents are unlikely to volunteer for professional assistance, because they are the cause of their child's injury or illness. Inasmuch as the referral is usually demanded by the juvenile court or child protection agency, the professional staff cannot expect to receive accurate medical and psychosocial information from the abusive parents, who fear criminal charges and/or the child's removal from the home, from abused infants who are incapable of reporting their plight, or from abused children who, fearing retaliation, may collude with the parents. Furthermore, the values, beliefs, and unconscious motivations of the staff play a more important role in the perception, management, and treatment of child abuse and neglect than in other pediatric or family problems.

INTERDISCIPLINARY COORDINATION

In light of the myriad psychosocial and medical factors associated with child abuse and neglect, it is not surprising that interdisciplinary cooperation and coordination are consistently stressed in the literature on management and treatment. Although social work and medicine have pioneered in the remediation of child abuse and neglect, no single discipline merits a special authoritative role on child abuse teams. Helfer (1975) has emphasized that "... if any of the disciplines begins to take on, or is given, responsibilities for which they are not prepared or trained, the program breaks down. The social worker who is forced to make legal, medical and psychiatric decisions while being a police officer finds it difficult to function ... Likewise, physicians who try to be a social worker or policeman generally find themselves well over their heads" (p. 2).

The U.S. Department of Health, Education and Welfare (HEW 1975, vol. 1) calls attention to the number of professionals required to help one family in which abuse or neglect has occurred:

> The abuse and neglect of children is a problem that cannot be managed by one discipline alone. A single case may involve social workers from both a hospital and the public child protection agency, a public assistance caseworker, one or more doctors, a psychiatrist or psychologist, both hospital and public health nurses, police, lawyers, a juvenile or family court judge, the child's schoolteacher and any of a number of other professionals (p. 50).

MANAGEMENT

The management of child abuse and neglect involves a number of practical arrangements and actions. These include identification and reporting of suspected abuse and neglect, diagnosis, crisis intervention, short- and long-term treatment planning, and follow-up. The U.S. National Center on Child Abuse and Neglect has established a number of federally funded demonstration projects across the United States and in Puerto Rico (Cohn, Ridge, and Collignon 1975; Besharov 1977). In general, they are based on the model, multidisciplinary, coordinated, community team philosophy developed by Helfer (1975) and elaborated by HEW (1975, vol. 3). All programs include management, treatment, education, coordination, and evaluation components. Arguably, their goal is to keep families together and to eliminate unnecessary placement of the child in a domicile outside the home. Inasmuch as there is a lack of knowledge about which interventions that purport to be therapeutic are, in fact, therapeutic, their programs vary, so that a variety of intervention strategies can be objectively evaluated.

The first steps in the management of child abuse and neglect are identification and reporting. Since neither the parents nor the child are likely to report, guidelines for identifying abused and neglected children have been developed by child protective and other agencies throughout the nation and have been circulated to hospitals, physicians, teachers, other professionals, and the public. In addition to such evidence from x-rays as multiple fractures in various stages of healing and other medical indicators, certain less obvious physical signs are suggestive of abuse. These include the child's wearing long-sleeved shirts or long pants in warm weather that hide injuries, cheek bruises, and unusual marks on the body, such as the oval scars formed by cigarette burns or the distinctive lash mark of an electric cord.

Behavioral characteristics of abused children may include some of the following: reluctance to play during recess because of unexplained soreness; behavioral extremes such as excessive fear or extreme aggressiveness; wariness of physical contact especially by adults; nonspecific behavioral pathology, including sudden expressions of regressive behavior, such as thumbsucking, whining, or disruptiveness; preference for remaining at school after class rather than returning home; and frequent fatigue. Signs of sexual abuse described by Kempe (1978) include behavioral pathology, such as intense fear, night terrors, clinging and developmental regression in children under five years old. In school-age children, there may be sudden onset of anxiety, school failure, or running away, as well as sudden weight loss or weight gain. Adolescents may show serious rebellion, especially against the mother, as well as delinquency and social isolation.

Behavioral characteristics of abusive parents may include delay in seeking medical attention for the child's injuries; seeking treatment for the child outside the neighborhood, which may indicate "hospital shopping"; conflicting or inappropriate explanations of a child's bruises or injuries; unexplained death of a sibling; few or no complimentary references to or about the child; a rigidly righteous belief in corporal punishment; fear of "spoiling" the child; social isolation; and an attitude of general mistrust.

Even though the child and/or parents manifest some of the characteristics associated with abuse or neglect, professionals and lay persons alike are reluctant to report their suspicion of these practices, despite provisions for anonymous reporting. Reasonable suspicion is sufficient to initiate an investigation of the home. Those who report are exempt from legal action, even if abuse or neglect is found to be absent. In many states, a 24-hour-a-day, statewide, toll-free hotline receives reports of suspicion of abuse and neglect, including anonymous phone calls. Although the aim is to check each report within 24 hours, case overloads and other factors often prevent such a rapid response to the report.

Helfer's (1975) multidisciplinary, coordinated approach to diagnosis, management, and treatment of child abuse and neglect involves several phases. First, someone—a physician, teacher, relative, or neighbor—reports suspected child abuse and neglect to a mandated agency, usually child protective services. The child is taken to a hospital emergency room where he or she is given emergency treatment and examined by the child abuse team in order to determine whether the injuries are nonaccidental. The parents are encouraged to remain in the hospital with their child. During the diagnostic assessment phase, the multidisciplinary team (consisting of a protective service worker from the community, a hospital social worker, the pediatrician or family physician, public health nurse, psychologist or psychiatrist, lawyer, law enforcement officer, and team coordinator) carry out a multitude of tasks. These include gathering data to make a diagnosis, supporting the family throughout the process and meeting regularly to collate information. Within four days after the case is recognized as child abuse or neglect, a review and planning conference is held by the team to determine the safety of the home, make plans for the short- and long-term phases of treatment and delegate responsibilities to various professionals and paraprofessionals to meet such needs as casework, psychotherapy, employment, housing, and homemaker services. If indicated, the juvenile or family court is petitioned to remove the child from the home and grant temporary custody to a designated agency.

Throughout the treatment, the team meets regularly to assess progress and problems. If the child was removed from a home which, after thorough study, is viewed as safe, the court is petitioned to return custody to the parents, who continue their psychotherapy and/or meetings with such self-help groups as Parents Anonymous. The team coordinator follows the family and coordinates all services throughout the treatment process.

Management problems related to the reporting of child abuse and neglect are often present even before the multidisciplinary team becomes involved in cases. As indicated in Chapter 1 of this book, there are a number of inconsistencies in state laws regarding abuse and neglect, and these may interfere with the reporting process. In addition to the lack of uniformity of definitions of child abuse and neglect, the maximum age for reporting ranges from twelve to eighteen years, depending on the state. Hospitals and a variety of persons are mandated by law to receive reports of suspected abuse and neglect. The mandated reporter, however, varies from state to state. Hospitals, institutions, physicians and nurses are mandated in most states. A number of states also mandate teachers, social workers, psychologists, and dentists. A few states mandate members of the clergy, pharmacists, religious healers, and chiropractors. The majority of states legally specify one agency to receive reports of suspected child abuse and neglect; such agencies include child protective and social service agencies and police departments. Some states specify as many as three agencies, a practice that fragments the reporting process. Some states penalize mandated persons for not reporting abuse and neglect; others do not. To add to the complexity of the management and coordination process, as many as fifteen states a year amend their child abuse and neglect reporting legislation.

The multidisciplinary approach to child abuse and neglect often produces serious problems. Wallen, Pierce, Koch, and Venters (1977) refer to some of the sources of interference with the functioning of the multidisciplinary team. These include internal problems within a member agency, such as rapid staff turnover or reorganization, power conflicts, funding problems, professional and personal frictions among team members, and lack of resources or cultural acceptance of the program in some communities. Inadequate salaries, staff shortages, and inordinately heavy caseloads contribute to the inability of some members of the team to perform necessary services. For example, the State Department of Children and Family Services in Illinois can respond to only 57 percent of the child abuse and neglect reports they receive (*St. Louis Globe Democrat* 1978).

While there appears to be general endorsement of the multidisciplinary community team approach in the diagnosis and crisis intervention phases of child abuse and neglect, its feasibility in the treatment process is sometimes questioned. Cohn and Miller (1977) cite the high cost of multidisciplinary treatment review teams and their inefficiency; i.e., only one or two cases can usually be reviewed at a team meeting.

TREATMENT

A number of questions arise in connection with the consideration of the treatment of child abuse and neglect. How is treatment defined? To whom is it applied? Is treatment successful? What are the criteria of successful treatment? Ideally, treatment involves a wide variety of modalities in addition to psychotherapy geared to the needs of abused and neglected children and their parents. These include hotlines, crisis nurseries, homemakers, self-help groups, parent aides, and other remedial resources characterizing such programs as the National Center for the Prevention and Treatment of Child Abuse and Neglect at the University of Colorado School of Medicine (Helfer and Kempe 1976; Kempe and Kempe 1978) and other federally funded child abuse and neglect projects (National Center on Child Abuse and Neglect 1976).

Cohn and Miller (1977) who are evaluating the nationwide treatment programs funded by the U.S. Office of Child Development and the National Center on Child Abuse and Neglect, state: "Based on our observations, we question whether the value of the multidisciplinary review team in treatment programs has been sufficiently established to warrant widespread endorsement. Indeed, while we believe that these teams have value in the initial diagnosis of severe cases, we question whether such a team ensures that an interdisciplinary approach is being taken toward actually treating families." They suggest that treatment is sometimes equated with casework, therapy or medical care, rather than with a broad range of remedial services.

Spinetta (1977) refers to the reality that "very little encouragement has been given to the therapist who does not have easy access to the new interdisciplinary treatment programs and who, in many instances, remains the sole therapeutic agent for a particular set of families" (p. 1). HEW (1975, vol. 3) states: "Of the three components of the community-team program—identification and diagnosis, treatment, and education—treatment tends to be the most notably lacking. It is not uncommon for a community to develop extensive identification and diagnostic resources and then to find itself ill-equipped to help identified families."

Even when a community has remedial resources, the agencies may be reluctant to modify their services to meet the unique needs of families in which child abuse and neglect have occurred. Galdston (1970) describes his experiences with agencies to which families were referred in connection with the Parents' Center Project for the Study and Prevention of Child Abuse:

> We have had patients who have been picked up by other agencies for day care treatment, night care treatment, job retraining, neighborhood activities, group therapy, psychotherapy, rehabilitation, Montessori training, and psychotropic pharmacotherapy. In many instances the patients were dropped by the agency involved when it became obvious that the patients' problems were not amenable or suitable for the treatment offered (p. 341).

Thus, even when treatment is broadly defined and agencies of a wide variety exist in a community, families in which child abuse and neglect are occurring are not necessarily served. Numerous problems arise in connection with a narrow definition of treatment as psychotherapy. The development of psychotherapeutic techniques specifically geared to these families has lagged behind the development of management strategies related to diagnosis and crisis intervention. Moreover, in the large majority of cases, the recipients of psychotherapy are the parents. For reasons to be discussed later in this chapter, treatment of abused and neglected children includes medical care, special education, and opportunities for socialization, but usually excludes psychotherapy.

At present, psychological treatment of abusive and neglectful parents is based primarily on trial-and-error efforts on the part of a therapist to develop an approach acceptable to these resistant parents. Furthermore, the selection of the therapist and the modality of therapy are usually dependent on the availability of psychotherapists, or on a number of other practical or extraneous considerations that lack a theoretical or empirical foundation. HEW (1975, vol. 3) indicates that "at present, there are no data derived from thorough, comparative studies indicating how or why any one mode of treatment is more effective than another for a particular parent" (p. 75). Lahey (1977) asserts:

Our review of the treatment literature (on child abuse and neglect) revealed that virtually no treatment evaluation research has been conducted that could appropriately be termed empirical, let alone experimental. Nearly all of the studies reviewed did not even have a defined dependent variable, especially not in quantified form. They merely reported subjective evaluations of the effectiveness of the treatment program.

The impressions of Steele and Pollack (1975) and Polansky and Polansky (1968) represent opposite poles of the optimism-pessimism continuum with regard to the efficacy of treatment of abusive and neglectful parents. Steele and Pollack (1975) state:

> The matching up of parent, worker, and treatment modality is difficult and is usually managed on a less than ideal scientific basis. Abusive parents are unique individuals, often with great reluctance to become involved in any form of treatment. Hence, the type of treatment may be selected under great influence of what the parent will go along with at the moment rather than any theoretical reason for a scientific method. It is known on the other hand, that even in the face of rather haphazard selection mechanisms, remarkably good results have come from parents who have been treated by many different methods (p. 21).

Polansky and Polansky (1968) are pessimistic about the prognosis of abusive parents who receive treatment: "Because of their dedication to the notion of 'the family,' or their zeal about 'rehabilitation,' the formal policies of social agencies in this field are sanguine to the point of being fatuous regarding the potentiality for change in a large proportion of the parents involved. The fact is that most hard-headed observers report *little success* with the methods of aggressive casework (or unaggressive psychiatry) now being practiced" (p. 44). They recommend measures to protect the child, such as permanent or long-term removal of the child from the home, surveillance of the home, the legal requirement that abusive parents take children to physicians for regular medical check-ups, imprisonment of parents convicted of child-battering, and abortion for pregnant women who do not want to bear a child.

The criterion of successful treatment is typically the elimination of physical abuse and neglect. According to Cohn and Miller (1977), reincidence of abuse and neglect is an inadequate measure of the impact of treatment for several reasons:

> (1) it may not be detected by treatment providers; (2) the child may have been removed from the home making reincidence impossible; or (3) reincidence may not occur until long after treatment (or the study) is over. The supportive treatment environment may serve to delay or inhibit abusive/neglectful behavior. Thus, while the presence of reincidence may give us clues about what is happening in the family, the absence may tell us nothing (p. 455).

Even if it could be assumed that reincidence of physical abuse and neglect were correctly assessed as absent, the matter of the continuation of emotional abuse and neglect is bypassed. Furthermore, the focus on parental variables as criteria of success can lead to the conclusion that a treatment program is successful, defined as elimination of abuse and neglect, while the child continues to suffer from untreated, severe, emotional problems resulting from the earlier parental abuse and neglect.

An evaluation of treatment based on eleven federally funded child abuse and neglect projects prepared for the National Center for Health Services Research (NCHSR 1978) indicated that current treatment programs can be successful in 40 to 50 percent of cases. Success was defined as no reincidence of child abuse and neglect. Thirty percent of the parents continued to maltreat the child while they were in treatment. "By the end of treatment an effective program may be able to count on only a 40 to 50 percent success rate" (Cohn and Miller 1977, p. 457). Treatment was more effective when it lasted more than six months and when "professional services are combined with carefully supervised lay therapy" (NCHSR 1978, p. 3).

Findings reported by Kempe and Kempe (1978), based on the work of the National Center for the Prevention and Treatment of Child Abuse and Neglect at the University of Colorado School of Medicine, indicate that abused and ne-glected children from the 80 percent of families considered treatable return home. They claim that children whose parents show the following changes have never been physically abused again: the parents' self-esteem has improved; they have made at least one friend; they express some affection for the abused child, whom they view as possessing some attractive qualities; they seek social support when crises occur; reunions with the child become increasingly enjoyable.

Kempe and Kempe stress that unless these criteria are met by the parents, the child is likely to be attacked even more severely. Furthermore, supportive treat-ment must continue for years with some parents, even after they meet these criteria. Emotional abuse of the child may continue, however, even after the physical abuse has stopped, a finding based on long-term follow-up for half the "successfully" treated families. The remaining successfully treated parents "do grow and develop, usually through prolonged contact with one or two reliable and uncritical adults who provide the mothering and fathering they have never known" (p. 109).

According to Helfer (1975) the 10 percent of abusive parents who are se-verely ill psychiatrically do not benefit from treatment. Another 10 percent "are those who believe that 'God told me that it was alright to beat my baby.' They produce Biblical references with which they justify their interpretation of child rearing" (p. 40). He believes that permanent termination of custody should be sought to protect children of these hard-core parents.

The number of reports on remedial interventions for abuse families has become so great that only the highlights can be presented in this chapter. Indi-vidual, marital, group, and family therapy and casework have been used with the parents, in addition to various family-strengthening services.

Although psychoanalysis has been used successfully with a few abusive parents, their mistrust, resistance, and primitive character structure make them poor candidates for this form of treatment. Individual therapy and casework are usually supportive and are aimed at replacing the parents' abusive child-rearing with behavior that is rewarding to all family members and at teaching the parent new ways of coping with crises. A major means of accomplishing these goals is reparenting the extremely nurturance-deprived parents and helping them ventilate their rage, dependence, loneliness, and despair—feelings they displace to the child or defend against through denial.

Beezley, Martin, and Alexander (1976) emphasize the need for much greater outreach toward abusive parents than is provided in traditional psychotherapy. These parents cannot wait their turn on a waiting list in order to receive help. In addition to needing psychotherapy, they often require immediate crisis intervention. The therapist must be available twenty-four hours a day and must accept frequent lateness and missed appointments. Furthermore, treatment must continue for at least a year, and contacts on an "as needed" basis must be available for an extended period of time after formal termination. These investigators believe that team support and consultation should be provided for the primary therapist and that the consultant may participate in the therapist's contacts with the parent.

Individual psychotherapy with abusive parents has many disadvantages. They may be too erratic to submit to regularly scheduled fifty-minute sessions. They may be insufficiently psychologically-minded to avail themselves of psychotherapy, and/or they may be so emotionally demanding or insatiable that treatment by one therapist is grossly inadequate. In light of these problems, it is not surprising that group therapy is the most widely used treatment modality for abusive parents. A greater number of parents can be reached. Confrontation can occur much earlier. Interpretations are usually accepted more readily from other abusive parents than from a professional psychotherapist.

Feinstein (1964) cited the advantages of group therapy over individual therapy for parents with murderous impulses toward their children. These include the group's correction of the view that a given parent is the only one with such impulses, support from the group, correction of perceptual distortions through consensual validation, interference with abusive parents' social isolation, and a mixing of defenses so that group members can learn different methods of adaptation from each other. Justice and Justice (1976) described a multifaceted approach to group therapy for abusive parents that includes behavior modification, transactional analysis, relaxation training, and parent education regarding appropriate responses to children at each developmental stage.

An important goal of therapy, regardless of modality, is to change the abusive parents' unrealistic perceptions of the child, but therapists disagree on the tactics to be used to accomplish this goal. Galdston (1965) believes that the therapist should tell the parents at the outset and repeatedly that their perception of the child is erroneous and colored by their own past experiences. He recommends urging them to review their memories in order to shift their focus from their externalizations on the child to their own memories and feelings. On the other hand, Steele (1975) believes that misperceptions should be dealt with cautiously and only after the therapist has a solid, trusting relationship with the parent. He contends that because of abusive parents' low self-esteem and fear of criticism, too rapid confrontations can sever the therapeutic alliance or prevent its formation.

The least applied treatment modality for abuse families is family therapy. This is understandable because the abused child may be reexposed to the traumatizing rage of parents, who may be unable to tolerate the child's candor or expression of anger. Beezley, Martin, and Alexander (1976) suggest that the readiness of parents to tolerate the child's anger must be carefully assessed before family therapy is implemented and that individual sessions may need to continue concurrently.

Paraprofessionals and self-help groups are important components of the multifaceted treatment services to abusive families. Parent aides are parents with very satisfactory family relationships who, under professional supervision, provide long-term support to abusive parents. Self-help groups, such as Parents Anonymous, are modeled after Alcoholics Anonymous. They have the advantage of ready availability in communities lacking adequate professional services. Furthermore, abusive parents feel more comfortable with other abusive parents than with professionals, who are often viewed as threatening authority figures.

Parents Anonymous and similar self-help groups have chapters across the nation. Parents may call their telephone hotlines at any time they feel they are in danger of losing control and abusing their child. Lieber and Baker (1977) attempted to evaluate the impact of membership in Parents Anonymous and concluded that the program improved parents' attitudes, knowledge, and behavior regarding their children. Inasmuch as the findings were based on self-reports to a questionnaire in which social desirability and a number of other pertinent test variables were not controlled, such conclusions may not be warranted. Furthermore, positive findings may be spurious in that other forms of treatment were likely to have occurred concurrent with membership in Parents Anonymous. As cited earlier, a combination of professional services and well-supervised lay therapy appears to be the most effective treatment (NCHSR 1978). Despite wide media coverage, the effectiveness of self-help groups is doubtful in the absence of the many and varied services needed by families in which child abuse and neglect have occurred. Although many abusive parents express gratification with these programs, there is no evidence that membership improves the parent-child relationship or increases positive feelings toward the child. Helfer (1975) quotes an abusive parent as saying; "Since I joined Parents Anonymous, I don't beat my kid anymore, but I don't like the little bastard any better." One shortcoming is that these groups contain no models of healthy parenting for the abusive parents to emulate. Another shortcoming is their lack of sponsorship of affiliated groups for abused and neglected children analogous to Al-Teen or Al-Anon for children of members of Alcoholics Anonymous.

Homemaker services is another component of the multidisciplinary program. Homemakers not only help organize the often chaotic home of the abused child, they also serve as models of good home management and child care and contribute to breaking up the abusive parents' pattern of isolation from the community.

All parents, especially abusive ones, require a recess from parenting. Beezley et al. (1976) describe "a respite for child and parent" in which they are separated for several hours a week. Kempe and Helfer (1972) recommend crisis nurseries, where parents can leave the child when they are unable to cope, and emergency shelters, where the family has an opportunity to resolve the crisis with the help of the shelter staff.

Education in child development and management is another service that is sometimes included in programs to curb child abuse. This approach has limited utility in families where one child is abused, while the other children receive adequate or better parental care. In addition to didactic courses, parent education based on practical behavior modification procedures is sometimes offered. A home-based "family training program," focused on strengthening appropriate parental and child behaviors, uses a token economy and other behavioral interventions (Christophersen, Kuehn, Grinstead, Barnard, Rainey, and Kuehn 1976). A systems approach to abuse families that assesses and attempts to modify negative parental affect, aversive behavior of the child, and unclear family communications is described as promising by Park and Collmer (1975) and Conger (1976).

Progress in the psychological treatment of abused and neglected children has lagged considerably behind that of abusive parents. Despite consistent findings of the high probability that child abuse and neglect are passed from one generation to the next, only adult members are receiving treatment services in the 85 percent of abuse families in the nationwide programs funded by the Office of Child Development and the National Center on Child Abuse and Neglect, according to Cohn and Miller (1977), who are evaluating their treatment programs. They state: ". . . while we must continue to test out innovative strategies for working with abusive parents, we clearly must spend more time implementing and testing methods for treating children who have been injured. We must more consciously learn ways of allowing these children to develop to their fullest potential, thereby breaking into the intergenerational pattern of abuse" (p. 458).

Major obstructions to the development of psychotherapeutic strategies geared to abused and neglected children have been the medical and social-legal models of child abuse (Beezley, Martin, and Alexander 1976). According to the first model, the child is viewed as suffering from physical injuries requiring medical treatment. The second model deflects attention from the child to the abusive parents, who are viewed as criminals who deserve punishment or are in need of rehabilitation. According to these models, the goals are medical treatment of the child and prevention of the repetition of the parents' criminal assault. Psychological treatment of abused children is bypassed by these models, which are too simplistic to encompass the intense psychological trauma to the child of physical abuse and neglect or the family dysfunction of which the abuse and neglect are manifestations.

Another barrier to the psychological treatment of abused children has been the abusive parents, even those in the process of rehabilitation. Although abused children show extensive personality problems and need psychotherapy, parents frequently feel too threatened to permit any but medical treatment and special education for the child they have abused. Even though parents' refusal to permit psychotherapy with the abused child suggests the continuation of abuse and neglect in more passive or subtle forms, or the substitution of emotional abuse and neglect for physical abuse and neglect, an agency usually has no recourse but to compromise its recommendations for the child (Williams 1976).

Regarding individual play therapy, Kempe and Kempe (1978) state:

> Individual therapy would undoubtedly benefit every abused child. It is tragic that we can bring this treatment to only a small proportion of those in need because we know that *all* abused children, not only those referred, have difficulties that affect their school performance as well as their relationships with adults and other children. Some of them show signs of severe disturbance. But the professional time needed and, therefore, the expense have thus far restricted individual play therapy to those few of the most disturbed whose behavior is particularly disruptive to those around them.

Another reason for the inadequate application of psychotherapy to abused and neglected children who are viewed by most investigators as in need of it is the aim of keeping the family together, an aim that directs treatment resources on the parents. Finally, ignoring the psychological needs of the victim may be part of the same unconscious processes in professionals that permitted them to ignore, until recently, the reality that parents abused and neglected their children.

Galdston (1965) offers the following suggestions for the psychological treatment of abused infants. At first the infants should be left unbothered on the hospital ward. When they show awareness of the environment by facial or vocal expression, some body contact may be offered by specially trained nurses. As the child responds, the nurse should provide maximal body contact by carrying the infant and humming and talking concurrently. As the infant moves from complete passivity to activity, another nurse with different nurturing skills may be required, because the infant's behavior may become extremely unappealing and include biting and poking. At this stage, the infant is likely to eat, a very important milestone because "the expression of appetite for food appears to be inextricably linked with appetite for contact with a nurse, as though they were the same."

Beezley et al. (1976), Martin (1976), and Kempe and Kempe (1978) describe a variety of therapeutic interventions for abused and neglected children. These include therapeutic play schools, day-care centers, or public schools where emotionally sensitive teachers can engender a sense of trust and confidence in the children and help them with handicapping personality traits; opportunities for socialization to counteract the effects of the poor parental models of interpersonal interaction; developmental stimulation and remediation of lags and deficits at special schools; and group therapy with preadolescent and adolescent children.

D'Ambrosio's (1970) successful, long-term psychotherapy with a savagely abused child demonstrates the degree of progress even a severely damaged child can make in a therapeutic milieu. The chapters in this book by Morrison and Brubakken and Flanzraich and Steiner describe specialized treatment approaches to abused and neglected children.

Separation from the parents and removal to another domicile may be the most therapeutic intervention for many abused children. Chapters in this book by Dennis, Kent, and Money and his associates demonstrate that placement of abused and neglected children in even moderately supportive environments results in at least partial reversibility of some of the psychological, hormonal, and statural effects of abuse and neglect. If the early finding (Cohn and Miller 1977) that only 40 to 50 percent of treated parents stop abusing their children is cross-validated, drastic revisions in planning for abused and neglected children are indicated. NCHSR (1978) states that "the findings suggest the need to identify more effective, early intervention methods of treatment" (p. 3). In addition to this strategy, the development of nonparental domiciles, earlier termination of parental rights (National Center for the Prevention and Treatment of Child Abuse and Neglect 1978), earlier adoption and government subsidies to low-income but child-enhancing adoptive homes are strategies that appear to be increasingly indicated.

In short, in many instances the community's resources will be more profitably spent on these strategies than on the manifold services required to bring the parental home up to even marginal standards of child care, where the prized goal of all these efforts is stopping the parents from abusing their children. Referring to the work of the National Society for the Prevention of Cruelty to Children in England, Jones (1977) states: "With the benefit of hindsight, we now realize that in several of our cases the child's interest might have been better served if the focus of our intervention had been on helping the parents to relinquish the child rather than on working toward rehabilitation" (p. 116).

REFERENCES

Beezley, P., Martin, H. P., and Alexander, H. "Comprehensive family oriented therapy." In R. E. Helfer and C. H. Kempe, eds., *Child Abuse and Neglect: The Family and the Community*. Cambridge, Mass.: Ballinger, 1976.

Besharov, D. J. "U. S. National Center on Child Abuse and Neglect: Three years of experience." *Child Abuse and Neglect—The International Journal* 1 (1977):173–77.

Christophersen, E. R., Kuehn, B. S., Grinstead, J. D., Barnard, J. D., Rainey, S. K., and Kuehn, F. E. "A family training program for abuse and neglect families." *Journal of Pediatric Psychology* 1 (1976):90–94.

Cohn, A. H., and Miller, M. K. "Evaluating new modes of treatment for child abusers and neglectors: The experience of federally funded demonstration projects in the USA." *Child Abuse and Neglect—The International Journal* 1 (1977):453–58.

Cohn, A. H., Ridge, S. S., and Collignon, F. C. "Evaluating innovative treatment programs." *Children Today* 4 (1975):10–12.

Conger, R. D. "A Comparative Study of Interaction Patterns between Deviant and Nondeviant Families." Doctoral dissertation, University of Washington, 1976.

D'Ambrosio, R. *No Language but a Cry*. Garden City, N.Y.: Doubleday & Co., 1970.

Feinstein, H. N. "Group therapy for mothers with infanticidal impulses." *American Journal of Psychiatry* 120 (1964):882–86.

Galdston, R. "Observations on children who have been abused by their parents." *American Journal of Psychiatry* 122 (1965):440–43.

————. "Violence begins at home: The Parents' Center Project for the Study and Prevention of Child Abuse." *Journal of the American Academy of Child Psychiatry* 10 (1970):336–50.

HEW. *Child Abuse and Neglect: An Overview of the Problems*, vol. 1. Washington, D.C. DHEW Publ. No. (OHD) 75-30073, 1975.

————. *Child Abuse and Neglect: The Roles and Responsibilities of Professionals*, vol. 3. Washington, D.C. DHEW Publ. No. (OHD) 75-30074, 1975.

Helfer, R. E. *Child Abuse and Neglect: The Diagnostic Process and Treatment Programs*. Washington, D.C.: U.S. Department of Health, Education and Welfare. Publ. No. (OHD) 75-69, 1975.

Helfer, R. E., and Kempe, C. H. *Child Abuse and Neglect: The Family and the Community*. Cambridge, Mass.: Ballinger, 1976.

Jones, C. O. "A critical evaluation of the work of the NSPCC's battered child research department." *Child Abuse and Neglect: The International Journal* 1 (1977):111–18.

Justice, B., and Justice, R. *The Abusing Family*. New York: Human Sciences Press, 1976.

Kempe, C. H. "Sexual abuse, another hidden pediatric problem." *Pediatrics* 62 (1978):382–89.

Kempe, C. H., and Helfer, R. E. *Helping the Battered Child and His Family*. Philadelphia.: J. B. Lippincott Co., 1972.

Kempe, R. S., and Kempe, C. H. *Child Abuse*. Cambridge, Mass.: Harvard University Press, 1978.

Lahey, B. Personal communication, 1977.

Lieber, L. L., and Baker, J. M. "Parents Anonymous—self-help treatment for child abusing parents: A review and an evaluation." *Child Abuse and Neglect: The International Journal* 1 (1977):133–48.

Martin, H. P. *The Abused Child: A Multidisciplinary Approach to Developmental Issues and Treatment*. Cambridge, Mass.: Ballinger, 1976.

National Center for Health Services Research. *Announcement*, 1978, May/June, p. 3.

National Center for the Prevention and Treatment of Child Abuse and Neglect. Legislation to terminate parent-child legal relationships. *National Child Protection Newsletter* 6 (May 1978):1–3.

National Center on Child Abuse and Neglect. *Federally Funded Child Abuse and Neglect Projects, 1975*. Washington, D.C.: U.S. Government Printing Office, DHEW Publ. No. OHD 76-30076, 1976.

Parke, R. D., and Collmer, C. W. "Child Abuse: An Interdisciplinary Analysis." In *Review of Child Development Research,* vol. 5. Chicago: University of Chicago Press, 1975.

Polansky, N., and Polansky, N. "The Current Status on Child Abuse and Child Neglect in This Country." Report to the Joint Commission on Mental Health for Children, February 1968. In Gil, D. G., *Violence against Children—Physical Child Abuse in the United States*. Cambridge, Mass.: Harvard University Press, 1970.

St. Louis Globe Democrat. "Editorial: Child Abuse Menace in Illinois," November 9, 1978.

Spinetta, J. J. "Parental Personality Factors in Child Abuse." Paper presented at the annual convention of the American Psychological Association, San Francisco, California, August 1977.

Steele, B. F. *Working with Abusive Parents from a Psychiatric Point of View.* Washington, D.C.: U.S. Department of Health, Education and Welfare, Publ. No. (OHD) 75-70, 1975.

Wallen, G., Pierce, S., Koch, M. F., and Nenters, H. D. "The interdisciplinary team approach to child abuse services: Strengths and limitations." *Child Abuse and Neglect: The International Journal* 1 (1977):359-64.

Williams, G. J. "Editorial." *Journal of Pediatric Psychology* 1 (1976):3-5.

CHAPTER 43

Aspects of Bonding Failure: The Psychopathology and Psychotherapeutic Treatment of Families of Battered Children

Christopher Ounsted, Rhoda Oppenheimer, and Janet Lindsay

INTRODUCTION

The battered child syndrome is a common one. Kempe and Helfer (1972) give a rate of 380 per million population per year for North America. This is probably a low estimate. If the same rate applies to England and Wales, we would have 19,000 new cases a year.

All workers agree that the syndrome has been diagnosed more frequently in recent years. Whether or not there has been a true secular increase is not known. Our impression is that the syndrome is truly increasing. In our own service in Oxford there has been a notable increase in the demand for treatment of the syndrome in the last few years. Our current rate is now about 110 per thousand referrals, whereas in the past it has been of the order of two or three per thousand.

Kempe and Helfer (1972) have given details of the sociology and the psychopathology of the syndrome.

In this paper we consider systems of treatment and of prevention that are evolving in our service. We shall deal with two series, one of approximately 86 families with an injured child referred to the Park Hospital for Children, the other of 24 selected mothers who were treated as out-patients because of fears that they might injure their babies, but who in fact had not done so when they were taken on for treatment.

Diagnosis

Diagnosis, as Kempe and Helfer have pointed out, is the first step in psychotherapy. It is an integral part of the classic syndrome that the babies will

Reprinted with permission from *Developmental Medicine and Child Neurology* 16 (1974):447–56. Copyright 1974, Spastics International Medical Publications.

have been brought by their parents to doctors on a number of occasions before the diagnosis is made. When the parents present their injured child at Casualty or to the pediatrician they give a confabulatory story: the explanation is colluded with by the spouse and the story is often accepted by the doctors and social workers. In spite of recent intensive propaganda, more than half of all our cases are known to have been injured on a number of occasions before they are finally diagnosed.

The first step in therapy is that the diagnosis should be made and maintained with equanimity. The parents are told at our first interview that the injuries are such that they must have been inflicted by an adult. We find that the parents often accept this with relief, though the relief may not be explicit until therapy has advanced.

Assessment of the Family Prognosis

About one-third of the families referred to us are found to be untreatable in the sense that permanent removal of the proband under a Care Order is required. A single example will suffice.

CASE 1

A female child aged 20 months was admitted to hospital with the classic syndrome. There were numerous bruises of different ages on all parts of the body. The child was dwarfed, being below the 3rd percentile in length and weight. Her skull circumference was just below the mean. She had a severe iron deficiency anemia. Radiological survey showed two recent fractures of the skull, probably of different dates. There were two fractured ribs, probably suffered three weeks before the time of the radiograph.

On admission, the child showed notable 'frozen watchfulness' (which syndrome we describe below). She did not raise her head or move her hands in any useful way. She was entirely silent, neither crying nor cooing. The only exception to this behavior was when she was approached by a male adult: she would gaze-fixate him and, as he picked her up, she would utter a brief piercing scream. Apart from this behavior she gave out no active signals. Two-and-a-half months after admission, during which time she had been given intensive care, she showed approximately ten months of developmental advance. She was attempting to walk with assistance, she was feeding well, her weight was rising, and her anemia was cured. She had formed selective affectional bonds with some members of the staff.

Investigation of the family background revealed that the mother, who was 21, had been harshly reared in another country. She had conceived the proband out of wedlock and had been deserted by her fiancé when she became pregnant. After the child's admission the mother was found to be suffering from pulmonary tuberculosis and to be pregnant by her second spouse. She was an inadequate, weak woman who refused to visit the child in hospital and refused to come into the Mother's Unit to be with her. These refusals were in response to the demands of her husband. The stepfather was the oldest of eleven children and came from a harsh background. He had been repeatedly in trouble with the police since he was twelve years old and had served sentences in detention centers, approved schools, borstals and, just before marrying the proband's mother, had completed a sentence of three years for infliction of grievous bodily harm.

The parents on one occasion expressed a weak wish to have the child returned to them for two days, but in practice made no steps to obtain care of her. Over a five-year period they have made no further contact.

In such cases there is an urgent need for the infant to be found fresh and safe surroundings where he can develop social bonds with healthy adults. Too often this decision is delayed, the maturational stage for bonding passes by and the child is left with a chronic deprivation syndrome which is likely to perpetuate itself in the next generation.

Both for separation and for therapy, early action is essential. In its absence we see that paragenetic perpetuation which Sir Keith Joseph (1973) named the 'cycle of deprivation'.

Diagnosis of Other Disease in the Proband

We have found that many children who are battered have unrecognized physical and/or behavioral abnormalities, or are thought to have them by their mothers. This obtained in about one-half of all the Park Hospital group of treated families. The abnormalities were very varied. For example, one child had had seven hospital admissions before it was found that he was blind and hence could not gaze-fixate his mother. The parents had maintained a totally defensive attitude until they were told that their child was blind, and had been from birth; then their defenses fell. 'He cried and cried and he never looked at me' said the mother. The father said 'It's my fault. I knew what was happening really. I should have stopped it.' They asked the physician—'Could you have done it?'' (battered the baby). He answered 'Yes', and this empathic answer led to an open relationship. This second stage in diagnosis is also therapeutic. One shares with the mother and father those features of the child's development and behavior which could provoke anyone to abuse.

Diagnosis of the Parents

A thorough, delicate and psychiatrically sophisticated diagnosis of both parents is essential. It must be a progressive process.

Serious mental illness, psychopathy and inadequate personalities were found. Precise statistics cannot be had and we think that statistical treatment of the data is likely to mislead more than to clarify.

Diagnosis of the Family

The family diagnosis, extending back into the pedigree, should be made in detail. It is well-recognized (and our own data confirm) that parents who abuse their children often come from families in which violence has been the rule for some generations. Both parents must be made conscious of this pattern, then they can see their task as one of breaking what often seems to them to be a family curse extending down the generations. The parents are themselves unloved children, specifically children to whom very little was given but from whom much was demanded. Many of the mothers have a dependent, yet angry and hating relationship with their own mothers. Since in therapy we give to these mothers the mothering of which they have been deprived, it is essential to elicit a clear and precise diagnosis of their own developmental experiences.

Diagnosis of Family Relationships

All these families are by definition disturbed, but it is desirable as treatment proceeds to try to define the nature of these different disturbances. For example, jealousy is relatively common, by which we mean that one of the parents is morbidly jealous of the other's feelings toward the baby. The father can often feel displaced by the baby in his wife's affections. In one case, a social class 1 father came into the maternity ward and saw his wife breast-feeding their new-born infant; he physically tore the infant from the breast and flung it violently across the ward, shouting 'those breasts are mine!'

IN-PATIENT SERVICE

Both the architecture and the setting of the in-patient service are essential aspects of the treatment we give. The mothers' house consists of a domestic dwelling, closely annexed to a children's hospital. The house contains three comfortable bed-sitting rooms, a communal sitting-room, a dining area, a kitchen, a laundry and the usual offices. It is set in a garden with peaceful views on every side. The hospital where the children and their brothers and sisters are treated has a great diversity of rooms and territories in it. There is an active school, and a large occupational therapy department with a number of environments. The play-rooms are equipped and furnished for children of all ages. There is a separate day-nursery, staffed with experienced nurses and removed from the rest of the day space. The night-nursery is in a different part of the hospital from the day space and from the mothers' unit.

Admission to the Unit

When the diagnosis is first made the parents are defensive, thus a crisis arises which must often be resolved by law. This can be a therapeutic action: the doctor and the parents know that the child has been injured, and the child must be put where such injuries will not recur. In the United Kingdom, this is done by obtaining a Place of Safety Order, either from the appropriate department of the social services or from the police. The Place of Safety Order names the hospital and gives 28 days in which the plan of treatment can be put into action.

When the order is obtained, we explain what it means and offer to admit the mother to the unit, together with any brothers and sisters of the injured child. In the great majority of cases the offer is accepted.

The first few days of therapy are crucial. The mothers and children have been living a life of extreme tension, punctuated often by outbursts of rage. Communication has been by shouts and blows. The families usually have been existing in social isolation.

Almost universally the mothers have felt trapped, unwanted, unloved, and unequal to their roles as children, as spouses, and as parents. These feelings must be reversed.

In the first few days, the mothers and children experience for the first time total care. Without having to ask, they are provided with food, warmth, privacy, tranquillity, and with an undemanding routine and the attentive care of varieties of mature adults.

The standard reaction of the mothers to this experience is one of astonishment. It is a situation quite new to them. We see at first the phenomenon which we have named 'second-day packing': on the second day after admission the mothers often panic and wish to leave. It is a situation analogous to the sudden cessation of chronic pain. Calm intervention by the staff soon overcomes this situation and the mothers settle down to a regular routine.

'Frozen Watchfulness'

The abused child must also receive his initial treatment. Once the injuries have received attention the behavioral syndrome remains to be treated. Repeatedly abused children show a characteristic behavior which we have named 'frozen watchfulness' (Ounsted 1972). Children with frozen watchfulness make no sounds. If they are toddlers they do not chatter in the presence of adults. If they are approached they stand quite still. They will gaze-fixate but do not smile. They are often silent, even when their wounds are dressed.

We see frozen watchfulness as an adaptation to situations in which the loving and loved parent unpredictably and without provocation becomes transformed into an aggressor, and then immediately reverts to good parental behavior. Treatment aims primarily to provide care that is predictable. Characteristically, the child with frozen watchfulness has been unable to establish basic trust in the regularity of his life, and this must now be given him. The routine is designedly regular; bed times, meal times, bath times and play times are all on a fixed schedule, and the behavior of the nurses is equally predictable.

An extreme example of frozen watchfulness and its change under treatment is exemplified by this case history.

CASE 2

The patient was admitted to hospital at the age of nine months, with his mother. The mother had a chronic schizophrenic illness which had been manifest for at least eight years. The father was unknown. The mother and infant had lived in isolation, and the mother had not allowed any interactions with the infant by any person other than herself. On admission, the child's physical measurements were on the 25th centile for his age. Examination revealed no stigmata. He was well washed. He lay completely immobile. When picked up he made no response, and his body was held in tonic extension. He showed no interest in toys; if a plaything was placed in his hands he would drop it without a glance. When food was placed in his hand he did not move it to his mouth. He did not react to sounds. There was no stepping response. If sat up, he lay down at once. He did not smile, nor did he vocalize or babble.

He was gently separated from his psychotic mother and given intensive mothering by the staff. His development was dramatic. Within a month he had made at least four months advance. At 25 months his skills were measured on the Griffiths Scale and he performed as follows:

locomotor scale	22 months
personal social scale	21 months
hearing and speech scale	21 months
eye/hand co-ordination	22 months
performance	20 months

Observation of the child in the presence of his foster-mother showed what appeared to be a natural and warm bonding between the two, and no significant abnormalities in their interactions. The child showed disturbed behavior at and after visits to his mother in a mental hospital. These were stopped when he was $2\frac{1}{2}$ years old. At the age of $3\frac{1}{2}$ years the foster-parents abruptly rejected him and ended the fostering. They gave no reason.

The 'Open Relationship'

The parents of battered babies usually have developed an overgrowth of fantasy, not only in respect of the battering, but also in respect of other matters in their lives. The fantasies protect the parents from a reality which they see as unbearable. This perception is often distorted. In the setting of the Unit, these fantasies are not needed. The situation moves forward and during the second week of treatment it is common for clarifications to occur in which, with relief, the parents will admit to the assaults and will abreact the emotions they have denied.

The timing of this crisis is critical. Behind the treatment is the Consultant, who does not interfere in the day-to-day therapy. He has to judge when the moment has arrived to see the parents. Both parents are seen together and in privacy. It is usual for them to condense what happened into a few emotive sentences. 'His crying' said the mother of one battered baby 'seemed to follow me round the house. I could not stop it. I could not escape.' They then go on to tell how alien to themselves the assaultive behavior seemed to be: 'It did not seem to be me that did it'. They express the feeling that they could not incorporate into their egos the alien behavior which they had shown.

During the interview, weeping, sobbing, and mutual comforting behaviors are prominent. Toward the end of the interview they begin to express their feelings of alienation: 'I did not think that I could be part of the human race'. At this point it is essential for the physician to make clear to them, with empathic communications, that cataclysmic breakdown in parental behavior is an integral part of the human ethogram. One has to convey that all of us, given adequate provocation, could batter babies. Later it is useful to go over each violent act and elicit in detail what really happened, so that the fantasies can be eliminated.

By the end of the second week of inpatient treatment we aim to have established an 'open relationship' with the families. By this we mean that:

a) We have released the proband from his frozen watchfulness. We have let him find a safe and predictable world, in which he can begin to explore, to learn, and to mature, both as an individual and as a social being.

b) We have helped the mother to feel free. She no longer feels trapped in a vicious circle. She begins to mature. She learns by precept and example how to care for her young.

c) We have helped the parental relationships and the intrafamilial dynamics to lose their quality of fantasy.

d) We have let the future be seen afresh with hope for growth and change.

We must here make a theoretical digression to explain our terminology. We use the terms 'closed relationship' and 'open relationship' as analogous to Bertalanffy's (1968) division of general systems into closed and open systems. In the former, the laws of classical thermodynamics apply—a closed system over time proceeds inevitably toward complete disorder, just because it is closed in on itself. These families seem similarly to have been closed in for generations. By removing, both physically and emotionally, all the constraints that have held the family closed, we allow an open relationship to develop. Open systems are those which show increasingly expressed orderliness as they develop over time. The classical example is the realization of the zygote's potential as it evolves into the adult organism through a series of metamorphoses.

We place the families in a highly regressive situation. They are fed, housed, and cared for as though they were infants. It might seem a paradox that, in this situation, they can change and mature. But consider how a caterpillar changes into a butterfly—the regression of pupation is essential. Thus we see the simultaneous occurrence of psychodynamic dissolution and psychodynamic developmental advance, not as a paradox but rather as the *coincidentia oppositorum* in Nicholas of Cusa's sense—a resolution by the coming together of opposites.

The Therapeutic Court

Court hearings need not damage the open relationship between the hospital and these families. Properly handled, the small drama of the Juvenile Court can itself be a useful catharsis. These parents have been dogged by guilt, denial, and fear of exposure. Their upbringing has often been unjust. They have fantasied another world of 'them'—of police, magistrates, and parental figures whom they must dread but obey.

They expiate their guilts in reality and this enables them for the first time to feel themselves to be responsible people (Ounsted 1968). After the court hearing the parents usually express relief. The court usually makes an order placing the child in the care of the local authority, but in treatable cases this does not mean separation from the parents. It does mean that the parents have an organization which protects both them and the child.

The Liberating Bond

Another apparent paradox is the notion that firm bonds to mature adults are preconditional for the capacity to choose freely and responsibly. Yet analogous concepts are basic to the physiology of stability and change: Claud Bernard's 'La fixité du milieu intérieur est la condition essentielle de la vie libre' expresses the matter precisely (Bernard 1895).

When part of a system is employed in choice, in idiosyncratic development or in movement, then another part of that same system must be stable. The stable bond for the battering parents is with the hospital and its staff. It is important that this trusting bond should not be seen as a kind of 'transference neurosis'. Specifically we make no attempt to end the families' relationship with us, nor do we interpret it to them. In an open relationship mutual courtesy between all parties is the goal. Verbal discussion has limited usefulness, and interpretations of private feelings are apt to destroy the self-respect which we aim to create.

The Outcome

No statistics of the results would be meaningful, since both our ideas and our practice are in a state of evolution. In most cases there has been a notable improvement in the intrafamilial dynamics.

Many cases still cannot be treated, and in others only palliation is possible. We now turn to the more hopeful area of prevention.

OUT-PATIENT SERVICE

Preventive Study

Kempe and Helfer (1972) showed that prevention is practicable and effective. We now describe a study of families treated on an out-patient basis.

Referral

The children were referred by their family doctors because of a grossly abnormal mother-child relationship, and because the doctors thought that the children were at risk for battering. From those referred to us as out-patients, we selected for detailed study and treatment 24 families in which the mother and child were of normal intelligence and the child was not older than four years.

Two-thirds of the mothers had complained to their family doctors that the child was driving them crazy. One-third had admitted to hitting the child too often and too hard. At the time of referral 22 of the mothers were on tranquillizers or anti-depressants and 16 of the children were receiving sedatives. Fifty-four separate factors were examined for each of the 24 families and were then arrayed in order of increasing frequency within the sample as a whole.

Parental Characteristics

The early biographies of both parents were often distorted. Fifteen of the mothers had had unhappy, emotionally deprived childhoods. The most striking aspect of their personalities was an extremely low tolerance to any form of pain or frustration. Two-thirds of the mothers were labile in mood. Migrainous attacks of sufficient severity to require withdrawal to bed had occurred in 16 of the mothers. Nineteen of the 48 parents had suffered from Besnier's syndrome (asthma, eczema). Ten of the fathers and 19 of the mothers showed immature and dependent personalities.

In general, the families were isolated and lonely. They had made few friends in their neighborhoods. Many had removed themselves from their own part of the country and were new settlers in the area. Not one of the 24 mothers went out to work.

The mothers were on average 24 years old at the time of the birth, which is two years younger than the median age of maternity in our region at the present time.

Parental Relationships

Parental relationships were generally bad. Four mothers had children by men other than their spouse. A further six mothers conceived by their spouse prior to marriage.

In about one-quarter of the sample, housing and work difficulties were prominent. In ten of the families one parent had been sterilized by the time of referral. Nearly two-thirds of the mothers complained that the fathers lacked understanding of their difficulties and were impatient and unhelpful. Sexual difficulties were an outstanding complaint by nineteen of the mothers.

Proband's Histories

From the beginning, most of these families had had an unhappy and disturbed mother-infant interaction. Nearly two-thirds of the mothers had complained of and were treated for puerperal depression. The 'colicky child' syndrome (Barrett 1971) was a prominent feature of most of the probands during infancy. One-third of the children were reported to have vomited frequently in the neonatal period. Complaints of tics and other displacement activities figured in ten of the children. Asthma and/or eczema afflicted eleven of the probands. Sleeping difficulties, 'crossness', excessive crying and irritability were present in two-thirds. This had led to the same proportion of children being treated with some form of sedation or tranquillizers before they were referred to the clinic.

State at Referral

At the time of referral the mothers had a multiplicity of complaints about the child. They saw the child as too clinging, too aggressive, too timid, too defiant, and disobedient. They made quite unrealistic demands on the children for obedience and for love. Two-thirds of the mothers complained that the child could not be cuddled.

As part of the general failure in communication which was evident in every case, it was striking that one-half of the children had selective speech retardation.

Thus we were faced in these families with a situation in which the interaction between all members had become distorted and fixed in the pattern of a closed system. This was made explicit by the mothers, often in terms that they felt trapped, or in prison, and were unable to break out except in outbursts of rage. The vicious circle of mal-communication was present in every case.

Treatment

On referral, the parents and the child were seen by the physician. Individual therapy by the social worker was begun for the parents and the child in their own home, as this made it easier to involve the father.

When judged to be ready, the mothers were introduced into a group of between five and eight other mothers. At the same time, the child was introduced into a toddler's group. The two groups were run simultaneously in adjoining rooms, with free access between the two. The goal of therapy was to help the mothers with their own problems and, at the same time, to teach them to cope in a more constructive way with all their children. The groups were found to be therapeutic. The mothers were able to receive support from each other.

The mothers were encouraged to telephone to the social worker whenever a crisis arose. As the mothers learned to cope, many of them reported that simply thinking of using the telephone was enough to enable them to regain control.

The mothers were helped to keep a daily diary of the situations in which their child drove them to explosive anger. This was brought along to the sessions with the therapist for detailed discussion.

The children soon learned to play and explore naturally, and associated these activities with the mothers' presence. The mothers came to be regarded by the children as bringing them to a place where they were safe and free. Babies who were too small to join actively in play activities were involved by being cuddled and loved by any staff member available. The mothers saw their children being handled cheerfully when they showed any signs of the 'colicky child' syndrome or when they soiled, vomited or were angry.

Outcome

The 24 mothers who attended regularly for between one and two years all showed some improvement. In no case did battering occur.

It must be emphasised that this group was a selected one. We deliberately chose those likely to respond to treatment and no generalizations can be made to all parents of battered infants.

SUMMARY

The authors discuss methods of treatment and prevention of child-battering in two groups of families: one group referred to their unit at the Park Hospital for Children, Oxford, and the second group treated on an out-patient basis in a clinic in another county.

The first (in-patient) group consisted of families in which the child was known to have been battered. Initial treatment consisted of: (a) a firm diagnosis that battering had occurred; (b) diagnosis of other diseases in the child; and (c) diagnosis of the parents, of the family's background and the family relationships. The mothers and children were admitted to a special unit in which a safe, therapeutic environment was organized to provide what had been lacking in the family's own environment. The authors' method of establishing relationships with and between the parents and children produced notable improvements in the family relationships.

The second (out-patient) group consisted of families in which a child was at risk of being battered. After investigation of the child and the family, the mothers were introduced into small groups for mutual support and the children were included in small play-groups, with free access between the groups. The mothers each kept a diary to record explosive situations, and were encouraged to telephone the social worker whenever a crisis arose. All the mothers showed some improvement and no cases of battering occurred, but the authors stress that no general conclusions applicable to all parents of battered children can be drawn from this small, selected group.

REFERENCES

Barrett, J. H. W. (1971) *in* Batstone, G. F., Blair, A. W., Slater, J. M. (eds.) *A Handbook of Prenatal Paediatrics*. Aylesbury: Medical & Technical Publishing Co.

Bernard, C. (1895) *Introduction à l'Etude de la Médicine Experimentale*. Paris: J. B. Ballière et Fils.

Bertalanffy, L. von (1968) *General System Theory*. London: Penguin Press.

Joseph, Sir K. (1973) *Extract from his speech at the Spring Study Seminar on the Cycle of Deprivation, Given to the Association of Directors of Social Services, Brighton*.

Kempe, C. H., Helfer, R. E. (1972) *Helping the Battered Child and His Family*. Philadelphia: Lippincott.

Ounsted, C. (1968) *in* de Reuck, A. V. S., Porter, R. (eds.) *The Mentally Abnormal Offender*. London: Churchill.

———. (1972) *in Proceedings of the 8th International Study Group on Child Neurology and Cerebral Palsy. (unpublished.)*

CHAPTER 44

Parent Surrogate Roles:
A Dynamic Concept in Understanding
and Treating Abusive Parents

Morris J. Paulson and Anne Chaleff

As early as 1922, Czerny demonstrated that institutional hospitalism was related to psychological neglect and lack of environmental stimulation in the first weeks of the infant's life. Goldfarb (1944), stated that children who experienced institutional deprivation during infancy were clearly differentiated from those whose total rearing has been in families. Brody (1956) affirmed that "the genesis of motherliness is to be sought primarily in the quality of the child's attachment to her own mother in the first five years of life." Heilbrun (1965), in discussing the importance of the concept of parental identification, stated: "Something occurs within the context of the family that leads to a degree of behavioral stimulation between a child and one or both parental models." Sandler and Torpie (1968) reported on procedures for improvement of residential care of infants and children, and in assessing the mother surrogate role stated that the primary need is to evaluate the "mothering" capacity of women as an initial step toward identifying who is and is not suitable for the mothering of young children.

Paulson, Lin *et al.* (1972) found that the absence of family harmony and isolation in the parent-child relationship were etiological factors in the alienation of young adults from their parents and from society. In a later paper, Hanssen and Paulson (1972) demonstrated that early child-rearing experiences and parental attitudes regarding the raising of infants and children were dynamic factors in the expression of later social activism and anti-establishment resistance. From these studies, it is evident that the presence of adequate mothering and parenting in general are essential needs for mature personal-social growth and development. The experiencing of a warm child-parent relationship, the identification with and modeling of parental behaviors and attitudes, the acceptance of and internalizing of parental values are all aspects of the early life history of the child which greatly influence later adult behaviors and become the dynamic genesis of future child-rearing practices.

Reprinted with permission from the *Journal of Clinical Child Psychology* 2(1973):38–40.

What then is the relationship between early impoverishment in parenting and later life style behaviors which express themselves through the neglect and abuse of children? Second, from a prophylactic point of view, if inadequate parenting does occur in infancy and early child growth, what remedial measures can be taken to ameliorate such inadequacy or absence of parenting before its consequences have a detrimental effect on the next generation of children? The present paper does not focus on the experience of children who have endured psychological and physical neglect, abuse, and parental violence. The paper directs itself to the concept of the parent-surrogate model and its role in the treatment and rehabilitation of abusive fathers and mothers, most of whom have themselves suffered chronic, severe emotional deprivation and absence of mature parenting in infancy.

THE NATURE OF THE STUDY

The authors, one a male clinical psychologist and the other a female psychiatric nurse, served as co-therapists on a multidisciplinary team of mental health professionals at the Neuropsychiatric Institute, U.C.L.A. Center for the Health Sciences. We developed and participated in a three-year program of group psychotherapy for parents fearful of, admitting to, or charged with neglect, abuse, and maltreatment of minor children. The subject population consisted of sixty-one fathers and mothers, most of whom were referred from the Department of Public Social Service, the Juvenile Courts, or other community agencies.

Resistance to group psychotherapy was expressed by many parents insofar as they initially maintained their innocence of any overly aggressive disciplining and many times compulsively affirmed the "accidental nature of the injury." Where an intact family existed, both parents were strongly encouraged to attend the weekly, evening, two-hour sessions. A preliminary one-half hour of time by the nurse-therapist was devoted to information giving and practical measures related to child care and infant development. The remaining one and a half hour session, with both co-therapists present, followed somewhat traditional lines of group therapy, but also incorporated significant use of confrontation, encouragement of abreaction and catharsis, and stimulation of group process. Both therapists, in their early fifties, were by age able to fulfill a surrogate parent role for the fathers and mothers in the group whose average age was twenty-six years.

Although none of the children involved in this study died from abuse and/or neglect, there was a range of violent parenting actions from mild bruising to multiple fractures, severe brain damage, and resulting mental retardation. Two-thirds of the children had confirmed histories of repeated abuse. The age range of children was from one month to ten years, with a mean average age at the time of the first identified abuse being approximately nineteen months. The sexes of the abusing parent were in our sample almost equally divided, as were the sexes of the identified victim.

THEORETICAL FORMULATIONS

The male-female, co-therapist relationship in our group allowed for identification and modeling of parent surrogate roles by the members. For many of our mothers and fathers, having experienced a lifetime of emotional isolation, parental rejection, and physical violence, the experience of interacting intimately with a group and with the male-female co-therapists was a pristine encounter with adults who were noncondemning and nonpunishing. The acceptance of verbally expressed rage, anger, and dependence, and at times even manipulations, without fear of rejection, were emotionally moving experiences both for the individual members as well as the group as a whole. What were the dynamic substrata that allowed for the positive development of parent-surrogate roles? The theoretical constructs we found most useful were those of intimacy, empathy, trust, and "mothering," used in the generic sense of mother-father parenting. Intimacy as the positive outgrowth of a willingness to risk a sharing of oneself with another is seen as an expression of a bond of affection and closeness between the group members and the co-therapists. Intimacy is the emotional touching that leads to affectional fulfillment in an inter-personal relationship. It is the foundation-stone to family harmony. For many of our parents, the life experience of personal and family estrangement reflected the emptiness in living and the absence of any degree of emotional closeness or sharing either with their peers or with their own biological parents and siblings.

To live through the experienced abreaction of a sobbing, violently distraught, guilt-ridden abusive parent is to undergo an experiential encounter that at one time may stimulate great empathy and compassion. Yet at another time, the nature and degree of the impulsive and at times, willfully inflicted injury can be so frightful and horrifying that great surges of negative feelings can be engendered even in those parents who themselves acknowledged some degree of severe disciplining. It is for this reason that the authors recommend homogeneity of group members insofar as the reason for referral is concerned. Such "oneness" in the identified reason for referral did contribute greatly to acceptance, group cohesiveness, and capacity for identification.

For the therapists to be judgmental and condemning is to be grossly antitherapeutic. To be empathetic is to realize that most of humanity, whether it be the patients, therapists, or "just plain parents," have at times experienced that moment of rage, that feeling of acute frustration, that anguish of aloneness and despair, that could have similarly erupted into a violent attack upon others. It is the nature of the positive early child-parent relationship and the quality of inner control that differentiate the overly disciplining and abusive parent from the parent who can exercise appropriate limit settings, yet fulfill the role of adequacy in parenting.

The concept of basic trust (Erikson 1950), and the role of early mothering experience as defined by Spitz (1945) and Harlow (1965) were additional essential constructs in the understanding and treatment of our parent population. It is evident that while learning the mechanics of motherhood is important, there is an even greater need to share with the child the positive emotional closeness of a warm, mature, affectional mothering experience. The anaclitic oneness of pregnancy symbolizes this closeness and intimacy in the sharing of a life experience. And, of course, following birth, there must of necessity be a continuation of this psychological caring and physiological fulfillment in order to assure maturity in emotional and physical development. Olden (1953), has suggested that the origins of empathy do lie in the biological mother-child relationship sustained during pregnancy and continued after birth. This first stage of infant development is thus the foundation-stone for the development of trust in a nurturing, omnipresent parent figure. It is within the symbiotic relationship of this early mother-child interaction that there then develops an awareness of others, the development of the "me," and the security that the mother as a source of environmental support will nurture and care. Without such affirmation, the child's feelings of hopelessness, the sense of isolation, the perception of the world as a potentially hostile and rejecting environment, can become the roots of what Horney (1945) calls "basic anxiety."

THE EXPERIENTIAL ENCOUNTER

For many of our parents, this virgin experience of a compassionate sharing of tenderness, the opportunity to literally cry out the agony of their emotional pain, the confirmation of feelings of understanding and acceptance within the group and by the co-therapists, were the first living experiences of acceptance from adults who were at that moment filling a parent-surrogate role. The nurse-therapist as a mother symbol allowed the parents to identify with a mature female figure and for many to experience a relationship of trust and sharing. Said one father whose severe disciplining included forcing his son to kneel on carpet tacks, "It may seem cruel to you, but as children this is the type of punishment we received, my wife and I. We were just using the same type of punishment. If we did not care about him, we would not do this." With this type of early, continual, childhood disciplining, it is understandable how such experiences as intimacy, empathy, trust, and adequacy of mothering can fail to develop, leaving the child fearful, angry, and distrustful.

Our experience has shown that the co-therapists as parent-surrogates can be a psychological antidote to those emotionally empty and at times violent relationships which characterize the early, chronic, life experience of our immature, impulsive, emotionally starved, and "unmothered" parents. One father, whose impulsive and violent disciplining resulted in major fractures in his infant child, said of the nurse-therapist, "To me, she is a warm bunny." For a soft-spoken, passive mother, whose breakthrough of frustration resulted in massive bruises from repeated kicking of her young stepdaughter, the female therapist was an emotionally fulfilling mother figure. At one critical moment in therapy this patient ran from the room in tears, followed moments later by the female-therapist. The patient, leaning against the wall, sobbing out her experienced rejection from her husband, threw her arms around the nurse-therapist, embraced her for a moment, gained comfort and solace from this mothering, then was able to return to the therapy. At this one moment in therapy this emotionally unfulfilled mother felt compassion and support from a parent-surrogate figure.

At times the male therapist was seen as authoritarian, stern, and judgmental; yet at other times the clasp of a handshake, the support and acceptance in spite of the expression of violent paranoid-like threats to the therapist, confirmed the feelings of faith, trust, and empathy. These examples are emotionally moving confirmations of an experienced acceptance of an adult, who at that moment as a parent-surrogate figure, was fulfilling all the longings for acceptance and understanding not achieved in the early life of these mothers and fathers.

In many respects the male-female, co-therapist relationship reconstituted the primary family unit. For almost all members, their own childhood was highly traumatic, fraught with punishment and severe disciplining, and lacking the experience of intimacy, sharing, and trust. Lacking in the fulfillment of these basic needs for security and faced with the responsibilities of parenting, for which they were ill-equipped, a sudden moment of stress frequently became the catalyst for violent acts of abuse against a scapegoat child.

THE PARENT SURROGATE ROLES IN RETROSPECT

During the initial phases of group therapy the individual patient frequently had a heightened level of suspicion toward the therapists. In spite of our clarifying our role as autonomous from any referral agency, the co-therapists were regarded as "on the side of establishment." The lifelong experience of many of our parents, in which their own mothers and fathers had not engendered trust and confidence in "authority" figures, was recapitulated in the early therapy sessions. We were the symbol of those "bad" parents, who did not understand, those who condemned rather than reached out a helping and compassionate hand. For those few parents who early in therapy had strong dependency needs and were searching for real or symbolic parent figures, there was an early decrease in distrust and a turning to the therapists for increasing help and support, both within the group and with situations in their outside life.

In contrast to the first few months of the group's life, where isolation and resistance characterized the inability of a number of the group members to reach out to the group as a whole, the latter months of our therapy experience have shown a marked change in the defined roles of the therapists. With greater feelings of trust, with an acknowledgment of the need for help in their marriage or individual life, and with the recognition that we were nonjudgmental and there to help, we were increasingly placed in this positive parent-surrogate role. While both therapists were regarded with increased warmth and consideration, the female nurse co-therapist was much more identified in the mothering role. Her responsibility for the parent training program, her information input in the important areas of child development, her practical knowledge in the caring and nursing of the infant and growing child, and her numerous home visits, all defined the greater degree of intimacy and personal involvement in the life experience of these families.

From a psychoanalytic frame of reference, one might be criticized for fostering dependency needs and for not "working through" the unresolved Oedipus complex. However, from our eclectic approach of intervention and understanding, the therapists felt that such giving of themselves was not the perpetuating of a neurosis but an opportunity for the group members to share intimacy and understanding with mature adult figures. Our results in the third year of this group experience confirm the positive outcomes from our role as parent surrogates. The capacity of the fathers and mothers to relate, especially to the female therapist in their own home environment, the ability to challenge the supposed authority position of the leaders, the handshaking warmth of an appreciative father and mother as they leave therapy, are testimonial to the importance of male-female co-therapists in the multidisciplinary, multitheoretical, and eclectic treatment of abusive parents through the vehicle of group psychotherapy.

The importance of the parent-surrogate role as a vital and dynamic concept in treating abusive parents has been affirmed. It was a significant prophylactic factor in the rehabilitating of many of the mothers and fathers to a more adequate and fulfilling role as parents.

REFERENCES

Brody, S. *Patterns of Mothering*. International Universities Press, New York, 1956.
Czerny, A. Der Artzt als erzicher des kindes, ed. 6, Franz Deuticke, Leipzig, 1922.
Erikson, E. *Childhood and Society*. New York. W. W. Norton & Co., 1950.
Goldfarb, W. Effects of early institutional care on adolescent personality: Rorschach data. *American Journal of Orthopsychiatry* 14:441–47, 1944.
Hanssen, C., and Paulson, M. Our anti-establishmentarian youth: Revolution or evolution. *Adolescence* 7, 27, 393–408, 1972.
Harlow, H. *Behavior of Non-human Primates*. Modern Research Trends. Academic Press, New York, 1965.
Heilbrun, A., and Fromme, D. Parental identification of late adolescents and level of adjustment: The importance of parent-model attributes, ordinal position, and sex of the child. *Journal of Genetic Psychology* 104, 49–59, 1965.
Horney, K. *Our Inner Conflicts*, New York. W. W. Norton & Co., 1945.
Olden, C. An adult empathy with children. *Psychoanalytic Study of the Child*, 8, 111–126, 1953.
Paulson, M., Lin, T., and Hanssen, C. Family harmony: An etiologic factor in alienation. *Child Development* 43:591–603, 1972.

Sandler, L. and Torpie, I. Improvement of residential care of infants and children from birth to age 3. *Archives of Environmental Health* 17, 80–90, 1968.

Spitz, R. Hospitalism, an inquiry into the genesis of psychiatric conditions in early childhood. *The Psychoanalytic Study of the Child.* Vol. 1, International Universities Press, New York, 1945.

CHAPTER 45

The Transmission of Psychopathology through Four Generations of a Family

Stanley J. Weinberg

INTRODUCTION

This paper results from a study of a family known to the Jewish Board of Guardians for over forty-two years, from 1928 to 1970, having received various outpatient and inpatient services. The family was first studied intensively in 1966, and followed up in 1970. An attempt to follow up again in 1976 failed, as the family could not be located.

Longitudinal family studies are of particular interest to those studying the vicious cycle of multigenerational "welfare families," and researching the borderline syndrome and schizophrenia. In regard to the latter, there is considerable evidence at this point from researchers such as Bowen, Kernberg, Kohut, Lidz, and Masterson, to support the theory that the borderline syndrome and schizophrenia are multigenerational phenomena.

Though conclusions cannot be drawn from this study because of the multiplicity of variables, and other factors, it can serve to further codify and explicate the observations and inferences of others, and demonstrate the need for a range of appropriate and sufficient services to children and families, in order to interrupt the transmission of psychopathology to successive generations.

The original study was undertaken in 1966, shortly after a member of the third generation of the T. family, Harold G., consulted the Child Development Center of the J.B.G. in relation to his son, Ben, then age 4, and daughter Jane, then age 2. Its purpose was to see if the agency's long experience and extensive knowledge of this family could enhance our understanding of the current generation in order to interrupt the pattern of psychopathology seen in preceding generations. The study focuses primarily on the original client's daughter, Ann T., her oldest son Harold, and his children, Ben and Jane, though almost all members of the original client's family received services at the Jewish Board of Guardians at various times.

Paper presented at the 54th annual meeting of the American Orthopsychiatric Association, April 1977. Reprinted with permission from the author.

Records on this family, dating back to 1928, were studied, and summaries of contacts with each of the family members discussed in the paper are presented under three topical headings: (1) Symptom Picture (diagnostic impressions, in the case of Ben and Jane); (2) Assessment of Environment; and (3) Goal of Therapeutic Intervention and Changes in Patient.

SUMMARY OF CONTACTS WITH THIS FAMILY

Mr. and Mrs. Harold G. contacted the Child Development Center in January 1966 because of their growing concern about the behavior of their son, Ben. They were particularly concerned because of the long history of emotional disturbance on both sides of their family. Mrs. G's parents were known to Mt. Sinai Hospital's O.P.D. Psychiatric Division since the 1930s. Mrs. G. was herself an outpatient at Mt. Sinai's Parent-Child Guidance Clinic from 1948 to 1953, and was also seen for treatment at Roosevelt Hospital, O.P.D. Psychiatric Division, in 1959. Harold G's mother, Ann T., and her parents had been known to the Jewish Board of Guardians with only brief interruptions since 1928. Ann T. first became known to J.B.G. in 1928, when she was ten years old. She was treated at the Child Guidance Institute from 1928 to 1930, when she was committed to the Cedar Knolls School, where she remained until 1933. From 1933 to the end of 1934, she was seen in the after-care unit, and for a very brief period during this time she was placed in an "opportunity home." The agency had no contact with her from 1935 until 1945, when she returned with her oldest son, Harold, who was eight years old at the time. From 1945 until 1957, with just a few interruptions, she was in treatment with the same social worker who had been her social worker as a child. For most of this period she was seen intensively for individual treatment. Agency records on her case end in 1957, though apparently she continued to be seen for a brief while longer. (From 1962 until 1966, she was in treatment at the Jewish Family Service.)

Harold G., Ann's oldest son, born in 1937, became the father of Ben and Jane. He was a patient at Child Guidance Institute for most of the period 1945 to 1949, when he was placed at Hawthorne Cedar Knolls School. He remained in placement at H.C.K. until 1953, when he was transferred to the Stuyvesant Residence Club, where he remained for a few months and then returned home. There was minimal contact with him in the after-care unit until 1958. His case was officially closed in 1961.

Harold's younger brother, Jack, born in 1942, was in placement at H.C.K. from 1953 to 1956. His younger twin sisters, Betty and Rachel, born in 1946, were known to the Child Development Center from 1950 to 1951, and to the Child Guidance Institute in 1957. The records do not indicate the extent of service offered to the sisters in 1957. Together with their mother, Mrs. G., they were in treatment at the Jewish Family Service from 1962 until 1966.

Ben and Jane G. were evaluated at the Child Development Center in 1966. Ben was reevaluated on several subsequent occasions, and counseling in relation to him was offered to his parents until 1970. Jane was initially placed in a prenursery program and Mrs. G. attended a prenursery mother's group. From 1967 to 1970, Jane attended the C.D.C. therapeutic nursery school. As mentioned, Mr. and Mrs. G. were seen for counseling during this period.

SUMMARY OF AGENCY CONTACTS (1928–1957) WITH ANN T.

Identifying data (at time of initial referral):
Patient: Ann T., born 3/25/18.
Mother: Betty, born in 1888 in Austria, employed as part-time domestic.
Father: Harold, died in 1918 of tuberculosis.
Stepfather: Sam, born in 1878 in Russia; employed as a rag picker.
Half-siblings: Jonathan, born in 1920, and Albert, born in 1922.
Socioeconomic factors: Family lived on a marginal income in substandard housing on the lower East Side of Manhattan.
Date of Referral: 10/25/28.

Ann, born in 1918, was referred to J.B.G. by her mother in 1928, when she was ten years, seven months old, because of unmanageable behavior at home and at school. She was the only offspring of Mrs. T's first marriage and had been an unwanted child, as her father was severely ill with tuberculosis at the time of conception. Her father died during her mother's eighth month of pregnancy, and shortly thereafter Mrs. T. married Mr. T., a widower with two grown children living in Russia. Two offspring were born of this marriage.

Information on Ann's birth and early development is sparse. Her mother is reported to have been in good health during the pregnancy, though she was anxious and insecure. Labor lasted two hours, and Ann weighed five pounds at birth and was reported to be normal and healthy. She was breast-fed for one year and was considered well nourished. Teething occurred at six months, and she walked and talked at one year. Weaning was accomplished at age one year. Toilet training was completed at two years of age.

Her early health history is essentially unremarkable except that, by self-report, at the age of two, she was ill and lost all her teeth. At age five, she was hospitalized for pneumonia, and following her hospitalization, she was sent for a brief period to a convalescent home in Riverdale. She later developed asthma.

At the time of referral, Ann lived with her mother, Betty, age forty, her stepfather, Sam, age fifty, and half-brothers, Jonathan and Albert, eight and six years of age, respectively.

Symptom Picture

At the time of the initial referral in 1928, Ann presented the picture of an extremely neglected child, physically and emotionally. She appeared to be intellectually dull, and tested on a retarded level (IQ 74). Psychological tests further revealed a limited capacity for sustained mental effort and limited ability to reason and abstract. Her reading and vocabulary were poor; affect flat; and she seemed generally apathetic. Behavioral problems in school, dating back to kindergarten, included: defiance, physical abuse of teachers, use of obscene language, and physical abuse of children. She had no friends and frequently assaulted children in the neighborhood. She was willful and defiant with her parents and often retaliated in kind when her mother hit her. She pursued men for money and cigarettes and was preoccupied with sex. She had a history of bronchial disturbances, which later developed into asthma.

In essence, the picture was one of a poorly socialized, depressed, and anxious girl with limited intelligence, dull affect, poor impulse control, and disturbed object relationships.

Assessment of Environment

Ann lived with her parents and half-brothers in a substandard tenement on the Lower East Side. The apartment was described as crowded, dark, malodorous, and filthy. The furnishings failed to meet any minimum standard, and Ann, her mother, and one of her brothers shared a bed.

Mrs. T. was described as an obese, slovenly, disorganized woman of low intelligence, who was superstitious and fearful. Her standards for herself and her children were extremely low, and she appeared markedly limited in her ability to manage her home and rear her children. She was employed as a domestic, and her children were frequently left unsupervised. Her treatment of Ann was inconsistent. She vacillated between overprotection and indulgence and indifferent, or sadistic behavior toward her. Her references to Ann as the dope, or stupid, led to her being known in the neighborhood by these terms.

Mrs. T. was subject to rather bizarre behavior at times, such as allowing children to witness, for a fee, her giving enemas to cats.

Mr. T. was described as a religious man of limited intelligence. He was seen as having a poor sense of responsibility and was an inadequate provider. He had always been overtly rejecting and often punitive in his attitude and behavior toward Ann.

At the time of referral, the half-siblings, Jonathan and Albert, were seen as functioning relatively well, though there was concern about their being overprotected by their father, and both had problems of nocturnal enuresis.

Therapeutic Intervention and Changes

The treatment goals and expectations as excerpted from a psychiatric report dated 11/26/28, were as follows:

> Inasmuch as the patient is willing to talk and become friendly, the examiner feels that she will establish a bond of friendship between herself and the worker. It is through

this that we may expect to obtain results with this girl. She will idealize the worker and attempt to imitate her. . . .

From the history, it is evident that much work will have to be done with the home in order to make it more pleasing for the child. Sleeping arrangements should be altered; her recreational time should be supervised, and, if possible, the girl should be gotten to join a club.

Since the mother is dull, has no understanding of the child, and is annoyed at her problems, the worker will have to be a substitute for the mother. . . . Recreation and helping this child develop interests are essential. . . . Prognosis would seem to be good.

The treatment plan was pursued for two years and ultimately was viewed as unsuccessful. The following excerpts from a letter to the Children's Court, dated May 9, 1930, reveal what were thought to be the reasons for the failure:

Work along these lines was unsuccessful due to the failure of the parents to respond in any way. The child showed a little response in the beginning but without the backing of the parents, has become indifferent and almost defiant to worker's interest. The only service that is acceptable to them is monetary relief. . . . The situation came to a climax on the evening of 5/6/30 when the child was raped on the roof of the building in which she lives.

It was learned at this time that Ann had been involved sexually with a number of men since she was eight years of age, and often received cigarettes and money from them. The agency recommended that Mrs. T. file a delinquency petition, which she willingly did, and Ann was arraigned in Children's Court on the following charges: sexual delinquency; being an inveterate cigarette smoker; truanting from school; and being altogether beyond control. The court ordered her committed to Cedar Knolls School.

The following excerpt from a psychiatric report dated May 1930, reveals the subsequent treatment plan: "Ann has had no training in her home and all of her experiences have been gathered from street life. She has been unduly interested in sexual matters from her fourth year, and at present, the only interest she displayed during the examination was when her sexual escapades were discussed. . . . As the home offers nothing and as the child needs intensive training and care, it is suggested that she be committed to Cedar Knolls."

During her stay at Cedar Knolls from May 1930 to January 1933, the therapeutic goals were to help her develop self-control, good manners, and educational and vocational skills. The means toward achieving these goals were those of providing her with fresh air, good food, strict discipline, and moral, educational, and vocational training.

In June 1930, a psychiatric report reveals Ann as unable to adjust to Cedar Knolls, mainly because of her immaturity, impulsivity, and feeblemindedness. The recommendation was to transfer her to an institution for the feebleminded. This recommendation, however, was not followed, and in September 1930, the director of Cedar Knolls reported that Ann had "blossomed out." She recommended that "at the earliest possible date that it can be arranged, this child should be placed in a foster home in the country where she can be outdoors to her heart's content, and where a foster mother will give her the love and affection which she needs in addition to good food and fresh air.''

During this period, work with the family consisted essentially in providing them with relief and other social services: coal, clothing, assisting in matters of health, summer camps for the younger siblings, etc.

On 1/30/33, Ann was discharged from Cedar Knolls and returned home. It was felt that she had matured, but that she would only be able to hold down the most simple, routine sort of job.

She and all members of her family continued to be seen in after-care until December 1934. The family was provided with a battery of welfare services to sustain and support their functioning as a unit. On a number of occasions, thought was given to placing the younger siblings, but apparently the many services offered this family enabled them to remain intact and function as a unit.

Work with Ann's family during this period included discussion of family problems provision of material assistance, and encouragement to utilize various social services: medical, recreational, etc. The family's dependence on the agency intensified, as they made increased demands, which apparently were met.

Work with Ann still seemed geared toward training her in manners and vocational skills. On 5/2/33, she was placed in an ''opportunity home'' and on 5/16/33, she was discharged because of ''poor manners and lack of training.''

Throughout this period there was concern about the possibility of sexual acting out, and it was known that she received money and clothing from a number of boyfriends. She continued her schooling at the Harlem Continuation School, but her attendance was poor, and it was felt that she learned nothing.

In 1934, the family was transferred to another social worker, at a time of conceptual and functional modifications within the agency. Psychotherapeutic approaches were further developed as relief functions were being abandoned. Operating within this new orientation, the worker experienced the T. family as most frustrating since they continued to demand concrete services and resisted discussion of problems and feelings. This soon resulted in termination in December 1934 on a note of mutual hurt and anger.

The worker's closing entry dated December 1934 states as follows:

> Ann has always been coming to us for things and her mother has done likewise. They have been accustomed to using this agency as a relief-giving source and at no time have they come in to discuss their problems. . . . Worker feels that the prognosis in this case is poor. It was difficult to work with Ann, not only because of the poor material in question, but Ann has rejected worker completely chiefly because she has not been coming here in order to discuss her difficulties and to gain insight into her problems, but rather coming here aimlessly and therefore, continuing to drift without a solution to her problem.
>
> A psychiatrist reported that Ann had tried to solicit him in the office. . . . He has stated that there is nothing further we can contribute to rehabilitate this client as she has no insight into her problem. . . . It was also suggested by the worker that should Ann get herself into further trouble, and become pregnant, or be arrested for soliciting, that this office should not reopen the case in view of the fact that Ann is not workable material—recommendation be made that the client be sent to Bedford.

Just prior to termination, Ann requested to be placed at a group residence because of the many difficulties she was experiencing at home. Apparently, this too was seen as another demand, and the request was never considered.

BRIEF SUMMARY OF SUBSEQUENT CONTACTS WITH MRS. G. (1945/1957)

Following Ann's discharge in 1934, the agency had no further contact with her until 1945, when she applied for help with her oldest son, Harold.

It was learned that shortly after her discharge she had married a seriously disturbed man twelve years her senior, whom she had known throughout her childhood. Both had been neighborhood scapegoats and were known as "dopes." She claimed to have married him because of his problems, and that she was afraid of educated men.

The marriage was fraught with conflict from its inception, and there were many separations, especially following the birth of their children. (During this time, Mrs. G. continued to live in the same tenement in which she had grown up.)

When she returned to the agency in 1945, she presented a host of social, economic, and psychological problems, and it was deemed advisable that she be seen for intensive treatment at the agency. (Interestingly, she was assigned to the same social worker she had previously seen in 1934.)

Mrs. G. was seen as extremely dependent, moody, subject to severe periodic depression, suicidal ideation, and plagued by the most primitive sexual and aggressive impulses and fantasies. She had strong impulses to kill her second son, Jack, and did act out sadistic impulses toward her children and other children in the neighborhood. Her ego boundaries were faulty and she was unable to separate her identity and the identities of her husband and parents from that of her children. Her thinking was, at times, delusional. She saw her hated husband in her son, Harold, and believed her daughter, Betty, to be the reincarnation of her mother. She had a history of prostitution dating from the time of her discharge from Cedar Knolls and acknowledged hatred of men and sexual frigidity. During the course of treatment, she acknowledged involvement in all sorts of perverse activities from the age of eight, which continued unabated throughout her stay at Cedar Knolls and continued to a lesser extent to the present time.

Throughout the period 1945 to 1957, she was seen in intensive treatment as often as three times a week when she was experiencing severe depression. Though at times the therapeutic task seemed futile and interminable, it was generally felt that it was serving to keep her out of a state hospital. In addition, she was provided with or assisted in obtaining a battery of social services. All of her children received services at the agency during this period. As detailed later, Harold received various services from 1945 to 1958. Jack was treated at H.C.K. from 1953 to 1956, and later in after-care. Betty and Rachel were in the Child Development Center Nursery Program from 1950 to 1951 and were later seen at the Child Guidance Institute in 1957.

The treatment goal was to help Mrs. G. achieve greater independence through fostering dependence on the social worker who provided emotional support and encouragement. She apparently responded to treatment and there was some abatement of symptoms, indications of a limited degree of self-understanding, and some greater awareness of and ability to meet the needs of her children. Throughout this period, the question of termination arose and frequently plans to terminate were made, only to be temporarily abandoned while another long period of treatment commenced.

During the 1950s, termination seemed to be contingent to rehabilitating the client vocationally. It was felt that this would serve to remove her from the welfare roles, and would be highly supportive on a psychological and emotional level as well. This goal was finally achieved in 1954, with the aid of the State Rehabilitation Bureau, and Mrs. G. passed a Civil Service examination and obtained a job with the federal government in the tax department.

Agency records on Mrs. G. end in 1957, and it is not clear how or when termination was effected. The final entries in the records indicate that her overall functioning had improved, though she was subject to recurrence of symptoms at times of crisis and stress. She continued to be employed, was dating a chiropractor, and was resisting the efforts of her friends to involve her in prostitution. She continued to live with her sons, daughters, and younger half-brother, in the same tenement apartment in which she had grown up.

In 1962, Mrs. G. and her daughters entered treatment at the Jewish Family Service. They were seen there until 1966, when they were terminated by the agency. The termination was arbitrary, since it was thought that there is no point of termination with Mrs. G., who is continually in need of tremendous support.

SUMMARY OF AGENCY CONTACTS WITH HAROLD G. (1945–1959)

Identifying data:
Patient: Harold, born 6/7/37.
Mother: Ann, born 3/25/18.
Father: Mark, born in 1906.
Siblings: Jack, born in 1942, and Betty and Rachel, born in 1946.
Socioeconomic factors: Parents separated; family on home relief; substandard housing on Lower East Side of Manhattan.
Date of Referral: 8/45.

Harold, born 6/7/37, was referred to J.B.G. by his mother in August 1945 because of acute upset and fears precipitated by his viewing the movie "A Portrait of Dorian Gray." His mother further complained that he was spoiled and difficult to control.

Harold lived with his mother and three-year-old sibling, Jack. The family was on home relief, since Mr. G., who was in and out of the home for shorter and longer periods of time since Harold's birth, did not support the family.

Harold was the first child born to Ann and Mark G., who were 19 and 31 years of age, respectively, at the time of his birth. He was an unplanned child, whose birth history is reported to have been normal. He was breast-fed, with bottle supplements, until the age of three months, when breast feeding was discontinued because of his mother's illness. (The record does not indicate the nature of the illness, though it is likely that it was depression.) Toilet training began at five months of age (not reliable), and it is not stated when it was accomplished. (At age 8, he still had nocturnal enuresis.) He began to walk and talk when he was 14 months old. He required surgery for a hernia at age 4 months and again at the age of one year. When he was eight months old, he was hospitalized for ten days for observation because of a "tear" in his throat which interfered with breathing. Shortly after a tonsillectomy at age 5, he was hospitalized for bronchial pneumonia. At age 7, he was hospitalized for two weeks because of sores in his mouth, which began to spread over his face. The nature of the sores is unknown.

Symptom Picture

Harold presented the picture of a bright, ingratiating, and inhibited child, who was extremely anxious, phobic, and withdrawn. He had an extremely rich and strange fantasy life, and his self-absorption was so great as to result in an almost total neglect of his personal appearance. His many fears included fear of death, dark, germs, and being left alone. He was hyperactive, distractible, and had a short attention span. He had no friends, and was extremely fearful of other children's aggression. The psychiatric report indicated hypochondriacal tendencies and paranoid trends. He spoke with a lisp and his speech was rapid and slurred.

In 1946, his diagnosis was that of "child psychosis." Evaluation in a psychiatric hospital was recommended.

Harold was admitted to Bellevue Hospital in December 1946 and their report indicated the following: IQ 146; no indications of organicity; disturbances in motility, speech, object relationships, identification, and thought processes; suspicion of auditory hallucinations; some paranoid elements; and hypochondriacal tendencies. Their diagnostic impression was that of "schizophrenia of a pre-puberty type," and they recommended electric shock treatment, which the mother declined.

Assessment of Environment

The home environment was extremely pathological, and Harold was physically and emotionally abused by his mother from the time of his birth. She was unable to view him as separate from her hated husband and tended to project her own negative feelings and unacceptable impulses onto the boy. Her treatment of him was either sadistic, seductive, or overprotective.

Mr. G., an intellectually limited, slovenly, disorganized, and irresponsible man, was also harsh and punitive toward the boy, beating him for crying and acting like a "sissy." (Mr. G. was thought to be psychotic.)

The parents first separated when Harold was born. Mr. G. returned when Harold was two, remained three months, and left again. There were many such separations and reconciliations for the next several years, with Mr. G. always abandoning the family after the birth of a child.

Following the birth of Jack in 1942, when Harold was five, Mrs. G. suffered a severe psychotic episode, with suicidal ideation and impulses to kill the new baby.

For a number of years prior to Harold's referral to J.B.G., Mrs. G. and her sons lived with the maternal grandmother and Mrs. G's younger brother. At the time of the referral, the maternal grandmother died of cancer and Mrs. G. suffered another depressive episode.

Therapeutic Intervention and Changes

Harold was seen at J.B.G. for treatment for the major part of 1946 to 1959. The records reveal considerable concern in regard to his diagnosis and minimal reference to treatment plans and goals. He had a number of social workers during this period and was without a worker for several months in 1949. In individual treatment prior to 1949, he seemed unable to establish a meaningful relationship with his workers and tended to use them as an audience for his own narcissistic involvement and productions—essentially in the realm of fantasy.

Though some improvement in his functioning is noted, it is not clearly documented.

Following his observation at Bellevue, placement at the Pleasantville Cottage School was considered but not effected for a number of reasons. The Jewish Child Care Association recommended that he be placed at the Children's Unit at Rockland State Hospital, if the hospital would accept him.

Just prior to 1949, it was decided that Harold could not be treated at the Jewish Board of Guardians because of the diagnosis of schizophrenia, which by then was clearly confirmed by various psychiatrists. Group therapy was recommended, but he was not accepted, since the group therapy consultant felt that the group was too aggressive and would be threatening to Harold.

In June 1949, a psychiatrist recommended placement at Hawthorne Cedar Knolls School, since he felt that Harold could best be treated in a "sheltered environment." Harold was admitted to H.C.K. on 12/2/49 and remained there until September 1953.

During the early part of his stay at Hawthorne, his self-absorption, absent-mindedness, and physical neglect were so extreme that his care approximated nursing care. Because of his self-absorption, rich fantasy life, which he readily shared, and his professorial manner, he was often scapegoated by the other boys. His object relationships were markedly impaired, and the goals of treatment were to help him relate more appropriately and to involve him more in reality issues.

Some improvement was gradually noted in his peer relationships and he received some status because of his academic success. Toward the latter part of his stay at Hawthorne, his involvement in fantasy diminished, and he attended the community high school, was successful academically, and participated in drama and other student activities.

On 11/29/53 he was transferred to the Stuyvesant Residence Club, where he stayed for a few months before returning home. His stay at the residence was an unhappy experience for him, since he was rejected by the other boys, who ridiculed him and called him "the professor." It was felt that he was rejected partly because he used his intellect to provoke and assault. He tried to engage counselors and other boys in conversations of an exceedingly abstract nature, but would not listen to what they had to say. This was characteristic of his treatment relationship as well; relating in a narcissistic manner, demanding total attention, and remaining essentially uninfluenced by the therapist.

From 1953 to approximately 1959, he was seen irregularly in the after-care department. His worker reported, in 1958, that "Harold continues to attend City College and to live with his family. He is a severely disturbed youth whose façade of good functioning could crumble under extreme stress, stimulation, or fatigue."

In 1959, it was reported that he was dropped from college because of extensive cutting and below standard grades. It was felt that his "total absorption in photography and his involvement with a girlfriend prevented him from studying."

There is no indication of any contact with the agency from 1959 to 1961, when his case was officially closed.

SUMMARY OF CONTACTS WITH BEN AND JANE G. (1966-1970)

Identifying data:
Children: Ben, born 9/21/62. Jane, born 11/64.
Father: Harold, born 6/7/37.
Mother: Ruth, born 11/28/41.
Address: Family resides in low-income housing project on the Lower East Side of Manhattan.
Socio-economic factors: Father employed by the Department of Welfare; both parents have had some college education.
Source of referral: Mother.

Mr. and Mrs. G. contacted the Child Development Center in January 1966 because of their growing concern over Ben's negativistic and deviant behavior. They felt he was unhappy, difficult to please, and in need of friends and opportunities for play. Additional concerns included poor eating habits and resistance to going to bed. They wanted to know whether he was becoming disturbed and, if so, what could be done for him on a preventive basis. More specifically, they desired assistance in providing him with an appropriate nursery school experience. They thought he was in need of an experience away from home, peer relationships, and educational stimulation.

Ben was an unplanned child, born at a time when his parents were neither emotionally nor financially ready to have a child. Pregnancy and delivery were reported to be normal, though instruments were used to assist in delivery. Ben weighed five pounds, two ounces at birth, and because of his low weight, circumcision was postponed until he was three weeks old.

Breast feeding, with supplements (because of insufficient supply), was discontinued after three months, since Mrs. G. was tense and anxious and the family was in the process of moving. He was weaned from the bottle at age two, and there were no eating or sleeping problems. He did not take a pacifier and sucked his thumb only briefly at four months. On occasion, he continued to express interest in a bottle.

Bowel and bladder training commenced at fifteen months and was completed easily shortly after he was two.

His general development was reported as normal, and his motor development was early. He walked alone at twelve months, and spoke his first word at seven months. He spoke full sentences at 1.6 years. His social-emotional development was seen as normal, and he was an alert, happy, and responsive child until age 3, when he became somewhat defiant and negativistic. His health was generally good.

Mr. and Mrs. G. admitted that their handling of Ben was inconsistent, and they varied from indulgence to physical punishment. They also felt that he might be reacting to their tension, anxiety, and marital conflicts. They related their marital conflicts to discontent with their socioeconomic condition.

Diagnostic Impressions of Ben

In his first visit to the Child Development Center, Ben appeared to be a well-endowed child, physically and intellectually. He was alert, interested, and enthusiastic, both in regard to involvement with the therapist and play activities. There was no evidence of negativism. He was interested in a wide range of age-appropriate play activities, and his skills were advanced for his age. Both his gross and fine motor coordination seemed equally advanced. His interest level and concentration span were good, as were his vocabulary, sentence structure, and reasoning. His speech was somewhat unclear at times. His affect was appropriate and he smiled readily. The only aspect of his behavior that was somewhat unusual was his need for precise boundaries in his drawings and exactness in drawing within the boundaries, coloring every speck of space.

The nursery observations essentially confirmed the initial impression. During the first visit, he seemed somewhat distractible and overstimulated by the materials and the setting. In the second nursery observation, he seemed more relaxed and functioned in a more organized fashion.

The following excerpts are taken from a psychiatric report dated 4/29/66:

[On the first visit to the nursery,] he was able to separate from his mother easily and became interested in everything very quickly. He is a rather good-looking, well-developed boy, with clear speech. At first he seemed overwhelmed by the plentitude of materials, and a great desire to experience the use of all the materials in the nursery. However, he soon settled down and was able to concentrate, and did puzzles well. His gross and fine motor coordination were good.

In general, he was cooperative and outgoing and the negativistic behavior described by the parents was in evidence only when he was unable to accept putting the toys away at the end of the session.

[On the second visit,] he participated well with the other boys. He was quite verbal, and his vocabulary is fairly large. His speech is not always clear. . . . He was able to separate from the group and play independently when he wanted to, always keeping an eye on what the others were doing. There was some competitiveness, but he was not inappropriately aggressive. . . .

Difficulty in communication was more apparent in testing than in the observation nursery, though it was detected. His social and emotional responses in the nursery seemed more appropriate and adaptive than was revealed in the testing situation. In view of the longstanding history of emotional disturbance in this family, one would have expected more overt manifestations in the observation nursery, and it is possible that continued observation may reveal this.

[The psychologist who tested Ben in March 1966 felt that he showed] unevenness in ego development. Given a well-structured situation, he is capable of excellent achievement and adequate control. Under the more ambiguous (and potentially more provocative) circumstances of the projective tests, he became overwhelmed by fantasy material with a concomitant loss of reality boundaries. He attempts to adapt on an anal level, employing isolation and obsessive-like controls. However, when pressures begin to mount, there ensues a massive anxiety reaction along with regression in thinking and behavior.

JANE

Jane G., born 10/31/64, was observed for a prenursery program when she was two years old. Her parents had not reported any problems with her but were most responsive to the suggestion that she be seen for prenursery.

Jane was a planned baby, and Mrs. G. reported that pregnancy and delivery were normal and easy. Labor lasted one hour and she was 4.6 lbs. at birth. There were no eating or sleeping problems and after one week, she slept through the night. Mrs. G. feels that Jane has always been easy to care for and she did not want any help in caring for her during infancy. She felt that she had been less anxious in caring for Jane and that she was more affectionate with her than she was with Ben when he was an infant.

Jane was breast-fed. Weaning began at five months, and was completed at eight months. She was a happy, active, and responsive baby, who began talking at eleven months (first word was "daddy"), and walked at age one. Toilet training commenced shortly prior to the referral and was almost complete.

Mrs. G. felt that Jane's infancy was similar to Ben's and that they had similar personalities. Both were easygoing, happy babies, who responded well to people. However, Jane was not as outgoing as Ben, and unlike Ben, she had shown stronger anxiety. Further, she was more dependent on Mrs. G. and tended to include her more in her activities than did Ben. Jane had more stimulation from other children than had Ben, who had no contact with other children until he was past age three. At age eighteen months, Jane burned her mouth after swallowing some chemicals her father used for photography. She was hospitalized for two days and had to be "tied down" for an esophagram. She was cheerful the following day and ate well. The only apparent reaction to the experience was increased clinging to her transitional object (doll or blanket) and mother.

Ben's initial reaction to Jane was positive. He tried to say her name and wanted to kiss her. Subsequently he resented her getting into his things and hit her on occasion. Mr. G. felt that Jane was too tolerant of Ben's abuse.

Diagnostic Impressions of Jane

In 1966, Jane was described as follows:

She is a good-looking, well-developed two year old with light brown hair and blue eyes. Though delicate in appearance, her gross motor coordination is good and she is quite sturdy in her movements. Her play with puzzles and crayons indicated good fine motor coordination, as well as an unusually long concentration span, and high frustration tolerance. Her use of materials further reflects her ability to sustain interest in an activity and exploit it to its fullest potential.

Her speech is limited, but she seems anxious to speak and is able to communicate her wishes with words, sounds, and gestures. Her affect is good, and she is a responsive, friendly little girl. She seems neither overly dependent nor independent of her mother, and quickly and easily related to her prenursery teacher.

In essence, Jane seems to be a well-endowed child, physically and intellectually, and her ego development appears to be age-adequate.

Assessment of Environment

The G. family resided in a four-room apartment in a low-income housing project on the Lower East Side. The ethnic composition within the project, according to the parents, was mainly Puerto Rican and black. The parents were the only young, white, Jewish couple in their building and they felt quite isolated. They had great difficulty making friends with young black and Puerto Rican couples and felt that few of them shared their intellectual and cultural interests.

Mrs. G. was particularly frustrated by their living situation, and both she and her husband were discouraged by the fact that they had not yet progressed socioeconomically. Both expressed resentment and envy of other young couples who had transcended their backgrounds and improved their lot, and they felt inadequate in comparison. Further, Mrs. G. was extremely fearful of living in the project, since she had been raped in the elevator of their building just prior to Jane's birth. Since that time, she would not go out alone at night and would not use the elevator after dark. This further limited her opportunities for social and intellectual activities. She had been taking courses at college at night prior to the incident, which she discontinued.

The G's could have moved to a low-income project in a different area, but Mr. G. did not want to leave the Lower East Side. He, his mother, and his father lived within three blocks of each other; the area in which four generations of his family had resided.

Mrs. G. was described as a short, slender, unattractive woman, with above-average intelligence. Initially she impressed the interviewer as being somewhat disorganized and disoriented. After a few sessions, she appeared well-related and in good contact with reality. She expressed warmth and sincerity, especially in relation to her children, and apparently derived a good deal of satisfaction from them, though at times she was easily frustrated and angered by Ben. She was an anxious, frightened, and frustrated young woman, extremely sensitive to criticism and quick to anger. She revealed feelings of inadequacy and seemed to expect to be criticized and rejected. She was unable to establish close relationships and led a rather isolated existence all of her life. She had no friends. She maintained the façade of a self-sufficient, strong, and capable person.

Mrs. G. was born on 11/28/41. She was the only child born to her parents when her mother was 41 and her father was 43 years of age. She described her father as an attractive, intelligent, personable man, with great superficial charm and little substance as a person. He came to the United States at age fourteen, drifted along, and never developed socially. He shirked responsibilities all of his life, was self-involved, and never seemed to have a sense of responsibility or feeling for his wife and child.

He was a musician "of sorts" and occasionally played the balalaika in small cafes. He never had a desire to work and never thought of the future. He would spend his days sitting around in cafeterias, impressing the circles of people he could gather around him. He was supposed to have had a heart attack some years prior to Mrs. G's birth, and the family had been on home relief since that time. (The family was known to the Department of Welfare since the early 1930s, and to Mt. Sinai Hospital's Social Service Department since the early 1940s.)

Mrs. G. described her mother as "an apologetic, self-effacing woman, who can get on your nerves." She was "an overly devoted wife and mother and tended to infantalize both her husband and child." She was a very dependent, frightened woman who used her responsibilities to her husband and child as rationalizations for not working or making more of a life for herself.

Mrs. G's father had wanted a son, and had always expressed disappointment with her and resentment of her close relationship with her mother. Though he was not much of a disciplinarian, when he did discipline her, he was inconsistent, and the "punishment never fit the crime."

Her childhood was a very lonely, troubled, and atypical one. She had practically no friends and was always in the company of older people. She always felt insecure, incompetent, and as though she had no aptitudes. In school, she experienced a profound sense of difference between her and other children. She was shy and unsure of herself, and friends retreated from her. She had one friend prior to her marriage—a young woman, much older than she, with whom she had lost contact. She had always wanted to be like other children and developed a system of conforming values very different from that of her parents.

At age seven, her parents felt that she was disturbed and brought her for help to Mt. Sinai Hospital, where she was in regular weekly treatment with a psychiatrist from 1948 through 1953, because of problems of enuresis, temper tantrums, poor eating, and unmanageable behavior at home. The parents, both severely disturbed, were simultaneously in treatment with separate workers. Though Mrs. G. showed some improvement at the point of termination of treatment, later reports from the parents indicated that she was seriously disturbed but that she refused help.

Mrs. G. sought help at Roosevelt Hospital when she was in her senior year at high school, because of anxiety, general discontent, and difficulty in getting along with her father. She was seen there only for several sessions.

She graduated from high school and attended Hunter College for one year prior to her marriage. She felt she was bright, but inhibited, and it was hard for her to concentrate on school work. She began dating Mr. G. when she was fourteen years old and he was eighteen. They dated for six years prior to their marriage. Their relationship created havoc in Mrs. G's family, since her father violently disapproved of Mr. G.

Mr. and Mrs. G. felt that they married precipitously and should have waited until they had finished school and had a better financial situation. They felt that they were forced to marry for fear that if they didn't, Mrs. G's father might succeed in breaking up their relationship.

Shortly after their marriage, they lived with Mrs. G's parents. Mr. G. had great difficulty holding down jobs, of which he had several within a year, and looking for jobs when he was unemployed. Prior to Ben's birth, they depended mainly on Mrs. G's wages and money they could borrow from their parents. They moved into their own apartment shortly before Ben's birth and lived there for one year following his birth, when they moved to a low-income project.

Mr. G. began working for the Health Department in 1963, and worked there until he obtained a position with the Department of Welfare. He was not satisfied with his work, which he felt was routine and below his potential.

Both Mr. and Mrs. G. felt that essentially they had a good marital relationship. They had always been close and could talk to each other about anything. They felt that the tensions between them and their frequent and, at times, violent quarrels resulted from their financial problems and dissatisfactions with their housing. However, it was apparent that they suffered from intense dissatisfaction with themselves and each other. Their major bond seemed to be their great dependency. Though they claimed to communicate well with each other, in their interviews, they had great difficulty communicating, and Mrs. G. ceded to Mr. G's verbal aggressiveness. Both were in constant states of anxiety, frustration, and discontent, and both were easily angered. Mr. G. was quick-tempered and volatile. He would become violently angry at his wife, slap her, storm out of the house, to return quickly, to make up and be loving. Mrs. G. felt she did not express her anger easily and tended to "stew for days." They both felt the tensions between them had increased, and they were quarreling more frequently. The G's had been to the Jewish Family Service for help with their marital problems, but discontinued after a few sessions, since Mrs. G. preferred to work things out on their own.

Therapeutic Interventions and Changes

BEN: Ben received a complete diagnostic evaluation in 1966 and periodic follow-up evaluations until 1970. No gross evidence of psychopathology was revealed, though there was evidence of unevenness in ego development; developmental lags were particularly noted in his object relationships and fantasy-reality balance. Though psychotherapy was considered on various occasions, his overall functioning did not warrant it.

Mr. and Mrs. G. received counseling in relation to Ben and assistance in obtaining appropriate educational and recreational experiences for him. At the time of termination, concern was still expressed in regard to some developmental lags, though his overall functioning appeared to be adequate.

JANE: Jane attended a prenursery program for several months and then attended the C.D.C. therapeutic nursery school until 1970, when she completed the kindergarten program.

Mrs. G. attended a mothers' group while Jane was in the prenursery group and was later seen with Mr. G. for counseling.

Jane utilized the programs and progress was noted in her development. Her good intelligence (tested within the bright-normal range on the Wechsler Pre-School and Primary Scale of Intelligence) was a major asset in utilizing educational and social experiences.

Developmental lags were noted primarily in object relationships, which in 1970, at age five years six months, were viewed as being on a one-year-old level. Separation-individuation had not proceeded beyond this level of development, though she was close to age-adequate in other areas of ego functioning. Psychological tests (1970) revealed independent strivings and interest in relating to others more appropriately. At the point of termination, she was seen as ready to utilize a first grade program in a public school, and in need of further assistance in individuating.

MR. & MRS. G.: Mr. and Mrs. G. were unable to utilize counseling on a regular basis, as Mrs. G. found it particularly threatening. She had difficulty tolerating her intense dependency needs which were stimulated by the therapeutic situation and the threat of invasion into her dependency relationship with her husband. Nonetheless, there were indications that their experience with the agency was emotionally supportive. They demonstrated increased relatedness to the needs of their children and utilized developmental opportunities for themselves and the children which were suggested to them. Mr. G. obtained a more self-enhancing and higher paying job; Mrs. G. returned to college; and the family moved to better living quarters outside of the neighborhood in which four generations of Mr. G's family had lived.

SUMMARY AND DISCUSSION

Families such as the one described confront our society with some of its most challenging social and philosophical issues, issues which go to the heart of a society's basic values and determine its vitality. In a speech to the American Orthopsychiatric Association in 1976, Kenneth Keniston stated that "There are children born in the cellar of our society and systematically brought up to remain there. Our sentiments in their behalf are always touching. Our treatment of them is heartbreaking . . . the tragic truth is that today, one-quarter of all American children are being brought up to fail . . . the reasons include race, poverty, handicaps, and being born of parents too overwhelmed by life to be able to care responsively and lovingly for their children." Dr. Keniston then went on to discuss the economic determinants of this deplorable phenomenon.

Measures being taken to deal with the current economic situation in our country clearly reveal the low priority given to mental health, educational, and social services to children, particularly to the children of the poor and minority groups. It is disturbing that preventive and rehabilitative services are in the greatest jeopardy and have already suffered severe cutbacks, while greater punitive measures of dealing with troubled children are being emphasized and instituted.

The determinants of the psychopathology seen in this family are multiple, and one has to consider the possibility of genetic factors. However, as genetic determinants are explored, it is important that it not deflect attention from the many other determinants which are currently remediable, or, as has been done, used to justify the neglect and abuse of those in need.

Each member of this family, with the exception of the current generation, presented severe psychopathology, at times, of psychotic magnitude, when they came to the attention of the agency. They all were being reared in extraordinarily pathological environments. Each achieved a level of functioning far beyond that which had been predicted, and although long-term institutionalization had been considered for both Ann and Harold, the battery of supportive services provided to them appears to have precluded its necessity. Further, a diminution of psychopathology in each successive generation is noted.

The level of knowledge at various points in the history of this case led to undue pessimism at times in relation to the clients, or unrealistically high expectations of them which obscured the gains that were being made. From the latter phases of Ann's treatment until work with the current generation commenced, the agency operated with a frame of reference and tools more appropriate for the treatment of neurotic children and adults with intact egos. The ego-supportive therapy and concrete services which were being provided were not yet conceptualized as appropriate and necessary services to individuals with major ego deficits and led to frustration and disappointment with the clients.

The work of Margaret Mahler and, more recently, of James Masterson, and Gertrude and Rubin Blanck, among others, is providing us with new insights as well as modalities and techniques for treating disorders of the ego, and new hope for interrupting the transmission of psychopathology to successive generations.

It is now well documented that disorders of the ego originate in the developmental phases within the first thirty-six months of life. Parents, who are themselves borderline or schizophrenic, withdraw emotional supplies in response to their children's efforts to separate and individuate, which they experience as deeply threatening. This suggests that preventive services to children of severely disturbed parents, or parents otherwise overwhelmed by life, would be best instituted at the time of their birth; or better still, during their prenatal period. Mothers who are limited or deficient in their capacity to mother, require mothering themselves during the crucial phases of their children's development. Beyond the first thirty-six months, supportive services to the family, including concrete services such as day-care centers, could well preclude the perpetuation of human misery in these families over generations. The hope lies in early detection and preventive services. For those having not received such services, a humane society must provide appropriate and sufficient rehabilitative services.

"The most important of all skills, that of living well with oneself and with others, can be acquired only by living in an emotionally stable and satisfying human environment. If too many families no longer provide it, a vicious circle is created because parents cannot convey to their children what they have never learned themselves. This vicious circle must be broken." Bruno Bettelheim— *Love Is Not Enough*.

CHAPTER 46

The Battered Child Rebrutalized: Ten Cases of Medical-Legal Confusion

Lenore C. Terr and Andrew S. Watson

Ten battered children and their families were followed by the authors over a two-year period. Medical, legal, and social work handling of each case was evaluated. It was found that confusion, delays, poorly coordinated efforts, and failure by agencies and individuals to assume responsibility for appropriate action produced serious emotional stresses to already traumatized youngsters. The authors offer several suggestions for improving the management of battered children.

Although the problem of the physically mistreated child is age-old and universal, attention to this problem has mounted sharply in the past ten years. This increase in public concern has stemmed from improved techniques of diagnosis and reporting to local authorities. In the late 1940s and the 1950s the problem of multiple fractures at various stages of healing was described by several radiologists (3, 12). The term "battered child" was first used by Kempe, Silverman, Steele, Droegemueller, and Silver in 1962, when they published a thorough medical-psychiatric report on the problem. It was suggested in their paper that physicians be alert to the possibility of this diagnosis and that cases be reported to the police or child protective service agency in the community (7).

In 1963, the Children's Bureau of the U.S. Department of Health, Education, and Welfare proposed model legislative language and guidelines to assist states in drafting mandatory reporting laws (14). This proposal suggested that doctors be required to report battered children, that they be immune from criminal and civil action stemming from such reporting, that failing to report be considered a misdemeanor, and that reports be made to the local police department.

Presently there are battered child statutes in almost every state, most of them similar to the legislation suggested by the Children's Bureau. There is considerable variation from state to state in the agency designated by law to receive battered child reports. Medical and legal authorities continue to be concerned about this matter, since there is a great philosophical and practical difference in the outcome of reporting to a law enforcement versus a child protective agency

Read at the 123rd annual meeting of the American Psychiatric Association, Detroit, Mich., May 8-12, 1967.

Reprinted with permission from the *American Journal of Psychiatry* 124 (April 1968): 1432-39.

(1, 8). In Michigan, physicians are required to report cases to both the prosecuting attorney and the state department of social welfare.

METHODS AND PURPOSES

Over a two-year period we studied ten cases of suspected child abuse at the University of Michigan. These cases were referred to us by our department of pediatrics or the local juvenile court. In each case we interviewed both parents and the child in question. Siblings were interviewed whenever indicated. In cases which came to court hearings, we provided reports and/or verbal testimony. In addition, we offered psychiatric treatment at our institution for those cases in which this was recommended. We continued to consult with the courts until our services were no longer required. Finally, all cases were reviewed at later dates for further developments or difficulties.

It is the purpose of this report to analyze the process of handling the battered child from the time he comes to the attention of a doctor, an agency, or a court. The effect of the handling process itself upon the child and family is the main focus of this study. We do not deal primarily with the individual or family dynamics of these cases, but rather with the dynamics of courtroom and examining room procedures as they influence the lives of abused children. In this report, the individual cases are used as examples of general problems seen in the group as a whole. Some cases appear in more than one section of the discussion because of the several types of mishandling which occurred in the single case.

In originating the term "battered child syndrome," Kempe and associates defined it as "a clinical condition in young children who have received serious physical abuse, generally from a parent or a foster parent" (7). We feel it is important to note that the child's injury or deformity may result not only from a willful act but also from an act of carelessness on the part of the parent or guardian. The injury need not be purposely or consciously inflicted upon the child for the child to be designated "battered."

ANALYSIS OF THE PROCEDURAL CONFUSION: LEGAL PROBLEMS

In each of the ten cases studied, we found confusion and lack of direction in both the legal and medical-social handling of the children and their families. Lawyers, prosecuting attorneys, juvenile court workers and judges, criminal court judges, divorce court workers, and legislators shared in this confusion and lack of direction.

1. Effects of the Adversary Process

In the heat of legal contest, lawyers representing the parents may ignore the interests of the child. For example, let us consider Denise, a recently adopted nine-year-old girl who had been subjected to 226 lashes with a belt for failure to bring home her homework papers. Denise's mother, in addition to doing most of the beating, had attempted to breast feed the nine-year-old, check her genitals daily for signs of masturbation, and engage her in games of *Sorry* whenever Denise confessed the impulse to masturbate.

The parents' lawyer chose to overlook all evidences of severe sexual and hostile provocations to this child. Instead, he threatened numerous appeals and delay tactics in the determination of custody in order to protect his clients' rights to Denise. In this case, countless delays would guarantee insecurity for this girl throughout most of her childhood, despite her desperate need for permanent roots.

It appears that a lawyer representing battering parents may find himself in a dilemma. If the lawyer *knows* of the child's injury but helps the parents avoid incrimination (or being found at fault), he may help perpetrate a truly dangerous situation for the child. On the other hand, if he decides to tell the juvenile court judge what he knows, he may be breaching, or at least feel he is breaching, his duty to the parents. (We must ask in this regard: If we wish to protect children fully, should not lawyers report child abuse too?) The lawyer's decision will probably depend upon his view of the community's treatment programs versus the community's punitive intentions.

2. Effects of Prosecution

A second important problem arises in the office of the prosecutor. The prosecutor feels he is "obliged" to prosecute the battering parent, but he has no similar sense of obligation to keep a family intact and functioning. Many factors enter into his decision to prosecute. First he needs sufficient evidence to "win" the case, preferably an admission by the parent or observation by eyewitnesses. For instance, prosecutors dropped two cases of severe brain injuries in babies because of "lack of evidence." In these cases, the offending parents vigorously denied purposeful abuse. In one, a mother recently released from a mental institution, insisted that her eight-month-old son Ricky's bilateral subdural hematomas were caused when he hit his own head with his bottle. This story was readily accepted by a prosecutor.

Prosecutors are also very concerned if the parents "did it on purpose." In our study, only five of the ten cases were known by us to be the result of purposeful, willful beatings or punishments. An example of the accidental type unappealing to prosecutors is the case of Chris, age three months. Little Chris had already met with two severe accidents in his short life, both at his mother's hand. At two months of age, he allegedly "slipped" from his mother's arms and suffered a badly twisted broken arm. At three months, he supposedly wiggled out of her arms again, this time sustaining a depressed skull fracture with severe acute brain syndrome. The prosecutor, convinced that Chris's mother really did not mean to do it, not only dropped the case but refused to refer the case to juvenile court for supervision. Chris's case was lost to treatment because his parents were unable to seek agency help voluntarily.

Unlike Chris's parents, others with strong guilt feelings who confessed "doing it on purpose" were prosecuted. One mother volunteered to take lie detector tests twice, failed both of them, and served two jail sentences.

In addition to self-admitted purposeful cases, prosecutors are attentive to cases which cause visible external disfigurement. Douglas, age two, who suffered a gangrenous leg that was eventually amputated, received much more response from prosecutors than did his baby brother who had been reported the year previously for a broken leg.

The decision to prosecute is also influenced by the amount of public attention a case receives. It is a strange irony that so much of the publicity which "forces" the prosecutor to act originates from the prosecutor's office itself. By permitting the police to release the story or by releasing the news themselves, prosecutors may in effect force their own hands.

Of the ten cases studied, three were prosecuted. All of these three were self-admitted, purposeful, visible, and publicly notorious. Four cases were reported but not prosecuted. In each of these, the abuse was denied or said to be "accidental." The wounds were well healed or hidden, and the stories had been kept out of the newspapers. The other three cases were not reported to the prosecutor.

Now let us consider the effect of legal punishment upon these cases. One mother, after serving a jail sentence for child abuse, committed three more similar offenses. A second mother who had served her jail sentence stood a good chance of getting her child back, despite numerous medical and social work opinions against return of the child. In general, then, prosecution and punishment when used alone served only to increase the child's time in psychological limbo and did nothing to help clarify the child's future status in regard to adequate parental care.

Prosecutors, by delaying their decision to prosecute, may cause the waste of considerable time and effort which had gone into treatment. One mother and father had received homemaker services, three months of intensive casework, and several psychiatric interviews by the time the prosecutor decided to initiate criminal action. Another couple two years after an alleged child abuse episode still await its legal resolution, even though they have undergone successful psychotherapy in the meantime.

As long as the issue of prosecution remains undecided, it is very difficult for parents to enter wholeheartedly into a treatment program. While a therapist should always inform parents that reports of their progress will be made available to the juvenile court, it is legally and medically self-defeating when such reports are sent to the prosecutor, who is seeking incriminating evidence.

Finally, a comment about obligatory reporting laws is in order. Although police or prosecutors taking statements from individuals suspected of crimes must by law inform them of their constitutional right to remain silent, the doctor who reports to the prosecutor offers the parents no such protection. In this way, doctors can be used to gain evidence for criminal prosecution without safeguarding the individual's constitutional rights. Needless to say, little dynamic understanding about the family could come from medical interviews forwarded to prosecutors.

3. Effects of Juvenile Court Procedure

The juvenile court contributes to the confusion in battered child cases. It appears to us that the crux of the difficulty in juvenile courts is the court's failure at the outset of a case to formulate a definite plan which sets forth all of the long- and short-range alternatives.

For example, let us return to Ricky, the eight-month-old who, according to his mother, had hit himself so hard with his bottle as to cause bilateral subdural hematomas. The prosecutor, when he dropped the case, informed the juvenile court about it. Although the juvenile court took temporary custody of Ricky, there was no initial consideration of whether the mother really wanted or ever could manage him. Originally, with careful juvenile court planning, a treatment plan could have been set up whereby the mother would be carefully supervised and helped while temporary custody was maintained. Instead, no initial plan was made, and over the next two years the child was abandoned by his mother three times and returned to her each time.

When one child has been battered it is very important that the juvenile court include all of the children in the family in the initial investigation and planning. In our study of eight couples with more than one child, three had been suspected of battering more than one youngster in the family.

A dramatic example of juvenile court failure in planning for the siblings occurred in the case of Jonathan, a five-year-old battered child. Jonathan had been tied up and beaten repeatedly by his stepmother, who considered him a rival for her new husband's affection. The juvenile court planned admirably for Jonathan, receiving voluntary permission from Jonathan's father for permanent termination of parental rights and arranging a fine foster home placement for Jonathan.

Beyond this, however, the court overlooked three sisters of Jonathan's who had been farmed out by the parents in a haphazard way to relatives. Two months after Jonathan's removal from the home, his stepmother came to the court-assigned psychiatrist complaining that she was about to murder Jonathan's two younger brothers. Both parents were unwilling to consider conjoint psychiatric treatment or casework. The juvenile court refused to intervene because the brothers had not been battered.

Immediately following the juvenile court's refusal, the stepmother gave the boys away to childless strangers who had heard of the family's predicament. The new parents were unacceptable by juvenile court standards, but with clever legal assistance they were able to proceed toward adoption of these youngsters. The juvenile court, finally aware of its failure to take the whole family into account, made permanent arrangements for the three "farmed-out" sisters.

Problems are often created in juvenile court when it overreaches or underextends itself. An extreme example of overreaching occurred in the case of two adopted children, Marcia and Susan. Marcia, a withdrawn retarded three-year-old, had been battered by her frustrated parents, while Susan, her bright, attractive baby sister, thrived in the same home. The juvenile court permanently removed not only the battered child but the normal child from the parents in this instance. This example of overreaching of authority is unusual.

Inadequate court intervention is more common. For example, two-year-old Douglas, already brain damaged from a previous, mother-inflicted injury, was refused the foster care requested by his frantic mother because the juvenile court worker noticed some opposition from Douglas's father. A few months later Douglas was near death at home from dehydration, starvation, and advanced gangrene.

Not only court workers but also juvenile court judges delay and fail to exert authority in battered child cases. Of seven cases handled in juvenile court hearings, final rulings of custody had not been obtained in four cases at the conclusion of the study. The shortest elapsed time had then been one year.

Courts of jurisdiction in criminal and divorce matters may greatly influence and interfere with the planning and disposition of cases by the juvenile court. For instance, five-year-old Nancy had been beaten by her stepfather several times when she visited his home. This had been reported to the divorce court over a two-year period by Nancy's grandmother and pediatrician. No forthcoming action or change in visiting arrangements had occurred, and the case was never mentioned by the divorce court to the juvenile court.

In another instance, a criminal court judge openly usurped juvenile court prerogatives when he ruled that a father could not see his battered child for five years as a condition of his probation. In this way, he tied the hands of the juvenile court, which had not yet settled the question of future parental contact with the child.

4. Effects of Legislation

Finally, in considering the law's confusion in regard to battered child cases, we note the effects of the legislation itself. Originally most states passed child-abuse reporting statutes for the purpose of remedying the problem by treatment of the families (9). Statutes which require that reports be made to police departments or prosecutor's offices interfere with these widely accepted treatment aims. When, as in Michigan, a state requires reporting to both a treatment agency and an agency concerned with punishment, a conflict is set up which impedes the effective management of cases.

Reinhart and Elmer pointed out that laws requiring reporting to police may increase parents' anger at the child and may cause the parents to keep the injured child away from the doctor's office (10). Furthermore, in a survey of doctors in the Washington, D.C. area, Silver learned from one-fourth of the answering doctors that they would not report battered children even with legal protection (11). This implies that legislative revisions may be necessary to allow more protective and therapeutic procedures than are presently in effect.

TREATMENT PROBLEMS

Doctors, social agencies, and nurses share responsibility with the law for the lack of communication and planning in battered child cases. Doctors frequently fail to report these cases. Of our ten cases, two were never reported to any authority. To the best of our knowledge this did not occur because the doctors wished to avoid court appearances. Rather, the failures to report were examples of either failure to diagnose child abuse or overconfidence in the voluntary nature of relationships with patients.

1. Effects of the Diagnostic Process

First let us consider diagnostic failures. Three-year-old Wendy was brought to a busy emergency room after her mother had tried to drown her in a bathtub. Her mother said that Wendy had slipped in the tub. The doctor accepted this story without question. Wendy's mother herself pointed out Wendy's bruises and Wendy's need for artificial respiration. Wendy's mother told us later that had she been asked any question about it she would have told the doctor of her homicidal intent.

Another example of diagnostic failure is the case of Janice, age five. She had been hospitalized for two weeks with malnutrition and growth failure before doctors suspected parental abuse or neglect. When parental abuse was finally considered, many old fractures, scars, and burns were noticed by the doctors. Failure to consider "battered child" in the initial differential diagnosis caused the doctors to lose the opportunity to check Janice's stools for protein and fat. This could have helped prove lack of food in Janice's diet.

Such proof is important for two reasons. First, medical proof can bring pressure to bear in order to move parents quickly and effectively into treatment. Second, if treatment should fail, the juvenile court, with medical proof, will be in a good legal position to arrange some alternative disposition.

Another part of the diagnostic process that doctors may neglect is documentation. One doctor who had diagnosed battered child syndrome twice in five-year-old Nancy had sent brief notes about it to the divorce court, but had failed to record the physical findings about her in his own files. Two years later, when Nancy's sister came home from a visit to her stepfather's house with a dislocated shoulder, there was no accumulation of evidence with which to put together a meaningful case on behalf of the children. The family doctor's notes were so rudimentary as to be almost worthless in court. In a case like this, where legal action is likely, the lack of complete notes and even photographs is a crucial failure to protect the vulnerable child.

Discussion with the patient's family about the nature of the disease and the recommended treatment is an important part of the diagnostic process. In three cases, the doctors who initiated the battered child reports to official agencies never told the parents they had done so. When these parents came to the psychiatrist and were told of the incipient court action, they were astounded and furious. Often it took several hours to calm them down to the point where they could begin to talk about their difficulties at home. Secrecy about court reports on the part of a physician will arouse very angry outbursts on the part of parents who already suffer from severe difficulties with hostility.

2. Effects of the "Voluntary" Nature of Doctor, Social Agency, and Patient Relationships

Besides failures in the diagnostic process, medical and social work failures occur in handling battered child cases because of confusion about the voluntary nature of relationships with patients. For example, both the family doctor and psychiatrist in the case of two-year-old Coleen purposely did not report an arm fracture, scalp laceration, and concussion, even though they were both convinced this was a battered child. Their rationale was that reporting would interfere with their treatment of Coleen and her family. This kind of confidence about the successful voluntary treatment of cases is doubtful, however, because parents can revert again to child beating if they are not closely followed for a sufficient period of time (2, 5).

Unwillingness to intervene without consent likewise affects the handling of battered children by community nursing and social agencies. In one striking example, a visiting nurse assigned to a family in which three reported batterings had already occurred failed to check two-year-old Douglas for several months. Week by week when the nurse came to visit she stayed out of the utility room where Douglas was kept, because Douglas's mother said she did not wish him to be disturbed while napping. The child developed gangrene of both legs, a protruding fracture of the thigh, and starvation without ever being seen by the visiting nurse. Similarly in Douglas's case, his mother, who had already served a jail sentence for child abuse, had been seeing a probation officer weekly for friendly chats, while Douglas's condition progressively went downhill.

Another failure by a community agency to accept responsibility because of confusion about voluntary relationships occurred in the previously cited case of the near-homicide in the bathtub. Wendy's mother, aware of her attempted murder, voluntarily told her story to the intake worker of a local service agency. The worker sent her away, telling her to admit herself to a psychiatric hospital. The agency did no follow-up on the case, and the mother delayed further action for two more months until she burned Wendy with a teakettle and again became frightened of her murderous impulses.

In another case, the juvenile court, after having very successfully worked with a severely disturbed family for many months, attempted to refer the case to a local agency for long-term supportive treatment. The agency refused because the parents were not "motivated enough" for casework.

Of six battered child cases which were considered by voluntary community social service agencies, three were flatly refused treatment. One was followed superficially through several child abandonments with no agency communication to the juvenile court. Another case was accepted for voluntary treatment, but the parents failed to keep appointments. Only one case was actively followed by a voluntary social agency.

PROPOSALS FOR HANDLING BATTERED CHILDREN

Having examined the many medical and legal stumbling blocks encountered by the battered child, we wish to offer some general proposals to relieve the confusion. Of course we are aware that every county and every state has its own statutes, courts, and treatment facilities. However, there are some principles which we believe transcend these differences.

First we wish to emphasize the importance of a treatment plan in the initial stages of working with the abused child and his family. The plan must allow for full and efficient use of the community's medical, social, and legal resources. One central agency is needed to set up the treatment plan, to facilitate interagency communication, and to bear ultimate responsibility for carrying out the plan. We feel that the juvenile court, or the child protective service agency working closely with the juvenile court, is the most appropriate unit to direct and coordinate this planning. Therefore, we would hope that every battered child case comes to the immediate attention of the juvenile court. (The term juvenile court will henceforth be used to include child-protective agency also.)

The sequence of planning is very important. The issue of prosecution must be settled before any treatment plan can go into effect. Prosecutors, when urged to do so, are able to decide within a few weeks whether or not to criminally prosecute a case. After the decision to prosecute is made, the juvenile court proceeds to weigh permanent termination of parental rights versus temporary placement of the child. Early planning is undertaken also for future juvenile court supervision and treatment of the parents if their child is to be returned to them at the time of acquittal or release from prison.

Let us assume that the prosecutor has decided not to initiate criminal action. What is the next step in planning? The juvenile court worker considers whether there is sufficient evidence of repeated abuse, a particularly severe injury, or parental disinterest in the child, to press immediately for permanent termination of parental rights. If termination appears to be necessary, the parents may be helped through casework to understand their inability to cope with the child, so that they voluntarily seek termination of their parental rights or at least desist from fighting such action in court.

On the other hand, there are a great many cases in which there is some doubt about eventual return of the child, or in which there is insufficient evidence to terminate parental rights. In these cases, there are two possible avenues of planning. One of these is removal of the battered child to a foster home or institution while the parents are treated to determine whether the child will eventually be returned to them (4). We take issue with this commonly used approach because we have found that after the disruptive child is removed, parents are no longer under stress and come to feel that they have changed, only to resume their former behavior when the child is returned to them.

We would propose a second approach in dealing with cases in which family restoration remains in doubt. After a reported battering, the child becomes a temporary ward of the juvenile court and returns to the parents, while certain safeguards are employed. The parents are required to undergo a few months diagnostic trial of penetrating conjoint interviews (15) to determine their capability for insight and change. Safeguards include almost daily checks of the child by community health, social work, and/or educational personnel, as well as provision of homemaker services (6, 13), if available, for the mother. Another desirable safeguard is the appointment by the court of an attorney to represent the child's interests.

The backbone of this plan, however, is the diagnostic trial of conjoint parental interviews previously mentioned. These sessions will offer the parents a chance to observe their interactions with each other and with the child and to come to grips with some of their unrealistic ideas about the child. Such interviews may be conducted by a psychiatrist, psychologist, or social worker. After several sessions the therapist will have a firm, well-documented opinion about the family's future chances with the abused child. Termination of rights may come about if abuse continues even under supervision or if the family is unable to begin to improve with treatment.

On the other hand, if some improvement comes about in the trial period, a strong basis has been laid for continuing parental conjoint or individual therapy with court worker, social agency, or physician. We feel it would be wise for the court to invoke temporary custody for at least a year in cases in which the child will continue to live at home.

Finally, in order to provide the best therapeutic chance for the battered child it is necessary to draft statutes aimed at rehabilitation, so that mandatory physicians' reports will result in treatment programs rather than punishment proceddures.

In summary, we wish to emphasize that the process of handling battered children must continue to be a complex multiagency process. One agency or one person cannot deal with the problems of the battered child alone. We have found that the handling will fail without the back-up of juvenile court jurisdiction. Parents who ordinarily are inaccessible to more traditional voluntary treatment approaches may respond to treatment if a court insists upon it.

REFERENCES

1. American Academy of Pediatrics, Committee on Infant and Pre-school Child. Maltreatment of children: The physically abused child. *Pediatrics* 37:377-382, 1966.
2. Boardman, H. A project to rescue children from inflicted injuries. *Social Work* 7:43-51, 1962.
3. Caffey, J. Multiple fractures in long bones of infants suffering from chronic subdural hematoma. *Amer. J. Roentgen.* 56:163-173, 1946.
4. Delsordo, J. Protective casework for abused children. *Children* 10:213-18, 1963.
5. Elmer, E. Identification of abused children. *Children* 10:180-84, 1963.
6. Foresman, L. Homemaker service in neglect and abuse: I. Strengthening family life. *Children* 12:23-26, 1965.
7. Kempe, C., Silverman, F., Steele, B., Droegemueller, W., and Silver, H. The battered child syndrome. *J.A.M.A.* 181:17-24, 1962.
8. Paulsen, M. The legal framework for child protection. *Columbia Law Review* 66:679-717, 1966.
9. Paulsen, M., Parker, G., and Adelman, L. Child abuse reporting laws—Some legislative history. *George Washington Law Review* 34:482-506, 1966.
10. Reinhart, J., and Elmer, E. The abused child: Mandatory reporting legislation. *J.A.M.A.* 188:358-62, 1964.
11. Silver, L., Barton, W., and Dublin, C. Child abuse laws—Are they enough? *J.A.M.A.* 199:65-68, 1967.
12. Silverman, F. Roentgen manifestations of unrecognized skeletal trauma in infants. *Amer. J. Roentgen.* 69:413-26, 1953.
13. Stringer, E. Homemaker service in neglect and abuse: II. A tool for case evaluation. *Children* 12:26-29, 1965.
14. U. S. Children's Bureau. The Abused Child—Principles and Suggested Language for Legislation on Reporting of the Physically Abused Child, 1963.
15. Watson, A. The conjoint psychotherapy of marriage partners. *Amer. J. Orthopsychiat.* 33:912-22, 1963.

CHAPTER 47

Social Isolation and Deprivation: An Environment of Rehabilitation

Helen L. Morrison and David M. Brubakken

Professional literature abounds with reports of experimental studies that investigate the deleterious effects of deprivation on later behavior (1-4). Most of the work has been reported in animals, as it would be unethical experimentally to induce this condition in humans. Thus, clinical research is often restricted to the study of "naturally occurring" case histories, using observational and retrospective methods. While data collected from such methodology may not be ideal, such reports have significant clinical and research value.

The clinical literature notes that deprivation has consequences in both physiological and psychological spheres (5-15). The lack of stimulation in many species has been noted to lead to deficits in perception, social behavior, activity level, emotional development, motor coordination, and intelligence (16-24). This has been observed most frequently in studies of investigators utilizing nonhuman primates in experiments studying this phenomena. Researchers are focusing their work on the development of social, intellectual, and physiological competence and the effects of varied early social environments on subsequent development. Total social isolation, or the primate deprivation syndrome, results in behavior characterized by lack of integration of motor patterns, communication difficulties, excessive arousal, and abnormal movements or posturing (25, 26). The time at which the animal is placed in isolation and the length of time of the isolation itself are important factors in the degree of behavioral abnormality subsequent to this environment. If the animal is placed in social situations with age-mate peers, there is evidence of absent or inappropriate social interactions with inappropriate aggressiveness and self-aggressiveness, behaviors not usually seen in the normal animal (27, 28). Many authors have postulated that the behavioral abnormalities in these animals are the results of learning deficits in critical periods. However, these theories have not been supported by the work reported in rehabilitation on this isolation syndrome in the primate (29-32). Space does not permit the discussion of the use and applicability of these animal models, and the reader is referred to comprehensive reviews of this work and discussions of its implications for experimental psychology (33, 34).

The human concept of feral man, or wild man, was first introduced by Linneaus in 1758, when he presented the cases of nine children who had been raised as "wild" children. Thirty-one cases, together with their histories and details of their behavior after capture by society, were described by Zingg (34). One of the most detailed cases ever reported was the study by Itard of the wild boy of Aveyron (35). Although many of the cases are poorly documented and the data are limited, it appears that isolation from normal social contact was devastating to subsequent adjustment. However, as is true in many situations we encounter in our field, there are multivaried and individual differences in the responses to this deprivation. This is illustrated by the case of Kaspar Hauser, reported in 1833 as a well-documented case of isolation (36). This boy had been confined after the age of three and for most of his seventeen years in a dungeon, alone for a great part of the time. When found, he could barely walk or talk, seemed to be intellectually defective and yet, after tutelage by von Feuerbach (1872), developed what has been said to be superior intellectual capacity. This case has been used to illustrate that he had some intellectual or human relationship in early life, before age three, and although the details of this stimulation will never be known, the concept has aided us in the subsequent study of the effects of isolation and its multifaceted components.

Many authors have reported cases of isolated or restricted children, with attempts made to explain the dynamics of their subsequent development in relationship to their early experience (37–41). Two of these cases, reported by Davis, were Anna and Isabella (42, 43). Anna was found at the age of five to be emaciated and immobile after being raised in an attic with minimal contact with her mother. At the age of ten, when she died, Anna had been able to attain speech near the two-year-old level, had clumsy locomotion and reasonable toilet habits. Isabella was confined for her first six years with her deaf-mute mother and upon emergence from isolation had a Stanford-Binet of nineteen months and a Vineland Social Maturity Scale of 2½ years, considerably superior to that of Anna. Isabella was systematically trained and attained vocalization in one week, spoke sentences in two months, read and could write within nine months, and developed a vocabulary of over 2,000 words in sixteen months. Of course, Davis questioned the differences between his two cases, and it was found that even though Isabella had been confined, her mother shared the child's isolation. Stone (44) discusses the question of whether the progress made by Isabella was more related to the presence of the attachment bond than to the training she had received when removed from isolation.

Most recently, reports of the consequences of social isolation have involved a case of monozygotic twins (45, 46). The discussion of this case notes that for the first year of their lives, following the death of their mother, these children had been placed in a group home and were noted to be normal in their development. Subsequent remarriage of the father led to what is described as a 5½-year period of deprivation, cruelty, and mistreatment. Rickets, difficulty in walking, reactions of "surprise and horror," and minimal language characterized them upon discovery. Their rehabilitation, described in a subsequent publication (47), shows that they had "no problems in the social sphere," and exhibited "no psychopathological symptoms." In addition, over the years of follow-up and exposure to a stimulating environment, they attained "average intelligence" and showed no problems with "timidity, shyness or aggression." The implications of these results will be discussed in the summary of this chapter.

The impoverished behavior observed in some of the reported cases of isolation seems similar to that of children diagnosed as autistic. Ferster (48) and Ferster and DeMeyer (49) present the argument that these children could be taught to comply with certain reality aspects of life. It had been noted previously by several authors that psychotherapy alone does not lead to change in these cases (50–52). Criteria that defined a poor prognosis for these children have been specified by several authors (53, 54). Those children with an IQ below 50 did not acquire speech, and 75 percent of them required long-term hospitalization. If there was no appropriate play, or mutism still existed at age five, the prognosis was extremely poor. In order for the child to make substantial gains, this improvement had to be evident before age seven, and, in almost all cases, there were declines in the child's condition. Rutter also noted that improvement was, in essence, unrelated to therapy.

Optimism in the treatment of the behavior of autistic children was really most evident in the work of the early behaviorists. Success in helping these children acquire more socially practical behavior was first reported by Wolf, Risley, and Mees, who worked with a 3.5-year-old boy in controlling self-destructive behavior, tantrums, lack of verbal communication, and inadequate social repertoire (55, 56). In the areas of imitation, reading, and language, many authors were able to achieve success with varied behavioral programs (57–63). But it has also been noted that there were little follow-up data on the generalization of treatment effects across environments. Some data had been reported to response generalization, along with a notable lack of the assessment of treatment effectiveness over time. Lovaas et al., have reported data regarding generalizations across situations and across time with the finding that the twenty children they studied still improved, but that post-treatment environment determined the maintenance of the improvement. Thus, those children who were institutionalized regressed, and those children whose parents were trained to use the techniques of behavior therapy continued to improve (64).

Stuecher in his reported treatment of an autistic child attempted, on the basis of Whitehorn's observations (65), to interact with the child in order to create a foundation for a behavior modification program (66). His contention was that before the child could be trained and educated there needed to be a consistent and predictable relationship and the development of trust. He further stated that the method for treating the behavior was by no means a simple, one factor technique.

CASE HISTORY

M was the fourth and last child born in his family. Father was born in the state, was the youngest of three siblings and the only son in his family. Paternal grandfather was a sheet metal worker on government projects and, as a consequence, father's family moved around a great deal. This frequent moving was felt to be partially responsible for the father's multiple school failures and his eventually leaving school in the ninth grade. At age eighteen, father joined the Navy and was trained as an electronics technician, work he continues in today. At age twenty-three, he married the patient's mother, a woman he met in Texas, who was of Mexican-American background. Mother had been married twice previously and had two children, but no information was available as to the status of these children.

There is essentially no early developmental or birth history for M until he reached age three. Indeed, there are no data for any of the siblings' early history. According to relatives, both M and his sister were left unattended for long periods of time during the parents' marriage. It was noted that the mother had difficulty with her husband's frequent absences from the home when he was working on a job. It was also reported that the mother was an alcoholic.

When the patient was three years of age, the family moved from the state of Washington into the home of the paternal grandparents. During the time of living with that family, M was essentially confined to a crib, would be fed when he cried "eat," and, aside from slight contact at feeding time, was not in social contact with the family. He was not fed solid food, but was given a bottle during at least the first four years of his life, the same pattern of feeding that had occurred with his sister. At the age of three years, nine months, his mother was killed in an automobile accident. The family remained with the paternal grandparents except for M who, because of reported uncontrollable behavior, was given to an aunt and uncle and their family of seven children. At the age of five, he was partially toilet trained, had some basically noncommunicative speech, and was quite overactive. He stayed with these relatives for the years just prior to his admission to the treatment unit described below. This family also had difficulties with marital instability, alcoholism, frequent separations, and their known reluctance to follow through on suggestions of the community agencies in the care of their children. Figure I shows the environments in which M has lived up to the present time.

M was admitted to the Project for Psychotic and Neurologically Impaired Children for the first time at the age of six years, eleven months. He was a thin, frail boy, weighing 40 pounds (3rd percentile for boys); height 46 inches (25th percentile for boys his age). Head circumference was 51 cm, considered to be normal. He was difficult to examine, but had a shuffling gait, could not grasp a pencil, and seemed grossly uncoordinated. His difficulty with motor movements was related to problems in balance and stability, in addition to difficulty in actual movement. No other abnormalities were noted on further physical or laboratory examinations, including electroencephalography.

Psychiatrically, M showed much repetitive behavior, little exploration of the playroom, fascination with water and keys, and apparent nonresponsiveness to the examiner. He accepted restraint from the examiner, but would not respond to a structured play situation. The Vineland Social Maturity Scale was under three years, except in the area of self-help skills, which were somewhat higher. Under

AGE		ENVIRONMENTAL CHANGE
Years	Months	
3		Parents move in with paternal grandparents
3	9	Death of mother
4	3	Moved to live with aunt, 7 other children
6	11	First admission to PPNIC[*]
7	7	Discharge to father and stepmother, 9 other children
7	9	Divorce of father and stepmother
7	11	Father and children move in with paternal grandparents
8		Second admission to PPNIC
8	2	Home visits to paternal grandparents
8	4	Death of paternal grandmother
8	6	Paternal grandfather remarries; father and children move out of paternal grandparent's home
8	8	Father and stepmother remarry
8	10	Discharge to father and stepmother, 7 other children
9	3	Father and stepmother separate

[*]Project for Psychotic and Neurologically Impaired Children

Figure I. Environments of Development (environmental change and age at which change occurred)

the stress of examination, he hit his head repeatedly with his hand and showed hand-flapping and screaming behavior. When given food, he looked at it but did not attempt to eat it. He did accept holding by the examiner, but only for very brief periods of time, and he would not mold to the examiner. The diagnostic impression at the time noted that he did not exhibit the pathognomonic behavior characteristic of early infantile autism (67). Although stereotypy and echolalia were present, this had not changed across the years. That he was psychotic was revealed in his severe impairment of emotional relationships with others, tendency toward preoccupation with inanimate objects, failure in speech development, disturbance in sensory perception, bizarre and stereotyped behavior, absence of a sense of personal identity, and fragmented intellectual development. The multifaceted effects of the social and environmental deprivation led us to the conclusion that no singular category of diagnosis was appropriate (68, 69).

Speech and language reports also are limited until age six. At the age of four he had two utterances, "eat" and "shut up." At age six, he used two- or three-word noun and verb phrases, noted to be inappropriate for the situation. He would communicate his needs by temper tantrums and there was much echolalia present. He was functioning at the two-year-old level of language development, with a great deal of egocentric speech.

During his first admission to the project, he was hospitalized for eight months, where focus was placed on the areas of eating, the development of communicative skills, self-help skills, and primary socialization. Gross motor skills were developed with a program of structured activities of crawling, climbing, swimming, and mastery of an obstacle course. Language work concentrated on increasing the length of his utterances, answering yes-no questions, vocabulary, and concepts such as big-little. Because of the eating difficulties, a program was designed to enable him to accept textured foods. He would initially eat only soft foods and would respond to the presentation of solid or textured foods with temper tantrums and spitting out the food. The program called for textured foods to be cut into small pieces and rewarding him with soft foods contingent on his swallowing the more textured foods. While he initially responded with temper tantrums, these were ignored, and he was praised when a textured bite was taken. Each meal required the recording of the number of textured bites taken, and he received a vitamin supplement tablet each day. He gained 6 pounds in four weeks on the program and responded extremely well to the social praise. This often led to his taking up to an hour to eat. The attention was slowly phased out, so that he had the same amount of time for eating and attention as the other children in the unit. He continued to eat well and tried foods with much less hesitation and resistance.

Initially, his behavior on the ward was noted to be nonactive. He would not play with toys, would not respond to staff interventions for involvement, and generally did not react to situations in the unit. The ward staff focused on engaging him in activities and discouraged his sitting in his favorite chair for long periods of time. They required that he play ball and interact with his peers, even though he cried initially during these times. He responded to times-out for noncompliance and temper tantrums, and by the time of discharge he also showed a great decrease in self-hitting behavior. He also began to approach the staff and his peers, could dress and undress himself, and was toilet trained by the time of discharge.

During this initial period of treatment his father had remarried. The parents were involved in a parent-training program that involved a group training program for parents in the general principles of the behavioral program. There was concentration on programing for specific behavior for M. Because of his progress, he was returned to his father and stepmother and placed in a prekindergarten program in a community school. Two months after discharge he was still speaking spontaneously and was easy to understand. He had less frequent temper tantrums and, there was continued decrease in the hand-flapping that often accompanied stress. The parents were having marital difficulties, but experienced no separations during these two months. Educational plans for the upcoming school year were that he would attend a regular kindergarten program that consisted of twenty-five children divided into groups on the basis of the ability of the child to learn and attend. The family was continuing to maintain the behavior program and M seemed to be stabilized.

Four months after discharge, the unit was contacted by the school principal, who stated that the parents had separated and that M was living with the father and paternal grandparents. A follow-up visit was scheduled and evaluation was made of his performance in the classroom. The special classroom had seven children, one teacher, and one aide. The need for referral was based on the observation that M was 100 percent nonattentive in the classroom and was preoccupied with keys and touching everything in the room. Eighty-six percent of his time was spent in being disruptive, 59 percent was spent in inappropriate yelling, and 57 percent in pulling on chairs and other furniture. Two weeks after this evaluation and the observation that regressive behavior was continuing M was readmitted to the unit.

READMISSION EVALUATION

Prior to this second admission, a requirement was made that father and grandmother would participate in an extensive, individualized parent-training program. The school also agreed to send its teachers for extensive training on M's behavior prior to his discharge.

Psychiatric evaluation at the time of the second admission noted that M's behavior had significantly regressed since the first discharge. He was aloof and distant, demonstrated echolalia, and displayed mannerisms of finger-flicking and hand-flapping. He was fascinated with keys and he toe-walked. Physical and laboratory examinations were again within normal limits, and there were no noted difficulties with walking or gross motor movements. In the areas of speech and language, he displayed a mental age of five years, five months on the Peabody Picture Vocabulary Test. In expressive skills, a sample analyzed a mean length of response equivalent to five years, five months. Structured complexity score placed him at five years, five months of age. Seventy percent of his utterances were appropriate to the situation, with the other 30 percent concerned with hurting himself, spelling words, or irrelevant comments. He could answer some abstract questions and had a poor attention span with very aggressive behavior. Verbal tantrums, screaming, crying, hand-flapping and rocking characterized his behavior during the speech evaluation. The summary data from that evaluation noted that he was 3½ years below age level. It was noted that he had developed language over the past five years, and it was felt that his language deficit was due primarily to the lack of environmental stimulation.

Occupational therapy noted that on the Frostig Developmental Test of Visual Perception, he had age equivalents of 3.9 on Eye Motor Coordination, 4.0 on Figure Ground, 2.6 on Form Consistency, 2.6 on Position in Space, and 4.0 on Spatial Relations. He was also noted to be independent on most self-help skills, but had a high degree of noncompliance, low attending behavior, and low frustration tolerance.

THE ENVIRONMENT OF REHABILITATION

Between M's first and second admissions, the reorganization of the project that began in June 1972 was completed. The present unit serves fifteen children ranging in age from three to eleven years. Admissions are carefully screened, so that only those children whose needs cannot be met in less intensive, less specialized, community-based treatment programs are admitted. These children are characterized by inappropriate social behavior, such as noncompliance, hyperactivity, aggressiveness, temper tantrums, and bizarre mannerisms or stereotypic behavior. Eye contact and attention to task are usually quite poor. In addition, the children have delayed language development, as well as delays in acquisition of academic skills and self-help skills. A multidisciplinary approach is employed. The project has a child-care worker-to-resident ratio of 1:2.2. In addition, psychologists, social workers, nurses, special education teachers, occupational therapists, and speech therapists, as well as consultants in psychiatry and neurology are involved with the total evaluation and treatment of the child while he is in the project. All of the staff work within a behavioral-educational framework, and all staff are trained on reliability weekly so that observation and treatment of behavior are consistent.

A primary goal of the residential treatment phase is to make the child more manageable. This involves increasing the child's compliance as well as reducing the negative behavior and bizarre mannerisms. Appropriate social behavior is followed by positive social and edible reinforcement, while negative social behavior is followed by a time-out. The program also focuses on the development of behavior in the area of language development, academic skills, and self-help skills. The staff works with the family and the child's teachers in the classroom, again with the objective of maintaining consistency of treatment. Follow-up is normally maintained on a child up to two years after discharge by the staff contacting the home and school at regular intervals. This is done to assist the family and school in new programs, to evaluate the treatment effects of the program, to assess maintenance and generalization of the programs to the community, and to evaluate the effectiveness of the parent- and school-training programs.

METHODS

An intensive program was defined for M in the areas of compliance, aggression, temper tantrums, bizarre behavior, eye contact, parallel and independent play, specific ward behavior for the dayroom and mealroom, parent training for all behavior, and school and community involvement in the learning of the programs used for M.

M's compliance during baseline was averaging 45 percent; aggressions averaged 239 for a twelve-hour period. A twelve-hour sample for temper tantrums showed 254 tantrums per day. Bizarre mannerisms were averaging 2,628 during a twelve-hour day, a rate of 219 per hour. Total success for eye contact was thirteen percent, with ability to hold contact for no more than one second. He was unable to play independently or spontaneously, even for brief periods of time.

M was started on an eye contact program to teach him to look at people during interactions. Initially this began with requiring only that he glance at a staff person at a distance of one foot. M quickly moved through the shaping steps that were conducted in session until he was able to look at an individual for 5 seconds from as far away as fifteen feet. After completion of this session, the program went to an *in vivo* format that was of a spontaneous nature. An initial goal was to develop noun identification and labeling, and eventually this was used to establish identification skills for commonly encountered environmental objects. In a similar manner, verb identification and labeling was also developed, with the eventual addition of adjectives. Upon completion of the program, one could call M's name, obtain eye contact and talk with him in a normal manner with appropriate language usage.

As mentioned previously, M's ability to play independently was quite low on admission. He was started on a program that had the staff model appropriate play for a period of time (5 minutes) followed by a period in which M would receive rewards or redirection if he were off the task. He was reinforced or redirected every 10 seconds for a period of 5 minutes initially and shaped to play more independently until he could play for 20 minutes appropriately with only one reinforcement. This program took approximately three months. He was then placed on a parallel play program with another child. Again, appropriate play was modeled and reinforced. The children were taught not to be aggressive or take things from one another. After two months of this program, M could play with other children. A final play program taught cooperative play among two children, where the children learned to share toys and interact appropriately.

Time-out and quiet-room shaping began two weeks after admission and consisted of an initial one-minute time-out in which M was required to sit on the floor. During this time, he was not allowed to slide, kick, lie down, or roll over. He was also not allowed to throw, dump, tear, or break objects on the way to time-out. Failure on any of these constituted a two-minute quiet-room back-up. While a time-out procedure was used in teaching M to control certain nonsocial behavior, over 98 percent of his interactions with staff were of a positive, rewarding nature. Only in a significantly rewarding environment will removal for one minute from that environment be an effective treatment technique.

M was engaged in numerous language development programs that were conducted spontaneously all day long. He was involved in many academic programs, began to enjoy school and frequently would attend for days, four hours per day, with no times-out, but was maintained completely on rewards of both an edible and social nature. Later the edible rewards were faded out so that he was self-initiating and rewarded by social interaction alone. Additionally, he participated in numerous dayroom activities, as well as gross motor exercises in the gym and frequent, community-oriented field trips, such as trips to the zoo, the circus, shopping centers, and ice cream parlors.

Parent training began one month after admission and involved the father, two sons, and the grandmother. The training was an intensive, behaviorally oriented effort designed to teach the family how to deal more effectively with M's behavior. The initial phase occurred at the unit and consisted of eight two-hour training sessions held on a bi-weekly basis and conducted by the occupational therapist and a nurse assigned to M. The behavior focused upon was compliance, aggression, temper tantrums, verbal temper tantrums, time-out shaping programs, eye contact, and independent play.

During the first phase of parent training, the grandmother died. At this point the father remarried. The stepmother began and continued the training program in the grandmother's place. The second phase of training involved sessions in the family home that continued on a bi-weekly basis with modifications made in the program when necessary to overcome other specific behavior. When M went home for visits, the parents conducted the same behavior program and collected data concerning his performance. This provided an indication of the family's ability to manage him and also provided feedback for the staff, who then designed subsequent training sessions to meet the specific needs of the family.

Since it was felt that M could return to school and would spend a significant amount of time in a classroom, the teacher was trained in the specific treatment methods that were effective with him. His teacher and the classroom aide came to the unit and observed him in the school program for two days. Training involved both preacademic as well as behavioral management. Through the use of staff demonstrations, role-playing, and coaching, as well as direct patient interaction, the teachers learned applicable programs found to be effective.

Following discharge, his teacher in the unit and the nurse assigned to M were present at his first day of school. They had continued training with the schedule of two days the first week after discharge, a half-day twice a week the second and third weeks after discharge, a half-day the fourth and sixth weeks, and a half-day each month thereafter, up to six months after discharge. This program was designed to help the teacher overcome specific problems in implementing treatment in M's classroom.

RESULTS

Figures II, III, IV, and V, respectively, illustrate the percentage compliance, rate of temper tantrums, rate of aggression, and rate of bizarre mannerisms per hour. These samples were taken at the time of admission (baseline), an average of four weeks prior to discharge (predischarge), and an average of two samples at the time of the four-month follow-up (Community A), six-month follow-up (Community B), and nine-month follow-up (Community C).

In the unit, behavior management with respect to compliance increased to 92 percent from the baseline of 46 percent; bizarre behavior decreased from 211 manifestations per hour to 24.5 per hour, aggressions from 17 occasions per hour to 1 per hour, and temper tantrums from 22 per hour to 2 per hour. Data collected on the four-month follow-up, as also illustrated in Figures II, III, IV, and V, indicate that M had maintained compliance at 92 percent, had had a further reduction in bizarre mannerisms to 4 per hour, had maintained aggressions at one outbreak per hour, and had decreased temper tantrums to 1.5 per hour. Six-month follow-up, also in Figures II, III, IV, and V reveals maintenance of

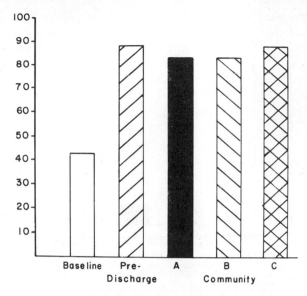

Figure II. Compliance Program

compliance at 90 percent, decrease of temper tantrums to 0.5 per hour, further decrease of aggression to 0.5 occasions per hour and no bizarre mannerisms noted. Nine-month follow-up data showed that M had maintained his progress and had proceeded to three-part commands.

Figure VI shows that in regard to expressive language, M's mean length of

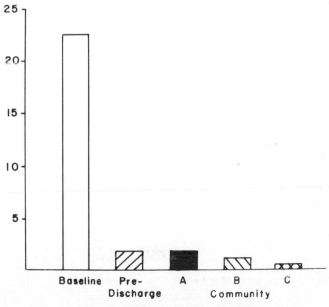

Figure III. Temper Tantrum Program

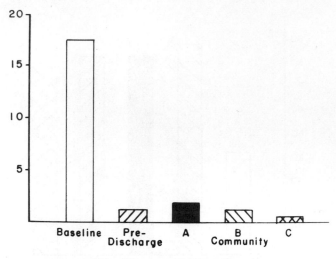

Figure IV. Aggression Program

response increased from a baseline of 4.6 to 5.2 words with the use of simple, compound, and complex structures. From a baseline of 30 percent of inappropriate comments at admission, at discharge only 10 percent of his utterances were inappropriate, and these were directed as threats to other children. Figure VII illustrates M's score on the Peabody Picture Vocabulary Test, a measure of

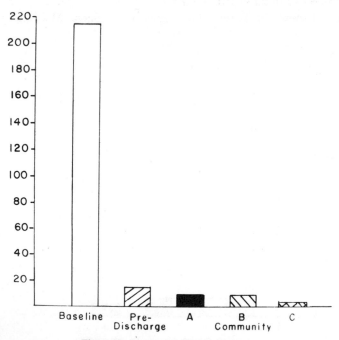

Figure V. Bizarre Mannerism Program

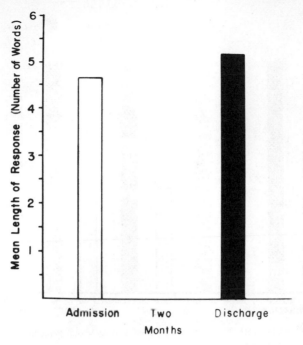

Figure VI. Expressive Language

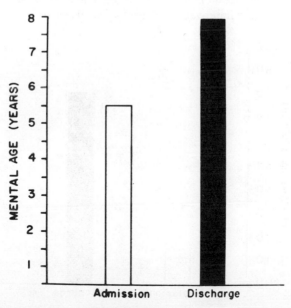

Figure VII. Receptive Language (Peabody Picture Vocabulary Test)

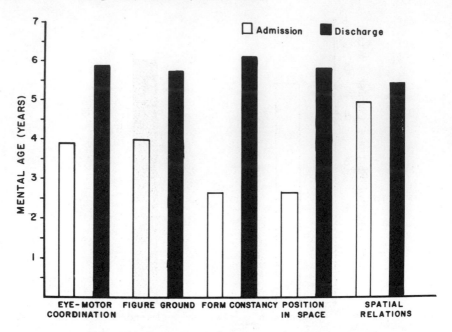

Figure VIII. Frostig Developmental Test of Visual Perception

receptive language, at the time of admission and upon discharge. He showed an increase of two years, five months in mental age over the ten months of residential treatment. At admission, he had a mental age of five years, five months, while upon discharge it had increased to seven years, ten months.

M's behavior had improved, with no hyperactivity or aggressive behavior

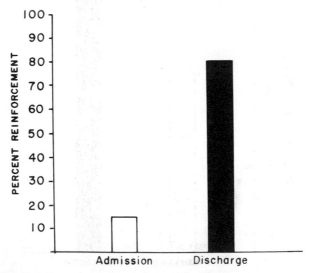

Figure IX. Father's Percent Response to Compliance—Reinforcement

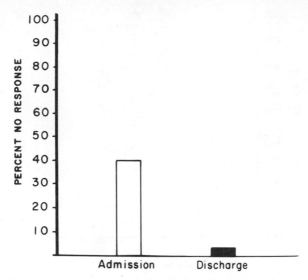

Figure X. Father's Percent Response to Compliance—No Response

seen, and he was compliant. The summary impression was that his language skills were two years below his chronological age, based on the Peabody, Carrow, and developmental data. His language was felt to have a continuing strong potential for development because of his rapid acquisition of concepts and his generalization of these concepts to new situations.

In the academic situation, he reached a sight vocabulary of forty-one words, learned preaddition skills, could count to twenty, knew the nine basic colors, five basic shapes, and the alphabet, both receptively and expressively. He could discriminate right and left, could print all his letters, and cursively write his first and last name. Initially, he could not work independently of the teacher, was easily frustrated, and if demands were placed on him, he responded with a tantrum. At discharge, he could work independently for one-half hour, had less difficulty with frustration and fewer tantrums.

In the occupational therapy program, M had improved in various aspects of visual performance. Figure VIII shows that from the baselines reported previously on the Frostig Developmental Test of Visual Perception, M had improved dramatically. Eye motor coordination increased from 3.9 to 5.8 years; figure ground from 4.0 to 5.6 years, form constancy from 2.6 to 6.2 years, position in space from 2.6 to 5.7 years, and spatial relations from 4.9 to 5.5 years.

Data collected in the home by the staff provided information on the effectiveness of the parents on M's behavior. Figures IX, X, XI, and XII show the parent–child interactions following parent training. While on admission, father reinforced M for compliant behavior only 15 percent of the time, at discharge he reinforced him 80 percent of the time, as shown in Figure IX. Figure X shows that no response to compliant behavior on admission occurred at a rate of 40

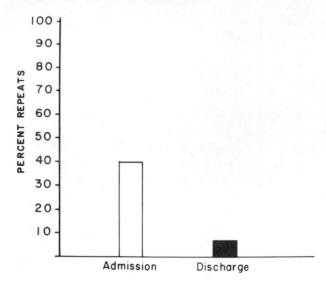

Figure XI. Father's Percent Response to Compliance—Repeats

percent and only 3 percent at discharge. As illustrated in Figure XI, even when M began to comply, the father repeated the command 40 percent of the time at admission, but only 8 percent of the time at discharge. The father's typical response to M's noncompliance was to repeat the command 75 percent of the time at admission and zero percent at discharge, as shown in Figure XII. Since M was so compliant, the father had few opportunities to repeat commands at discharge, and he also effectively used times-out for noncompliance, even though it

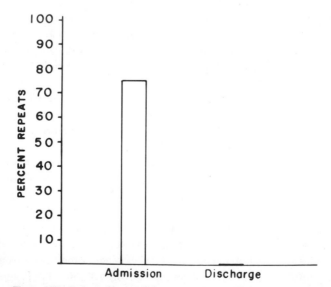

Figure XII. Father's Percent Response to Noncompliance—Repeats

was on an extremely low rate during the two-hour sampling period and, therefore, is not reflected in the data.

DISCUSSION

This report discusses the development and behavioral improvement in a child with a history of severe social isolation/deprivation and the maintenance of this improvement through a coordinated, multi-disciplinary approach to treatment in the residential, home, and school environment. The intensive remedial program significantly altered his behavior, as is obvious from the results section. Follow-up data in regards to compliance, temper tantrums, aggressions, and bizarre mannerisms show that the community transitioning program has assisted M in maintaining his progress. The period of treatment also noted that M went from low rates of play behavior to parallel-cooperative play. Language programs provided improvement in all areas of language functioning. These data have enabled us to conclude that M's initial functioning was related to a primarily environmental defect. The results reported from this study support other research evidence in both the human and the animal field that maintenance of progress is dependent on the environment. We cannot state unequivocally that the most important and effective factor in his progress was the support of the family, as has been noted by Koluchová (1976). We can note that the environment of the unit was such that it provided a growth-oriented, predictable context through a combination of positive social interaction and reinforcement, together with negative contingencies. It is also apparent that this environment needed to be generalized to the parents' home as well as the school to maximize the potential for success.

The early environmental deprivation that M experienced resulted in severe deficits in social, motor, and cognitive areas. The deficits in motor and cognitive areas responded to treatment and improved markedly. In the primate and human literature, the results of isolation and rehabilitation tend to support the theory that the social area is most affected by social isolation. Such is true with M. Although no direct program dealt with affective expression, M would seek out those staff members with whom he had developed some transient attachment. These staff persons were most often the more spontaneous members of the unit. Their own spontaneous behavior often drew M's attention and enabled him to concentrate on the particular task, indicating his need for appropriate social approval. This agrees with reports by several different authors that an adult's posture need not be intrusive in treating a severely disturbed child and can provoke less avoidance behavior on the part of the child (70, 71). However, the range and appropriateness of his affective responses vastly differ from the norm for his present age.

Attachment behavior remains clearly elusive. Although M has been able to develop motor skills and control his hyperactivity, maintain interest in tasks of learning, comprehend stories, and develop language without echolalia, he continues to remain affectively unattached. It is noted that he evidences a minimal capacity for self-object differentiation, play ability with other children, and "purposeful" activity in learning, but has only developed object relations of a transient nature. All of the reported intellectual advances have not been sufficient in and of themselves in the socialization of this child. What can be concluded is that adequate social experience in early development is of primary importance in subsequent self and other differentiation and object relatedness. We do not mean to imply that because M responded positively to the environmental intervention he did not have associated organic deficits. There has never been overt evidence of organic damage in any of the multiple evaluations that he received. Also, M continues to exhibit the need for support in the community, and although it is hopeful that he will gain more independent functioning, we question his ability to attain total independence. As he maintains his progress and functions in the community, he requires less specialized environment for the maintenance of this progress. However, we feel that he will require some continuing structure to maintain his progress.

A final issue is that of a less than clear-cut diagnosis of autism and social isolation. Initially, M showed a syndrome clinically indistinguishable from that of early infantile autism. Inclusion of his early history, as well as his rapid response to treatment, made us consider that in spite of reports that maternal deprivation or social isolation does not cause the syndrome of autism, M exhibited this combined classification. We must emphasize, however, that we are speaking of similarities in behavior and are not assuming a causal nature. Evaluation of a child with the diagnosis or signs of early infantile autism warrants detailed investigation of early developmental history, especially in regards to early socialization. Only in this manner will appropriate treatment and subsequent response to this treatment allow for the best approach to management and prognosis.

REFERENCES

1. D. O. Hebb, "The mammal and his environment." *American Journal Psychology* 111 (1955): 826–31.
2. C. B. Brownfield, *Isolation: Clinical and Experimental Approaches*. New York: Random House, 1965.
3. M. D. Ainsworth and J. Bowlby, "Research strategy in the study of mother-child separation." *Courrier* 4 (1954): 2.
4. J. Bowlby, *Maternal Care and Mental Health*. Geneva: World Health Organization. Monograph Series, Number 2, 1952.
5. H. Lewis, *Deprived Children: The Mersham Experiment. A Social and Clinical Study*. London: Oxford University Press, 1954.
6. H. M. Skeels and E. A. Fillmore, "The mental development of children from under-privileged homes." *Journal Genetic Psychology* 50 (1937): 427.

7. D. Burlingham and A. Freud, *Infants without Families*. London: Allen and Unwin, 1944.
8. W. Goldfarb, "Emotional and Intellectual Consequences of Psychologic Deprivation in Infancy: A Re-evaluation." In P. Hoch and J. Zubin, eds. *Psychopathology of Childhood*. New York: Grune and Stratton, 1955.
9. R. A. Spitz, "The role of ecological factors in emotional development in infancy." *Child Development* 20 (1949): 145.
10. L. J. Yarrow, "Maternal deprivation: Toward an empirical and conceptual reevaluation." *Psychological Bulletin* 58 (1961): 459.
11. R. A. Spitz and K. M. Wolf, "Anaclitic Depression." In *Psychoanalytic Study of the Child*, volume 2. New York: International Universities Press, 1946.
12. D. A. Freedman and S. L. Brown, "On the role of coenesthetic stimulation in the development of psychic structure." *Psychoanalytic Quarterly*, 37 (1968): 418–38.
13. D. A. Freedman, "Congenital and perinatal sensory deprivations: Their effect on the capacity to experience affect." *Psychoanalytic Quarterly* 44 (1975): 62–80.
14. W. R. Thompson, "Psychosocial and Cultural Deprivations in Psychobiological Development: Dimensions of Early Experience." In *Deprivation in Psychobiological Development*. Pan American Health Organization, 1966.
15. World Health Organization. "Deprivation of Maternal Care: A Reassessment of Its Effects." Geneva: World Health Organization, 1962.
16. B. Evans, "The wolf child." *New Republic* 104 (1941): 892.
17. A. Gesell, *Wolf Child and Human Child*. London: Methuen, 1941.
18. D. A. Hamburg, ed. *Psychiatry as a Behavioral Science*, Englewood Cliffs, N.J.: Prentice Hall, 1970.
19. J. H. Hutton, "Wolf children." *Folk Lore* 51 (1940): 9–31.
20. D. G. Mandelbaum, "Wolf-child histories from India." *Journal Social Psychology* 17 (1943): 25–44.
21. A. H. Reisen, "Stimulation as a Requirement for Growth and Function in Behavioral Development." In D. W. Fiske and S. R. Maddi, eds. *Functions of Varied Experience*. Homewood, Ill.: Dorsey Press, 1961.
22. R. A. Spitz, "Unhappy and Fatal Outcomes of Emotional Deprivation and Stress in Infancy." In I. Gladston, ed., *Beyond the Germ Theory*. New York: Health Education Council, 1954.
23. R. M. Zingg, "India's wolf children." *Scientific American* 164 (1941): 135–37.
24. U. Bronfenbrenner, "Early Deprivation in Mammals: A Cross-Species Analysis." In G. Newton and S. Levine, eds., *Early Experience and Behavior: The Psychobiology of Development*. Springfield, Ill.: Charles C Thomas, 1968.
25. W. T. McKinney, Jr. "Primate social isolation: Psychiatric implications." *Archives General Psychiatry* 31 (1974): 422–26.
26. H. F. Harlow, K. A. Schultz, and M. K. Harlow, "Effects of Social Isolation on the Learning Performance of Rhesus Monkeys." In C. R. Carpenter, ed., *Proceedings Second International Conference of Primatology*, volume 1. New York: Karger, 1969.
27. H. F. Harlow, M. K. Harlow, R. O. Dodsworth, and G. I. Arling, "Maternal behavior of Rhesus monkeys deprived of mothering and peer associations in infancy." *Proceedings of American Philosophical Society* 110 (1966): 58–66.
28. H. F. Harlow, G. L. Rowland, and G. A. Griffen, "The effect of total social

deprivation on the development of monkey behavior.'' *Psychological Research Reports* 19 (1964): 116-35.

29. S. J. Suomi and H. F. Harlow, "Social rehabilitation of isolate reared monkeys.'' *Developmental Psychology* 4 (1972): 487-96.

30. S. J. Suomi, H. F. Harlow, and W. T. McKinney, "Monkey psychiatrists.'' *American Journal of Psychiatry* 128 (1972): 927-32.

31. S. J. Suomi, "Surrogate rehabilitation of monkeys reared in total social isolation.'' *Journal Child Psychology and Psychiatry* 14 (1973): 71-77.

32. H. F. Harlow, and S. J. Suomi, "Social recovery by isolation reared monkeys.'' *Proceedings National Academy of Science* 68 (1971): 1534-38.

33. H. L. Morrison and W. T. McKinney, Jr. "Environments of Dysfunction: The Relevance of Primate Animal Models.'' In R. N. Walsh and W. T. Greenough, eds., *Environments as Therapy for Brain Dysfunction*. Advances in Behavioral Biology, volume 17. New York: Plenum Press, 1976.

34. R. M. Zingg, "Feral man and extreme cases of social isolation.'' *American Journal Psychology* 53 (1940): 487-517.

35. J. M. G. Itard, *The Wild Boy of Aveyron*. Translated by G. And M. Humphrey. New York: Appleton-Century-Crofts, 1932.

36. E. E. Evans, *The Story of Kaspar Hauser from Authentic Records*. London, 1892.

37. W. Dennis, "Infant development under conditions of restricted practice and of minimum social stimulation: A preliminary report.'' *Journal of Genetic Psychology* 53 (1938): 149-58.

38. W. Dennis, "Infant development under conditions of restricted practice and of minimum social stimulation.'' *Genetic Psychology Monographs* 23 (1941): 143-89.

39. W. Dennis and M. G. Dennis, "Development under Controlled Environmental Conditions.'' In W. Dennis, ed., *Readings in Child Psychology*. New York: Prentice-Hall, 1951.

40. J. C. Hill and B. A. Robinson, "A case of retarded mental development associated with restricted movements in infancy.'' *British Journal of Medicine* 10 (1929): 268-77.

41. W. Goldfarb, "Infant rearing as a factor in foster home replacement.'' *American Journal of Orthopsychiatry* 14 (1944): 162-66.

42. K. Davis, "Extreme social isolation of a child.'' *American Journal of Sociology* 1 (1940): 554-65.

43. K. Davis, "Final note on a case of extreme isolation.'' *American Journal of Sociology* 52 (1947): 432-37.

44. L. J. Stone, "A critique of studies of infant isolation.'' *Child Development* 25 (1954): 1-20.

45. J. Koluchová, "Severe deprivation in twins: A case study.'' *Journal of Child Psychology and Psychiatry* 13 (1972): 107-14.

46. A. D. B. Clarke, "Commentary on Koluchová's 'Severe deprivation in twins: A case study.' '' *Journal of Child Psychology and Psychiatry* 13 (1972): 103-106.

47. J. Koluchová, "The further development of twins after severe and prolonged deprivation: A second report.'' *Journal of Child Psychology and Psychiatry* 17 (1976): 181-88.

48. C. B. Ferster, "Positive reinforcement and behavioral deficits of autistic children.'' *Child Development* 32 (1961): 437-56.

49. C. B. Ferster and M. K. DeMeyer, "The development of performance in autistic

children in an automatically controlled environment." *Journal of Chronic Disease* 13 (1961): 312–45.

50. L. Kanner and L. Eisenberg, "Notes on the Follow-up Studies of Autistic Children." In P. Hoch and J. Zubin, eds., *Psychopathology of Childhood*. New York: Grune and Stratton, 1955.

51. J. L. Brown, "Prognosis from presenting symptoms of pre-school children with atypical development." *American Journal of Orthopsychiatry* 30 (1960): 389–90.

52. M. Havelkova, "Follow-up study of 71 children diagnosed as psychotic in pre-school age." *American Journal of Orthopsychiatry* 38 (1968): 846–57.

53. M. Rutter, "Prognosis: Psychotic Children in Adolescence and Early Adult Life." In J. K. Wing, ed., *Early Childhood Autism: Clinical, Educational and Social Aspects*. London: Pergamon Press, 1966.

54. F. M. Ornitz and E. R. Ritvo, "The syndrome of Autism: A critical review." *American Journal of Psychiatry* 133 (1976): 609–21.

55. M. Wolf, T. Risley, and H. Mees, "Application of operant conditioning procedures to the behavior problems of an autistic child." *Behavior Research and Therapy* 1 (1964): 305–12.

56. M. Wolf, T. Risley, M. Johnston, F. Harris, and E. Allen, "Application of operant conditioning procedures to the behavior problems of an autistic child: A follow-up and extension." *Behavior Research and Therapy* 5 (1967): 103–12.

57. F. M. Hewett, "Teaching reading to an autistic child through operant conditioning." *Reading Teacher* 17 (1964): 613–18.

58. F. M. Hewett, "Teaching speech to an autistic child through operant conditioning." *American Journal Orthopsychiatry* 35 (1965): 927–36.

59. R. Leff, "Behavior modification and the psychoses of childhood: A review." *Psychological Bulletin* 69 (1968): 396–409.

60. I. O. Lovaas, "A Program for the Development of Speech in Psychotic Children." In J. K. Wing, ed., *Early Childhood Autism*. New York: Pergamon Press, 1966.

61. G. R. Patterson and G. G. Bechtel, "Formulating the Situational Environment in Relation to States and Traits." In R. B. Cattell, ed., *Handbook of Modern Personality Study*. Chicago: Aldine Publishing Co., 1970.

62. R. G. Wahler, "Setting generality: Some specific and general effects of child behavior therapy." *Journal Applied Behavioral Analysis* 2 (1969): 239 46.

63. T. Risley and M. M. Wolf, "Experimental Manipulation of Autistic Behaviors and Generalization into the Home." In R. Ulrich, T. Stachnik, and J. Mabry, eds., *Control of Human Behavior*. Glenview, Ill.: Scott, Foresman and Co., 1966.

64. I. O. Lovaas, R. Koegel, J. O. Simmons, and J. S. Long. "Some generalizations and follow-up measures on autistic children in behavior therapy." *Journal of Applied Behavioral Analysis* 6 (1973): 131–66.

65. J. C. Whitehorn, "Problems of Communication between Physicians and Schizophrenic Patients." In P. Hoch and J. Zubin, eds., *Psychopathology of Communication*. New York: Grune and Stratton, 1958.

66. V. Stuecher, *Tommy: A Treatment of an Autistic Child*. Virginia: Council for Exceptional Children, 1972.

67. L. Kanner, "Autistic disturbances of affective contact." *Nervous Child* 2 (1943): 217–50.

68. Group for the Advancement of Psychiatry, Committee on Child Psychiatry. *Psychopathological Disorders in Childhood: Theoretical Considerations and a Proposed Classification*. GAP Report 62. New York, 1966.

69. L. Bender, "Diagnostic and Therapeutic Aspects of Childhood Schizophrenia." In P. W. Bowman and H. V. Mautner, eds., *Mental Retardation*. New York: Grune and Stratton, 1960.
70. J. M. Richer and B. Richards, "Reacting to autistic children: The danger of trying too hard." *British Journal Psychiatry* 127 (1975): 526–29.
71. E. Tinbergen and N. Tinbergen, "Early Infantile Autism: An Ethological Approach." In *Advances in Ethology* (Supplement to *Z. Tierpsychology*) 10 (1972): 1–53.

CHAPTER 48

Therapeutic Interventions That Foster Ego Development in Abused/Neglected Children

Mark Flanzraich and Gloria L. Steiner

INTRODUCTION

Observations of abused/neglected children have led to the identification of associations between parental practices, ego development, and specific behavioral phases. This paper presents descriptions of these behavioral phases, a conceptualization of their origins, and various interventions that were effective in the moderation and progression of the children's behavior.*

In a program designed to treat families identified as abusive/neglectful of their children, there are three therapeutic components consisting of the following staff: social workers, who meet with parents and focus on emotional functioning; family enablers, who provide concrete services; and activity therapists (a male/female team), who conduct therapeutic groups for children. The goal of these therapeutic interventions is the prevention of further abuse/neglect and the stabilization of family relationships.

Sixty children between the ages of two and sixteen years have attended the program to date during a period of eighteen months. Therapeutic intervention with the children has focused on fostering ego development, with additional attention paid to their educational, social, and medical needs. Play therapy as well as organized activities are utilized by the therapists, with the goal of moving the children to more mature and therefore more complex levels of ego development.

Previous research (Morris and Gould 1975; Steele and Pollock 1974; Minuchin et al. 1967) has identified abusive/neglectful parents as immature and impulsive, intolerant of delay and apt to relinquish authority. These studies, however, have not pinpointed a direct relationship between these parental characteristics and the ego developmental problems of their children or the personality disorders resulting from such ego distortion.

*All the families herein described participate in the Family Life Education Center of Children's Hospital, at United Hospitals of Newark, New Jersey.

Pollock and Steele (1974) suggest a generalized pattern of behavior, or parental style, which incorporates the inability to mother and the presence of a severe superego as the primary etiology of the abuse/neglect cycle. However, this position does not fully explain the ego developmental problems observed in the children or the formation of future parental character disorders that lead to abuse/neglect of their children.

The view of this paper is that parental abuse/neglect of children during specific ego stages, transitions or crises, affects the character formation of the child in such a way as to develop a personality that is disordered at extremely infantile levels and that, in turn, is prone to inflict abuse and neglect.

CHILDREN'S BEHAVIOR

Three specific behavioral phases, with a progressive pattern, have been observed during the treatment of these abused/neglected children: a depressive phase, a negativistic phase, and an aggressive phase. Each phase is distinct in the behavior manifested, its duration, predictability, and sequence.

The depressive phase is typically manifested when the children enter the nursery group. Lethargy, fearfulness, dullness, and lack of communication are displayed. After varying lengths of time in the program, a new phase becomes evident, characterized by impulsivity, negativism, and narcissism. At a later period the negativistic behavior tends to subside and an aggressive phase appears, with aggressiveness, competitiveness, and controlling, power-oriented behavior.

It is postulated that these behavioral phases are related to the normal ego developmental stages that surround the periods of attachment, separation/individualization, and identification. Developmental theorists, such as Loevinger (1976, pp. 15–19), have considered that all children pass through a symbiotic stage with the process of differentiating self from nonself, an impulsive stage where identity begins to be asserted, and a conformist stage where the child starts to identify his welfare with other significant persons or groups. It is our observation that abused/neglected children tend to exhibit behavioral phases that are distortions and exaggerations of these normal processes and that last well beyond normal developmental lines.

The following are some examples of typical cases:

A) Gary exhibits behavior characteristic of the depressive phase. He is 3½ years old and the 3rd sibling in a family of 4 children. When Gary enters the nursery he finds a spot on the floor and lies there sucking his thumb. Many times he will crawl under a table and stay there for the entire nursery session. He does not verbalize his thoughts, feelings, or needs. He does not show initiative, curiosity, or use motility. At times Gary appears almost catatonic, seldom using his body.

B) Bobby, who is almost 4 years old, is the youngest child in a family of five. He exhibits characteristics of the negativistic phase. He will say "No" to almost every request. When limits are placed on him, he will go into a temper tantrum; he will kick, bite, scratch, knock over objects, and scream. He has little impulse control. He gets caught in the sheer momentum of his actions and, with increasing motility and affect, soon loses all control. He rarely recognizes or interacts in a social or group situation.

C) Angelo, who is 6 years old, is the middle child of a family of 3 boys. He exhibits characteristics of the aggressive phase. He will always try to assume control, give purpose and direction to any situation in which he finds himself. When he enters the group he immediately says, "I'm the boss. I'll do what I want. I'm the boss." Angelo will harass, manipulate, physically remove himself, or create a disturbance to assume authority.

As previously stated, the three phases appear intricately related. Thus, when Gary's nurturance and support needs had been met consistently over a substantial period of time, he began to show characteristics of the negativistic phase and became active, impulsive, and markedly destructive. Bobby, who had exhibited negativistic behavior for the past year, was first observed to be withdrawn and unresponsive, characteristics that are typical of the depressive phase. He is presently beginning to show characteristics of the aggressive phase and has demonstrated a need to share and be with the therapist. Angelo, who exhibits characteristics of the aggressive phase is gradually becoming part of his juvenile peer group. Each of these phases may be differentiated from each other and follows a specific sequence or progression of development.

TREATMENT PLAN

After a year of clinical observation, the staff evolved a treatment plan focused on the lack of progressive ego development in the children. Accordingly, each child is evaluated as to his/her ego developmental stage with respect to the three behavioral phases outlined above.

The therapists become parental models and provide the "parental input" necessary to help the child move to higher and more complex levels of ego functioning. Three crucial parental inputs are identified in the treatment plan: nurturance/support, direction/limits, and power-esteem sharing.

The supportive/nurturing role is used with children manifesting depressive behavior. Body contact, food, and verbal communication are used as tools to support this role. Children are touched while they are talked to, physically played with, and picked up at their request; however, care must be taken not to initiate the latter interaction for fear of creating rescue fantasies within the children. Food is also an extremely important tool; snack time is a major activity and is used to encourage verbalization and interpersonal interaction. All the children are required and encouraged to ask for food presented to them. Initially, the children are monosyllabic, but after a few weeks they typically begin to use sentences. Planned play activities and the use of puzzles, balls, and blocks are found to be effective in the building of interpersonal communication and the lessening of depressive behavior.

It is relatively easy and gratifying to the therapist to provide nurturance/support for the children who are depressed and withdrawn, for these children usually make substantial progress in a matter of weeks. It is much more difficult and emotionally taxing, however, to provide limits and authority for the children who display the negativistic phase. We have found that the children who either progress to, or enter the program in, the negativistic phase, remain in this state longer than a year. Intervention directed to the alleviation of the negativistic phase centers around structure and firm direction. Organized activities and authority intervention are used to bring greater social awareness. Techniques such as mirroring and consistent and corrective discipline are effective. Mirroring is frequently beneficial because it creates both motivation and frustration as forces of change within the children. For example, many times following a disruptive incident a child will quickly forget the impact of his/her behavior and approach the therapist for fulfillment of a need. At this time the therapist mirrors back to the child saying, "I won't get the toy for you; when I needed you to do something for me, you didn't listen." A hierarchy of consistent signals is used to decrease negative behavior; verbal commands, physical restraint, and removal are utilized. Corrective discipline facilitates the development of social consequences; that is, the children have to experience the consequences of their disruptive behavior, for example, by picking up toys knocked over in rage, apologizing for physical or verbal abuse, or completing an interrupted activity. Although these techniques may be extremely frustrating to the children, they serve to heighten social awareness. Another important technique that is used in association with the above is the substitution of words of affect (e.g., "anger," "hate," or "love") for actions. For example, when a therapist notes a child becoming disruptive, he/she might respond, "You look so angry. Are you angry?" and encourage the child to verbally communicate the problem, frustration, or impulse. The child's gradual acceptance of words in place of action is a long and frustrating process for both child and therapist. The establishment of limits many times necessitates the use of physical restraint, which is frequently difficult for the therapist to implement because of his/her mistaken notion and fantasy as a child rescuer.

Modifying the aggressive phase requires a great deal of patience and sensitivity on the part of the therapist, because the children typically enter the group ready and willing for a confrontation. It is very difficult to avoid engaging in a power struggle or a game of control and at the same time to devise ways of giving and sharing power. The therapist has to act before the interpersonal dynamics can be acted out. For example, one child would stand by the door, refusing to come in, screaming, "I'll do what I want," and wait for the therapist to act. The child, however, was countered by the therapist who simply said, "I'm so glad you're here. I really need you to help me move something heavy." Thus the confrontation was averted and the child happily came to the group. Every time a therapist shares a task (and power) confrontations are averted. Compliments given along with the sharing are additionally helpful in the building of self-esteem. Any sharing of responsibility, task, or chore, whether it be model-building, an art project, or washing a car, accomplishes the building of a more positive self-image and sense of identity within the children.

Each behavioral phase reflects a normal ego developmental stage that has become distorted and exaggerated through the lack of appropriate parental participation. The most important dynamic in this relation is the interpersonal dialectic operating between the child's needs and the parent's needs (Loevinger 1976, pp. 270–73). It is this dialectic, occurring constantly throughout the development of the child, and the resulting synthesis, which is the dynamic necessary for ego development.

Parents of abused/neglected children generate great psychological distance from their children and, as a consequence, the children are isolated from this interpersonal dialectic so necessary for emotional growth. Because parental affection, protection, and authority are seldom experienced by the children as they develop, they need to rely on their own infantile resources and to use their peer group or siblings to form a new dialectic that does not create motivation or frustration, but instead reinforces infantile levels of ego functioning.

Thus, abused/neglected children do not experience the acceptance, support, limits, and sharing that is necessary for ego development. One can understand how a depressed child, who does not experience basic nurturance/support, will lack the ability within his ego to conceptualize meaningful interpersonal relationships. Narcissistic, negativistic, and impulsive children, who do not experience limits or appropriate authority, develop into adults with narcissistic personalities, who are characteristically insensitive, demanding, and self-indulgent at the expense of their children. One can also see that identification that comes from a fear of aggression may result in a parent's becoming aggressive to his/her child.

Personality traits that cause abuse/neglect are observable in children as young as two years. In the nursery, children as young as three and a half years can be seen to reverse roles with their mothers and assume total care of their younger siblings. These three-year-olds feed, clothe, speak for, and fight for their brothers and sisters. In older groups, children with aggressive behavior fight for every inch of esteem; they must always be first, receive total attention, and be the recipient of total praise. These children do not show trust, caring, or the capacity to share. Amoral behavior, which so often shocks the public, can be seen forming in the negativistic, impulsive, narcissistic behavior of the children in the negativistic phase where the children behave according to their own inner drives.

In the treatment of ego-impaired children, the therapist attempts to reconstruct the parent-child dialectic with the hope of creating a relationship that will provide both the motivation in need fulfillment and frustration in social/personal expectations for future and continuous ego development.

CONCLUSION

In summary, two observations stand out: first, behavioral characteristics of parents are transmitted across generations either through specific parental inputs or deprivations; second, in the treatment of abusive/neglectful families, attention must be focused on the distortions in ego development in the child, inasmuch as they are the precursors of future character disorders.

The abusive/neglectful parent is to be recognized as having a special character disorder developed through certain parental inputs and deprivations during the period of attachment, separation/individuation, and identification. The narcissistic, impulsive, negativistic, and aggressive characteristics of these parents are character traits that are associated with early ego stages, transitions, and crises. To say that child abuse/neglect is a child-rearing style, practiced, learned, and transmitted, is insufficient.

Abuse/neglect is an experience that touches the deepest part of a child's developing ego. New expanding and appropriate experiences must be given to these children, guided by an understanding of the ego distortion they developed in interaction with their home environment. Such interventions enable them to grow more aware, more complex, more fully human, and thus help reduce the abuse/neglect cycle.

REFERENCES

Loevinger, J. *Ego Development: Conceptions and Theories.* San Francisco: Jossey-Bass, pp. 15–19, 270–274, 1976.

Minuchin, Salvador, et al. *Families of the Slums.* New York: Basic Books, p. 223, 1967.

Morris, M. G., and Gould, R. W. "Role Reversal: A Concept in Dealing with Neglected/Battered-Child Syndrome." In *The Neglected/Battered Child-Syndrome—Role Reversal in Parents.* New York: Child Welfare League of America, p. 28, 1975.

Steele, B. F. and Pollock, C. B. "Psychiatric Study of Abusive Parents." In *The Battered Child,* edited by Ray E. Helfer and C. Henry Kempe, Chicago: University of Chicago Press, p. 96, 1974.

CHAPTER 49

Approaches to Preventing Child Abuse: The Health Visitors Concept

C. Henry Kempe

A better title for this lecture would be "A Vindication of the Rights of Children," after the classic essay, "A Vindication of the Rights of Woman," written in 1792 by Mary Wollstonecraft, which set forth the plight of women in those days.

Children in the Western world (though not yet in the southern hemisphere) have made striking progress in the past two hundred years. Seen against a background of virtually being nonpersons, they are slowly emerging as citizens with rights of their own. In 1763, the poor-law governors (that is, the welfare department) of the parishes of St. Andrew's and St. George's in London were entrusted with fifty-nine infants: of these, all but two had died two years later. But not only the poor died. Between 1767 and 1769 in London, in the absence of epidemic disease, there were 16,000 baptisms and 8,000 infant burials reported—half the children died. Because of this appalling mortality in the first years of life, George Armstrong opened his clinic for poor children in 1769, focusing on the period from birth to age four. He quickly achieved success in lowering the mortality of his patients, though it was at great personal and financial sacrifice. He was what in this day would be called a "bleeding heart," but he did not just show constant pity for the needy young; he also possessed three other qualities: he was a hard worker, he was an activist, and he was a visionary. He worked very hard, making his rounds on his paying patients in Hampstead in the morning and then, generally, walking five miles to his clinic downtown. He saw over 4,000 patients each year, spending about 2½ hours in his clinic each day. He was greatly concerned with the importance of ensuring easy access to care. He was an activist in instituting the first infant clinic anywhere. Early on, when he sought support from patrons, each paid one guinea per child per year to sponsor a child and then two guineas for the second child per sponsored year. In time, the overworked clinic helpers tried to limit his patients to those with

Read as the Armstrong lecture before the annual meeting of the Ambulatory Pediatric Association, Toronto, June 9, 1975.

Reprinted with permission from the *American Journal of Diseases of Children* 130 (September 1976). 941–47. Copyright 1976, American Medical Association.

sponsorships in hand, excluding those without—in other words, those patients who didn't have their clinic card. Let me quote Armstrong: "This hindered their coming more than can well be imagined. The circumstance, by the by, may afford a useful hint: to be very cautious of any obstacle that is thrown in the way if we mean to render charity generously useful." He was primarily concerned with "a good start," the time from birth to age four years. And he was a visionary: preventive medicine was his long suit—good hygiene, feeding, health care of the youngest.

A hundred years later, in 1874, Mary Ellen, a child living with step-parents in New York, was cruelly treated, and it required the Society for the Prevention of Cruelty to Animals (there was no Society for Prevention of Cruelty to Children) to intervene on her behalf as a member of the animal kingdom. She was removed to safer quarters. Soon came child labor laws and universal, free education. In the last fifty years increasing attention is being paid to the health of young children and we are now, in 1975, addressing the civil rights of children.

PRENATAL, PERINATAL, AND POSTNATAL OBSERVATIONS

Throughout the Western world it has become almost routine for children to have periodic health assessments. As part of this assessment, we do a standard history and physical examination, the technique of which is pretty well accepted all over the world. I propose that these be supplemented by standardized observations in the prenatal, perinatal, and postnatal care of families. Table 1 lists ten warning areas in prenatal care indicative of need for extra services.

You will note that none of these observations, nor those made during and after delivery, has anything to do with social class, education, or financial status. They deal with attitudes and feelings.

Table 1. Observations of parents-to-be in physician's office or prenatal clinic

---

1. Are the parents overconcerned with the baby's sex?
2. Are they overconcerned with the baby's performance? Do they worry that he will not meet the standard?
3. Is there an attempt to deny that there is a pregnancy (mother not willing to gain weight, no plans whatsoever, refusal to talk about the situation)?
4. Is this child going to be one child too many? Could he be the "last straw"?
5. Is there great depression over this pregnancy?
6. Is the mother alone and frightened, especially by the physical changes caused by the pregnancy? Do careful explanations fail to dissipate these fears?
7. Is support lacking from husband and/or family?
8. Where is the family living? Do they have a listed telephone number? Are there relatives and friends nearby?
9. Did the mother and/or father formerly want an abortion but not go through with it or waited until it was too late?
10. Have the parents considered relinquishment of their child? Why did they change their minds?

Table 2. Observations to be made at postpartum checkups and pediatric checkups

1. Does the mother have fun with the baby?
2. Does the mother establish eye contact (direct in face position) with the baby?
3. How does the mother talk to her baby? Is everything she expresses a demand?
4. Are most of her verbalizations about the child negative?
5. Does she remain disappointed over the child's sex?
6. What is the child's name? Where did it come from? When did they name the child?
7. Are the mother's expectations for the child's development far beyond the child's capabilities?
8. Is the mother very bothered by the baby's crying? How does she feel about the crying?
9. Does the mother see the baby as too demanding during feedings? Is she repulsed by the messiness? Does she ignore the baby's demands to be fed?
10. What is the mother's reaction to the task of changing diapers?
11. When the baby cries, does she or can she comfort him?
12. What was/is the husband's and/or family's reaction to the baby?
13. What kind of support is the mother receiving?
14. Are there sibling rivalry problems?
15. Is the husband jealous of the baby's drain on the mother's time and affection?
16. When the mother brings the child to the physician's office, does she get involved and take control over the baby's needs and what's going to happen (during the examination and while in the waiting room) or does she relinquish control to the physician or nurse (undressing the child, holding him, allowing him to express his fears, etc)?
17. Can attention be focused on the child in the mother's presence? Can the mother see something positive for her in that?
18. Does the mother make nonexistent complaints about the baby? Does she describe to you a child that you don't see there at all? Does she call with strange stories that the child has, for example, stopped breathing, turned color, or is doing something "on purpose" to aggravate the parent?
19. Does the mother make emergency calls for very small things, not major things?

If prenatal observations are not possible, then much of this information can be obtained, along with delivery room observations, on the first postpartum day.

During delivery, mother, doctor, and nurses are very busy. But they are busy with the perineal end of the mother, and birth is often a struggle between the obstetrician and the uterus from which he skillfully extracts the child. The mother's head is three miles upstream.

I and my colleagues encourage fathers to be present in the delivery room, and more than 90% come. We ask our nurses to look at the mother (and the father, if he is present) and answer just three questions: How does she look? What does she say? What does she do? The parents' reactions to their newly born child are carefully observed. Are the parents passive, showing no active interest in the baby, not holding it? Are they disappointed in its sex? Are their reactions hostile or their comments inappropriate? Is there eye contact?

Observation of reactions after the baby goes home is also important. Significant warning signals are listed in Table 2. Positive factors, which may partially offset these, are listed in Table 3.

Table 3. Positive family circumstances

1. The parents see likeable attributes in the baby and perceive him as an individual.
2. The baby is healthy and not too disruptive to the parents' life-style.
3. Either parent can rescue the child or relieve one another in a crisis.
4. The parents' marriage is stable.
5. The parents have a good friend or relative to turn to, a sound "need-meeting" system.
6. The parents exhibit coping abilities, i.e., the capacity to plan, and understand the need for adjustments because of the new baby.
7. The mother is intelligent and her health is good.
8. The parents had helpful role models when they grew up.
9. The parents can have fun together and with their personal interests and hobbies.
10. The parents practice birth control; the baby was planned or wanted.
11. The father has a steady job. The family has its own home, and living conditions are stable.
12. The father is supportive of the mother and involved in the care of the baby.

My colleagues and I have tried to determine whether our child abuse and "failure to thrive" patients came from the group we thought to be in need of extra services. We studied 300 consecutive births and concluded that 20% of them seemed to be in need of extra services. We divided these families into two groups by random numbers: The control risk group received the best care that is routinely provided, including a single visit by a visiting nurse, regular well-baby appointments, and, also, a telephone call to the physician caring for the family, in which we voiced our concern about the parents' attitude toward the baby. The second risk group received active intervention through the extra services shown in Table 4. Detailed results of this study will be reported separately, but we found no instance of child abuse by the 240 mothers about whom we had no concern, and that the modest intervention given to half of our risk families significantly reduced the incidence of many problems including abuse and "failure to thrive."

Similar efforts are in progress in California, New York, Colorado, North Carolina, the District of Columbia, and elsewhere, using mostly visiting nurses,

Table 4. Special well-child care for high-risk families

1. Promote maternal attachment to the newborn.
2. Phone the mother during the first two days at home.
3. Provide more frequent office visits.
4. Give more attention to the mother.
5. Emphasize nutrition.
6. Counsel discipline only for accident prevention.
7. Emphasize accident prevention.
8. Use compliments rather than criticism.
9. Accept phone calls at home.
10. Arrange for regular home visits by a public health nurse or a lay health visitor.

although a number of these programs have begun to utilize lay health visitors. The intervention we propose can be carried out simply. It is available to each of us in our current pediatric settings. However, since a large percentage of children who need help are not brought to us for "check-ups" and do not have meaningful contact with any type of health personnel on a regular and ongoing basis, it is clear that something else is needed.

THE HEALTH VISITORS SYSTEM

I propose that we in the United States develop a system of lay health visitors, although nurses can be used when available, and that these health visitors work with traditional health professionals in assuring that the basic health needs of every child are met, especially during the first four years of life.

This program for utilization of health visitors should be a national one, but any state, or any one of our 3,362 counties, could start right now. Any county could—but no county yet has. In most places the health visitor will not be a nurse. Instead, the ideal candidate will be a successful mother who is able and interested in sharing her experience and goodwill with less experienced young families. She could well be chosen by her neighbors as one of their trusted own. The health visitor will form a bridge between these families and the health care system.

It is true that virtually all European child health visitors are trained nurses and that they do very much good, but it must also be said, in all candor, that their orientation is largely toward mother-crafting skills. They tend to shy away from matters of feelings, and they are relatively passive in dealing with the families who don't want their services. Recently, one experienced European health visitor told me, "If they won't let me in, I don't do a thing. It's their kid, after all, and I have no right to interfere." She said that this was the general feeling of the nurses in her local district. This attitude is also often found in Scandinavian countries where I visited: all have good health visitor systems; nobody wants to violate the rights of parents.

So the system itself is not enough. One has to have meaningful access. Lay health visitors can be trained in a period of a few days, because they will be learning just a few facts to be grafted on the important foundation that they already have, namely, their success as mothers and their intimate knowledge of the community that they serve.

Our first concern has to do with the parent-child relationship. We know that difficulties are often encountered when there is a prolonged separation such as in prematurity or early illness in infancy, when there are obstetrical complications such as cesarean section or maternal illness—all these interfere with bonding in some families. I was taught that some mothers couldn't love their newborn babies because they suffered from postpartum depression. I now know that as many postpartum depressions are caused by the mother's finding that she doesn't love her baby. The health visitors will also be involved in helping to fulfill the health needs of siblings, fathers, grandparents, and others.

Ideally, the health visitor should get to know the family during the pregnancy period. She should have knowledge of what happened at delivery and during the first few postpartum days, so that she may be more able to assist effectively when she makes postnatal visits. The physician may want to notify the health visitor very early in the pregnancy so that she can be of support to the mother-to-be. She can provide advice on how to prepare for the child's arrival, types of supplies that will be needed, and she may even provide some supplies. Many of our mothers have greatly benefited by gifts of disposable diapers and infant formula so they could have one hour of rest each day. To be more specific, we should subsidize young mothers. We are the only Western nation that does not do so.

If the health visitor's first contact with mother and father is in the hospital, she can gain critical information at that time. On the first or second day after the arrival of the family at home, she will visit, leave her telephone number, and encourage calls. This will be the essential lifeline between the family and herself. It is nonthreatening and therefore useful.

If the need is there, visits will be frequent. Doctors will have an invaluable resource in the health visitor when they are troubled about the progress of a young infant, and they will be able to gain great insight into the possibility of a postpartum depression, serious marital problems, financial crises, or existing attachment difficulties. Such problems are more likely to come to the attention of the trusted lay health visitor as she visits in the home than in the brief, well-child visit in a busy office or clinic.

I propose that health visitors be utilized regularly, not only in the first months of life, but at least twice yearly in the second year of life and until the child reaches school age. At that time many of the health visitor's duties will be taken over by the teacher, the school nurse, or the school nurse practitioner.

On the basis of our experience to date, my co-workers and I think that one health visitor can care for fifty to sixty children, provided she works about four or five hours a day. Since there are millions of mature women whose children are in school and who are otherwise not gainfully employed, we already have a large number of excellent candidates for a very worthwhile career in which they would make a maximum contribution by helping others. These women have developed important skills of mothering, and I would rather that they share these skills than take jobs in a bakery. On the basis of the current birth rate of 3.2 million per year, we would gradually plan to phase in, over five years, 60,000 health visitors—a goal that could be easily attained.

What would such a program cost? It would cost less than 1% of our defense budget or less than 6% of the requested increase in military spending for next year. But, since most of us don't like to hear what we spend on defense, let me say instead that it would cost one-third of the money already set aside for stand-by authority for the bureaucracy needed for gas rationing, if that unhappy event should come to pass.

ROLE OF THE HEALTH VISITOR

What will the health visitor do and where will she function? She will go out to the home where she will weigh the child and graph its progress on a weight chart, but most importantly she will look at the child, at the mother, at the setting in which the family lives, and determine how things are going, what problems exist, and how the family is coping with these problems. It has been found that health visitors are fully capable of determining which children are at risk, whether they are thriving adequately or not doing well, whether the child is unloved or deprived, whether the mother's experience or the father's lack of support are interfering with the care of the child. Is the child seeing a health professional on schedule? Have recommendations been carried out? Does the family understand what services are available and can they be induced to obtain them?

The health visitor will help to educate the family on the need for basic immunization, good nutrition for the whole family, and periodic examinations by the physician. The health visitor can also see the child when it is brought to her office, which may be in a local grammar school, a fire station, a health department office, a neighborhood shopping center, a high-rise apartment house, or a housing development—anyplace.

Of great importance is the fact that the health visitor can, between visits, be available by telephone for parents who are in need of advice and assistance. If the family moves, she can be the one who assists in a transfer to a health facility in another city as well as arranging for a health visitor from the new neighborhood.

CHILDREN'S RIGHTS TO PROTECTION AND HEALTH CARE

It should be emphasized that the use of health visitors should be a universal phenomenon. This is not a kind of detection service to identify child abuse. It is not a service for the poor or the minorities but rather an expected, tax-supported right of every family along with fire protection, police protection, and clean water—societal services that we all deserve to have and from which no one can be easily excluded.

The concept of the health visitor as a compulsory, universal service for the child is similar to the concept of compulsory, universal schooling. In preparation for this talk, I've been reading about how public education came about, a hundred years ago. All the hue and cry that we hear about this concept of free, universal, adequate health care for children were precisely the ones raised against the concept of free, universal public education a hundred years ago. But that debate is over; today, free, effective basic education is a right. This came about because society decided that each young person must be able to take his place in the labor force as an independent, self-supporting citizen and, in order to do so, he had to read and write.

By the same token we must now insist that each child is entitled to effective comprehensive health care, and that when parents are not motivated to seek it, society, on behalf of the child, must compel it. It seems incomprehensible that we have compulsory education, with truancy laws to enforce attendance and, I might add, imprisonment of parents who deny their child an education, and yet we do not establish similar safeguards for the child's very survival between birth and age six.

A free society does not want to interfere with the rights of parents to be let alone and to raise their children in any way that they desire. But, far too often, children are considered the property or chattel of their parents, many of whom think that they are entitled to dispose of them at will. Unfortunately, such a system ignores the rights of children and results in tragic failures that will adversely affect the children's lives or even result in their deaths.

When an airplane takes off, the pilot is required to go through an unvaried series of safety checks. He has no choice—they must be carried out. Often there are double checks of those things that are considered especially important. If the successful operation of an airplane requires such routine supervision, it is all the more important that the takeoff and subsequent passage of a young family be similarly supervised to assure a safe arrival.

Under our traditional system of pediatric care, which depends on parent motivation, we often find that we are spending a good deal of our time and effort in giving excellent service to many families who don't really need much of it. We do so because they come to us for such care, they are delighted to keep their appointments, they are a joy for us to have in our offices, and they make our days pleasant and fulfilling ones. Such motivated families provide a sunny interval in our work and are a great boon to our mental health: in fact we couldn't practice without it, and they do deserve excellent care. But it is the very isolated families—those who are unmotivated, who break appointments, who are unappreciative and unresponsive—to whom we must reach out protectively. When we see such a family, instead of saying: "Well, we tried..." and giving up, we must say, "This behavior is so unusual and worrisome that we must intervene actively." We must do this first by persuasion and education and trying to be as helpful as we can, but if that fails, we must initiate active intervention through child protection services. We cannot sit helplessly by and mistakenly believe that there is nothing we can do. In a very well-organized infant care service, such as is provided by Sweden, where over 95% of all newborns are followed up in child health centers for periodic care in the first year, only 2.5% of the battered babies were reported from these centers. The assumption is that either routine well-baby care, as we know it, misses a lot or the 5% who elect not to be in the system account for most of the problems.

Curiously, professionals are far behind the citizenry in their desire to provide effective protection to the threatened child. Will the health visitor be seen as someone who can be truly useful and accepted like a member of the old, lamented, extended family, particularly to those who are frightened and alone, or will they be looked on as another bureaucratic layer of busybodies who come between those who need help and those who can provide it? I believe that, to a large extent, this will depend on whether the program is started for all people, rich or poor, black or white, brown or red, or whether it is limited, once again, to the disadvantaged or the minorities. To my mind, only a universal program will develop quality and be successful. I think private practitioners will welcome the health visitor as a universal outreach program of their practice that will become operative when patients miss appointments and when follow-up visits in the home seem desirable and more social information is needed. Let me stress that this is not a program to bring every child to a clinic. It is a program to facilitate and make sure there is *access to comprehensive health care for each child.*

Everybody agrees that every child should be under the care of somebody in the health field, particularly in the first years of life, and I think the health visitor plan is the only way to bring this about.

If it should turn out that local or state health departments are not very interested or are unwilling to undertake the health visitor program, there may be other approaches for its implementation. The state of Michigan, for example, has placed the charge on the Department of Education to assure that everyone is "educable." In theory this gives the Department the right to provide screening procedures and comprehensive health care to make every child school-ready. But if neither the Department of Health nor the Department of Education in a given state can be brought to be involved in this program we might then fall back on a system that already exists in many places.

We can utilize our hospitals as a base to establish a system of after-care. Admittedly, it is after-care that lasts five years. Once we decide that a skilled delivery is only the beginning and that we then must provide follow-up, then, I think, it's very easy to see that the hospital could extend its postnatal care into the health visitor concept. Some do so now for premature infants and for certain chronic diseases.

It is economically quite feasible to insist that the young child have access to health care in the broad sense. France actually pays families to seek regular and compulsory child care; such a subsidy is thought to be a very good investment in the ultimate health of its citizens. Similarly, a program to prepare all children for regular school in Amsterdam and in other Dutch cities provides excellent, comprehensive day care for a great number of children who are mentally disturbed or emotionally deprived. In many countries, government leaders believe that it is better to invest money in the first five years of a child's life than to have to develop special programs and institutions for the provision of special education for those whose problems were not recognized early in life. Although the United States spends a lot of money to detect preventable disease, to a considerable degree these funds are misdirected. For example, it is hard to believe that there is currently in Congress a bill that proposes that all our newborns be screened for adenine deaminase deficiency disease, which occurs in approximately one in 200,000 births. This would, of course, be an important screening test for the fifteen children in whom this condition is detected each year, but even among those fifteen children, it would only matter for those who are also lucky enough to have an identical tissue-type twin as a transplant donor—an unlikely event.

THE COST OF CHILD ABUSE

We need to bring some order to our priorities. It would seem to be more important that we give sufficient emphasis to the assessment of the child who might be neglected or abused, since suspected child abuse and neglect is now being reported approximately 300,000 times each year in our country. About 60,000 children end up with significant injuries; some 2,000 of them die and 6,000 have permanent brain damage. The cost of institutional care for a severely brain damaged child in our country is $700,000 for a lifetime. Many other children are scarred by sexual abuse, incest, and rape. Those who do recover are likely to have significant emotional difficulties and most manifest this in the form of serious learning problems in school. Although in most fatal cases of child abuse the family's problems have been recognized before the child's death, many others have never been active participants in any segment of the health care system.

The late effects of child abuse may manifest themselves in ways that are not generally recognized. My associates, Brandt Steele, M.D., and Joan Hopkins, R.N., studied delinquent children on the first occasion they were seen in a detention center in a mixed urban-rural county near Denver. The population of youngsters was approximately 85% Caucasian, 14% Chicano, and 1% black. Of 100 well-documented cases, which involved interviews with not only the delinquent young but also their parents, all the hospitals, physicians, and schools, it was found that 84 of those youngsters had been abused before the age of six years. Ninety-two had been bruised, sustained lacerations or fractures, or were involved in incest in the preceding year or so prior to being identified by the authorities. Only one of this group of 100 delinquents came from a family on welfare, and only three had an alcoholic parent. These were not children from broken homes or the ghettos, but the type all of us are likely to see.

Our country literally wastes hundreds of thousands of our precious children. Even though we confess that they are our future and therefore our most valuable national asset, we don't act as if they were.

Recently, considerable emphasis has been placed on the provision of "early periodic screening, diagnosis, and treatment" (EPSDT), but for only those Medicaid clients who are motivated to present their children for screening. It is another helpful attempt to provide health care for many children. One would expect that this would include extensive attention to the emotional growth and development of the child. But that is not to be. Most of our screening tests ignore the significant problems of parent-child interaction. To a considerable degree the emphasis is on those conditions and diseases that had had the greatest attention from various pressure groups or lend themselves to a quick checklist. It has been argued that it is far easier to have a checklist and a screening test when you are dealing with easily quantitated observations and that in the field of maternal attachment and the child's emotional health such observations cannot be readily made. Nonsense! Pediatricians have for years made such observations competently, and to exclude them from instruments sanctioned as national policy in the health care field of children does not make sense.

Specific diseases, even those that are quite uncommon, should be prevented whenever possible, but this should not be done at the expense of giving adequate attention to the whole child, his family, their total health status, including those emotional as well as physical factors that might affect the child's welfare. There is something I know about every battered child I've seen— he does not have phenylketonuria. There is more to a child's life than teeth, hearing, and vision.

In many ways it would be better to start this program at the grass roots level; perhaps our state governors should take the lead. The people in the community, laymen as well as health professionals, will have to work together in developing an understanding that health is a personal asset that every child deserves and should have even if it would require limited intrusion into family privacy by society. Just as any fireman will enter a burning house and try to put out the fire even though he doesn't receive a specific request to do so by the owners, so those of us who are qualified to assess and correct the problems that produce child abuse and "failure to thrive" should have the authority to intervene effectively for the good of the suffering child. Let us face the fact that there are large numbers of American children living with troubled families whose emotional house is on fire. Something must be done before their lives are forever distorted and destroyed.

When marriages fail, we have an institution called divorce, but between parent and child, divorce is not yet socially sanctioned. I suggest that voluntary relinquishment should be put forth as a desirable social act—to be encouraged for many of these families. When that fails, legal termination of parental rights should be attempted. However, such termination is a difficult thing to achieve in our country because the laws are so vague. In my state of Colorado, for example, parents must be proved to be untreatable, and remain so, before the state will uphold terminations by our juvenile court judges, a process that could take five to ten years. But each child is on a schedule of his own emotional development. He doesn't give us the luxury of waiting five years. He needs loving parents right now, and the same parents, not a series of ten foster homes. For twenty years, courts have lectured me on the rights of parents, but only two judges in my state have spoken effectively on the rights of children. Courts only interpret laws passed by legislators and the actions of legislators reflect us and our communities—they reflect the voters. Regrettably, children don't vote. Unless we change the conscience of our adult voting communities, child abuse will continue to be managed by partial, Band-Aid solutions. I think all of us have the duty to educate and to be a conscience for our communities. It is significant that not one of our nation's presidents nor any one of our many governors in our 200-year history is remembered as a champion of children.

Where the state is supreme, this particular problem is easily managed: in a dictatorship each child belongs to the state and you may not damage state property. The really first-rate attention paid to the health of all children in less free societies makes you wonder whether one of our cherished democratic freedoms is the right to maim our own children. When I brought this question to the attention of one of our judges, he said, ''That may be the price we have to pay.'' Who pays the price? Nobody has asked the child.

''A man's home is his castle,'' but all too often the child is a prisoner in its dungeon. It is a dungeon of constant anger, dislike, aggression, or even hatred. We must guarantee that the child will be saved when there is danger to his health and life resulting from failure in parenting. In order to do this we must see the child, and the child must have access to us.

Current national health insurance proposals are largely directed toward sickness care and financial management of the high cost of hospitalization. None specifically provide for universal and outreach health care for our young children as a right. For every federal dollar spent on our older citizens, just 5 cents goes to the preschool-age child. Obviously, people of all ages need good health care, but the investment in our children's health care has been tight-fisted, fragmented, devoid of planning, and therefore in many instances has never accomplished what it set out to do. In the coming battles for health insurance we must be absolutely certain to advance the cause of comprehensive child care; otherwise, most of the money will go to the hospitals. The state of California, to its credit, has mandated a health evaluation for all its five- and six-year-old children in order to receive a school health certificate before the child can enter first grade. But, obviously, this new change is far too late for many children.

In the past we have accepted inadequate and limited programs—EPSDT, Mother and Child, and Children and Youth, as well as many other categorical efforts—hoping that, like pieces of a jigsaw puzzle, there would evolve a complete picture when the last piece fell into place. We have settled for small steps in the belief that something is better than nothing and that a comprehensive system would eventually result. Instead we have a nonsystem, fragmented, oriented not toward comprehensive health care, but at the very best, gradually moving from episodic sickness care to screening only for organic disease. But that has never been the philosophy of pediatrics as we know it. It has especially not been the philosophy of this distinguished organization. Let us, therefore, now ask for what really makes sense by placing our priority on ''the good start,'' as George Armstrong suggested, on the infant from conception to school age with the understanding that ''the good start'' has to involve attention to the rights of the child for tender care and love. No child can thrive without it.

CONCLUSION

1. In a free society the newborn child does not belong to the state nor to his parents, but to himself in care of his parents. When parenting is defective or blatantly harmful, prompt effective intervention by society is essential on behalf of the suffering child and also his suffering parents.

2. Universal, egalitarian, and compulsory health supervision, in the broadest sense of the term, is the right of every child. Access to regular health supervision should not be left to the motivation of the parents but must be guaranteed by society.

3. Predicting and preventing of much child abuse is practical, if standard observations are made early.

4. As a bridge between the young family and health services, the utilization of visiting nurses or, more often in most places, indigenous health visitors who are successful, supportive, mature mothers acceptable to their communities, is to my mind, the most inexpensive, least threatening, and most efficient approach for giving the child the greatest possible chance to reach his potential.

It is truly grand that we can pay tribute here to a modest and innovative man, 200 years after his time. George Armstrong serves as a model for us. May we, like him, strive to be "bleeding hearts," hard workers, activists, and visionaries. We are, after all, the principal health advocates of all our children. Let us now resolve to fight for their total civil rights. Let us not, I beg of you, settle for anything less.

This work was supported by the Commonwealth Fund, the Grant Foundation, the Robert Wood Johnson Foundation, and grant 90-C-409 (C) from the Office of Child Development, Department of Health, Education, and Welfare.

Brandt Steele, M.D., Ruth S. Kempe, M.D., Barton D. Schmitt, M.D., Jane Gray, M.D., Christy Cutler, Janet Dean, and other staff members of the National Center for the Prevention of Child Abuse and Neglect assisted in this project.

CHAPTER 50

Toward the Eradication of Child Abuse and Neglect at Home

Gertrude J. Williams

Although the Child Abuse Prevention and Treatment Act specifies prevention as a major goal, prevention has received minuscule attention in child abuse and neglect programs. There are many reasons for this state of affairs. The health care system in the United States is focused on the treatment of illness rather than its prevention and the maintenance of health. In addition, community agencies cannot meet even the chronic and emergency needs of the community and certainly lack the well-coordinated service delivery systems required for preventive action. Furthermore, preventing child abuse and neglect lacks concreteness, drama, and sensationalism, whereas treatment evokes the graphic images and rescue fantasies that inspire public support.

Most important, emphasis on the treatment of child abuse and neglect deflects attention from the changes required for prevention, which are bound to be unpopular. This chapter examines the transformations in attitudes, practices, and programs that are suggested by data and theory and that must occur if child abuse and neglect in the home are ever to be eradicated. The term "primary prevention" is replaced in this chapter by the stronger, more affirmative term "eradication," derived from the Latin *ex* + *radix* and denoting "rooting out or annihilating."

RECIDIVISM RATES AND THE MOTHERHOOD MYSTIQUE

Major revisions in treatment programs are indicated by findings that a sizable percentage of parents who received an array of multidisciplinary professional and lay services continued to abuse and neglect their children. Reporting on their evaluation of federally funded nationwide demonstration projects, Cohn and Miller (1977) state:

> All treatment programs strive to eliminate reincidence of abuse and neglect in their client families. Many assume that they are doing just that. However, we have found

that in at least 25 percent of the cases in our study, there has been some form of reincidence while the client is receiving services. Indeed, by the end of treatment an effective program may only be able to count on a 40–50 percent rate (p. 457).

The National Center for Health Services Research (NCHSR 1978) reports on the findings for eleven federally funded demonstration projects:

> Treatment for child abuse and neglect proves more effective when professional services are combined with carefully supervised lay therapy and when treatment extends for more than six months. . . . Thirty percent of the clients were identified as abusing or neglecting their children while in treatment. According to the investigators, current treatment programs can be successful in 40 to 50 percent of all cases (p. 3).

It can be assumed that recidivism rates are even higher among abusive and neglectful parents in programs that do not have the benefits of the funding, consultation, and other support of these demonstration projects.

Findings that current programs do not prevent reincidence of abuse and neglect in at least half the families served calls into question the guiding philosophy of such programs; namely, the overriding goal of keeping the child with the parents and a view of placement outside the home as a last resort. This philosophy is based on the assumption that children are always better off in their own homes and that separation from the mother (i.e., maternal deprivation) leads to dire consequences. These assumptions require reexamination, for they are misapplications of the findings of Bowlby (1951), Spitz (1945), and others who have investigated the vicissitudes of infancy.

In his reassessment of this classic research, Rutter (1972) concludes that the term "maternal deprivation" is misleading because it implies a single set of experiences related to a single condition, loss, in regard to a single individual, the mother. He states:

> . . . it appears that in most cases the deleterious influences are *not* specifically tied to the mother and are *not* due to deprivation. . . . While loss is probably an important factor in one of the syndromes associated with "maternal deprivation," a review of the evidence suggests that in most cases the damage comes from "lack" or "distortion" of care rather than any form of "loss." Bowlby's claim in 1951 that "mother-love in infancy and childhood is as important as are vitamins and proteins for physical health" was probably correct, but unfortunately it led some people (mistakenly) to place an almost mystical importance on the mother and to regard love as the only important element in child rearing. This is nonsense and it has always been a *mis*-interpretation of what was said in the 1951 report. Nevertheless, this view has come to be widespread among those involved in child care (p. 123).

If distortion and lack of care characterize the relationships of abusive and neglectful mothers with their children and damage the children more than separation, then removal from the home must be viewed, not as a last resort, but as the less damaging option. From this perspective, the major decision would be, not treatment of the mother, but the selection and support of a domicile outside the home that offered optimal quality and sufficiency of care for the child.

In her review of Bowlby's (1951) work, Ainsworth (1965) states:

> It does not follow that separating a child from his mother necessarily entails that he will then experience insufficient care and interaction. Mother-child separation *may* provide the occasion for such when a child goes to a setting, institutional or otherwise, where he has insufficient interaction with a substitute mother. Provided a child is offered a substitute mother with whom he can sufficiently interact, however, a separation experience need not have this result (p. 192).

A major basis for confusion lies in the failure to distinguish the different effects on the child of various interactions with the mother and other caretakers. These interactions, inaptly subsumed under the single term "maternal deprivation," refer to insufficiency of interaction, distorted interaction, and discontinuity of relations resulting from separations, each of which has different effects on the child.

From this more refined perspective, children may be damaged in institutions because of insufficient interactions with the new primary caretakers and not necessarily because of separation from the mother. Children may be damaged in foster homes as a result of a combination of effects: insufficient and/or distorted interactions with the mother as well as the foster parents, in addition to discontinuities in relationships resulting from repeated separations from various caretakers. Children are also damaged by insufficiencies and distortions in their relationships with mothers who abuse and neglect them. It is erroneous to conclude that continuing to expose children to maternal sources of damage is less damaging than separating them from this maternal source of damage and exposing them to nonmaternal sources of sufficient and adequate care. Yet this seems to be the assumption underlying the goal of current treatment programs for child abuse and neglect.

The view of the mother, regardless of how inadequate and emotionally unavailable, as indispensable to the child is a misapplication of the concept of attachment. It is assumed that separating children from their mothers is damaging because of the child's exclusive attachment to the mother, which is qualitatively different from attachments to others. Yet it cannot be assumed that a child has formed a bond with an abusive or neglectful mother. For example, insufficiency of early nurturance may lead to the formation of affectionless character, a formation mediated by bonding failure. Klaus and Kennell (1976) have called attention to bonding failure as a partial explanation of maternal abuse and neglect. It is possible that a mother's lack of attachment to the infant may interfere with the infant's attachment to her.

Furthermore, the quality of the attachment to the mother must be considered. An abused child's wish to remain or return to the mother may stem from a masochistic rather than a growth-enhancing attachment. In such a case, a child's attachment to an abusive or neglectful mother may be more damaging than the effects of separation. Some investigators (Schaffer and Emerson 1964; Schaffer 1971) question whether special attachment inevitably occurs to one person, the mother, and whether such an attachment is qualitatively different from that to others. It may be, for example, that attachment to the siblings is stronger than to the mother, and that distress at being removed from the home may relate as much or more to separation from the siblings than from the mother. In addition, the effects of separation from the mother must be distinguished from the effects of exposure to a new environment. Douglas and Blomfield (1958) found that damaging effects on a child followed separation from the mother only when separation was accompanied by environmental change. In all probability, separation of abused and neglected children from their parents would be less damaging if the parents left the home and moved to another therapeutic domicile, while the child remained at home with another adequate caretaker.

Other lines of research call into question the assumption that placement of the child in a nonparental home should be a last resort. Several investigators (Browder 1975; Moss and Moss 1975; Tizard 1974) have described the therapeutic contributions to children of some foster homes. Dennis (1973), Kent (1976), Money and Annecillo (1976), and Money and Needleman (1976) have reported improvements in psychological functioning and statural growth in abused and neglected children after they were removed from parental homes and placed in other domiciles.

Clearly, the matter of the least damaging placement of abused and neglected children is far from settled. The evidence does not support the single goal underlying current programs for child abuse and neglect: to keep the child with the parents except in dire circumstances. Such a unilateral stance forecloses the development of child-focused strategies that may accomplish more in the way of prevention of child abuse and neglect than bringing the parental home to barely minimal child-care standards.

These strategies include earlier termination of parental rights, earlier adoption of the child, government subsidies to low-income but child-enhancing adoptive homes, the development of nonparental domiciles in which sufficient and adequate care of the child is assured over an extended period of time, and removal of the abusive parents from the home while the children remain at home with a better caretaker.

The Department of Health, Education and Welfare (HEW 1975) refers to the fact that adoption is rarely viewed as an alternative by child welfare agencies, even when there is little likelihood of the parents ever being able to care adequately for the child. Recommendations to facilitate the adoption process include training workers to handle adoptions, reimbursement of agencies for the legal fees involved in terminating parental rights and arranging adoptions, and the enactment of laws to free children for adoption when return to the parental home is improbable. A project funded by the Children's Bureau, *Freeing Children for Adoptive Placement,* is involved in helping children who have remained in "temporary" foster care for years.

The National Center for the Prevention and Treatment of Child Abuse and Neglect (1978) describes a model Parent-Child Legal Relationship Termination Act which assumes that: "... parents and children are equal in their right to the satisfaction of a permanent and sustaining family life, and that they are also equal in their rights to life, liberty and the pursuit of happiness. No room is left for the presumption that children are the property of their parents. This Act further states that the court shall give primary consideration to the needs of the child" (p. 1).

Many professionals are guided by the expression of affection for the child by abusive and neglectful parents in making often ill-advised recommendations that the child remain in the parents' custody, or return to the parental home after a brief placement elsewhere. In some instances, this expression may represent genuine affection and be a prime motivator in the parents' authentic rehabilitation and development of dormant child-care skills. In other cases, the expressed affection and wish for the child's return may be part of the narcissistic attachment and pathological collusion that research has demonstrated to be characteristic of many abusive parents.

Polansky and Polansky (1968) make recommendations "some of which may seem rather shocking to people accustomed to viewing with genial detachment the sufferings of children outside their own families" (p. 44). These recommendations include immediate removal from the home of children abandoned by their parents or neglected to the point of starvation "with the expectation that they will not be removed for a considerable period of time" (p. 44). They believe that child abuse is a felony that should be punishable by imprisonment rather than probation, "because of the known instances in which a parent, fixed in this pattern, has still murdered his child even while supposedly on probation—a typically loosely administered gesture at this stage of our national development" (p. 44). Parents of children suffering from "failure-to-thrive" syndrome should be required by law to bring these children to a clinic or hospital regularly for medical check-ups. Finally, they recommend: "Wherever there is either clear evidence, or even persuasive evidence, of abuse of a child under the age of three, he should be permanently removed from the parental home. Return to the original parental home should be regarded as the rare exception, rather than the hoped-for norm" (p. 45).

In referring to the abuse families who are not treatable and for whom termination of parental rights is sought, Kempe and Kempe (1978) emphasize that they do not mean that the parents are not deserving of treatment, but that "the child should not be used as the instrument of treatment." They maintain:

> Quite commonly, a professional who is treating a parent and who has overidentified with the needs of his patient will say that losing custody of the child will harm the parent and set back his progress in treatment. But we firmly believe that a child's rights must be independently recognized. A child's developmental timetable simply does not allow undue delay. A parent may require three or four years of treatment before he can safely look after a child, but the child cannot wait that long in "temporary placement." There must be a more civilized way of dealing with incurable failures than providing a martyred child (p. 105).

UNWANTED PREGNANCY AND CHILD ABUSE

In view of the high reincidence of abuse and neglect among treated parents and in view of the high probability of maltreatment of all children in the family, the likelihood of maltreatment of subsequently born children is extremely high. Consequently, family planning and abortion counseling are crucially needed components of any program that purports to prevent child abuse and neglect; and these services have been recommended by Gil (1970, 1973) and Light (1974). Their availability to the general population, as well as the provision of authentic sex and family life education in the schools, is indispensible for the eradication of child abuse and neglect. The paucity of attention paid to such services in preventive planning is especially noteworthy because the circumstances of the conception and attitudes toward the pregnancy have been linked to child abuse and neglect by a number of investigators.

Blumberg (1974), Gil (1970), Prescott (1976), Spinetta and Rigler (1972), and Steele and Pollock (1968) refer to a significant association between child abuse and unwanted pregnancy, pregnancy occurring shortly after the birth of a previous child, and/or being a member of a large family with four or more children. Steele and Pollock (1968) state: "An infant born as the result of a premaritally conceived pregnancy or who comes as an accident too soon after the birth of a previous child, may be quite unwelcome to the parents and start life under a cloud of being unrewarding and unsatisfying to the parents. Such infants may be perceived as public reminders of sexual transgression or as extra, unwanted burdens rather than as need-satisfying objects" (p. 128).

Wasserman (1967) contends that the child conceived out of wedlock often becomes the "hostility sponge" for the unwanted marriage, or reminds the mother of the man who deserted her during pregnancy, or the stepfather beats the child for reminding him of his wife's transgression. The abusive parents beat out their own "badness," or that of the person who injured them, when they beat the child.

Green (1976) found that a significant number of abusive and neglectful mothers reported that the children they maltreated were unplanned. The relationship between unplanned pregnancy and child abuse and neglect is found in New Zealand as well as the United States. Ferguson, Fleming, and O'Neill (1972) reported that child abuse and neglect rates in that country are higher for illegitimate children and in larger families.

After reviewing the world literature on the murder of the newborn, Resnick (1970) concluded that the majority of murders were attributed simply to not wanting the child. In a review of the world literature on filicide, Resnick (1969) found that 18 percent of the murders were attributed to the child's being unwanted. Mothers who commit neonaticide are younger, less frequently psychotic, and more often unmarried than mothers who commit filicide. Passivity is a prominent characteristic of these women who tend to deny the pregnancy and make no preparations for either the birth or the murder. However, "when reality is thrust upon them by the infant's first cry, they respond by permanently silencing the intruder'' (p. 1416). Resnick (1970) contrasts neonaticidal women with those who seek abortions; the latter recognize the reality of the unwanted pregnancy early and actively cope with the problem.

In 1969, Dr. Lester Breslow, president of the American Public Health Association, asserted:

> Can anyone estimate how much physical harm is a byproduct of our rigid abortion laws? The unwanted child, resulting from contraceptive failure or failure to abort, may be born only to be victimized by hostile parents. . . . Not only are battered children sometimes killed and often disabled but they are usually psychologically distorted. An enlightened policy on abortion would prevent much of this callous pain and waste.

Although the relationship between child abuse and enforced pregnancy by denied abortion has not been directly assessed yet, findings indicate that children born to women denied abortion have a high potential for problems in a number of areas. The landmark study by Forssman and Thuwe (1966) on Swedish children born after applications to abort them were refused, indicated that by age twenty-one, they were more likely than other groups to have emotional problems, engage in antisocial and criminal actions, and to be on public assistance.

Dytrych, Materjcek, Schuller, David, and Friedman (1975) studied Czechoslovakian children born of women twice denied legal abortion for the same pregnancy and compared them to matched control children whose mothers did not apply for abortion. The authors conclude: "The higher incidence of illness and hospitalization . . . slightly poorer school marks and performance, somewhat worse integration in the peer group—all point to a higher risk situation for the (unwanted) child and the family, as well as for society. . . . These higher risks concern, above all, the emotional and social development of the children'' (p. 171).

Adolescent child-bearing is associated with a multitude of variables related to child abuse and neglect (Green and Pottzeiger 1977; Friedrich and Boriskin 1976; Lynch and Roberts 1977). These variables include a high risk of complications during pregnancy, labor, and delivery; and high incidence of prematurity and low birth weight and high risk of mental retardation, cerebral palsy, and epilepsy among infants of adolescent mothers. Despite these facts, teenagers bear 20 percent of the babies born in the United States, and two-thirds of their pregnancies are unplanned. Half the sexually active teenage females in this country receive no family planning services, and only 30 percent of them use contraception consistently. The level of sexual ignorance among adolescents is incredibly high. For example, 70 percent of sexually active teenage females who use no contraception believe they cannot become pregnant (Green and Potteiger 1977).

In light of the relationship between sexual ignorance, unwanted pregnancy, and child abuse and neglect, the provision of sex education at school and contraceptive and abortion services would be rationally based programs. Not only is there popular support for the eradication of child abuse and neglect, a large majority of Americans favor legal abortion, as well as sex education, including birth control information, in schools; 60 percent support the provision of contraceptives to teenagers. Catholics are just as likely as non-Catholics to approve all these services (Family Planning Perspectives 1978; Gallup 1978*a*, 1978*b*).

Despite the crucial need for such services to prevent child abuse and neglect, a small, vocal, organized, lavishly funded, fanatical minority promotes suppression of ideas and the violation of free choice by the majority. These antidemocratic groups attempt to foist their so-called morality on the majority by sensationalizing and distorting objective issues about sexuality, harassing and intimidating schools, clinics, and citizens who often fearfully withdraw active support of contraceptive and abortion services and sex education.

Cassell (1978) refers to the defunding of Planned Parenthood of Niagara County's Peer Outreach program because of the opposition of these groups, who threatened to sabotage the United Way campaign if Planned Parenthood were allowed to remain a member agency. The great importance of countering these extremist tactics and increasing subsidies to family planning agencies is shown by the fact that three and a half million women of low and marginal income are without access to family planning services. These women are at risk for child abuse and neglect because of the stresses of poverty. Between 20 and 25 percent of all births are unplanned or unwanted by parents at the time of conception, again the proportion being higher among the poor (Hatcher, Stewart, Guest, Finklestein, and Godwin 1976).

Attempts to prohibit public spending for abortions (Alan Guttmacher Institute 1976; Petitti and Cates 1977) increase the probability of child abuse and neglect in already chronically stressed, low-income groups. Many of them already have a large number of children (National Center for Health Statistics 1978), another predisposing characteristic for child abuse and neglect.

The 50 percent of adolescents who are sexually active are not going to stop because of the antisex pietists. Their moralizing is harmful, however, because, ironically, by provoking guilt, they encourage reluctance to use contraception among sexually active youth. Cutright (1971) refers to the finding that many young, unmarried women refuse to use contraceptives because of their "moral objections." He describes this attitude as "a pseudo-moral barrier inhibiting both male and female contraceptive use. The term *pseudo*-moral seems appropriate because, if one wishes to take a moral stance on nonmarital coitus, then actual behavior indicates that traditional morality has already been abandoned" (p. 47). Thus, the irrational belief that contraceptive planning is sexually immoral has been assimilated by adolescents who, nevertheless, continue their sexual activities without contraception, and the proportion of unwanted pregnancies in this child abuse prone group increases.

Polansky and Polansky (1968) refer to situations in which contraceptive information is ineffective. They state:

> The correlation between a low level of child care and large family size is unmistakable, regardless of the cultural or presumed religious backgrounds of those involved. For many couples of low intelligence, or otherwise psychologically inadequate, the

provision of birth control information is inadequate to prevent the *intergenerational treadmill*. It is recommended that the excellent laws in North Carolina regarding sterilization be adopted by the other states as constituting the most effective, if late, preventative they can make available. . . . Sterilization should be made available free to those unable to pay, with the county bearing the cost. We have seen improvement in some women following this operation alone! (p. 46)

SEXISM, PRONATALISM, AND CHILD ABUSE

Not wanting pregnancy or a child is one parental attitude related to child abuse and neglect. Wanting to bear a child for irrational reasons is another. Martin and Beezley (1974) described parents who "want" the child they subsequently abuse and adoptive parents who abuse recently adopted, much wanted children. Lenoski (1974) described a group of abusive mothers who had wanted the child intensely. They had donned maternity clothes earlier than a control group of nonabusive mothers and were more likely to name the child after a parent.

Martin and Beezley (1974) explain these seemingly paradoxical results as an extension of Steele and Pollock's (1968) finding that abusive parents characteristically expect the child to meet their own intense emotional needs. This egocentric expectation forms the basis for wanting the child, who is incapable of meeting it, and the parent lashes out at the child, who is irrationally perceived as withholding love and care. A similar conclusion was drawn by Walsh (1977) for adolescent mothers who believed the baby would establish the security they lacked with their own parents. They also viewed pregnancy and motherhood as a way of defining their lives and solving their identity problems. When the baby fails to meet these needs, the adolescent mother expresses her frustrated rage by abusing the child.

The relationship between child abuse and wanting the child intensely has also been reported by Helfer (1975). He described a group of abusive young women who refused contraception and abortion because of their strong desire to become pregnant and with whom "family planning and birth control measures must be pursued even though frequently resisted" (p. 29). He recommended special counseling for such women, because referral to a family planning agency is insufficient.

These abusive mothers have experienced the "World of Abnormal Rearing (WAR)", a pattern of damaging childhood experiences and negative parental attitudes toward them that they transmit to their children who, in turn, transmit the damaging pattern to their own children. Having been belittled and criticized as children for not meeting the irrational expectations of their parents, these abusive mothers have low self-esteem and distrust people, attitudes that lead to social isolation and a choice of mate determined by the desire to escape from home. They tend to marry emotionally unsupportive men and, hence, increase their sense of emptiness and frustrated dependency as they attain adulthood.

All these factors draw them to a view of motherhood as a panacea. According to Helfer (1975), the motivations for the pregnancy are ". . . to free them from their unhappy home, prove to their parents and themselves they can indeed be good parents, provide them with someone to keep them company, or (they expect) the baby to role reverse and begin to parent the parents" (p. 34).

The relationship between child abuse and wanting the child highlights the importance of competent, ethical, nonpropagandistic counseling for women, especially adolescents, with unplanned pregnancies. Antiabortion agencies, which violate ethical standards when they exhort conflict-ridden women with problem pregnancies to carry the child to term, often emphasize the ease with which these women discover that they really want the child. Inasmuch as few place their children for adoption, antiabortion agencies may be inadvertantly contributing to child abuse and neglect; for although not wanting the pregnancy and lack of planning for an unwanted child are related to child abuse and neglect, wanting the child in no way rules out the maternal abuse and neglect of that "wanted" child after it is born.

The finding that some women abuse and neglect the child they wanted also demonstrates the importance of transforming attitudes toward women's roles, child-bearing, and the definition of the family, if child abuse and neglect are ever to be eradicated. The abysmal failure of these women in a role they sought with apparently joyous expectations poignantly depicts the destructiveness of sexist and pronatalist upbringing. In all likelihood, they learned to accept without question the major tenets of sexism and pronatalism; namely, sex role stereotyping and the views that anatomy is destiny, that the only fulfilling life style for women is motherhood, and that a woman becomes validated as a person only when she bears a child.

Despite their harsh backrounds, these women need not have become child abusers. Had the culture offered them a range of socially sanctioned options, in addition to marriage and motherhood, they might have become contributors to the community rather than a drain on its resources.

Clearly, adoption of the tenets of the Women's Liberation Movement and the National Alliance for Optional Parenthood would significantly contribute to the eradication of child abuse and neglect at home. These tenets include the view that anatomy is not destiny for either women or men, that a wide variety of life styles can be equally fulfilling, that the family should be defined as a unit that may or may not include children, and that child-free marriage and remaining single merit social sanctions equal to marriage and parenthood.

As Peck and Senderowitz (1974) indicate, pronatalist as well as sexist ideologies are promoted in textbooks, advertising, and sex education courses. Such ideologies contribute indirectly but powerfully to child abuse and neglect, because they assume that the ability to bear children equips women, in some mysterious way, with the ability to rear them adequately. Not only must textbooks depict Dick and Jane as equally proficient in social and occupational roles; they must include stories about families in which neither Dick, Jane nor any other children are part of the household. A positive step toward preventing the abuse and neglect of children by their parents is the development of the Optional

Parenthood Questionnaire, a well-constructed test to measure attitudes and goals regarding parenthood, which can be used to aid couples in reflecting on the consequences of a decision to have a (another) child (Beach, Townes, Campbell, and Keating 1976; Townes, Beach, Campbell, and Martin 1977).

The distorted, sentimental view of children as always cute, clean, and quiet, a pronatalist depiction presented by the media in order to sell products, must be corrected if child abuse and neglect are ever to be eradicated. Unrealistic expectations of children, a primary characteristic of abusive and neglectful parents, are continually reinforced by commercials that portray children as adorable, cuddly, ever fulfilling cherubs whose disposable diapers are never soiled, who gurgle quietly, and who never utter the shrill, ear-piercing wails that many abusive parents report is a trigger for their loss of self-control.

The destructiveness of romanticizing children is incisively discussed by Holt (1974):

> The trouble with sentimentality and the reason why it always leads to callousness and cruelty is that it is abstract and unreal. We look at the lives and concerns of children as we might look at actors on a stage, a comedy as long as it does not become a nuisance. And so since their feelings and their pain are neither serious nor real, any pain we may cause them is not real either. . . . People who treat children like living dolls when they are feeling good may treat them like unliving dolls—fling them into a corner or throw them downstairs or out of the window—when they are feeling bad. "Little angels" quickly become "little devils" (p. 81).

A massive campaign, including persuasive contacts with advertisers by child advocates, will be required to correct the harmful distortions of children inflicted on the public by the media. Such a campaign would also need to include unsentimentalized courses in family life education that realistically present the ugly, dirty, unrewarding, unfulfilling, frustrating aspects of children. Parenting courses would need to give equal time to nonparenting life styles. Indeed, the substitution of courses on life styles for the much touted parenting courses would present youth with the varied range of their relational options, teach them realistic expectations of children, and help them make an informed choice, rather than one determined by social pressures, if parenthood is eventually selected.

CORPORAL PUNISHMENT: SOCIALLY SANCTIONED VIOLENCE AGAINST CHILDREN

The eradication of child abuse cannot be accomplished if the attitude persists that corporal punishment of children is a right of parents. Gelles's (1977) survey on normative samples of parents in the United States reveals that, despite the public furor over child abuse, violence against children is socially sanctioned.

The conflict between protecting children from abuse and protecting the presumed right of parents to assault their children is clearly depicted in Texas law. After passing a law to protect children from abuse by their parents, Texas passed another law that states: "The use of force, but not deadly force, against a child younger than 18 years is justified: (1) if the actor is the child's parent or stepparent . . . (2) when and to the degree that the actor reasonably believes the force is necessary to discipline the child" *(Texas Penal Code* 1974, pp. 22–23). Providing that they do not kill their child, Texan parents can legally justify abuse on the grounds of "discipline."

It is usually overlooked that corporal punishment and child abuse are on the same continuum of violence. Most abusive parents do not plan to abuse their children. They start out to physically punish them, and the violence intensifies. Frequently, the right hip of the battered child is injured because blows are directed primarily to the right buttock when the subsequently abused child is laid over the parent's knees for a "spanking."

The extent of social sanctions for violence against children in America is attested to by the United States Supreme Court ruling in the case of Ingraham vs. Wright (1977). The Court ruled that corporal punishment of children in public schools, regardless of how excessive, does not come within the scope of constitutional protection against "cruel and unusual punishment," a protection reserved for incarcerated criminals. Thus, in the midst of efforts to implement the much touted Child Abuse Prevention and Treatment Act, violence against children has been sanctioned by the highest court in the land. Thus, a major social institution in America, the schools, now serve as a model of legally sanctioned child abuse, especially to marginal and brutal parents.

Assaults on teachers and vandalism by students have often been used to justify physical coercion of children at school. The issue of self-defense by a teacher against assault by a student, however, is an entirely different issue from the use of corporal punishment in the education of children. Preliminary data (Hyman 1979) indicate that younger, smaller children are likely to be hit, many of them physically disabled and emotionally fragile, a significant number of them from ghettoes and barrios. There is some evidence that schools that practice corporal punishment are more likely to be vandalized than schools that do not use physical force on students, and that children who were corporally punished in school when they were too weak to defend themselves may retaliate when they are older and stronger by assaulting teachers and vandalizing schools.

Corporal punishment is not a necessity in the teaching of children. It has been abolished in schools in Denmark, Finland, Holland, Israel, Japan, Norway, the Soviet Union, and Sweden. It is practiced in such English-speaking countries as Australia and Britain, as well as the United States.

Violence against children at home and at school is usually denied in the face of evidence of its use in American society, by means of illogical thinking. Violence against children by parents and teachers is discipline; violence against parents and teachers by children is assault. The lack of discipline by parents and teachers, manifested by their use of physical punishment, is irrationally transformed into a means of assuring the discipline of children. A child who strikes a teacher creates disorder in the classroom; a teacher who strikes a child is presumed to create order. Penal codes of several states exclude corporal punishment from the definition of assault and battery, even though an identical violent action against adults, inherently more able to defend themselves, would consitute assault and battery. In short, striking adults is assault and battery; striking children is good for them.

Corporal punishment has its roots in slavery, and its proponents unwittingly retain vestiges of a master-slave ideology when they defend it; for example, "a stick is the only way to make them behave"; "they aren't able to understand anything else." Indeed, it was the alleged "child-like" characteristic of slaves that was often used to justify the practice of physically punishing them. Above all, as with slavery and other tyrannies, corporal punishment is sustained by the righteous assertion that the violence benefits the victim. In this connection, G. B. Shaw advised:

> If you strike a child, take care you strike it in anger. . . . A blow in cold blood neither can be, nor should be forgiven. If you beat children for pleasure, avow your object frankly, and play the game according to the rules, as a fox hunter does. . . No fox hunter is such a cad as to pretend he hunts the fox to teach it not to steal chickens, or that he suffers more acutely than the fox at death. Remember that even in child beating there is the sportsman's way and the cad's way.

Medical data document spinal cord and whiplash injuries, sciatic nerve damage and central nervous system hemorrhage as a result of corporal punishment (Friedman 1976). Furthermore, physical punishment perpetuates what Piers (1978) calls "the chain reaction of violence." In reporting on their studies on the effects of parental child-rearing practices on children's behavior, Sears, Maccoby, and Levin (1957) stated: "The unhappy effects of punishment have run like a dismal thread through our findings . . . Mothers who punished aggressive behavior severely had more aggressive children than mothers who punished lightly. . . . Harsh physical punishment was associated with high childhood aggressiveness" (p. 57).

Innumerable investigators have emphasized the ineffectiveness and irrationality of the corporal punishment of children and have suggested effective, growth-inducing, nonviolent alternatives to disciplining and instructing children (American Civil Liberties Union 1972; Bakan 1971; Button 1973; Divosky 1973; Feshbach 1973; Feshbach and Feshbach 1973, 1976; Hagebak 1973; Hyman 1979; Kozol 1967; Maurer 1973; 1974; National Education Association 1972; Skinner 1976; Valusek 1974; Welsh 1976a, 1976b).

In his testimony at the Senate hearings on the Child Abuse Prevention and Treatment Act, Gil (1973) referred to findings that child abuse occurred in all income groups and in ordinary families. He stated that this was not surprising because: ". . . the use of physical force in the rearing and disciplining of children is widely accepted in our country. Common sense suggests that whenever corporal punishment is widely used, extreme cases are bound to occur and children will be injured. . . . Our studies indicate that the widespread acceptance in our culture of physical discipline of children is the underlying factor of physical child abuse." (p. 15).

Despite data and informed opinion regarding the important role played by corporal punishment in the perpetuation of child abuse, proponents of corporal punishment vehemently resist its abolition because it is so deeply entrenched in American society. Many of these proponents piously bemoan violence "in society" and "the death of spiritual values." Paradoxically, it is the assassins who deliver the funeral oration.

CHILD ABUSE AND NEGLECT AT HOME: ERADICATION OR STOPGAP MEASURES?

It has been stated thus far that the eradication of child abuse and neglect will require substantial changes in attitudes, practices, and programs. In order to make many of these changes, more funds will be needed than the relative pittance currently allotted to child abuse and neglect programs. For example, large subsidies will be required for the development and evaluation of innovative, child-oriented programs besides those aimed at keeping the family together. Additional funds will be needed to broaden the scope of child-protection agencies to include arrangements for adoption and family planning counseling as integral components of their services, and to reimburse agencies for the legal fees required for adoptions.

Accordingly, the eradication of child abuse and neglect will require a reordering of financial priorities in the United States. Despite the furor over child abuse and self-congratulatory statements by politicians that America is a child-caring nation, funds for child abuse programs amount to roughly sixty million dollars for a four-year period; and the combined budget of Child Welfare Services, Child and Maternal Health, and Crippled Children Services totals 900 million dollars. In impressive contrast, the 1979 military budget of 126 *billion* dollars was another installment in the 1.8 *trillion* dollars spent on the military since the end of World War II (SANE 1978).

This country clearly has the resources to nourish and enhance its children. Yet there is simply no financial profit in investing in children as there is in investing in the military industrial complex. For example, industry profited by 6,684 percent in the Nike missile system. Major military contractors frequently earn profits 70 percent higher than nonmilitary contractors (Johnson 1972). Furthermore, children lack the political power to protest, for instance, the trading off of a child nutrition program for two destroyers, or the fact that the total federal funds appropriated for elementary and secondary education is no greater than the cost of two Trident submarines (SANE 1978). As for using America's resources for its children, there is much less here than meets the eye. "We spend less than 10% of our gross national product on children, who represent 40% of our population, and 100% of our future" (Kempe 1978, p. 260).

Unless radical transformations in programs, practices, and financial priorities take place in America, child abuse and neglect will not be eradicated, and programs purporting to treat and prevent abuse and neglect will be little more than stopgap measures and window dressing.

The emphasis on temporary expediency as the implicit guideline for child abuse and neglect programs is reminiscent of a people described in Jewish legend, the Fools of Chelm, a community of smug simpletons who lacked insight into their incredible stupidity. They lived at the top of a steep mountain from which they had to traverse a narrow, winding path in order to go to the market at the foot of the mountain. In the course of their frequent journeys to the market, droves of Chelmsians were killed or maimed as they dropped off the narrow path into the deep valley below. After decades of ignoring the carnage, the survivors finally took action against the problem. They voted funds to build a hospital at the bottom of the valley to treat those unfortunates who dropped off the mountain into the valley.

REFERENCES

Ainsworth, M. S. "Further Research into the Adverse Effects of Maternal Deprivation." In J. Bowlby, *Child Care and the Growth of Love*. Baltimore: Penguin Books (2nd edition), 1965.

Alan Guttmacher Institute. "Supreme Court to review restrictions on abortion by Medicaid." *Family Planning/Population Reporter* 5 (1976): 58-62.

American Civil Liberties Union. *Report of the National Conference on Corporal Punishment in the Public Schools*. New York, 1972.

Bakan, D. *Slaughter of the Innocents*. San Francisco: Jossey-Bass, 1971.

Beach, L. R., Townes, B. D., Campbell, F. L., and Keating, G. W. "Developing and testing a decision aid for birth planning decisions." *Organizational Behavior and Human Performance* 15 (1976): 99-116.

Blumberg, M. L. "Psychopathology of the abusing parent." *American Journal of Psychotherapy* 28 (1974): 21-29.

Bowlby, J. *Maternal Care and Mental Health*. Geneva: World Health Organization, 1951.

Breslow, L. Paper presented at the First National Conference on Abortion Laws, Chicago, Illinois, February 1969.

Browder, J. A. "Adoption and foster care of handicapped children in the United States." *Developmental Medicine and Child Neurology* 17 (1975): 614-19.

Button, A. "Some antecendents of felonious and delinquent behavior." *Journal of Clinical Child Psychology* 2 (1973): 35-37.

Cassell, C. "The opposition." *Impact* 1 (1978): 19-21.

Cohn, A. H., and Miller, M. K. "Evaluating new modes of treatment for child abusers and neglectors: The experience of federally funded demonstration projects in the USA." *Child Abuse and Neglect—The International Journal* 1 (2-4) (1977): 453-58.

Cuttright, P. "Illegitimacy: Myths, causes and cures." *Family Planning Perspectives* 3 (1971): 43-47.

Dennis, W. *Children of the Crèche*. New York: Appleton–Century–Crofts, 1973.

Department of Health, Education and Welfare. *Child Abuse and Neglect: The Community Team, An Approach to Case Management and Prevention*. Vol. 3. Washington, D.C.: DHEW Publ. No. (OHD) 75-30075, 1975.

Divosky, D. "Corporal punishment in U. S. schools." *Learning* 5 (1973): 54–58.

Douglas, J. W. B., and Blomfield, J. M. *Children under Five.* New York: Allen and Unwin, 1958.

Dytrych, Z., Matejcek, Z., Schuller, V., David, H. P., and Friedman, H. L. "Children born to women denied abortion." *Family Planning Perspectives* 7 (1975): 165–71.

Family Planning Perspectives. "Large majority of Americans favor legal abortion, sex education and contraceptive services for teens." *Family Planning Perspectives* 10 (1978): 159–60.

Feshbach, N. D. "The effects of violence in childhood." *Journal of Clinical Child Psychology* 2 (1973): 28–31.

Feshbach, N. D., and Feshbach, S. "Parent Rites vs. Children's Rights." In G. P. Koocher, ed., *Children's Rights and the Mental Health Professions.* New York: John Wiley, 1976.

Feshbach, S., and Feshbach, N. D. "Alternatives to corporal punishment: Implications for training and controls." *Journal of Clinical Child Psychology* 2 (1973): 46–48.

Forssman, I. H., and Thuwe, I. "One hundred and twenty children born after therapeutic abortion refused." *Acta Psychiatrica Scandinavica* 42 (1966): 71.

Friedman, D. B. "Corporal punishment in the schools—Discipline or abuse?" Paper presented at the Annual Convention of the American Psychological Association, Washington, D.C., September 1976.

Friedrich, W. N., and Boriskin, J. A. "The role of the child in abuse: a review of the literature." *American Journal of Orthopsychiatry* 46 (1976): 580–90.

Gallup, G. "Seventy-five percent back abortions but most say only in certain circumstances." *The Gallup Poll,* news release, Princeton, New Jersey, January 22, 1978a.

————. "Reflects epidemic of teenage pregnancies: Growing number of Americans favor discussion of sex in classroom." *The Gallup Poll,* news release, Princeton, New Jersey, January 23, 1978b.

Gelles, R. J. "Violence toward children in the United States." Paper presented at the Annual Convention of the American Association for the Advancement of Science, Denver, Colorado, February 1977.

Gil, D. G. *Violence against Children: Physical Child Abuse in the United States.* Cambridge, Mass.: Harvard University Press, 1970

————. *Testimony.* Hearing before the Subcommittee on Children and Youth of the Committee on Labor and Public Welfare, United States Senate, 93rd Congress, First Session on S. 1191, Child Abuse Prevention Act, 1973. Washington, D.C.: U.S. Government Printing Office, 1973.

Green, A. "A psychodynamic approach to the study and treatment of child abusing parents." *Journal of Child Psychiatry* 15 (1976): 414–29.

Green, C. P., and Potteiger, K. "Teenage Pregnancy: A Major Problem for Minors." Washington, D.C.: Zero Population Growth, 1977.

Hagebak, R. "Disciplinary practices in Dallas contrasted with school systems with rules against violence against children." *Journal of Clinical Child Psychology* 2 (1973): 14–16.

Hatcher, R. A., Stewart, G. K., Guest, F., Finkelstein, R., and Godwin, C. *Contraceptive Technology 1976–1977.* Eighth revised edition. New York: Irvington Publishers, 1976.

Helfer, R. E. *Child Abuse and Neglect: The Diagnostic Process and Treatment Programs.* Washington, D.C.: U.S. Department of Health, Education and Welfare, Publ. No. (OHD) 75-69, 1975.

Holt, J. *Escape from Childhood—The Needs and Rights of Children.* New York: Ballantine Books, 1974.

Hyman, I. A. *Corporal Punishment in American Education: Readings in Practice and Theory.* Philadelphia: Temple University Press, 1979.

Ingraham v. Wright. 498 F. 2d 248 (5th Cir. 1977).

Johnson, R. N. *Aggression in Man and Animals.* Philadelphia: W. B. Saunders Co., 1972.

Kempe, C. H. "Child abuse—The pediatrician's role in child advocacy and preventive pediatrics." *American Journal of Diseases of Children* 132 (1978): 255-60.

Kempe, R. S., and Kempe, C. H. *Child Abuse.* Cambridge, Mass.: Harvard University Press, 1978.

Kent, J. T. "A follow-up study of abused children." *Journal of Pediatric Psychology* 1 (1976): 25-31.

Klaus, M., and Kennell, J. *Maternal-Infant Bonding.* St. Louis: Mosby Co., 1976.

Kozol, J. *Death at an Early Age.* Boston: Houghton Mifflin Co., 1967.

Lenoski, E. F. "Translating Injury Data into Preventive and Health Care Services—Physical Child Abuse." Paper presented at Seminar on Child Abuse, Denver, Colorado, September 1974.

Light, R. J. "Abused and neglected children in America: A study of alternative policies." *Harvard Educational Review* 43 (1973): 556-98.

Lynch, M. A., and Roberts, J. "Predicting child abuse: Signs of bonding failure in the maternity hospital." *British Medical Journal* 1 (1977): 624-26.

Martin, H. P., and Beezley, P. "Prevention and the consequences of child abuse." *Journal of Operational Psychiatry* 6 (1974): 68-77.

Maurer, A. "Spare the child!" *Journal of Clinical Child Psychology* 2 (1973): 4-6.

———. "Corporal punishment." *American Psychologist* 29 (1974): 614-26.

Money, J., and Annecillo, C. "IQ change following change of domicile in the syndrome of reversible hyposomatotropinism (psychosocial dwarfism): Pilot investigation." *Psychoneuroendocrinology* 1 (1976): 421-29.

Money, J., and Needleman, A. "Child abuse in the syndrome of reversible hyposomatotropic dwarfism (psychosocial dwarfism)." *Journal of Pediatric Psychology* 1 (1976): 20-23.

Moss, S. Z., and Moss, M. S. "Surrogate mother relationships." *American Journal of Orthopsychiatry* 45 (1975): 382-90.

National Center for Health Services Research. *Announcement* (1978, May/June), p. 3.

National Center for Health Statistics. "Wanted and Unwanted Child-bearing in the United States—1968, 1969, and 1972 National Natality Surveys." *Vital and Health Statistics,* 1978. Series 21, No. 32, DHEW Publ. No. (PHS)78-1918.

National Center for the Prevention and Treatment of Child Abuse and Neglect. "Legislation to terminate parent-child legal relationships." *National Child Protection Newsletter* 6 (1978): 1-3.

National Education Association. "Report of the Task Force on Corporal Punishment." Washington, D.C., 1972.

Peck, E., and Senderowitz, J. *Pronatalism: The Myth of Mom and Apple Pie.* New York: Crowell Co., 1974.

Petitti, D. B., and Cates, W. "Restricting Medicaid funds for abortions: Projections of excess mortality for women of childbearing age." *American Journal of Public Health* 67 (1977): 860-62.

Piers, M. W. *Infanticide Past and Present.* New York: W. W. Norton Co., 1978.

Polansky, N., and Polansky, N. "The Current Status on Child Abuse and Child Neglect in This Country. Report to the Joint Commission on Mental Health for Children, February 1968." In Gil, D. G., *Violence against Children—Physical Child Abuse in the United States.* Cambridge, Mass.: Harvard University Press, 1970.

Prescott, J. "Abortion or the unwanted child: A choice for a humanistic society." *Journal of Pediatric Psychology* 1 (1976): 62–67.

Resnick, P. J. "Child murder by parents: A psychiatric review of filicide." *American Journal of Psychiatry* 126 (1969): 325–34.

———. "Murder of the newborn: A psychiatric review of neonaticide." *American Journal of Psychiatry* 126 (1970): 1414–20.

Rutter, M. *Maternal Deprivation Reassessed.* New York: Penguin Books, 1972.

SANE. "Do You Know What Your Tax Dollar Buys?" Washington, D.C.: SANE, 1978.

Schaeffer, H. R. *The Growth of Sociability.* New York: Penguin Books, 1971.

Schaeffer, H. R., and Emerson, P. E. "The development of social attachments in infancy." *Monographs of the Society for Research in Child Development,* 29 (1964): 94.

Sears, R. E., Maccoby, E. E., and Levin, H. *Patterns of Childrearing.* New York: Harper and Row, 1957.

Skinner, B. F. "Corporal Punishment of Children in the Schools." Paper presented at the Annual Convention of the American Psychological Association, Washington, D.C., September 1976.

Spinetta, J. J., and Rigler, D. "The child-abusing parent: A psychological review." *Psychological Bulletin* 77 (1972): 296–304.

Spitz, R. A. "Hospitalism: An Inquiry into the Genesis of Psychiatric Conditions in Early Childhood." In *The Psychoanalytic Study of the Child,* vol. 1, pp. 53–74. New York: International Universities Press, 1945.

Steele, B. F., and Pollock, C. B. "A Psychiatric Study of Parents Who Abuse Infants and Small Children." In R. E. Helfer and C. H. Kempe, eds. *The Battered Child,* pp. 103–47. Chicago: University of Chicago Press, 1968.

Tizard, J. "The upbringing of other people's children." *Journal of Child Psychology and Psychiatry* 15 (1974): 161–73.

Townes, B. D., Beach, L. R., Campbell, F. L., and Martin, D. C. "Birth planning values and decisions: The prediction of fertility." *Journal of Applied Social Psychology* 7 (1977): 73–88.

Valusek, J. E. *People Are Not for Hitting.* Wichita, Kan.: Valusek, 1974.

Walsh, T. "Premature parenting and child abuse." Paper presented at the Workshop on Teen Parenthood. Onondaga Community College, New York, March 1977.

Wasserman, S. "The abused parent of the abused child." *Children* 14 (1967): 175–79.

Welsh, R. S. "Severe parental punishment and delinquency: A developmental approach." *Journal of Clinical Child Psychology.* 5 (1976a): 17–23.

———. "Violence, permissiveness and the overpunished child." *Journal of Pediatric Psychology* 1 (1976b): 68–71.

CONTRIBUTORS

Thomas R. Anderegg, M. A., clinical psychologist, Dubuque-Jackson County Mental Health Center, Dubuque, Iowa 52001.

Charles Annecillo, M.A., graduate student, Johns Hopkins University School of Hygiene and Public Health, Baltimore, Maryland 21205.

Alan S. Appelbaum, Ph.D., assistant professor, Division of Child and Adolescent Psychiatry, University of Texas Medical Branch, Galveston, Texas 77550.

Jerry A. Boriskin, M.A., doctoral candidate in clinical psychology, University of North Dakota, Department of Psychology, Grand Forks, North Dakota 58202.

Stuart L. Brown, M.D., medical director, Mental Health Unit, and chief, Department of Psychiatry, Mercy Hospital, San Diego, California 92103.

David M. Brubakken, Ph.D., director, Child-Adolescent Programs, Mendota Health Institute, Madison, Wisconsin 53704.

Ann Buchanan, Dip. Social Studies, research social worker, Burderop Hospital, Swindon, Wiltshire, England.

Jessica Cameronchild, consultant on child abuse for various agencies, San Francisco Child Abuse Council, 4093 24th Street, San Francisco, California 94114.

Anne Chaleff, R.N., psychiatric nurse and coordinator, Child Sexual Abuse Program, Department of Child Psychiatry, Center for Health Sciences, University of California, Los Angeles, California 90024.

Sheldon Cotler, Ph.D., associate professor, Department of Psychology, De Paul University, 2219 North Kenmore, Chicago, Illinois 60614.

Lloyd DeMause, Ph.D., training staff member, New York Center for Psychoanalytic Training, editor and founder, *History of Childhood Quarterly—The Journal of Psychohistory,* 2315 Broadway, New York, New York 10024.

Wayne Dennis, Ph.D., formerly professor of psychology, Brooklyn College, and visiting professor, University of Beirut, now deceased. c/o Margaret Dennis, Route #1, Box #180, Doswell, Virginia 23047.

Charles Dickens, British novelist.

William Droegemueller, M.D., professor, Department of Obstetrics and

Gynecology, University of Colorado Medical Center, 4200 East 9th Avenue, Denver, Colorado 80262.

Mark Flanzraich, M.S., M.S.W., director of Youth and Family Services, Emanu-el Midtown YM–YWHA, 344 East 14th Street, New York, New York 10003.

David A. Freedman, M.D., professor of psychiatry, Baylor College of Medicine and Training, and supervising analyst, Houston–Galveston Psychoanalytic Institute, 5300 Jacinto, Houston, Texas 77004.

William N. Friedrich, M.P.H., doctoral candidate in clinical psychology, University of North Dakota, Department of Psychology, Grand Forks, North Dakota 58202.

Lytt I. Gardner, M.D., professor of pediatrics, State University of New York, Upstate Medical Center, 750 East Adams Street, Syracuse, New York 13210.

Henry Giarretto, M.S.W., director of Child Abuse Treatment Program, Santa Clara County Juvenile Probation Department, San Jose, California 95113.

D. James Henderson, M.D., director of psychiatric services, Royal Victoria Hospital of Barrie, 76 Ross Street, Barrie, Ontario L4N 1G4, Canada.

Irwin A. Hyman, Ed.D., professor of school psychology, and director, National Center for the Study of Corporal Punishment and Alternatives, Temple University, 833 Ritter Hall South, Philadelphia, Pennsylvania 19122.

Irving Kaufman, M.D., faculty member, Harvard University School of Medicine and Smith College School of Social Work, 40 Williston Road, Auburndale, Massachusetts 02166.

C. Henry Kempe, M.D., editor-in-chief, *Child Abuse and Neglect—The International Journal,* and professor of pediatrics and director, National Center for the Prevention of Child Abuse and Neglect, University of Colorado Medical Center, 4200 East 9th Avenue, Denver, Colorado 80220.

John P. Kemph, M.D., clinical director, Children's Psychiatric Hospital, University of Michigan, Ann Arbor, Michigan 68104.

John H. Kennell, M.D., professor of pediatrics, Case Western Reserve University, 2103 Adelbert Road, Cleveland, Ohio 44106.

James Kent, L.L.D., former chief justice, New York Supreme Court and professor of law, Columbia University, now deceased.

James T. Kent, Ph.D., director of Family Development Project, Los Angeles Children's Hospital, and associate clinical professor of pediatrics (psychology), University of Southern California School of Medicine, Los Angeles, California 90027.

Marshall H. Klaus, M.D., professor of pediatrics and director of nurseries, Rainbow Babies and Children's Hospital, 201 Adelbert Road, Cleveland, Ohio 44106.

Michael Klein, M.D., associate professor of family medicine and assistant professor of pediatrics, McGill University, and director, Herzel Family Practice Center, Jewish General Hospital, 5750 Côte des Neiges Road, Montreal, Quebec H3T 1EZ, Canada.

Jarmila Koluchová, Ph.D., faculty member, Department of Psychology and Psychiatry, Palacký University, Olomouc, Czechoslovakia.

Janet Lindsay, M.D., M.R.C. Psych., D.P.M., consultant in psychiatry, The Park Hospital for Children, Old Road, Headington, Oxford OX3 7LQ, England.

Harold P. Martin, M.D., associate professor of pediatrics, University of Colorado Medical School, and associate director, John F. Kennedy Child Development Center, 4200 East 9th Avenue, Denver, Colorado 80220.

Roy Meadow, M.D., senior lecturer and consulting pediatrician, University of Leeds, Department of Pediatrics and Child Health, Medical Education Centre, Seacroft Hospital, York Road, Leeds LS146UH, England.

John Money, Ph.D., professor of medical psychology and associate professor of pediatrics, Johns Hopkins University and Hospital, Baltimore, Maryland 21205.

Helen L. Morrison, M.D., faculty member, Department of Psychiatry, Loyola University, Stritch School of Medicine, Maywood, Illinois 60153.

Andrea Needleman, student, Psychohormonal Research Unit, Johns Hopkins University and Hospital, Baltimore, Maryland 21205.

J. E. Oliver, M.B., B.S., D.P.M., M.R.C. Psych., consulting psychiatrist, Pewsey Hospital, Peusey, Wiltshire, England.

Rhoda Oppenheimer, B.Sc. (Econ.), C.Q.S.W., senior social worker (teaching), University Department of Psychiatry, Clinical Sciences Building, Leicester Royal Infirmary, Leicester, England.

Christopher Ounsted, M.A., D.M., F.R.C.P., F.R.C. Psych., D.P.M., D.C.H., psychiatrist, The Park Hospital for Children, Old Road, Headington, Oxford OX3 7LQ, England.

Morris J. Paulson, Ph.D., professor of medical psychology and principal investigator, Child Trauma Intervention Project, Department of Psychiatry, University of California Center for Health Sciences, Los Angeles, California 90024.

Alice L. Peck, M.S.W., former social worker, Guidance Center, Boston, Massachusetts.

Thomas J. Reidy, Ph.D., clinical psychologist, Mental Health Center, Community Hospital of the Monterey Peninsula, Box HH, Carmel, California 93921.

Domeena C. Renshaw, M.B., Ch.B., M.D., professor of psychiatry, Loyola University of Chicago. 85 South 3rd Street, Lombard, Illinois 60148.

Robert H. Renshaw, Ph.D., assistant professor of economics, Northern Illinois University in Dekalb, 85 South 3rd Street, Lombard, Illinois 60148.

Phillip J. Resnick, M.D., assistant professor and director, Division of Forensic Psychiatry, Case Western Reserve University, 2040 Abington Road, Cleveland, Ohio 44106.

David Rigler, Ph.D., professor of clinical psychology, University of Southern

California, and professor of pediatrics and psychiatry, Los Angeles Children's Hospital, 4650 Sunset Boulevard, Los Angeles, California 90027.

Martha A. Rodeheffer, Ph.D., assistant professor, University of Colorado Medical Center, and clinical child psychologist, National Center for the Prevention and Treatment of Child Abuse and Neglect, 4200 East 9th Avenue, Denver, Colorado 80220.

Charles Schwarzbeck III, Ph.D., clinical instructor in psychiatry, George Washington University School of Medicine, and chief clinical psychologist, Child and Adolescent Services, Professional Associates of the Psychiatric Institute, 5454 Wisconsin Avenue, Suite 610, Chevy Chase, Maryland 20015.

Winifred J. Scott, Ph.D., clinical psychologist, Ramsey County Mental Health Department, St. Paul-Ramsey Hospital, Division of Child Psychiatry, St. Paul, Minnesota 55101.

Henry K. Silver, M.D., professor of pediatrics, University of Colorado Medical Center, 4200 East 9th Avenue, Denver, Colorado 80220.

Frederic N. Silverman, M.D., visiting professor, Department of Radiology, Stanford University Medical Center, Stanford, California 94305.

Nicole Simon, Ph.D., senior systems programmer, American Science and Engineering, Inc., 955 Massachusetts Avenue, Cambridge, Massachusetts 02139.

John J. Spinetta, Ph.D., associate professor of psychology, San Diego State University, 5300 Campanille Drive, San Diego, California 92182.

Brandt F. Steele, M.D., professor of psychiatry, University of Colorado Medical Center, 4200 East 9th Avenue, Denver, Colorado 80220.

Gloria L. Steiner, Ed.D., clinical associate professor, Division of Child and Adolescent Psychiatry, The New Jersey Medical School, 100 Bergen St., Newark, New Jersey 07103.

Leo Stern, M.D., chairman and professor, Department of Pediatrics, Brown University, 97 Waterman, Providence, Rhode Island 02902.

Consuelo K. Tagiuri, M.D., former psychiatrist at the Judge Baker Guidance Center, Boston, Massachusetts.

Lenore C. Terr, M.D., assistant clinical professor of psychiatry, University of California Medical School, 450 Sutter, San Francisco, California 94108.

Robert J. Tracy, Ph.D., associate professor, Department of Psychology, De Paul University, 2219 North Kenmore, Chicago, Illinois 60614.

Andrew S. Watson, M.D., professor of psychiatry and law, University of Michigan, Children's Psychiatric Hospital, Ann Arbor, Michigan 48104.

Stanley J. Weinberg, M.S.W., director of clinical services, Hawthorne Cedar Knolls School, 226 Linda Avenue, Hawthorne, New York 15032.

June Werlwas, M.M.H., assistant in medical psychology, Johns Hopkins University and Hospital, Baltimore, Maryland 21205.

Gertrude J. Williams, Ph.D., diplomate in clinical psychology, ABPP; independent practice of clinical and consulting psychology, 9378 Olive Street Road, Suite 202, Premier Building, St. Louis, Missouri 63132.

George Wolff, Ph.D., psychologist, Hannover, West Germany.

Logan Wright, Ph.D., associate professor, University of Oklahoma Health Sciences Center, Division of Pediatric Psychology, 1616 N.E. 15th Street, P.O. Box 26910, Oklahoma City, Oklahoma 53190.

Atalay Yorukoglu, M.D., faculty member, Ankara University, Hacettepe Medical Faculty, Ankara, Turkey.

Index

Index

The Johns Hopkins University Press

This book was composed in VIP Times Roman by The Composing Room of Michigan Inc., from a design by Charles West. It was printed on 50-lb. Decision Opaque paper and bound by The Maple Press Company.